An Intermediate Text

Price Theory

David D. Friedman
A.B. Freeman School of Business
Tulane University

Published by
HO5 **SOUTH-WESTERN PUBLISHING CO.**

CINCINNATI   WEST CHICAGO, IL   DALLAS   PELHAM MANOR, NY   LIVERMORE, CA

Copyright © 1986

by SOUTH-WESTERN PUBLISHING CO.
Cincinnati, Ohio

ALL RIGHTS RESERVED

ISBN: 0–538–08050–7

Library of Congress Catalog Card Number: 85–62461

1   2   3   4   5   D   9   8   7   6   5

Printed in the United States of America

Foreword

Modern economics is above all a way of thinking about social behavior. When a person decides to engage in any activity, the economist instinctively looks for benefits to that person that exceed his costs; conversely, if he decides not to engage in an activity, the economist looks for costs that exceed the benefits. Moreover, if two persons voluntarily engage in a transaction or trade, the economist looks for gains to *both* participants, not gains to one and losses to the other.

Recent decades have seen growing confidence that this economic way of thinking provides important insights into human behavior under quite different economic systems and institutions. It has been used to help understand primitive societies studied by anthropologists as well as advanced economies of the modern day; capitalist countries like the United States as well as Communist countries like China and Cuba; personal interactions that do not use explicit markets, like marriage and gift giving, as well as transactions in organized markets, like the stock market; decisions to engage in crime as well as decisions to study economics; and decisions by college graduates with high IQ's as well as decisions by illiterates with low IQ's.

Although the range of behavior analyzed with the economic way of thinking has been greatly extended during the past several decades, textbooks on economic principles generally have taken a much narrower view of the scope of economics. This is not surprising since recent developments in a scientific field usually do not find their way into textbooks for many years. Fortunately, several economics texts in recent years have begun to take a broader view, and this text by David Friedman does so in the most thoroughgoing and satisfactory manner of any that I have seen. Every chapter shows evidence of a skilled and imaginative economist applying his tools to the world around him. Perhaps I can whet the reader's appetite for the book with a few examples culled from different chapters.

Travelers have long recognized that homes in Los Angeles are cooler and less comfortable during the winter than are homes in cities like Chicago, even though Los Angeles has a milder winter climate than Chicago does. Chapter 21 explains this by showing why indoor temperature can be raised more cheaply in Chicago than in Los Angeles, notwithstanding the lower outdoor temperatures in Chicago. The reason is that home owners in Chicago invest in much better insulation, more powerful and more efficient heating units, and so forth. *Given* these investments, it is cheaper to raise indoor temperatures there than in Los Angeles.

Plea bargaining occurs when prosecutors agree to lighter sentences in return for guilty pleas by defendants. Plea bargaining has been frequently criticized for permitting guilty criminals to escape with excessively light sentences, but Friedman shows in Chapter 19 that the system of plea bargaining indirectly may raise the punishments to defendants who bargain! Plea bargaining avoids costly trials for some defendants and thereby enables prosecutors to spend more of their limited budgets on trials of defendants without plea bargains. By spending more on each trial, the prosecutor raises the likelihood of getting a conviction with a stiffer sentence.

The crucial point is that these stiffer sentences also *raise* the sentences of defendants who plea bargain. Prosecutors can now refuse to plea bargain unless a defendant accepts a relatively stiff sentence because defendants who refuse to bargain can expect a stiffer sentence. This is a good example of the so-called "Prisoner's Dilemma," or of the conflict between individual and group incentives. By bargaining *alone,* defendants are forced to accept less favorable terms than they could extract by bargaining *together.*

Since radio and television programs are costly to produce but are "free" to viewers, each station must find indirect ways to cover the cost of producing programs. The most common way is to advertise products of companies that pay for commercials. A less common way, mainly used by "educational" radio and television, is to ask viewers for contributions. However, efforts to raise contributions encounter the same conflict between group and individual incentives found in plea bargaining. Viewers could get better programming by contributing together, but each one separately has an incentive to view without contributing.

Religious programming can provide proper incentives by claiming that contributions to support a religion or preacher improve the standing of the contributor with his God. Therefore, each viewer cannot free-ride by shifting the burden of support to others because he then fails in his duty to God, who is aware of the behavior of everyone. Friedman advances this argument to explain why religious preaching on radio appears to be more common than religious preaching through written media.

As a final example, consider tariffs, quotas, and other protection against imports. Almost 200 years ago, Alexander Hamilton argued that "infant" industries in the United States should be protected by tariffs so that the growth of these industries would not be stifled by competition from imports. Yet the evidence is clear that import protection is mainly given not to growing infant industries but to what Friedman calls "senile" industries, like steel and shoes (see Chapter 18). He shows how competition for political influence among special interest groups provides political support for tariffs and other trade restrictions that mainly benefit old declining industries. This is an excellent example of how the economic way of thinking is used to explain political behavior.

Economic theory is a powerful engine that permits a more rapid and deeper application of the economic way of thinking to behavior. Concepts like utility, cost, production functions, investment, equilibrium, and strategic behavior are useful in building this engine. Since the economic way of thinking is quite foreign to ordinary ways of thinking about behavior, command of economic theory requires dedication and systematic study to master its logic and structure. These are developed in the first 15 chapters of this text, although applications are also liberally sprinkled throughout these chapters. Friedman relies on geometry and verbal reasoning and generally avoids mathematics. Nevertheless, the discussion is sufficiently rigorous and also considers various weaknesses as well as strengths of economic theory.

I highly recommend this text to students and others with curiosity about our economic and social world. David Friedman obviously enjoys his work, for his enthusiasm is manifest on practically every page. You may find his enthusiasm contagious and also have fun as you use your new way of thinking to understand, and perhaps improve, the world around you.

Gary S. Becker
University Professor of Economics and Sociology
University of Chicago

Preface

INSTRUCTOR'S INTRODUCTION

This book is intended primarily for intermediate micro courses taken by students who have already had principles. It is, however, entirely self-contained; no previous knowledge of economics is assumed. I hope that it will also be used as an introductory text for especially well qualified students, such as honors undergraduates and students taking their first economics course in business or law school.

The main difference between this book and other intermediate price theory books is the emphasis in this book on economic intuition, on learning to think like an economist. A common complaint about students entering graduate school is that they are competent technicians with no understanding of economics. My objective is, while teaching the essential technical tools, to concentrate the student's attention on understanding what he is doing and why. There is no point in following a mathematical proof step by step if, at the end, you know that the conclusion has been proved but have no idea why it is true.

The emphasis on economic intuition is responsible for the somewhat unconventional organization of the book. The first two chapters are designed to show the student what economics is and why it is interesting and useful. The next six chapters introduce the traditional tools—indifference curves, utility functions, consumer surplus, and the like—and use them to analyze a very simple economy. Once the students clearly understand how that simple economy fits together, they are prepared to add, one by one, such complications as firms, monopoly, change, and uncertainty.

In trying to teach economic intuition, especially at the very beginning of the book and near the end, I make heavy use of unconventional applications of economics—to warfare, love, marriage, theft, and many other "uneconomic" issues. My objective is to present economics as economists see it—not a collection of facts about the economy but a powerful approach to understanding almost all human behavior.

Pedagogical Details

In organizing this book, I have <u>arranged the chapters by subject</u> matter rather than cutting the material into convenient 20-page chunks. While this is a convenient arrangement for both author and reader, it creates some difficulties for the instructor, especially if he has never taught the book before and so has no very clear idea of how long each chapter is going to take.

The problem has been dealt with in two ways. The chapters, especially the longer chapters, have extensive internal divisions, making it possible to assign Part 1 of a chapter for one lecture and Part 2 for the next. In addition, the *Instructor's Manual* contains an annotated table of contents and a number of suggested syllabi, designed for courses of varying length and emphasis.

The book will, I hope, be used by a considerable variety of students and teachers. To accommodate variation in the backgrounds of the students, I have included in many of the chapters optional sections at the end, containing somewhat more advanced material. Only in those sections do I assume a familiarity with calculus. Optional sections can be identified by a thin blue line running down the margin.

To accommodate variations in the taste of instructors (and the length of courses), I have included in the book more material than I expect anyone to actually teach in a one-quarter or one-semester course. While almost all of the early chapters are essential, many of the later ones are not. Especially in the applications section, instructors should feel free to teach those chapters that are most interesting to themselves or their students and omit the rest.

I hope instructors will also make use of the computer programs associated with the text and available from the publisher. They are designed to teach economic concepts that can be understood more easily in that form than in the more conventional form of text or lecture. Within the text, discussions which have associated programs are marked in the margins by a blue icon of a computer diskette. The programs are self-documenting.

STUDENTS' INTRODUCTION

Many students have been persuaded, by their academic experience in high school and college, that taking a course consists of memorizing a set of conclusions. Reading a textbook then becomes an exercise in creative highlighting, designed to extract from 500 pages of verbiage the 30 or 40 pages containing the answers to the questions that will appear on the final exam.

Such a collection of answers is about as easy to remember as a collection of random numbers, and not much more useful. Students who take such courses generally forget shortly after the final most of what they have learned.

This book is based on a different idea of how economics (and most other things) should be taught—the idea that since <u>answers are hard to remember and easy to look up</u>, one should instead concentrate on <u>learning ways of thinking</u>. The book has two central purposes. The first is to introduce you to what one of my competitors has called "the economic way of thinking." Economists—even economists with widely differing political views—have in common an approach to understanding human behavior that seems natural to them and very odd indeed to most non-economists. This book is designed to introduce you to that way of thinking, in the hope that many of you will find it interesting and at least some may find it irresistible. I am in that sense a missionary.

The second central purpose of the book is to teach you the analytical core of economics as it now exists. One of the features of economics which distinguishes it from most of the other social sciences is that it has such a core—a set of well-worked-out and closely related ideas which underlie almost everything done in the field. That core is price theory—the analysis of why things cost what they do and of how prices function to coordinate economic activity.

This book is organized into six sections. Section I is a general introduction to what economics is and why it is worth learning. Section II shows how the prices at which goods and services are sold and the quantities produced and consumed are determined in a simple economy. It is the most important part of the book. If you completely understand it you will know economics, in the same sense that a French six-year-old knows French. You may still be missing many details and complications, but you will understand the essential logic of how an economy works. Section III adds the most important of the complications omitted in the previous section, including firms, monopoly, change, and uncertainty. Section IV introduces the idea of economic efficiency and shows how it can be used to evaluate the outcome of different economic arrangements. Section V presents a number of real-world applications of the ideas of the previous sections, some of them conventional, most not. The final chapter of the book discusses why economics is worth knowing and what sorts of things economists do.

Many of the individual chapters have special sections at the end identified by a thin blue line running down the margin. These sections contain material which, while relevant to what is being discussed in the chapter, is not essential to understanding the rest of the text. In some cases, they assume that you already know things, such as calculus, which are not required for the rest of the text. When I use the textbook to teach economics (to MBA students at Tulane), these sections are optional; whether they are optional for you is, of course, up to your instructor. They are intended for students who find the material sufficiently interesting to want to pursue it further.

One thing I hope you will pay attention to as you go through the book is the importance of understanding things rather than merely remembering them. You should try to develop (if you have not already developed) a built-in alarm which goes off whenever I say "It follows that" and you see no particular reason *why* it follows or whenever I say that the answer is a particular point on a graph and you see no good reason why it should be that point instead of some other point. Whenever the alarm goes off, go back over the argument to see if you have missed something. If what I am saying still does not make sense, ask your instructor, or another student, or someone. It is all supposed to make sense, and if it does not, one of us is making a mistake. You may eventually conclude that the mistake is mine (or the typesetter's) but you should start out by assuming that it is yours.

① economic way of thinking
② analytical core of econ

Dedication

This book is dedicated to

A. S.,

D. R.,

A. M.,

and M.F.,

from whom I learned economics and to

Linda,

Ruben,

and all others who have made the value of teaching it greater than the cost.

I would also like to thank all the people who helped me write this book—the producers of the LNW computer on which it was written; Peter Ray of Anitak Software Products, author of my favorite LNW-compatible word processor (*Le Script*); Apple Computer, Inc., producer of the Macintosh computer used to draw the figures; and Bill Atkinson and Mark Cutter, authors of software that makes drawing figures fun. Special thanks are due to Wolfgang Mayer for assistance in finding and correcting defects on the manuscript above and beyond what an author may reasonably expect from a reviewer.

Contents

Economics for Pleasure and Profit

Chapter 1

What Is Economics?

Economics is often thought of as the answers to a particular set of questions: How do you prevent unemployment? Why are prices rising? How does the banking system work? Will the stock market go up? A slightly better view would be that economics is not the answers themselves but rather the method by which such answers are found. Neither definition adequately defines what is or is not economics, both because there are ways to answer such questions that do not involve economics (astrology, for example, might give answers to some of the questions given above, although not necessarily the right answers) and because economists use economics to answer many questions that are not usually considered "economic" (What determines how many children people have? How can crime be controlled? How will governments act?).

I prefer to define economics as a particular way of understanding behavior; what are commonly thought of as "economic questions" are simply questions for which this way of understanding behavior has proved particularly useful in the past:

Economics is that way of understanding behavior that starts from the assumption that people have objectives and tend to choose the correct way to achieve them.

The second half of the assumption, that people tend to find the correct way to achieve their objectives, is called *rationality*. This term is somewhat deceptive, since it suggests that people find the correct way to achieve their objectives by *rational analysis*—the process of using formal logic to deduce conclusions from assumptions, analyzing evidence, and so forth. No such assumption about how people find the correct means to achieve their ends is necessary.

One can imagine a variety of other explanations for "rational" behavior. To take a trivial example, most of our objectives require that we eat occasionally, so as not to die of hunger (exception—if my objective is to be fertilizer). Whether or not people have deduced this fact by logical analysis, those who do not choose to eat are not around to have their behavior analyzed by economists. More generally, evolution may produce people (and other animals) who behave "ration-

2

ally" without knowing why. The same result may be produced by a process of trial and error; if you walk to work every day, you may by experiment find the shortest route even if you do not know enough geometry to calculate it. Rationality in this sense does not necessarily require thought—or even life. In the final section of this chapter, I describe a simple device—a "matchbox computer"—which consists of nothing but matchboxes filled with black and white marbles and yet exhibits "rationality."

Half of the assumption in my definition of economics was "rationality"; the other half was that people have objectives. In order to do much with economics, one must strengthen this part of the assumption somewhat by assuming that people have *reasonably simple objectives*. The reason for this additional assumption is that if one has no idea at all about what people's objectives are, it is impossible to make any prediction about what people will do. Any behavior, however peculiar, can be explained by assuming that the behavior itself was the person's objective. (Why did I stand on my head on the table while holding a burning $1,000 bill between my toes? I *wanted* to stand on my head on the table while holding a burning $1,000 bill between my toes.)

To take a more plausible example of how a somewhat complicated objective can lead to apparently "irrational" behavior, consider someone who has a choice between two identical products at different prices. It seems that for almost any objective we can think of, he would prefer to buy the less expensive item. If his objective is to help the poor, he can give the money he saves to the poor. If his objective is to help his children, he can spend the money he saves on them. If his objective is to live a life of pleasure and luxury, he can spend the money on Caribbean cruises and caviar. Hence we are confident that he will choose the less expensive item.

But suppose you are taking a date to a movie. You know you are going to want a candy bar, which costs $.50 in the theater and $.25 in the Seven-Eleven grocery you pass on your way there. Do you stop at the store and buy a candy bar? Do you want your date to think you are a tightwad? You buy the candy bar at the theater, impressing your date (you hope) with the fact that you are the sort of person who does not have to worry about money.

One could get out of this problem by claiming that the two candy bars are not really identical; the candy bar at the theater includes an additional characteristic (impressing your date) which the other does not. But if you follow this line of argument, no two items are identical and the statement that you prefer the lower priced of two identical items has no content. I think it more reasonable to say that the two items are identical enough for our purposes but that in this particular case your objective is sufficiently odd that our prediction (based on the assumption of reasonably simple objectives) turns out to be wrong.

WHY ECONOMICS MIGHT WORK

Economics is based on the assumption that people have reasonably simple objectives and choose the correct means to achieve them. Both halves of the assumption are false; people sometimes have very complicated objectives and they sometimes make mistakes. Why then is the assumption useful?

Suppose we know someone's objective and also know that half the time that person correctly figures out how to achieve it and half the time he acts at random. Since there is generally only one right way of doing things (or perhaps a few) but very many wrong ways, the "rational" behavior can be predicted but the "irrational" behavior cannot. If we predict this person's behavior on the assumption that he is rational, we will be right half the time. If we assume he is irrational, we will almost never be right, since we still have to guess *which* irrational thing he will do. We are better off assuming he is rational and recognizing that we will sometimes be wrong. To put the argument more generally, the tendency to be rational is the consistent (and hence predictable) element in human behavior. The only alternative to assuming rationality (other than giving up and concluding that human behavior cannot be understood and predicted) would be a *theory* of irrational behavior—a theory that told us not only that someone would not always do the rational thing but also *which particular irrational thing* he would do. So far as I know, no satisfactory theory of that sort exists.

There are a number of reasons why the assumption of rationality may work better than one would at first think. One is that we are often concerned not with the behavior of a single individual but with the aggregate effect of the behavior of many people. Insofar as the *irrational* part of their behavior is random, its effects are likely to average out in the aggregate.

Suppose, for example, that the rational thing for people to do is to buy more hamburger the lower the price. Suppose people actually decide how much to buy by first making the rational decision then flipping a coin. If the coin comes up heads, they buy a pound more than they were planning to; if it comes up tails, they buy a pound less. The behavior of each individual will be rather unpredictable, but the total demand for hamburger will be almost exactly the same as without the coin flipping, since on average about half the coins will come up heads and half tails.

A second reason why the assumption works better than one might expect is that we are often dealing not with a random set of people but with people who have been selected for the particular role they are playing. Consider the heads of companies. If you selected people at random for the job, the assumption that they want to maximize the company's profits and know how to do so would not be a very plausible one. But people who do not want to maximize profits, or do not know how to, are unlikely to be chosen for the job; if they are, they are unlikely to keep it; if they do, their companies are likely to become increasingly unimportant in the economy, until eventually the companies go out of business. Hence the simple assumption of profit maximization plus rationality turns out to be a good way to predict how firms will behave.

A similar argument applies to the stock market. We may reasonably expect that the "average" investment is made by someone with an accurate idea of what companies are worth—even though the average American, and even the average investor, may be poorly informed about such things. Investors who consistently bet wrong on the stock market soon have very little to bet with. Investors who consistently bet right have an increasing amount of their own money to risk— and often other people's money as well. Hence the well-informed investors have an influence on the market out of proportion to their numbers as a fraction of the population. If we analyze the workings of the market on the assumption that all investors are well informed, we may come up with fairly accurate predictions in spite of the inaccuracy of the assumption. In this as in all other cases, the ultimate test of the method is whether its predictions turn out to describe reality correctly. Whether something is an "economic question" is not something we know in advance. It is something we discover by trying to use economics to answer it.

SOME SIMPLE EXAMPLES OF ECONOMIC THINKING

So far, I have talked of economics in the abstract; it is now time for some concrete examples. I have chosen ones involving issues not usually considered "economic" in order to show that economics is not a particular set of questions to be answered but a particular way of answering questions. I will begin with two very simple examples and then go on to some slightly more complicated ones.

You are laying out a college campus as a rectangular pattern of concrete sidewalks with grass between them. You know that one of the objectives of many people, including many students, is to get where they are going with as little effort as possible; you suspect most of them realize that a straight line is the shortest distance between two points. You would be well advised to take precautions against students cutting across the lawn. Possible precautions would be constructing fences or diagonal walkways, adding tough ground cover, or replacing the grass with cement and painting it green.

One point to note. It may be that everyone will be better off if no one cuts across the lawn (assuming the students like to look at green lawns without brown paths across them). Rationality is an assumption about individual behavior, not group behavior. The question of under what circumstances individual rationality does or does not lead to the best results for the group is one of the most interesting questions economics investigates. Even if a student is in favor of green grass, he may correctly argue that his decision to cut across provides more benefit (time saved) than cost (slight damage to the grass) *to him*. The fact that his decision provides additional costs, but no additional benefits, to other people who also dislike having the grass damaged is irrelevant unless making those other people happy happens to be one of his objectives. The total costs of his action may be greater than the total benefits; but as long as the costs to him are less than the benefits to him, he takes the action. This point will be taken up at much greater length in Chapter 17, when we discuss public goods and externalities.

A second simple example of economic thinking is Friedman's Law for Finding Men's Washrooms—"Men's rooms are adjacent, in one of the three dimensions, to ladies' rooms." One of the builder's objectives is to minimize construction costs; it costs more to build two small plumbing stacks (the set of pipes needed for a washroom) than one big one. So it is cheaper to put washrooms close to each other in order to get them on the same stack. That does not imply that two men's rooms on the same floor will be next to each other (although men's rooms on different floors are usually in the same position, hence adjacent vertically). While putting them next to each other reduces the cost, separating them gets them close to more users. But there is no advantage to having men's and ladies' rooms far apart, since they are used by different people; hence they are almost always put on the same stack. The law does not hold for buildings constructed on government contracts at cost plus 10 percent.

As a third example, consider someone making two decisions—what car to buy and what politician to vote for. In either case, the person can improve his decision (make it more likely that he acts in his own interest) by investing time and effort in studying the alternatives. In the case of the car, his decision determines with certainty which car he gets. In the case of the politician, his decision (whom to vote for) changes by one ten-millionth the probability that the candidate he votes for will win. If the candidate would get elected without his vote, he is wasting his time; if the candidate would lose even with his vote, he is also wasting his time. He will rationally choose to invest much more time in the decision of which car to buy—the payoff to him is enormously greater. We expect voting to be characterized by "rational ignorance"; it is rational to be ignorant when the information costs more than it is worth.

This is much less of a problem for a concentrated interest than for a dispersed one. If you, or your company, receives almost all of the benefit from some proposed law, you may well be willing to invest enough resources in supporting that law (and the politician who wrote it) to have a significant effect on the probability that the law will pass. If the cost of the law is spread among many people, no one of them will find it in his interest to discover what is being done to him and oppose it. Some of the implications of that will be seen in Chapter 18, where we explore the economics of politics.

The distinction between a concentrated interest and a dispersed interest is *not* the same as the distinction between rich and poor. The same person who is in a concentrated interest on one issue (the president of U.S. Steel with regard to a steel tariff) is in a dispersed interest in many others (that same president as an airline passenger with regard to government regulations that affect the cost of flying or as a driver with regard to oil import restrictions that affect the cost of gasoline). There is a crucial difference between how much someone *can* spend and how much it is in his interest to spend. A billionaire certainly could spend $10,000 deciding which car to buy—but if the difference among cars is not very great, it is not worth it for him to do so. Still less is it worth it to him to spend that much deciding to oppose a politician because of some small cost that the politician imposes on the billionaire, such as paying more for gasoline because of import restrictions.

In the course of this example, I have subtly changed my definition of rationality. Before, it meant making the right decision about what to do—voting for the right politician, for example. Now it means making the right decision about *how to decide* what to do—collecting information on whom to vote for only if the information is worth more than the cost of collecting it. For many purposes, the first definition is sufficient. The second is necessary where an essential part of the problem is the cost of getting and using information.

A final, and interesting, example is the problem of winning a battle. In modern warfare, many soldiers do not fire their guns in battle, and many of those who fire do not aim. This is not irrational behavior—on the contrary. In many situations, the soldier correctly believes that nothing he can do is very likely to determine who wins the battle; if he shoots, especially if he takes time to aim, he is more likely to get shot himself. The general and the soldier have two objectives in common. Both want their army to win. Both also want the soldier to survive the battle. But the relative importance of the second objective is much greater for the soldier than for the general. Hence the soldier rationally does not do what the general rationally wants him to.

Interestingly enough, studies of U.S. soldiers in World War II revealed that the soldier most likely to shoot was the member of a squad who was carrying the Browning Automatic Rifle. He was in a situation analogous to that of the concentrated interest; since his weapon was much more powerful than an ordinary rifle (an automatic rifle, like a machine gun, keeps firing as long as you keep the trigger pulled), his actions were much more likely to determine who won—and hence whether he got killed—than the actions of an ordinary rifleman.

The problem is not limited to modern war. The old form of the problem (which still exists in modern armies) is the decision whether to stand and fight or to run away. If you all stand, you will probably win the battle. If everyone else stands and you run, your side may still win the battle and you are less likely to get killed (unless your own side notices what you did and shoots you) than if you fought. If everyone runs, you lose the battle and are quite likely to be killed—but less likely the sooner you start running.

One traditional solution to this problem is to "burn your bridges behind you." You march your army over a bridge, line up on the far side of the river, and burn the bridge. You then point out to your soldiers that if your side loses the battle, you will all be killed, so there is no point in running away. Since your troops do not run and the enemy troops (hopefully) do, you win the battle. Of course, if you lose the battle, a lot more people get killed than if you had not burned the bridge.

We all learn in high school history how during the revolutionary war, the foolish British dressed their troops in bright scarlet uniforms and marched them around in neat geometric formations, providing easy targets for the heroic Americans. My own guess is that the British knew what they were doing. It was, after all, the same British army that less than 40 years later defeated the greatest general of the age at Waterloo. I suspect the mistake in the high school history texts is in not realizing that what the British were worried about was controlling their own troops. Neat geometric formations make it hard for a soldier to unobtrusively advance to the rear; bright uniforms make it hard for soldiers to hide after their army has been defeated, which lowers the benefit of running away.

The problem of the conflict of interest between the soldier as an individual and the soldiers as a group is nicely illustrated by the story of the battle of Clontarf, as given in *Njal Saga*. Clontarf was an eleventh century battle between an Irish army on one side and a mixed Irish-Viking army on the other side. The Vikings were led by Sigurd, the Jarl of the Orkney Islands. Sigurd had a battle flag, a raven banner, of which it was said that as long as the flag flew, his army would always go forward, but whoever carried the flag would die.

Sigurd's army was advancing; two men had been killed carrying the banner. The Jarl told a third man to take the banner; the third man refused. After trying unsuccessfully to find someone else to do it, Sigurd remarked, "It is fitting the beggar should bear the bag," tied the banner around his own waist, and led the army forward. He was killed and his army defeated. The story, whether true or not, illustrates nicely the essential conflict of interest in an army, and the way in which individually rational behavior can prevent victory. If one or two more men had been willing to carry the banner, Sigurd's army would have won the battle— but the banner carriers would not have survived to benefit from the victory.

And you thought economics was about stocks and bonds and the unemployment rate.

PUZZLE

You are a hero with a broken sword (Conan, Boromir, or your favorite Dungeons and Dragons character) being chased by a troop of bad guys (bandits, orcs, . . .). Fortunately you are on a horse and they are not. Unfortunately your horse is tired and they will eventually run you down. Fortunately you have a bow. Unfortunately you have only 10 arrows. Fortunately, being a hero, you never miss. Unfortunately there are 40 bad guys. The bad guys are strung out behind you.

Problem: Use economics to get away.

Note: You cannot talk to the bad guys. They are willing to take a reasonable chance of being killed in order to get you—after all, they know you are a hero and are still coming. They know approximately how many arrows you have.

SOME HARDER EXAMPLES— ECONOMIC EQUILIBRIA

So far, the examples of economic reasoning have not involved any real interaction among the rational acts of different people. Either we dealt with a single rational individual—the architect deciding where in the building to put washrooms—or with a group of rational individuals all doing more or less the same thing. Very little in economics is this simple. Before we start developing the framework of price theory in the next chapter, you may find it of interest to think through some more difficult examples of economic reasoning, examples in which the outcome is an equilibrium produced by the interaction of a number of rational individuals.

I will use economics to analyze two familiar situations (supermarket lines and crowded expressways), showing how economics can produce useful and nonobvious results and how the argument can be expanded to deal with successively higher levels of complexity. The logical patterns that appear in these examples reappear again and again in economic analysis. Once you clearly understand when and why supermarket lines are all the same length and lanes in the expressway equally fast, and why and under what circumstances they are not, you will have added to your mental furniture one of the most useful concepts in economics.

Supermarket Lines

You are standing in a supermarket at the far end of a row of checkout counters with your arms full of groceries. The line at your end blocks your view of the other lines; you know your line is long, but you do not know if the others are any shorter. Should you stagger from line to line looking for the shortest line, or should you get in the nearest one?

The first and simplest answer is that all the lines will be about the same length, so you should get into the one next to you; it is not worth the cost of searching for a shorter one. Why?

Consider any two adjacent lines in Figure 1-1, say Lines 4 and 5. Some shoppers will approach the checkout area not from one end, as you did, but from the aisle that lies between those two lines. Since those shoppers can easily see both lines, they will go to whichever one appears shorter. By doing so, they will lengthen that line and shorten the other; the process continues until both lines are the same length. The same argument holds for every other pair of adjacent lines—thus all lines will be the same length. So it is not worth it for you to make a costly search for the shortest line.

There are a number of implicit assumptions in this argument. When these assumptions are false, or only approximately true, the argument may break down. Suppose, for example, that you are at the far end of the row of checkout counters because that is where the ice cream freezer and the refrigerator with the cold beer are located. Many other customers also choose to get these things last and so enter the checkout area from that end. Even if *everyone* who comes in between Lines 1 and 2 goes to Line 2, there are not enough such people to make Line 2 as long as Line 1. So if everyone understands the argument of the above paragraph and acts accordingly, Line 1 will be longer than Line 2 (and probably much longer than the other lines), and the conclusion of the argument will be wrong.

Imagine that you program a computer with the argument of the previous paragraph and tell it that 10 people per minute are entering the checkout area at one end (where they can only see Line 1) and that 6 per minute are entering between Lines 1 and 2. You ask the computer to assign customers to lines in a way that equalizes the length of the two lines.

The computer replies that of the 6 customers coming in between the two lines, 8 go to Line 2 and -2 go to Line 1. Since 10 customers are going to Line 1 from the end, the total number going to Line 1 is 10 plus -2, which equals 8—the number going to Line 2. The computer, having solved the problem you gave it, sits there with a satisfied expression on its screen.

You then reprogram it, pointing out that fewer than zero customers cannot go anywhere. Mathematically speaking, you are asking the computer to solve the problem subject to the condition that a certain number (the number of customers coming in between the two lines and going to one of them) cannot be negative. The computer replies that in that case, the best it can do is to send all 6 customers to Line 2—leaving the lines still unequal.

This sort of situation is called a "corner solution" because it corresponds to the mathematical situation where the maximum of a function is not at the "top" of its graph but instead at a corner where the graph ends, as shown in Figure 1-2a. In such a situation, the normal conclusion (that all the lines must be the same length) no longer holds. The corresponding result in Figure 1-2a is that the graph is not horizontal at its maximum—as it would be if the maximum were at

Figure 1-1

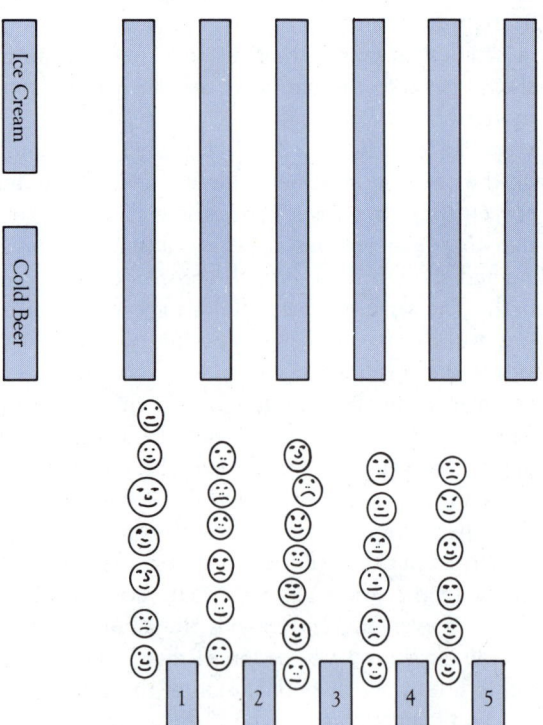

Supermarket, viewed from above.   Lines tend to be equal; Line 1 is a special case because many customers get ice cream and cold beer last.

an "interior solution," as it is in Figure 1-2b. In economics—especially mathematical economics—the usual role of corner solutions is to provide annoying exceptions to general theorems.

Are there other situations in which the conclusion—that all lines will be the same length—does not hold? Yes.

So far, I have assumed that for people coming in between two lines, it is costless to see which line is shorter. This is not always true. The relevant length, after all, is not in space but in time; you would rather enter a line with 10 customers each of whom has only a few items than a line with 8 customers with full carts. Estimating which line is shorter requires a certain amount of mental effort. If the system works so well that all lines are exactly the same length (in time), then it will never be worth that effort. Hence no one will make it; hence there will be nothing keeping the lines the same length. In equilibrium the "length" of lines must differ by just enough to repay (on average) the effort of figuring out which line is shorter. If it differed by more than that, everyone would look for the shortest line—making all lines the same length (assuming no corner solution). If it differed by less than that, nobody would.

It may have occurred to you that I am assuming all customers have the same ability to estimate how long a line will take. Suppose a few customers know that the checker on Line 3 is twice as fast as the others. The experts go to Line 3. Line 3 appears to be longer than the other lines (to non-experts, that is; allowing for the fast checker, the line is actually shorter, in time although not in length). Non-experts avoid Line 3 until it shrinks back to the same length as the others. The experts (and some lucky non-experts—the ones who are still in Line 3) get out twice as fast as everyone else.

Word spreads; the number of experts increases. As long as, with all the experts going through Line 3, Line 3 can still be as short (in appearance) as the

Figure 1-2

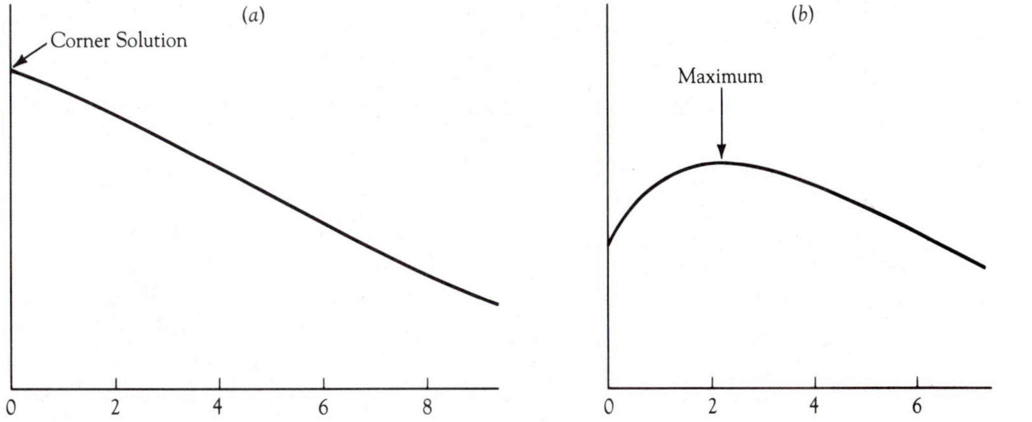

Two maxima—a corner solution (a) and an interior solution (b).   At the interior maximum, the slope of the curve is zero; at the corner maximum, it need not be.

other lines, the increasing number of experts does not reduce the payoff to being an expert. Every time one more expert enters the line (making it appear slightly longer than the others), one more non-expert decides not to enter it.

Eventually the number of experts becomes large enough to crowd out all the non-experts from that line. As the number of experts increases further, Line 3 begins to lengthen. It cannot be brought back to the same length as the other lines by the defection of non-experts (who mistakenly believe that it is longer in waiting time as well as length) because there are none of them going to it and the experts know better. Eventually the number of experts becomes so great that Line 3 is twice as long as the other lines and takes the same length of time as they do; the gain from being an expert has now vanished.

To put the same argument in more conventional economic language, rational behavior (in the sense of "making the right decision") requires information. If that information is itself costly, rational behavior consists of acquiring information ("paying information costs") only as long as the return from additional information is at least as great as the cost of getting it. If certain minimal information is required to equalize the time-length of lines, then the time-length of lines must be sufficiently unequal to just pay the cost of acquiring that information. That principle applies to both the cost of looking at lines to see which is shortest and the cost of studying checkers to learn which ones are faster. The initial argument was given in an approximation in which information was costless; such an approximation greatly simplifies many economic arguments but should be used with care.

There is at least one more hidden assumption in the argument as given. I have assumed that everyone in the grocery store wants to get out as quickly as possible. Suppose the grocery store ("Westwood Singles Market") is actually the local social center; people come to stand in long lines gossiping with and about their friends and trying to make new ones. Since they do not *want* to get out as fast as possible, they do not try to go to the shortest line, so the whole argument breaks down.

Rush Hour Blues

A similar analysis can be applied to lanes on the freeway. When you are driving on a moderately crowded highway, it always seems that some other lane is going faster than yours; the obvious strategy is to switch to the faster lane. If you actually try to follow such a strategy, however, you discover to your amazement that a few minutes after you switch lanes, the battered blue pickup which was behind you in the lane you switched out of is now in front of you.

To understand why it is so difficult to follow a successful strategy of lane changing, consider that by moving into a lane you slow it down. If there is a "faster" lane then people will move into it, equalizing its speed with that of the other lanes, just as people moving into a short line equalize its length. Hence a lane remains fast only as long as drivers do not realize it is.

Here again, a more sophisticated analysis would allow for the costs (in frayed nerves and dented fenders) of continual lane changes. On average, if everyone is rational, there must be a small gain in speed from changing lanes—if there were not, nobody would do it and the mechanism described above would not work. The payoff must equal the cost for the "marginal" lane changer—the least well qualified of those following the lane-changing strategy. If the payoff were less than that, he would not be a lane changer; if it were more, someone else would. In principle, if you knew how much a strategy of lane changing cost each driver (in dents and nerves—less for those with strong nerves and old cars) and how many lane changers it took to reduce the benefit from lane changing by any given amount, you could figure out who would be the marginal lane changer and how much the gain from lane changing would be. By the end of the course, you should see how to do this. If you see it now, you are already an economist—whether or not you have studied economics.

Even More Important Applications To Think About

Doctors make a lot of money. Doctors also spend many years as medical students and interns. The two facts are not unrelated. Different wages in different professions are set by a process similar to that described above. If one profession is, on net, more attractive than another (taking account of wages, risks, costs of learning the profession, etc.), people go into the more attractive profession and by so doing drive down the wages. All professions are in some sense equally attractive—to the marginal person. Hence, in deciding what profession you want to enter, it is not enough to ask what profession pays the highest wage. Not only are there other factors, there is also reason to expect that the other factors will be worst where the wage is best. What you should ask instead is what profession you are particularly suited for in comparison to other people making similar choices. This is like deciding whether to follow a lane-switching strategy by considering how old your car is compared to others, or deciding whether to look for a shorter line in the grocery store according to how much you are carrying.

A similar argument applies to the stock market. It is often said that if a company is doing very well, you should buy its stock. But if everyone else knows that the company is doing well, then the price of its stock already reflects that information. If buying it were really such a good deal, who would sell? The company you should buy stock in is one which you know is doing better than most other investors think it is—even if in some absolute sense it is not doing very well.

A friend of mine has been investing successfully for several years by following almost the opposite of the conventional wisdom. He looks for companies that are doing very badly and calculates how much their assets would be worth if they went out of business. Occasionally he finds one whose assets are worth more than their stock. He buys stock in such companies, figuring that if they do well their stock will go up and if they do badly they will go out of business, sell off their assets—and the stock will again go up.

If all of this is obvious to you the first time you read it (or even the second), then in your choice of careers you should give serious consideration to becoming an economist.

NEGATIVE FEEDBACK

Several of the situations described in this chapter involved a principle called *negative feedback*. A familiar example of negative feedback is driving a car. There is some position of the steering wheel which makes the car go in the direction you want. Cars could be designed with a mark on the steering wheel for "straight ahead," another mark for "15° to the right," and so on. One could imagine driving such a car with one's eyes on the steering wheel, glancing at the road only to look for curves and stoplights. One can also imagine the consequence if the steering wheel were just a little bit out of alignment—an error of 1° would put you off the road in less than a quarter of a mile.

Actual cars have unmarked steering wheels and depend on negative feedback to stay on the road. If the car is going to the right of where you want it, you turn the wheel a little to the left; if it is going to the left of where you want, you turn it a little to the right. This is called feedback because an error in what direction you are going "feeds back" into the mechanism that controls the direction you are going (through you to the steering wheel). It is negative feedback because an error in one direction (right) causes a correction in the other direction (left). An example of positive feedback is the shriek when the amplifier attached to a microphone is turned up too high. A small noise comes into the mike, is amplified by the amplifier, comes out of the speaker, and feeds back into the mike. If the amplification is high enough, the noise is louder each time around, resulting in the familiar shriek.

In the supermarket line example, the lines are kept at about the same length by negative feedback—if a line gets too long people stop going to it, which makes the line get shorter. Similarly, when a lane on the expressway speeds up, cars move into it—slowing it down. In each case, what we are mostly interested in are not the details of the feedback process but rather the nature of the stable equilibrium—the situation such that deviations from it cause correcting feedback.

RATIONALITY WITHOUT MIND

In defending the assumption of rationality, I pointed out that it is not the same as the assumption that people reason logically. Logical reasoning is not the only, or even the most common, way of getting a correct answer. In this appendix, I will give two extreme examples of this—cases in which we observe rationality in something that cannot reason, since it has no mind to reason with. In the first case, I will show how a mindless object—a collection of matchboxes filled with marbles—can learn to play a game rationally. In the second, I will show how the rational pursuit of objectives by genes—mindless chains of atoms inside your cells—explains a striking fact about the real world, something so fundamental that it never occurred to you to find it surprising.

The Matchbox Computer

Consider some simple game in which two players take turns moving and in which at each stage there are only two possible moves. Diagram the game as a set of branching lines, as shown on Figure 1-3; each fork represents a decision. Each

Figure 1-3

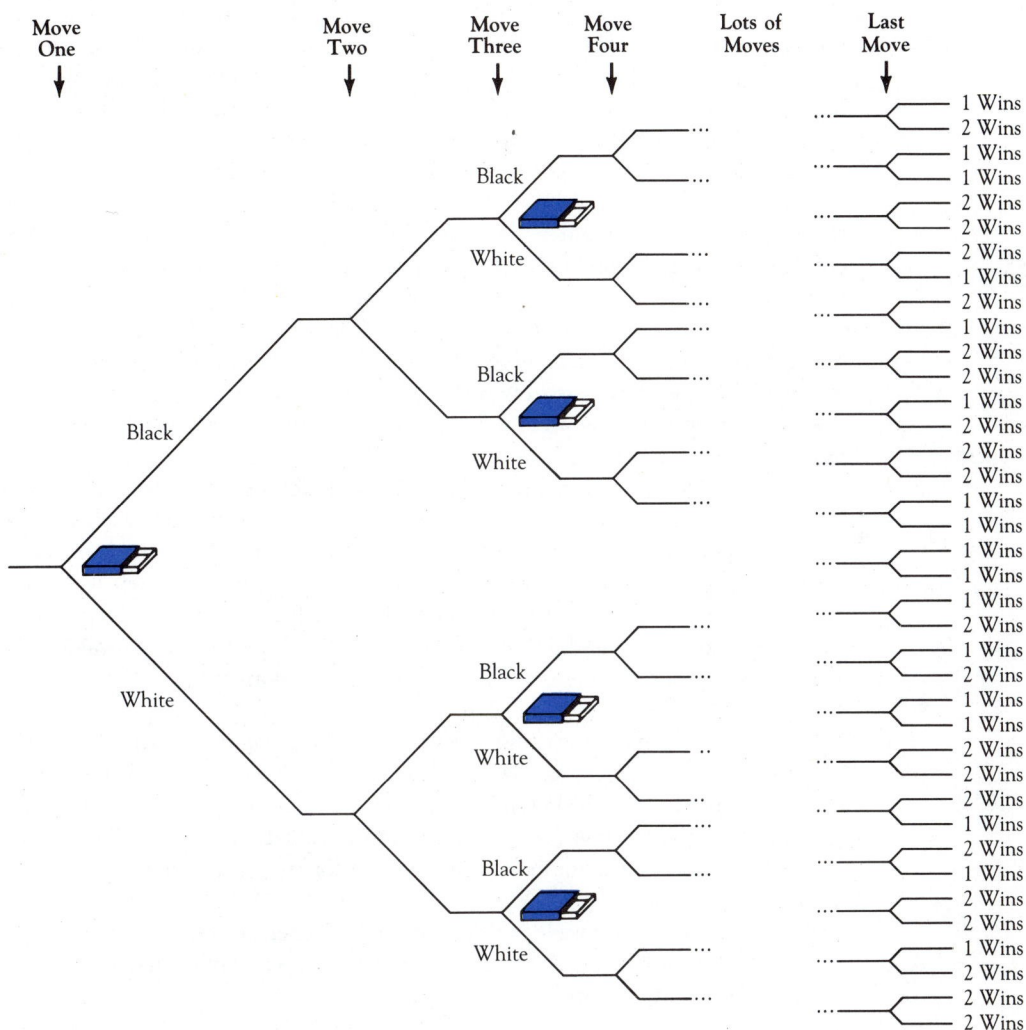

Move One		Move Two	Move Three	Move Four	Lots of Moves	Last Move	

Diagram of a two-person game and a matchbox computer to play it. The moves of Player 1 are determined by drawing marbles from matchboxes. The computer "learns" because the number of black and white marbles in each matchbox changes according to whether each move ultimately led to a win or a loss for Player 1.

series of decisions ultimately leads to one player or the other winning. Instead of describing the rules of a particular game, the figure simply shows the outcomes—who wins as the result of any series of moves.

At each fork, label one of the two possible moves "black" and the other "white." To build a "matchbox computer" that will replace the first player, procure a number of matchboxes equal to the number of different situations the first player can find himself in during the course of the game (i.e., the number of forks at which it is his move). This is much greater than the number of moves, since at the second move, there are two possible forks the second player could be at (according to which first move was made); at the third move, 4 that the first player could be at (according to what the first two moves were); at the fourth move, 8 possible situations for the second player, etc. Put 5 white marbles and 5 black marbles in each matchbox, and put each matchbox down on the diagram of the game, sitting at one of the first player's decision forks.

Now play the game, using a human as second player and the matchbox computer as first player. Begin by drawing a marble at random from the matchbox corresponding to the first move. If it is black, first player makes the "black" move; if it is white, the "white move"; on the diagram, the black move is the upper branch of the fork and the white move is the lower. Leave the marble you have drawn sitting beside the matchbox. Second player makes his move. For first player's second move, draw a marble from the matchbox at the fork corresponding to the situation you are now in (i.e., defined by the first two moves). Continue the procedure until one side has won the game.

If Player 2 (the human) won, take all the marbles sitting beside the matchboxes (corresponding to "decisions" the computer made) and throw them away. Each of the decisions the matchbox computer made, decisions which ultimately led it to lose, is now somewhat less likely (4 marbles of that color left in the box, 5 of the other) next game. On the other hand, if Player 1 (the computer) wins, you take each of the marbles which was drawn, add another of the same color, and put both back in the matchbox. Now the decision, which led to a win, is *more* likely than before (6 marbles to 5).

As you play game after game, decisions by the computer which lead to wins become more likely, decisions which lead to losses become less likely; thus the computer plays better and better. Of course, if the game is at all complicated, it may take a very long time (and require a starting situation with a million marbles of each color in each matchbox, instead of 5) for the computer to learn to play well.

The point of this example is that "rationality" does not mean a particular way of thinking but rather the ability to get the right answer, and it may be the result of many things other than "rational thinking."

Economics and Evolution

There is a close historical connection between economics and evolution. Both of the discoverers of the theory of evolution (Darwin and Wallace) said they got the idea from Thomas Malthus, an economist who was also one of the originators of the so-called Ricardian Theory of Rent (named after David Ricardo, who did not invent it), one of the basic building blocks of modern economics.

There is also a close similarity in the logical structure of the two fields. The economist expects people to choose correctly how to achieve their objectives; he does not concern himself very much with the psychological question of how they do so. The biologist expects *genes*—the fundamental units of heredity which control the construction of our bodies—to construct animals whose structure and behavior are such as to maximize their reproductive success (roughly speaking, the number of their descendants), since the animals which presently exist are descended from those animals which were reproductively successful in the past and carry the genes which made them successful. He does not concern himself very much with the detailed biochemical mechanisms by which the genes control the organism. Many of the same patterns appear in both economics and evolutionary biology; the conflict between individual interest and group interest which I mentioned briefly in Chapter 1 reappears in the conflict between the interest of the gene and the interest of the species.

A nice example is Sir R. A. Fisher's explanation of observed sex ratios. In many species, including ours, male and female offspring are produced in roughly equal numbers. There is no obvious reason why this is in the interest of the species; one male suffices to fertilize many females. Yet the sex ratio remains about 1:1, even in some species in which only a small fraction of the males succeed in reproducing. Why?

Fisher's answer is as follows. Imagine that two thirds of offspring are female, as shown in Figure 1-4. Consider three generations. Each individual in the third generation has both a father and a mother, so if there are twice as many females as males in the second generation, the average male must have twice as many children as the average female. This means that an individual in the first generation who produces a son will, on average, have twice as many grandchildren as one who produces a daughter. Individual A on Figure 1-4, for example, has 6 children, while Individual B only has 3. Hence A's parents got twice as great a return in grandchildren for producing A as B's parents did for producing B.

If there are more women than men in the population, couples who produce sons have more descendants than those that produce daughters. Since couples who produce sons have more descendants, more of the population is descended from them and has their genes—including the gene for having sons. Genes for producing male offspring increase in the population.

The initial situation, in which two thirds of the population in each generation was female, is unstable. As long as more than half of the children are female, genes for having male children spread faster than genes for having female children, so the percentage of female children falls. Similarly, if more than half the children were male, genes for having female children would have the advantage and spread. Either way, the situation must swing back towards an even sex ratio.

In making this argument, I implicitly assumed equal cost for producing male and female offspring. In a species with substantial sexual dimorphism (i.e., male and female babies of different size), the argument implies that the total weight of female offspring (weight per offspring times number of offspring) will be about the same as that for male offspring. One could add further complications by considering differences in the costs of raising male and female offspring to maturity. Yet even the simple argument is strikingly successful in explaining one of the observed regularities of the world around us by the "rational" behavior of microscopic entities. Genes cannot think—yet in this case and many others, they behave *as if* they had carefully calculated how to maximize their own survival in future generations.

Figure 1-4

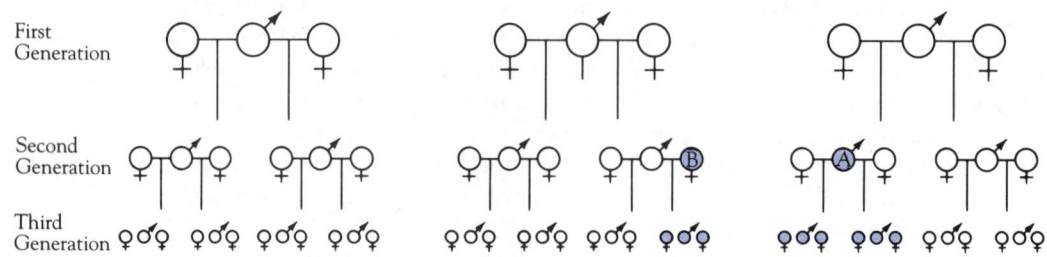

First Generation
Second Generation
Third Generation

Three generations of a population with a male:female ratio of 1:2. Members of the first generation who have a son produce twice as many grandchildren as those who have a daughter, so genes for having sons increase in the population, swinging the sex ratio back toward 1:1.

PROBLEMS

1. In defending the rationality assumption, I argued that while people sometimes make mistakes, their correct decisions are predictable and their mistakes are not. Can you think of any alternative approaches to understanding human behavior that claim to predict the mistakes? Discuss.

2. Give examples (other than buying candy for your date—the example discussed in the text) of apparently "irrational" behavior which consists of choosing the correct means to achieve an odd or complicated end.

3. Friedman's Law for Finding Men's Washrooms could be described as *fossilized rationality*—whether the architect lives or dies, his rationality remains "set in concrete" in the building he designed.

   a. Can you think of other examples? Discuss.

   b. Can you describe any cases where instead of deducing the shape of something from the rationality of its maker, we deduce the rationality of its maker from its shape? Discuss.

4. What devices (other than those discussed in the text) are used by armies, ancient and modern, to prevent soldiers from concluding that it is in their interest to run away, not aim, or in some other way act against the interest of the army of which they are a part?

5. The problem I have discussed exists not only in your army but in the enemy's army as well. Discuss ways in which a general might take advantage of that fact, giving real-world examples if possible.

6. In a recent conversation with one of our deans, I commented that I was rather absent-minded—I had missed two or three faculty meetings that year—and wished I could get him to make a point of reminding me when I was supposed to be somewhere. He replied that he had already solved that problem, so far as the (luncheon) meetings he was responsible for. He made

sure I would not forget them by always arranging to have a scrumptious chocolate dessert.

a. Is this an "economic solution" to the problem of getting me to remember things? Discuss.

b. In what sense does or does not the success of this method indicate that I "choose" to forget to go to meetings? Discuss.

The following problems refer to the optional section:

7. The analyses of supermarket lines, freeway lanes, and the stock market all had the same form. In each case, the argument could be summarized as "the outcome has a particular pattern because if it did not, it would be in the interest of people to change their behavior in a way that would push the outcome closer to fitting the pattern." Such a situation is called a *stable equilibrium*. Can you think of any examples not discussed in the text?

8. Analyze express lanes in supermarkets. Is the express lane always faster? If not, when is it and when is it not?

9. In the supermarket example, I started by assuming that you had your arms full of groceries. Why? How does that assumption simplify the argument?

10. In discussing supermarket lines, I mentioned an "impossible" solution in which -2 people entered a line. Can you suggest a sensible interpretation of that—a way in which 6 people can be added to two lines, with 8 of them going to 1 and -2 to the other? Explain.

11. Describe some "corner solutions" on the freeway.

12. The friend whose investment strategy I described is a very talented accountant. When I met him, he was in his early twenties and was making a good income *teaching* accounting to people who wanted to pass the CPA exam. Does this have anything to do with his investment strategy?

13. Is there any reason why my accountant friend should prefer that this book, or at least this chapter, not be published?

14. Give some examples of negative and positive feedback in your own experience.

15. Certain professions are very attractive to their members and very badly paid. Consider the stereotype of the starving artist—or a friend of mine who supports herself as a part-time secretary while trying to make a living as a dancer and actress. Is the association between job attractiveness and low pay accidental, or is there a logical connection? Discuss.

16. Suppose that in Floritania, the total cost of bringing up a son is three times the cost of bringing up a daughter, since Floritanians do not believe in educating women. Floritanians simply love grandchildren and want to have as many as possible. Due to a combination of modern science and ancient witchcraft, Floritanian parents can control the gender of their offspring. What is the male/female ratio in the Floritanian population?

17. The principal foods of the Floritanians are green eggs and ham. It costs exactly twice as much to produce a pound of green eggs as a pound of ham. The more green eggs that are produced, the lower the price they sell for, and similarly with ham.

a. You are producing both green eggs and ham. Green eggs sell for $3/pound; so does ham. How could you increase your revenue without changing your production cost?

b. What will be the result on the prices of green eggs and ham?

c. If everyone acts rationally, what can you say about the eventual prices of green eggs and ham in Floritania.

FOR FURTHER READING

For a good introduction to the economics of genes—*sociobiology*—I recommend Richard Dawkins's *The Selfish Gene* (New York: Oxford University Press, 1976).

A more extensive discussion of the economics of warfare can be found in my essay, "The Economics of War," in J. E. Pournelle (ed.), *Blood and Iron* (New York: Tom Doherty Associates, 1984).

For a very different application of economic analysis to warfare, I highly recommend Donald W. Engels's *Alexander the Great and the Logistics of the Macedonian Army* (Berkeley: University of California Press, 1978). The author analyzes Alexander's campaigns while omitting all of the battles. His central interest is in the problem of preventing a large army from dying of hunger or thirst and the way in which that problem determined much of Alexander's strategy. Consider, as a very simple example, the fact that you cannot draw water from a well, or 5 wells, or 20 wells, fast enough to keep an army of 100,000 people from dying of thirst.

The relationship between individual rationality and group behavior is analyzed in Thomas Schelling's *Micromotives and Macrobehavior* (New York: W. W. Norton and Co., 1978).

Chapter 2

How Economists Think

This chapter consists of three parts. The first describes and defends some of the fundamental assumptions and definitions used in economics. The second attempts to demonstrate the importance of price theory, in large part by showing, for a number of different cases, that the "obvious" analysis of the situation is wrong and that the mistake comes from not having a consistent theory of how prices are determined. The third part briefly describes how, in the next few chapters, we are going to create such a theory.

PART 1 · ASSUMPTIONS AND DEFINITIONS

There are a number of features of the economic way of analyzing human behavior that many people find odd or even disturbing. One such feature is the assumption that the different things a person values can all be measured on a single scale, so that even if one thing is much more valuable than another, a sufficiently small amount of the more valuable good is equivalent to some amount of the less valuable. A car, for example, is probably worth much more to you than a bicycle, but a sufficiently small "amount of car" (not a bumper or a headlight but rather the use of a car one day a month, or one chance in a hundred of getting a car) has the same value to you as a whole bicycle—given the choice, you would not care which of them you got.

This sounds plausible enough when we are talking about cars and bicycles, but what about really important things? Does it make sense to say that a human life—as embodied in access to a kidney dialysis machine or the chance to have an essential heart operation—is to be weighed in the same scale as the pleasure of eating a candy bar or watching a television program?

Strange as it may seem, the answer is yes. If we observe how people behave with regard to their own lives, we find that they are willing to make trade-offs between life and quite minor values. One obvious example is someone who smokes even though he believes that smoking reduces life expectancy. Another is the overweight person who is willing to accept an increased chance of a heart attack in exchange for some number of chocolate sundaes.

Perhaps you neither smoke nor overeat; is it still the case that you trade off life against other values? Yes. Every time you cross the street to go to a movie theater or speak to a friend, you are (slightly) increasing your chance of being run over. Every time you spend part of your limited income on something that has no effect on your life expectancy (instead of using it for a medical checkup or to add safety equipment to your car) and every time you choose what to eat on any basis other than what food comes closest to the ideal diet a nutritionist would prescribe, you are choosing to give up, in a probabilistic sense, a little life in exchange for something else.

Those who deny that this is how we do and should behave assume implicitly that there is such a thing as "enough" medical care, that people should (and wise people do) first buy "enough" medical care and then devote the rest of their resources to other and (infinitely) less valuable goals. The economist replies that since additional medical care (or caution in crossing streets or nutrition or some other good that increases life expectancy) produces benefits well past the point at which one's entire income is spent on it, the concept of "enough" as some absolute amount determined by medical science is meaningless. The proper economic concept of "enough" medical care is that amount of medical care such that if you spent less on medical care and more on other things, the additional goods you got would be worth less to you than the reduction in your health, while if you spent more on medical care and less on other things, the increase in your health would be worth less to you than the reduction in your consumption. "Too much" medical care is that amount where you would be better off (as judged by your own preferences) buying less medical care and spending the money on something else.

I have given the definition of "enough" in terms of money only because the choice you face with regard to the goods and services you buy is whether to give up a dollar's worth of one in exchange for getting another dollar's worth of something else. But market goods and services are only a special case of the general problem of choice. You are buying "enough" safety when the pleasure you get from running across the street to talk to a friend just balances the value to you of the resulting increase in the chance of getting run over.

So far, I have considered the trade-off between small "amounts" of life and ordinary "amounts" of other goods. Perhaps it has occurred to you that we would reach a different conclusion if we considered trading a large amount of life for a (very) large amount of some other good. My argument seems to imply that there should be some price for which you would be willing to let someone kill you!

There is a good reason why most people would be unwilling to sell their entire life for any amount of money or other goods—they would have no way of collecting. Once they are dead, they cannot spend the money. This is evidence not that life is infinitely valuable but that money has no value to a corpse.

Suppose, however, we offer someone a large sum of money in exchange for his agreeing to be killed in a week. It still seems likely he would refuse. The reason (seen from the economist's standpoint) is that as we increase the amount we consume in a given length of time, the value to us of additional amounts decreases. I am very fond of Baskin-Robbins ice cream cones, but if I were consuming them at a rate of a hundred a week, an additional cone would be worth very little to me. I weigh life and the pleasure of eating ice cream on the same scale, yet there is no quantity of ice cream which I can consume in a week that is worth as much to me as the rest of my life. That is why, when I initially defined the idea that everything can be measured on a single scale, I put the definition in terms of a comparison between the value of a given amount of the less valuable good and a sufficiently small amount of the more valuable, instead of comparing a given amount of the more valuable to a sufficiently large amount of the less valuable.

Wants or Needs?

The economist's assumption that all (valued) goods are in this sense comparable shows itself in his use of the term *wants* rather than *needs*. The word *needs* suggests things that are infinitely valuable. You "need" a certain amount of food, clothing, medical care, or whatever. How much you "need" could presumably be determined by the appropriate expert and has nothing to do with what such things cost or what your particular values are. This is the typical attitude of the non-economist, and it is why the economist's way of looking at things often seems unrealistic and even ugly. The economist replies that how much of each of these things you will, and should, choose to have depends on how much you value them, how much you value other things you must give up to get them, and how much of such other things you must give up to get a given amount of clothing, medical care, or whatever. Your choices depend, in other words, on your tastes and on the costs to you of the alternative things that you desire.

One reply the non-economist (perhaps I mean the anti-economist) might make is that we ought to have enough of everything. If you have enough movies and enough ice cream cones and enough of everything else you desire, you no longer have any reason to choose less medical care or nutrition in order to get more of something else (although combining good nutrition with enough ice cream cones could be a problem for some of us). Perhaps our objective should be a society where everybody has enough. Perhaps, it is sometimes argued, the marvels of modern technology, combined with the right economic system, could bring such a society within our reach, making the problems of choosing among different values obsolete.

This particular argument was more popular last decade than this. Currently the fashion has changed and we are being told that limitations in natural resources (and in the ability of the environment to absorb our wastes) impose stringent limitations on how much of everything we can have. Yet even if that is not true, even if (as I suspect) resource limits are no more binding now than in the past, "enough of everything" is still not a reasonable goal. Why?

It is often assumed that if we could only produce somewhat more than we do, we would have everything we want. In order to consume still more, we would have to each drive three cars and eat six meals a day. This argument confuses increasing the value of what you consume with increasing the amount you consume. A modern stereo is no bigger and consumes no more power than its predecessor of thirty years ago, yet moving from one to the other represented an increase in "consumption." I have no use for three cars, but I would like a car three times as good as the one I now have. There are many ways in which my life could be improved if I consumed things that are more costly to create but no larger than those I now have. My desire for pounds of food is already satiated and my desire for number of cars could be satiated with a moderate increase in my income, but my desire for quality of food or quality of car would remain even at a much higher income, and my desire for more of *something* would remain unsatiated as long as I remained alive and conscious under any circumstances I can imagine.

From both introspection and conversation, I have formulated a general law on this subject. Everyone feels that there is a level of income above which all consumption is frivolous. For everyone, that level is about twice his own. An Indian peasant living on $500/year believes that if only he had $1,000/year, he would have everything he could want with a little left over. An American physician living on $50,000/year (after taxes) doubts that anyone can really have any use for more than $100,000/year.

Both the peasant and the physician are wrong, but both opinions are the result of rational behavior by those who hold them. If you are living on $500/year, the consumption decisions you make, the goods you consider buying, are those appropriate to such an income. Heaven would be a place where you could "afford" all of the things which you have considered buying and decided not to. There is little point to your wasting your time learning or thinking about consumption goods that cost ten times your yearly income, so the possession of such goods is not part of your picture of the good life. The same is true if you are living on $50,000/year.

Value

So far I have discussed, and tried to defend, two of the assumptions that go into economics: *comparability*, the assumption that the different things we value are comparable, and *non-satiation*, the assumption that in any plausible society, present or future, we cannot all have everything we want and must give up some things we desire in order to have others. In talking about value, I have also implicitly introduced an important definition—that *value* (of things) means how much we value them and that how much we value them is properly estimated not by our words but by our actions. In discussing the trade-off between the value of life and the value of the pleasure of smoking, my evidence that the two are comparable was that people choose to smoke, even though they believe doing so lowers their life expectancy. This definition is called *the principle of revealed preference*—meaning that your preferences are revealed by your actions.

The first part of the definition of value embodied in the principle of revealed preference might be questioned by those who prefer to base value on some external criterion—what we should want or what is good for us. The second might be questioned by those who believe that their values are not fairly reflected in their actions, that they value health and life but just "cannot resist" one more cigarette. But economics is supposed to describe how people act, and we are therefore concerned with value as it relates to action. A smoker's statement that he puts infinite value on his own life may help to explain what he believes, but it is less useful for understanding what he will do than is the kind of value expressed when he takes a cigarette out and lights it.

Even if revealed preference is a useful concept for our purpose, should we call what it reveals *value*? Does not the word carry with it an implication of something beyond mere individual preference? That is a philosophical question that goes beyond the subject of this book. If using the word *value* to refer equally to a crust of bread in the hands of a starving man and a syringe of heroin in the hands of an addict makes you uncomfortable, then substitute the term *economic value* instead. But remember that the addition of "economic" does not mean "having monetary value," "being material," "capable of producing profit for someone," or anything similar; economic value is simply value to a person as measured by him and observed in his actions.

Economics Joke #1: *Two economists walked past a Porsche showroom. One of them pointed at a shiny car in the window and said, "I want that." "Obviously not," the other replied.*

Choice or Necessity?

The difference between the approaches to human behavior taken by economists and by non-economists comes in part from the economist's assumptions of comparability and insatiability, in part from the definition of value in terms of revealed preference, and in part from the fundamental assumption of rationality that I made and defended in the previous chapter. One form in which the difference often appears is the economist's insistence that virtually all human behavior should be described in terms of choices. To many non-economists, this seems deceptive. What, after all, is the point of saying that you "choose" not to buy something you cannot afford?

When you say that you cannot afford something, you usually mean only that there are other things you would rather spend the money on. Most of you would say that you could not afford a $1,000 shirt. Yet most of you could save up $1,000 in a year if it were sufficiently important—important enough that you were willing to spend only a dollar a day on food (roughly the cost of the least expensive full-nutrition diet—powdered milk, soy beans, and the like), share a one-room apartment with two roommates, and buy your clothing from Goodwill.

Consider an even more extreme case, in which you have assets of only a few hundred dollars and there is something enormously valuable to you that costs $100,000 and will only be available for the next month. In a month, you surely cannot earn that much money. It seems reasonable, in this case at least, to say that you cannot afford it. Yet even here, there is a legitimate sense in which what you really mean is that you do not want it.

Suppose the object were so valuable that getting it made your life wonderful forever after and failing to get it meant instant death. Assuming you could not earn, borrow, or steal $100,000, the sensible thing to do would be to get as much money as possible, go to Reno or Las Vegas, work out a series of bets which would maximize your chance of converting what you had into exactly $100,000, and make them. If you are not prepared to do that, then the reason you do not buy the object is not that you cannot afford its $100,000 price. It is that you do not want it—enough.

In part, the claim that people do not really have any choice confuses the lack of alternatives with the lack of attractive or desirable ones. Having chosen the best alternative, you may say that you had little choice; in a sense you are correct. There may be only one *best* alternative.

One example of this confusion that I find particularly disturbing is the argument that the poor should be "given" essential services by government even if (as is often the case) they end up having to pay for the services themselves through increased taxes. Poor people, it is said, do not really "choose" not to go to doctors—they simply cannot afford to. Therefore a benevolent government should take money from the poor and use it to provide the medical services they "need."

If this argument seems convincing, try translating it into the language of choice. Poor people choose not to go to doctors because to do so they would have to give up things still more important to them—food, perhaps, or heat. It may sound heartless to say that someone chooses not to go to a doctor when he can do so only at the cost of starving to death, but putting it that way at least reminds us that if you "help" him by forcing him to spend *his* money on doctors, you are compelling him to make a choice—starvation—which he rejected because it was even worse than the alternative—no medical care—that he chose.

The question of how much choice individuals really have reappears on a larger scale in discussions of how flexible the economy as a whole is—to what extent it can vary the amount of the different resources it uses. Our tendency is to look at the way things are now being done and assume that that way is the only possible one. But the way things are now done is the solution to a particular problem— producing goods as cheaply as possible given the present cost of various inputs. If some input—unskilled labor, say, or energy or some raw material—were much more or less expensive, the optimal way of producing would change.

A familiar example is the consumption of gasoline. If you suggest that someone should use less gasoline, his initial response is that using less gasoline means not taking trips. Indeed, when oil prices shot up a decade ago, many people argued that Americans would continue to use as much gasoline as before at virtually any price, unless the government forced them to do otherwise.

There are many ways to save gasoline. Car pooling and driving more slowly are obvious ones. Buying lighter cars is less obvious. Workers choosing to live closer to their jobs or employers choosing to locate factories nearer to their workers are still less obvious. Petroleum is used to produce both gasoline and heating oil; the refiners can, to a considerable degree, control how much of each is produced. One way of "saving" gasoline is to use less heating oil and make a larger fraction of the petroleum into gasoline instead. Insulation, smaller houses, and moving south are all ways of "saving gasoline."

PART 2 · PRICE THEORY— WHY IT MATTERS

This book has two purposes—to teach you to think like an economist and to teach you the set of ideas that lie at the core of economic theory as it now exists. That set of ideas is *price theory*—the explanation of how relative prices are determined and how prices function to coordinate economic activity.

There are at least two reasons to want to understand price theory (aside from passing this course). The first is to make some sense out of the world you live in. You are in the middle of a very highly organized system with nobody organizing it. The items you use and see, even very simple objects such as a pen or pencil, were each produced by the coordinated activity of millions of people. Someone had to cut down the tree to make the pencil. Someone had to season the wood and cut it to shape. Someone had to make the tools to cut down the trees and the tools to make the tools and the fuel for the tools and the refineries to make the fuel. While small parts of this immense enterprise are under centralized control (one firm organizes the cutting and seasoning of the wood, another actually assembles the pencil), nobody coordinates the overall enterprise.

Someone who visited China told me about a conversation with an official in the ministry of materials supply. The official was planning to visit the U.S. in order to see how things were done there. He wanted, naturally enough, to meet and speak with his opposite number—whoever was in charge of seeing that U.S. producers got the materials they needed in order to produce. He had difficulty understanding the answer—that no such person exists.

A market economy is coordinated through the price system. Costs of production—ultimately, the cost to a worker of working instead of taking a vacation or of working at one job instead of at another, or the cost of using land or some other resource for one purpose and so being unable to use it for another—are reflected in the prices for which goods are sold. The value of goods to those who ultimately consume them is reflected in the prices purchasers are willing to pay. If a good is worth more to a consumer than it costs to produce, it gets produced; if not, it does not.

If new uses for copper increase demand, that bids up the price, so existing users find it in their interest to use less. If supply decreases—a mine runs out or a harvest fails—the same thing happens. Prices provide an intricate system of signals and incentives to coordinate the activities of several hundred thousand firms and several billion individuals. How this is done you will learn in the next few months. That it is done somehow and that it is worth learning how should be obvious to anyone who opens his eyes.

Four Wrong Answers

The first reason to understand price theory is to understand how the society around you works. The second reason is that an understanding of how prices are determined is essential to an understanding of most controversial "economic" issues; and a misunderstanding of how prices are determined is at the root of many, if not most, economic errors. Consider the following four examples of cases where the "obvious" answer is wrong and where the error is an implicit (wrong) assumption about price theory. I shall not prove what the right answer is, although I shall give you some hints about where the counterintuitive result comes from.

Rental Contracts. Tenants rent apartments from landlords. In addition to agreeing on rent, the two parties agree on other conditions of rental, such as how much notice the landlord must give the tenant if he wishes to evict him, how much notice the tenant must give if he wishes to leave, etc. Cities often have laws restricting what lease agreements are legal. For example, the law may require the landlord to give the tenant three months' notice before evicting him.

It seems obvious that the effect of such a law is to benefit tenants and hurt landlords. That may be true for those tenants who have already signed leases when the law goes into effect. For most other tenants, it is false. The law either has no effect or it injures both tenants and landlords (on average, that is; there may be particular tenants, or particular landlords, who are benefitted).

The reason you expect the law to benefit tenants is that you have, without realizing it, assumed that the law does not affect how much rent the tenant must pay. If you are paying the same rent and have a more favorable lease, you are better off. But this assumption is implausible. While the law *says* nothing about rents, it indirectly affects both the operating costs of landlords (they are higher, since it is harder to get rid of bad tenants) and the attractiveness of the lease to tenants (who are now guaranteed three months' notice). With both supply conditions and demand conditions for rental housing changed, you can hardly expect the market rent to remain the same—any more than you would expect the market price of cars to be unaffected by a law that forced the manufacturers to produce cars that were more costly to build and more desirable to buy. It turns out that either the law has no effect at all (the landlords would have chosen to offer the guarantee anyway in order to attract tenants and so be able to get more rent) or it injures both parties (the advantage of greater security does not compensate the average tenant for the resulting increase in his rent). I am asserting this, not proving it; the argument will be worked out in detail in Chapter 7.

Popcorn Prices. The second counterintuitive result concerns popcorn. Movie theaters normally sell popcorn (and candy and sodas) for substantially higher prices than they are sold for elsewhere. You know why—the movie theater has a captive audience. You are wrong. Assuming that both customers and theater owners are rational, a straightforward economic argument can be constructed to show that selling food at above-cost prices lowers the net income of the theater owner. Explaining the observed prices requires a more complicated argument.

Here again, the trick is to realize that you are assuming a price—this time the price the theater can get for a ticket—is fixed, when it will in fact depend (among other things) on how much the theater charges for food. If that does not seem plausible to you, imagine that instead of exploiting its "captive market" with high food prices, the theater exploits it by charging an additional dollar per customer for "seat rental." Just as the customers have nowhere else to buy their popcorn so they have nowhere else to rent seats in the movie theater. If the price the theater can sell tickets for is unaffected by the price of popcorn, why should it be affected by the availability or price of other "amenities"—such as seats.

Obviously the conclusion is absurd. Assuming that customers are not willing to watch the movie while standing, the new charge is exactly equivalent to raising the ticket price by a dollar. But if the theater could have made more money with higher ticket prices, it would already have higher ticket prices. The reason it charges the price it does is because any increase costs the theater more in lost customers than it gains from the higher price per ticket. Hence charging an additional fee for seats will lower, not raise, the theater's profits.

The effect of raising popcorn prices is more complicated than the effect of renting seats, since it is easier to vary the amount of popcorn you eat according to its price than to vary the number of seats you sit in; we will return to the question of why popcorn in theaters is expensive in later chapters. But the error in the obvious explanation of expensive popcorn—assuming the price at which tickets can be sold is unaffected by changes in the quality of the product—is the same.

Why Price Control Makes Gasoline More Expensive. A third counterintuitive result is that price control on gasoline lowers the price consumers pay for gasoline in dollars per gallon but raises the cost to consumers of getting gasoline, where the cost includes both price and nonmonetary costs such as time spent waiting in line.

To see why this is true, imagine that the uncontrolled price is $1/gallon. At that price, producers want to produce exactly as much gasoline as consumers want to consume (which is why it is the market price). The government imposes a maximum price of $.80/gallon. As a first step in the argument, assume producers continue producing the same quantity as before. At the lower price, consumers want to consume more. But you cannot consume gasoline that is not produced, so stations start running out. Consumers start coming to the stations earlier in the day, just after the stations have received their consignments of gasoline. But although this may enable one driver to get gasoline instead of another, it still does not allow drivers as a group to consume more than is produced, so the stations still run out. As everyone tries to be first, lines start to form. The cost of gasoline is now a cost in money plus a nonmonetary cost—waiting time (plus getting up early to go to the gas station); you can think of the latter as equivalent, from the consumer's standpoint, to an additional sum of money. As long as the money equivalent of the nonmonetary cost is less than $.20, the total cost per gallon (waiting time plus money) is less than $1/gallon. Hence consumers still want to consume more than is being produced (remember that $1/gallon was the market price at which quantity demanded and quantity supplied were equal), and the lines continue to grow. Only when the cost—time plus money—reaches the old price are we back in a situation where the amount of gasoline that consumers want to buy is equal to the amount being produced.

So far, we have assumed that the producers produce the same amount of gasoline when they are receiving $.80/gallon as when they are receiving $1/gallon. That is unlikely. At the lower price, producers produce less—marginal oil wells close down, older and more inefficient refineries that were worth running at \$1/gallon but not at \$.80 go out of use, and so on. Since less is being produced than at a price of \$1/gallon, consumers are still trying to consume more than is being produced even when the cost to them (price plus time) reaches \$1/gallon, so at that point the lines have to grow still longer to reduce quantity demanded to quantity now being supplied. Hence price control raises the cost of gasoline. In Chapter 16, this analysis is applied in more detail to price control under a variety of arrangements.

Improved Light Bulbs. The final example concerns light bulbs. It is sometimes argued that if a company has a monopoly of selling light bulbs and invents a new bulb that will last ten times as long as the old kind, the company will be better off if it suppresses the invention. After all, it is said, if the new bulb is introduced, the company can only sell one tenth as many bulbs as before, so its revenue and profit will be one tenth as great.

The mistake in this reasoning is the assumption that the company will sell the new bulb, if introduced, at the same price as the old. If consumers were willing to buy the old light bulbs for \$1 each, they should be willing to buy the new ones for about \$10 each. What they are really buying, after all, are "light bulb hours," which are at the same price as before. If the company sells one tenth as many bulbs at ten times the price, its revenue is the same as before. Unless the new bulb costs at least ten times as much to produce as the old, costs are less than before, and profits therefore are higher. It is worth introducing the new bulb.

In all of these cases, when I say something is true on average, what I mean is that it is strictly true if all consumers are identical to each other and all producers are identical to each other. This is often a useful approximation if you wish to distinguish distributional effects within a group from distributional effects between groups.

Naive Price Theory

All four of these examples have one element in common. In each case, the mistake is in assuming that one part of a system will stay the same when another part is changed. In three of the four cases, what is assumed to stay the same is a price. I like to describe this mistake as *naive price theory*—the theory that the only thing determining tomorrow's price is today's price. Naive price theory is a perfectly natural way of dealing with prices—if you do not understand what determines them. In each of the three cases—theater tickets, light bulbs, and apartments—we were considering a change in something other than price. In each case, a reader unfamiliar with economics might argue that when the problem was stated, I said nothing about the price changing, so he assumed it stayed the same.

If that seems like a reasonable defense of naive price theory, consider the following analogy. I visit a friend whose one-month-old baby is sleeping in a small crib. I ask him whether he plans to buy a larger crib or a bed when the child gets older. He looks puzzled and asks me what is wrong with the crib the child is sleeping in now. I point out that when the child gets a little bigger, the crib will be too small for him. My friend replies that I had asked what he planned to do when the child got older—not bigger.

It makes very little sense to assume that as a baby grows older he remains the same size. It makes no more sense to assume that the market price of a good remains the same when you change its cost of production, its value to potential purchasers, or both. In each case, the assumption that "if you did not say it was going to change, it probably stays the same" ceases to make sense once you understand the causal relations involved. That is what is wrong with naive price theory.

Why, you may ask, do I dignify this error by calling it a price theory? I do so in order to point out that in each of these cases, and many more, the alternative to correct economic analysis is not doing without economics (sometimes referred to as "just using common sense"). The alternative to correct economics is incorrect economics. In order to analyze the effect of introducing longer lasting light bulbs (or the other cases I have just discussed), you must, explicitly or implicitly, assume something about the effect on the price; you do not avoid doing so by assuming that there is no effect.

PART 3 · THE BIG PICTURE OR HOW TO SOLVE A HARD PROBLEM

In order to understand how prices are determined, we must somehow untangle a complicated, intricately interrelated problem. How much of a good a consumer chooses to consume depends both on the total resources available to him—his income—and, as the earlier discussion suggested, on how much of other things he must give up to get that good—in other words, on how much it costs. How much it costs depends, among other things, on how much he consumes, since his demand affects what producers can sell it for. How much producers sell and at what price will affect how much labor (and other productive resources) they choose to buy, and at what price. Since consumers get their income by selling their labor (and other productive resources they own), this will in turn affect the income of the consumers, bringing us full circle. It seems as though we cannot solve any one part of the problem until we have first solved the rest.

The solution is to break the problem into smaller pieces, solve each piece in a way sufficiently general that it can be combined with whatever the solutions of the other pieces turn out to be, then reassemble the whole in such a way that all of the solutions are consistent with each other. First, in Chapters 3 and 4, we consider a consumer with either a given income or a given endowment of goods, confronted with a market and a set of prices, and analyze his behavior. Next, in Chapter 5, we consider a producer producing either for his own consumption or for sale; the producer can transform his labor into goods and either consume them or sell them on the market. In Chapter 6, we consider trade among individuals, mostly in the context of a two-person (or two-country) world. In Chapter 7, we put together the material of Chapters 3, 4 and 5, showing how the interaction of (many) consumers who wish to buy goods and (many) producers who wish to sell them produces market prices. Finally, in Chapter 8, we close the circle, combining the results of the previous five chapters to recreate the whole interacting system.

PROBLEMS

1. The principle of revealed preference may be summarized in which of the following ways:
   a. Economists must accept preferences as they find them; they cannot tell people what their preferences ought to be.
   b. Believe what he does, not what he says.
   c. Preferences are learned, not inherited.
   d. Firms cannot affect what people prefer.
   e. None of the above.
2. The assumption of comparability may be summarized in which of the following ways:
   a. There is some rate of trade-off between any two goods you value.
   b. Different people's value for the same goods may be compared.
   c. Different people's value for the same goods may not be compared.
   d. None of the above.
3. The assumption of non-satiation implies which of the following:
   a. If you can earn more income by working more hours, it is always rational to do so.
   b. However much steak you are eating, if the price of steak goes down or your income goes up, you should eat more.
   c. If you can get more income without giving up anything else of value, you should always do so.
   d. None of the above.
   e. All of the above.
4. State the assumption of comparability in your own words. Suppose we were talking not about what people *do* value but about what they *should* value. Do you think comparability would still hold? Discuss. If your answer is no, give examples of incomparable values.
5. State the principle of revealed preference in your own words. Give an example, in your own or your friends' behavior, where stated values are different from the values deduced from revealed preference.
6. State the principle of non-satiation in your own words.
   Briefly describe how you would live if your after-tax income were $30,000/year; $60,000/year; $200,000/year; $30,000/week? Which of your answers do you think is most accurate? Why?
7. You are an economist, you have a child, and you decide you should make him wash out his mouth with soap whenever he uses a "bad" word or phrase. The first forbidden word on your list is *need*. What would other words or phrases be? If possible, give examples that have not been discussed in the chapter.
8. In the popcorn problem discussed in this chapter, what do you think the numerical relation is between the price charged for popcorn and the price for which the theater owner can sell a ticket? Consider the case of a single customer who is willing to pay a $3 admission price to a theater where popcorn costs $1/carton. Imagine that the cost of producing popcorn to the theater is only $.50/carton. At $1/carton, the customer buys one carton of pop-

corn. What can you say about how much he would buy, how much he would pay for a ticket, and how much money the theater would make, if the price of popcorn were reduced to cost? (This is a hard problem.)

9. Which of the principles discussed in the chapter did the Porsche joke illustrate? Explain.

10. I recently received a letter from a credit card company (call it ACCCo) urging me to support a law that would make it illegal for merchants to charge a higher price to customers who used credit cards. Such a law currently exists but is about to expire. The letter argues as follows:

> To begin with, present law already permits merchants to offer discounts to customers who choose to pay with cash. Such discounts can benefit customers—and we have long been for them. They allow you to either pay the regular price and have the convenience of using your credit card, or pay cash and receive a discount.
>
> We think you and all consumers should have this freedom of choice. It is a choice with no penalty and numerous benefits.
>
> *A credit card surcharge, however, is entirely different. It would penalize you whether you used cash or a credit card. If you paid cash, you would be charged the full price. If you wanted—or needed—to use your credit card, you would be charged a penalty over and above the regular price.*
>
> I am especially troubled by supporters of the surcharge who claim that if merchants no longer had to bear the cost of processing credit card sales, they would lower their prices across the board. (When did you last see that happen?)

   a. Is the distinction made by ACCCo. between permitting cash discounts and permitting a surcharge for use of a credit card a legitimate one? Discuss.

   b. ACCCo. apparently believes that it is in *its* interest to have credit card surcharges prohibited (how do I know that?). Is it obvious that it is right? From the standpoint of credit card companies, what are the *advantages* of permitting such surcharges?

11. Figure 2-1 shows how the total pleasure I get from eating ice cream cones varies with the number of ice cream cones I eat each week. Figure 2-2 shows how the total pleasure I get from all the goods I buy varies with the number of dollars worth of goods I buy each week. Discuss and explain the similarities and the differences in the two figures.

12. At least one of the examples in this chapter involved negative feedback. Which was it? (This question is for students who have read the optional sections of Chapter 1.)

13. While negotiating with a firm that wished to publish this book, I got into a conversation on the subject of the secondhand market for textbooks. The editor I was talking with complained that sales of a textbook typically dropped about 35 percent in the second year because students were buying secondhand copies from other students who had bought the books new the year before. While she had no suggestions for eliminating the secondhand market, she clearly regarded it as a bad thing.

I put the following question to her and her colleagues. Suppose an inventor walks in your door with a new product—"timed ink." Print your books in timed ink and activate it when the books leave the warehouse. Twenty months later, the pages will go blank. Students can no longer buy second-hand textbooks. Do your profits go up—or down?

To make the problem more specific, assume that presently textbooks are sold for $30 each, that students resell them to other students for $15, and that each textbook costs the publisher $20 to produce. Discuss.

Figure 2-1

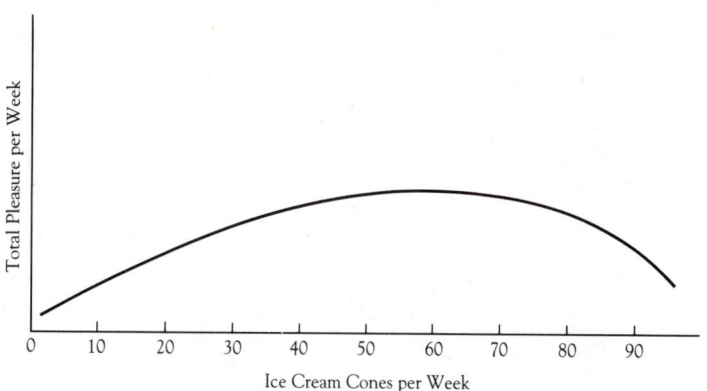

Total pleasure per week from eating ice cream cones, as a function of the rate at which they are eaten.

Figure 2-2

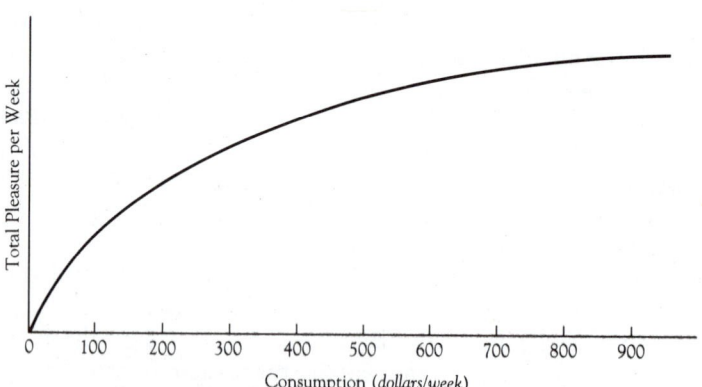

Total pleasure per week from all consumption, as a function of weekly expenditure.

Price = Value = Cost: Competitive Equilibrium in a Simple Economy

Chapter 3

The Consumer:
Choice and Indifference Curves

PRICE, COST, AND VALUE

A very old puzzle in economics is the relation between price, value to the consumer, and cost of production. It is tempting to say that the price of a good is determined by its value to the user. Why, after all, would anyone buy a good for more or sell it for less? But if this is so, why are diamonds, which are relatively unimportant (most of us could get along quite well if they did not exist), worth so much more per pound than water, which is essential for life? If the answer is that diamonds are rare and that it is rarity rather than usefulness that determines price, I reply that signatures of mine written in yellow ink are even rarer than original autographs of Abraham Lincoln but bring a (much) lower price.

Perhaps it is cost of production that determines price. When I was very young, I used to amuse myself by shooting stalks of grass with a BB gun. That is a costly way of mowing the lawn, even considering that the cost per hour of a nine-year-old's time is not very high. I think it unlikely that anyone would pay a correspondingly high price to have his lawn mowed in that fashion.

This puzzle—the relation between value to the consumer, cost of production, and price—was solved a little over 100 years ago. The answer is that price equals both cost of production and value to the user, both of which must therefore be equal to each other. How market mechanisms arrange that triple equality will be discussed in the next few chapters. In this chapter and the next, we shall analyze the behavior of a consumer who must decide what to buy with his limited resources; among the things we shall learn in the process is why, as a consequence of rational behavior by the consumer, price equals (marginal) value.

LANGUAGES

There are several different "languages" in which the problem of consumer behavior—and many other problems in economics—can be analyzed. Each of these languages has advantages and disadvantages. One may use the language of calculus, making assumptions about the form of the "utility function" which describes, in a very general way, the individual's preferences among different goods, and deducing the characteristics of the bundle of goods that maximizes it. This has the advantage of allowing compact and rigorous mathematical arguments and of producing very general results, applicable to a wide range of possible situations. It has the disadvantage that even if you know calculus, you probably do not know it in the same sense in which you know English. Unless you are very good at "intuiting" mathematics, you can follow a proof step by step from assumptions to conclusions and still not know *why* the result is true. For these reasons, calculus and utility functions will be used only in some of the optional sections of this text. The ordinary sections will not assume any knowledge of either, although a few concepts borrowed from calculus will be explained in simple terms and used where necessary.

Another possible language is geometry. Most of us can understand abstract relations better as pictures than as equations; hence geometric arguments are easier to intuit. One disadvantage of geometry is that it limits us to situations that can be drawn in two dimensions—typically, for example, to choices involving only two different goods. A second disadvantage is that we may, in drawing the picture, inadvertently build into it assumptions about the problem—possibly false ones.

The third language is English. While not as good as mathematical languages for expressing precise quantitative relations, English has the advantage of being, for most of us, our native tongue. Insofar as we think in words at all, it is the language we are used to thinking in. Unless we have very good mathematical intuition, all mathematical arguments eventually get translated, in our heads, into words, and it is only then that we really understand them. Alfred Marshall, possibly the most important economist of the past century, wrote that economics should be worked out and proved in mathematical form and then translated into words; if you cannot put your analysis into words, you should burn your mathematics. Since it is often hard to keep track of quantitative relations in a verbal argument, explanations given in English will frequently be supplemented by tables.

This chapter presents the logic of a consumer, first in verbal form, then in a simple geometrical form suitable for describing the choice between two different goods. The analysis is continued in the next chapter, which uses a somewhat more complicated geometric argument, designed to produce "calculus results" without actually using calculus. Among the results are the answers to three interesting questions: How does the amount you buy depend on price? How much do you benefit by being able to buy something at a particular price? What is the relation between price and value?

THE CONSUMER I: ENGLISH VERSION

Your problem as a consumer is to choose among the various bundles of goods and services you could purchase or produce with your limited resources of time and money. There are two elements to the problem—your preferences and your opportunity set. Your preferences could be represented by a gigantic table showing all possible "bundles"—collections of goods and services that you could conceivably consume—and showing for every possible pair of bundles which one you prefer. Your opportunity set can be thought of as a list containing every bundle that you have enough money to buy. Your problem as a consumer is to decide which of the bundles in your opportunity set you prefer.

I will simplify the problem in most of this chapter by considering only two goods at a time—in this part of the chapter, apples and oranges. We may imagine either that these are the only goods that exist or else that you have already decided how much of everything else to consume. We assume that both apples and oranges are goods, meaning that you prefer more to less. Things that are not goods are either *neutral* (you do not care how much you have) or *bads* (garbage, strawberry ice cream, acid rock).

Preferences: Patterns on a Table

Table 3–1

Bundle	Apples	Oranges	Utility	Bundle	Apples	Oranges	Utility
A	10	0	5	F	2	8	5
B	7	1	5	G	10	1	6
C	5	2	5	H	8	2	6
D	4	3	5	I	7	3	6
E	3	5	5	J	9	1	?
				K	7	5	?

Table 3-1 is a small part of a list of bundles of apples and oranges. For each bundle, the table shows its name (A-K), how many apples and oranges it contains, and its *utility*—an abstract measure of how much you value the bundle. The statement "Bundle A and bundle C have the same utility" is equivalent to the statement "Given a choice between A and C, I would not care which I got." The statement "Bundle G has greater utility than bundle B" is equivalent to "Given a choice between B and G, I would choose G." Listing a utility for each bundle is a simple way of describing your preferences; by comparing the utilities of two bundles, we can see which you prefer.

Bundles A-F have the same utility (5), so you are indifferent among them. If you started with 4 apples and 3 oranges (D) and somehow gained an apple and lost an orange, moving from D to C, you would be neither better nor worse off. We will say that in such a situation an apple and an orange "have the same value to you" or alternatively "The value of an apple is 1 orange; the value of an orange is 1 apple."

It is important to note that the statement "The value of an apple is 1 orange" is true only between C and D. As we move up or down the table, values change. If you start with 5 apples and 2 oranges, you must receive not 1 but 2 apples to make up for losing 1 orange; in this situation (between B and C), the value of an orange is equal to that of 2 apples. An orange is worth 2 apples; an apple is worth half an orange.

The numbers in bundles *A-F* follow a pattern—as you move up the table, it takes more and more apples to equal 1 orange; as you move down, it takes more and more oranges to equal 1 apple. The numbers are set up this way because, as a rule, the more you are consuming of something, the less you value consuming one more. If you have very few oranges, you will be willing to give up a good deal to have one more (assuming you like oranges). If you are already consuming 12 oranges per day, you will be willing to give up very little to have 13 instead. As we move up the column, we are considering situations in which you have fewer oranges and more apples; hence each orange is worth more to you and each apple less; hence each orange is worth more apples.

You can see the same pattern if you compare the move from *A* to *B* with the move from *G* to *H*. In each case, you are gaining 1 orange; in each case, your utility is staying the same (5 from *A* to *B*, 6 from *G* to *H*). To balance the loss of 1 orange in the first case, you must lose 3 apples; in the second, only 2. The reason is that in the first case, you start with no oranges, so getting an orange is more valuable to you (worth more apples) than in the second, where you start with 1 orange.

Yet another way of seeing the pattern is to ask how many oranges it takes to raise your utility by 1. If you start at *A*, the answer is that it takes 1 orange; adding 1 orange to your bundle puts you at *G*, with a utility of 6, up 1 from 5. If you start at *B*, it takes 2 extra oranges to move you to *I*, increasing your utility by 1. At *B* you already have 1 orange, so the extra utility you get from an additional orange (the "marginal utility" of an orange) is less than at *A*, where you start with no oranges at all.

The name for this pattern is the Principle of Declining Marginal Utility — *marginal* utility because what is declining as you have more and more oranges is the additional utility to you of having *one more* orange. It is the same principle that was introduced in the previous chapter when I discussed why I would not trade my life for any quantity of Baskin-Robbins ice cream cones. Figure 2-1 showed that as the rate at which I consumed ice cream cones increased, the additional utility from each additional cone became less and less. Eventually I reached a rate of consumption at which increased consumption resulted in decreased utility—the additional utility from additional ice cream cones was negative.

Trading Toward an Optimal Bundle

Suppose you start with bundle *A* on Table 3-1, and someone offers to trade oranges for your apples at a rate of 1 for 1. You accept the offer, and trade 1 apple for 1 orange. That gives you bundle *J*. Since *J* has more apples than *B* and as many oranges, and since apples are a good, you prefer *J* to *B*, which is equivalent to *A*; it has more utility. We do not know what *J*'s utility is, but it must be more than 5 (and less than 6. Why?).

To figure out *how many* apples you would be willing to exchange for oranges at a rate of 1 for 1, we would need to add many more bundles to Table 3-1. That problem is more easily solved using the geometric approach, which will be introduced in the next part of the chapter. There are, however, a number of lessons that can be drawn from this rather simple analysis of consumer choice.

The first is that the "value" of something is whatever we are (just) willing to give for it. Two things have the same value if gaining one and losing the other leaves us neither better nor worse off—meaning that we are indifferent between the situation before the exchange and the situation after the exchange. This is an application of the principle of revealed preference discussed in the previous chapter—our values are defined by the choices we make.

A second lesson is that the value of goods (to you) depends not only on the nature of the goods and your preferences but also on how much of those goods you have. If you have 1 apple and 12 oranges, an orange will be worth very little (in apples). If you have 10 apples and no oranges, an orange is worth quite a lot of apples—3, according to Table 3-1.

The third lesson is that the price (or *cost*) of a good is the amount of something else you must give up to get it. In our example, where someone is willing to trade oranges for apples at a rate of 1 for 1, the price of an apple is 1 orange and the price of an orange is 1 apple. This is called *opportunity cost*—the cost of getting one thing, whether by buying it or producing it, is what you have to give up in order to get it. The cost of an A on a midterm, for example, may turn out to be 3 parties, 2 football games, and a night's sleep. The cost of living in a house that you already own is not, as you might think, limited to expenditures on taxes, maintenance, and the like; it also includes the interest you could collect on the money you would have if you sold the house to someone else instead of living in it yourself.

Opportunity cost is not a particular *kind* of cost but rather the correct way of looking at all costs. The money you spend to buy something is a cost only because there are other things you would like to spend the money on instead; by buying A, you give up the opportunity to buy B. Not getting the most valuable of the B's that you could have bought with the money—the one you would have bought if A had not been available—is then the cost to you of buying A. That is why, if you were certain that the world was going to end at midnight today, money would become almost worthless to you. Its only use would be to be spent today—so you would "spend as if there were no tomorrow."

The final lesson is that you buy something if and only if its cost is less than its value. In the example we gave, the cost of an orange was 1 apple. The value of an orange, between Bundles A and B, was 3 apples. So we bought it. That put us at Bundle J. If, starting from there, the value of an orange was still more than 1 apple, we would have bought another. As we trade apples for oranges, the number of apples we have decreases and the number of oranges increases. Because of the principle of declining marginal utility, additional oranges become less valuable and apples become more valuable, so the value of (one more) orange measured in apples falls. When, as a result of trading, we reach a bundle for which the value of yet another orange is no more than its price, we stop trading; we have reached the best possible bundle, given our initial situation (bundle A) and the price at which we could trade apples for oranges.

So far, I have only considered trading (and valuing) whole apples and oranges. As long as we limit ourselves in this way, concepts such as "the value of an apple" are somewhat ambiguous. If you have 4 apples and 3 oranges, is the value of an apple the number of oranges you would give up in order to get 1 *more* apple (1 orange) or the number of oranges you would accept in exchange for having 1 *fewer* apple (2 oranges)? This ambiguity disappears if we consider trading very small amounts of the two goods—if this sounds messy with apples and oranges, substitute apple juice and orange juice. If we move from 4 quarts of apple juice either up or down by, say, a teaspoon, the value to us of apple juice changes only very slightly, and similarly with the value of orange juice, so the rate at which we are just willing to exchange apple juice for orange juice should be almost exactly the same whether we are giving up a little apple juice in exchange for a little orange juice or giving up a little orange juice in exchange for a little apple juice. This is the sort of relation that is hard to put into words. It should become a little clearer in the next section, where the same argument is repeated in a geometric form, and clearer still to those of you familiar with calculus.

THE CONSUMER II: GEOMETRY AND INDIFFERENCE CURVES

Figure 3-1 shows another way of describing the preferences shown in Table 3-1. The horizontal axis represents apples; the vertical axis represents oranges. Instead of showing utility, we show "indifference curves" I_a, I_b, and I_c. Each indifference curve connects a set of bundles which have the same utility—bundles among which the consumer is indifferent. "Higher" indifference curves represent preferred bundles. Note, for instance, that point H on I_b is a bundle containing more apples *and* more oranges than point B in I_a. Since we have assumed that apples and oranges are both "goods" (you would rather have more than less), you prefer H to B. Since all bundles on I_a are equivalent to B (by definition of an indifference curve) and all bundles on I_b are equivalent to H (ditto), any bundle on I_b is preferred to any bundle on I_a. Similarly any bundle on I_c is preferred to any bundle on either of the other two indifference curves. This conclusion depends only on assuming that apples and oranges are goods; it does not require us to know the actual utilities of the different bundles.

A table such as Table 3-1 can show only a finite number of bundles; one of the advantages of the geometric approach is that one indifference curve contains an infinite number of points representing an infinite number of different bundles. Another advantage is that looking at the blank space between the indifference curves shown on a figure such as Figure 3-1 reminds us that the indifference curves we draw, or the bundles on a table such as Table 3-1, are only a tiny selection from an infinite set. Any point on the figure, such as I, J, or K, is a bundle of goods—so many apples, so many oranges—a bundle you prefer to those on the indifference curves below it and to which you prefer those on the indifference curves above it. Through any such point, you could draw a new indifference curve containing all the bundles you regard as equivalent to it.

Figure 3-1

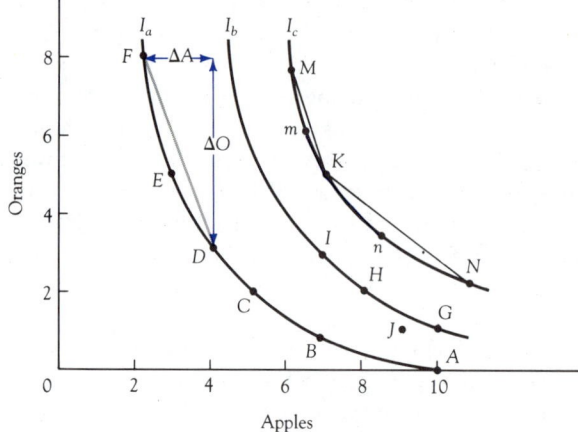

Indifference curves showing your preferences among different bundles of apples and oranges.   The slope of an indifference curve shows the value of one good measured in terms
of the other. $\Delta O/\Delta A$ is the average slope of indifference curve I_a between F and D. The
slopes of mK and Kn are almost equal, indicating that it does not matter whether you
measure value in terms of a little more of a good or a little less, provided you consider
only very small changes.

Preferences: The Shape of Indifference Curves

All of the indifference curves I have drawn have a similar shape—they slope
down and to the right, and the slope becomes less steep the further right you go.
Why?

The curves slope down to the right because both apples and oranges are
goods. If one bundle (I) has more of both apples and oranges than another (C),
so that a line through them would slope up and to the right, both points cannot
be on the same indifference curve. You would obviously prefer I, which has more
of both goods, to C. But an indifference curve connects bundles among which
you are indifferent. So if a bundle (C) has more apples than another on the same
indifference curve (D), putting it further right, it must have fewer oranges—
putting it lower. So indifference curves must slope down to the right, up to the
left.

What about the shape of the curve? As you move from point F to point D
along I_a, the number of apples increases by ΔA and the number of oranges decreases by ΔO. F and D are on the same indifference curve (I_a), so you are
indifferent between them. That implies that ΔA apples have the same value to
you as ΔO oranges; hence one apple is worth $\Delta O/\Delta A$ oranges.

$\Delta O/\Delta A$ is the value of an apple measured in oranges. It is also (minus) the
slope of the line FD—which is approximately equal to the slope of I_a (more
nearly equal the smaller ΔO and ΔA are). The slope gets less steep as you move

down and to the right along the indifference curve, because the value of apples measured in oranges becomes less as you have more apples (further right) and fewer oranges (lower). This is the same pattern we already saw in Table 3-1.

Figure 3-1 also allows us to see geometrically why the meaning of the value of apples becomes less ambiguous the smaller the changes (in quantity of apples and oranges) we consider. Suppose we start at point K on indifference curve I_c. For large changes in both directions, the two ways of calculating the value of an apple (how many oranges would you have to get to make up for losing one apple versus how many oranges would you be willing to lose in exchange for getting one apple) correspond to finding the slopes of the lines KM and KN, which are substantially different. For small changes, they correspond to finding the slopes of the colored lines Km and Kn, which are almost equal. As the change approaches zero, the two slopes approach equality with each other and with the slope of the indifference curve.

Numerical Example

In Figure 3-1, point D is a bundle of 4 apples and 3 oranges, and point F is a bundle of 2 apples and 8 oranges. ΔA is 2 apples and ΔO is 5 oranges. The slope of the line connecting D and F is (minus) $\frac{5}{2}$. $\frac{5}{2}$ is also the value of an apple— 2 apples are worth 5 oranges, so an apple is worth $\frac{5}{2}$ of an orange.

Finding the Optimal Bundle

In the previous section, we considered an individual who started with a particular bundle of apples and oranges (A) and could trade apples for oranges at a rate of 1 for 1. In this section, we will analyze essentially the same situation, starting out in a slightly different way. We begin by assuming that you have an income (I) which you can use to buy apples and oranges; the price of apples is P_a and the price of oranges is P_o. If you spend your entire income of $100 on apples at $.50 apiece, you can buy I/P_a ($100/$.50 = 200$) apples and no oranges, putting you at point K on Figure 3-2a. If you spend your entire income on oranges at $1 apiece, you can buy I/P_o ($100/$1 = 100$) oranges and no apples, putting you at point L. You should be able to convince yourself, by either algebra or trial and error, that the line B, connecting L and K, represents all of the different combinations of apples and oranges that you could buy—assuming you spent your entire income. Its equation is $I = a(P_a) + o(P_o)$ where a is the quantity of apples you buy and o is the quantity of oranges. Put in words, that says that the amount you spend on apples and oranges equals quantity of apples times price of apples plus quantity of oranges times price of oranges—equals your entire income. Remember that at this point, apples and oranges are the only goods.

Numerical Example

Suppose your income is $100/month; P_a = $.50/apple; P_o = $1/orange. The following bundles all add up to $100. Figure 3-2a shows the corresponding budget line.

Apples	Oranges	Expenditure
200	0	200 apples × $.50 + 0 oranges × $1 = $100
160	20	160 apples × $.50 + 20 oranges × $1 = $100
120	40	120 apples × $.50 + 40 oranges × $1 = $100
100	50	100 apples × $.50 + 50 oranges × $1 = $100
60	70	60 apples × $.50 + 70 oranges × $1 = $100
20	90	20 apples × $.50 + 90 oranges × $1 = $100
0	100	0 apples × $.50 + 100 oranges × $1 = $100

Indifference curves, like those of Figure 3-1, show a consumer's preferences; the budget line shows the alternatives available to him. Figure 3-2a shows both a budget line and a set of indifference curves.

The bundles on indifference curve I_5 are preferred to those of the other two curves; unfortunately there is no point which is both on I_5 and on the budget line—no bundle on I_5 which the consumer can buy with his income. There are two points on I_1 which are also on the budget line (M and N), representing two bundles which the consumer could buy; in addition, the portion of I_1 between the two points is below the budget line and therefore represents bundles which the consumer could buy and still have some money left over. Should the consumer choose one such point? No. Points O and P are on both the budget line and I_2; since I_2 is above (hence preferred to) I_1, the consumer prefers O (or P) to M or N.

Figure 3-2

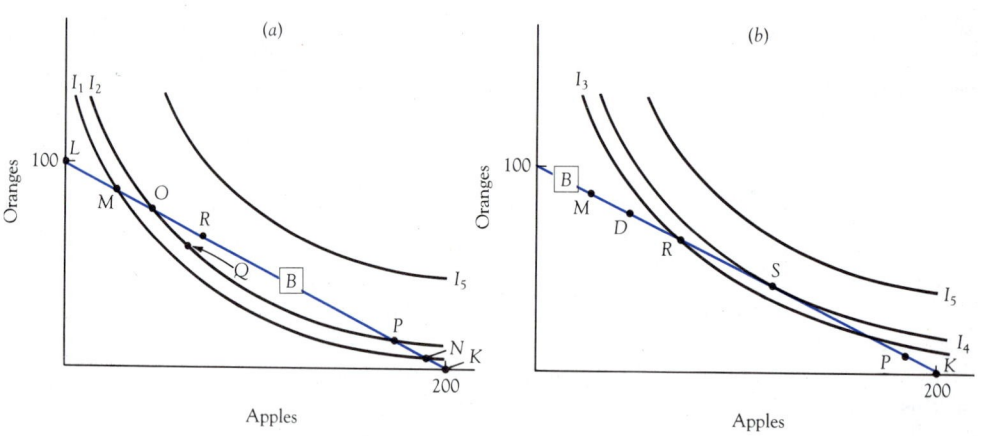

The solution to the consumer-choice problem for a world of only 2 goods. B is the budget line for a consumer who has $100 and can buy oranges at $1 each or apples at $.50 each. The optimal bundle is S, where the budget line is tangent to an indifference curve, since there is no point on B that is on a higher indifference curve than I_4.

Should the consumer choose a bundle represented by O, P, or one of the points in between, such as Q? Again the answer is no. Remember that the three indifference curves are merely the three I have chosen to draw out of the infinite number needed to describe the consumer's preferences. Consider point R. It represents a bundle containing more of both goods than Q; hence it is preferable to Q. Since all points on I_2 are equivalent, R must also be superior to O and P. To find out whether it is the best possible bundle, we draw the indifference curve on which it lies—I_3 on Figure 3-2b. As I have drawn it, there is another point, S, which lies on a still higher indifference curve and is also on the budget line.

How do we know that S is the optimum? Note that its indifference curve, I_4, just touches the budget line. Any higher indifference curve must be above I_4, so it cannot intersect the budget line.

It appears that the highest indifference curve consistent with the consumer's income is the one that is just tangent to the budget line, and the optimal bundle is at the point of tangency. This is the usual solution; Figures 3-3a and 3-3b show two exceptions. In each case, the budget line is the same as in Figures 3-2 but the indifference curves are different; the figures represent the same income and prices as Figures 3-2 but different preferences.

On Figure 3-3a, the consumer's optimal point is X on indifference curve I_2. He could move to a still higher indifference curve by moving down and to the right along the budget line—except that to do so, he would have to consume a negative quantity of oranges! Similarly, in Figure 3-2b, in order to do better than point Y, he would have to consume a negative quantity of apples. These are both "corner solutions." In the normal case ("interior solution"), where the optimal bundle contains both apples and oranges, the result of the previous paragraph holds—the optimal bundle is at the point of tangency.

Figure 3-3

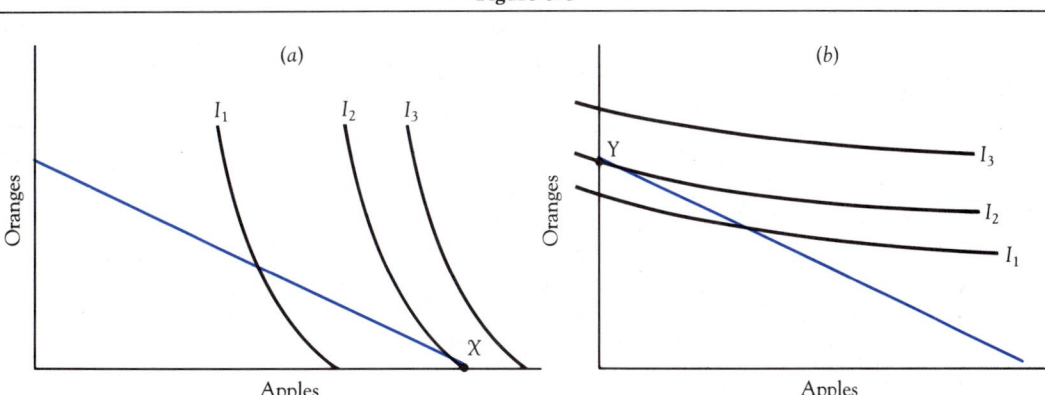

Corner solutions on an indifference curve diagram.   X shows a situation in which the consumer's preferred bundle contains only apples; Y shows a situation in which it contains only oranges.

Price = Value

If two lines are tangent, that means that they are touching and their slopes are the same. The budget line runs from the point $(0, I/P_o)$ to the point $(I/P_a, 0)$, so its slope is $-(I/P_o)/(I/P_a) = -P_a/P_o$. The rate at which you can "trade" apples for oranges (while keeping your total expenditure fixed) is simply the ratio of the price of an apple to the price of an orange. That is the same thing as the price of an apple measured in oranges; if apples cost \$.50 and oranges \$1, then the price of an apple (measured in oranges) is half an orange. So the slope of the budget line is minus the price of an apple measured in oranges.

The slope of the indifference curve, as I showed earlier in this chapter, is minus the *value* of an apple measured in oranges. So the *price* of an apple measured in oranges (*the marginal rate of transformation*—the rate at which you can transform oranges into apples by selling one and buying the other) is equal to the *value* of an apple measured in oranges (*the marginal rate of substitution*—the rate at which oranges substitute for apples as consumption goods, the number of oranges you are willing to give up in exchange for an apple). This is the same result that I sketched verbally at the end of the first part of the chapter, when I said that you would keep trading until you reached a point where the value of an additional orange (in apples) was equal to its cost (also in apples).

One possible reaction to this result is "that's obvious; of course the value of something is the same as its price." Another is "this is a bunch of meaningless gobbledygook." Both are wrong.

To see why the first reaction is wrong, consider what we mean by price and value. Price is what you *have to* give up in order to get something. Value is what you are *just barely willing* to give up to get something. Nothing in those two concepts makes it obvious that they are the same.

The second reaction is much more defensible. You have just been bombarded with a considerable junkpile of abstractions; it may take a while to dig yourself out. You may find it useful to go through the argument in each of the four ways it is presented (two so far, two in the next chapter) until you find one that makes sense to your intuition. Once you have done that, you should be able to go back over the other three and make sense out of them too. One of the reasons for using several different languages is that different people learn in different ways.

This equality between relative prices and relative values is one example of a very general pattern which we will see again and again. I will refer to it as the *equimarginal principle*—"marginal" because the values being compared are values for *one more* apple, orange, or whatever. It is a statement not about our tastes but about equilibrium—where we are when we stop trading. The same pattern has already appeared several times, in a very different context, in the optional sections of Chapter 1, where we saw that in equilibrium all lines in a supermarket and all lanes on a freeway are equally attractive—provided that the "cost" of getting to them is the same.

The Invisible World—A Brief Digression

Another response you may have at this point is "Where do all these tables and indifference curves come from, anyway? How can you possibly know what my preferences are? How, for that matter, can *I* know exactly how many apples I would give for an orange? Are economists people who go around asking people what bundles they are indifferent among—and are they fools enough to believe the answers?"

I shall answer the five questions in order. The tables and figures all came out of my head—I made them up, subject to the requirement that the numbers in the table have a certain pattern and the curves a certain shape. I cannot tell what your preferences are. You do not know exactly what your preferences are. No. No.

If we cannot find out what indifference curves are, what good are they? The answer is that indifference curves—like much of the rest of economics—are tools used to help us think clearly about human behavior. By using them, we can show that if people have preferences and rationally pursue them (the assumptions which I made and defended in Chapter 1), certain consequences follow. So far in this chapter, I have concentrated on one particular consequence—the equality between relative values and relative prices. I will show others later. Indifference curves and the like are useful as analytical tools; it is a serious error to think of them as things we actually expect to go out and measure.

Income and Substitution Effects

Now that we know what indifference curves are, we shall use them to show how the amount you consume of a good varies with your income and with the price of the good. Figure 3-4 shows what happens as income rises, with price held constant. B_1 is the same budget line we have seen before, corresponding to an

Figure 3-4

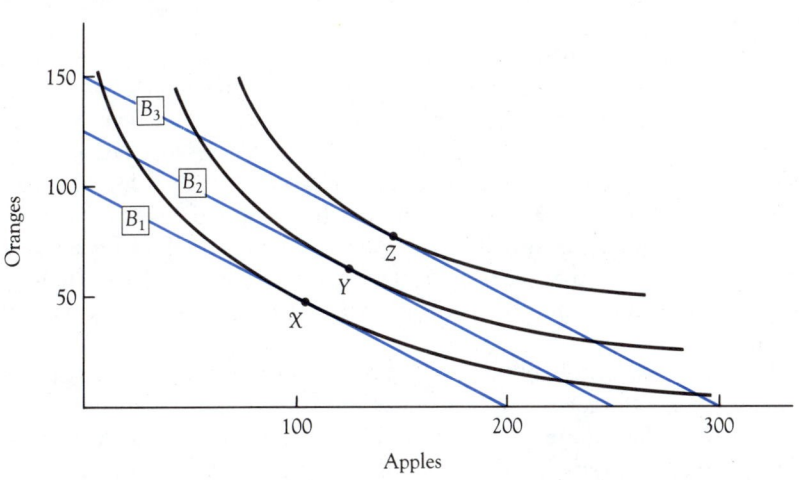

Optimal bundles for 3 different incomes—2 normal goods.   X is the optimal bundle for an income of $100, Y for an income of $125, and Z for an income of $150—as shown by B_1, B_2, and B_3. Consumption of both apples and oranges increases with increasing income.

income of $100 and prices of $1/orange and $.50/apple. B_2 is the budget line for the same prices but for an income of $125, B_3 for an income of $150. Since relative prices are the same in all three cases, all three budget lines have the same slope, making them parallel to each other. In each case, I have drawn in the indifference curve that is just tangent to the budget line. As income rises, the consumption bundle shifts from X to Y to Z; in the case illustrated, consumption of both apples and oranges rises with income.

Figure 3-5 shows the same pattern of income and prices but a different set of indifference curves, corresponding to an individual with different preferences. This time, as income increases, the consumption of oranges increases but the consumption of apples decreases! In such a situation, apples are an *inferior good*— a good of which we consume less the richer we are. Hamburger and beans are both plausible examples of inferior goods, for some ranges of income. As a very poor person becomes less poor, he eats hamburger instead of beans; his consumption of beans goes down as his income goes up, so for that range of incomes beans is an inferior good. As his income becomes still higher, he starts eating steak instead of hamburger. His consumption of hamburger goes down as his income goes up, so for that range of incomes, hamburger is an inferior good.

In describing the budget lines B_1, B_2, and B_3, I gave specific values for income and prices. I could just as easily have told you that income was $200, $250, and $300 and that prices were $2/orange and $1/apple; that would have produced exactly the same budget lines. The reason is obvious: If you double your income and simultaneously double the price of everything you buy, your real situation is unchanged—you can buy exactly the same goods as before.

I could also have told you that income was $100 for all three budget lines and that the price of an orange was $1 for B_1, $.80 for B_2, and $.66\frac{2}{3}$ for B_3, with corresponding prices ($.50, $.40, $.33\frac{1}{3}$) for apples. A drop in the price of everything you consume has the same effect on what you can buy as an increase in income.

It is not obvious when we should describe changes on an indifference curve diagram—or changes in the situations that such diagrams represent—as changes in prices and when we should describe them as changes in income. That is not because there is something wrong with indifference curves but because the distinction between a change in income and a change in price is less clear than it at first seems. We are used to thinking of all prices and incomes in terms of money, but money is important only for what it can buy; if all prices go down and my income stays the same, my real income—my ability to buy things—has risen in exactly the same way as if prices had stayed the same and my money income had gone up.

If income and prices all change at once, how can we say whether my *real income* has gone up, gone down, or stayed the same? Income is useful for what it can buy; the value to me of the bundle of goods that I buy is indicated, on an indifference curve diagram, by what indifference curve it is on. It therefore seems natural to say that a change in money income and prices that leaves me on the same indifference curve as before has left my "real income" unchanged. A change that leaves me on a higher indifference curve has increased my real income; a change that leaves me on a lower indifference curve has lowered my real income.

Figure 3-5

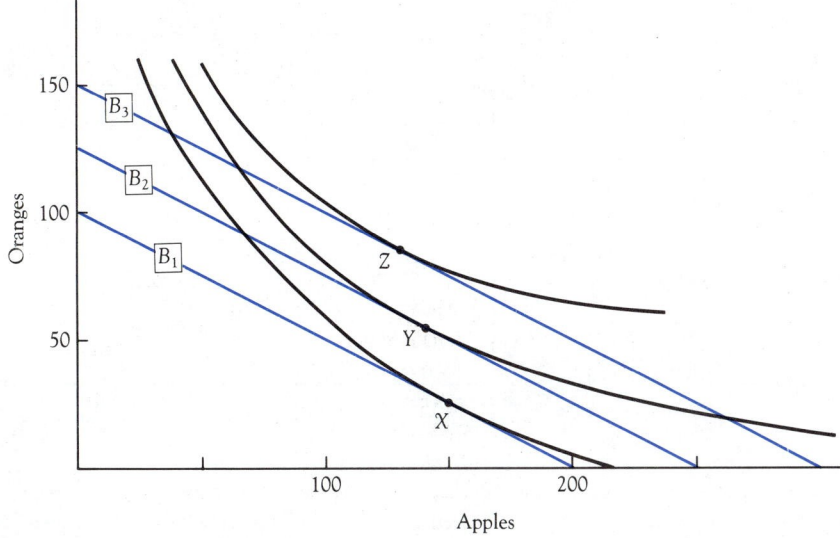

Optimal bundles for 3 different incomes—a normal good and an inferior good.   As income increases, consumption of oranges increases, but consumption of apples decreases; so apples are an inferior good.

The prices that are important are *relative prices*—how much of one good I must give up to get another. As I showed earlier, the price of one good in terms of another corresponds to (minus) the slope of the budget line. So a change in money income and money prices that alters the slope of the budget line while leaving me on the same indifference curve is a pure change in prices—prices have changed and (real) income has not. A change which leaves the slope of the budget line the same but changes the indifference curve is a pure change in income—real income has changed but (relative) prices have not. An example of the former is shown on Figure 3-6*a*; an example of the latter, on Figure 3-6*b*.

Figure 3-7 shows the effect of a decrease in the price of apples. B_1 is our usual budget line; A is the optimal bundle on B_1. B_2 is a budget line for the same income ($100) and the same price of oranges ($1/orange), but for a new and lower price of apples (.33⅓/apple). C is the optimal point on that budget line. We can decompose the movement from point A to point C into two parts, as shown in Figure 3-7. A pure change in price with income held fixed would keep us on the same indifference curve, changing the budget line from B_1 to B' and the optimal bundle from A to B. A pure change in income would keep relative prices (the slope of the budget line) unchanged, while moving us to a different indifference curve. That is the movement from bundle B on budget line B' to bundle C on budget line B_2. The first change is called the *substitution effect* (we substitute apples for oranges because they have become relatively cheaper); the second is the *income effect.*

Figure 3-6

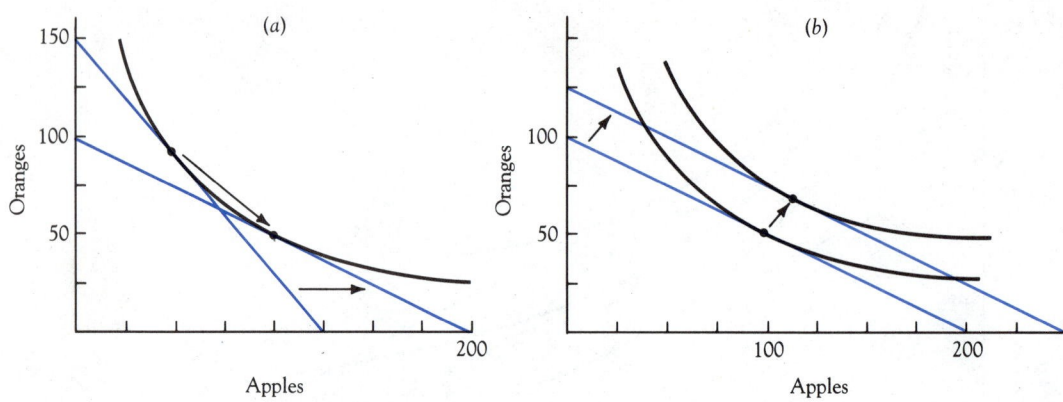

A pure change in price (*a*) and a pure change in income (*b*).   On Figure 3-6*a*, relative prices change, but real income does not, since the individual ends up on the same indifference curve after the change. On Figure 3-6*b*, relative prices stay the same but real income increases.

Figure 3-7

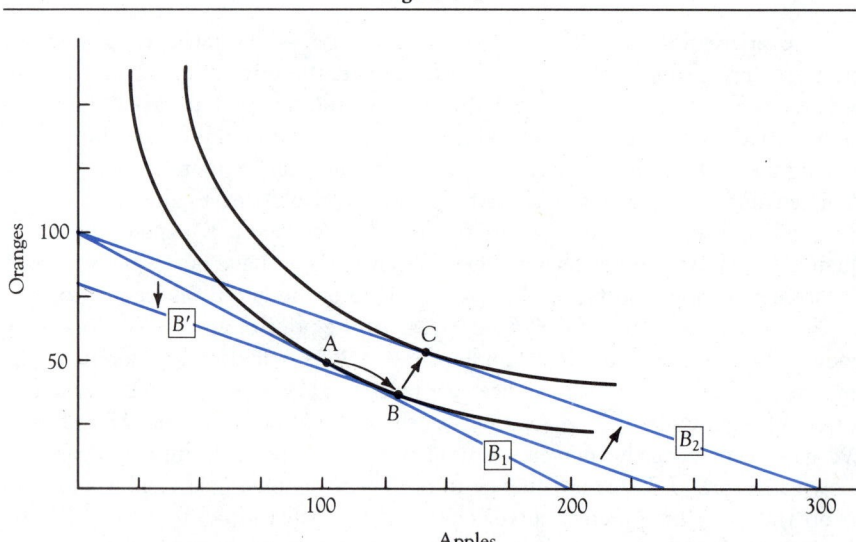

The effect of a fall in the price of apples.   When the price of apples falls, the optimal bundle changes from A to C. The movement from A to B is a substitution effect—relative prices change; real income does not. The movement from B to C is an income effect; real income changes, and relative prices do not.

A pure substitution effect always increases the consumption of the good that has become relatively cheaper. You can see that by looking at the shape of the indifference curve and imagining what happens as the budget line "rolls along it" (as it does from B_1 to B'). This corresponds to lowering the price of one good while at the same time cancelling out the gain to the consumer by either raising the price of the other good or lowering income. On net, the consumer is neither better off nor worse off. The result is to increase the consumption of the good that has become cheaper. The pure income effect from a decrease in the price of a good, on the other hand, may either increase or decrease its consumption, according to whether it is a normal or an inferior good.

A drop in the price of one good without any compensating change in income or other prices produces both a substitution effect and an income effect, as shown on Figure 3-7; apples are cheaper than before relative to oranges, and the lower price of apples makes the consumer better off than before. The substitution effect always increases the consumption of the good whose price has fallen; the income effect may increase or decrease it. This suggests the possibility of a good so strongly inferior that the income effect more than cancels the substitution effect—as its price falls, its consumption goes *down*.

Imagine, for example, that you are spending almost your whole income on hamburger. If the price of hamburger falls by 50 percent while your income and all other prices remain the same, your real income has almost doubled. Since you are, in effect, much richer than before, you may decide to buy some steak and reduce your consumption of hamburger. The substitution effect tends to make you consume more hamburger; at the lower price of hamburger, the money required to buy an ounce of steak would buy twice as much hamburger as before the price change, so steak is more expensive in terms of hamburger than before. But you are now much richer—so you may choose to eat more steak in spite of its higher relative cost.

A good whose consumption goes down instead of up when its price goes down is called a *Giffen good*. It is not clear whether any such goods actually exist. The reason they are (at least) very rare is that most of us consume many different goods, spending only a small part of our income on any one. A drop in the price of one good has a large effect on its relative price (hence a large substitution effect) but only a small effect on our real income. A Giffen good must either consume a large fraction of income or be so strongly inferior that the effect of a small change in income outweighs that of a large change in relative price.

Students frequently confuse the idea of an inferior good with the idea of a Giffen good. An inferior good is a good which you buy less of when *your income* goes up. There are many examples—for some of you, McDonald's hamburgers or bicycles. A Giffen good is a good that you buy less of when *its price* goes down. A Giffen good must be an inferior good, but most inferior goods are not Giffen goods.

If a Giffen good is rare or nonexistent, why have I spent time describing it? The main reason is that in much of economic analysis (including a good deal of this book), we assume that demand curves slope down—that the higher the price of something is, the less of it you buy. If I am going to use that assumption over and over again, it is only fair to give you some idea of how solid it is—by describing the circumstances in which it would be false.

Application: Housing Prices—A Paradox

You have just bought a house. A month after you have concluded the deal, the price of houses goes up. Are you better off (your house is worth more) or worse off (prices are higher)? Most people will reply that you are better off; after all, you own a house and houses are now more valuable.

You have just bought a house. A month after you have concluded the deal, the price of houses goes down. Are you worse off (your house is worth less) or better off (prices are lower)? Most people, in my experience, reply that you are worse off. The answers seem consistent, even to those who are not sure what the right answer is. It appears obvious that if a rise in the price of housing makes you better off, then a fall must make you worse off, and if a rise makes you worse off, then a fall must make you better off.

Although it appears obvious, it is wrong. The correct answer is that either a rise or a fall in the price of housing makes you better off!

Before proving this, I will first describe the situation a little more precisely. I am assuming that you have an income (I), part of which went to buy the house. One may imagine either that your income is from a portfolio of stocks and bonds, part of which you sold in order to buy the house, or that you have a salary, part of which must now go for interest on the mortgage. In either case, you have bought housing and, as a result, have less to spend on other goods.

I am also assuming that none of the circumstances determining how much housing you want are ever going to change, except for the price of housing; if the price of housing stayed the same, so would the amount of housing you want. You are not, in other words, planning to have children and move to a bigger house or planning to retire, sell your house, and move to Florida. To simplify the argument, I will ignore any costs of buying and selling housing other than the price— sales taxes, realtor's commissions, and the like.

Now that I have described the situation more precisely, you may want to stop and try to figure out how my answer—that a change in either direction benefits you—can be true.

The situation is shown in Figure 3-8. The vertical axis represents housing; the horizontal axis represents expenditure on all other goods. The budget line B_1 shows the different combinations of quantity of housing and quantity of other expenditure you could have chosen at the initial price of housing ($50/square foot). Point A_1 is the *optimal bundle*—the amount of housing you bought. It is on indifference curve I_1.

Line B_2 shows the situation after the price of housing has risen to $75/square foot. B_2, your new budget line, must have a slope of (minus) 1 square foot of housing/$75, since that is the new price of housing—the rate at which you can exchange "dollars spent on all other goods" for "housing," or vice versa. The new budget line must go through point A_1, since one of the alternatives available to you is to do nothing—to keep the bundle (of "housing" and "all other consump-

Figure 3-8

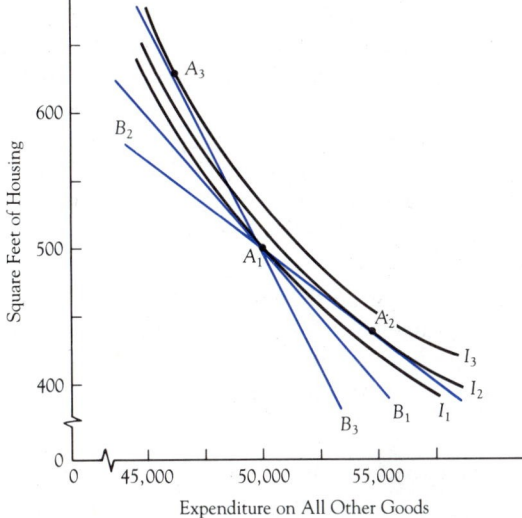

The effect on a homeowner of a change in the price of housing. B_1 shows the alternatives available at the original price of housing; B_2 shows those available if the price of housing rises after the house is bought; B_3 shows the alternatives available if the price falls. A_1 shows the homeowner's bundle of housing and all other consumption after the house is built and before there is any change in housing prices.

tion") that you had before the price change. You can choose to move away from point A_1 along the budget line either up (buy more housing, trading dollars for housing at a rate of \$75/square foot) or down (sell your house and move to a smaller one—sell some of your housing for money at \$75/square foot). So your new budget line, B_2, is simply a line with slope $-1/75$ drawn through point A_1.

The figure shows what you choose to do; your new optimal point is at A_2. Since housing is now more expensive than before, you have chosen to sell your house and buy a smaller one—the gain in income is worth more to you than the reduction in the amount of housing you consume. You are now on indifference curve I_2, which is above (preferred to) I_1.

Line B_3 shows the situation if the price of housing goes down rather than up after you buy your house—to \$30/square foot. It is drawn in exactly the same way except that the price ratio is now $1/40$. Again you have the choice of keeping your original house, so the line has to go through A_1. Your new optimal point is A_3; you have adjusted to the lower price of housing by selling your house and buying a bigger one. You are now on I_3—which is above I_1! The drop in the price of your house has made you better off.

By looking at the figures, you should be able to convince yourself that the result is a general one; whether housing prices go up or down after you buy your house, you are better off. The same argument can be put in words as follows:

What matters to you is what you consume—how much housing and how much of everything else. Before the price change, the bundle you had chosen—your house plus whatever you were buying with the rest of your income—was the best bundle of those available to you. If prices had not changed, you would have continued to consume that bundle. After prices change, you can choose to still consume the same bundle. The house belongs to you, so as long as you choose to keep it, the amount of money you have to spend on other things is unaffected by the price of the house. Hence you cannot be worse off as a result of the price change—at worst you continue to consume the same bundle (of housing and other goods) as before. But since the optimal combination of housing and other goods depends, among other things, on the price of housing, it is unlikely that the old bundle is still optimal. If it is not, that means there is now some more attractive alternative, so you are now better off; a new alternative exists which you prefer to the best alternative (the old bundle) which you had before.

This somewhat paradoxical result is interesting in part for what it shows us about the relative virtues of our different languages. In solving the problem geometrically, the drawing tells us the answer. All we have to do is look at Figure 3-8, in order to see that any budget line which goes through A_1 with a different slope than B_1 has to intersect some indifference curve higher than I_1—whether the slope is steeper (lower price of housing) or shallower (higher price of housing). What the drawing does not tell us is why it is true. When we solve the problem verbally, we are likely to get the wrong answer (as at the beginning of this section, where I concluded that a fall in the price should make you worse off). But once we do get the right answer (possibly with some help from the figures), we not only know what is true, we also understand why.

I have ignored the transaction costs associated with buying and selling houses—realtor's commissions, sales taxes, the time spent finding a satisfactory house, and so on. If such costs are included, the result is that small changes in housing prices have no effect at all on you—it is not worth paying the transaction costs necessary to increase or decrease your consumption of housing. Large changes in either direction still benefit you.

If you still find the result puzzling, the reason may be that you are confusing two quite different questions—whether a change in price makes you better off, given that you have bought a house, and whether having bought a house made you better off, given that the price is going to change. I have been discussing the first question. I asked whether, given that you had bought a house, a subsequent change in price made you better or worse off. The conclusion was that it made you better off, whether the price went up or down. That does not mean that buying the house was a good idea; if the price is going to go down, you would have been still better off if you had waited until it did so before you bought. The alternatives we have been comparing are "buy a house and have the price go down (or up)" versus "buy a house and have the price stay the same," not "buy a house and have the price go down (or up)" versus "have the price go down (or up) and then buy a house."

Application: Subsidies

Figure 3-9 shows your preferences between potatoes and "expenditure on all other goods." You have an income of $100/week; the price of potatoes is $2/pound. If you spend all your income on potatoes, you can consume 50 pounds per week of potatoes and nothing else. If you spend nothing on potatoes, you have $100/week left to spend on all other goods. Line B is your budget line; point D is the bundle you choose.

The potato lobby convinces the government that potatoes are good for you and should therefore be subsidized. For every $2 you spend on potatoes, the government gives you $1. So for each pound of potatoes you buy, you have $1 less to spend on other goods—in effect, the price of potatoes to you is now only $1/pound instead of $2/pound.

If you choose to buy no potatoes, you are unaffected by the subsidy and can spend your entire income of $100/week on other goods. If you choose to spend your entire income on potatoes, you can now buy 100 pounds per week. B_1 is your new budget line. Your optimal bundle is D_1. Your consumption of potatoes has risen. Since you are on a higher indifference curve than before—I_4 instead of I_2—you are better off than before. You are happier (and, if the potato farmers are right, healthier), the potato farmers are selling more potatoes, all is well with the world.

Figure 3-9

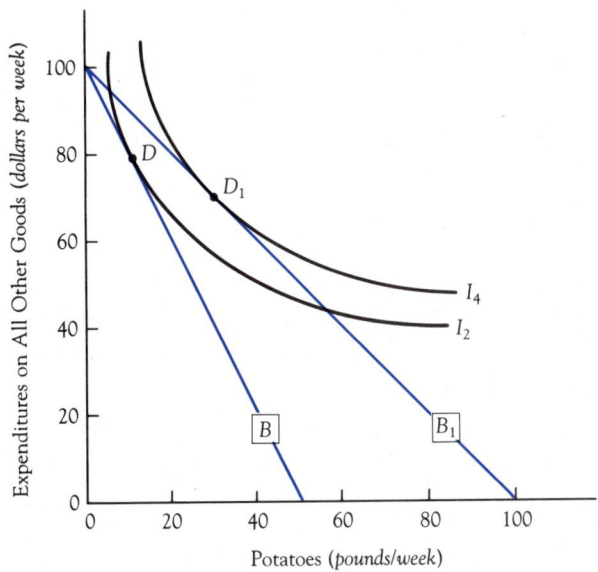

The effect of a potato subsidy that someone else pays for. B is the initial budget line; B_1 is the budget line after the government announces that it will pay half the cost of the potatoes you buy.

There is one problem. At point D_1 you are consuming 30 pounds per week of potatoes (if that seems unreasonable, you may assume that some of the potatoes are converted into vodka before you consume them). Each pound costs $2, of which you pay only $1; the other dollar is provided by the subsidy. So the total subsidy is $30/week. Some taxpayer somewhere is paying for that subsidy. Before we conclude that the potato subsidy is a complete success, we should include his costs in our calculations.

To do so, I will assume that consumers and taxpayers are the same people. For simplicity I will also assume that everyone has the same income and the same preferences, as shown on Figures 3-9 and 3-10. Each individual has a pretax income of $I = \$100$/week and an aftertax income of $I - T$, where T is the amount of tax paid. While we do not yet know what T is, we do know that the total amount collected in taxes must be the same as the amount paid out in subsidy (we ignore the cost of collecting taxes and administering the subsidy).

For the population as a whole, tax collected equals subsidy paid, and the amount of subsidy paid depends on how many pounds of potatoes people buy. But from the standpoint of each individual in a large population, the quantity of potatoes *he* buys has a negligible effect on the total subsidy and hence on his taxes. So each individual takes T as given and finds his optimal bundle, as shown on Figure 3-10. Since the effective price of potatoes is still $1/pound (pay $2 and get $1 back as subsidy), the corresponding budget line (B') has the same slope as B_1 on Figure 3-9.

Figure 3-10

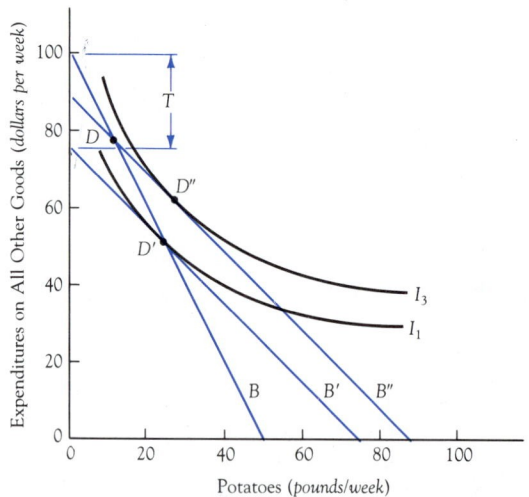

The effect of a potato subsidy that you pay for. T is the tax that pays for the subsidy; B' is the budget line for a consumer who pays the tax and can receive the subsidy. At D', the optimal point on B', the consumer pays exactly as much in tax as he receives in subsidy—and is worse off than he would be, at D, if neither tax nor subsidy existed.

How do we know that the budget line is B', instead of some other line with the same slope? B' is the only budget line for which the tax collected *from* each taxpayer (T = \$22/week) is exactly equal to the subsidy paid *to* each taxpayer—as it must be, since everyone is identical and total taxes paid must equal total subsidy received.

When Is a Wash Not a Wash? D', the bundle you choose to consume, lies on both B', your budget line given the tax and subsidy, and B, your original budget line. This is not an accident. In the simple case I have described, everyone buys the same amount of potatoes, receives the same amount of subsidy, and pays the same amount of taxes, so taxes and subsidy must be equal not only for the population as a whole but for each individual separately. If you pay as much in taxes as you receive in subsidy, tax and subsidy cancel; the bundle (potatoes plus expenditure on all other goods) that you purchase is one you could have purchased from your original income if there had been neither tax nor subsidy. Hence it must be on B, your initial budget line.

D' is on a lower indifference curve than D—the combination of tax and subsidy makes you worse off. This is not accidental. Since D' is on your original budget line, it is a bundle that you could have chosen to consume if there had been no subsidy and no tax. In that situation, you chose D instead, so you must prefer D to D'. Hence the combination of a subsidy and a tax which just pays for the subsidy must make you worse off.

In accounting, a transaction which results in two terms that just cancel—a \$1,000 gain balanced by a \$1,000 loss—is referred to as a wash. Your first reaction on reading the previous few paragraphs may be that the sort of tax/subsidy combination I have described is a wash; since you are getting back just as much as you are paying, there is no net effect at all.

In one sense, that is true; in another and more important sense, it is not. The total dollar value of your consumption bundle is the same with or without the tax/subsidy combination; in that sense, there is no effect. But, as you can see on Figure 3-10, the bundle you choose is different in the two cases; with the tax and subsidy, you end up choosing a less attractive consumption bundle—one on a lower indifference curve—than without it.

The reason for the difference goes back to a point I made earlier—that although the amount of the tax is determined (for the population as a whole) by how many pounds of potatoes are consumed, each individual will and should treat the amount of the tax as a given when deciding how many potatoes to buy. Given what everyone else is doing, your budget line (with the tax and subsidy) is B', not B. B' does not include D, so you do not have the option of choosing that bundle. If somehow everyone could get together and agree to consume 13 pounds of potatoes apiece, the new budget line would be B'' on Figure 3-10. These people could all choose bundle D and all be better off than in the solution shown by B' and D'. But if they did so, each individual would find that he could do better by moving from D to D'', the optimal bundle on B''. Each would (correctly) believe that his defection from the agreement would have a negligible effect on the taxes he had to pay. Unless there was some way of enforcing the agreement (to consume only 13 pounds of potatoes apiece), everyone would defect. The solution would again be D'—leaving everyone worse off.

This "paradoxical" result—that in some situations, rational behavior by every individual leaves each individual worse off—is not new. We encountered it before when we were explaining why armies run away and traffic jams.

Fine Point. One assumption which has been implicit throughout this discussion is that the tax/subsidy does not affect the market price of potatoes; that was always assumed to be $2/pound. The assumption is a reasonable one if we imagine that the subsidy and tax are occuring for only a small part of the population—say, a single town. Changes in the potato consumption of Podunk are unlikely to have much effect on the world market price of potatoes. It is less reasonable if we consider a program applying to, say, the entire population of the U.S. One effect of the subsidy is to increase the demand for potatoes, which should produce an increase in their price. That is one of the reasons why the potato farmers are in favor of the subsidy.

This raises a second question. So far, in analyzing the problem, we have only considered the interests of the consumers and the taxpayers; what about the producers? Is it possible that if we take them into account as well, the net effect of the subsidy is positive?

Insofar as we can answer that question—insofar, in other words, as we have a way of "adding up" different people's gains and losses—the answer is no. Even including the effect on the producers, the net effect of the subsidy is negative. You will have to wait until Chapter 15 to learn why.

OPTIONAL SECTION

UTILITY FUNCTIONS

Utility

Utility and the utility function were important ideas in the development of economics and remain useful as tools for thinking about rational behavior. The idea of utility grows out of the attempt to understand all of an individual's choices in terms of a single thing he is trying to maximize—happiness, pleasure, or something similar. We call this his *utility*. Utility is observed only in choices. The statement "The utility to you of a Hawaiian vacation is greater than the utility to you of a moped" is equivalent to the statement "Given the choice between a Hawaiian vacation and a moped, you would choose the vacation." It does *not* mean "A vacation is more useful to you than a moped." Used as a technical term in economics, "utility" does not have the same meaning as in other contexts.

A utility *function* is a way of describing your preferences among different bundles of goods. Suppose we consider only two goods—apples and pears. The statement "Your utility function is 3 × (number of pounds of apples) + 2 × (number of pounds of pears)," which we write mathematically as

$$U(a,p) = 3a + 2p,$$

means that if you have to choose between two bundles of apples and pears, you will choose the bundle for which that function is greater. You will prefer 4 pounds of apples plus 3 pounds of pears (total utility = 18) to 3 pounds of apples plus 4 pounds of pears (total utility = 17).

If you are not familiar with the idea of functions, you may find the expression $U(a,p)$ confusing. All it means is "utility, which depends on a (the number of pounds of apples) and p (the number of pounds of pears)." The form of the dependence is then shown on the other side of the equality sign.

Several things are worth noting about such functions. The first is that we are very unlikely to know what someone's utility function actually is—we would have to know his preferences among all possible bundles of goods. The purpose of utility functions is to clarify our thinking by allowing us to build simplified pictures of how people act. Such "models" are *not* attempts to describe reality; they are attempts to set up a simplified situation with the same logical structure as the much more complicated reality in order to use the former to understand the latter. You should not confuse such models with *econometric models*—complicated sets of equations used (not very successfully) to try to predict the behavior of some real-world economy.

The second point to note is that the same pattern of behavior can be described by many different utility functions. In the example given above, if the utility function had been

$$U'(a,p) = 6a + 4p = 2 \cdot U(a,p),$$

we would have predicted exactly the same behavior. The second function (U') is just twice the first (U); hence if the first is larger for one combination of apples and oranges than for another, so is the second.

So far, we have assumed that your utility depends on only two goods. More generally, we can write $U(\vec{x})$, where $\vec{x}$ is a *bundle* of goods. In the simple two-good case, $\vec{x}$ is the number of apples and of oranges; we could write $\vec{x} = (2,3)$ to describe a bundle of 2 apples and 3 oranges. In the more general case of n goods, $\vec{x}$ is a longer list, describing how much of each good is in the particular bundle being considered. If we call the first good $\vec{X}_1$ and the amount of the first good x_1, the second good $\vec{X}_2$ and the amount of the second good x_2, and so on, and if the price of the first good is P_1 and similarly for the other goods, your income constraint—the requirement that the total bundle you purchase is worth no more than your total income—is the equation

$$I \geq P_1 x_1 + P_2 x_2 + \ldots + P_n x_n,$$

where the right-hand side of the equation is the amount you have to spend to buy that quantity of the first good (the quantity times its price—3 pounds of apples at \$1/pound equals \$3) plus the amount for the quantity you are buying of the second good, etc.

The point I made above about equivalent utility functions can be made more general by observing that if there are two functions, $U(\vec{x})$, $U'(\vec{x})$, and if for any two bundles of goods, $\vec{x}_1, \vec{x}_2$, whenever $U(\vec{x}_1) > U(\vec{x}_2)$ then $U'(\vec{x}_1) > U'(\vec{x}_2)$ and vice versa, then the two utility functions describe exactly the same behavior and are equivalent. The purpose of a utility function is to tell which bundle of goods I prefer (the one for which the utility function gives a higher utility). Two different functions that always give the same answer to that question are equivalent—they imply exactly the same preferences.

My income and the prices of the goods I want define the alternatives from which I can choose; my utility function defines my preferences. Mathematically speaking, the "problem" of consumption is simply the problem of choosing the bundle of goods that maximizes your utility, subject to the *income constraint*—the requirement that the bundle you choose cost no more than your income. This, of course, is what we were doing earlier in the chapter. The utility function simply provides a more mathematically precise way of talking about it.

Calculus

We have a utility function $U(x,y,z, \ldots)$ depending on the amount consumed of goods X, Y, Z, etc. We assume that the quantities $x, y, z, \ldots$ can be continuously varied; that for $x, y, z, \ldots > 0$, U is a continuous function with continuous first derivatives, and that U is an increasing function of all its arguments (since they are goods, utility increases with increased consumption). U obeys the *principle of declining marginal utility*: dU/dx decreases as x increases (and similarly for y, z, etc.), so $d^2U/dx^2 < 0$. Our problem is to maximize U subject to the income constraint:

$$I \geq xP_x + yP_y + zP_z + \ldots$$

The general approach to solving such a problem (a constrained maximization) is by the use of a mathematical device called a Lagrange multiplier, with which you may already be familiar. In this particular case, we can use a simpler and (to me) more intuitive approach. To begin with, note that $\geq$ in the income constraint can be replaced by $=$; since the only thing money is good for is buying goods and since more goods are always preferred to fewer goods, there is never any reason to spend less than your entire income.

We now consider varying x and y, while holding fixed the quantities of all other goods. If utility is at a maximum, an infinitesimal increase in x combined (because of the income constraint) with an infinitesimal decrease in y (such that total expenditure on x and y is unchanged) must leave utility unchanged, or in other words:

$$0 = dU(x,y,z, \ldots)/dx = \partial U/\partial x + \partial U/\partial y \cdot dy/dx \qquad \text{(Eqn. 1)}$$

To find dy/dx I solve the income constraint for y in terms of x, then take the derivative, thus:

$$y = (I - zP_z - \ldots - xP_x)/P_y$$

$dy/dx = -(P_x/P_y)$.

Substituting this into Equation 1, we have

$$0 = \partial U/\partial x - (P_x/P_y) \cdot \partial U/\partial y$$

Rearranging this gives us

$$(\partial U/\partial x)/P_x = (\partial U/\partial y)/P_y$$

which is the same relation that we derived earlier in the chapter, when we concluded that the price of an apple measured in oranges (P_a/P_o) is equal to the value of an apple measured in oranges. $\partial U/\partial x$ is the marginal utility of x and $\partial U/\partial y$ the marginal utility of y; their ratio is the value of x measured in y. If a pound of X has a marginal utility of 3 and a pound of Y has a marginal utility of 1, then on the margin a pound of X is worth 3 pounds of Y. We could have made the same argument for X and Z instead of X and Y, or for any other pair of goods (holding consumption of everything else constant), so the equimarginal principle holds for all goods we consume.

It does *not* hold for goods we do not consume. As you may remember from a calculus course, the normal condition for a maximum, which is that the derivative is zero, does not apply if the maximum occurs at one end or the other of the variable's range. The situation is shown in Figure 3-11; $f(x)$, which is only defined for $x > 0$, has its maximum value at $x = 0$. Its derivative there is negative, but we cannot find higher values of f at lower values of x because there are no lower values of x. This is called a corner solution; the maximum occurs at the corner (point A on Figure 3-11), where the function runs into the barrier at $x = 0$.

Figure 3-11

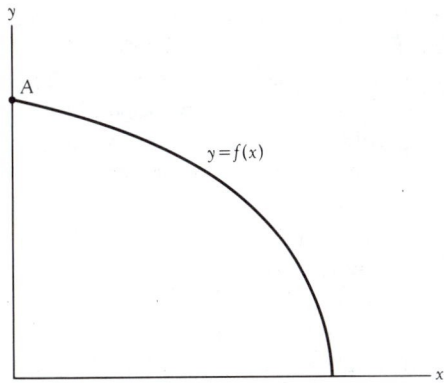

A corner solution.   At A, $f(x)$ is maximum, but df/dx is not zero.

A corner solution arises in consumption if there is a good X such that your maximum utility occurs when you are consuming none of it—$x = 0$. Since it is a corner solution, the derivative of utility need not be zero even though utility is at a maximum, so Equation 1 need not hold. Put in words, that means that utility is still increasing as you decrease consumption of the good (and spend the money on other goods) up to the point where your consumption of X reaches 0. The marginal utility of X is less per dollar than the marginal utility of other goods, but you cannot increase your utility by consuming a dollar less of X and a dollar more of something else since you have already reduced your consumption of X to zero. So the equimarginal principle does not apply to goods you do not consume. This is the same point I made earlier and illustrated on Figures 3-3a and 3-3b. The picture of the corner is different, since it involves a utility function here and an indifference curve there, but the situation is the same.

Indifference Curves and Utility Functions

Next let us look at indifference curve analysis in terms of the utility function. Since we have only two dimensions, we will limit ourselves to a utility function with only two goods. Even in that case, showing two goods "uses up" the two dimensions we have available, leaving no place to show the utility function itself. With a third dimension, we could draw it as a surface, letting the height of the surface above any point (x,y) represent $U(x,y)$. Unfortunately this book is written on two-dimensional paper; Figure 3-12a is an attempt to overcome that limitation.

This is not a new problem; mapmakers face it whenever they try to represent a three-dimensional landscape on two-dimensional paper. The solution is a contour map. A contour map has one line through all points 100 feet above sea level, another through all points 200 feet above, and so on; by looking at the map you can, with practice, figure out the shape of the land in the third dimension. Where it is rising steeply, the contours are close together (the land rises 100 feet in only a short horizontal distance); where it is gently sloped, they are far apart.

The economist's equivalent of the contour on a topographical map is an indifference curve; it represents all of the points among which you are indifferent— or in other words, all of the bundles which give you the same utility. Figure 3-12a shows indifference curves I_1, I_2, and I_3 corresponding to utility values of U_1, U_2, and U_3. U_1 is less than U_2, which in turn is less than U_3, so points on I_3 are preferred to points on I_2, which are in turn preferred to points on I_1. The X-Y plane of Figure 3-12a corresponds to the indifference curve diagrams done earlier in the chapter.

Indifference curves contain only incomplete information about the utility function from which they come. A curve is not labeled; it does not say "utility equals 9" on it. All the indifference curves tell us is which bundles we are indifferent among and which we prefer to which. They are in this sense less informative than the lines on a contour map, which tell us not only where the contour is but which contour (how many feet above sea level) it is. Hence one set of indifference curves may correspond to many different utility functions. The fact

Figure 3-12

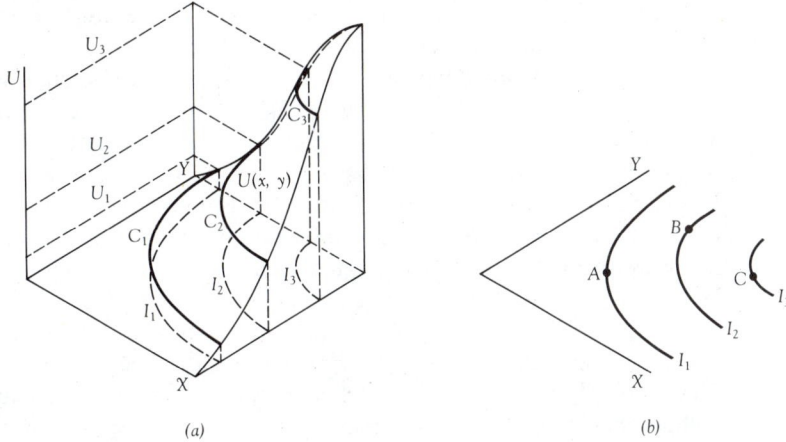

(a)   (b)

A utility surface, contours, and indifference curves. $U(x,y)$ shows how utility varies with consumption of X and Y. C_1, C_2, and C_3 are contours on U; I_1, I_2, and I_3 are the corresponding indifference curves. C_1 is the contour at a "height" of U_1; I_1 is the indifference curve joining all bundles with utility U_1. The same is true for C_2, I_2 and C_3, I_3.

that, in spite of that, we can analyze consumption completely in terms of indifference curves corresponds to a point I made earlier—that different utility functions may describe exactly the same behavior.

As we move along an indifference curve, utility stays the same. Suppose (x,y) and $(x + dx, y + dy)$ are two points on the same indifference curve. We have:

$$U(x,y) = U(x + dx, y + dy) \cong U(x,y) + dx \cdot \partial U/\partial x + dy \cdot \partial U/\partial y.$$

As dy, $dx \to 0$, their ratio becomes the slope of the indifference curve, and the approximate equality becomes an equality. In that case,

$$dx \cdot \partial U/\partial x + dy \cdot \partial U/\partial y = 0, \text{ and}$$

$$-(\partial U/\partial x)/(\partial U/\partial y) = dy/dx = \text{slope of the indifference curve.}$$

This is equivalent, as you should be able to show, to the conclusion we reached earlier—that minus the slope of the indifference curve was equal to the value of apples (Y) measured in oranges (X).

I_1 in Figure 3-12b, like the indifference curves discussed earlier, slopes down to the right; in other words, its slope is negative. To keep utility constant, a reduction in the amount of one good must be balanced by an increase in the amount of another. Indifference curves sloping the other way would describe your preferences between two things, one of which is a good and one a bad—something for which $dU/dy > 0$. If this seems an odd thing to graph, consider representing your utility as a function of number of hours worked and number of dollars of income, the first a bad and the second a good, and deducing how many hours you will work at any given wage. Or consider the situation where production of a good results in undesirable waste products.

The *slope* of an indifference curve is usually negative because we are usually representing preferences between two goods. Its *curvature*, the fact that the slope of the indifference curves becomes shallower (i.e., less negative) as you move right or down on the diagram and steeper as you move left or up, is suggested by the principle of declining marginal utility but is not, strictly speaking, implied by it. Imagine that you move straight to the right on the Figure 3-12*b*, from A to C. Quantity of Y stays the same and quantity of X increases, so $\partial U/\partial x$ must decrease. The slope of the indifference curve is $-(\partial U/\partial x)/(\partial U/\partial y)$, so the slope of the indifference curve through C is shallower than the slope of the indifference curve through A—*unless $\partial U/\partial y$ decreases even faster than $\partial U/\partial x$ as x increases.* There is no obvious reason why it should, but nothing in our assumptions makes it impossible. Similarly, as you move up from A to B, y increases, x stays the same, $\partial U/\partial y$ decreases, and the slope of the indifference curves becomes steeper—unless, for some reason, an increase in the quantity of Y decreases the marginal utility of X even faster than it decreases the marginal utility of Y.

Here again, as several times before, our analysis is complicated by the possibility that consumption of one good may affect the utility of another. In most real-world situations, we would not expect such effects to be very large—we consume many different goods, most of which have little to do with each other. The exceptions are pairs of goods which are closely related—cars and bicycles, bread and butter, bananas and peanut butter.

In such cases, we may expect indifference curves to be oddly shaped—some examples are given in the problems at the end of this chapter. In most other cases, we assume the principle of "declining marginal rate of substitution"—which means that the slope of the indifference curves becomes shallower as we move to the right on the diagram and steeper as we move up. As you can see from the previous discussion, the two principles are close enough that for most practical purposes, we may think of them as the same.

We have now derived the equimarginal principle directly from utility functions and shown the connection between utility functions and indifference curves.

It is worth noting that although the argument is made in terms of money income and money prices, money has nothing essential to do with the argument. We could just as easily have started with a bundle of goods $(x_0, y_0, \ldots)$, and allowed you to exchange X for Y at a price (of Y in terms of X) of P_y/P_x, for Z at a price of P_z/P_x, and so on.

PROBLEMS

1. Near the beginning of the chapter, I gave some examples of bads. Do you agree with them? If not, is one of us necessarily wrong? Discuss.
2. Suppose my preferences with regard to hamburger and pens are as shown.

Options	Hamburger (pounds/year)	Pens	Utility
A	100	30	50
B	108	29	50
C	118	28	50
D	200	30	75
E	?	29	75

    a. What is the value of hamburger to me (between points A and B)?

    b. In choosing between bundles A and B, which do I prefer? Between C and D?

    c. About how much hamburger should there be in E to make me indifferent between it and D? Explain briefly.

3. Figure 3-13 shows your preferences between brandy and champagne. Which (if any) of the bundles shown do you prefer to point A? To which is A preferred? Which are equivalent to A? For which bundles can you not tell whether they are equivalent, better, or worse than A?

4. Answer the same questions for point B.

5. Figure 3-14 shows your indifference curves for cookies and bananas. You have an income of $100, the price of cookies is $1, and the price of bananas is $.25. How many of each do you choose to consume?

6. Figure 3-15a shows a set of indifference curves; Figure 3-15b shows a set of budget lines. Your income is $12/week, the price of good X is $2, and the price of good Y is $4.

    a. Which line on Figure 3-15b is your budget line?

    b. Which point on Figure 3-15a do you prefer, among those available to you? In other words, how much of X and of Y do you choose to consume?

Figure 3-13

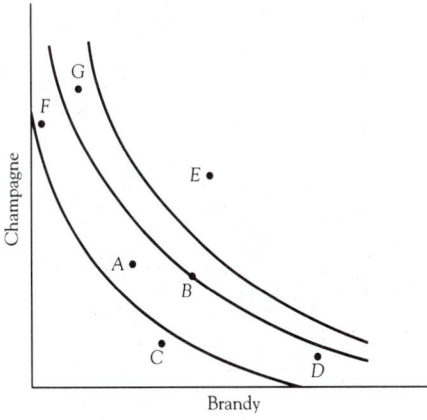

Indifference curves showing your preferences between brandy and champagne. For Problems 3 and 4.

Figure 3-14

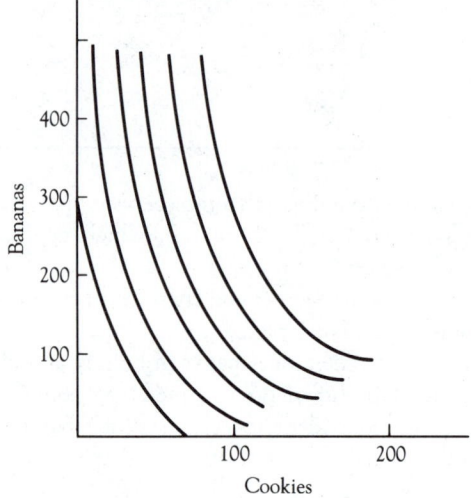

Indifference curves showing your preferences between cookies and bananas.   For Problem 5.

Figure 3-15

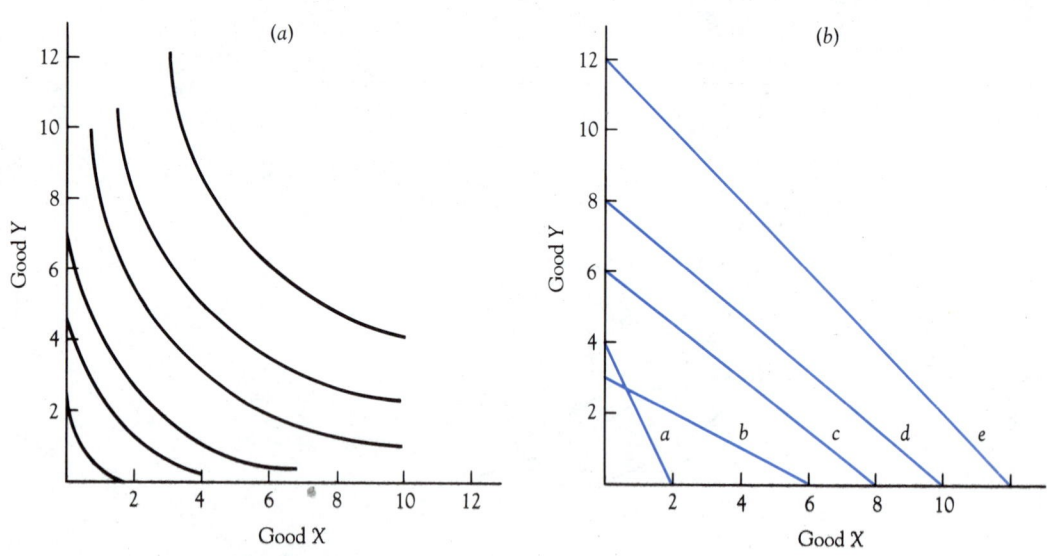

Indifference curves (*a*) and budget lines (*b*).   For Problem 6.

7. Figures 3-16*a*, 3-16*b*, and 3-16*c* show three different sets of indifference curves; in each case, points on I_4 are preferred to points on I_3, points on I_3 are preferred to points on I_2, and points on I_2 are preferred to points on I_1. Describe verbally the pattern of preferences illustrated in each case. Yes, they are odd.

8. Figure 3-16*d* shows your preferences with regard to bread and butter. Explain why the indifference curves have the shape shown.

9. Suppose that instead of subsidizing potatoes, as discussed in the text, we tax them; for every $2 you spend on potatoes, you must give an additional $1 to the government. The tax collected is then returned to the consumers as a *demogrant*: everyone gets a fixed number of dollars to add to his income. We assume that everyone has the same income and the same tastes.

Would people be better or worse off than if there were no tax (and no subsidy)? Prove your answer.

Figure 3-16

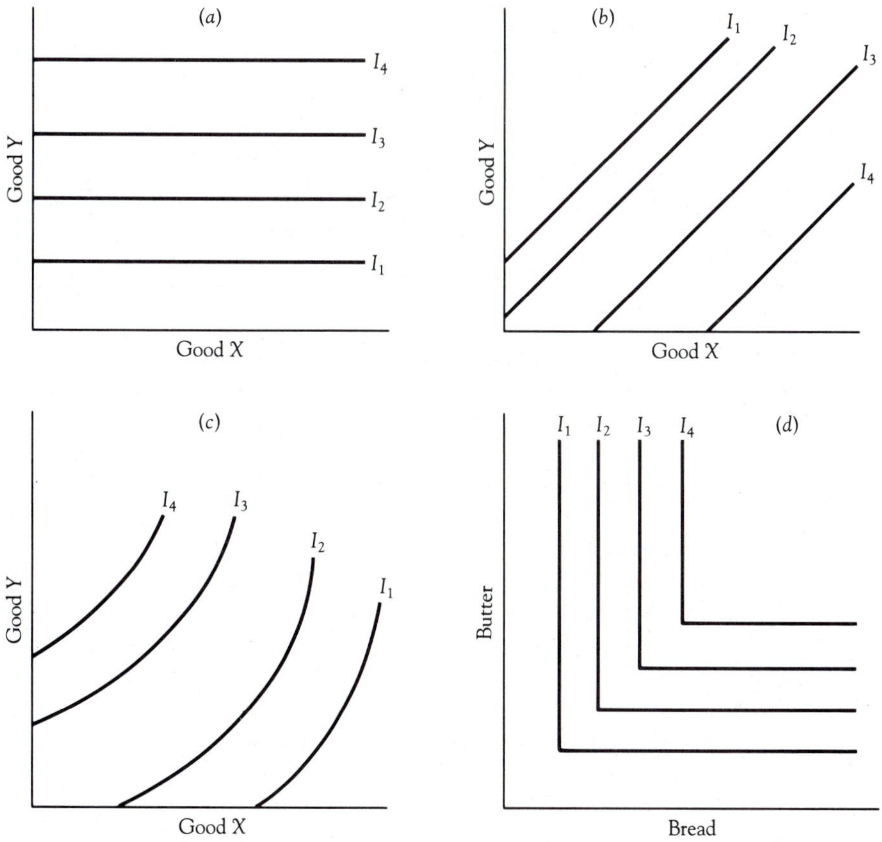

Some odd indifference curves.   For Problems 7 and 8. I_4 is always preferred to I_3, I_3 to I_2, and I_2 to I_1.

The following problems refer to the optional section:

10. What testable proposition is suggested by the statement "A has more utility than B to me?"

11. Do each of (a-d), both geometrically (you need not be precise) and using calculus. There are only two goods; x is the quantity of one good and y of the other. Your income is I. $U = xy + x + y$.

    a. $P_x = 1$; $P_y = 1$; $I = 10$. Suppose P_y rises to 2. By how much must I increase in order that you be as well off as before?

    b. In the case described in part (a), assuming that I does not change, what quantities of each good are consumed before and after the price change? How much of each change is a substitution effect? How much is an income effect?

    c. $P_x = 1$. Draw the demand curve for Y for prices from 0 to 10; $I = 10$.

    d. With both prices equal to 1, show how consumption of each good varies as I changes from 0 to 100.

12. Answer the following questions for the utility function:

    $$U = x - 1/y$$

    $$P_x = 1 = P_y; I = 10.$$

    a. Draw the demand curve for good Y, $1 < P_y < 100$.

    b. P_y increases from 1 to 2. Show the old and the new equilibria. The income effect could be eliminated either by changing I or by changing P_x and P_y while keeping relative prices the same. What would the necessary change in I be? What would the necessary change in the prices be? Diagram both.

    c. Draw the income-compensated demand curve (the demand curve showing how quantity demanded changes as price changes, with income adjusted to keep utility constant) for good Y. $0 < P_y < 100$.

    d. Graph Y against I for $0 < I < 10$.

    Do each of Problems 13-16 both geometrically and using calculus. Do each for both of the following utility functions. There are only two goods; x is the quantity of one good and y of the other. Your income is I.

    a. $U = xy$.

    b. $U = (x + y)^2$.

13. $P_x = 1 = P_y$; $I = 10$. Suppose P_y rises to 2. By how much must I increase in order that you be as well off as before?

14. In the case described in Problem 13, assuming that I does *not* change, what quantities of each good are consumed before and after the price change? How much of each change is a substitution effect? How much is an income effect?

15. $P_x = 1$. Draw the demand curve for Y for prices from 0 to 10; $I = 10$.

16. With both prices equal to 1, show how consumption of each good varies as I changes from 0 to 100.

    Do each of Problems 17 and 18 either geometrically or using calculus. Do each for both of the following utility functions. In case (a), there are only two goods—x is the quantity of one good and y of the other. In case (b), there are three goods—X, Y, and Z. Your income is I.

a. $U = x + xy + 2y; P_y = 10$
b. $U = xyz; P_y = 10; P_z = 1$.

17. $I = 10$, construct the demand curve for X, $0 < P_x < 10$.
18. Starting with $I = 10$, $P_x = 1$, construct the income-compensated demand curve for X, $1 < P_x < 50$. As P_x increases, P_y should decrease, or I increase, by just enough so that the utility of the new optimal bundle after the change is the same as the utility of the old optimal bundle before the change.

Chapter 4

The Consumer: Marginal Value, Marginal Utility, and Consumer Surplus

In the first part of this chapter, we will develop the concepts of marginal utility and marginal value and show how they can be used to analyze the behavior of a consumer. The most important result of that analysis will be that the consumer's demand curve is identical to his marginal value curve. In the second part of the chapter, that result will be used to derive the concept of *consumer surplus*—the answer to the question "How much is it worth to me to be able to buy some good at a particular price—how much better off am I than if the good did not exist?" The remainder of the chapter is a collection of loosely related sections in which I rederive the equimarginal principle, examine more carefully exactly what we have been doing in the past two chapters, and use consumer surplus to analyze the popcorn puzzle discussed in Chapter 2.

MARGINAL UTILITY AND MARGINAL VALUE

So far, we have considered the consumption of only two goods—simple to graph but hardly realistic. We shall now consider the more general case of many goods. Since we only have two-dimensional graph paper, we imagine varying the quantity of one good while spending whatever income we have left on the optimal bundle of everything else.

Table 4-1 shows bundles, each of which contains the same quantity of all goods other than oranges, plus some number of oranges. In addition to showing the utility of each bundle, it also shows the *marginal utility* for each additional orange—the increase in utility as a result of adding that orange to the bundle. Figure 4-1 shows the same information in the form of a graph, with number of oranges on the horizontal axis and total utility and marginal utility on the vertical axes. In comparing the table to the figure, you will note that on the figure, marginal utility changes smoothly with quantity, while on the table, there is one value of marginal utility between 1 orange and 2, another between 2 and 3, and so forth. The marginal utility shown on the table is really the *average* value over the corresponding range. For example, 20 is the average of marginal utility between 1 and 2 (oranges)—bundles B and C.

Table 4-1

Bundle	Oranges	Utility	Marginal Utility
A	0	50	
B	1	80	30
C	2	100	20
D	3	115	15
E	4	125	10
F	5	133	8
G	6	139	6
H	7	144	5
I	8	146	2
J	9	147	1
K	10	147	0
L	11	147	0
M	15	147	0
N	20	147	0

Figure 4-1

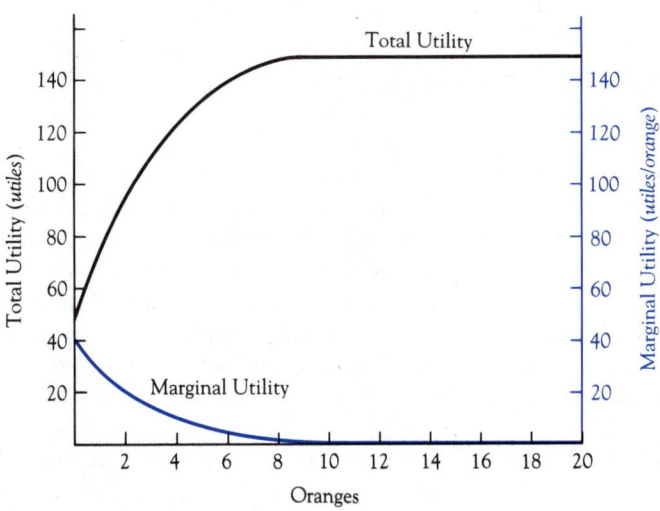

Total utility and marginal utility of oranges, assuming that it costs nothing to dispose of them. Total utility is shown in black, and marginal utility is shown in color. Because surplus oranges can be disposed of, marginal utility is never negative, and total utility never decreases with increasing number of oranges.

On a table such as Table 4-1, marginal utility is the difference between the utility of 1 orange and none, between 2 and 1, and so forth. On a graph such as Figure 4-1, it is the *slope* of the total utility curve. Both represent the same thing—the rate at which total utility increases as you increase the quantity of oranges. Since marginal utility is the slope of total utility, it is high when total utility is rising steeply, zero when total utility is constant, and negative if total utility is falling.

Total utility is stated in *utiles*—hypothetical units of utility. Marginal utility is an increase in utility divided by an increase in oranges, so it is measured in utiles per orange. That is why Figure 4-1 has two different vertical axes, marked off in different units. Both marginal utility and total utility depend on quantity of oranges; hence both have the same horizontal axis. By putting them on the same graph, I make it easier to see the relationship between them.

The idea of total and marginal will be used many times throughout this book and applied to at least five different things—utility, value, cost, revenue, and expenditure. In each case, the relation between total and marginal is the same—marginal is the slope of total, the rate at which total increases as quantity increases. In this chapter, we use marginal utility and marginal value in order to understand consumer choice; in later chapters, production (both by individuals and by firms) will be analyzed in a similar way, using marginal cost.

Declining Marginal Utility

You are deciding how many oranges to consume. If the question is whether to have one orange a week or none, you would much prefer one. If the alternatives are 51 oranges a week or 50, you may still prefer the additional orange, but the gain to you from one more orange is less. The marginal utility of an orange to you depends not only on the orange and you, but also on how many oranges you are consuming. Even if you are sufficiently fond of oranges that the utility to you of a bundle of oranges keeps increasing with the number of oranges in the bundle, we would expect it to increase more and more slowly with each additional orange. Total utility increasing more and more slowly means marginal utility decreasing, as you can see from Table 4-1, so marginal utility decreases as the quantity of oranges increases. This is what I earlier called the Principle of Declining Marginal Utility. There may be some point (9 oranges a day on Table 4-1 and Figure 4-1), at which you have as many oranges as you want. At that point, total utility stops increasing; additional oranges are no longer a good. Their marginal utility is 0.

As long as one of the things we can do with oranges is throw them away, we cannot be *worse off* having more oranges; hence oranges cannot be a bad. If it were costly to dispose of oranges (imagine yourself buried in a pile of them), then at some point, the marginal utility of an additional orange would become negative—you would prefer fewer to more. Figure 4-2 shows your total and marginal utility for oranges as a function of the quantity of oranges you are consuming, on the assumption that it is costly to dispose of oranges.

Figure 4-2

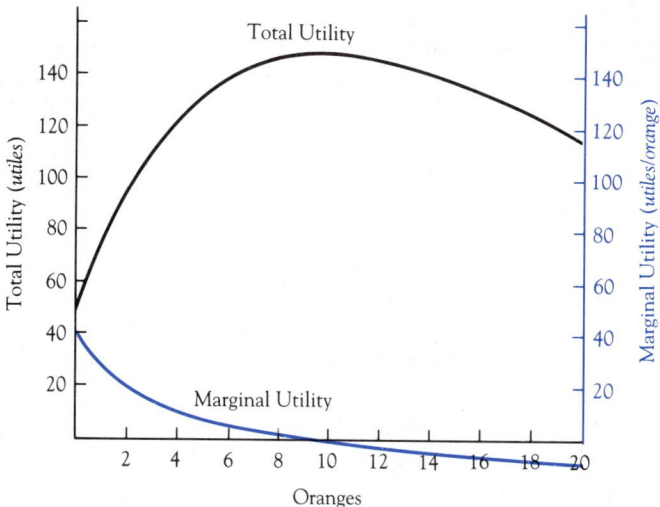

Total utility and marginal utility of oranges, assuming that it is costly to dispose of them. I want to eat only 10 oranges, so additional oranges have negative marginal utility. Total utility falls as the number of oranges increases beyond 10.

From Marginal Utility to Marginal Value

Utility is a convenient device for thinking about choice, but it has one serious limitation—we can never observe it. We can observe whether bundle X has *more* utility to you than bundle Y by letting you choose between them and seeing which you choose, but that does not tell us *how much more* utility the bundle you prefer has. Since utiles are not physical objects that we can handle, taste, trade, and measure, we can never try the experiment of offering you a choice between an apple and 3 utiles in order to see whether the marginal utility of an apple to you is more or less than 3.

What we can observe is the relative marginal utilities of different goods. If we observe that you prefer 2 apples to 1 orange, we can conclude that the additional utility you get from the 2 apples is more than you get from the orange; hence the marginal utility per apple must be more than half the marginal utility per orange. If instead of measuring utility in utiles we measure it in units of "the marginal utility of 1 apple," we can then say that the marginal utility of 1 orange is less than 2. If we observe that you are indifferent between 3 apples and 1 orange, we can say that the marginal utility of an orange is exactly 3.

What we are now dealing with is called *marginal value*; it is what one more unit of a good is worth to you in terms of other goods. Unlike marginal utility, it is in principle (and to some extent, in practice) observable. We cannot watch you choose between apples and utiles, but we can watch you choose between apples and oranges. It is what I referred to in the previous chapter as "the value of an orange" (measured in apples). A more precise description would have been "the value of one more orange."

While we could discuss marginal value in terms of apples, it is easier to discuss it in terms of dollars. "The value to you of having one more orange is $1" means that you are indifferent between having 1 more orange and having 1 more dollar. Since the reason we want money is to buy goods with it, that means that you are indifferent between having 1 more orange and having whatever goods you would buy if your income were $1 higher. A graph showing total and marginal utility (Figure 4-2) and the corresponding graph showing total and marginal value (Figure 4-3) appear the same, except for the scale; the vertical axis of one has utiles where the other has dollars, and $1 does not necessarily correspond to 1 utile. In drawing the figures, I have assumed that the marginal utility of $1 is 2 utiles, so a marginal utility of 20 utiles per orange corresponds to a marginal value of $10/orange, and a total utility of 60 utiles corresponds to a total value of $30.

This is an adequate way of looking at the relation between marginal value and marginal utility so long as we only consider situations in which the marginal utility of $1 does not change. If it does, then measuring utility in dollar units is like measuring a building with a rubber ruler. The resulting problems will be discussed in the optional section at the end of this chapter. For the moment, we will assume that the marginal utility of $1 can be treated as a constant. In that case, marginal value is simply marginal utility divided by the marginal utility of an additional dollar of income;

$$MV(\text{oranges}) = MU(\text{oranges})/MU(\text{Income}).$$

How Are Marginal Eggs Different From Other Eggs? You eat some number of eggs each week. Suppose that the marginal value of the fifth egg (per week) is $.50 (per week). This does not mean that there is a particular egg which is worth $.50; it means that the *difference* between having 5 eggs per week and having 4 is worth $.50/week. If we imagine that 5 eggs per week means 1 egg/day from Monday through Friday (cereal on the weekend), there is no reason why any one of those eggs should be valued more than another—but it seems likely that the extra value of 5 eggs a week instead of 4 is less than the extra value of 4 instead of 3. There is a "marginal value of egg," not a "marginal egg."

While this is the correct way of looking at marginal value in general, there are some particular cases in which one can talk about a *marginal* unit—a specific unit which produces the marginal value. Considering such cases may make it easier to understand the idea of marginal value and its applications to economics. Once the idea is understood, it can then be applied to more general cases.

The Declining Marginal Value of Water. Suppose, for example, that we use water for a number of different uses—drinking, washing, flushing, watering plants, swimming. The value of a gallon of water used in one way does not depend on how much water we are using in another; each is independent. To each use, we can assign a per-gallon value. If the price of water is $1/gallon, we use it only for those uses where it is worth at least that much; as the price falls, the number of uses expands. If water is worth $1/gallon to us for washing but

Figure 4-3

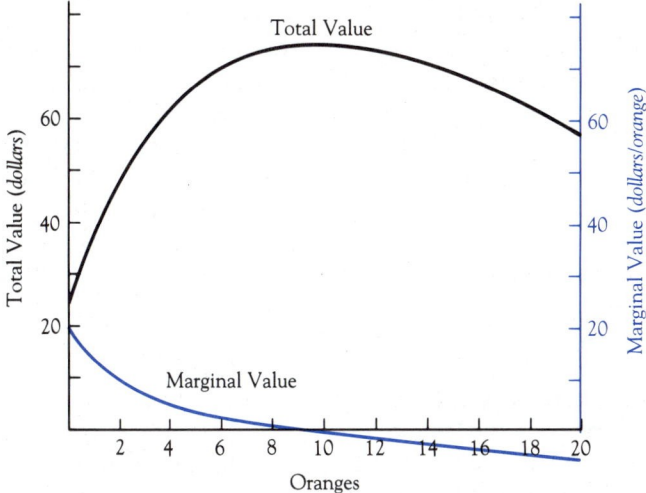

Total value and marginal value of oranges.   The marginal utility of income is assumed to be 2 utiles per dollar, so total value is half as many dollars as total utility is utiles. The same is true for marginal value and marginal utility.

only $.10/gallon for swimming and $.01/gallon for watering the lawn, then if its price is between $.10 and $1, we wash but do not swim, if it is between $.01 and $.10 we wash and swim but do not water, and if it is below $.01 we do all three. We can then talk of the "marginal use" for water—the use which is just barely worthwhile at a particular price.

If each additional unit of water goes for a different and independent use, there is an obvious justification for the principle of declining marginal utility. If you have only a little water, you use it for the most valuable purposes—drinking, for example. As you increase your consumption, additional water goes into less and less important uses; hence the benefit to you of each additional gallon is less than that of the gallon before. In this particular case, declining marginal utility is not merely something we observe but also something implied by rationality. The difference between this and the egg case is that using water for a swimming pool does not, by assumption, change the value to us of using water to drink or to water the lawn; whereas eating an egg every Wednesday, in addition to the Monday, Tuesday, Thursday, and Friday eggs, makes us enjoy the other 4 eggs a little less.

The Declining Marginal Value of Money. Consider, instead of water, money. There are many different things you can buy with it. Imagine that all of the things come in $1 packages. You could imagine arranging the packages in the order of how much you valued them—their utility to you. If you had $100, you would buy the 100 most valuable packages. If you had $1,000, you would buy the 1,000 most valuable, and so forth. The more money you had, the further down the list of packages you could go, hence the less valuable the "marginal" package. This way of looking at things provides a simple intuitive way of understanding why additional money is worth less to us the more money we have. While this way of looking at things is useful, it is not entirely correct, since goods are not independent; the possession of one may make another more or less valuable. One can imagine situations in which increasing your income from $3,000/year to $3,001 was more important than increasing it from $2,000 to $2,001. You may find it interesting to think up such a situation for yourself and see how it depends on a violation of the simple assumptions with which I started this paragraph. I will return to the subject in a later chapter.

Marginal Value and Demand

One of the objectives of this chapter is to derive a *demand curve*—a relation between the price of a good and how much of it a consumer chooses to buy. We are now in a position to do so. Imagine that you can buy all the eggs you want at a price of $.80/egg. You first consider whether to buy 1 egg per week or none. If the marginal value to you of the first egg is more than $.80 (in other words, if you prefer an additional egg to whatever else you could buy with $.80), you are better off buying at least 1 egg. The next question is whether to buy 2 eggs or 1. Again, if the marginal value of one more egg is greater than $.80, you are better off buying the egg and giving up the money. Following out the argument to its logical end, you conclude that you want to consume eggs at a rate such that the marginal value of an egg is $.80. If you increased your consumption above that point, you would be paying $.80 for an additional egg, when consuming one more egg per week was worth less than $.80 to you (remember declining marginal utility). You would be consuming an egg that was worth less than it cost. If you consumed less than that amount, you would fail to consume an egg which was worth more to you than it cost. This implies that (if you act rationally) the same points describe both your marginal value for eggs (value of having one more egg as a function of how many eggs per week you are consuming) *and* your demand for eggs (number of eggs per week you consume as a function of the price of eggs), since at any price you consume that quantity for which your marginal value of eggs equals that price. The relation is shown in Figures 4-4*a* and 4-4*b*. Note that your marginal value for eggs shows value per egg as a function of quantity of eggs. Your demand curve shows quantity of eggs as a function of price per egg.

Figures 4-4*c* and 4-4*d* show the same relation for a continuous good. As long as you are consuming a quantity of wine such that the marginal value of additional wine is greater than its price, you can make yourself better off by increasing your consumption. So you buy that quantity for which marginal value equals price. Since you do that for any price, your demand curve and your marginal value curve are the same.

By the principle of declining marginal utility, the marginal value curve should slope down; the more we have, the less we value additional quantities. I have just demonstrated that the demand curve is identical to the marginal value curve. It follows that demand curves slope down.

Figure 4-4

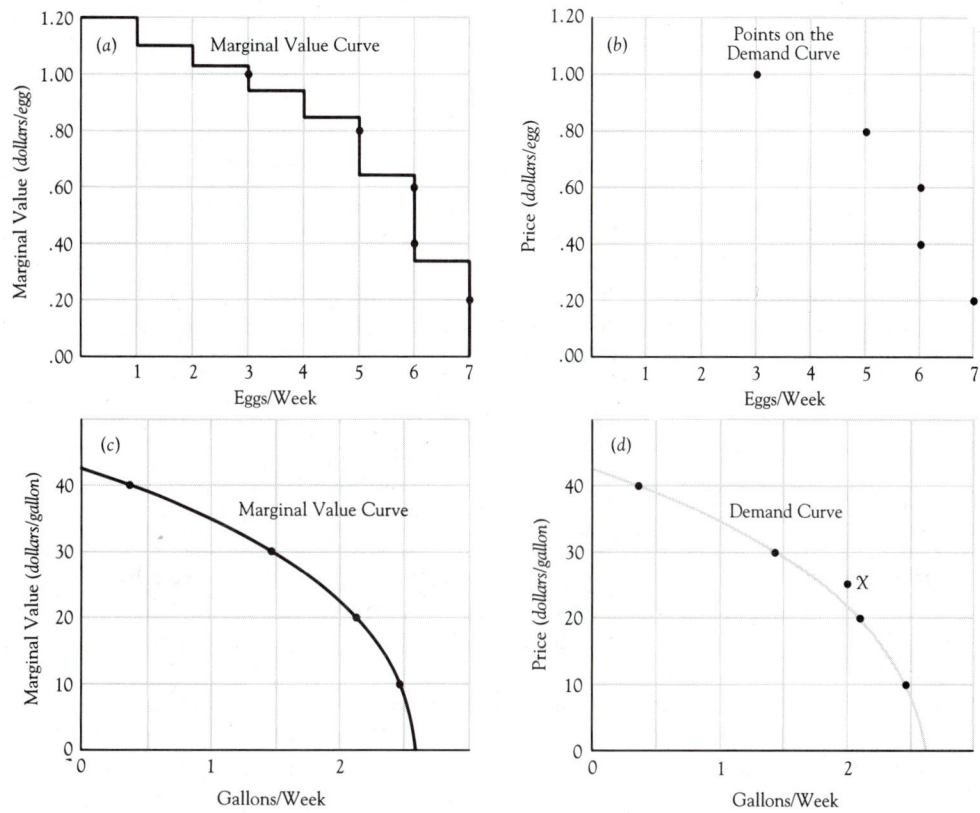

Marginal value and points on the demand curve.   Panels (a) and (b) show a lumpy good. At any price, you buy a quantity for which marginal value equals the price, so the (price, quantity) points on the demand curve are the same as the (marginal value, quantity) points on the marginal value curve.

Panels (c) and (d) show a continuous good. At any price, you buy a quantity for which marginal value equals the price; that is true for every price, so the demand curve is identical to the marginal value curve.

Some Problems. There is one flaw in this argument. So far, I have been assuming that the marginal utility of income—the increased utility from the goods bought with an extra dollar—is constant. But just as the marginal utility of apples depends on how many apples we have, the marginal utility of income depends on how much income we have. If our income increases, we will increase the quantities we consume (for normal goods), reducing the marginal utility of those goods. The marginal utility of a dollar is simply the utility of the additional goods we could buy with that dollar; so as income rises, the marginal utility of income falls.

A marginal value curve shows us what happens when we increase our consumption of one good *while holding everything else constant*. This does not quite correspond to what is shown by the demand curve of Figure 4-4d. That curve graphs quantity against price. As the price of the good falls and the quantity consumed increases, the total amount spent on that good changes—and so does the amount left to spend on other goods. Since the marginal value curve shows the value of a good measured in money, it should shift slightly as the change in that good's price changes the amount we have left to spend on other goods, and hence the marginal utility of money.

A similar difficulty in the analysis arises when the value to us of one good depends on how much we have of some other good. Bread is more valuable when we have plenty of butter, and butter less valuable when we have plenty of margarine. As price falls and quantity consumed rises in Figures 4-4b and 4-4d, the quantities of other goods consumed changes—which may affect the value of the good whose price has changed.

The problems here are the same as in the case of the Giffen good discussed earlier; a change in the price of one good affects not only the cost of that good in terms of others but also the consumer's total command over goods and services—a drop in price is equivalent to an increase in income. A full discussion of this would involve an "income-compensated" demand curve—a demand curve which shows how the quantity you demand of a good changes as its price falls while all other prices rise (or alternatively, while your income falls) in such a way as to hold your real income constant. This would be the demand curve corresponding to the "pure changes in price" discussed earlier in the context of indifference curves.

A simpler solution, adequate for most practical purposes, is the one we used to justify the downward-sloping demand curve in the previous chapter. Since consumption is usually divided among many different goods, with only a small part of our income spent on any one, a change in the price of one good has only a very small effect on our real income and our consumption of other goods as compared to its effect on the cost of the good whose price has changed. If we ignore the small income effect, the complications of the last few paragraphs disappear. The demand curve is then exactly the same as the marginal value curve; since the latter slopes down (because of diminishing marginal utility), so does the former. The indifference curve argument gave us a downward-sloping demand curve for a consumer choosing between two goods; this argument gives one in the general case of a consumer buying many goods.

Warning. When I ask students taking an exam or quiz to explain why the demand curve is the same as the marginal value curve, most of them think they know the answer—and most of them are wrong. The problem seems to be a confusion based on an imprecise verbal argument. It sounds very simple: "Your demand is how much you demand something, which is the same as how much you value it" or alternatively "Your demand is how much you are willing to pay for it, which is how much you value it." But both of those explanations are wrong. Your demand curve shows not how much you demand it but how much of it you demand—a quantity, not an intensity of feeling.

Your demand curve does *not* show how much you are willing to give for the good. On Figure 4-4d, the point X (price = $25/gallon, quantity = 2 gallons/week) is above your demand curve. But if you had to choose between buying 2 gallons of wine a week at a price of $25/gallon or buying no wine at all, you would buy the wine. The demand curve shows the quantity you would *choose to buy* at any price, given that (at that price) you were free to buy as much or as little as you chose. It does not show the highest price you would pay for any quantity if your choice were that quantity or nothing.

What the height of your demand curve at any price *is* equal to is the amount you would be willing to pay for *a little more of the good*—your marginal value. That is true—but not because demand and value mean the same thing. The reason was given in the discussion of eggs and wine a few paragraphs earlier. It is also important; as you will see later in the chapter, the relation between demand and marginal value is essential in deriving consumer surplus, and as you will see later in the book, consumer surplus is an important tool in much of economics. I have emphasized the relationship between the two curves so strongly because it is easy to skip over it as obvious and continue building the structure of economics with one of its foundations missing.

Price, Value, Diamonds, and Water

In addition to the downward-sloping demand curve, another interesting result follows from the analysis of marginal value. As I pointed out earlier, there is no obvious relation between price (what you must give up to get something) and value (how much it is worth to you—what you are *willing*, if necessary, to give up to get it), a point nicely summarized in the saying that the best things in life are free. But if you are able to buy as much as you like of something at a per-unit price of P, you will choose, for the reasons discussed above, to consume that quantity such that an additional unit is worth exactly P to you. Hence *in equilibrium* (when you are dividing your income among different goods in the way that maximizes your welfare), the marginal value of goods is just equal to their price! If the best things in life really are free, in the sense of being things of which you can consume as much as you want without giving up anything else (true of air, not true of love), then their *marginal* value is zero!

This brings us back to the "diamond-water paradox." Water is far more useful than diamonds, and far cheaper. The resolution of the paradox is that the total value to us of water is much greater than the total value of diamonds (we would be worse off with diamonds and no water than with water and no diamonds), but the marginal value of water is much less than that of diamonds. Since water is available at a low cost, we use it for all its valuable uses; if we used a little more, we would be adding a not very valuable use, such as watering the lawn once more just in case we had not watered it quite enough. Diamonds, being rare, get used only for their (few) valuable uses. Relative price depends on relative *marginal* value, so diamonds are much more expensive than water.

CONSUMER SURPLUS

This brings us to another (and related) paradox. Suppose you argued that "since the value of everything is equal to its price, we are no better off buying things than not buying, hence would be just as happy on Robinson Crusoe's island with nothing for sale as in the U.S. in 1986." You would be confusing marginal value and average value; you are no better off buying the last drop of water at exactly its value but are far better off buying (at the same price) all the preceding (and to you more valuable) drops. Note that "preceding" describes order in value, not in time.

Can we make this argument more precise? Is there some sense in which we can define *how much* better off you are by being able to buy as much water as you want at \$.01/gallon or as many eggs as you want at \$.80/egg? The answer is shown in Figure 4-5a. By buying one egg instead of none, you receive a marginal value of \$1.20 and give up \$.80; hence you are better off by \$.40. Buying a second egg provides a further increase in value of \$1.10, at a cost of another \$.80. Hence buying two eggs instead of none makes you better off by \$.70.

This does not mean you have \$.70 more than if you bought no eggs—on the contrary, you have \$1.60 less. It means that buying 2 eggs instead of none makes you as much better off as would the extra goods you would buy if your income were \$.70 higher than it is. You are indifferent between having your present income and buying 2 eggs (as well as whatever else you would buy with the income) and having an income of \$.70 more but being forbidden to buy any eggs.

Continuing the explanation of Figure 4-5a, we see that as long as you are consuming fewer than 5 eggs per week, each additional egg you buy makes you better off. When your consumption reaches 5 eggs per week, any further increase involves buying goods that cost more than they are worth to you. The total gain

Figure 4-5

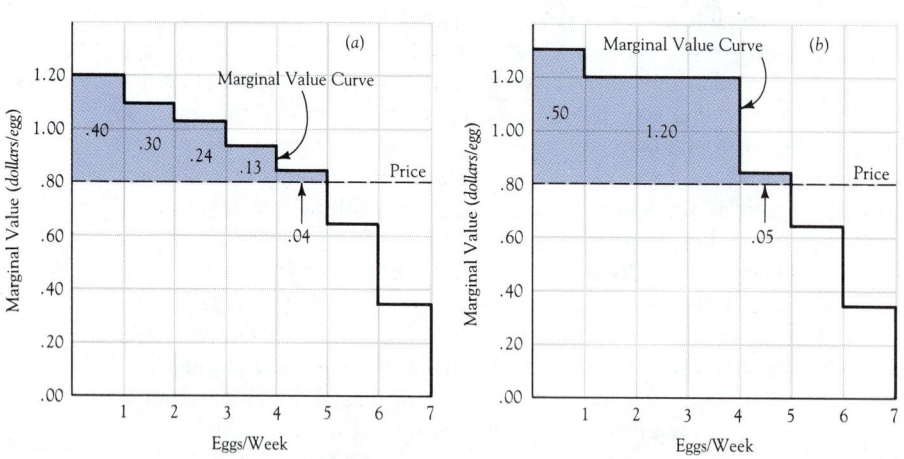

Marginal value curve and consumer surplus for a lumpy good.   The shaded area under the marginal value curve and above the price equals the benefit to you of buying that quantity at that price. It is called *consumer surplus*.

to you from consuming 5 eggs at a price of $.80 each instead of consuming no eggs at all is the sum of the little rectangles shown in the figure. The first rectangle is a gain of $.40/egg times 1 egg, for a total gain of $.40; the next is $.30/egg times 1 egg, and so on.

Summing the area of the rectangles may seem odd to you. Why not simply sum their heights, which represent the gain per egg at each stage? But consider Figure 4-5b, which shows a marginal value curve for which the rectangles no longer all have a width of 1 egg per week. Gaining $.40/egg on 3 eggs is worth 3 times as much as gaining $.40/egg on 1.

Finally, consider Figure 4-6a, where instead of a "lumpy" good such as eggs we show a "continuous" good such as wine (or apple juice). If we add up the gain on buying wine, drop by drop, the tiny rectangles exactly fill the shaded region. The total advantage of being able to buy wine at $8/gallon is then the area of the shaded region.

Like many things in economics, this area—representing the gain to a consumer from what he consumes—has a name. It is called *consumer surplus*. It equals the area under the demand curve and above the price—area A on Figure 4-6a. You will meet consumer surplus again—its derivation was one of the main purposes of this chapter. Its traditional use in economics is to evaluate the net effect on consumers of some change in the economic system, such as the introduction of a tax or a subsidy. As we will see in Chapters 10 and 15, it is also useful for helping a firm, under certain circumstances, to decide how to price its product.

Your consumer surplus from buying wine at some price is the value to you of being able to buy as much wine as you wish at that price—the difference between

Figure 4-6

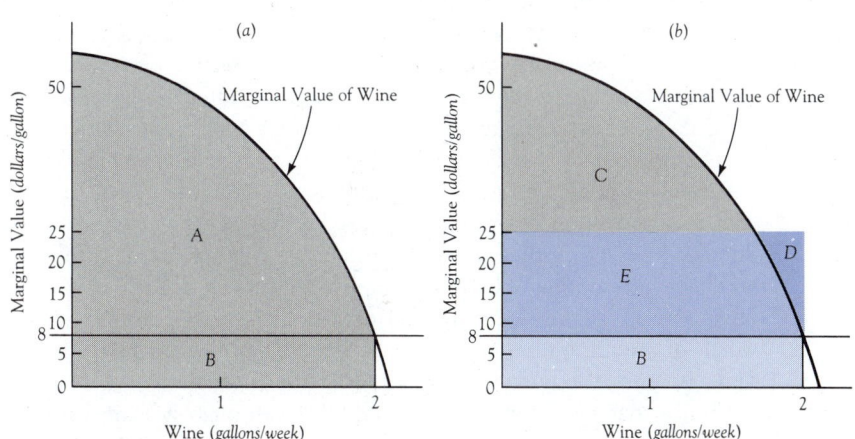

Marginal value and consumer surplus for a continuous good.   A is the consumer surplus from being able to buy all the wine you want at $8/gallon. B is what you pay for it. A + B is the total value to you of 2 gallons per week of wine. B + E + D is what you would pay if you bought 2 gallons per week at $25/gallon.

what you pay for the wine and what it is worth to you. The same analysis can be used to measure the value to you of other opportunities. Suppose, for example, that you are simply *given* 2 gallons per week, with no opportunity to either sell any of it or buy any more. The value to you of what you are getting is the value of the first drop of wine, plus the second, plus . . . adding up to the whole area under your demand curve—region A plus region B on Figure 4-6a. The situation is just the same as if you bought 2 gallons per week at a price of $8/gallon and were then given back the money. Area A is the consumer surplus on buying the wine; area B is the $16/week you spend to get it. The total value to you of the wine is the sum of the two, which is the area under the marginal value curve; total value is simply the area under marginal value.

If area A plus area B is the value to you of being given 2 gallons of wine per week, it is also the largest sum you would pay in order to get 2 gallons per week if the alternative were having no wine at all. Figure 4-6b shows that situation. Your surplus from buying 2 gallons per week for $25/gallon is the value to you of the wine—areas A plus B on the previous figure, which is equal to $C + E + B$ on Figure 4-6b—minus what you spend for it. You are spending $25/gallon and buying 2 gallons, so that comes to $50/week—the colored rectangle $D + E + B$ on Figure 4-6b. Subtracting that from the value of the wine ($C + E + B$) gives a surplus equal to region C minus region D. Your surplus is positive, so you buy the wine. This is the case mentioned earlier in the chapter, where you buy a price/quantity combination which is above your demand curve—given that your alternative is buying nothing at all.

ODDS AND ENDS

Again the Equimarginal Principle

You are consuming a variety of goods; being rational, you have adjusted the amount you consume of each until you are consuming that bundle you prefer among all those bundles you can afford. Consider two goods—apples and cookies. For each, consider the marginal utility to you *of an additional dollar's worth* of the good. Suppose it were larger for apples than for cookies. In that case, by spending $1 less on cookies and $1 more on apples, you could get a bundle you prefer to the bundle you are presently consuming while spending exactly the same amount of money as before! But you are supposed to have already chosen the best possible bundle. If so, no further change can improve your situation. It follows that when you have your optimal bundle, the utility to you of a dollar's worth of apples must be the same as the utility to you of a dollar's worth of cookies—or a dollar's worth of anything else. If it were not, there would be a better bundle with the same price, so the one you had would not be optimal.

Since that may seem confusing, I will go through it again with numbers. We start by assuming that you are consuming your optimal bundle of apples and cookies. Suppose apples cost $.50 each and cookies (the giant size) cost $1 each. You are consuming 4 cookies and 9 apples each week, and at that level of consumption, the marginal utility of a cookie is 3 utiles and the marginal utility of an apple is 2 utiles (remember that the marginal utility of something depends both on your preferences and on how much you are consuming). A dollar's worth of apples is 2 apples; a dollar's worth of cookies is 1. If you increased your consumption of apples by 2, your utility would increase by four utiles; if you then decreased your consumption of cookies (Kroger's chocolate chip, from the deli section—free plug) by 1, your utility would go back down by 3 utiles. The net effect would be to make you better off by 1 utile (4 − 3 = 1). You would still be spending the same amount of money on apples and cookies, so you would have the same amount as before to spend on everything else. You would be better off than before with regard to apples and cookies and as well off with regard to everything else. But that is impossible; since you were already choosing the optimal bundle, no change in what you consume can make you better off.

I have proved that if the marginal utility per dollar's worth of the different goods you are consuming is not the same, you must not be choosing the optimal bundle. Hence if you *are* choosing the optimal bundle, the marginal utility of a dollar's worth of any of the goods you consume must be the same. In other words, the marginal utility of each good must be proportional to its price. If butter costs $4/pound and gasoline $2/gallon, and a dollar's worth of butter (¼ pound) increases your utility by the same amount as a dollar's worth of gasoline (½ gallon), the marginal utility of butter (per pound) must be twice the marginal utility of gasoline (per gallon)—just as the price of butter (per pound) is twice the price of gasoline (per gallon).

This is now the fourth time I have derived this result. The third time was when, in the process of showing that the marginal value curve and the demand curve are the same, I demonstrated that you consume any good up to the point where its marginal value is equal to its price. While I did not point out then that marginal value equaling price implied the equimarginal principle, it is easy enough to see that it does. Simply repeat the argument for every good you consume. If marginal value is equal to price for every good, then for any two goods, the ratio of their marginal values is the same as the ratio of their prices. Since marginal value is simply marginal utility divided by the marginal utility of income, the ratio of the marginal values of two goods is the same as the ratio of their marginal utilities.

This may be clearer if it is stated using algebra instead of English. Consider two goods x and y, with marginal values MV_x and MV_y, marginal utilities MU_x and MU_y, and prices P_x and P_y. We have

$$MV_x = P_x;$$

$$MV_y = P_y, \text{ and}$$

$$MV_x = MU_x/MU(Income);$$

$$MV_y = MU_y/MU(Income).$$

Therefore,

$$P_x/P_y = MV_x/MV_y = MU_x/MU_y.$$

This is the final derivation of the principle in this chapter, but you will find it turning up again in economics (and elsewhere). The form in which we have derived it this time makes more obvious the reason for calling it the equimarginal principle. A convenient, if sloppy, misstatement of it is "Everything is equal on the margin."

It is important, in this and other applications of the equimarginal principle, to realize that it is a statement not about the initial situation (preferences, market prices, roads, checkout counters, or whatever) but about the result of rational decision. You may (as I do) vastly prefer Kroger chocolate chip cookies (the kind they bake in the store) to apples; if so, you may buy many more cookies than apples. What the equimarginal principle tells you is that you will buy just *enough more* cookies to reduce the marginal utility per dollar of cookies to that of apples.

Continuous Cookies

It may occur to some of you that there is a problem with the most recent argument by which I "proved" the equimarginal principle. I originally defined the marginal utility of something of which I have n units as the utility of $n + 1$ units minus the utility of n units (and similarly for marginal value). Applying this to my example of 9 apples and 4 cookies, the marginal value of an apple involves the difference between 9 and 10 and the marginal value of a cookie involves the difference between 4 and 5. But the change that I considered involved increasing the consumption of apples from 9 not to 10 but to 11, and *decreasing* the consumption of cookies from 4 to 3. Unless the marginal value of the eleventh apple is the same as that of the tenth (which it should not be, by our assumption of declining marginal utility) and the marginal value of the fourth cookie the same as that of the fifth (ditto), the argument as I gave it is wrong!

The answer to this objection is that although I have described the marginal utility of an apple or an orange as the difference between the utility of 10 and the utility of 9, that is only an approximation. Strictly speaking, we should think of all goods as consumed in continuously varying quantities (if this suggests apple sauce and cookie crumbs, wait for the discussion of time in the next section). We should define the marginal utility as the increased utility from consuming a tiny bit more, divided by the amount of that tiny bit (and similarly for marginal value). The marginal value is then the slope of the graph of total value—$\Delta V/\Delta Q$ in Figure 4-7. If, when we are consuming 100 gallons of water per week, an additional drop (a millionth of a gallon) is worth one hundred-thousandth of a cent, then the marginal value of water is \$.10/gallon (.00001 cents/.000001 gallons). The argument of the previous section can then be restated in terms of an increase in consumption of .002 apples and a decrease in consumption of .001 cookies. Since we do not expect the marginal value of cookies to change very much between 4 cookies and 3.999 cookies, the argument goes through.

The precise definitions of marginal utility and marginal value require calculus—the marginal value of apples is the partial derivative of total value with respect to quantity. Since I am not assuming that all of my readers know calculus, I use the sort of imprecise language given above. Precisely the same calculus concept (a derivative) is implicit in such familiar ideas as speed and acceleration.

You might carelessly say that having driven 50 miles in an hour, your speed was 50 miles per hour—but you know that speed is actually an instantaneous concept and that 50 miles per hour is only an average (part of the time you were standing still, part of it going at 50, part of it at 65). A precise definition of speed must be given in terms of small changes in distance divided by the small amounts of time during which they occur, just as a precise definition of marginal value is given in terms of small changes in value divided by the small changes in quantity which cause them.

Economics and Time

In talking or writing about economics, it is often convenient to describe consumption in terms of quantities—numbers of apples, gallons of water, and so forth. But 100 apples consumed in a day are not of the same value to me as 100 apples consumed in a year. The easiest way to deal with this problem is to think of consumption in terms of rates instead of quantities—6 apples per week, 7 eggs per week, and so on. Income is not a number of dollars but rather a number of dollars per week. Value is also a flow—6 apples per week are worth, not $3, but $3/week.

If we think of all quantities as flows and limit ourselves to analyzing situations in which income, prices, and preferences remain the same for long periods, we avoid most of the complications that time adds to economics. Many of these complications are important to understanding the nonstatic world we live in. But in solving a hard problem, it is often wise to solve the easier parts first; so in this section of the book, the problems associated with change are mostly ignored. Once we have a clearly worked-out picture of static economics, we can use it to

Figure 4-7

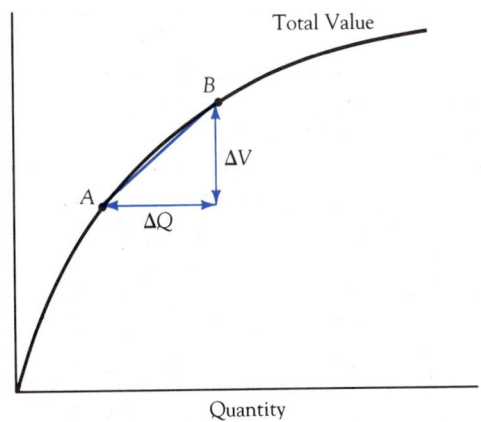

Total value and its slope. $\Delta V/\Delta Q$ is the average slope of total value between A and B. As ΔV and ΔQ become very small, A and B move together, and $\Delta V/\Delta Q$ approaches the slope of total value at a point—which is marginal value.

understand more complicated situations—and will, starting in Chapter 11. Until then, we are doing economics in a perfectly static and predictable world, in which tomorrow is always like today and next year is always like this year. That is why, in drawing indifference curve diagrams, we never considered the possibility that the consumer would spend only part of his income in order to save the rest for a rainy day; either it is raining today or there are no rainy days.

Problems associated with time and change are not the only complications ignored at this point; you might find it interesting to make a list as we go along, and see how many get dealt with by the end of the book.

One advantage to thinking of consumption in eggs per year instead of just eggs is that it lets us vary consumption continuously. There are severe practical difficulties with changing the number of eggs you consume by $\frac{1}{10}$ of an egg at a time—what do you do with the rest of it? But it is easy enough to increase the *rate* at which you consume eggs by $\frac{1}{10}$ of an egg per week—eat, on average, 5 more eggs per year. Thus lumpy goods become continuous—and the consumption of continuous goods is, for mathematical reasons, easier to analyze than the consumption of lumpy goods. That is how I can talk about marginal utility and marginal value in terms of very small amounts of apples and cookies without first converting the apples into apple sauce and the cookies into a pile of crumbs. From this point on, we will treat all goods as continuous.

There is a second problem associated with time that we should also note. In describing the process of choice, I talk about "doing this, then doing that, then . . . ." For example, I talk about increasing consumption from 4 apples to 5, *then* from 5 to 6, *then* from . . . and so on. It sounds as though the process happens over time, but that is deceptive. We are really describing not a process of consumption going on out in the real world but rather something happening inside your head—the process of solving the problem of how much of each good to consume. A more precise description would be "First you imagine that you choose to consume no apples and consider the resulting bundle of goods. Then you imagine that you consume 1 apple instead of none and compare *that* bundle with the previous one. Then 2 instead of 1. Then . . . . Finally, after you have figured out what level of consumption maximizes your utility, we turn a switch, the game of life starts, and you put your solution into practice."

If you find it difficult to distinguish "time" in the sense of an imaginary series of calculations by which you decide what to do from the "time" in which you actually do it, you may instead imagine (as suggested before) that we are considering a situation (income, preferences, prices) that will be stable for a long time. We start by spending a few days "experimenting" with different consumption bundles to see which we prefer. The loss from consuming "wrong" bundles during the experiment can be ignored, since it is such a short period compared to the long time during which the solution is put into practice.

Money, Value, and Prices

Although prices and values are often given in terms of money, money has nothing essential to do with the analysis. In demonstrating the equimarginal principle, for example, I converted cookies into money (bought 1 less cookie, leaving me with an extra dollar to spend on something else) and then converted the money into apples (bought 2 apples for $1). The argument would have been exactly the same if there were no such thing as money and a cookie simply exchanged for 2 apples.

We are used to stating prices in money, but prices can be stated in anything of value. We could define all our prices as apple prices. The apple price of a cookie, in my example, is 2 apples—that is what you must give up to get a cookie. The apple price of an apple is 1 (apple). Once you have the price of everything in terms of apples, you also have the price of everything in terms of any other good. If a peach exchanges for 4 apples, and 4 apples exchange for 8 cookies, then the cookie price of a peach is 8.

There are two ways of seeing why this must be true. The simplest is to observe that someone who has cookies and wants peaches will never pay more than 8 cookies for a peach, since he could always trade 8 cookies for 4 apples and then exchange the 4 apples for a peach. Someone who has a peach and wants cookies will never accept fewer than 8 cookies for his peach, since he could always trade it for 4 apples and then trade the 4 apples for 8 cookies. If nobody who is buying peaches will pay more than 8 cookies and nobody selling them will accept less, the price of a peach (in cookies) must be 8. The same analysis applies for any other good. So once we know the price of all goods in terms of one good (in this example—apples), we can calculate the price of each good in terms of any other good.

This argument depends to some extent on an assumption that has so far been implicit in our analysis—that we can ignore all costs of buying and selling other than the price paid. This assumption, sometimes called *zero transaction costs*, is a reasonable approximation for much of our economic activity and one that will be retained through most of the book. Exceptions are discussed in parts of Chapters 6 and 17. It is not clear that the assumption is reasonable here. Imagine, for example, that you have 20 automobiles and want a house. The cookie price of an automobile is 40,000; the cookie price of a house is 800,000. It seems, from the discussion of the previous paragraph, that all you have to do to get your house is trade automobiles for cookies and then cookies for the house.

But where will you put 800,000 cookies while you wait for the seller of the house to come collect them? How long will it take you to count them out to him? What condition will the cookies be in by the time you finish? Clearly, in the real world, there are some problems with such indirect transactions.

This brings us to the second reason why relative prices—prices of goods in terms of other goods—must fit the pattern I have described. Trading huge quantities of apples, cookies, peaches, or whatever may be very costly for you and me. It is far less costly for those in the business of such trading—people who routinely buy and sell carload lots of apples, wheat, pork bellies, and many other outlandish things and who make their exchanges not by physically moving the goods around but merely by changing the pieces of paper saying who owns what, while the goods sit still. For such professional traders, the assumption of zero transaction costs is close to being correct. And such traders, in the process of making their living, force relative prices into the same pattern as would consumers with zero transaction costs—even if they never consume any of the goods themselves.

To see how this works, imagine that we start with a different structure of relative prices. A peach trades for 2 apples and an apple trades for 4 cookies, but the price of a peach in cookies is 10. A professional trader in the peach-cookie-apple market appears. He starts with 10,000 peaches. He trades them for 100,000 cookies (the price of a peach is 10 cookies), buys 25,000 apples with the 100,000 cookies (the price of an apple is 4 cookies), trades the apples for 12,500 peaches (the price of a peach in apples is 2). He has started with 10,000 peaches, shuffled some pieces of paper representing ownership of peaches, apples, and cookies, and ended up with 2,500 peaches more than he started with—which he can now exchange for whatever goods he wants! By repeating the cycle again and again, he can end up with as many peaches—and exchange them for as much of anything else—as he wants.

So far, I have assumed that such a transaction—the technical name for it is *arbitrage*—has no effect on the relative prices of the goods traded. But if you can get peaches, in effect, for nothing, simply by shuffling a few pieces of paper around, there is an unlimited number of people willing to do it. When the number of traders—or the quantities each trades—becomes large enough, the effect is to change relative prices. Everyone is trying to sell peaches for cookies at a price of 10 cookies for a peach. The result is to drive down the price of peaches. Everyone is trying to buy apples with cookies at 4 cookies for an apple. The result is to drive up the price of apples measured in cookies and, similarly, to drive up the price of peaches measured in apples. As prices change in this way, the profit from arbitrage becomes smaller and smaller. If the traders have no transaction costs at all, the process continues until there is no profit. When that point is reached, relative prices exactly fit the pattern described above—you get the same number of cookies for your peach whether you trade directly or indirectly via apples. If the traders have some transaction costs, the result is almost the same but not quite; discrepancies in relative prices can remain as long as they are small enough so that it does not pay traders to engage in the arbitrage trades that would eliminate them.

I have now shown that the price of peaches in terms of cookies is determined once we know the price of both goods in apples—precisely, if transaction costs are zero, approximately, if they are not. By similar arguments, we could get the exchange ratio between any two goods (how many of one must you give for one of the other) starting with the price of both of them in apples, or in potatoes, or in anything else. The equimarginal principle then appears as "the ratio of marginal utilities of two goods is the same as their exchange ratio." In other words, if two apples exchange for one cookie, then in equilibrium a cookie must have twice the marginal utility of an apple.

I used money in talking about values as well as in talking about prices. Here too, the money is merely a convenient expository device. The statement that the marginal value of something is $.80 means that you are indifferent between one more unit of it and whatever else you would buy if you had an additional $.80. Just as in the case of prices, the money serves as a conceptual intermediate—we are really comparing one consumption good with another. The arguments of this chapter could be made in "potato values" just as easily as in "dollar values." Indeed potato values are more fundamental than dollar values, as you can easily check by having a hamburger and a plate of french-fried dollars for lunch.

It is often asserted that "economics is about money" or "what is wrong with economics is that it only takes money into account." That is almost the opposite of the truth.

A similar error is the idea that economists assume everyone wishes to maximize his wealth or his income. Such an assumption would be absurd. If you wished to maximize your wealth, you would never consume anything except things (such as food) that you required in order to continue to earn money. If you wished to maximize your income, you would take no leisure (except that needed for your health) and always choose the highest paying job, independent of how pleasant it was. What we almost always do assume is that everyone prefers more wealth to less and more income to less, *everything else held constant*. To say that you would like a raise is not the same thing as to say that you would like it whatever its cost in additional work.

Conclusion: Consumption, Languages, and All That

In my analysis of consumption (Chapters 3 and 4), I have tried to do two things. The first is to show how rational behavior may be analyzed in a number of different ways, each presenting the same logical structure in a different language. The second is to use the analysis to derive three interrelated results.

The simplest of the three, derived once with indifference curves and once with marginal value, is that demand curves slope down—the lower the price of something, the more you buy. In both cases, the argument depended on declining marginal utility. In both cases, there was a possible exception, based on the ambiguity between a fall in (one) price and a rise in income; in both cases, the ambiguity vanishes if we insist on a "pure" price change—a change in one price balanced by either a change in the other direction of all other prices or a corresponding change in income. It also vanishes if we assume that any one good makes up a small enough part of our consumption that we may safely ignore the effect on our real income of a change in its price.

A second result was that the value to a consumer of being able to buy a good at a price, which we call consumer surplus, equals the area under the demand curve and above the price. At this point, that may seem like one of those odd facts that professors insist, for their own inscrutable reasons, on having students memorize. I suggest that instead of memorizing it, you go over the derivation of that result (eggs and wine) until it makes sense to you. At that point, you will no longer need to memorize it, since you will be able to reproduce the result for yourself. It is worth understanding, and not just for passing economics courses. As we will see in later chapters, consumer surplus is the essential key to understanding arguments about policy ("should we have tariffs?") as well as to figuring out how to maximize profits at Disneyland.

The third result from these chapters is the equimarginal principle, which tells us that, as a result of our own rational behavior, the ratio of the marginal utilities of goods is the same as the ratio of their prices. In addition to helping us understand consumption, the equimarginal principle in this guise is one example of a pattern that helps us understand how the high salaries of physicians are connected to the cost of medical school and the labors of interning, why we do not get ahead by switching lanes on the freeway, and how not to make money on the stock market.

POPCORN—AN APPLICATION

In Chapter 2, I asked why popcorn is sold at a higher price in movie theaters than elsewhere. While we will not be ready to discuss possible right answers until Chapter 10, we can at this point use the idea of consumer surplus to show that the obvious answer is wrong. The obvious answer is that once the customers are inside the theater, the owner has a monopoly; by charging them a high price, he maximizes his profit. What I will show is that far from maximizing profits, selling popcorn at a high price results in lower profits than selling popcorn at cost!

To do this, I require the usual economic assumption that people are rational, plus an important simplifying assumption—that all consumers are identical. While the latter assumption is unrealistic, it should not affect the monopoly argument; if the theater owner charges high prices because he has a monopoly, he should continue to do so even if the customers are all the same. Here and elsewhere, the assumption of identical consumers (and identical producers) very much simplifies our analysis. It is frequently a good way of getting a "first approximation" solution to an economic problem.

The theater owner is selling his customers a package consisting of the opportunity to watch a film, plus associated goods such as comfortable seats, clean rest rooms, and the opportunity to buy popcorn. He charges his customers the highest price at which he can sell the package. Since the customers are identical, there is one price which everyone will pay and a slightly higher price which no one will pay.

In order to decide what to put into the package, the owner must consider how changes will affect its value to the customers and hence the maximum he can charge the customers for a ticket. Suppose, to take a trivial case, he decides to improve the package by giving every customer a quarter as he comes in the door. Obviously this will increase the amount the customers are willing to pay for a ticket by exactly $.25. The owner is worse off by the time and trouble spent handing out the coins.

Suppose the theater owner decides that since he has a monopoly on providing seats in the theater, he might as well charge $1 for each seat in addition to the admission price. Since everyone wants a seat, the consumer is paying (say) $4 for an admission ticket and another $1 for a seat. That is the same as paying $5 for admission. If the customer was not willing to pay $5 for the movie, he will be no more willing when the payment is divided into two pieces; if he was willing to pay $5, the theater owner should have been charging $5 in the first place.

Now suppose the theater owner is trying to decide whether to sell popcorn in the theater at $1/carton or not sell it at all. One advantage to selling popcorn is that he gets money for the popcorn; another is that customers prefer a theater that sells popcorn to one that does not and are therefore willing to pay more for admission. How much more?

Figure 4-8 shows a customer's demand curve for popcorn. At $1/carton, he buys 1 carton. The shaded area is his consumer surplus—$.25. That means (by the definition of consumer surplus) that the customer is indifferent between being able to buy popcorn at $1/carton and being unable to buy any popcorn but being given $.25; the opportunity to buy popcorn at $1/carton is worth $.25 to him. Making the popcorn available at that price is equivalent to handing each customer a quarter as he walks in the door; it makes the package offered by the theater (movie plus amenities—including popcorn) $.25 more valuable to him, so the theater owner can raise the admission price by $.25 without driving off

Figure 4-8

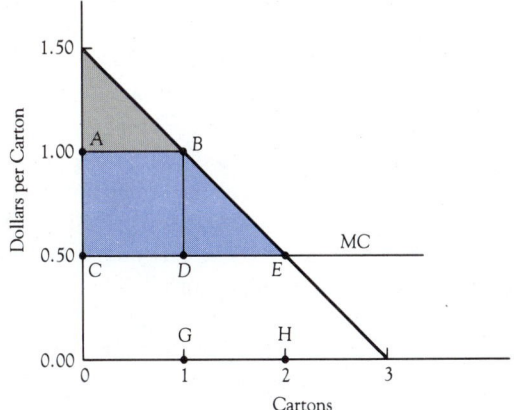

One theater customer's demand curve for popcorn.   The lightly shaded triangle is the customer's consumer surplus from buying popcorn at $1/carton. The darkly shaded region (ABEDC) is the increase in his consumer surplus if price falls from $1/carton to $.50/carton.

the customers. The owner should start selling popcorn, provided that the cost of doing so is less than $1.25/customer. That is what he gets from selling the popcorn—a dollar paid for the popcorn plus $.25 more paid for admission because the opportunity to buy popcorn is now part of the package.

Is $1/carton the best price? Assume that, as shown on Figure 4-8, the *marginal cost* to the owner of producing popcorn (the additional cost for each additional carton produced) is $.50/carton. He can produce as many cartons as he likes, at a cost of $.50 (for popcorn, butter, wages, and so forth) for each additional carton. Suppose he lowers the price of popcorn from $1 to $.50. He is now selling each customer 2 cartons instead of 1, so his revenue is still $1/customer. His costs have risen by $.50/customer, since he has to produce 2 cartons instead of 1. Consumer surplus, however, has risen by the colored area on Figure 4-8, which is $.75; he can raise the admission price by that amount without losing customers. His revenue from selling popcorn is unchanged, his costs have risen by $.50/customer, and his revenue from admissions has risen by $.75/customer, so his profits have gone up by $.25.

The argument is a general one; it does not depend on the particular numbers I have used. As long as the price of popcorn is above its cost of production, profit can be raised by lowering the price of popcorn to its production cost (MC on Figure 4-8) and raising the price of admission by the resulting increase in consumer surplus. The reduction in price reduces the owner's revenue on the popcorn that he was selling already by its quantity times the reduction—rectangle *ABDC*. The increase in production cost due to producing the additional popcorn demanded because of the lower price is just covered by what the consumers pay for it, since the price is equal to the cost of production; on Figure 4-8, both the additional cost and the additional revenue from selling popcorn are rectangle *DEHG*. Consumer surplus goes up by the colored area in the figure—rectangle *ABDC* plus triangle *BDE*. Since the owner can raise his admission price by the increase in consumer surplus, his revenue goes up by (*ABDC* + *BDE*) (increased admission) + (*DEHG* − *ABDC*) (change in revenue from selling popcorn). His cost goes up by *DEHG*, so his profit goes up by the area of triangle *BDE*.

The same argument can be put in words, without reference to the diagram: "So far as the popcorn already being sold is concerned, the price reduction is simply a transfer from the theater owner to the customer, so revenue from selling popcorn goes down by the same amount that consumer surplus goes up (*ABDC*). So far as the additional popcorn sold at the lower price is concerned, the customer pays the owner its production cost (*DEHG*) and is left with its consumer surplus (*BDE*). So if we lower the price of popcorn down to its cost of production, consumer surplus goes up by more than revenue from popcorn goes down. The theater owner can transfer the consumer surplus to his own pocket by raising the admission price to the theater; by doing so (and reducing popcorn to cost), he increases his profit by the consumer surplus on the additional popcorn (*BDE*)."

This shows that any price for popcorn above production cost lowers the profits of the theater owner, when the effect of the price of popcorn on what customers are willing to pay to come to the theater is taken into account.

We are now left with a puzzle. We have used economics to prove that a theater owner maximizes his profits by selling popcorn at cost. Economics also tells us that theater owners should want to maximize their profits and know how to do so. That implies that they will sell popcorn at cost. Yet they apparently do not. Something is wrong somewhere; there must be a mistake either in the logic of the argument, in its assumptions, or in our observation of what theaters actually do. We will return to that puzzle, and two possible solutions, in Chapter 10.

OPTIONAL SECTION

CONSUMER SURPLUS AND MEASURING WITH A (SLIGHTLY) RUBBER RULER

In using the equality between the marginal value curve and the demand curve to derive a downward-sloping demand curve earlier in this chapter, I discussed some of the problems of measuring value in goods instead of in utility. We are now in a position to see how the same problem affects the concept of consumer surplus.

Suppose a new good becomes available at price P. Consumer surplus, the area under the demand curve for the new good and above a horizontal line at P, is supposed to be the net benefit to me in dollars of being able to buy the new good—the increase in my utility divided by my marginal utility for a dollar. But as I increase my expenditure on the new good, I must be decreasing my expenditure on all old goods. The less I spend on something, the less I consume of it; the less I consume, the greater its marginal utility. So after I have adjusted my consumption pattern to include the new good, the marginal utility of all other goods has risen. Since the marginal utility of a dollar is simply the utility of what I can buy with it, the marginal utility of a dollar has also increased. But the original discussion of marginal utility, marginal value, and consumer surplus treated the marginal utility of a dollar (usually called the marginal utility of income) as a constant.

The reason this is a good approximation for most purposes is shown in Figure 4-9. I assume that I am initially consuming 25 different goods, A-Y, and a twenty-sixth good, Z, becomes available at a price P_z. The graphs show my marginal utility for goods A, B, and Z. In the initial situation (shown by the dashed lines), I am dividing all of my income among goods A-Y in such a way that the marginal utility of an additional dollar's worth of each good is the same. The price of good A is assumed to be $1/unit (the units could be pounds, gallons, or whatever, depending on what sort of good it is); of B, $2/unit.

After good Z becomes available, I rearrange my expenditure so that I again have the same marginal utility per dollar on each unit. Since some of my income is now going to Z, I must be spending less on each other good, as shown by the solid lines in the figure. If I simply transferred all of the expenditure away from one good, its marginal utility per dollar would rise, the marginal utility per dollar of the other goods would stay the same, and I would no longer be satisfying the equimarginal principle, and hence no longer maximizing my utility. So instead, I reduce my expenditure a little on each good, raising the marginal utility of each by the same amount. The result is that I am now consuming $Q_a - \Delta Q_a$ of good A, $Q_b - \Delta Q_b$ of good B, and so forth; by the equimarginal principle we have

$$MU(Q_a - \Delta Q_a)/P_a = MU(Q_b - \Delta Q_b)/P_b = \ldots = MU(Q_z)/P_z. \qquad \text{(Eqn. 1)}$$

Since total expenditure is unchanged, the reduction in expenditure on goods A-X must equal the new expenditure on good Z, so

$$\Delta Q_a P_a + \Delta Q_b P_b + \ldots = Q_z P_z. \qquad \text{(Eqn. 2)}$$

Figure 4-9

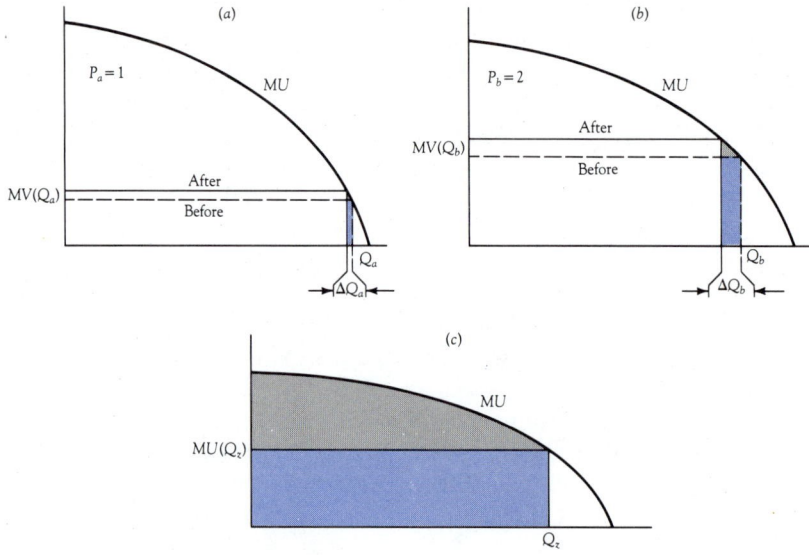

Marginal utility curves for 3 goods, showing the situation before and after the third good becomes available. When good Z becomes available, the consumer buys less of goods A-Y and spends the money on Z instead. Colored regions show utility losses on goods A and B which (with similar losses on C-Y, not shown) add up to the colored region representing expenditure on good Z.

Since I am consuming 25 other goods, the decrease in consumption of each of them when I start consuming the new good as well is probably very small, as shown on the figures. So the marginal utility of a dollar's worth of the good is almost the same after the change as before.

To put the derivation of consumer surplus in terms of utility rather than in dollars (and so make it more precise), consider the narrow shaded areas (mostly but not entirely colored) in Figures 4-9a and 4-9b. They represent the utility loss as a result of the decreased consumption of goods A and B. They are made up almost entirely of the narrow colored rectangles whose height is $MU(Q - \Delta Q)$

and whose width is ΔQ, where "Q" is Q_a in Figure 4-9a and Q_b in Figure 4-9b. If you sum the areas of those rectangles (for all of goods A-Y), you get

$$\text{Total area} = MU(Q_a - \Delta Q_a)\Delta Q_a + MU(Q_b - \Delta Q_b)\Delta Q_b + \ldots$$

Substituting in from Equation 1 we have

$$= (MU(Q_z)/P_z) \times \{P_a\Delta Q_a + P_b\Delta Q_b + \ldots,$$

which by Equation 2

$$= (MU(Q_z)/P_z)(P_zQ_z) = MU(Q_z)Q_z = \text{colored area on Figure 4-9c.}$$

Since the total utility I get from consuming Q_z of Z is the area under the MU curve—the shaded area plus the colored area—my net gain is the shaded area— my consumer surplus measured in utiles.

The one approximation in all of this was in ignoring the part of the narrow shaded areas on Figures 4-9a and 4-9b that was not colored. That difference be- comes smaller, relative to the colored part, the larger the number of different goods being consumed.

PROBLEMS

1. Figure 4-10a shows a number of total utility curves and Figure 4-10b shows marginal utility curves.
   a. Which total utility curves correspond to goods? (There may be more than one.)

Figure 4-10

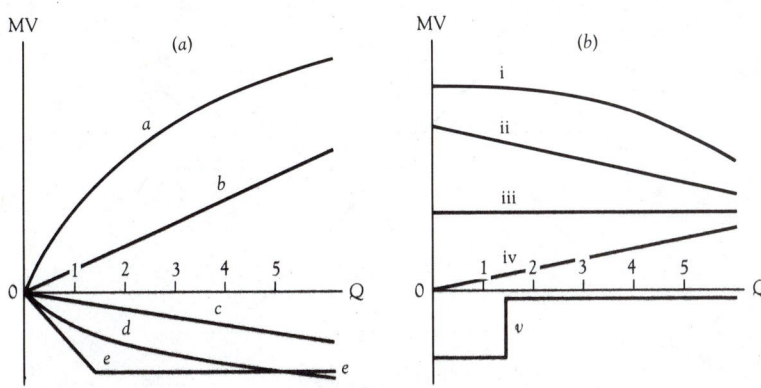

Total and marginal utility curves.   For Problem 1.

b. Which marginal utility curve corresponds to total utility curve *b*? to total utility curve *e*?

c. Which total utility curves and which marginal utility curves are consistent with declining marginal utility?

2. Figure 4-11 shows your demand curve for Tab.

a. Approximately how much better off are you being able to buy all the Tab you want at $5/gallon than not being able to buy any?

b. How much better off are you being able to buy all the Tab you want at $3/gallon than at $5/gallon?

3. Fill in the first blank in the following sentence from part (a) and the second from part (b):

If you are a rational consumer, _____ has the same _____.

a.
  i. everything you consume
  ii. everything you could consume

b.
  i. value
  ii. marginal value
  iii. average value
  iv. average value per dollar's worth
  v. marginal value per dollar's worth

Figure 4-11

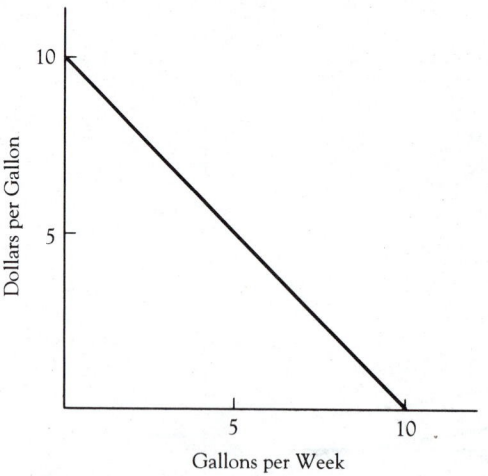

Your demand curve for Tab.   For Problem 2.

4. Estimate, to within a factor of 10, what percentage of all water used in the U.S. is used to drink. Give your sources. Is the common conception of a "water shortage" as a situation where people are going thirsty an accurate one? What does this tell us about the difference between the marginal value of water at a quantity of a few gallons a week and the marginal value of water at the quantity we actually consume? (The numerical part of this cannot be answered from anything in the book; it is intended to give you practice in the useful art of "back-of-the-envelope" calculations—very rough estimates of real-world magnitudes—while at the same time connecting the abstract examples of the chapter to something real.)

5. Figure 4-12 shows your demand curve for sapphires. For religious reasons, sapphires can neither be bought nor sold. You accidentally discover 100 carats of sapphires. How much better off are you?

6. Figure 4-13 shows your demand curve for red tape. There is no market for red tape, but the government, which is trying to reduce its inventory, orders you to buy 50 pounds of it at $.20/pound. How much better or worse off are you as a result?

7. In discussing Figure 4-4, I asserted that "if you had to choose between buying 2 gallons of wine a week at a price of $25/gallon or buying no wine at all, you would buy the wine." How can I tell that from the figure?

8. In the example worked out in the text, how would profit be changed by a further reduction in the price of popcorn to $.25/carton?

Figure 4-12

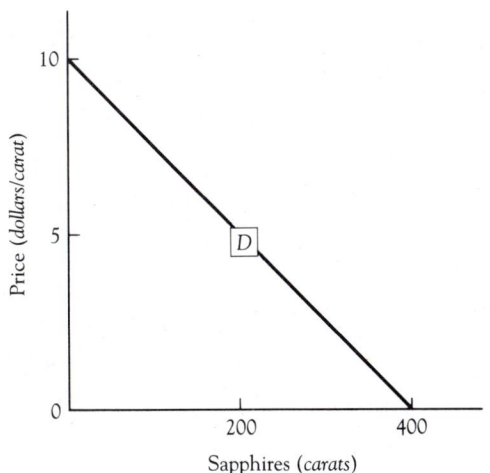

Your demand curve for sapphires.   For Problem 5.

Figure 4-13

Figure 4-13

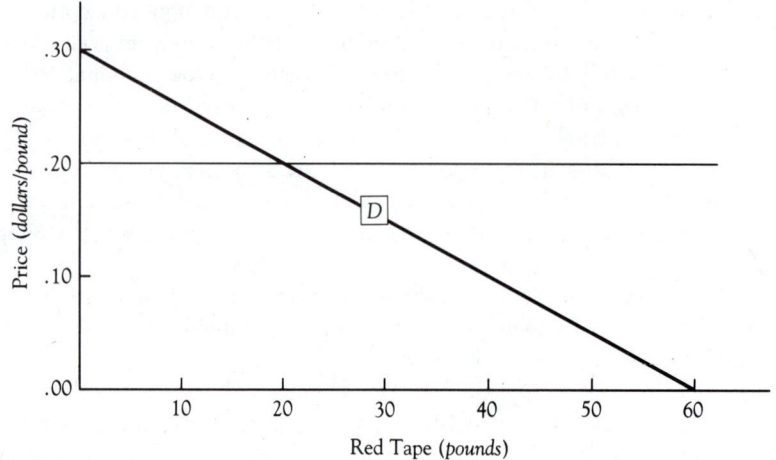

Your demand curve for red tape.   For Problem 6.

Chapter 5

Production

The preceding two chapters discussed consumption; this chapter discusses production, using some of the same tools. For simplicity we assume that there is only a single input to production, the producer's time, which he may use to produce any one of a variety of goods. You may think of these goods either as services, such as lawn mowing or dish washing, or as objects produced from raw materials that are freely available.

Implicit in the assumption is that the producer is indifferent between an hour spent mowing lawns and an hour spent washing dishes. Otherwise there would have to be either an additional input ("unpleasantness of mowing lawns") or an additional (perhaps disvalued) output ("getting grass all over my clothes"); since we assume that at any one time only one input is being used and only one output produced, neither is possible.

PART 1 · THE ARGUMENT

In Chapters 3 and 4, we derived the demand curve for a good from the preferences of the consumer; in this chapter, we will be deriving supply curves from the preferences and abilities of the producers. The first step is to see how a potential producer decides which good to produce. The next is to see how he decides how many hours to work. The final step is to consider the situation in which there are many different producers, so that the supply curve is the sum of their individual supply curves.

Choosing a Good to Produce

Table 5-1 shows the output per hour, the price, and the implicit wage for each of 3 goods—mowed lawns, washed dishes, and meals. The price for a mowed lawn is $10 and the producer can mow 1 lawn per hour, so the implicit wage is $10/hour. Similarly, washing 70 dishes per hour at $.10/dish yields a wage of $7, and cooking 2 meals per hour at $3/meal yields $6/hour. Since the only difference among the alternatives (from the standpoint of the producer) is the implicit wage, he chooses to mow lawns. Note that this decision depends on (among other things) the price he gets for each lawn. If the price for mowing a lawn were less than $7 (and the other prices were as shown in the table), he would wash dishes instead.

Table 5-1

	Lawn Mowing	Dish Washing	Cooking
Output	1 lawn/hour	70 dishes/hour	2 meals/hour
Price	$10/lawn	$.10/dish	$3/meal
Wage	$10/hour	$7/hour	$6/hour

The Supply of Labor

Figure 5-1a shows a graph of the marginal *dis*value of labor as a function of the number of hours worked. If you were enjoying 24 hours per day of leisure, it would take only a small payment ($.50 in the figure) to make you willing to work for a single hour; you would be indifferent between 0 hours a day of work and 1 hour plus $.50. If, on the other hand, you were already working 10 hours a day, it would take a little over $10 to make you willing to work an additional hour.

Suppose the wage is $10/hour and you are working 5 hours per day. You would be willing to work an additional hour for an additional payment of about $3; since you can actually get $10 for it, you are obviously better off working the extra hour. The same argument applies as long as the marginal disvalue of labor to you is less than the wage, so you end up working that number of hours for which the two are equal. The number of hours of labor you supply at a wage of $10 is the number at which your marginal disvalue for labor is equal to $10. The same relation applies at any other wage, so your marginal disvalue for labor curve is also your supply curve for labor, just as, in Chapter 4, your marginal value curve for a good was also your demand curve.

Presumably, leisure (like other goods) is worth less to you the more of it you have—it has declining marginal value. The cost to you of an hour of labor is giving up an hour of leisure—the less leisure you have, the greater that cost. So if leisure has decreasing marginal value, labor has increasing marginal disvalue. That fits my experience, and probably yours; the more hours a day I am working, the less willing I am to work an additional hour.

Producer Surplus

We can now define producer surplus in a way analogous to consumer surplus. Suppose the wage is $10/hour. You are willing to work the first hour for $.50; since you actually receive $10 for it, your net gain is $9.50. The next hour is worth about a dollar to you; you receive $10 for a gain of 9. Summing these "profits" over all the hours you work gives us the colored area of Figure 5-1a.

Note that the benefit to you of being able to work for $10/hour—your producer surplus—is not the same as the salary you get. Working 10 hours at a wage of $10/hour gives you a salary of $100/day. This is not, however, your gain from working. To find that, you must subtract out the cost to you of working—the value to you of the time that you spend working instead of doing something else. Your salary is the area of a rectangle ten hours/day wide by ten dollars/hour high—the sum of the shaded and the colored regions on Figure 5-1a. The value to you of your time—the total disvalue to you of working 10 hours a day—is the shaded area *under* the supply curve; you might think of it as how much worse off you would be if you were forced to work 10 hours per day and paid nothing. The rectangle minus the area under the supply curve is the area *above* the supply curve—your producer surplus, the amount by which you are better off working at $10/hour than not working at all.

The result, as you can see, is very much like the result for consumer surplus in the previous chapter. The consumer buys goods which have a certain total value to him, measured by the area under his marginal value curve—which equals his demand curve. He pays for them an amount equal to the rectangle price times quantity. His consumer surplus is the difference between the value of what he gets and what he pays—the area under the demand curve and above the price.

Figure 5-1

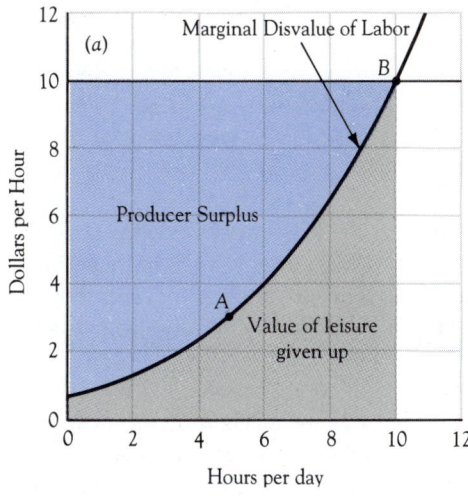 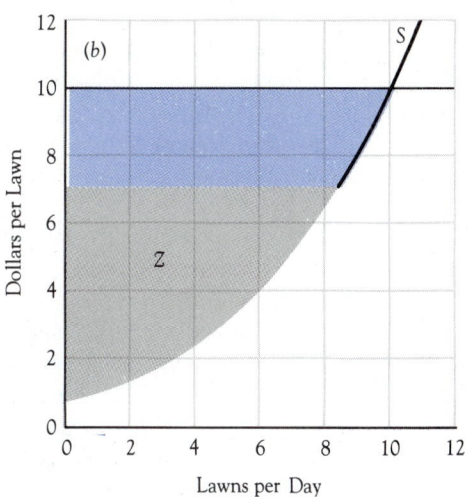

Producer surplus, the marginal disvalue for labor, and the supply curve for lawn mowing. The area above the marginal disvalue for labor curve and below $10/hour is the producer surplus from being able to work at $10/hour. The shaded area above the supply curve for lawns and below the price is the producer surplus from mowing lawns at that price ($10/lawn). The supply curve is horizontal at the price at which you are indifferent between lawn mowing and your next most profitable production opportunity (dish washing).

The producer "sells his leisure," which has a value to him measured by the area under his marginal value for leisure curve, which is the same as his marginal disvalue for labor curve. He receives in exchange the rectangle wage times number of hours worked—the price for selling his leisure (working) times the amount of leisure sold (number of hours worked). His producer surplus is the difference between what he gets for his work and what it cost him—the value of the leisure he gives up—which is the area below the wage and above the marginal disvalue of labor curve. The marginal disvalue for labor curve is the supply curve for labor—just as the marginal value for apples curve is the demand curve for apples.

The Supply of Goods—One Producer

We now have the supply curve for labor, but what we want is the supply curve for mowed lawns. Since I can mow 1 lawn per hour, a price of $10/lawn corresponds to a wage of $10/hour and a labor supply of 10 hours per day corresponds to mowing that many lawns. It appears that the supply curve for lawns and for labor are the same; all I have to do is to relabel the vertical axis "price in $/lawn" and the horizontal axis "lawns/day."

Appearances are deceiving; the supply curve for lawns is not the same as for labor. My decision to mow lawns instead of spending my time producing something else depended on the price I could get for doing so. If that price drops below $7/lawn, my output of mowed lawns drops to 0; I am better off washing dishes instead. The resulting supply curve is shown on Figure 5-1b. The colored area is my producer surplus from producing mowed lawns at $10/lawn. To see why my producer surplus does not include the lightly shaded area Z below the line at $7/lawn, consider what my producer surplus would be if I could get $7 for each lawn I mowed. How much better off am I being able to mow lawns at $7 than not mowing lawns? I am not better off at all; at that wage, I can do just as well washing dishes.

Going from the supply curve for labor to the supply curve for mowed lawns was particularly simple because the rate at which I mow is 1 lawn per hour. Suppose the grass stops growing, someone invents an automatic dishwasher, and I become a cook. Figure 5-2 shows my supply curve for meals, given that my supply curve for labor is as shown on Figure 5-1a.

To derive Figure 5-2, we note that each hour of work produces 2 meals (Table 5-1). Hence I earn $10/hour cooking if the price for meals is $5/meal. Working 10 hours/day, which is what I do if I get $10/hour, produces 20 meals/day. So point B on Figure 5-1a ($10/hour and 10 hours/day) corresponds to point b on Figure 5-2 ($5/meal and 20 meals/day); similarly point A corresponds to point a. The supply curve for meals is the same as the supply curve for labor except that it is "squished" vertically (by a factor of 2) and "stretched" horizontally (by a factor of 2). Unlike the supply curve for mowed lawns shown on Figure 5-1b, it has no horizontal segment—because, by assumption, meals are the only thing left to produce.

Figure 5-2

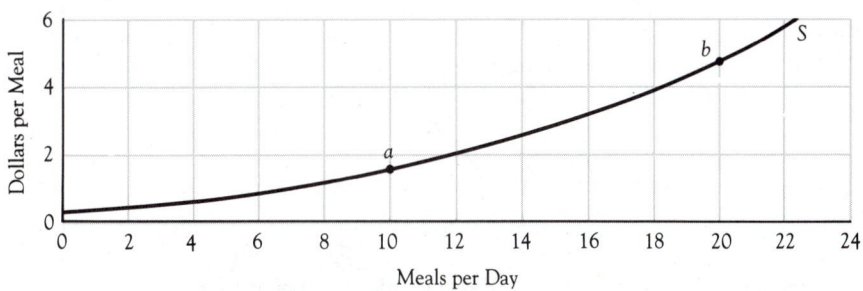

The supply curve for cooking meals. This supply curve is the same as the supply curve for labor, except that each hour worked corresponds to 2 meals cooked and each dollar per meal corresponds to $2/hour. Points *a* and *b* correspond to points A and B on Figure 5-1*a*.

More Than One Producer

So far, I have considered the supply curve of a single producer. If we have more than one, there is no reason to assume they will all be equally good at producing the different goods, nor that they will all have the same supply curves for labor. If they do not, then their supply curves for mowed lawns—or other goods—will also be different, with the horizontal sections occurring at different prices according to their relative skills at different kinds of production. A producer who is very good at mowing lawns (many mowed per hour) or very bad at doing anything else will choose to mow lawns even if the price is low. A producer who is bad at mowing lawns (many hours per lawn) or good at something else will mow lawns only when the price is high. Figure 5-3*a* shows the supply curves for two such producers, A(nne) and B(ill), and their combined supply curve.

As long as the price is below $5/lawn, only Anne produces; the combined supply curve is the same as her supply curve. At a price of $5, Bill abruptly enters the market, mowing 6 lawns per day; adding that to Anne's output of 9 gives a total output of 15. When the price goes from $5 to $6, Anne increases her output by another unit and so does Bill, so total output goes up by 2 to 17.

The combined supply curve is a *horizontal* sum. The summation is horizontal because we are summing *quantities* (shown on the horizontal axis) at each price. Both A and B can sell their products at the same price; whatever that price is, total supply is the (horizontal) sum of what they each produce. The same would be true if we were deriving a total demand curve from two or more individual demand curves. All consumers in a market face the same price, so total quantity demanded at a price is the *quantity* consumer A demands plus the *quantity* consumer B demands plus . . . .

The sum of the producer surplus that B receives at a price of $6 plus the producer surplus that A receives is equal to the producer surplus calculated from the combined supply curve—the area above their combined supply curve and below the horizontal line at $6. The reason is shown on Figures 5-3a through 5-3c. Consider the narrow horizontal rectangle R shown in Figure 5-3a. Its height is ΔP, its width is $S_{A+B} = S_A + S_B$, so its area is $\Delta P \times (S_{A+B}) = \Delta P \times S_A + \Delta P \times S_B = R_A + R_B$ on Figures 5-3b and 5-3c. The same applies to all of the other little horizontal rectangles that make up the producer surplus; in each case, the area of the rectangle on Figure 5-3a, showing the summed supply curve, is the sum of the areas of the rectangles on Figures 5-3b and 5-3c, which show the individual supply curves. So the shaded area on Figure 5-3a equals the sum of the shaded areas on 5-3b and 5-3c. The shaded areas are not precisely equal to the corresponding surpluses, since the rectangles slightly over-lap the supply curve; but the thinner the rectangles are, the smaller the discrepancy. In the limit as the height of the rectangles (ΔP) goes to 0, the shaded areas become exactly equal to the corresponding producer surpluses, so the producer surplus calculated from the summed supply curve is the sum of the producer sur-pluses from the individual supply curves.

The result applies to any number of producers, as does a similar result for the consumer surplus of any number of consumers. So we can find the sum of the surpluses received by consumers or producers by calculating the surplus for their combined demand or supply curve just as if it were the demand or supply curve for a single individual. This fact will be important in Chapter 7, where we analyze the cost that taxes impose on producers and consumers, and elsewhere.

Figure 5-3

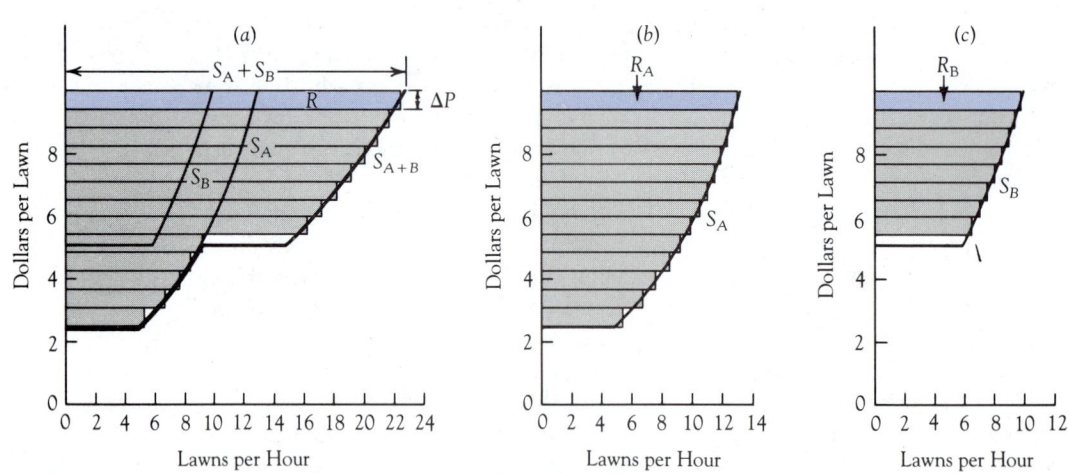

The producer surplus for a two-producer supply curve. The colored rectangle R is the sum of R_A and R_B, and the same is true for the other rectangles. So the shaded area on Figure 5-3a is the sum of the shaded areas on Figures 5-3b and 5-3c. As ΔP approaches zero, the shaded area on each figure becomes exactly (instead of approximately) equal to the corresponding producer surplus. Hence the producer surplus calculated from the summed supply curve S_{A+B} is the sum of the producer surpluses calculated from S_A and S_B.

We now have two different reasons to expect that supply curves will slope up. The first is the increasing marginal disvalue of labor. The second is that as the price of a good rises, more and more people find that they are better off producing it than producing anything else. As each new producer comes in, the supply curve gets a new horizontal segment—the increased price results in increased quantity above and beyond any increased production by existing producers. This will prove important in the next section, where we see that the first reason for expecting supply curves to slope up is less powerful than it at first appears.

PART 2 · SOME PROBLEMS

Look again at Figure 5-1a, and think about what it means. At a wage of $1/hour, the producer is working for 2 hours per day and earning $2/day. It may be possible to live on an income of $730/year, but it is not easy. At a wage of $15/hour, the same individual chooses to work 12 hours per day and earn $65,700/year. There are probably people earning that kind of money who work those hours for 365 days per year, but I suspect that for most of them the reason is more that they like working than that they want the money.

Income Effects in Production and the Backward-Bending Supply Curve for Labor

The mistake in the analysis that produced Figure 5-1a is the omission of what was described in Chapter 3 as the "income effect." An increase in wages (say, from $10/hour to $11/hour) has two effects. It makes leisure more costly—each hour not worked means $11 less income instead of $10. That is an argument for working more hours at the higher salary. But at the same time, the increased wage means that the producer is wealthier—and hence inclined to purchase more leisure. It is possible for the second effect to outweigh the first, in which case the increased wage causes a decrease in hours worked, as shown in Figure 5-4. This is called a "backward-bending" supply curve for labor; the backward-bending portion is from F to G (and presumably above G). The result, in the case of a single producer, would be a supply curve for goods that sloped in the wrong direction; for some range of goods, higher prices would generate less output instead of more.

This is not the first time we have seen a conflict between income and substitution effects; in Chapter 3, the same situation generated a Giffen good—a good whose demand curve sloped in the wrong direction. I argued that there were good reasons not to expect to observe Giffen goods in real life. Those reasons do not apply to the backward-bending supply curve for labor.

One of the reasons was that while we generally expect consumption of goods to go up when income goes up, a Giffen good must be an inferior good—a good whose consumption goes down with increasing income. Indeed, a Giffen good must be so strongly inferior that the income effect of a decrease in its price (which is equivalent to an increase in real income) outweighs the substitution effect. The backward-bending supply curve for labor, on the other hand, only requires that leisure be a normal good; an increase in the wage rate makes the producer richer and hence inclined to buy more leisure. The other reason was that a Giffen good must also be a good on which we spend a large fraction of our income, in order that the decrease in its price can have a substantial effect on real income. This is implausible in the case of consumption, but not in the case of production. Most of us diversify in consumption but specialize in production; we divide our income among many consumption goods, but we get most of that income from selling one kind of labor. If the price we get for what we sell changes substantially, the result is a substantial change in our income. Hence the backward-bending supply curve for labor is far more likely to occur than is the Giffen good.

<hr>

Figure 5-4

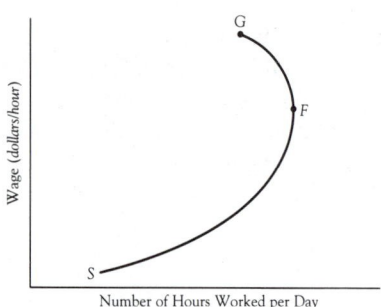

A backward-bending supply curve for labor.   As the wage increases, the number of hours worked first increases (up to point F), then decreases.

<hr>

Economics is considerably simpler if demand curves always slope down and supply curves always slope up than if they insist in wriggling about as in Figure 5-4. Fortunately the argument for upward-sloping supply curves for goods does not entirely depend on upward-sloping supply curves for labor. If individuals supply less labor, and hence mow fewer lawns, as the price of lawn mowing rises, their individual supply curves will slope backward. But if an increase in the price increases the number of people who find that lawn mowing yields a higher wage than any other alternative, the aggregate supply curve for lawns may still slope normally. It is particularly likely to do so in a large and complicated society. If many different goods are being produced, with the production of each employing only a small part of the population, even a small rise in the price of a good can induce some people to switch to producing it. It is still more likely if, as seems likely, only some of the producers are on the backward-bending portion of their supply curve for labor.

Marginal Value vs Marginal Utility

Another way of looking at the problem of the backward-bending supply curve for labor is as a result of the effect of a change in income on the relation between marginal value and marginal utility. When your wage increases from $10/hour to

$11, you are being offered more dollars for your time than before, but since at the higher income each dollar is worth less to you (the "marginal utility of income" has fallen), you may actually be being offered less utility—eleven dollars at the higher income may be "worth less" to you than $10 was before. If so, and if the marginal utility of leisure to you has not been changed by the increase in your income, you will choose to sell less of your time at the higher wage, and so to work fewer hours. If the marginal utility of leisure has *increased* (you now have more money to spend on golf games and Caribbean vacations), the argument holds still more strongly.

The analysis of production given in the first part of this chapter (ignoring income effects) would correctly describe a producer whose income from other sources was large in comparison to his income from production. Changes in his wage would have only a small effect on his income, so we could legitimately ignore the income effect and consider only the substitution effect. The result would be the sort of curves shown in Figures 5-1a, 5-1b, and 5-2.

The question of whether the supply curve for labor was or was not backward bending was a matter of considerable controversy 200 years ago, when Adam Smith wrote *The Wealth of Nations*, the book that founded modern economics. Some employers argued that if wages rose, their employees would work shorter hours and the national income would fall; Smith argued that higher wages would mean better fed, healthier employees willing and able to work more in exchange for the higher reward. It is worth noting that Smith, who is usually described as a defender of capitalism, consistently argued that what was good for the workers was good for England and almost as consistently that what was good for the "merchants and manufacturers" (high tariffs and other special favors from government) was bad for England. He was a defender of capitalism—but not of capitalists.

Whether the supply curve for labor is backward bending is also one of the issues in the current controversy over "supply-side economics" and the "Laffer curve." If tax reductions increase after-tax income, will people work more hours because they are getting more for their labor, or fewer because with the higher income they feel less need to work?

PART 3 · INDIFFERENCE CURVES AND THE SUPPLY OF LABOR

So far, we have analyzed the supply curve for labor, or for goods or services produced by labor, by using marginal value curves. Another way is by using indifference curves. The indifference curves on Figure 5-5a show an individual's preferences between leisure and income. Using such a diagram, we can derive a supply curve for labor in a way which allows for the possibility that it may be backward bending. Figure 5-5a shows the production possibility sets (possible combinations of leisure and income) corresponding to prices (for lawn mowing) of $5, $10, and $15/lawn, along with the corresponding indifference curves and optimal bundles. In each case, one possibility is 24 hours per day of leisure and no income. Another is no leisure and a daily income of 24 times the hourly wage; the fact that working 24 hours per day is not a serious alternative corresponds to

Figure 5-5

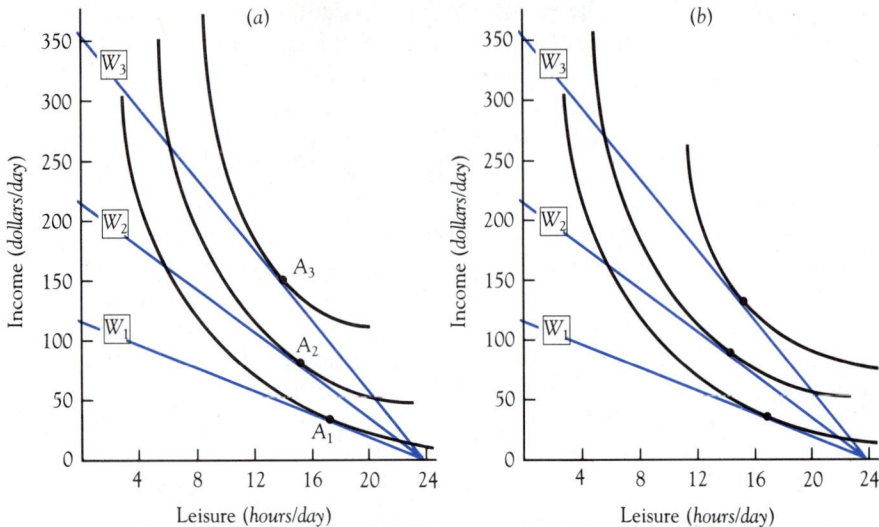

Indifference curve/budget line diagrams for calculating the supply curve of labor. The budget lines show the alternative bundles of leisure and income available to a producer at different wage levels; the indifference curves show his preferences among such bundles. The indifference curves of Figure 5-5a lead to a normally sloped supply curve for labor; those of Figure 5-5b lead to a backward-bending supply curve for labor.

its being on a *very* low indifference curve (not actually shown). The available combinations of leisure and income on Figure 5-5a correspond to the points on the line between those two extremes. As the wage moves from $5 to $10 to $15/hour, the line moves from W_1 to W_2 to W_3 and the optimal bundle from A_1 to A_2 to A_3.

The indifference curves illustrated in Figure 5-5a imply a normal supply curve for labor, at least over the range of wages illustrated; as the wage rises, so does the number of hours worked (shown by a fall in the number of hours of leisure). Figure 5-5b illustrates a different set of indifference curves, leading to a backward-sloped supply curve. Figure 5-6 shows the two supply curves, S_1 (obtained from Figure 5-5a) and S_2 (from Figure 5-5b).

Students who try to redo the calculations shown on Figures 5-5a, 5-5b, and 5-6 in homework (or exam) problems frequently make the mistake of assuming that they can simply connect points such as A_1, A_2, and A_3 with a line, and then redraw the same line on another graph as the supply curve for labor. But the vertical axis of Figures 5-5a and 5-5b is income, while the vertical axis of Figure 5-6 is the wage rate; income is wage (dollars/hour) times number of hours worked. The wage on Figure 5-5a is not the height of a point but the slope of a line. W_1, for example, has a slope of (minus) $5/hour and shows the alternatives available to someone who can work at that wage. The point on Figure 5-6 that corresponds to A_1 on Figure 5-5a is C_1; its vertical coordinate is $5/hour (corresponding to the slope of W_1) and its horizontal coordinate is 7 hours per day (corresponding to the number of hours worked at A_1—24 hours per day total minus 17 hours per day of leisure). You may want to check for yourself the correspondence between A_2 and C_2 and between A_3 and C_3.

You may have realized by this point that what we are analyzing in this chapter is simply a special case of what we already analyzed in Chapters 3 and 4. Instead of talking about a supply of labor and a marginal disvalue for labor, we could have started with an individual who had an endowment of a good called "leisure" (24 hours per day) which he could sell at a price (his wage) and for which he had a marginal value curve. Just as in Chapter 4, the marginal value curve is identical to the demand curve. The marginal value for leisure curve is the same as the marginal disvalue for labor curve, and the demand curve for leisure is the same as the supply curve for labor, except that in each case the direction of the horizontal axis is reversed—increasing leisure corresponds to decreasing labor.

Figure 5-6

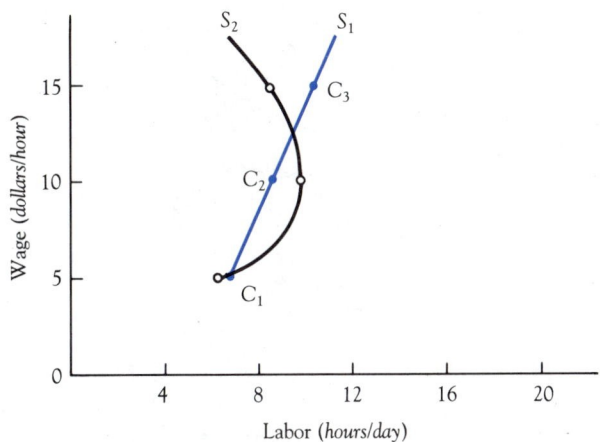

The supply curves for labor implied by Figures 5-5a and 5-5b. Points C_1, C_2, and C_3 correspond to points A_1, A_2, and A_3 on Figure 5-5a. Note that the vertical axis of this figure shows wage, not income; wage on Figures 5-5a and 5-5b is not the height of a point but the slope of a line.

OPTIONAL SECTION

PRODUCTION—MORE COMPLICATED CASES

So far, we have considered production under relatively simple circumstances. Producers sell their output on the market, so all they have to know in order to decide what to produce is how much it sells for. Amount of production, for any good, is simply proportional to amount of time spent producing it. In this section, we will consider some more complicated cases.

Production Without a Market

So far in my discussion of production, I have assumed that the producer sells his output rather than consuming it himself. Figure 5-7a shows one way of analyzing the alternative—a situation where you consume your own output. MV is the marginal value to you of mowed lawns; MdV is the marginal disvalue of your labor. Your rate of output is 1 lawn per hour. The horizontal axis shows how many mowed lawns you produce and consume. You consume a mowed lawn by enjoying the view—I am not assuming that you eat grass.

Figure 5-7

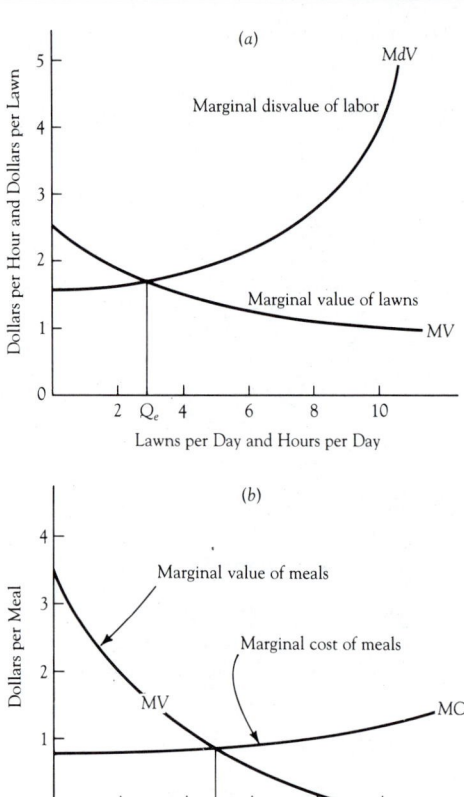

Marginal value/marginal cost diagrams for a producer who consumes his output himself.
On Figure 5-7a, the marginal cost of production is the marginal disvalue of labor; since the output rate is 1 lawn per hour, the vertical axis can be read as either dollars per hour or dollars per lawn, and the horizontal axis can be read as either lawns per day or hours per day. The output rate for meals is 2 per hour; the marginal cost curve for meals is derived by compressing the marginal cost (disvalue) curve for labor by a factor of 2 and stretching it horizontally by a factor of 2.

If the quantity is less than Q_e, where the two curves cross, then the marginal value of the good is greater than the marginal disvalue of the labor used to produce it. That means that if you produce an additional unit, the value to you of the good would be more than the cost to you of the labor used to produce it, so you would be better off producing it. That remains true as long as quantity is less than Q_e, so you keep increasing your level of output (and consumption) until it reaches Q_e. Beyond that, additional units cost you more in labor than they are worth, so any further increase in output would make you worse off.

Figure 5-7a shows a particularly simple case; with an output rate of 1 unit per hour, the number of hours and the quantity produced are the same and so are the disvalue of an hour of labor and the cost of producing 1 unit of the good. Figure 5-7b shows a case where your marginal disvalue for labor curve is the same as on Figure 5-7a, but you are producing 2 meals per hour instead of 1 lawn per hour. Instead of showing marginal disvalue of labor, we show marginal cost of production; if an hour's labor has a disvalue of $4 and produces 2 meals, then the cost of producing meals is $2/meal. The marginal cost curve on Figure 5-7b is derived from the marginal disvalue curve of Figure 5-7a in the same way that, earlier in this chapter, the supply curve of Figure 5-2 was derived from the marginal disvalue curve of Figure 5-1a. The horizontal axis was stretched by a factor of 2, since an hour's work corresponds to producing 2 meals; the vertical axis was squished in half, since a marginal disvalue of labor of $4/hour corresponds to a marginal cost of $2/meal. Just as in the case shown on Figure 5-1a, you maximize your net benefit by producing up to the point where the two curves cross; if you produce less than that, each additional unit costs less than it is worth to you, so you should increase your production. If you produce more than that, each unit by which you reduce production saves you more in labor than it costs you in consumption, so you should decrease production.

Figures 5-7a and 5-7b show cases where only one kind of good can be produced. Figure 5-8 shows one way of analyzing a situation where that is no longer true. Two goods can be produced—meals and mowed lawns. The individual's preferences between them are shown by indifference curves, as in Chapter 3. If he chooses to work 10 hours per day, he can produce 10 lawns, or 20 meals, or any intermediate bundle; his "production possibility set" is the colored area on Figure 5-8. The optimal bundle is the point in the set which intersects the highest indifference curve—point A on the figure. The diagram is exactly the same as for an individual with an income of $10/day who is able to buy lawn mowing at $1/lawn and meals at $.50/meal. In each case, the individual chooses the best bundle from a collection which includes 10 lawns (and no meals), 20 meals (and no lawns), and everything in between.

If you move back from the picture, however, and think about what it means, there is one important difference between the two cases. In discussing a consumer spending money, I argued that he would always spend his entire income, since the only thing money is good for is buying goods. The equivalent in the case of time is always working 14 hours per day—or perhaps 24!

The problem is that in drawing Figure 5-8, I implicitly assumed that the only things which matter to you are meals and mowed lawns—in particular, I assumed that you have no value at all for your own leisure. If that were true, you *would* work 24 hours per day. In drawing the figure, I have correctly translated the assumption into geometry without pointing out, until now, that the assumption itself is absurd. That is an example of why it is a good idea to move back and forth between mathematical and verbal descriptions, in order to make sure you know what your mathematics actually stands for. It is not unusual for articles to be submitted to economics journals that, when translated into English, turn out to make no sense. Some of them get published.

What the figure can be used for is to show what combination of the two goods the individual will choose to produce *if* he decides to work a certain number of hours. To find out how many hours he would choose to work, we would need to add a third dimension in order to show his preferences among meals, lawns, and leisure.

Figure 5-8

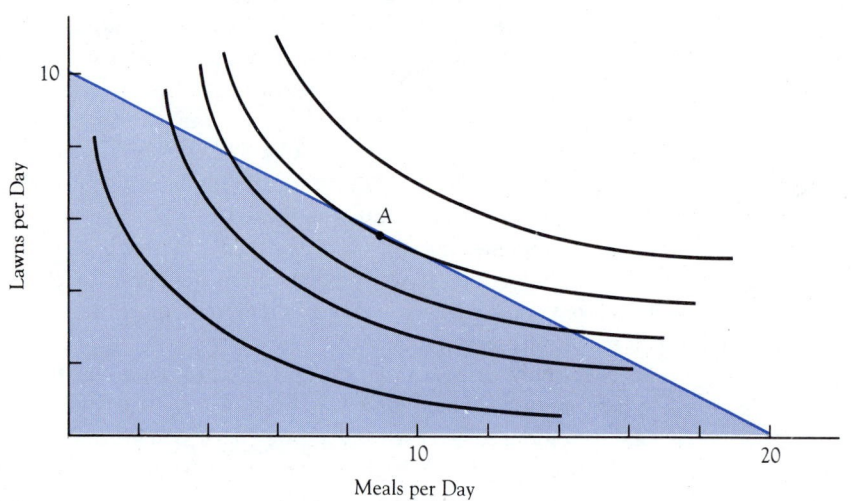

Indifference curves and production possibility set for an individual working 10 hours per day. The individual can produce 1 lawn per hour and 2 meals per hour; different points on the line between 10 lawns and 20 meals represent different divisions of time between producing lawns and producing meals. A is his optimal point.

Nonlinear Production

Let us now drop another assumption. So far, the producer has spent his time producing either one good or another, and the output of each good has been proportional to the time spent producing it. As a result, the frontier of the production possibility set for any pair of goods (total hours worked held constant, as in Figure 5-8) is a straight line, like a budget line. The similarity is not accidental. In Chapter 3, the consumer got goods by spending money; in this chapter, he gets them by spending time. In both cases, total "expenditure" is simply the sum of the price of one good—in money or in time—multiplied by the quantity of that good "bought" plus the price of the other good multiplied by the quantity of it "bought."

Figure 5-9a shows a more complicated case—the production possibility set of someone who is more productive if he specializes. If he spends all his time mowing lawns, he can maintain his lawn-mowing skills at a high level and mow more lawns per hour than if he spends much of his time cooking. If he spends all his time cooking, he can maintain his culinary skills at a high level and produce far more meals per hour than if he spends most of his time mowing lawns. (Perhaps our measure of "quantity" of meals cooked should include some allowance for quality as well, so that a meal cooked by a professional mower of lawns is equivalent to $1/10$ of a meal cooked by a Cordon Bleu chef). Point J shows what happens if he tries to divide his time between lawn mowing and cooking, making himself "a jack of all trades and a master of none."

Figure 5-9b shows a production possibility set whose boundary curves in the opposite way. You may think of this as describing someone who could engage in two quite different kinds of production—digging ditches and writing sonnets. Digging ditches uses the producer's muscles; writing sonnets uses his mind. He can compose a few more sonnets per day if his mind is not distracted by ditch digging, and he can dig a few more ditches if he is not trying to find three more words that rhyme with "world" for the octave of a Petrarchan sonnet. But the two activities compete with each other only mildly, producing the curve shown in the figure.

Figure 5-9

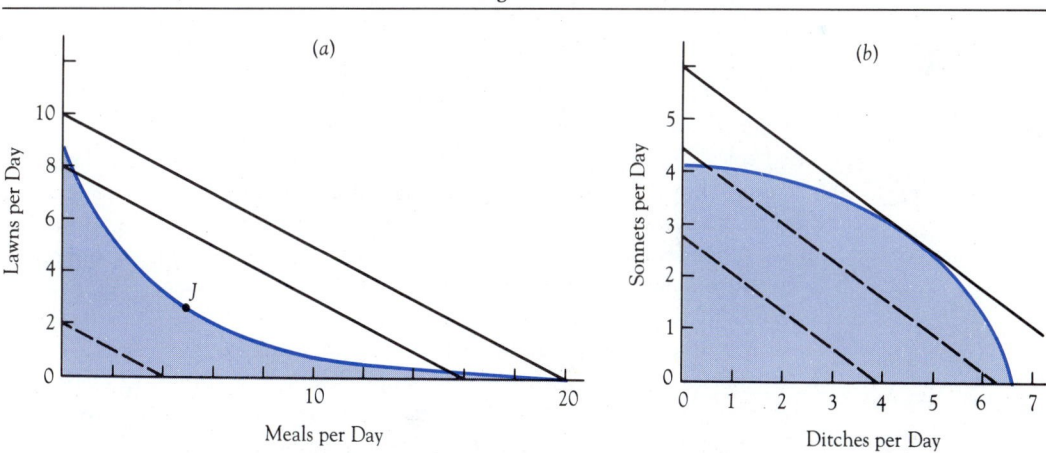

Two cases of nonlinear production. The individual is producing goods to sell. The shaded areas are the different bundles that he can produce. The straight lines are "indifference curves"; each shows all the different bundles that sell for a given amount of money. The producer wants to produce the bundle that sells for the largest amount. That will be the point in the shaded region that touches the highest "indifference curve."

Let us now go back to the problem with which we started this chapter—which good to produce. As in the earlier discussion, we assume the individual is producing goods to sell on the market rather than producing for his own consumption. We can reproduce the argument of Table 5-1, in this more complicated situation, by adding to our figure *equi-income lines*—lines which show the different bundles of goods that can be sold for the same total amount. These are indifference curves from the standpoint of the producer, since all that matters to him about his output is what he can sell it for. Unlike our usual indifference curves, these are straight lines. If lawn mowing sells for $10/lawn and meal cooking for $5/meal, then if you start with a bundle of 10 lawns and want to construct other bundles that will bring you the same amount of money ($100), you find that each time you subtract 1 lawn, you must add 2 meals. The result is a straight line, as shown on Figures 5-9a and 5-9b. The slope of the line depends on the relative prices of the two goods. Picking the optimal set of goods to produce is easy. For any number of hours you consider working, find the highest line that touches the corresponding production possibility set; the point where they touch is the most valuable bundle you can produce with that amount of labor.

By looking at Figure 5-9a, you should be able to convince yourself that whatever the slope of the equi-income lines, the highest equi-income line that touches the production possibility set touches either at one end of the curve (all lawns) or at the other (all meals) or possibly at both, but never anywhere in the middle. This corresponds to what we usually observe—people specialize in production, spending all their time (aside from home production—cooking your own food and washing your own face) producing a single good or service. The situation of Figure 5-9b, on the other hand, while it can lead to specialization (if the slope of the line is either very steep or very shallow, implying that one of the goods has a very high price compared to the other), can also lead to diversified production, as in the case shown.

Figures 5-9a and 5-9b look very much like indifference curve diagrams, especially Figure 5-9a. In a way they are, but the straight line and the curve have switched roles. In an ordinary indifference curve diagram, the straight line is a budget line, showing what bundles of goods the consumer can choose among. The curve is an indifference curve, showing what bundles are equally attractive to him. On Figure 5-9, the curves are the equivalents of budget lines—they show the different bundles of goods the consumer can choose to produce. The straight lines are indifference curves—since the goods are being produced for sale, the producer is indifferent between any two bundles that bring the same price.

From another standpoint, the straight line "indifference curves" of Figure 5-9 and the straight budget lines of Chapter 3 are the same—seen from opposite sides. Both represent all of the bundles of goods that cost a given amount of money. From the standpoint of the consumer with a certain amount of money to spend, the line represents alternative bundles that he can buy with that amount of money. From the standpoint of the producer, it represents alternative bundles that he can sell to get that amount of money. It is the same transaction seen from opposite sides.

In the first part of the optional section of this chapter, I analyzed the situation of a producer producing for his own consumption instead of for the market. Just as in the earlier part of the chapter, I assumed that the amount he produced of any good was simply proportional to the time spent producing it. In the second part of the optional section, I analyzed the situation of a producer producing for the market, but with a more complicated relation between how he spent his time and how much he produced. One could combine the two cases, analyzing the situation of a producer with the production possibility set of Figure 5-9a or 5-9b and the indifference curves of Figure 5-8. I will leave that as an exercise.

PROBLEMS

1. "At a cost of only $10,000,000 of public expenditure, this administration has brought $20,000,000 of jobs into the state. The citizens should be grateful; for every dollar of tax money they give us, we are providing them $2 of income." Assume the facts are correct; discuss the conclusion in terms of the ideas of this chapter. You may want to assume that the numbers given are all totals over a period of, say, 4 years.

2. You are consuming two services—meal cooking and dish washing. Assume that the alternative to having meals cooked for you is dieting, going to restaurants, eating TV dinners, or doing something else that does not produce dirty dishes. There is not much point to washing dishes if they are not dirty, and if you eat meals and never get the dishes washed, the house rapidly becomes intolerable for everyone but the cockroaches. Draw a plausible set of indifference curves to show your preferences for bundles of cooking and washing. Explain why the indifference curves have the shape you show.

3. In the text, I prove that the producer surplus calculated from the summed supply curve for two producers is the sum of the producer surpluses calculated separately. Prove the same result for consumer surplus.

4. Prove the same result for 3 producers.

5. Prove that the result applies to any number of producers.

6. Figure 5-10 is an indifference map showing your tastes for leisure and income. Draw the corresponding supply curve for labor over a range of wages from $1-$10/hour. How does it slope?

7. Table 5-2 shows outputs and prices for two goods—A and B. Figure 5-11 shows your supply curve for labor. Draw your supply curve for good A (assuming that B has the price shown in the table) and your supply curve for good B (assuming that A has the price shown).

Table 5-2

	Good A	_Good B_
Output	3/hour	5/hour
Price	$4	$2

Figure 5-10

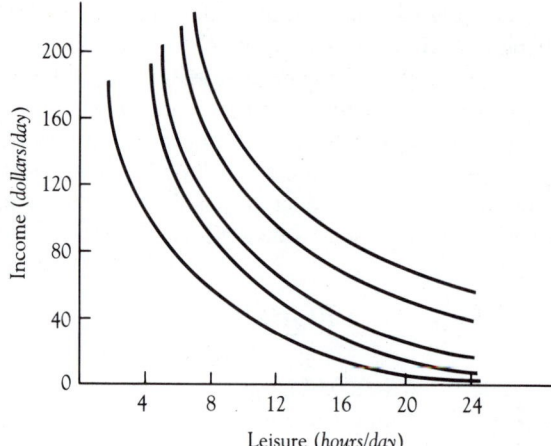

Indifference curves showing preferences with regard to income and leisure. For Problem 6.

Figure 5-11

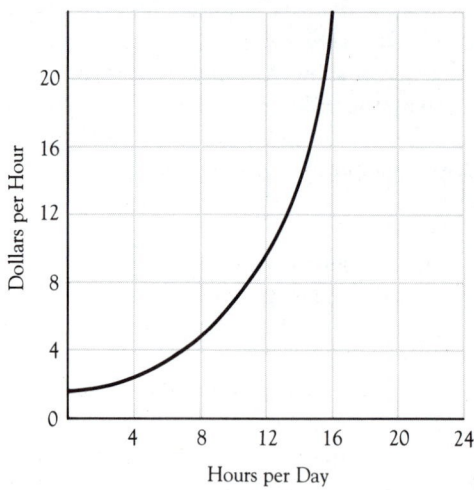

A supply curve for labor. For Problem 7.

8. Some people, such as scoutmasters and PTA officials, are willing to work at jobs that pay nothing—even, in some cases, at jobs that pay less than nothing. Draw a labor supply curve for such a person.

The following problems refer to the optional section:

9. In the situations shown in Figures 5-7a and 5-7b, how much worse off would you be if you were forbidden to produce anything? Discuss your answer in terms of producer surplus and consumer surplus.

10. Use indifference curves to explain why we usually do not specialize in consumption. Use indifference curves to show a situation where an individual does specialize in consumption. This particular kind of solution to the decision problem illustrated on an indifference curve diagram has a name; what is it?

11. Draw an indifference curve diagram showing the producer of Figure 5-9a producing goods for his own consumption. Where is his optimal point? Is he specializing or diversifying?

12. Draw an indifference curve diagram showing the producer of Figure 5-9b producing goods for his own consumption. Where is his optimal point? Is he specializing or diversifying?

Chapter 6

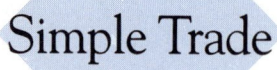

Simple Trade

PART 1 · POTENTIAL GAINS FROM TRADE

Individuals exchange goods. The benefits they receive depend on how much they exchange and on what terms—obviously I am better off (and you worse off) if you buy this book for $100 than if you buy it for $1. We do not yet know how market prices are determined—that is the subject of the next chapter—so we cannot say much about how the gains from trade will be divided among the traders. We do, however, know enough to understand why gains from trade are possible—why one person's gain is not necessarily another person's loss. In this part of the chapter, I will examine the origin of such gains—first in the case where each individual has a stock of goods which he can either consume or trade for someone else's goods and then in the case where individuals produce goods in order to exchange them.

Trade Without Production

I have 10 apples. You have 10 oranges. We have identical tastes, shown in Figure 6-1 and in Table 6-1. Point F is my initial situation, point A is yours; the same indifference curves describe us both. The table shows the bundles equivalent (for both of us) to 10 oranges plus no apples in column 1 (corresponding to indifference curve I_1 on Figure 1) and the bundles equivalent (for both of us) to 10 apples and no oranges in column 2 (corresponding to I_2).

Suppose I trade 5 of my apples for 5 of your oranges. We are now both at point U, with 5 apples and 5 oranges each. Since point U is on a higher indifference curve than either A or F, we are both better off. The same result can be seen from the table. I was indifferent between my initial 10 apples and a bundle of 5 apples plus 2 oranges. Since oranges are a good, I prefer more of them to fewer. It follows that I prefer 5 apples and 5 oranges to 5 apples plus 2 oranges; I am indifferent between having 5 apples plus 2 oranges and having 10 apples, hence I prefer 5 apples plus 5 oranges to my original 10 apples. Similarly, you were indifferent between having your original 10 oranges and having 4 apples plus no oranges; obviously you are better off with 5 apples plus 5 oranges. We have both gained by the trade. That is why we were both willing to make it.

Table 6-1

| Bundle | Column 1 | | Utility | Bundle | Column 2 | | Utility |
	Apples	Oranges			Apples	Oranges	
A	0	10	5	F	10	0	10
B	1	6	5	G	7	1	10
C	2	3	5	H	5	2	10
D	3	1	5	K	4	3	10
E	4	0	5	L	3	5	10
				M	2	8	10
				N	1	12	10
				O	0	17	10

Figure 6-1

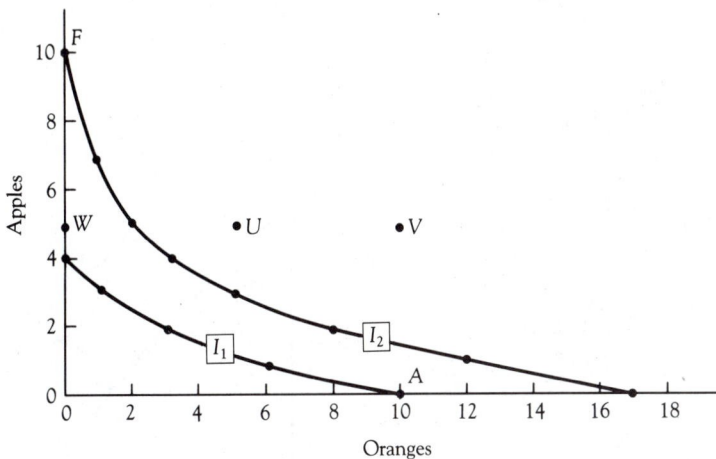

Indifference curves between apples and oranges, showing the same preferences as Table 6-1.

There are many other trades we could have made instead which would also have benefited both of us. Since I am indifferent between my initial situation (10 apples) and having 5 apples plus 2 oranges, I gain by trading away 5 apples as long as I get more than 2 oranges in exchange. Similarly you gain by trading away all of your oranges as long as you get more than 4 apples in exchange. So if you give me 10 oranges for 5 apples, we are both better off than when we started (I am at point V on the figure; you are at point W). If you give me 3 oranges for 5 apples, we are also better off than when we started. Obviously I would prefer to get 10 oranges for my 5 apples, and you would prefer to give only 3. There is a *bargaining range*—a range of different exchanges, some more favorable to me and less favorable to you than others, but all representing improvements on our original situation. One consequence of the existence of a bargaining range is discussed in the section of this chapter on bilateral monopoly. Other consequences—and ways of dealing with the ambiguity as to which trade will actually occur—are discussed later in the optional section.

In the example I have been using, the gains from trade come about because we start with different *endowments*—different initial quantities of goods. The same gains could also occur if we had identical endowments—5 apples plus 5 oranges each, for example—but different preferences. Figure 6-2a shows my preferences (the colored indifference curves) and your (the black indifference curves). We both have the same initial endowment—5 apples and 5 oranges apiece. The arrows show the results of my trading 4 of my apples for 4 of your oranges; both of us are better off. As in the previous case, there are a variety of alternative trades which would also benefit both of us.

It is even possible to draw indifference curves which allow two people with identical preferences *and* identical endowments to gain by trade. In order to do so, however, I must give the indifference curves a shape inconsistent with our usual assumptions, as shown in Figure 6-2b. The goods shown are beer and apples. G is just enough beer to get drunk (you are not interested in being half drunk),

Figure 6-2

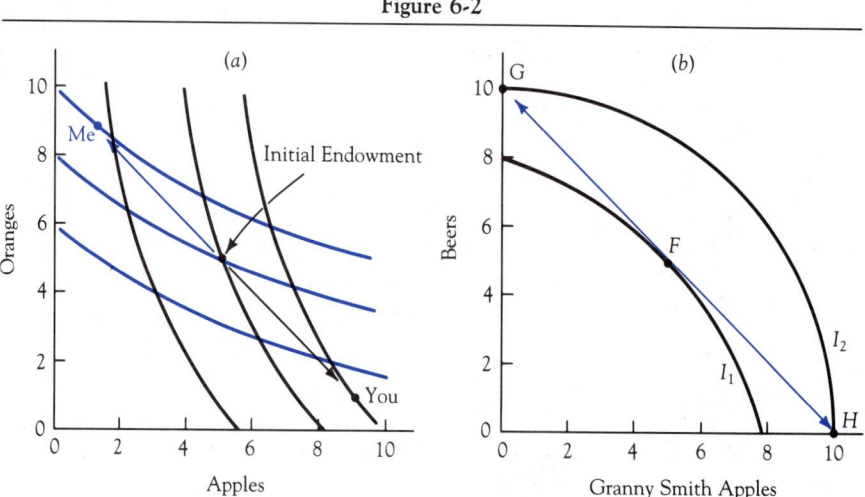

Indifference curves, endowments, and trade.   Panel (*a*) shows a situation for two individuals with different tastes but the same initial endowment. The colored indifference curves show my tastes; the black curves show yours. The figure shows a trade (you give me 5 oranges in exchange for 5 apples) which benefits both of us.

In panel (*b*), we have the same tastes and identical endowments. The trade of 5 apples for 5 beers makes both parties better off, since both point G (10 beers) and point H (10 apples) are preferred to point F (5 of each).

and H is just enough apples to make a big enough pie for your dinner party. F, your original endowment, includes enough apples for too small a pie and enough beer to get you just drunk enough to burn it. You would prefer either G (all beer) or H (all apples) to F. This is not an impossible situation, since marginal utility can increase with quantity for some range of quantities—if it takes a gallon of gasoline to get where you are going, increasing the amount you have from ½ gallon to 1 gallon benefits you more than increasing it from zero to ½ gallon did. But it is a situation we usually prefer to assume away, since it adds complications to the analysis that are usually unnecessary.

Trade and Production—English Version

So far, we have been trading a fixed endowment of goods; now we will consider the combination of trade with production, first in a verbal form and later using geometry. We will find it convenient to consider only two traded goods while holding constant our consumption of all other goods (except leisure). In order to simplify the discussion, we assume that over the range of alternatives considered, we always consume the same amount of the traded goods. (Our demand for them is "perfectly inelastic," to use a term with which you will later become familiar.) The benefit of trade then takes the form of increased leisure; if it takes less time to produce consumption goods, we have more time to spend enjoying them.

Assume it takes me 1 hour to mow my lawn and ½ hour to cook a meal. You are a better cook; you can cook a meal in 15 minutes. You are also a worse mower; it takes you 2 hours to mow the same lawn.

Initially I am mowing my lawn once per day (the grass grows fast around here) and cooking 3 meals per day, for a total of 2½ hours of work. You are doing the same, for a total of 2¾ hours.

I offer to mow your lawn in exchange for your cooking my meals. It will take me 2 hours to mow both lawns; it will take you 1½ hours to cook all 6 meals. Thus we are both better off. Just as in the earlier examples, there are a variety of other trades which would also be improvements on the initial situation. For example, I could offer to mow your lawn once in exchange for 4 meals (you would cook all my meals; I would mow your lawn three days out of four). Since it takes you 1 hour to cook 4 meals and 2 hours to mow the lawn, you are still better off making the trade.

I am better at mowing lawns than you are, so I mow the lawns; you are better at cooking, so you cook. Since "better" appears to mean "can do it in less time," it seems that I could be better than you at both cooking and mowing, and that if I were, there would be no way in which I could benefit from trading with you.

This seems to make sense, but it is wrong—as a simple example will show. Suppose I can cook a meal in 15 minutes and mow a lawn in ½ hour. It takes you ½ hour to cook a meal and 2 hours to mow a lawn. I am better at everything; what can you offer me to trade?

Just as before, you offer to cook my meals in exchange for my mowing your lawn. Before the trade, you spent 1½ hours cooking 3 meals and 2 hours mowing your lawn, for a total of 3½ hours. After the trade, you spend 3 hours cooking meals for both of us. You are better off by ½ hour. What about me?

Before the trade, I spent 45 minutes per day cooking and ½ hour mowing, for a total of 1¼ hours. After the trade, I spend 1 hour per day mowing both lawns, for a total of 1 hour. I am better off too! How can this be? How can it pay me to "hire" you to do something I can do better?

The answer is that the relation between cost to me and cost to you *in time* has nothing to do with the opportunity for trade; time is not what we are trading. The relevant question is what it costs me to mow the lawn *in terms of meals cooked* in comparison to what it costs you to mow the lawn in the same terms. We are, after all, trading meals for mowed lawns, not meals (or lawns) for time.

In the first example I gave, the cost to me of mowing a lawn was 2 meals, since mowing 1 lawn took the time in which I could have made 2 meals. The cost to you of mowing a lawn was 8 meals. Since lawn mowing cost much more to you (in terms of meals) than to me, it was natural for you to buy lawn mowing from me, using meals to pay me.

A different way of describing the same situation is to say that the cost to me of producing a meal was ½ lawn and the cost to you was ⅛ lawn. Since meals cost you much less than they cost me (in terms of lawns), it was natural for me to buy meals from you, using lawn mowing to pay you. These are two descriptions of the same transaction; when we trade lawn mowing for meal cooking, we can describe it as buying lawns with meals or meals with lawns, according to whose side we are looking at it from.

Since a lawn costs you 8 meals, you are willing to buy lawn mowing for any price less than 8 meals per lawn—it is cheaper than producing it yourself. Since it costs me 2 meals, I am willing to sell for any price higher than 2. Obviously there is a wide range of prices at which we can both benefit—any price of more than 2 meals per lawn and less than 8 will do.

Now consider the second example, where I can cook a meal in 15 minutes and mow a lawn in 30, while you take 30 minutes to cook a meal and 2 hours to mow a lawn. The cost of mowing a lawn to me is 2 meals; the cost of mowing a lawn to you is 4 meals. I benefit by trading lawns for meals as long as I get more than 2 meals per lawn; you benefit by trading meals for lawns as long as you have to give fewer than 4 meals per lawn. Again, there is room for both of us to benefit by trade.

Once we realize that the relevant cost of producing one good is measured in terms of other goods, it becomes clear that I *cannot* be better than you at everything. If I am "better" at producing lawns (in terms of meals), then I must be "worse" at producing meals (in terms of lawns). If this is not obvious when put into words, consider it algebraically.

Let L be the time it takes me to mow a lawn and L' the time it takes you. Let M be the time it takes me to cook a meal and M' the time it takes you. The cost to me of mowing a lawn (in terms of meals) is L/M; if a lawn takes 30 minutes and a meal 15, then a lawn takes the time in which I could produce 2 meals. The cost to you is L'/M'. But the cost to me of a meal in terms of lawns is, by the same argument, M/L; the cost to you is M'/L'. If $L/M > L'/M'$ then $M'/L' > M/L$. If you are better than I am at mowing a lawn, I must be better than you at cooking a meal.

To put the same argument in numbers, imagine that it costs me 3 meals to mow a lawn and costs you 2. 3 > 2, hence I am a worse mower than you—it costs me more meals to mow a lawn. But ⅓ < ½. I am a better cook than you—it costs me only ⅓ lawn to cook a meal, and it costs you ½ lawn.

Comparative Advantage. The general principle I have been explaining is called the *Principle of Comparative Advantage*. It is usually discussed in the context of foreign trade. The principle is that two nations, or individuals, can gain by trade if each produces the goods for which it has a comparative advantage. Nation A has a comparative advantage over Nation B in producing a good if the cost of producing that good in A relative to the cost of producing other goods in A is lower than the cost of producing that good in B relative to the cost of producing other goods in B.

The error of confusing absolute advantage ("I can do everything better than you can") with comparative advantage typically appears as the claim that because some other country has lower wages, higher productivity, lower taxes, or some other advantage, it can undersell our domestic manufacturers on everything, putting our producers and workers out of work. This is used as an argument for *protective tariffs*—taxes on imports designed to keep them from competing with domestically produced goods.

There are a number of things wrong with this argument. To begin with, if we were importing lots of things from Japan and exporting nothing to them (and if no other countries were involved), we would be getting a free ride on the work and capital of the Japanese. They would be providing us with cars, stereos, computers, toys, and textiles, and we would be giving them dollars in exchange— pieces of green paper which cost us very little to produce. A good deal for us, but not for them.

Here, as in many other cases, thinking in terms of money obscures what is really happening. Trade is ultimately goods for goods—although that may be less obvious when several countries are involved, so that the Japanese can use the dollars they get from us to buy goods from the Germans who in turn send the dollars back to get goods from us. In terms of goods, the Japanese *cannot* be better at producing everything. If it costs them fewer computers to produce a car (translation: If the cost in Japan of all the inputs used to produce a car divided by the cost in Japan of all the inputs used to produce a computer is smaller than the corresponding ratio in the U.S.), then it costs them more cars to produce a computer. If they trade their cars for our computers, both sides benefit.

A full explanation of how the logic of this argument works itself out in a world of many nations and many goods would take us far beyond the material of this course. If you still find the claim that tariffs on Japanese automobiles are a way of "protecting us from the Japanese in order to keep American workers from being replaced by Japanese workers" plausible, consider the following fable.

Growing Hondas. "There are two ways we can produce automobiles. We can build them in Detroit, or we can grow them in Iowa. Everyone knows how we build automobiles. To grow automobiles, we begin by growing the raw material from which they are made—wheat. We put the wheat on ships and send the ships out into the Pacific. They come back with Hondas on them."

From our standpoint, "growing Hondas" is just as much a form of production—using American farm workers instead of American auto workers—as building them. What happens on the other side of the Pacific is irrelevant; the effect would be just the same for us if there really were a gigantic machine sitting somewhere west of Midway turning wheat into automobiles. Tariffs are indeed a way of protecting American workers—from other American workers.

In Chapter 18, we will discuss tariffs again, demonstrating under what circumstances and in what sense American tariffs impose net costs on Americans and in what special cases they do not. At that point, we will also discuss why tariffs exist—and why the industries that actually get protected by tariffs are not the same as the industries which one might be able to argue, on economic grounds, ought to get protected.

Trade and Production—Geometric Version

There is a problem in using indifference curves to represent our preferences among two produced goods. With only two dimensions, there is no place to put leisure; if we are not careful, we may find that we are treating leisure as if it had no value at all. One way of solving the problem is to put leisure on one axis and "all other goods"—shown as the income available to buy them—on the other. This is what we did in Chapter 5 in order to use indifference curves to derive a supply curve for labor. While this was a useful diagram for analyzing the division of time between production and leisure, it is of no use for analyzing trade. In order to have trade, we must have two different goods to exchange. Since leisure itself cannot be traded, we need two goods *in addition to* leisure. With two-dimensional paper, we cannot graph three goods.

If we want to use the geometric approach to analyze trade, we will have to go back to graphing two different tradeable goods (or services) on the axes. We justify this by letting the indifference curves represent our preferences with regard to those two goods, given that we are also consuming some fixed amount of leisure (and possibly other goods). Such diagrams can be used to analyze the choice between two goods while ignoring decisions about how much of other goods (including leisure) we wish to consume.

Figure 6-3 shows the production possibility sets for me and you in the first example of the previous section. The only addition is the assumption that each of us is going to spend exactly 6 hours per day working. Both of us are assumed to have the same preferences, represented by indifference curves I_1, I_2, and I_3. Point A is on the highest indifference curve that touches my opportunity set, point B on the highest curve that touches yours.

The entire shaded area on Figure 6-3 shows the production possibility set available to the two of us together. The colored inner section shows how much each of us can have if we choose to split our output evenly, with each of us getting half of the lawns and half of the meals. C is the optimal point (for each of us) on that assumption. Note that it is on a higher indifference curve than either A or B. Obviously many other divisions are possible. The point to note is how much bigger the opportunity set becomes for each of us when we combine

Figure 6-3

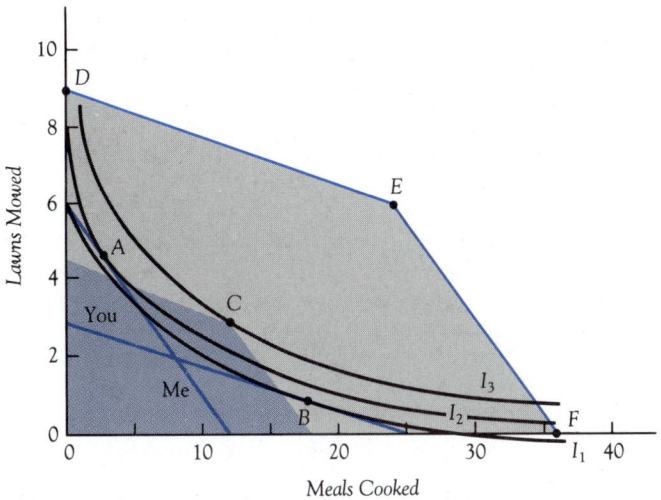

Production possibility sets for 2 individuals.   The entire shaded region shows the production possibility set for the combined output of two producers. The dark region shows the alternatives available to each producer if they divide their output evenly. C, the optimal point with joint production and even division, is preferred to A, my optimal point if I produce alone, and to B, your optimal point if you produce alone. This shows the possibility of mutual gains from trade.

our efforts through trade. I am (relatively) good at mowing lawns, and you at cooking meals. Without trade, I cannot make full use of my comparative advantage—there are too many meals I want cooked and not enough lawns I want mowed. Similarly (in the opposite direction—too many lawns and not enough meals) for you. Through trade, we solve the problem.

To see why our combined opportunity set is as I have drawn it and why it is so large, imagine that we start in the upper left-hand corner, at point D on Figure 6-3. All we are doing is mowing lawns—9 of them a day.

How much must we give up (in terms of lawns mowed) in order to produce 1 meal? If I cook it, we must give up ½ lawn mowed (it takes me 1 hour to mow a lawn, ½ hour to cook a meal); if you do it, only ⅛ of a lawn. Obviously we get the meal at lower cost by having you cook it. As we move down and to the right along the boundary of the opportunity set, we are giving up only ⅛ lawn per meal—that is why the line slopes down so slowly.

Eventually we reach point E, where you are spending all of your 6 hours of working time cooking. We are producing 24 meals and 6 mowed lawns per day (if this seems like more than we have any use for, remember that the nonsatiation assumption becomes more plausible when we expand our simple examples to fit a world with many more than two goods in it). If we wish to produce still more meals, I must cook them—at a cost of ½ lawn per meal. The boundary turns abruptly down, since my cost for cooking meals is higher than yours. Eventually we reach point *F*, where we are both cooking full time and producing 36 meals per day.

PART 2 · COMPLICATIONS OF TWO-PERSON TRADE

In the first part of this chapter, we saw why individuals can gain by trade. In this part, we will look a little more carefully at some of the problems associated with two-person trade—in particular, at problems associated with the conflict between the two traders over the division of the gains.

Bilateral Monopoly—The Serpent in the Garden

So far, I have presented an entirely optimistic view of trade, with individuals cooperating to their mutual benefit. There is one problem which may have occurred to you. In each of these cases, there are many different trades which benefit both parties; some are preferred by one, some by the other. What decides which trade actually occurs?

Consider the following very simple case. I have a horse that is worth $100 to me and $200 to you. If I sell it to you, there is a net gain of $100; the price for which I sell it determines how the gain is divided between us. If I sell it for $100, you get all the benefit; if I sell it for $200, I do. Anywhere in the bargaining range between these two extremes we divide the $100 surplus between us.

Bargaining Costs. If I can convince you that I will not take any price below $199, it is in your interest to pay that; gaining $1 is better than gaining nothing. If you can convince me that you will not pay more than $101, it is in my interest to sell it for that—for the same reason. Both of us are likely to spend substantial real resources—time and energy, among other things—trying to persuade each other that our bargaining positions (the amounts we say we will pay or take) are real.

One way I can do so is by trying to deceive you about how much the horse is really worth to me; similarly, you can try to deceive me about how much it is worth to you. When I set up the problem, I (the author of this book) told you (the reader of this book) what the real values were, but the you and I inside the problem do not have that information. Each of us has to guess how much the horse is worth to the other—and each has an incentive to try to make the other guess wrong. If I believe the horse is worth only $101 to you, there is no point in my trying to hold out for more.

One danger in such bargaining is that we may be too successful. If I persuade you that the horse is really worth more than $200 to me (and I may try to do so, in the false belief that you will, if necessary, pay that much for it), then you stop trying to buy it. If you persuade me that it is worth less than $100 to you (ditto, mutatis mutandis), then I stop trying to sell it. In either case, the deal falls through and the $100 gain disappears.

Strikes and Wars—Errors or Experiments? Consider a strike. When it is over, union and management will have agreed to some contract. Typically, both the stockholders whose interest management is supposed to represent and the workers whose interest the union is supposed to represent would be better off if they agreed, on the first day of bargaining, to whatever contract they will eventually sign, thus avoiding the cost of the strike. The reason they do not is that the union is trying to persuade management that it will only accept a contract very favorable to it and management is trying to persuade the union that no such contract will be offered. Each tries to make its bargaining position persuasive by demonstrating that it is willing to accept large costs—in the form of a strike—rather than give in.

Much the same is true of wars. When the smoke clears, there will be a peace treaty; one side or the other will have won, or some compromise will have been accepted by both. If the peace treaty were signed immediately after the declaration of war and just before the first shot was fired, there would be an enormous savings in human life and material damage. The failure of the nations involved to do it that way may in part be the result of differing factual beliefs; if each side believes that its tanks and planes are better and its soldiers braver, then the two sides will honestly disagree about who is going to win and hence about what the terms of the peace treaty will be. In this situation, one may regard the war as an (expensive) experiment to settle a disagreement about the military power of the two sides.

But there are other reasons why wars occur. Even if both sides agree on the military situation, they may have different opinions about how high a price each is willing to pay for victory. It is said that when the Japanese government consulted its admiralty on the prospects of a war with the U.S., prior to Pearl Harbor, the admiralty replied that they could provide a year of victories, hold on for another year, and would then start losing—a reasonably accurate prophecy. The Japanese attacked anyway, in the belief that the U.S.—about to become engaged in a more difficult and important war in Europe—would agree to a negotiated peace sometime in the first two years. An expensive miscalculation.

While bilateral monopoly bargaining is a common and important element in real-world economies, it is not the dominant form in which trade occurs. Fortunately (from the standpoint of both saving bargaining costs and simplifying economic analysis), there are other and more important mechanisms for determining on what terms goods are exchanged, mechanisms that lead to a less ambiguous result as well as considerably lower transaction costs.

Getting "Ripped Off"

There seems to be a widespread belief that if someone sells something to you for more than he could have—if, for example, he could make a profit selling it to you for $5 but charges $6—he is somehow mistreating you, "ripping you off" in current jargon. This is an oddly one-sided way of looking at such a situation. If you pay $6 for the good, it is presumably worth at least $6 to you. (I am not now considering the case of fraud, where what you think you are getting and what you are really getting are different things). If it costs him $5 and is worth $6 to you, then there is a $1 gain when you buy it; your claim that he "ought" to sell it to you for $5 amounts to claiming that you are entitled to get all of the benefit from the transaction. It would seem to make just as much (or as little) sense to argue that he should get all the benefit—that if you buy a good for $6 when you would, if necessary, have been willing to pay $7, then you are "ripping him off." Yet I know very few people who, if they see a price of $3 on a new book by their favorite author for which they would gladly pay $10, feel obliged to volunteer the higher price—or even to offer to split the difference.

As it happens, substantial bargaining ranges are not typical of most transactions, for the same reasons that bilateral monopoly is not the dominant form of trade. Most of the goods you buy are sold at about cost (if cost is properly computed) for reasons you will learn in the next few chapters. Nonetheless, bilateral monopolies and bargaining ranges do exist. I am myself a monopolist; I give speeches and write articles on a variety of topics and believe that nobody else's speeches and articles are quite the same as mine. I enjoy writing and speaking. I would give some speeches and write some articles even if I did not get paid for them; indeed I do (sometimes) write articles and give speeches for which I am not paid. That is no reason why I should not charge for my services if I can. If someone is willing to pay me $500 for a speech I would be willing to give for free, then that is evidence that giving the speech produces a net gain of at least $500. I see no reason why I should feel obliged to turn all of that gain over to my audience.

OPTIONAL SECTION

The Edgeworth Box

In the case of two-person trade, there may be many different exchanges, each of which would be beneficial to both parties; some exchanges will be preferred by one person, some by the other. There are then two different questions to be settled. One is how to squeeze as much total gain as possible out of the opportunities for trade; the other is how that gain is to be divided. The two individuals who are trading have a common interest in getting as much total gain as possible but are likely to disagree about the division.

An ingenious way of looking at such a situation is the Edgeworth Box, named after Francis Y. Edgeworth, the author of a nineteenth century work on economics called *Mathematical Psychics* (which does not mean what it sounds like).

In the simplest two-person trading situation (such as the one discussed at the beginning of this chapter), there are only two goods and no production. There are then four variables—how much of good X I have (x_1), how much you have (x_2), how much of good Y I have (y_1), and how much you have (y_2). Since exchange does not change the total amounts of the two goods, we have $x_1 + x_2 = x$ and $y_1 + y_2 = y$, where x and y are the total amounts of X and Y.

Since we have four variables and two constraints, the constraints can be used to eliminate two of the variables, leaving us with two; the remaining two variables can be plotted on a two-dimensional surface, such as this page. Here is how you do it.

How to Build a Box. First draw a box, such as Figure 6-4, with length x and height y. Any division of x and y between you and me can be represented by a point, such as point A. The horizontal distance from the left-hand edge of the box to A is x_1, the vertical distance from the bottom of the box is y_1, so A represents the amount of x and y I have, seen from the lower left-hand corner of the box (which is where the origin of a graph usually is). Since the length of the box is x, the horizontal distance from A to the *right-hand* edge of the box is $x - x_1 = x_2$; the vertical distance from A to the top edge of the box is $y - y_1 = y_2$. Hence A also represents your holdings of X and Y—as seen, in an upside-down sort of way, from the upper right-hand corner of the box. Any point inside the box represents a possible division of the total quantity of X and Y, with my share seen from the lower left-hand corner, yours from the upper right-hand corner. Any possible trade is represented by a movement from one point in the box, such as A, to another, such as B. The particular trade that moves us from A to B consists of my giving you 2 units of X in exchange for 1 unit of Y.

Figure 6-4

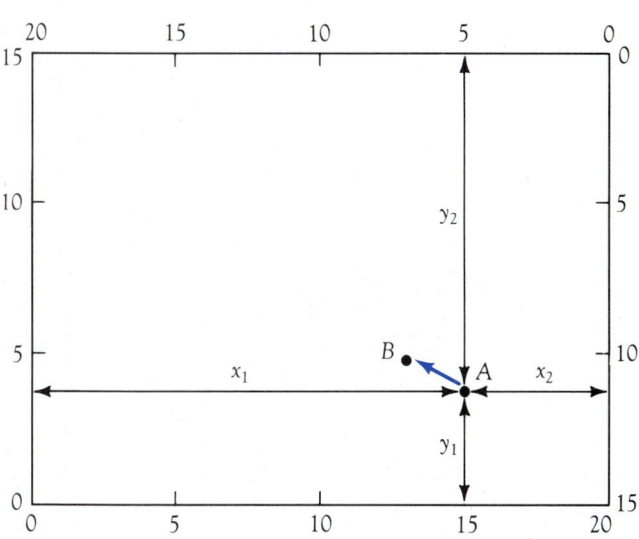

An Edgeworth Box.   A point, such as A or B, represents a division between us of the total quantity of X and Y. x_1 is how much X I have, and x_2 is how much you have; similarly y_1 is how much Y I have, and y_2 is how much you have. My quantities are measured from the bottom left corner of the box; your quantities are measured from the top right corner.

The Edgeworth Box is the opportunity set of the two traders; it shows all the ways in which the existing stock of goods could be divided between them. Any trade simply moves them from one point in the box to another. In order to see what trades they will be willing to make, we also need their preferences. Figure 6-5 shows the same box, with my indifference curves (the thin lines—I_1, I_2, I_3) and yours (the thick lines—J_1, J_2, J_3) drawn in. Note that my indifference curves are shown in terms of my consumption (x_1, y_1), while yours are shown in terms of your consumption (x_2, y_2). Hence mine are oriented towards my origin at the bottom left-hand corner and yours towards your origin at the top right-hand corner. My utility increases as I move up and to the right (increasing my consumption); yours increases as you move down and to the left (increasing your consumption).

Trading. This makes it sound as though any trade must help one of us and hurt the other, but that is not the case. A trade which moves us down and to the right or up and to the left may put both of us on higher indifference curves. Consider the move from point A to point B on Figure 6-5. B is on a higher indifference curve for both of us than A, hence the trade benefits both of us. If we start at point A, any point in the shaded area bounded by I_1 and J_1 is preferred by both of us; we might both agree to a trade that moved us from A to such a point.

Suppose we make the trade that moves us from A to B. The points which are preferred to B make up a smaller area bounded by I_2 and J_2, shown colored in the

Figure 6-5

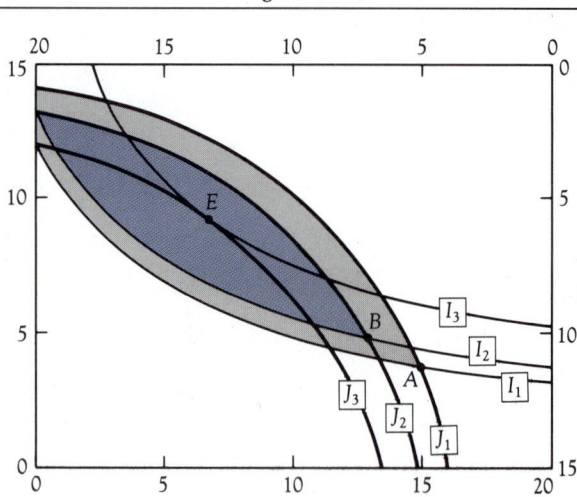

An Edgeworth Box showing indifference curves and possible gains from trade. Thin indifference curves show my preferences; thick ones show yours. The entire shaded area is preferred to A by both of us; the colored area is preferred to B by both of us. Once we reach point E, no further trade can benefit both of us.

figure. It is in our interest to make another trade. The process stops only when we reach a point such as E. At E our indifference curves are tangent. Since they curve in opposite directions, this means that starting from point E, any point which is on a higher indifference curve for me must be on a lower curve for you; any trade which makes me better off makes you worse off. This is easier to see on the diagram than to explain in words.

The Contract Curve. The point E is not unique; Figure 6-6 shows the same box with the indifference curves drawn in such a way as to show the *contract curve*—the set of all points from which no further mutually beneficial trading is possible. As we saw in the previous paragraph, these are the points where one of my indifference curves is tangent to one of yours. If we continue trading as long as there is any gain to be made, we must eventually end up at some point on the contract curve. The arrows in the figure show two different series of trades, each starting at point A, leading to different points on the contract curve. Once we reach the curve, there is no further trade that can make both of us better off.

Figure 6-6

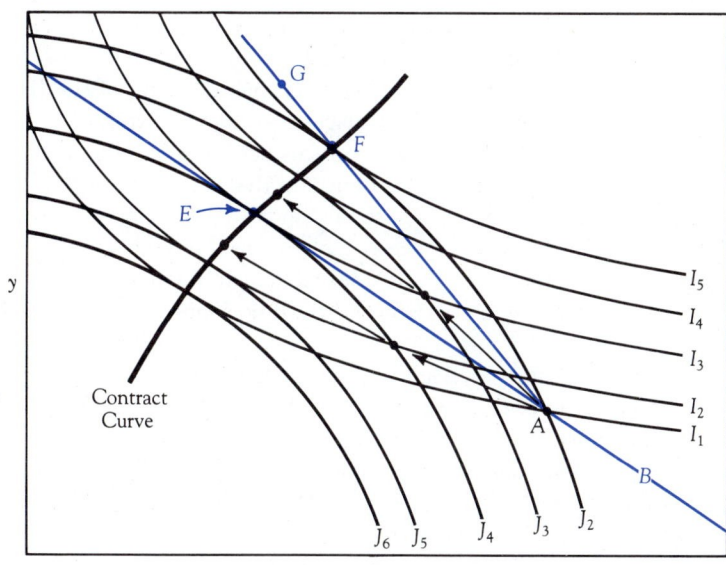

An Edgeworth Box showing the contract curve and ways of reaching it.   Starting at point A, the arrows show two possible sequences of trades that reach the contract curve. Line B shows a possible trade corresponding to the normal conditions of many-person markets; each of us is exchanging, at a constant price, the quantities of X and Y that we wish to exchange at that price. The line goes through E and must be tangent at E to both of our indifference curves, since otherwise one of us would want to trade more (and the other less) than the amount that gets us to E.

Is there any way to predict which of these series of trades will occur? No. But there is one series of trades, one particular way of getting from an initial distribution to the contract curve, which is of particular interest—although it may not be any more likely than the others.

We have so far been considering only two-person trading. In the much more typical case of a market with many buyers and sellers, trading does not usually involve a long series of exchanges. If, for example, you want to buy groceries, you do not expect to first haggle over the price of the first apple you buy, then again (with a different result) over the price of the second, and so on. The typical market has a market price for any good. At that price, you can buy as much as you want. The condition which determines the price, as you will see in the next few chapters, is that it is the price at which the amount sellers wish to sell is the same as the amount buyers wish to buy.

There is no reason to expect two-party trade to follow the same pattern—a single price at which the buyer buys all he wants, the seller sells all he wants, and the buyer turns out to want to buy just as much as the seller wants to sell. But since we are going to go on to discuss ordinary markets, it is interesting to see how two-party trade would turn out if it did follow the same pattern. The result is shown on Figure 6-6. Starting at point A, there is only one possible trade which meets the conditions. It must go to a point E on the contract curve, where the line from A is tangent to both indifference curves.

To see why this is so, think of the lower left-hand section of the box as an ordinary indifference curve-budget line diagram—which is what it is from my standpoint (as a trader, not as the author of this book). The indifference curves are $I_1, I_2, \ldots I_5$, the budget line is B. I am told that I can buy or sell all the X I want at a price P (measured in units of Y). Since I am starting out at A, I can (by either trading X for Y or vice versa) move anywhere I like along B, a line drawn through A with slope $-P$. For reasons explained in Chapter 3, my optimal point, where I must end up, is where the budget line is tangent to an indifference curve—E.

Now look at things from your standpoint—hanging upside down in the upper right-hand corner of the box. To you too, the line B is your budget line. You too are starting at A. Since you too are told that you can sell all you wish at a price P, that means that you can move anywhere you wish along a line that runs through A with slope $-P$. You also must end up at a point where your indifference curve is tangent to your budget line.

But a point in the Edgeworth Box represents both my holdings and yours, so we must both always be at the same point. Hence we must end up at a point such as E, a point where the line from our starting situation A is tangent to both of our indifference curves—which are therefore tangent to each other.

This is not the only possible trade—not even the only trade which takes us to a point from which no further trades are possible. The arrow from A to F does that too. But in that case, having traded a certain amount of X for Y in order to get from A to F, I would like, if I could, to trade even more at the same rate. If you look at the diagram, you will see that doing so would get me onto a higher indifference curve, say at G. You are not willing to agree to that since the additional trade would get you to a lower indifference curve. At that rate of exchange (price), I want to trade more than you do. So, it is not a point reached from A by each of us trading, at a given price, as much as we each wish to trade at that price—which is what does happen in an ordinary (many-trader) market.

PROBLEMS

1. Table 6-1a shows bundles of apples and oranges that A regards as equivalent; Table 6-1b similarly shows bundles that B regards as equivalent. Tables 6-2 and 6-3 are similar to Table 6-1; the bundles on any one table are not equivalent to those on another. Apples and oranges are goods for both A and B.
   a. Draw indifference curves for A and B.
   b. Suppose A starts with 10 apples and can trade apples for oranges at a price of 2 apples per orange. How many of each will he end up with?
   c. Suppose B starts with 10 oranges and can trade apples for oranges at a price of ½ apple per orange. How many of each will he end up with?
   d. A starts with 10 apples (and 0 oranges) and B with 10 oranges (and 0 apples). They engage in voluntary trade with each other. What can you say about the bundles they will end up with?

Table 6-1a			**Table 6-1b**	
A			*B*	
Apples	*Oranges*		*Apples*	*Oranges*
10	0		10	0
6	1		7	1
4	2		5.5	2
2	3		4	3
1	4		3	4
0	5		2.5	5
			2.1	6
			1.6	8

Table 6-2a			**Table 6-2b**	
A			*B*	
Apples	*Oranges*		*Apples*	*Oranges*
10	1		6.5	0
6	2		5	1
4.5	3		3.9	2
3	4		3	3
2.2	5		2.2	4
1.5	6		1.5	5
1	7		1	6
0	10		0	10

Table 6-3a			Table 6-3b	
A			B	
Apples	Oranges		Apples	Oranges
10	2		9	2
8	3		7.2	3
6.2	4		6	4
5	5		5	5
3.9	6		4.1	6
3	7		3.4	7
1.5	10		2.3	10

2. Person A of Problem 1 starts with 1 apple and 9 oranges. He can trade apples for oranges (or oranges for apples) at a rate of 2 apples for each orange. What bundle does he end up with?
3. Table 6-4 shows how many hours it takes each of three people to produce a table or a chair.
   a. If only A and B exist, will A buy chairs from B, sell chairs to B, or neither.
   b. If only A and C exist, will A buy chairs from C, buy tables from C, or neither.
   c. If only B and C exist, will B buy chairs from C, sell tables to C, or neither.

Table 6-4			
Time to Produce	A	B	C
1 Table	10 hours	15 hours	12 hours
1 Chair	2 hours	5 hours	6 hours

4. I am better than my wife at bargaining with contractors, repair people, and the like; with a given amount of time and effort, I am likely to get a lower price. Also, I rather enjoy such bargaining, while she dislikes it. Are these two separate reasons why I should do the bargaining and she should do other family work, or are they two parts of one reason? Discuss. Does the fact that my wife and I are not "selfish" with regard to each other (i.e., I have a high value for her happiness, and she for mine) mean that we should ignore the principle of comparative advantage in allocating household jobs? Does it simplify any of the problems normally associated with exchange (between us)?
5. Figure 6-3 corresponds to the first example in the verbal discussion of trade with production. Draw a similar figure corresponding to the second example (where I can cook a meal in 15 minutes and mow a lawn in ½ hour; it takes you ½ hour to cook a meal and 2 hours to mow a lawn.)
6. Figure 6-7 shows the opportunity, or production possibility, sets for three producers. Draw their combined production possibility set.
7. Figures 6-8a and 6-8b correspond to two possible situations discussed in the optional section of Chapter 5. Use them to show how two people with identical production possibility sets and identical preferences can still gain from trade. (Hint: It only works with one of the figures.)

8. "Of course, leisure can be traded; when I do your work for you, I give up leisure and you get it." Why does this not refute the statement that leisure cannot be traded?
9. State the principle of comparative advantage in your own words.

Figure 6-7

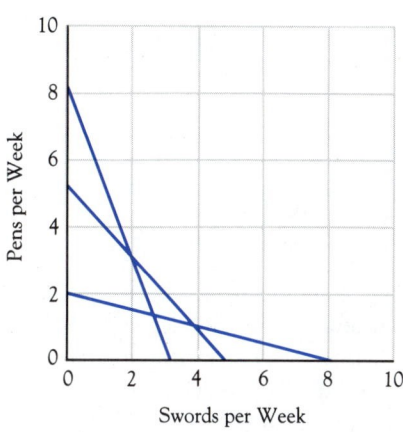

The production possibility frontiers of 3 producers.   For Problem 6.

Figure 6-8

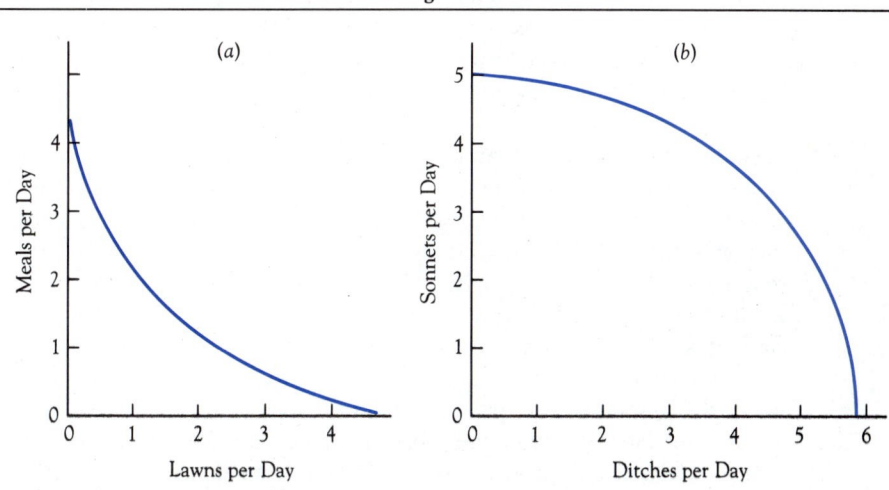

Nonlinear production possibility frontiers.   Figure 6-8a represents the production possibility frontier for each of two identical individuals with identical preferences; so does Figure 6-8b.

Chapter 7

Markets—Putting It All Together

PART 1 · EQUILIBRIUM PRICE AND QUANTITY

In this chapter, we will combine what we learned about demand and supply curves in Chapters 3, 4, and 5 with the idea of trade discussed in Chapter 6, in order to understand how prices and quantities are determined.

In Chapter 3, we saw how the behavior of an individual consumer led to a demand curve, a relation between the price at which he could buy a good and the quantity he chose to buy. In most markets, all customers pay about the same price, so we can talk of a single market price and a single demand curve, representing the total demand of all consumers for the good as a function of its price. Since total quantity demanded at any price is the amount I want to buy at that price plus the amount you want to buy at that price plus the amount he wants to buy at that price plus . . . , the market demand curve is the *horizontal* sum of the individual demand curves, as shown in Figure 7-1.

In Chapter 4, I argued that we could analyze consumption in terms of continuously variable goods, even though some goods are not actually continuous, by thinking in terms of rate of consumption rather than number of units consumed—cookies per week rather than cookies. When we are considering, not individual demand curves, but the combined demand of a large number of people, we have a second reason for treating goods, and curves, as continuous. For "lumpy" goods such as automobiles, for which individual demand curves are step functions rather than curves (you buy one automobile or two, not 1.32 automobiles), even a very small drop in price will make a few consumers (out of millions) decide to buy a car instead of not buying one.

In Chapter 5, I showed how individual supply curves could be derived, starting with a producer's output rates for different goods plus either his marginal disvalue for labor curve or the indifference curves showing his preferences with regard to leisure and income. Just as the total demand curve is the horizontal sum of individual demand curves, so the total supply curve is the horizontal sum of the individual supply curves; having seen how to derive the individual supply curves for a good, we also know how to derive its total supply curve.

136

Figure 7-1

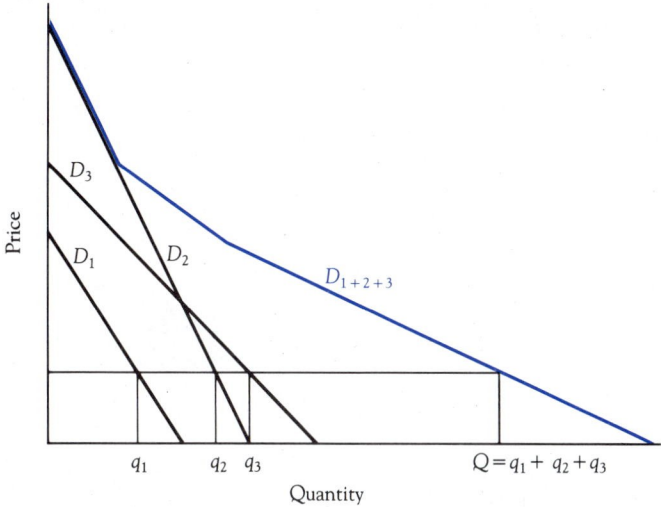

Market demand curve. The market demand curve is the *horizontal* sum of individual demand curves, since at any price, total quantity demanded is the sum of my quantity demanded at that price plus your quantity demanded at that price plus . . . .

We are now ready to put supply curves and demand curves together. Figure 7-2a shows supply and demand curves for "widgets," a hypothetical commodity consumed mostly by the authors of economics textbooks. The particular "curves" shown in the figure happen to be straight lines; as you may have guessed by now, the term "curve," in the language of economists and mathematicians, includes straight lines. The vertical axis of the diagram is price, the horizontal axis is quantity; any point on the diagram, such as A, represents a quantity and a price (Q_A and P_A). What will the market price be and what quantity will be produced and consumed at that price?

As any experienced guesser could predict, the answer is point E, where the supply and demand curves cross. The interesting question is why.

Suppose the price were P_1 on Figure 7-2a. At that price, producers wish to produce a quantity Q_1, while consumers only wish to purchase a (smaller) quantity Q_1'. Some of the producers find themselves with widgets on their hands that they cannot sell. In order to get rid of them, the producers are willing to cut the price. Price falls. It continues to do so as long as the quantity supplied is greater than the quantity demanded.

Suppose, instead, that the price were P_2 on Figure 7-2a. Now producers wish to produce a quantity Q_2, while consumers wish to purchase a (larger) quantity Q_2'. Consumers cannot consume goods that are not produced, so some of them are unable to buy what they want. They are willing to offer a higher price, so they bid the price up. Figure 7-2b shows what is happening in terms of the marginal value curve of one such consumer. At P_2 he would like to buy q_2' but finds he can only buy q_2. At that quantity, his marginal value for another widget is $P' > P_2$; he is willing to pay any price up to P' in order to get another widget, so the price is bid up.

Figure 7-2

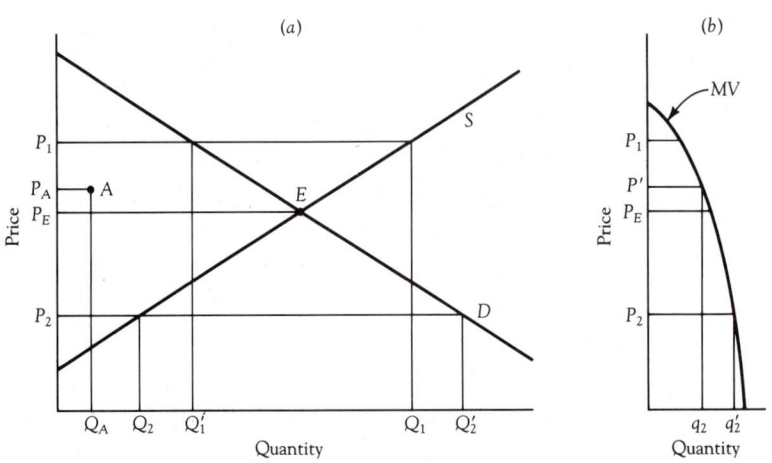

Market equilibrium.   At point E, price $= P_E$; quantity demanded equals quantity supplied. At lower prices, less is supplied; individuals are consuming quantities for which $MV > P$, as shown on Figure 7-2b, and so are willing to offer a higher price for additional quantities.

So if the price is below P_E, the price for which quantity supplied and quantity demanded are equal, it will be driven up; if it is above P_E, it will be driven down. Hence P_E is the equilibrium price. But P_E is the price for which quantity supplied (at price P_E) equals quantity demanded (at price P_E), so it is the price at the point where the two curves cross.

The idea of an *equilibrium*—a situation in which a system generates no forces that tend to change it—is common to many different sciences. It is often useful to distinguish three different sorts of equilibria. A *stable equilibrium* is one in which, if something does move the system slightly away from the equilibrium, forces are set in motion which move it back again. An *unstable equilibrium* is one in which, if something moves the system slightly away from the equilibrium, forces are set in motion which move it even further away. A *metastable equilibrium* is one in which, if something moves the system slightly away from the equilibrium, no forces are set in motion at all—it remains in the new position, which is also an equilibrium.

The three sorts of equilibrium can all be illustrated with a pencil. Hold the pencil by the point, with the eraser hanging down. It is now in a stable equilibrium—if someone nudges the eraser end to one side or another, it swings back. Balance the pencil on its point on your finger. It is now in an unstable equilibrium—if someone nudges it, it will fall over. Lay the pencil (a round one) down on the table. It is now in a metastable equilibrium—nudge it and it rolls over part way and remains in its new position. One sometimes encounters people, either feline or human, who appear to be in metastable equilibrium.

The equilibrium illustrated in Figure 7-2a and again in Figure 7-3a is stable—if you move the price and quantity away from E, forces are set in motion which move them back. In zone I (on Figure 7-3a), quantity demanded is greater than quantity supplied, so price goes up; in zone III, quantity demanded is less than quantity supplied, so price goes down. In zone II, the quantity being produced is more than producers want to produce at that price, so they reduce their output; in zone IV, for similar reasons, they increase their output. The "restoring forces" are shown by the arrows in Figure 7-3a.

Figure 7-3b is a similar but less plausible diagram in which the supply curve is falling rather than rising. The result is an unstable equilibrium. If price is above P^*, quantity demanded is larger than quantity supplied, which drives the price up even further; similarly, if price is below P^*, quantity demanded is less than quantity supplied, driving the price down. Figure 7-3c is an (implausible) diagram showing a range of metastable equilibria, with quantity equal to Q^* and price between P_1 and P_2.

We now have a simple rule for combining a supply curve and a demand curve to get a market price and quantity. The equilibrium occurs at the intersection of the two curves and is stable if the demand curve is falling and the supply curve rising—as we shall always assume that they are, for reasons discussed in Chapters 3, 4, and 5. We shall now use this rule to analyze the effects of shifts in demand and supply curves.

Figure 7-3

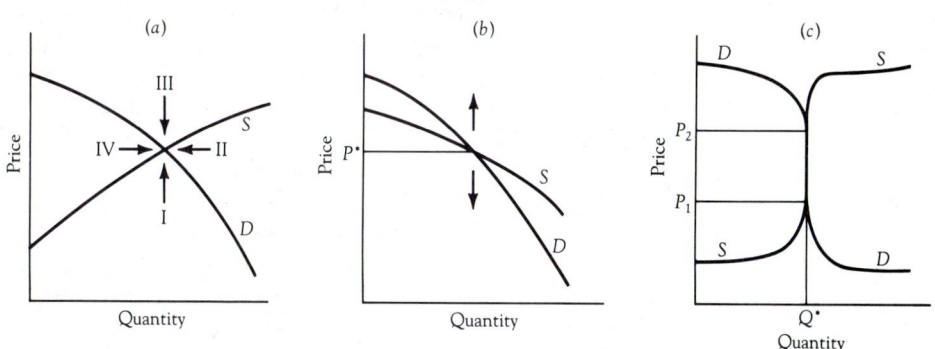

Stable, unstable, and metastable equilibrium.   The arrows show the directions of the forces moving the system back to equilibrium (Figure 7-3a) or away from equilibrium (Figure 7-3b). In Figure 7-3c, there is a range of equilibrium prices between P_1 and P_2.

Elasticity—A Brief Digression

The effect on price and quantity of shifts in supply and demand curves depends, among other things, on how steep the curves are. For reasons that will be discussed in Chapter 10, economists find it useful to discuss the steepness of curves in terms of their "elasticity." The elasticity of a demand or supply curve, at a point, is defined as the percentage change of quantity divided by the percentage change in price. If, for instance, a 1 percent increase in price results in a 1 percent increase in quantity supplied, we have:

$$\text{Percent change in quantity/percent change in price} = 1\%/1\% = 1.$$

The elasticity of supply is 1.

For the purposes of this chapter, all you need to know is that "very elastic" means "a small change in price results in a large change in quantity" while "very inelastic" means "a large change in price results in only a small change in quantity." The limiting cases are "perfectly elastic" (a horizontal supply or demand curve) and "perfectly inelastic" (a vertical curve).

Shifting Curves

Figure 7-4a shows a supply-demand diagram with a shift in the demand curve from D_1 to D_2. One can imagine this resulting from a change in tastes (widgets become more popular), weather (it has been a hot summer and widgets work better in hot weather), the price of other goods (widgets use a lot of widget oil, the price of which has just fallen), or whatever. The demand curve has "shifted out." Demand has "increased"—at every price, the new quantity demanded is larger than the old. The result is to move the equilibrium point from E_1 to E_2. Both equilibrium price and equilibrium quantity increase.

In Figure 7-4b, the shift occurs in the supply curve. Supply has increased; at every price, the new quantity supplied is larger than the old. The result is an increase in quantity but a *decrease* in price. These results are completely general; as long as demand curves slope down and supply curves up, an increase in demand will increase both price and quantity, while an increase in supply will increase quantity but decrease price. Decreases in demand or supply have the opposite effects. You should be able to convince yourself of these relationships by examining Figures 7-4a and 7-4b.

It is important, in order to avoid confusion, to distinguish between changes in *supply* (the supply curve shifting, as in Figure 7-4b) and changes in *quantity supplied*. In Figure 7-4a, the supply curve stays fixed, but the quantity supplied increases from Q_1 to Q_2. A supply curve (or a demand curve) is a relation between price and quantity; if the price changes because of a shift in the demand curve, the new price results in a new quantity supplied, even if the supply curve does not change. In Figure 7-4c, on the other hand, both the supply curve and the demand curve shift, while the quantity supplied stays exactly the same. The shift in the supply curve just cancels the effect of the change in price, so the new price on the new supply curve yields the same quantity supplied as the old price on the old supply curve.

Figure 7-4

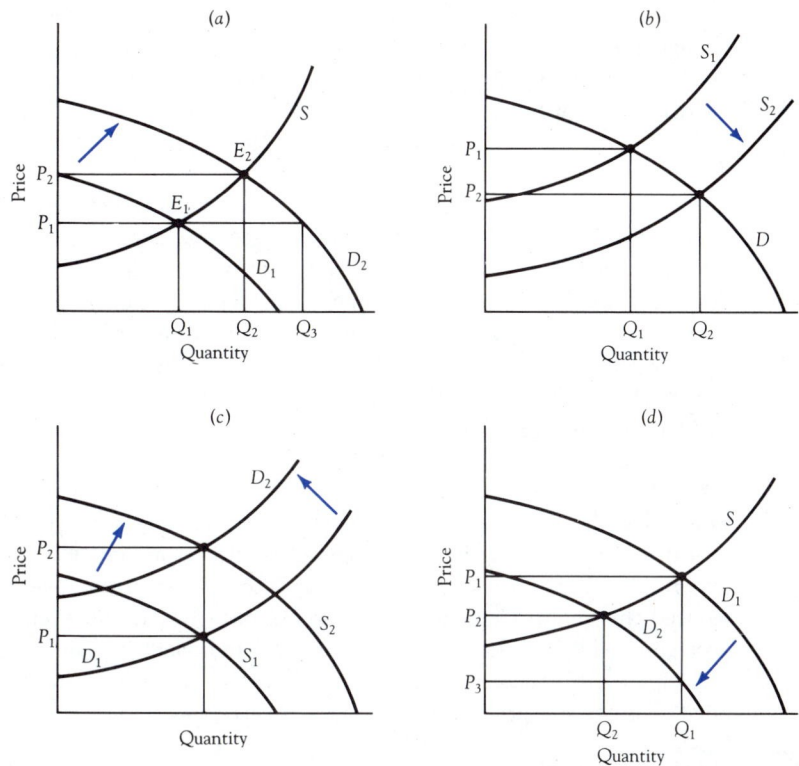

(a) (b) (c) (d)

The effects of shifts in supply and demand curves.   In Figures 7-4a and 7-4d, the demand curve shifts. In Figure 7-4b, the supply curve shifts. In each case, quantity demanded, quantity supplied, and price all change as a result. In Figure 7-4c, both the demand curve and the supply curve shift; price changes, but quantity stays the same.

One should distinguish similarly between changes in *demand* and changes in *quantity demanded*. By being careful about both distinctions, one can avoid some of the worst absurdities of newspaper discussions of economics. Consider, for example, the following paradoxes:

"If demand increases, that bids up the price, so increased demand is associated with increased price. But if price rises, that decreases demand, so decreased demand is associated with increased price."

Or: *"If demand increases, that bids up the price, but the increased price drives demand back down again."*

Or: *"If demand decreases, that drives down the price, which drives down the supply, which brings the price back up."*

Most such confusions can be avoided by drawing the relevant curves and distinguishing carefully between shifts of the curves (demand or supply moving up or down) and movements along the curves (quantity demanded or supplied changing because of a change in price). If the demand curve shifts, as in Figure 7-4a, while the supply curve stays fixed, that is a change in demand, which changes price, which changes *quantity supplied*—but supply (the supply curve) is still the same. A change in supply, as in Figure 7-4b, changes price and *quantity demanded* but not demand.

The first two "paradoxes" are illustrated on Figure 7-4a. An increase in demand (the demand curve shifts out) raises price; the increased price reduces quantity demanded below what it would have been if the demand curve had shifted but the price had remained the same (Q_3). The resulting quantity demanded (Q_2), although less than Q_3, is more than the old quantity demanded (Q_1). Q_2 must be greater than Q_1 because quantity demanded is equal to quantity supplied, the supply curve has not shifted, and a higher price applied to the same supply curve must result in a larger quantity supplied.

The third paradox is illustrated on Figure 7-4d. A decrease in demand (the demand curve shifts in) lowers the price; quantity supplied is now lower than it would have been at the old price ($Q_2 < Q_1$). But quantity supplied is equal to quantity demanded (at the new price on the new demand curve), so there is no reason for the price to go back up. What is true is that if the lower price had not reduced the quantity supplied, price would have had to fall even further (to P_3 on Figure 7-4d) in order for quantity supplied and quantity demanded to be equal. It is only in this sense that the "reduced supply" (actually reduced quantity supplied) "brings the price back up" (i.e., reduces the amount by which the price falls).

Figures 7-5a through 7-5f show some interesting extreme cases. In Figures 7-5a and 7-5b, the supply curves are "perfectly elastic". On Figure 7-5a, the industry will produce any quantity at a price P (or any higher price, but the price can never get higher since as soon as it does quantity supplied exceeds quantity demanded) and no quantity at any lower price. A shift in demand (Figure 7-5a) has no effect on price; it simply results in a different quantity at the old price. A shift in supply from S_1 to S_2, both perfectly elastic (Figure 7-5b), changes the price by the (vertical) amount of the shift and the quantity by the effect of that price change on quantity demanded along the old demand curve.

In Figures 7-5c and 7-5d, *demand* is perfectly elastic. Consumers are willing to buy an unlimited quantity at a price P on Figure 7-5c (or any lower price, of course, but . . .) and nothing at any higher price. A shift in supply (Figure 7-5c) leaves price unaffected but changes quantity by the (horizontal) amount of the shift. A shift in demand (Figure 7-5d) changes price by the vertical amount of the shift and quantity by the effect of the price change on the supply curve.

In Figure 7-5e, the supply curve is perfectly *inelastic*—the quantity supplied does not depend on price. The supply of land is often thought of as perfectly inelastic—there are a certain number of square miles on the earth's surface, and that is that. The supply of labor is also perfectly inelastic—if your desire for your own time (i.e., for leisure) is included in the demand curve for labor. From this standpoint, the supply of labor is 24 hours per day times the population. It is fixed, at least over the short term. What we normally call the supply of labor is this minus the demand by the owners of the labor—I do not work 24 hours per day, because I choose to "consume" some of my labor myself. Both of these examples will come up again in Chapter 13.

With a perfectly inelastic supply curve, a shift in the demand curve results in a corresponding change in price and no change in quantity, as shown in Figure 7-5e. With a perfectly inelastic demand curve (a "need" in the sense discussed and rejected in Chapter 2), a shift in the supply curve has a similar effect, as shown in Figure 7-5f.

One of the differences between economics as done by economists and economics as done by journalists, politicians making speeches, and others, is that the non-economists often speak as though all supply and demand curves were perfectly inelastic. This is the same disagreement which I discussed earlier in the

Figure 7-5

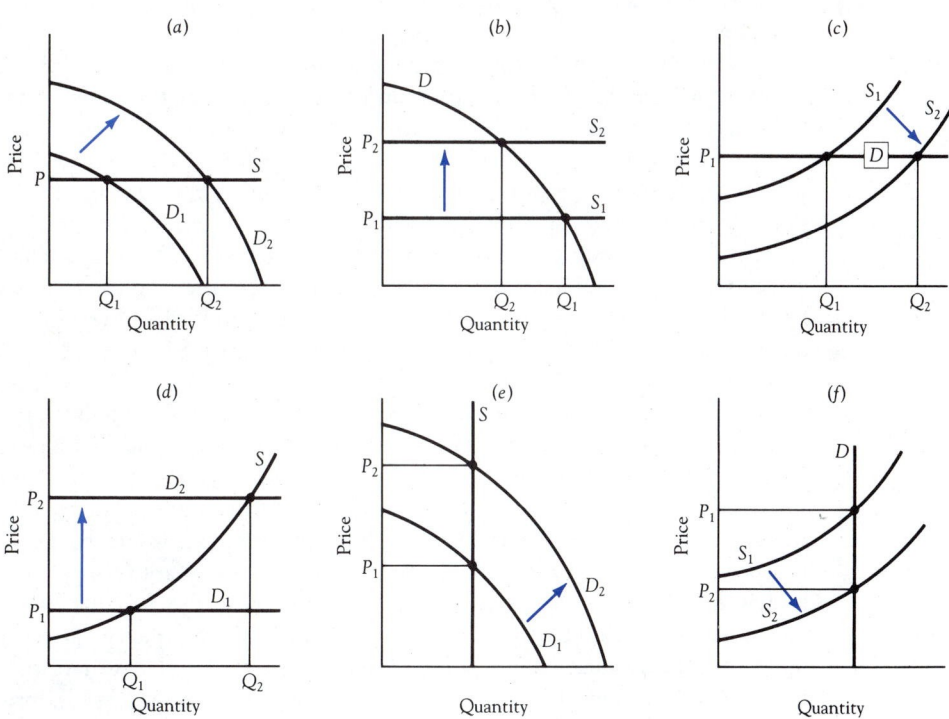

The effect of shifts when one curve is either perfectly elastic or perfectly inelastic. When one curve is perfectly elastic, a shift in the other changes quantity but not price (Figures 7-5a and 7-5c); when one curve is perfectly inelastic, a shift in the other changes price but not quantity (Figures 7-5e and 7-5f).

context of "needs" vs "wants." The non-economist tends to think of the "demand for water" as "the amount of water we need" and assumes that the alternative to having that amount of water is people going thirsty. But, as you should know from answering one of the questions in Chapter 4, only a tiny fraction of the water we consume is drunk. While the demand for drinking water may be highly inelastic over a wide range of prices, demand for other uses is not. If the price of water doubles, it pays farmers to use water more sparingly for irrigation, chemical firms to use less of it in their manufacturing processes, and homeowners to fix leaky faucets more quickly than before. Nobody dies of thirst, but total consumption of water falls substantially.

Who Pays Taxes?

We are ready to start answering one of the questions frequently asked of economists; the number of weeks and pages it has taken us to get this far may explain why answers that fit in a newspaper column or a 30-second news report are generally unsatisfactory. The question is "Who really pays taxes?" When the government imposes a tax on some good, does the money come out of the profits of those who produce the good or do the producers "pass it along" to the consumers in higher prices?

Suppose, for example, that the government imposes a sales tax of $1/widget; for every widget that is sold, the producer (assumed to be the seller—there are no middlemen at this stage of the analysis) must pay the government $1. The result is to shift the supply curve up by $1, from S_1 to S_2, as shown in Figure 7-6. What matters to the producer is how much he gets, not how much the consumer pays. A price of $6/widget with the tax gives the producer the same amount for each widget sold as a price of $5/widget without the tax. Hence he will produce the same quantity of widgets at $6/widget after the tax is imposed as he would have produced at $5 before, and similarly for all other prices. Each quantity on the new supply curve corresponds to a price $1 higher than on the old; the supply curve is shifted up by $1.

This does not mean that the market price goes up $1. If it did, producers would produce the same amount as before the tax; consumers, at the higher price, would consume less than before, so quantity supplied would be greater than quantity demanded. If, on the other hand, price did not rise at all, quantity demanded would be the same as before the tax. Quantity supplied would be less (since producers would be getting a dollar less per widget), so quantity supplied would be less than quantity demanded. As you can see on Figure 7-6, the price rises, but by less than a dollar. All of the tax is "paid" by the producer in the literal sense that the producer hands the government the money, but in fact the price paid by the consumer has gone up by a and the price received by the producer has gone down by b.

To see why b on the figure equals the decrease in the price received by the producer, note that if the market price had gone all the way up to $P_3 = P_1 + \$1$, the producer's receipts, after paying the $1 tax, would still be P_1 per widget, just as before the tax was imposed. Since the price only goes to

Figure 7-6

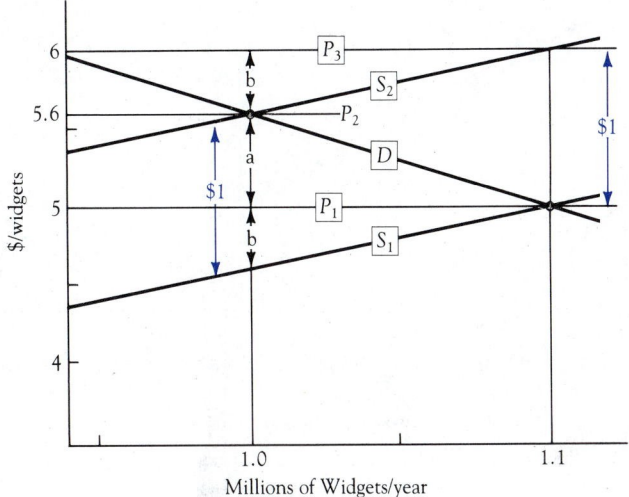

The effect of a $1 tax on widgets "paid" by the producers. The supply curve shifts up from S_1 to S_2 due to the tax; equilibrium price rises by a, from $5/widget to $5.6/widget. Quantity falls from 1.1 million widgets per year to 1 million widgets per year.

$P_2 = P_1 + a$, the producer's receipts per widget (after tax) have fallen by the difference between P_3 and P_2, which is b. Put algebraically, we have:

$$P_3 - P_2 = (P_1 + \$1) - (P_1 + a) = \$1 - a = b.$$

As you can see by examining Figure 7-6, the way in which the "burden" of the tax is divided between consumers and producers depends on the slopes of the supply and demand curves. Figures 7-7a and 7-7b show two extreme cases. In Figure 7-7a, the supply curve S is perfectly inelastic; you cannot see the shift in S, since shifting a vertical line up moves it onto itself. Since quantity and the demand curve stay the same, the price must stay the same, so the entire burden of the tax is borne by the producers; it is sometimes asserted that this is true of a tax on land. In Figure 7-7b, the demand curve is perfectly inelastic, and the price increases by the full dollar; the entire burden of the tax is borne by the consumers. Most real-world cases fall between these two extremes.

In Figure 7-8a, the initial demand and supply curves for widgets are the same as in Figure 7-6; what has changed is the form of the tax. Instead of taxing producers, the government has decided to tax consumers. For every widget you buy, you must pay the government $1. The result is to shift the demand curve instead of the supply curve—from D_1 down to D_2. The number of widgets you choose to buy depends on what it costs you to buy them—the price plus the tax.

Figure 7-7

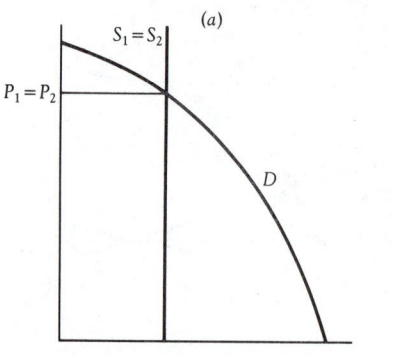 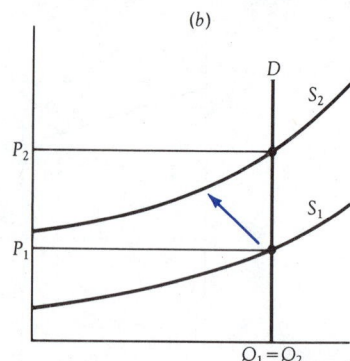

The effect of a tax when demand or supply is perfectly inelastic.   In Figure 7-7a, the supply curve is perfectly inelastic, and the entire burden of the tax is borne by the producers. In Figure 7-7b, the demand curve is perfectly inelastic, and the entire burden is borne by the consumers.

Figure 7-8

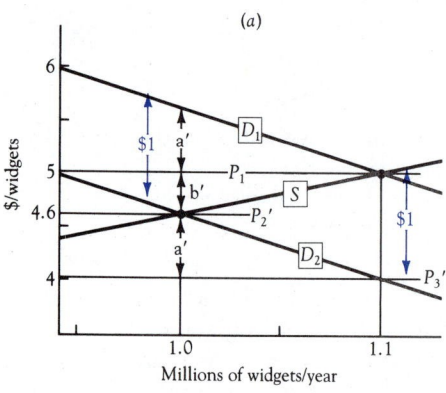 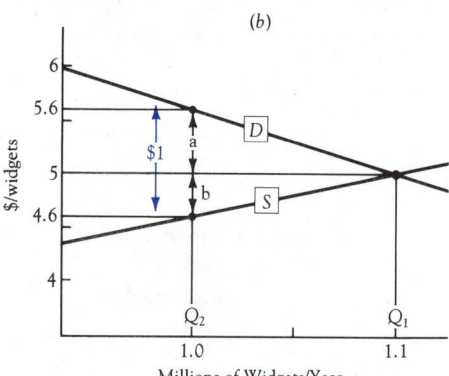

Two ways of graphing the effect of a $1 tax on widgets.   In Figure 7-8a, the tax is collected from consumers, shifting the demand curve down from D_1 to D_2. In Figure 7-8b, the demand curve is a function of price paid (market price plus any tax on consumers), and the supply curve is a function of price received (market price minus any tax on producers). The figure could show a $1 tax on either producer or consumer.

If before the tax was imposed you were willing to buy 12 widgets at $5 apiece, you will now be willing to buy 12 at a "price" of $4 each, since that means that you are again actually paying $5/widget—$4 to the producer and $1 to the government. Hence the demand curve shifts down by $1.

This is an application of the principle that costs are opportunity costs, discussed in Chapter 3. The cost to you of buying a widget for $5 is the loss of the goods you would otherwise have bought with the money. So widgets at $5 with no tax cost you the same amount as widgets at $4 with a $1 tax, payable by the consumer; in each case, you give up, for each widget purchased, the opportunity to buy $5 worth of something else. Since the cost to you of each widget is the same in both cases and since you decide how many widgets to purchase on the basis of cost and value, as described in the derivation of the individual demand curve in Chapter 4, you buy the same quantity in both cases. So, for the same reason, does everyone else. So the total quantity demanded is the same with the tax at a price of $4 as it would be without the tax at a price of $5, and similarly for all other prices. The demand curve shifts down by $1—the amount of the tax.

Looking at Figure 7-8a, you can see that as a result of the shift in the demand curve, the price received by the producer has gone down by an amount b' and the amount paid per widget by the consumers has gone up by a'. To see why a' is the increase in what consumers are paying per widget, note that if price had fallen by a full dollar, to P'_3, the consumers would have been no worse off—what they paid on the tax they would have made up on the lower price, making the cost to them of each widget the same as before. In fact, price has only fallen to $P'_2 > P'_3$; hence the consumers are paying $P'_2 - P'_3 = (P'_1 - b') - (P'_1 - \$1) = \$1 - b' = a'$ more than before for each widget.

If you compare Figure 7-8a with Figure 7-6, you can see that they are essentially the same figure; $b = b'$ and $a = a'$. Figure 7-8a is simply Figure 7-6 with everything shifted down by $1. The reason is that in Figure 7-6, the price shown on the vertical axis is price after tax, since the tax is paid by the producer; in Figure 7-8a, it is price before tax, since the tax is paid by the consumer. The difference between price before tax and price after tax is the amount of the tax—$1. In both cases, quantity supplied is determined by price received by the producer, quantity demanded by price paid by the consumer, and the effect of the tax is to make price paid by the consumer $1 higher than price received by the producer.

A third way of describing the same situation is shown in Figure 7-8b. Here supply is shown as a function of price received, demand as a function of price paid. Before the tax was instituted, market equilibrium occurred at a quantity (Q_1) for which price received was equal to price paid; after the tax was instituted, market equilibrium occurs at a quantity (Q_2) for which price received is a dollar less than price paid, with the difference going to the government.

If you look carefully at Figures 7-6, 7-8a, and 7-8b, you should be able to see that they are all the same; the only thing that changes from one to another is what is shown on the vertical axis. The figures are the same not just because I happen to have drawn them that way but because they have to be drawn that way; all three describe the same situation. The cost of widgets to the consumers (which is what matters to them), the amount received by the producers per widget sold (which is what matters to them), and the quantity of widgets sold are all the same whether the tax is "paid" by producers or consumers. How the burden of the tax is really distributed is entirely unaffected by who actually hands over the money to the government!

And for the Real Cost of Taxes . . .

The previous section started with the question of who "really pays" taxes. It seems we now have the answer. Using a supply-demand diagram, we can show how much of the amount of the tax is "passed along" to the consumer in the form of higher prices and how much appears as a reduction in the (after-tax) receipts of the producer. In any particular case, the answer depends on the relative elasticity of the supply and demand curves—on how rapidly quantity demanded and quantity supplied change with price, as indicated by the slope of the curves S and D on our diagrams.

We have answered *a* question, but it is not quite the right question. We know by how much the tax raises the cost of widgets to the consumer and by how much it lowers the revenue received by the producer for each widget he sells, but that is not quite the same thing as how much *worse off* it makes them. The cost to the consumer is not merely a matter of how much money he spends; it also depends on what he gets for it.

To see this in a particularly striking way, imagine that the government decides to impose a tax of $1,000/widget. Production and consumption of widgets drop to zero. The government receives nothing; producers and consumers pay nothing. Does that mean that a tax of $1,000/widget costs consumers (and producers) nothing?

Obviously not. The consumers could have chosen to consume zero widgets before the tax increase—the fact that they actually consumed 1,100,000 widgets at a price of $5/widget (Figure 7-9) indicates that they preferred that number of widgets at that price to zero widgets; hence the tax has made them worse off. Our mistake was in assuming that the cost of the tax to the consumers was simply the number of widgets they bought times the increase in the price of the widgets. We should have also included the loss associated with the reduced consumption of widgets.

Let us now consider imposing a more reasonable tax—$1/widget instead of $1,000/widget. This makes the cost of widgets to consumers $5.60 and the quantity demanded and supplied 1,000,000, as shown by P_2 and Q_2 on Figure 7-9. Before there was any tax at all, consumers bought 1,100,000 widgets per year; after the $1 tax was imposed, their consumption went down to 1,000,000. The extra 100,000 widgets were worth at least $5 apiece (which is why consumers bought them before the tax was imposed, when the price of widgets was $5 each) but less than $5.60 (which is why they no longer buy them when the price goes up to $5.60). The consumers are worse off by the benefit they no longer get from purchasing those 100,000 widgets per year at $5 apiece, as well as by the increased price they must pay for the 1,000,000 widgets per year they continue to purchase. Similarly, the producers are worse off by the profits they would have made on the additional 100,000 widgets, as well as by lost revenue on the 1,000,000 widgets they still produce.

What we left out of our initial analysis of the cost of taxation was consumer (and producer) surplus, which was introduced in Chapter 4 (and 5) to measure the benefit to a consumer (producer) of being able to purchase (sell) as much as he wanted of a good at a particular price. Before the tax, the consumer could

Figure 7-9

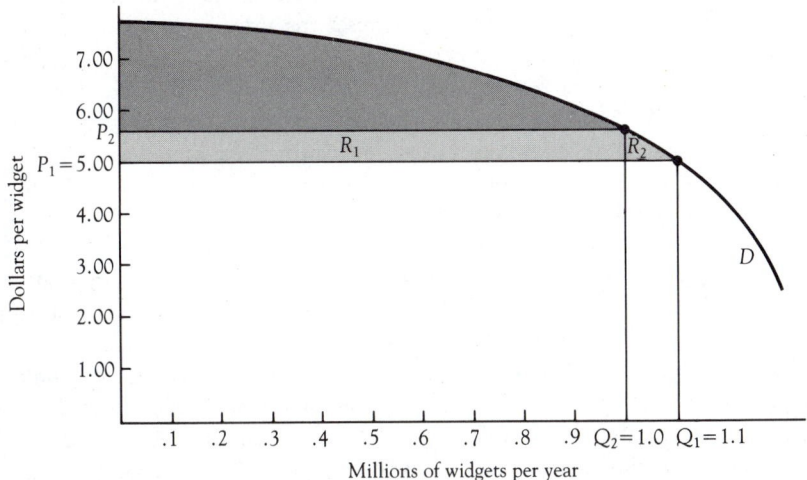

The effect on consumer surplus of a \$1 tax on widgets. The entire shaded area is consumer surplus before the tax; the dark shaded area is consumer surplus after the tax. The lightly shaded area is the cost the tax imposes on consumers. R_1 is revenue collected by the tax; R_2 is excess burden.

purchase as many widgets as he wanted at \$5 apiece; afterwards he could purchase as many as he wished at \$5.60 apiece. The cost to him of the tax is the difference between the consumer surplus he received in the first case and the consumer surplus he received in the second. This is shown in Figure 7-9. The entire shaded area of Figure 7-9 is the consumer surplus received before the tax. The darkly shaded area is the consumer surplus received after the tax. The lightly shaded area is the difference between the two—the cost of the tax. It is divided into two regions. R_1 is a rectangle whose height is the increase in the price and whose width is the quantity of widgets being consumed after the tax (1,000,000 per year). R_2 is an (approximate) triangle representing the lost consumer surplus on the 100,000 widgets per year which were consumed before the tax and are not consumed after the tax. R_1 is the amount of the tax paid by the consumers, in the sense discussed earlier in this chapter—the price increase times the quantity being consumed after the tax is imposed. R_2 is part of what is called the "excess burden" of the tax. R_1 is a loss to the consumers and an equal gain (in tax revenue) for the government; R_2 is a loss for the consumers with no corresponding gain for anyone. It has often been argued that the "ideal" system of taxes is that which minimizes excess burden.

Figures 7-10a and 7-10b show that the relation between R_1 and R_2 depends on the shape of the demand curve. If it is very flat (demand is "highly elastic"), then the increased price due to the effect of the tax (from P_1 to P_2) results in a large reduction in quantity demanded and a large loss of consumer surplus relative to the amount of tax revenue collected. P_3 on the diagram is the price at which quantity demanded is zero; for a tax that raises the price of the good that high, R_2 is substantial (the entire consumer surplus at P_1) and R_1 is zero. The effect of such a tax is all excess burden and no revenue at all.

If, on the other hand, the slope of the demand curve is very steep (demand is "highly inelastic"), as shown in Figure 7-10b, then the increased price results in only a small decrease in consumption, and R_2 is small compared to R_1. In the limiting case of pefectly inelastic demand, there is no reduction in consumption and hence no excess burden.

This has sometimes been used as an argument for taxing "necessities" instead of "luxuries." The idea is that demand for necessities is very inelastic (you "have to have them") while demand for luxuries is very elastic; hence taxes on necessities produce little excess burden compared to taxes on luxuries. Attempts to actually measure elasticity of demand for different goods do not always bear out this presumption; the demand for cigarettes, for example, which are usually thought of as luxuries (and sinful ones at that—hence the object of "sin taxes"), seems to be relatively inelastic. In any case, even if taxes on necessities do minimize excess burdens, there remains the objection that taxes on necessities "hurt the poor" while taxes on luxuries "soak the rich"—and that the latter is generally more popular, at least as a political slogan, than the former.

So far in this discussion, I have concentrated on the cost of the tax to the consumer. A similar analysis could be applied to the producer, with "producer's surplus" substituted for "consumer's surplus." The result would be similar; for con-

Figure 7-10

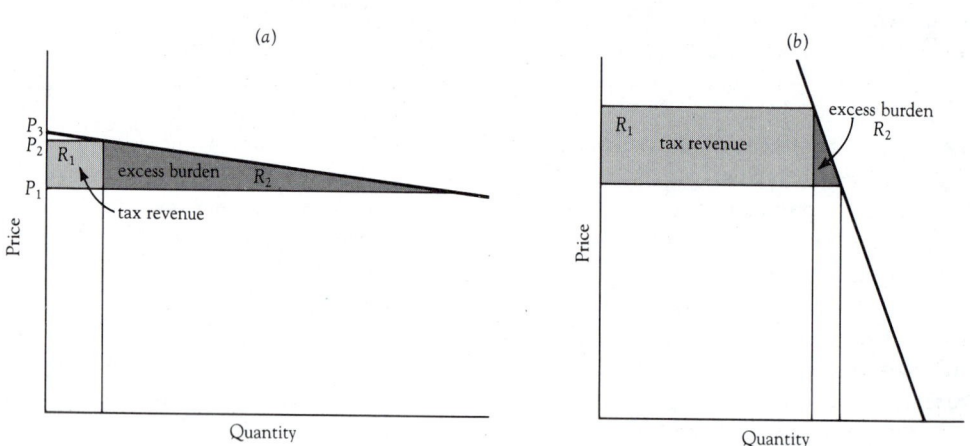

The effect of elasticity of the demand curve on the relation between revenue and excess burden. A very elastic demand curve (Figure 7-10a) produces a high ratio of excess burden to revenue; a very inelastic demand curve (Figure 7-10b) produces a low ratio.

sumers as well as for producers, the cost of the tax includes an element of excess burden, and the relation between excess burden and the rest of the cost to the producers depends on the elasticity of the supply curves.

In discussing the excess burden imposed by taxes, or anything else that depends on elasticity of supply and demand, it is important to distinguish between short-run and long-run effects. Typically, elasticities of both supply and demand are greater in the long run than in the short. If the price of gasoline rises, the immediate response of the consumer is to drive less; given a longer time to adjust, he can also arrange a car pool, buy a smaller car, or move closer to his job. If the price of heating oil rises, he can adjust, in the short run, only by turning down his thermostat. In the long run, he can improve the insulation of his house or move to a warmer climate.

In the short run, the producer is stuck with his existing factory. If price falls, he may still prefer producing at the lower price to scrapping his machinery. In the longer term, supply is more elastic; at the lower price, it will no longer be worth maintaining the machines or buying new ones as the old ones wear out. If, on the other hand, price rises, his short-run response is limited to trying to squeeze more output from the existing factory. In the longer run, he can build a bigger factory.

For all of these reasons, elasticities are generally greater in the longer run. High elasticity implies high excess burden, so the excess burden of a tax is likely to become larger, relative to the amount collected, as time goes on. A famous example is the window tax in London some centuries ago, which led to a style of houses with few windows. A similar and more recent example was a tax on houses in New Orleans which depended on the number of stories at the front of the house. That is supposed to be the origin of the "camelback" houses—one story in front, two in back. In the long run, dark houses in London and higher building costs in New Orleans were part of the excess burden of those taxes.

Landlords and Tenants—An Application of Price Theory

Suppose the government of Santa Monica decides that since landlords are bad and tenants good, every landlord must pay each of his tenants $10/month. In the short run, this benefits the tenants and hurts the landlords, since rents are set by contracts that usually run for a year or so; as long as the tenant is paying the same rent as before and receiving an additional $10, he is better off than before. In the longer run, however, the supply and demand curves for apartments are shifted by the new requirement, changing the equilibrium rent. The effect is shown in Figure 7-11a.

From the standpoint of the landlord, the new requirement is simply a tax of $10/month on each apartment rented. What matters to the landlord in deciding whether to rent out an apartment (as opposed to occupying it himself, turning it into a condominium, letting the building fall apart, not building it in the first place, or whatever other alternatives he has) is how much he ends up getting, not how much the tenant initially pays him. Since he has to give $10 back to the tenant, he actually gets $10 less than the amount the apartment is renting for. So the supply curve is shifted up by $10; at a rent of $510 per apartment per month, the quantity of apartments offered to rent is the same as it would have been before at a rent of $500/month.

From the standpoint of the tenant, the $10 he gets paid is a subsidy—a *negative* tax. A positive tax would shift the demand curve *down* by the amount of the tax, so the effect of the negative tax is to shift the demand curve *up* by $10. Whatever quantity of housing each tenant would before have chosen to rent at a price of $500/month (instead of buying a house, sharing an apartment with a friend, or moving to Chicago), that is now the quantity he will choose to rent if the rent is $510, since $510 in rent minus $10 from the landlord is a net cost to

Figure 7-11

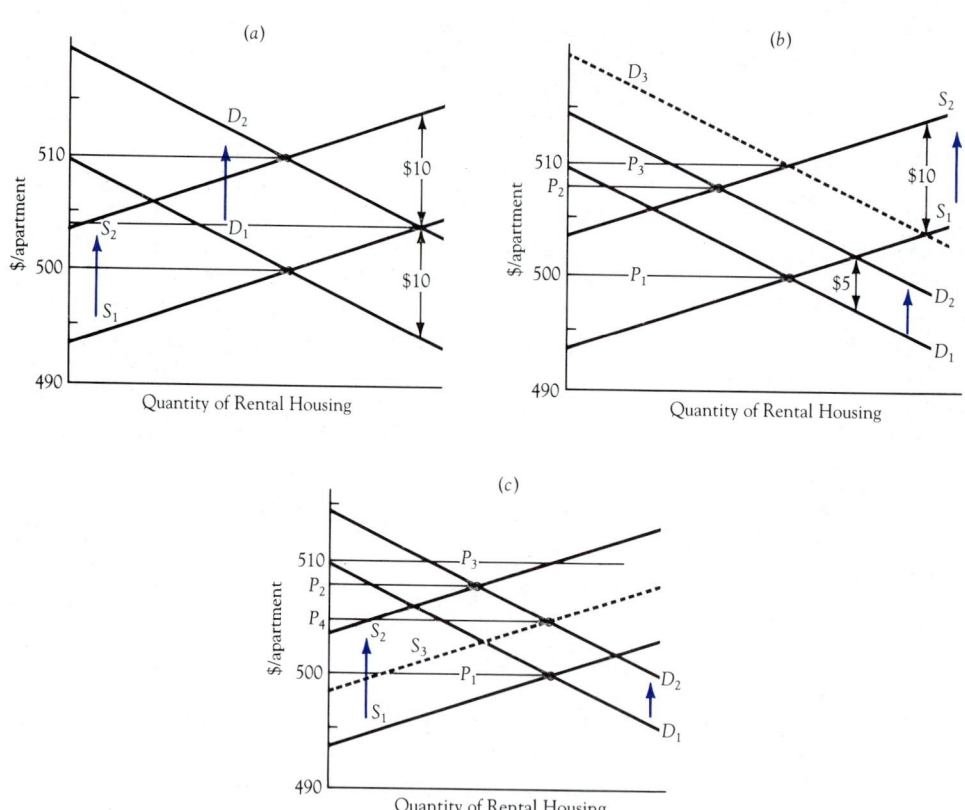

Effect of regulations on the rental market.   Figure 7-11a shows the effect of a compulsory $10 transfer from landlords to tenants. Figures 7-11b and 7-11c show the effect of requiring landlords to provide tenants with six months' notice. The requirement is equivalent to a $10 tax on landlords and a $5 subsidy to tenants.

him of $500. If the rent is less than $510, he will choose to rent more housing than he rented before at $500; if the rent is more than $510, he will rent less.

Figure 7-11a shows the result; since both supply and demand curves shift up by $10, their intersection shifts up by $10 as well. The new equilibrium rent is precisely $10 higher than the old, so the law neither benefits the tenant nor hurts the landlord. If this result seems paradoxical to you, you are a victim of what I earlier called "naive price theory." Once the assumption that prices are handed down from heaven in some mysterious manner is replaced by an understanding of how they are determined, the result is not only possible but obvious. If every time you pay the rent, the landlord is required to go through a ceremony of extracting one $10 bill and giving it back to you, there is no reason why that requirement should affect the real rent you pay and he receives.

Let us now consider a different law—one which seems at first less arbitrary. The city government decides that it is unfair for landlords to "force" tenants to sign lease contracts that are "biased" in favor of the landlords, so it passes a law requiring landlords to give tenants six months' notice before evicting them, even if the tenants have agreed in the lease to some shorter period. Again we consider the effect after enough time has passed so that rents have had a chance to adjust themselves to the new equilibrium, as determined by the supply and demand curves after the change.

Suppose the landlords are all identical. The requirement of six months' notice increases their operating costs, since it means that they will occasionally have an undesirable tenant whom they cannot evict for six months. From their standpoint, it is equivalent to a tax. Suppose it is equivalent to a tax of $10. Suppose, in other words, that landlords are indifferent between having to provide each tenant with six months' notice and having to pay a $10/month tax on each apartment. The supply curve for apartments shifts up by $10, as shown in Figure 7-11b.

From the standpoint of the tenants (who we will also assume are all identical to each other), the additional security of the six months' requirement is worth something; an apartment with that security is worth more than one without it. It is thus equivalent to them to receiving a subsidy—a negative tax. Suppose that it is equivalent to a subsidy of $5/month. Just as in the previous case, the result is to shift the demand curve up; the same tenant who was willing to pay $500/month for an apartment without six months' tenure is willing to pay $505 for one with the additional security. The curve shifts up by $5, as shown in Figure 7-11b. The result is similar to the $10 transfer shown on Figure 7-11a, but the demand curve shifts up only $5 instead of $10.

Looking at the figure, you can see that the new price is higher than the old by more than $5 and less than $10. To prove this, consider the dashed line D_3, which is D_1 displaced upward by $10 (as in the previous example, shown in Figure 7-11a). The intersection of D_3 with S_2 (the supply curve, given the new law) occurs at a price P_3 which is exactly $10 higher than the original price, P_1, just as on Figure 7-11a. D_2, the demand curve which actually results from the law (D_1 shifted up by only $5) is below D_3; hence it intersects with S_2 at a lower price, P_2. Hence P_2, the new equilibrium price, is between P_1 and $P_1 + \$10 = P_3$; price has gone up, but by less than $10.

To show that price goes up by more than $5, one makes a similar argument using D_2 and S_3, as shown in Figure 7-11c. Here S_3 is the supply curve S_1 shifted up by only $5. Its intersection with D_2 (the original demand curve shifted up $5) is at a price P_4, $5 higher than P_1, the original price. Since S_2, the supply curve resulting from the new law, is higher than S_3 (the curve has been shifted up $10 instead of only $5), it intersects D_2 at a price P_2 above P_4. So price has gone up by more than $5. We have shown that the effect of the law is to increase rents by more than $5 and less than $10. Since the law increases the costs to landlords by more than it increases rents, landlords are worse off. Since it increases the value of the apartment to tenants by less than it increases rents, tenants are also worse off!

In setting up the problem, I assumed that the six months' notice requirement cost the landlords more than it was worth to the tenants; specifically, I assumed that it cost the landlords $10 and was worth $5 to the tenants. What happens if we make the opposite assumption? Suppose the law imposes a cost of $5 (shifting the supply curve up by $5) and a benefit of $10 (shifting the demand curve up by $10) as shown in Figure 7-12. In that case, as you should be able to demonstrate, the increase in rent is again between $5 and $10. Both parties are *better* off as a result of the law—the landlord gets an increase in rent greater than the increase in his costs, while the tenant pays an increase in rent less than the value to him of the improved contract.

In this case, however, the law is unnecessary. If there is no law setting the terms for rental contracts, a landlord who is renting out his apartment (without six months' security) for $500/month will find it in his interest to offer his tenant the alternative of the same apartment with six months' security at, say, $509/month. The tenant will accept the offer, since (by our assumption) he prefers $509 with security to $500 without; the landlord will be better off, since it only costs him, on average, $5/month to provide the security. Hence, even without the law, all rental contracts will provide for six months' notice before eviction. So in this case, the law has no effect; it forces the landlords to do something they would do anyway.

More generally, it will pay the landlord to include in the lease contract any terms that are worth more to the tenant than they cost him—and adjust the rent accordingly. Given that he has done so, any requirement that he provide additional security (or other terms in the contract) will ultimately result in a rent increase that leaves both landlord and tenant worse off than before.

In proving this result, I made a number of simplifying assumptions. One was that the cost per apartment imposed by such a requirement on the landlord did not depend on how many apartments he was renting out, or in other words that the requirement, like a tax, shifted the supply curve up by the same amount all along its length. I also made the equivalent assumption for the tenants—that security was worth the same amount per apartment independent of how "much" apartment was consumed (the horizontal axis of the diagrams should really represent not "number of apartments" but "amount of housing rented" —rooms, square feet of apartment space, or some similar measure). Dropping these assumptions would make the diagrams and the analysis substantially more complicated.

Figure 7-12

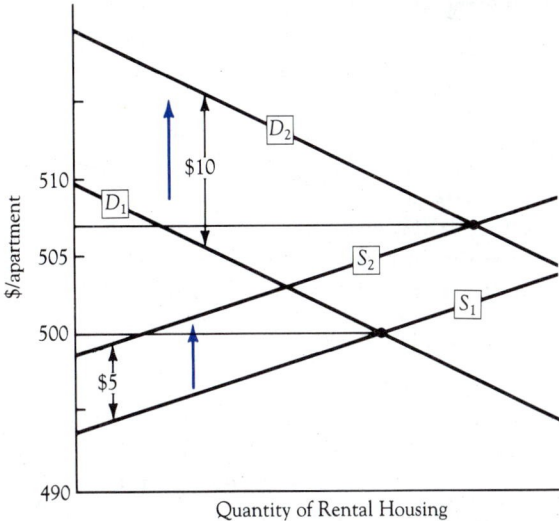

Effect of regulations on the rental market. This is like Figures 7-11b and 7-11c except that the requirement is equivalent to a $5 tax on landlords and a $10 subsidy to tenants.

A second assumption was that all landlords were identical to each other, and similarly for all tenants. Dropping these assumptions does change the results somewhat. To see why, imagine that you are a landlord who is unusually good at recognizing good tenants. Offering six months' security costs you nothing—you never rent an apartment to anyone you will ever want to evict. Assume that the situation, with regard to the tenants and the other landlords, is as shown in Figure 7-11b. If there is no legal restriction on contracts, you find that by offering security you can get a rent of $505/month instead of $500; since the security costs you nothing, you do so. After the law changes to force all landlords to offer security, you find that the market rent, for apartments with the (required) six months' security, is *more than* $505 (as shown in Figure 7-12). The restriction has actually helped you, by forcing your competitors (the other landlords) to add a feature (security) to their product that was expensive for them to produce but inexpensive for you. Their higher costs decreased the market supply curve and increased the market price, benefiting you.

One could construct similar cases involving tenants. The interesting point to note is that the effect of legal restrictions on contracts between landlords and tenants is not, as one might at first expect, a redistribution from one group (landlords) to another (tenants). Insofar as the groups are uniform, the restrictions either have no effect or injure everyone; insofar as the members of the groups differ from each other, the restriction may also result in redistribution *within* the groups—benefiting some members of one or both of the groups at the expense of other members of the same group.

One of the difficulties in teaching (and learning) economics is that so much of it seems to be simply plausible talk about familiar subjects. That is an illusion. In the course of this chapter, I have given proofs of two very implausible results—that it does not matter whether a tax is collected from producers or consumers and that restrictions on rental contracts "in favor" of tenants actually hurt both tenants and landlords.

The fact that economics seems to be merely plausible talk about familiar things poses a serious danger to the student. He may go through the first half of the course nodding his head from time to time at what seem like reasonable statements by the text or the professor, only to discover at the midterm that he has somehow failed to learn most of the structure of ideas that the lectures and text were supposed to be teaching—even though it all seemed to make sense when he heard it.

The best way to find out for yourself whether you really understand the ideas is to try to apply them to numerical examples. That is the significance of such examples. Whether you do or do not become an economist, it is unlikely that you will ever be faced with any real-world equivalent of a numerical problem on an economics exam; as I explained earlier, the real world rarely provides us with accurate graphs of supply and demand curves. What you will be faced with—whether as an economist or a participant in the economy—are problems similar to the problem of figuring out whether a restriction on lease contracts benefits or harms tenants. To do so, you must learn economics, not merely learn about economics; numerical problems are a way in which you can check whether or not you have done so. In exactly the same sense, the right way to find out whether you have learned typing is not to see if you can tell someone about it, or remember what you have been taught, but to try to type something—even if it is only "The quick brown fox jumped over the lazy dog." Many of the problems in an economics text are about as closely related to the ways in which you will actually use economics as the quick brown fox is to the things you eventually expect to type—and serve much the same function.

PART 2 · SUPPLY AND DEMAND— SOME GENERAL POINTS

In the first part of this chapter, we put together what we had done in Chapters 3-6 in order to show how equilibrium price and quantity are determined by demand and supply curves. We then applied the analysis to a variety of real-world issues. In the second part of the chapter, we will look back at what we have just done in order to clarify some points and avoid some common misunderstandings.

Mechanism vs Equilibrium

In economics (and elsewhere), there are often two different ways of approaching a problem—one way is to work through a (possibly infinite) series of changes; the other is to look at what the situation must be when all changes have ceased. The latter is often much easier than the former.

Consider a simple supply-demand problem. At a market price of $1, purchasers of eggs wish to buy 1,000 eggs per week and producers wish to produce 900. The first way of analyzing the problem might go as follows:

Step 1: There are only 900 eggs to be purchased. The consumers bid against each other until they have driven the price up to $1.25; at that price, they only want to buy 900 eggs.

Step 2: At the new price, producers want to produce 980 eggs per week. They do so. They find that at $1.25, they cannot sell that many, so they compete against each other (by cutting the price) until the price falls to $1.05; at that price, consumers will buy 980 eggs.

Step 3: At $1.05, producers only want to produce 910 eggs per week. They do so. Consumers bid against each other . . .

As you can see, there are several things wrong with this approach. To begin with, the series may go on forever, with the prices gradually converging; indeed, with some demand and supply curves, the series would diverge—the swings in price would get wider and wider. Furthermore, the process as I have described it depends on producers and consumers always basing their decisions on what the price just was instead of trying to estimate what it is going to be. Once you drop that assumption, there are many possible sequences of events, depending on the detailed assumption you make about how producers predict the future. The alternative approach goes as follows:

If quantity supplied is greater than quantity demanded, the price will fall; if less, the price will rise. Hence price will tend toward the point at which the two are equal. This is the equilibrium market price—the intersection of supply and demand.

Shortages, Surpluses, and How to Make Them

To most non-economists, a shortage is a fact of nature—"there just isn't enough." To an economist, it has almost nothing to do with nature. Diamonds are in very short supply—yet there is no diamond shortage. Water is very plentiful; the average American city dweller "consumes" more than 100 gallons per day. Yet we see water shortages.

The mistake is in assuming that "enough" is a fact of nature—that we need a particular amount of land, water, diamonds, oil, or whatever. In fact, the amount we choose to consume (and that producers choose to produce) depends on the price; what we think of as our "need" is usually our quantity demanded at the price we are used to paying. A shortage occurs not when the amount available is small but when it is less than the amount we want; since the latter depends on price, a shortage is equivalent to a below-market price. Typically this is the result of either government price control (gas and oil prices in the early seventies, for example) or the refusal by government to charge the market price for something it supplies (urban water). Sometimes it is the result of producers who misestimate demand (particular models of cars) and are unwilling or unable to adjust price or output quickly. An obvious example is where the seller is bound by an advertised price and finds that at that price he runs out.

One interesting case of a relatively stable supply-demand disequilibrium occurred many years ago in Hong Kong. Rickshaws are small carts drawn by one person and used to transport another—a sort of human-powered taxi. They used to be common in Hong Kong. Casual observation suggested that the drivers spent most of their time sitting by the curb waiting for customers—quantity supplied was much larger than quantity demanded. Why?

The explanation appears to be that many of the customers were tourists from countries where the wage level was, at that time, much higher than in Hong Kong. The price it seemed natural to them to offer to pay was far above the price at which supply would have equaled demand. Hence people were attracted into the rickshaw business until the daily income (one fourth of the day working for a high hourly payment, three fourths of the day sitting around) was comparable to that of other Hong Kong jobs. It is worth noticing that the tourists who paid $4HK for a ride that represented $1HK worth of labor were worse off by $3HK than if they had paid the lower price but that there was no corresponding gain to the recipients.

The Invisible Demand Curve

A careless reading of an economics textbook may give the impression that economists are people who go around measuring supply and demand curves and calculating prices from them. This is a complete misunderstanding. What we observe are prices and quantities. To the extent that we know anything about particular demand curves, it is mostly deduced from such observations. For the most part, supply curves and demand curves are used not as summaries of information (like a table of atomic weights) but as analytical tools, ways of understanding the mechanism by which prices are determined.

Indeed, demand (and supply) curves are in a sense unobservable. We observe that this year there was a certain amount of wheat grown and it sold at a certain price. We make similar observations for other years. Can we plot the corresponding points on a graph and call them a demand curve ("When price was $1, demand was 4,000,000 bushels; when price was . . .")? No. If the demand curve and supply curve had stayed the same from year to year, price and quantity would have stayed the same as well. Since they did not, at least one of the curves must have shifted, and perhaps both. If the demand curve stayed the same and the supply curve shifted around (perhaps because of varying weather), then the observed points trace out the demand curve (Figure 7-13a), but if it was demand that shifted and supply that stayed fixed, then we have a graph of the supply curve instead (Figure 7-13b). If both curves shifted, we have a graph of neither (Figure 7-13c).

Demand or Supply?

One of the original puzzles of economics was whether price was determined by the value of a good to the purchaser (demand) or the cost of production (supply). You are now in a position to see that the answer is both. If the supply curve is horizontal at a price P, then P is the market price, whatever the demand curve

Figure 7-13

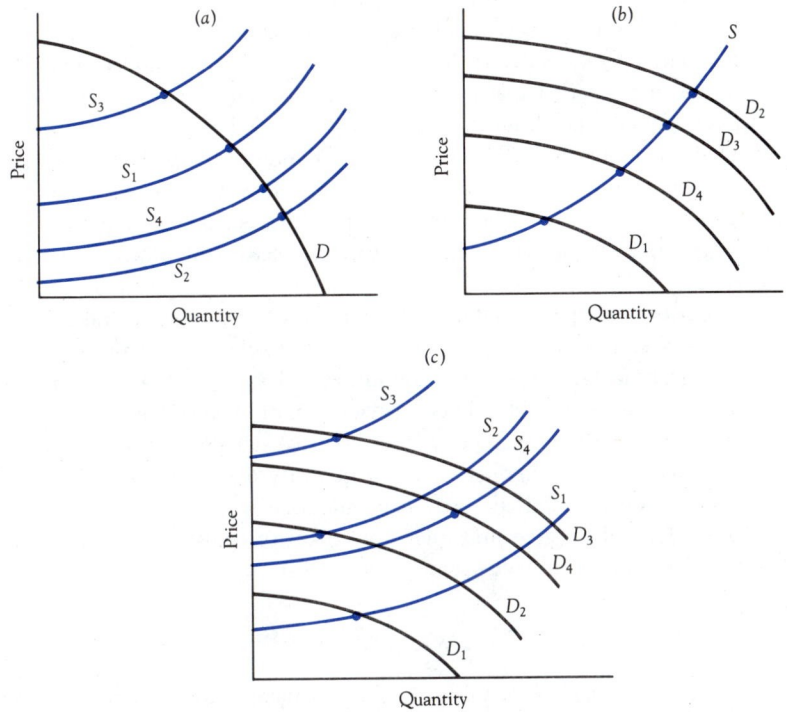

Invisible curves. What we observe is only the intersection of a supply and a demand curve. If the supply curve is shifting (Figure 7-13a), the intersections map out the demand curve; if the demand curve is shifting (Figure 7-13b), they map out the supply curve; and if both are shifting (Figure 7-13c), they show neither.

may be—unless the quantity demanded at that price is zero, in which case nothing is sold and there is no market price. If *demand* is horizontal at a price P, then that will be the market price—whatever the supply curve (with the same exception). In the normal case, where neither line is horizontal, a shift in either will change the price.

The statement "Price is determined by both value to the consumer and cost of production" is also true in a more complicated sense; it is in a sense true that "Price is equal to both value to the consumer and cost of production"—even in the extreme case of a horizontal supply curve, where price is *determined* entirely by supply.

How can this be true? It is true if what we mean by value is marginal value, and by cost, marginal cost (of production). The consumer, faced with the opportunity to consume as much as he wants at a price P, chooses to consume that quantity of the good at which his marginal value for an additional unit is just equal to P. We saw that in Chapter 4, where we derived the demand curve from the consumer's marginal value curve. Hence price equals value—not because value determines price but because price (at which the good is available) determines quantity (which the consumer chooses to consume) and quantity consumed determines (marginal) value. Seen from the other side, the producer, able to sell all he wants at a price P, expands output until his marginal cost of production (the marginal disvalue per hour of labor to him divided by the number of units he produces in an hour) is P. We saw that in Chapter 5 and will see it again, in the case of a firm rather than an individual producer, in Chapter 9. Hence price equals cost—not because cost determines price but because price (at which he can sell the good) determines quantity (that he produces) which determines (marginal) cost.

In considering a single consumer or a single producer, we may take price as given, since his consumption or production is unlikely to be large enough to influence it significantly. Considering the entire industry (made up of many producers) and the entire demand curve (made up of many individual demand curves), this is no longer true. The market price is that price at which quantity demanded equals quantity supplied. At the quantity demanded and supplied at that price, price equals marginal cost equals marginal value. Demand and supply curves jointly determine price and quantity; quantity (plus demand and supply curves) determines marginal value and marginal cost.

Warning

There are two somewhat subtle mistakes which I have found that students often make in "interpreting" the material of this chapter. The first is a verbal mistake with regard to "demand." It is easy to think of "my demand increasing" as meaning "I want it more." But demand (the demand curve) is a graph of *quantity demanded* vs price. If your demand increases, that means that at any price, you want more of it—not that you "want it more." *How much* you want it is your marginal value, not your demand; it depends, among other things, on how much of it you have. That the two curves (demand and marginal value) are the same is not a matter of definition (they mean quite different things) but something that we proved in Chapter 4.

The other mistake has to do with why supply curves shift. We are used to thinking of prices as the result of bargaining between buyer and seller, with each claiming that the price he wants is "fair." It is tempting to imagine that when a tax is imposed, the reason price rises is that the seller tells the buyer, "Look here. My costs have gone up, so it is only fair for you to let me raise my price." The buyer replies, "I agree that it is fair for you to raise your price, but I should not have to bear the whole cost of the tax, so let us compromise on a price increase that transfers part of the tax to me and leaves you paying the rest."

Such an imaginary dialogue has *nothing* to do with the process I have been describing in this chapter, and almost nothing to do with how prices are really determined. To begin with, I am assuming a market with many buyers and many sellers; each individual, in deciding how much to buy or sell, takes the price as given, knowing that nothing he does can much affect it. In such a context, bargaining has no place. If you do not like my price, I will sell to someone who does; if nobody will buy at the price I am asking, I must have made a mistake about what the market price was.

When a tax is imposed on the producers, each producer revises his calculation about how large a quantity it is in his interest to produce. Before the tax, when the price was, say, $10, he produced up to the point where producing an additional widget cost him as much, in time and effort, as $10 was worth to him. When a $1 tax is imposed, he finds that each additional widget is bringing him only $9 —$10 for the widget minus $1 for the tax. He is in the same situation as if there were a $9 price and no tax, so he reduces his production to what he would have produced if the price were $9 and there were no tax. He is not trying to bargain with anyone—he is simply maximizing his welfare under changed circumstances. All other producers act similarly. Quantity supplied (at $10) is now less than quantity demanded, so price rises. As it rises, producers increase the amount they find it in their interest to produce; consumers decrease the amount they find it in their interest to consume. The price continues to rise until it reaches a level at which the quantity producers wish to produce is the same as the quantity consumers wish to consume.

PROBLEMS

1. Figures 7-14a and 7-14b each show demand curves for two individuals; in each case, draw the combined demand curve.
2. One crucial step in the analysis of this chapter was to show that a tax on producers shifts the supply curve up by the amount of the tax, while a tax on consumers shifts the demand curve down by the amount of the tax. The argument was made verbally; restate it (for consumers) using budget lines and indifference curves. (This is a hard problem.)

Figure 7-14

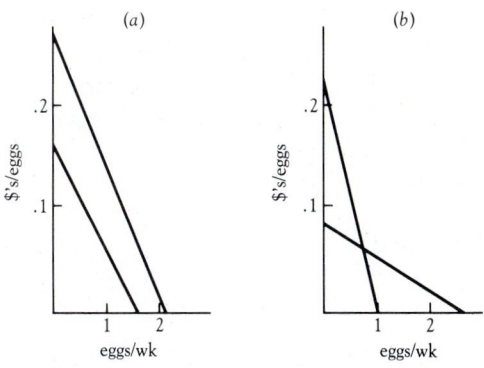

Demand curves for Problem 1.

3. Figure 7-15 shows the supply curve for avocados. A tax of $.50/avocado is imposed. Draw the new supply curve.
4. Figure 7-16 shows the demand curve for peanut butter. A consumption tax is imposed; every purchaser must pay the government $.40 for every jar of peanut butter purchased. Draw the new demand curve for peanut butter.

Figure 7-15

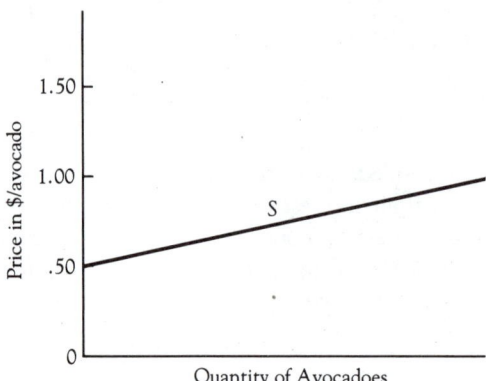

Supply curve for Problem 3.

5. The only way anyone eats peanut butter is on bananas; the only way anyone eats bananas is with peanut butter. One jar of peanut butter is just the right amount for eating with 10 bananas. The demand curve for peanut butter used to be as shown in Figure 7-16; the price of bananas used to be $.20 apiece. Due to a revolution in Central America, the supply curve for bananas changes; their market price goes up to $.30. Draw the new demand curve for peanut butter. You may assume that the new supply curve for bananas is parallel to the old. (This is a harder problem; you have to work out for yourself a point that has not been explained in the chapter.)
6. In drawing the demand curve for peanut butter in Problem 5, what did you assume happened to the price of bananas as you varied the amount of peanut butter? Explain. Does the demand curve you draw depend on this assumption? Discuss. (This is a hard problem.)
7. Figure 7-17 shows the supply and demand curves for bananas (from this point on, forget about peanut butter).
   a. What are the equilibrium price, quantity, and total consumer expenditure? For parts (b-g), answer the following questions:
      i. What is the equilibrium price? Quantity? Consumer expenditure for bananas?
      ii. How much better or worse off are consumers than in part (a) (no tax)? Producers?
      iii. How much revenue does the government get?

Figure 7-16

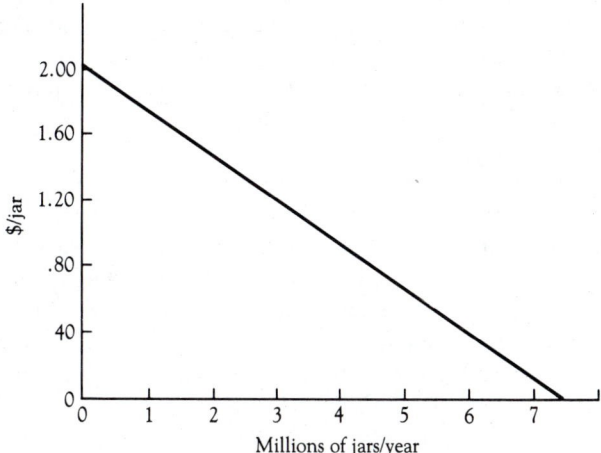

Demand curve for Problems 4 and 5.

Figure 7-17

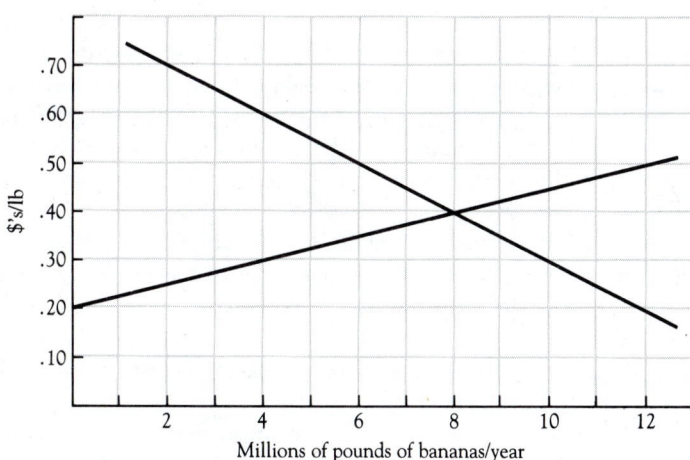

Supply and demand curves for Problem 7.

b. Consumers must pay a tax of $.10/pound on bananas.
c. Producers must pay a tax of $.10/pound on bananas.
d. Producers pay and consumers receive a tax of $.10/pound.
e. Producers and consumers each pay a tax of $.05/pound.

f. The government requires all bananas to be labeled with the date they were picked. This results in an increased cost to producers of $.08/pound. Consumers are indifferent between unlabeled bananas at a price P and labeled bananas at a price P plus $.03.

g. As in (f), except that the cost to the producers is $.03 and the value to the consumers $.08. Comment on your results.

h. The government imposes price control at $.30/pound. How large is the resulting shortage? If the "insufficient supply" is rationed by the sellers accepting bribes, what will the bribe be per pound of banana purchased?

i. Can a tax lower the total expenditure of consumers on bananas and at the same time hurt the consumers? If so, give an example. Explain.
(Note: Each of parts (*b-h*) is independent; in each case, we start with the same initial situation, make one change, and evaluate the result.)

8. Work out the effect of a tax in the case of a perfectly elastic supply curve. In the case of a perfectly elastic demand curve.

9. Demonstrate that if *supply* is perfectly inelastic, there will be no excess burden to the consumers.

10. What are the relations between elasticity of demand and supply and excess burden to the *producers*? Demonstrate your results with figures similar to Figures 7-5a through 7-5f, 7-10a, and 7-10b.

11. What is the exact mathematical relation between P_2 and P_3 in Figure 7-6 and P_2' and P_3' in Figure 7-8a?

12. Social Security taxes are paid half by the employer and half by the worker. What do you think is the significance of that division; how would things be different if the tax were entirely on the worker or entirely on the employer or divided in some other way between them? Prove your answer.

13. In discussing the costs and benefits of the Social Security program, it is common to compare the amount "contributed" by the worker with the benefits he receives. Is this appropriate? Can you suggest a better comparison—specifically, one more appropriate to a worker trying to decide if he would be better off if the program were abolished? What about a worker trying to decide if he would be better off if he opted out of the program (supposing he were allowed to do so). Are the two questions the same? (Hint: The answer is no. Why?)

14. Why do you think the present division of Social Security payments between employer and employee exists?

15. In discussing the surplus of rickshaws, I claimed that the high price paid by customers to rickshaw drivers was a cost to the customer but not a gain to the driver. Explain. Describe what the situation would be like if customers paid a price at which the number of rickshaw rides which the producers wished to sell was equal to the number that the customers wished to buy.

Chapter 8

The Big Picture

SOLVING AN ECONOMY

Several chapters back, I described the economy as a complicated interdependent system and proposed to solve it by separately solving the parts. I have now done so, at least for a simple economy. The separate pieces are the consumer, the producer, and the market in which they interact. In discussing the consumer's behavior, in Chapters 3 and 4, we saw how the attempt to achieve his objectives leads to an individual demand curve, describing how much he will buy of a good at any price. The shape of this demand curve depends on the preferences of the individual, his income, and the prices of all other goods. Once we have the individual demand curves, we can sum them to get a market demand curve.

In Chapter 5, we saw how a similar argument leads to a supply curve. One new element was the addition of a *production function*—a relation between the time a particular producer spends producing things and how much he produces. In Chapter 5, the production function took the form of a table showing the rates at which a producer could produce each of various combinations of goods. The producer could use his time to produce goods, sell the goods for money, and, as a consumer, use the money to buy the goods he wished to consume.

Here, as in most of economics, money is not essential to the analysis, although it makes its presentation easier. We could analyze production and consumption in essentially the same way even if all trade occurred by barter, with individuals producing goods and exchanging them directly for other goods. The only difference would be that the system would appear more complicated, both to us and to the people inside it. Instead of talking about "the price of apples," "the price of meals," and so forth, we would have to talk about "the price of apples measured in meals," "the price of lawn mowing measured in oranges," and so on; this would complicate both our description of the economy and the lives of the participants.

Another complication of barter, from the standpoint of individual traders, is the *double coincidence problem*. In an economy with money, an individual can sell the goods he produces to one person and use the money to buy what he wants from another. In a barter economy, the trader must find one person who both has what he wants and wants what he has. In almost all of the analysis so far, I have neglected the *transaction costs* associated with a market—the costs of finding someone to trade with and negotiating an exchange. That useful simplification would be less plausible in a barter market.

Having gotten demand curves (and consumer surplus) from the chapter on consumption, and supply curves (and producer surplus) from the chapter on production, I combined the two in Chapter 7 to describe how market prices are determined, how they are affected by changes in supply and demand, and the effects of the resulting changes in price and quantity on the welfare of consumers and producers. It appears that we now have all the pieces of an economy—supply, demand, and their combination. Let us see if we can assemble them.

Putting It Together: The First Try

Putting the pieces together appears very simple; indeed, it seems that we have already done so. We start with individual preferences—represented by indifference curves or utility functions—and the ability of individuals to produce goods—production functions. The preferences of consumers (and their incomes) give us demand curves, the preferences of producers (between leisure and income) plus production functions give us supply curves, the intersections of supply and demand curves give us prices (and quantities), and we are finished. We have derived prices and quantities from preferences and production functions.

It is not so simple. The intersection of supply and demand curves gives us prices. Prices (of the goods the individuals produce and sell) give us incomes. But we needed incomes to start with, since they were one of the things that determined demand curves!

The same problem appears if we stop talking about "prices" in general and talk instead about particular prices. We run through our supply and demand argument to get the price of widgets. We then do the same to get the price of cookies. But one of the things affecting the demand for widgets is the price of cookies (if cookies are inexpensive, you spend your money on them instead of on widgets). We could solve that problem by solving for cookies first—but one of the things affecting the demand for cookies might well be the price of widgets.

Why would we expect the demand curve for one good to depend on the price of another? There are two reasons. The first is that the goods may actually be related in consumption; this is the case of what are called "complements" and "substitutes." Bread and butter, for example, are commonly used together, so the value of bread to you depends in part on the price of butter, and vice versa. Your demand curve for bread goes up when the price of butter goes down. Bread and butter are complements; so are peanut butter and bananas in Chapter 7, Problem 5. Trains and airplanes both provide the same service—transportation. Your demand curve for rail travel goes down when airline fares go down. Trains and airplanes are substitutes.

These possibilities may be assumed away when we are trying to describe a very simple economy; we can limit ourselves, if we wish, to people for whom the usefulness of one good never depends on how much they have of another, and then reintroduce such complications at a later stage of the analysis. We may assume, in other words, that the individual's utility function is simply the sum of a lot of little utility functions—utility of apples (which depends only on how many apples he has) plus utility of oranges plus utility of water plus . . . . There is a second sort of interdependence which cannot be dealt with so easily. The demand curve of a good is identical to its marginal value curve, which tells us how many dollars are equivalent to a little more of the good. But dollars are valuable for the (other) goods that they can buy; hence the value of a dollar depends on the price of those goods. If all prices go down, a unit of a good is still equivalent to the same amount of some other good but to fewer dollars, so the demand curve for one good depends on the prices of the other goods that money could be spent on. As I have pointed out before, a drop in the price of everything is just like an increase in income—and has similar effects on the demand curve for any particular thing.

In thinking about what determines the price of one good, it is convenient, and often correct, to treat all other prices as "given" and work through the effect of some change in demand or supply on the particular good we are interested in. We cannot follow the same procedure in understanding the whole interdependent system. Each price depends on all other prices, both directly, because the price of one good to a consumer may affect his demand curve for other goods, and indirectly, since the price of a good to its producer affects his income, which in turn affects both his supply and demand curves for other goods.

Nailing Jelly to a Wall

The interdependence of the different elements that make up the economic system is not wholly new; it is a more complicated example of a problem we have already met and dealt with. The mistake is in thinking that, having worked out the separate parts of the problem, we can then assemble them one part at a time— solve for one part of the system, then for another, then . . . The discussion of the egg market in Chapter 7 started with a simpler form of the same mistake. I tried to solve the problem in a series of stages; at each stage, I solved part of the system while ignoring its effect on the rest. I started with a given quantity of eggs being produced, then found the price at which that was the quantity consumers wished to consume. At that point, I was solving for price, given the requirement that price must be such that quantity demanded (at that price) equals quantity produced. I next found the quantity which would be produced at that price; in other words, I solved for quantity, given the condition that quantity produced must be the quantity producers choose to produce, using the price derived in the previous stage of the argument. That gave me a different quantity produced, which had to be plugged back into the demand side of the analysis (the first step), yielding a different price, which must be plugged back into the supply side, yielding a different quantity . . . The logical tangle that results is a (simple!) case of an attempt to solve an interacting system one piece at a time while ignoring the effect on all the other pieces.

The solution was to stop treating it as a mechanism and instead look for the equilibrium point. That occurs at the one price and quantity combination for which quantity supplied equals quantity demanded. In the more complicated case of the whole economy, we will follow essentially the same procedure.

Putting It Together: The Second Try

Our problem is to start with individual preferences and production functions and derive a complete set of equilibrium prices and quantities. The first step is to consider some list of prices—a price for every good. This initial list is simply a first guess, a set of prices chosen at random.

Since each supply curve is determined by the prices of the goods the producer would like to buy and of the other goods he could sell (and preferences and production functions, which we know), we can calculate all supply curves. Since quantity supplied of any good is determined by the supply curve and the price of that good, we can calculate the quantity supplied of every good. Since income is determined by the prices of the goods we produce and the quantities we produce of them, we can calculate every producer's income. Since the demand curve for any particular good is determined by income (of the consumers, which they get as producers) and prices (of other goods), we can calculate all demand curves; since quantity demanded of any good is determined by the demand curve and the price of that good, we can calculate the quantity demanded of every good.

So, starting with preferences, production functions, and a list of prices, we can calculate all quantities supplied and demanded and compare the quantity demanded of every good with the quantity supplied. If the two are equal (for every good), we have the right list of prices—the list which describes the equilibrium of the system. If they are not equal, we pick another list of prices and go through the calculation again. We continue until we find the right list of prices. The logical sequence is diagrammed in Figure 8-1.

In practice, this would be a slow way of finding the right answer, rather like putting a thousand monkeys at a thousand typewriters and waiting for one of them to type out *Hamlet* by pure chance. After the first million years, the best result you would get might be "To be or not to be, that is the grglflx." There are faster ways, provided you have explicit descriptions of everybody's preferences and productive abilities; the general mathematical problem is that of "solving a set of n simultaneous equations in n unknowns." Our simple egg example was a problem of two equations (quantity equals quantity producers choose to supply at the price; quantity equals quantity demanded at the price) in two unknowns (quantity and price). Since a problem in two variables can be solved in two dimensions, which happened to be the number we had available, we were able to solve the problem graphically by looking for the point where two lines (the supply and demand curves) intersected.

I have gone through right and wrong ways of solving an economy so fast that you may have lost the former in the latter. I will therefore repeat the very simple result.

To solve an economy, find that set of prices such that quantity demanded equals quantity supplied for all goods and services.

That simple result—contrasted with the previous hundred and some pages—may remind you of the mountain that gave birth to a mouse. But without those pages, we would not have known how prices (and preferences) generate supply and demand curves, nor how supply and demand curves in turn determine prices.

Solving even a very simple real-world economy would involve thousands of equations; in practice, the problem is insoluble even with advanced mathematics and modern computers. But the point of the analysis is not actually to solve an economy and come up with a set of prices and quantities. Even if we could solve the equations, we could not write them down in the first place, since we do not know everyone's preferences and abilities. What we observe are prices and quantities; we see the solution, not the problem. The point of the analysis is to learn how the system is interrelated, in order that we can understand how some particular change (a tariff, a tax, a law, an invention) affects the whole system. Also for the fun of understanding the logical structure of the interrelated world around us.

Your response may be that we do not understand a system if our "solution" requires information and calculating abilities we do not have. But as I tried to make clear in Chapter 1, economists do not expect to know what people's objectives are, only what the consequences are of people rationally pursuing them. Nor, I might have added, are economists experts in the technology of production.

If you think economics is useless if it cannot actually "solve" an economy—predict what the entire set of prices and quantities is going to be—consider what we have already done. The book so far contains demonstrations of at least four

Figure 8-1

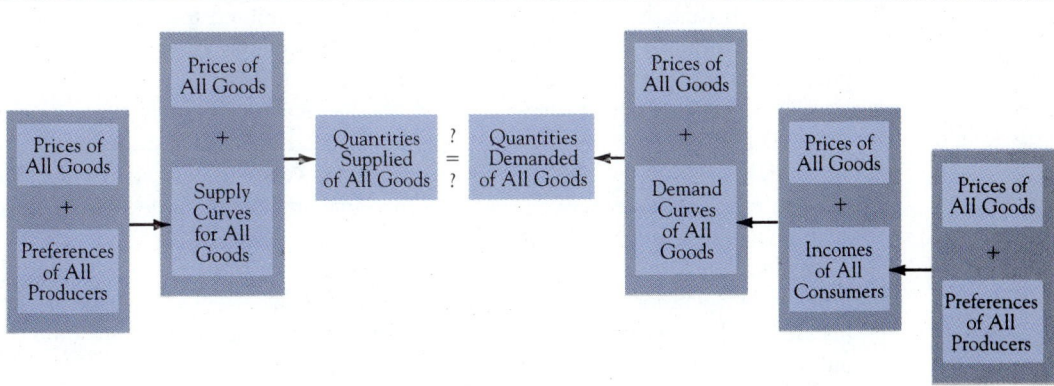

<u>How to solve an economy.</u> Starting with prices of all goods, production functions, and preferences of all consumers, one can derive quantities supplied and demanded. If they are equal for all goods, the initial set of prices describes a possible market equilibrium—a solution for that economy.

strikingly counter-intuitive results: (1) that a theater owner maximizes his profit by selling popcorn at cost, (2) that for a nation or individual to be better at producing one thing is logically equivalent to its being worse at producing something else (the principle of comparative advantage), (3) that the costs imposed by taxes on producers and consumers are unaffected by who pays the taxes, and (4) that legal restrictions on leases "in favor of tenants" either have no effect or hurt both tenants and landlords. Not one of those conclusions depended on our knowing any real-world demand or supply curve, nor any of the preferences and abilities from which those curves might have been derived.

Economics is not the only science that analyzes systems which it cannot actually solve. The "three-body problem"—the problem of determining the behavior of three objects interacting by gravitational attraction according to the laws of Newtonian physics—has not yet been solved, but that does not prevent astronomers from studying the solar system, which contains at least nine planets, the sun, and a considerable number of moons, comets, and asteroids.

OPTIONAL SECTION

PARTIAL AND GENERAL EQUILIBRIUM

The kind of economics that we did in Chapter 7 is what economists call "partial equilibrium" analysis; we analyzed the effect of changes in the market for one good, whether widgets or apartments, while ignoring the effects on other goods. The kind of economics that we did in this chapter, when we saw how, in principle, an economy can be solved, is called "general equilibrium" analysis.

Most economic analysis, in this book and elsewhere, is partial equilibrium; one assumes that the effects one is interested in are limited to one or at most a few goods. In many situations, this is a legitimate assumption—not because it is precisely correct but because it leads to correct conclusions.

Consider a case where some change shifts the demand or supply curve for one good. The result is to change the price of the good and the quantity produced and purchased, as described in Chapter 7. It is very unlikely that, after the change, each consumer will be spending the same amount of money on the good at the new price as he did at the old.

If a consumer is spending more (or less) on the good whose price has changed, he must be spending less (or more) on all other goods. Hence the quantity demanded of those goods has changed. Hence the initial assumption, that only the one good was affected, is wrong.

It is wrong but, like the assumptions on which economics is built, useful. In most cases, such effects are spread among a large number of other goods, each of which is only slightly affected (this is not true in the special case of two goods which are close substitutes or close complements, which is why such goods must be treated together in such an analysis). Small changes in prices generally produce very small effects on total surplus—the sum of consumer and producer surplus. Roughly speaking, a $.10 increase in price produces not one tenth the effect of a $1 increase but one hundredth. The reason is that when a price goes up, most of the resulting loss in consumer's surplus is a gain in producer surplus; only that part of the loss of (consumer and producer) surplus associated with the reduction in quantity produced and consumed is a net loss. Since the reduction in quantity associated with a price increase of $1 is about 10 times as great as that associated with a price increase of $.10 (exactly 10 times if the relevant curve is a straight line) and since the average consumer surplus per unit on the lost consumption is also about 10 times as high, the product is 100 times as great.

That is a verbal explanation of why partial equilibrium analysis, while not rigorously correct, gives almost exactly the correct solution to many problems. Figures 8-2a and 8-2b present the same argument geometrically for one particular example. They show the effect on those already buying and selling a particular good of an increase in its price due to an additional demand by a new consumer—someone who has entered the market due to an increase in his income, the change of the price of some other good he was consuming, or some other change elsewhere in the economy. S is the supply curve, D the demand curve of the original consumers, and D' the new demand curve, including the demand by the new consumer. P and Q are the price and quantity before the change, P' and Q' after the change. Q' is made up of two parts—the quantity purchased by the original consumers, Q'', and the quantity purchased by the new consumer, Q_n. $Q' = Q'' + Q_n$.

If we consider only the effect of the new consumer on the transactions among the original traders, we observe that consumer surplus (to the original demanders) has been reduced from BHF to BJC; those consumers are worse off by the two shaded areas, $CJGF$ and JHG. Producer surplus (on goods sold to the original

Figure 8-2

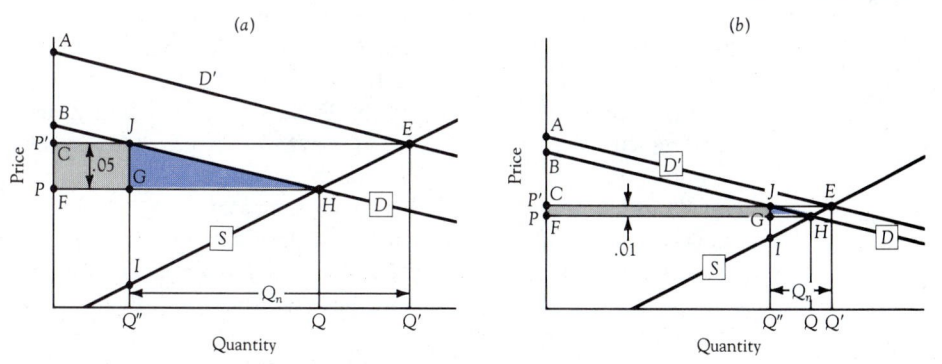

The effect of a change in demand on the market for one good. The shift is 5 times as great in Figure 8-2a as in Figure 8-2b; the resulting net change in surplus (the darkly shaded region) is 25 times as great.

demanders) has been reduced by *GHI* (due to a reduction in quantity of goods they buy) but increased by *CJGF* (due to an increase in the price they pay). The net effect on the original traders is to reduce their total surplus by *JHI*, while *CJGF* is transferred from consumer to producer surplus. The producers receive an additional surplus of *JEI* on Q_n, the output sold to the new demander.

What is important for our present purposes is not the particular division of the changes among the participants but the observation that the *net* changes in surplus are equal to the areas of triangles (*JHI*, *JEI*). Since both the height and the width of each triangle is proportional to the size of the change introduced by the new consumer, the area is proportional to its square. Comparing Figure 8-2a to Figure 8-2b, you can see that when the change in price is reduced from \$.05 to \$.01, all of the areas involved in the analysis (except for *CJGF*, which is a transfer rather than a net gain or loss) are reduced by a factor of not 5 but 25. The heights go down by a factor of 5 because the price change in Figure 8-2b is one fifth as great as in Figure 8-2a, and the widths because the change in quantity produced by the price change in Figure 8-2b is one fifth as large as the corresponding change in quantity in Figure 8-2a.

It follows from this argument that while it may be important that a change in the price and quantity of one good results in a change of \$1 in the price of another good, it is much less important if the change in one good results in a change of \$.10 in 10 other goods, and still less if it results in a \$.01 change in each of 100 other goods. Since such effects are typically spread over thousands of goods, it is usually legitimate to ignore them. This is the justification for using partial equilibrium analysis. The *reason* for doing so is that, as you have probably realized at this point, general equilibrium analysis is usually much harder.

IS THIS CHAPTER REALLY NECESSARY?

I have spent most of this chapter showing that the way in which we have been doing economics is not quite correct, explaining what the correct way would be, and then explaining why I am going to keep on using the "not quite correct but much easier" approach. It would seem that if I omitted the whole discussion, the book could continue in exactly the same way, saving the reader a chapter of work and a considerable amount of confusion. In that sense, this chapter is unnecessary; there is not a single problem anywhere else in the book which depends on understanding this chapter for its solution—and this chapter has no problems.

The justification for this chapter—and complications elsewhere which may seem equally unnecessary—is my belief that lying to students is bad pedagogy. If I am going to teach you a particular way of doing economic analysis, I ought to point out its problems and inconsistencies—as I have done in this chapter—instead of passing quietly over them in the hope that you will not notice. The argument by which I have tried to justify the way in which I am doing economics is really only a sketch of a much more complicated argument, one which those of you who decide to become economists will probably encounter again in a few years. In the rest of this book, I will limit myself to partial equilibrium theory; the purpose of this chapter was to explain why.

Halftime

WHAT WE HAVE DONE SO FAR

In Section I of this book, I defined economics as that approach to understanding behavior that starts from the assumption that people have objectives and tend to choose the correct ways of achieving them. I went on to add several additional elements—the assumption that objectives were reasonably simple, the definition of value in terms of revealed preference, and the idea that the different things we value are all comparable. In Section II, I used economics to analyze individual behavior in order to show how prices and quantities are determined in a simple economy. The connections between the two sections may not always have been obvious; while Section II applied the ideas discussed in Section I, I usually did not bother interrupting the analysis to point out what assumption or definition was being applied where. Since we are now at a sort of halfway point, finished with the analysis of a simple economy and about to launch ourselves into a sea of complications, this is a convenient place to look back at what we have done and trace out some of the connections.

The central assumption of rationality—the assumption that people tend to choose the correct means to achieve their objectives—has been applied throughout Section II. The approach used over and over again was first to figure out what a rational person would do—how he could best achieve his objectives—and then to conclude that that is what people *will* do.

In the analysis of production, for example, we first figured out which good it was in the individual's interest to produce, then concluded that that was the good he would produce. We went on to figure out how much it was in his rational interest to produce, given his preferences, and again concluded that that was what he would do. Similarly, in the analysis of consumption, the demand curve was equal to the marginal value curve because the individual took the actions that maximized his net benefit. In the analysis of trade, each individual only made those exchanges that benefited him, and two individuals continued to trade as long as any exchanges that benefited both of them remained to be made.

One part of the assumption of rationality discussed in Chapter 1 was that people have reasonably simple objectives. This too has been used, although rarely mentioned, several times in Section II. Consider, for example, the discussion of budget lines and indifference curves in Chapter 3. Throughout that discussion, I assumed that the only reason someone wanted money was for the goods it would buy. Thus, in discussing the location of the optimal bundle, I argued that the individual would spend his entire income—that, after all, is what money is for (the possibility of saving for future consumption did not come up, since we were assuming a static world in which each day was just like the next). But one could imagine an individual who liked the idea of living below his income—forever— and so chose to buy fewer goods than he might, while accumulating an ever-increasing pile of money. That may seem irrational to you, but remember that we have no way of knowing what people *should* want. Economics deals with the consequences of what they *do* want. I ignored the possibility of such behavior not because it was irrational in the normal sense of the word but because it violated the assumption that individual objectives were reasonably simple.

I again assumed that one desired money only for what it could buy, when I discussed income effects and substitution effects; I asserted, as you may remember, that if your income doubled and the prices of everything you consumed also doubled, you would be in the same situation as before. But suppose that at some point in your life, you fell in love with the idea of being a millionaire. What you wanted was not a particular level of consumption but the knowledge that you "had a million dollars." Doubling all incomes and prices would make it considerably easier for you to reach that goal. Here again, I assumed such situations away on the grounds that they would violate my assumption of reasonably simple objectives.

The definition of value in terms of revealed preference was also used in Section II. One could argue that it is revealed preference, not rationality, which implies that demand curves are equal to marginal value curves; your values are revealed by how much you choose to consume at any price—your demand curve. The principle of revealed preference and the assumption of rationality are closely connected; if we did not believe that people tended to choose the actions that best achieved their objectives, we would have a hard time relating their objectives to the actions they chose. To say that you value an additional apple at a dollar means that given the choice between the apple and some amount of money less than a dollar, you will choose the apple; given the choice between an apple and some amount of money larger than a dollar, you will choose the money. From that, it follows that you will keep increasing your consumption of apples until you reach the point where the marginal value of an apple is equal to its price; since you do that at any price, the graph of how much you buy at any price is the same as the graph of your marginal value at any quantity. The demand curve and the marginal value curve are identical.

Revealed preference appeared again in the derivation of consumer surplus. Later in Chapter 4, the combination of consumer surplus and rationality was used to prove that a profit-maximizing theater owner would sell popcorn at cost. The argument depended on the assumption that consumers would correctly allow for the price of popcorn in deciding how much they were willing to pay for a ticket. In classroom discussions of the popcorn problem, I find that students are frequently unwilling to accept that; they believe that consumers (irrationally!) ignore the price of popcorn and simply decide whether or not "the movie is worth the price." Perhaps so. The applicability of economics to any form of behavior is an empirical question. What I demonstrated was that if the assumptions of economics apply to popcorn in movie theaters, then the "obvious" explanation of why it was expensive had to be wrong.

The assumption of rationality was used yet again in the popcorn problem, applied this time to the theater owner rather than to his customers. If the theater owner's rational policy is to sell popcorn at cost, then according to the economic assumptions, that is what he will do. The observation that theater owners apparently sell popcorn for considerably more than it costs them to produce it provides us with a puzzle. One may, of course, conclude that economics is wrong. In Chapter 9, I hope to persuade you that there are more plausible solutions to the puzzle.

One more economic idea was discussed in Section I—comparability, the idea that none of the goods we value is infinitely important in comparison to the others. While comparability was never mentioned in Section II, it was implicit in the way in which we drew up the tables and figures of Chapters 3, 4, and 5. Imagine drawing an indifference diagram for two goods, a "need" A on the horizontal axis and a "want" B on the vertical axis. Since no amount of B could make up for even a tiny reduction in A, the indifference curves would have to be vertical. But vertical indifference curves imply that you are indifferent between a bundle consisting of 5 units of A and 5 of B and a bundle consisting of 5 units of A and 10 of B—which is inconsistent with the assumption that you value B. It is possible to analyze such a situation—but not with indifference curves.

I have now shown you some examples of how the assumptions of Section I were used in the analysis of Section II. The same assumptions will continue to be applied throughout the rest of the book; just as in Section II, I will only occasionally point out which assumptions go into which arguments. One of the things I have learned in writing this book is that economics is considerably more complicated than I thought it was. In such an intricately interrelated system of ideas, pointing out every connection whenever it occurs would make it almost impossible to follow the analysis. Much of the job of tracing out how and where the different strands of the analysis are connected you will have to do for yourself.

That is not entirely a bad thing. It has been my experience that I only really understand something when I have figured it out for myself. Reading a book, or listening to a lecture, can tell you the answer. But until you have fitted the logical pattern together yourself, inside your own head, what you have read or heard is only words.

AND FOR OUR NEXT ACT

This brings us to the end of the first half of the book. The second half will be devoted to expanding and applying the ideas worked out so far. In Section III, I will introduce a series of complications to our simple model. The first, in Chapter

9, is the existence of the firm, an enterprise which serves as an intermediary between the ultimate producers and the ultimate consumers, buying productive services from the individuals who own them and selling consumption goods. Next, in Chapter 10, I drop the assumption that we are dealing with markets in which each individual producer and consumer is too small a part of the whole for his decisions to have a significant effect on market price; this will get us into discussions of monopoly and related complications. In Chapters 11 and 12, I add time and uncertainty to the analysis, thus bringing the world we are analyzing noticeably closer to the one we live in. Finally, having expanded the theory to include most of the essential complications of a real economy, I use it in Chapter 13 to answer one of the questions that economists are frequently asked—how the distribution of income is determined in a market economy.

Section IV begins by making explicit the criteria of "economic welfare," "efficiency," "desirability," and the like, which I have introduced, or at least suggested, in the discussion of consumer and producer surplus. I then go on to show how such criteria can be used to judge alternative economic arrangements. Expanding on that subject, and on the results of dropping our normal assumption that prices are free to reach their supply/demand equilibrium, I will discuss the effects of various interferences in the workings of the market, some touched on already in earlier chapters.

At the end of Chapter 16 ("Market Interference"), you may be left with the impression that the market is a perfect mechanism for satisfying our desires and that there are no possible (legitimate) arguments for interfering with its natural workings. In Chapter 17, I attempt to dispel that impression by discussing "market failures"—ways in which failures of the market to conform to assumptions we have made (often implicitly) may result in its failure to function as we would expect (and wish). This chapter is, in a way, an expansion of a point I made in Chapter 1—that rational behavior by individuals does not necessarily produce rational behavior by groups.

By the end of Section IV, all of the essential ideas of the course will have been covered. Section V consists of a series of chapters applying those ideas. A few of the applications will be conventional ones, such as the analysis of the effects of tariffs in Chapter 18 and the discussion of inflation and unemployment in Chapter 22. More of the applications will be of the sort that I find especially interesting—using economics to analyze the dating/sex/marriage market of which most of us are a part, for example, or to explain why people in Chicago keep their houses warmer than people in Los Angeles, or to analyze the economics of theft.

The book ends with a final chapter in which I discuss how economics is done, what economics is good for—why, aside from passing a course, you should want to learn what I want to teach—and what economists do.

Complications
or
Onward to Reality

Chapter 9

The Firm

So far, we have discussed production in the context of one person converting his time into some service such as lawn mowing. While that is a useful place to start, it ignores two important features of production—the use of more than one input in producing an output and the cooperation of more than one person in production. In this chapter, we will explore production in the more complicated case of the firm—a group of people combining inputs to produce an output.

Why do firms exist? Part of the reason is suggested by Figures 6-5 and 6-6 of Chapter 6—because two people coordinating their production can do better for themselves than if they act independently. In Chapter 6, the coordination occurred through trade. Individuals produced independently but decided how much to produce of what by taking into consideration the possibility of trading it for something else. In a firm, the cooperation is closer. Typically many individuals work together to produce a single item. The obvious reason is that they produce more that way. This is, in large part, a result of the principle of division of labor—if each of us specializes in a particular part of the productive process, he can be much better at it, hence more productive, than if each of us has to do everything. It is difficult to imagine one man, however skillful and well equipped, producing an automobile in a year entirely by himself, yet the average auto worker "produces" several automobiles per year.

In the production of automobiles, some of the division of labor occurs within the firm and some between firms; General Motors does not, for example, produce the steel from which its cars are made. One could imagine a society in which there was a high degree of division of labor, all of which occurred between firms, with each firm participating in only one part of the productive process and perhaps consisting of only one person. That possibility, and the difficulties which it would produce, are discussed in the optional section at the end of this chapter.

In discussing consumption, we reduced the individual to a set of preferences and his environment to a set of prices and a budget constraint. In discussing the

178

firm, we follow a somewhat similar process—how similar will be clearer by the end of the chapter. We start with a production function, which describes the ways in which the firm can convert inputs (labor, raw materials, the use of machinery) into its output (the product it produces); we assume, for simplicity, that each firm produces only one product. The production function, plus the statement that the firm is trying to maximize its profits, "describe" the firm; the prices the firm faces, for both its inputs and its output, describe its environment. The combination of the two tells us what the firm will do—how much it will produce and how.

PART 1 · FROM PRODUCTION FUNCTION TO COST CURVES

We begin with a production function, which tells how a firm can transform its inputs into the goods it produces. You can think of a production function as an explicit function, $Q(x_1, x_2, x_3, \ldots)$, where Q is the amount produced and $x_1, x_2, \ldots$ are the amounts of all the different inputs that can be used to produce it. Alternatively, you can think of a production function as a very large table listing all possible combinations of inputs and, for each combination, the resulting quantity of output. Table 9-1 is part of such a table for a firm manufacturing clay pots; the explicit production function is given at the bottom. Each row of Table 9-1 shows the number of pots that can be produced with a particular collection of inputs—so much labor, so much use of capital, so much clay.

Table 9-1

Input Bundle	Labor (hours) ($10/hr.)	Cost of Labor	Capital ($-years) (.05/yr.)	Cost of Capital	Clay (pounds) ($4/lb.)	Cost of Clay	Total Cost	Output of Pots
A	1.00	$10.00	100	$ 5.00	1.00	$ 4.00	$19.00	1
B	0.25	2.50	400	20.00	4.00	16.00	38.50	1
C	4.00	40.00	25	1.25	0.25	1.00	42.25	1
D	2.00	20.00	200	10.00	2.00	8.00	38.00	2
E	4.00	40.00	100	5.00	1.00	4.00	49.00	2
F	1.00	10.00	100	5.00	16.00	64.00	79.00	2
G	1.00	10.00	1,600	80.00	1.00	4.00	94.00	2
H	3.00	30.00	300	15.00	3.00	12.00	57.00	3
I	9.00	90.00	100	5.00	1.00	4.00	99.00	3
J	4.00	40.00	100	5.00	5.06	20.24	65.24	3
K	4.00	40.00	225	11.25	2.25	9.00	60.25	3
L	1.00	10.00	8,100	405.00	1.00	4.00	419.00	3
M	4.00	40.00	400	20.00	4.00	16.00	76.00	4
N	9.00	90.00	178	8.89	1.78	7.12	106.01	4
O	0.945	9.45	94.5	4.72	1.18	4.72	18.94	1
P	1.89	18.90	189	9.45	2.36	9.44	37.79	2
Q	2.84	28.40	284	14.20	3.55	14.20	56.80	3
R	3.78	37.80	378	18.90	4.73	18.92	75.62	4

$$\text{Output} = \text{Labor}^{1/2} \times (\text{Capital}/100)^{1/4} \times \text{Clay}^{1/4}$$

The table also shows the cost of the inputs. The price of labor is $5/hour, the price of clay is $4/pound, and the price to use capital (strictly speaking, its rental) is .05/year. The meaning of the first two is obvious; the third, the price of capital, is an interest rate. If the interest rate is .05/year (or, more conventionally stated, "5% per annum"), then using $100 worth of capital for a year costs you $5—the interest you would pay if you borrowed the money to buy the $100 worth of machinery which you must use for a year ($100 × 1 year = 100 dollar-years of capital) in order to produce a pot using input bundle A. At the end of the year, you could either resell the machinery and pay back the loan or keep the machinery for another year and use another 100 dollar-years worth of capital to produce another pot—at a cost, for capital, of another five dollars interest on your loan. If you find it odd that your inputs consist of pounds of clay but dollar-years of capital, and that you have used capital as an input even if you give back the machine when you have finished with it, consider that exactly the same thing is true of the third input—labor. Your input is not workers but man-hours, and you return the worker (to himself) when you have finished employing him.

The firm must figure out how much to produce and how to produce it. A sensible first step, on the principle of dividing hard problems into manageable pieces, is to pick a level of output and figure out, given the production function and the prices of inputs, how to produce that quantity at the lowest possible cost. To do so, you start by considering all of the different combinations of inputs that would produce that quantity of output. On Table 9-1, for example, input bundles H, I, J, K, L, and Q can each be used to produce three pots. Next you calculate the cost of each bundle. This is just like calculating the cost of a consumption bundle; you multiply the quantity of each input by its price to find out how much you spend on that input, then add the figures for all the inputs to find the cost of the whole bundle, as shown on the table. Mathematically this gives us

$$C = P_1 x_1 + P_2 x_2 + P_3 x_3 + \ldots$$

C is the cost of that particular bundle. But there are usually many different combinations of inputs that will produce the same output. By using more labor, for example, you can minimize wastage, and so reduce your consumption of raw material; whether that is worth doing depends on how expensive raw material is in comparison to labor. By using machinery (ultimately capital—you will have to wait until Chapter 13 for a clearer explanation of what capital is), you may be able to economize on labor, raw material, or both. There are many kinds of raw material you can use (substituting among plastic, aluminum, and steel, for example, in making an automobile), and each of them comes in many different forms at different prices. Hence figuring "how to produce 73 television sets" is an immensely complicated process which does not have a single answer—there are many ways to do it. Typically, however, there is only one least expensive way, and it is that which the firm is looking for.

Comparing, on Table 9-1, the different bundles that can be used to produce one pot, you find that bundle O does it at the lowest cost; similarly bundle P is the least expensive way of producing 2 pots, Q of producing 3, and R of producing 4. Figure 9-1 shows the total cost curve implied by Table 9-1.

Figure 9-1

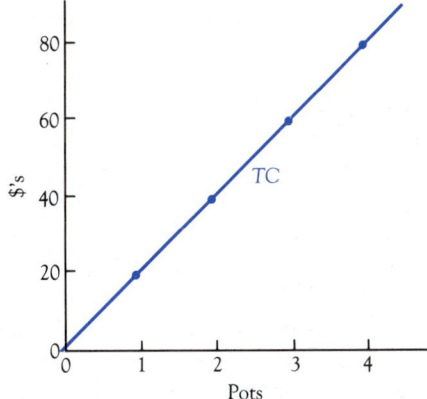

Total cost for producing clay pots.   The figure shows the cost of the least cost bundle of inputs for producing each quantity of pots.

Since the table shows only a few of the possible ways of producing any particular number of pots, you cannot tell from it whether you have found the least costly input bundle or only the least costly of those shown. That is one of the problems with using a finite table to represent an infinite number of alternatives. In the optional section of this chapter, I show how one can use calculus to find the lowest cost bundles of inputs to produce various levels of output. The results of those calculations, for output levels of 1, 2, 3, and 4, are bundles O, P, Q, and R. It is worth noting that they represent only a slight improvement over bundles A, D, H, and M, the lowest cost bundles which I found, without calculus, by simple trial and error. In this case, at least, one can come fairly close to achieving the "perfectly rational" decision by using a fairly simple trial and error method.

It may have occurred to you that the way in which we use Table 9-1 to find the least cost way of producing pots is very similar to the way in which a similar table was used in Chapter 3 to find the most attractive consumption bundle. The logic of the two problems is almost exactly the same. In Chapter 3, we compared all the bundles with the same cost to find out which produces the greatest utility; in this chapter, we compare all the bundles producing the same output to see which has the lowest cost.

In Chapter 3, after recognizing that the table showed only a tiny sample of the possible consumption bundles, we went on to analyze the same problem geometrically, using budget lines and indifference curves. The same approach applied to production is shown on Figure 9-2; just as in the case of consumption, the fact that we are drawing our curves on two-dimensional paper means that we can only show two variables at a time. In Chapter 3, the two variables were consumption goods—apples and oranges. Here they are inputs. Here, as there, we may imagine either that there *are* only two variables—that only two inputs are used to produce the output—or that we have already decided on the amount of the other inputs to be used.

In Chapter 3, the individual maximizes his utility subject to a budget constraint; here the firm minimizes its "budget"—its total expenditure—subject to a fixed level of production. These represent essentially the same process. The individual consumer tries to get as much of something (utility, happiness, "his objectives") as possible while spending a given amount of money; the firm tries to spend as little money as possible while getting a given amount of something (output). Figure 9-2 is the equivalent, for a firm, of the indifference curve diagrams of Chapter 3.

The contour I_1 is called an *isoquant*. It shows the different combinations of the two inputs, X_1 and X_2, which can produce a given quantity of output (73 television sets). In Chapter 3, we had a given budget line and were looking for the highest indifference curve that touched it; here we have a given isoquant and are looking for the *lowest* budget line that touches it (implying the lowest possible cost for the input bundle). That is why the figures in Chapter 3 showed one budget line and several indifference curves, while here Figure 9-2 shows one isoquant and several possible budget lines. In Chapter 3, the solution was to find the (indifference) curve that was tangent to the (budget) line; the optimal consumption bundle was at the point of tangency. Here the solution is to find the (iso-expenditure) line that is tangent to the (isoquant) curve; the optimal input bundle is at the point of tangency.

Figure 9-2

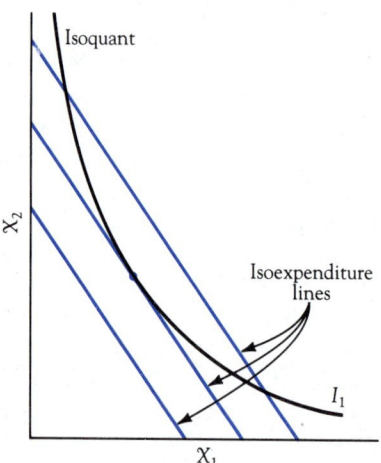

Isoquant/isoexpenditure diagram for two inputs.   Each isoexpenditure line shows the different bundles of inputs that have the same cost. The isoquant, I_1, shows the different bundles of inputs needed to produce a given quantity of output. The point of tangency is the optimal (i.e., lowest cost) input bundle for producing that quantity of output.

Suppose the firm has figured out the lowest cost way of producing a particular output—73 television sets, a million cars per year, 3 pots, or whatever. It repeats the calculation for every other level of output it might consider producing—74 television sets, 50 television sets, 900 television sets, and so forth. At the end of the process, it has converted its production function into a *total cost function*—a function that tells it how much it will cost to produce any level of output. Figure 9-1 shows the total cost function for the pottery of Table 9-1. A total cost function is enormously simpler than a production function, since it has only one variable; you may, if you wish, think of it as the "production function" for producing automobiles (or anything else), using only one input—money. The single input is used to hire labor and machinery and to buy steel, glass, and other inputs which are then used to produce automobiles. For most of the rest of this chapter, it is only the cost function and not the full production function that we will need in order to understand the firm's behavior.

Before going on, I should first clarify what I have so far done in order to prevent a possible misunderstanding. You should not interpret this section as implying that an actual firm, say General Motors, has a list somewhere describing every possible way of producing every conceivable quantity of output and a room full of computers busy twenty-four hours a day figuring the least cost way of doing so. GM is profoundly uninterested in the cost of producing 7 automobiles per year or 7 billion, and equally uninterested in the possibility of making them out of such bizarre inputs as bubble gum, lettuce, or the labor services of phrenologists.

Just as in the case of consumer behavior, our assumption is that people (and firms) tend to end up making the right decision, which in this case means producing goods at the lowest possible cost so as to maximize their profit. To figure out what that decision is, we imagine how it would be made by a firm with complete information and unlimited ability to process it. In practice, the decision is made by a much more limited process involving a large element of trial and error—but we expect that it will tend to produce the same result. If it does not, and some other practical method does, then some other firm will produce cars at lower cost than GM. Eventually GM will either imitate its competitor's method or go out of business.

I Knew I Had an Equimarginal Principle Lying Around Here Somewhere

The same argument that led us to the equimarginal principle in consumption applies in production as well, if we replace *marginal value* with *marginal product*—after first defining the latter. The marginal product of an input is the rate at which output increases as the quantity of that input increases; you may think of it as the increase in output as a result of one additional unit of that input. If adding one man to a factory employing 1,000, while keeping all other inputs fixed, results in an additional 2 cars per year, then the marginal product of labor is 2 cars per man-year.

How can you produce two more cars with no more steel? The answer is that for small variations in inputs, one factor can substitute for another—in this case, labor for raw materials. One of the things the additional labor may do is improve quality control, so that fewer cars have to be scrapped; another is to make possible a more labor-intensive production process which produces cars with slightly less steel in them. Table 9-1 shows the same thing happening with the manufacture of pots. As you go from bundle A to bundle E, for example, the amount of clay and of capital used stay the same; the amount of labor quadruples, and the output rises from 1 pot to 2. Perhaps what is happening is that in A, many of the pots crack when they are fired; in E, the workers are spending four times as much time on each pot, and as a result they have doubled the percentage that survive firing. Going from A to E, labor input increases by 3 man-hours and output by 1 pot, so the marginal product of labor is $\frac{1}{3}$ pot/man-hour.

If we consider large changes in inputs, this becomes less plausible—it is hard to see how one could produce either pots or cars with no raw materials at all, however much labor one used. This is an example of the *law of diminishing returns*, which plays the same role in production as does the law of declining marginal utility in consumption. If you hold all factors but one constant and increase that one, eventually its marginal product begins to decline. Each additional man-year of labor increases the number of cars produced by less and less. However much fertilizer you use, you cannot grow the world's supply of wheat in a flowerpot. In just the same way, as you hold all other consumption goods fixed and increase one, eventually the additional utility from each additional unit becomes less and less. I will not trade my life for any number of ice cream cones.

The equimarginal principle in consumption tells us that if you have chosen the optimal consumption bundle, the value to you of an additional dollar's worth of any good in the bundle—anything you consume—is the same. The equimarginal principle in production tells us that if the firm is minimizing its costs for a given quantity of output, the additional output produced by a dollar's worth of *any* input it uses is the same.

The argument, which should seem familiar, goes as follows: If the firm is already producing its output at the lowest possible cost, there can be no way of reducing its cost any further while producing the same quantity of output. Suppose there are two inputs whose marginal product per dollar's worth is different—an additional dollar's worth of input A increases output by 3 units; an additional dollar's worth of input B increases output by 4 units. To reduce cost while producing the same amount of output, use \$.75 more of input B and \$1 less of input A. Output goes up by (4 units/\$'s worth) $\times$ ($\frac{3}{4}$ \$'s worth) = 3 units, because of the increased input of A. It goes down by 3 units because of the decreased input of B. So the net effect is to produce the same output with \$.25 less of expenditure—which is impossible if the firm is already producing at minimum cost.

If you find it confusing to use a "dollar's worth" as a unit to measure the quantity of input, we can use physical units instead. Good A costs \$1/pound and its marginal product is 4 units per pound; good B costs \$2/pound and its marginal product is 6 units per pound. Use $\frac{3}{4}$ of a pound more of A, $\frac{1}{2}$ pound less of B; output remains unchanged and expenditure has fallen by \$.25.

In this case, just as in the similar proof in Chapter 4, the argument only works precisely if the amount of the change is infinitely small, so that the marginal product of an input is the same whether we consider an increase or a decrease. The larger the size of the changes in inputs we consider, the less precise the argument becomes. But in order to prove that the firm is not producing at minimum cost, all we need show is that there is some change which lowers cost while maintaining output—even a very small change will do.

What we have shown is that if the marginal product of a dollar's worth of input is not the same for all inputs, or in other words if the marginal products of inputs are not proportional to their prices, it is possible to alter the bundle of inputs in such a way as to reduce cost while maintaining the same output. It follows that for the *least cost bundle*—the bundle which a profit-maximizing firm will choose—the marginal products of inputs are proportional to their prices. That is the equimarginal principle in production.

Income ultimately comes from owning factors of production, such as your own labor, your savings, land, or the like. The amount of income you get from the factors you own depends on how much you can sell or rent them for. The equimarginal principle in production, which tells us the relation between the prices of factors and their marginal product, will turn out to be of considerable interest when we discuss the distribution of income in Chapter 13.

Cost Curves

Figure 9-3 shows total cost as a function of output for a hypothetical firm producing widgets. Fixed cost (FC) is the height of the total cost curve where it runs into the vertical axis—total cost as we approach zero output from the right. For the firm shown by TC_2, total cost goes to zero as output goes to zero. For the firm whose total cost curve is TC_1, the ability to produce anything at all involves a substantial cost (FC_1), perhaps because there is a minimum size of factory in which it is practical to produce the product.

One of the things not shown on the figure is the influence of time on costs. Cost of production really depends on *rate of production* (automobiles per year) as well as on *amount of production* (automobiles); the cost of producing 1,000,000 automobiles in 10 years is very different from the cost of producing them in one year. The cost of producing different levels of output also depends on how much time the firm is given to adjust to changes. If General Motors has been producing 5,000,000 cars per year and suddenly decides to reduce output to 2,000,000, there will be many costs it cannot get out of—expensive factories standing empty, executives with long-term contracts who must be paid whether or not there is any work for them, and so on. If General Motors decides that over the next ten years its output will gradually fall to 2,000,000/year, it can gradually reduce its scale of operations to something more appropriate to the new rate of production.

Going in the other direction, if GM finds that it wishes to double its rate of output over a period of a few months, it will find it difficult and expensive; factories will be running all night, workers will have to be paid for overtime, and suppliers will have to be paid premium prices to get them to provide large quantities at short notice. If the same increase occurs gradually over a period of years, the cost is much less. In general, we would expect the total cost curve to rise

Figure 9-3

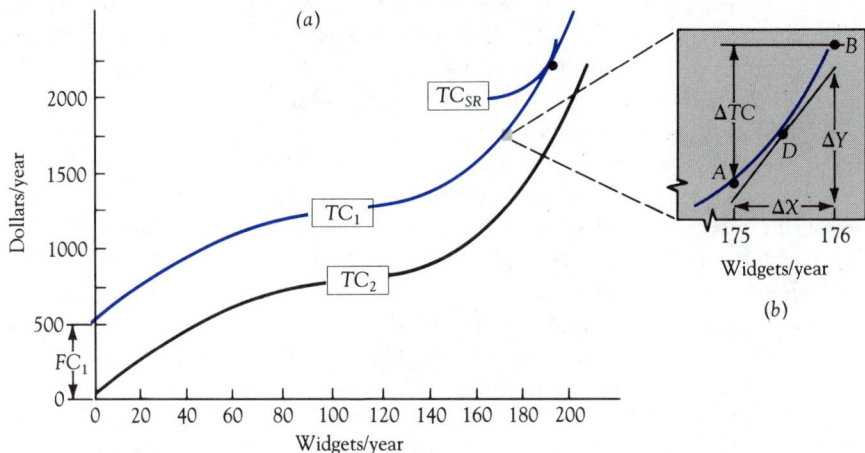

Total cost curves with (TC_1) and without (TC_2) fixed cost. *3b* is an expanded view of the section of *3a* inside the square, showing the relation between the precise definition of marginal cost (slope of total cost) and the approximate definition (increase in total cost with a one-unit increase in quantity).

more steeply with increasing quantity, and fall more gently with decreasing quantity, for short-term changes than for long-term changes. Curve TC_{SR} on Figure 9-3a shows such a pattern, with A the point at which the firm is presently producing.

While the distinction between long-run and short-run cost curves is worth noting at this point, it need not be dealt with here. At this point, we are still considering a perfectly static and predictable world in which tomorrow is always just like today. In such a world, production decisions are made once and for all and never changed. The cost curves in this chapter describe costs for a firm that expects to produce the same quantity of output in the same way forever. In Chapter 12, we will finally drop that assumption. At that point, it will be necessary to return to the distinction between long-run and short-run cost curves; until then, we can ignore it.

Figure 9-4 shows the marginal cost curve corresponding to TC_1 on Figure 9-3a. The relation between total cost and marginal cost is the same as the relation between total utility and marginal utility, total value and marginal value, or total product (quantity of output) and marginal product. Marginal cost is the rate at which total cost changes with output; it may be thought of, somewhat imprecisely, as the increase in total cost when output is increased by one unit. Just as marginal value is the slope of the total value curve, so marginal cost is the slope of the total cost curve.

Expressed in numbers, marginal cost at an output rate of 1,000 is the difference between the cost of producing 1,001 units and the cost of producing 1,000.

Figure 9-4

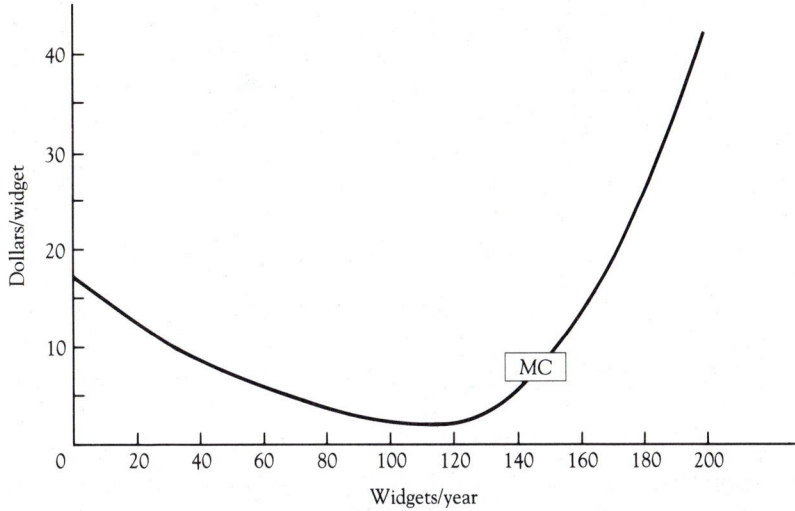

A marginal cost curve.   MC is the marginal cost curve corresponding to TC_1 in Figure 9-3.

Just as with marginal value, you should not try to associate marginal cost with a particular identifiable unit—a particular car, say. All the cars rolling off the assembly line are identical; the marginal cost of another car is the cost of making the total number of cars coming off that line larger by one.

Figure 9-3b is an expanded view of the part of Figure 9-3a inside the square; it shows the relation between the precise definition of MC (the slope of TC) and the approximate definition (increase of cost with a one-unit increase in quantity). The slope of TC at the point D is $\Delta y/\Delta x$; the increase in cost per unit increase in quantity, the slope of the dashed line AB, is $\Delta TC/\Delta x$. Δx is one unit. The solid and the dashed line are almost exactly parallel, so their slopes are almost exactly equal.

So far, I have defined total cost (TC) and marginal cost (MC). There is a third kind of cost curve which we will find useful—average cost (AC). The average cost to produce any quantity of output is simply the total cost divided by the quantity; if it costs $10,000 to produce 500 widgets, then the average cost is $20/widget. Figure 9-5 combines Figures 9-3a and 9-4, putting TC, MC, and AC on one graph so as to make it easier to see the relations among them.

One thing you may notice about AC on Figure 9-5 is that it goes to infinity as quantity goes to zero. Why? As quantity goes to zero, TC does not; the firm whose cost curves we are looking at has some fixed costs. Average cost is total cost divided by quantity; as quantity goes to zero and total cost does not, the ratio goes to infinity. Figure 9-6 shows TC, MC, and AC for the firm represented by TC_2 on Figure 9-3; there are no fixed costs, and AC does not go to infinity as quantity goes to zero.

Figure 9-5

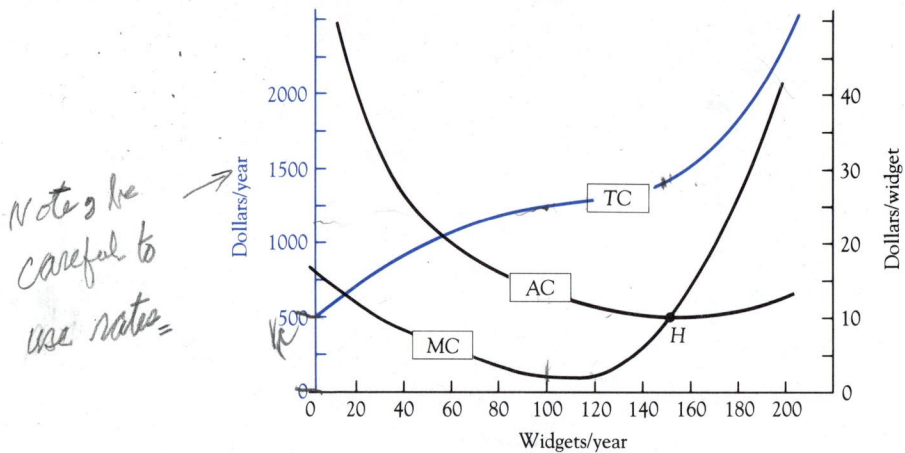

Note, be careful to use rates.

Total cost, marginal cost, and average cost for a firm. Because the firm has positive fixed cost, average cost goes to infinity as quantity goes to zero. Average and marginal cost intersect at point H, which is the minimum of average cost.

Figure 9-6

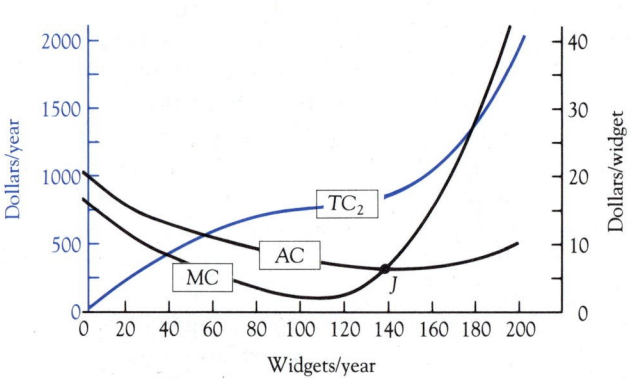

Total cost, marginal cost, and average cost for a firm with no fixed cost.

There is also a useful relation between AC and MC which you may have noticed on Figures 9-5 and 9-6. Where marginal cost is above average cost, average cost is rising; where marginal cost is below average cost, average cost is falling. Where marginal cost is equal to average cost, at point H on Figure 9-5 and J on Figure 9-6, average cost is neither rising nor falling; it is horizontal.

Why? Suppose that at an output of 150 widgets, total cost is $1,500 and marginal cost is $10/widget. Average cost is $1,500/150 widgets = $10/widget. If you increase output to 151, total cost increases by $10—that is what MC = $10 means. But if the present average is $10 and you increase quantity by 1 and cost by $10, the average stays the same; you are averaging in one more unit whose cost is exactly the average of the previous units. If average cost does not change when you add another unit, then at that point, average cost is independent of quantity—the line is horizontal, as at points H and J.

Consider a different point on the graph, one at which output is 100 widgets, total cost is $1,100, and marginal cost is $9/widget. Average cost is $1,100/100 widgets = $11/widget. If you increase output to 101, total cost increases by $9— that is what MC = $9 means. But if the present average is $11 and you increase quantity by 1 and cost by $9, the average must go down; you are averaging in one more unit whose cost is less than the average of the previous units—hence you are pulling the average down. The same thing would happen if you calculated the average height of a basketball team and then decided to average in the coach as well.

If MC is below AC, each additional unit of output pulls down the average. If an increase in quantity lowers average cost, then the AC curve must be falling. So when marginal cost is below average cost, average cost is going down. Similarly, if marginal cost is higher than average cost, then increasing quantity means adding more expensive units to the average, which pulls the average up. So if marginal cost is above average cost, average cost is rising (getting higher as output gets higher).

Average cost is rising when it is below marginal cost, falling when it is above marginal cost, and level when it is equal to marginal cost. Now that you know the pattern, you should be able to see it easily enough on Figures 9-5 and 9-6. You should also be able to see that when average cost is at its minimum, it intersects marginal cost.

Why? Just before it reaches its minimum, average cost is falling; just after, it is rising. When it is falling, marginal cost must be below it; when it is rising, marginal cost must be above it, so marginal cost must cross average cost from below just at the minimum of average cost. A similar argument demonstrates that at a *maximum* of average cost, marginal cost crosses it from above. Running the same argument in the opposite direction, it is easy enough to show that these are the only two situations in which marginal cost can cross average cost; if the two curves cross, it *must* be at a minimum or maximum of average cost.

Students who try to memorize these relations frequently find them confusing; there are, after all, three different curves involved (TC, MC, AC) and two different kinds of characteristics (above/below, rising/falling). A better policy is to go over the argument until you can reproduce it for yourself, then do so when necessary. There are lots of relations that *could* exist among the curves, but only a few rather simple ones that *do*. While at this point, they may seem to be the sort of thing that only a professor or textbook author could find of interest, they turn out to be surprisingly useful. In Chapter 15, the fact that marginal cost intersects average cost at the latter's minimum turns out to be a key element in the proof of what may be the most surprising, and important, result in all of economics. Stay tuned.

PART 2 · FROM COST CURVES
TO SUPPLY CURVES

We have now derived the cost curves of the firm from its production function and the costs of inputs. The next stage is to use the cost curves to derive the firm's *supply curve*—the relation between the price it can sell its output for and the amount it chooses to produce. The final step in the analysis is to combine the supply curves of many firms into a supply curve for the entire industry; doing this will turn out to involve some additional complications.

The Firm's Supply Curve

In Chapter 4, we derived the demand curve of the consumer from his marginal value curve; now we will use almost exactly the same argument to derive the supply curve of the firm from its marginal cost curve. Figure 9-7a shows the same curves as Figure 9-5; the only addition is the price P at which the firm can sell its output. We will assume that the firm is producing only a small fraction of the industry's total output, so that its decision of how much to produce has a negligible effect on P; from the firm's point of view, it can sell as much as it wishes at P and nothing at any higher price. For the same reason, we will assume that the quantity of inputs the firm buys has no significant effect on the price it must pay for them. Each input has a market price; the firm can buy as much as it likes at that price and none at any lower price. These two assumptions—that the firm cannot affect the price it can get for its output or the price it must pay for its input—are the central features of what economists call "perfect competition."

The firm considers producing a quantity, q_1, at which MC is lower than price. If it increased its output from q_1 to $q_1 + 1$, it would sell one more unit, increasing its revenue by P and its cost by MC. Since P is larger than MC, revenue would go up by more than cost; hence *profit*, which is revenue minus cost, would increase. Obviously q_1 is the wrong amount to produce. The same argument applies at q_2. It continues to apply as long as marginal cost is less than price—MC $< P$. So the firm should expand its output up to the point at which MC $= P$. That is q_3 on Figure 9-7a.

If a firm always produces that quantity at which MC $= P$, then its supply curve—the amount it produces as a function of price—is equal to its MC curve, just as a demand curve is equal to an MV curve for a consumer. This is almost correct, but not quite. Typically, MC first falls (as the increasing size of the firm produces advantages—more efficient production on a larger scale), then rises (the firm has taken full advantage of large-scale production; further increases in size mean more and more levels of administration between the president and the factory floor, leading to less efficient production). There may be prices at which, rather than producing a quantity for which MC $= P$, the firm prefers not to produce at all, thus saving the expense of producing units for which MC is higher than P. This occurs when, at the "optimal" quantity of output (MC $= P$), profit is still negative.

The firm's profit is the difference between what it takes in (total revenue—the quantity produced times the price for which it is sold) and what it spends (total cost). If there were no fixed cost, then total profit from producing quantity q_3 on Figure 9-7a would be the shaded area F minus the shaded area G. The reason is the same as in the derivation of consumer surplus in Chapter 4. Starting at an output level of 0 and expanding output up to q_0, each additional unit costs more to produce than the price it sells for, contributing a (negative) profit of $P - MC$; adding all those little rectangles together gives us the area G. If the firm chose to produce a quantity q_0, its profit would be minus G. As it continues expanding output beyond q_0, the additional units sell for more than they cost to produce; again each unit increases profit by $P - MC$—but this time it is positive, since between q_0 and q_3 marginal cost is less than P. The profit from expanding output from q_0 to q_3 is the sum of all *those* little rectangles—the area F. So the total profit from producing a quantity q_3 is $F - G$.

Seen this way, it becomes obvious why producing the quantity for which $P = MC$ results in the maximum profit. If you produce less, you are giving up the opportunity to produce units that will sell for more than they cost to produce; if you produce more, expanding output to q_4, the additional units cost more than they sell for, lowering profit by the area H.

So far, we have calculated what profit would be if there were no fixed cost. Fixed cost is the amount you have to pay in order to produce anything at all; it does not depend on how much you produce. Total cost is fixed cost plus variable cost; $TC = FC + VC$. Since fixed cost does not depend on how much you produce, it has no effect on the marginal cost curve, which shows the additional cost of producing one more unit. It does affect the average cost curve, since

Figure 9-7

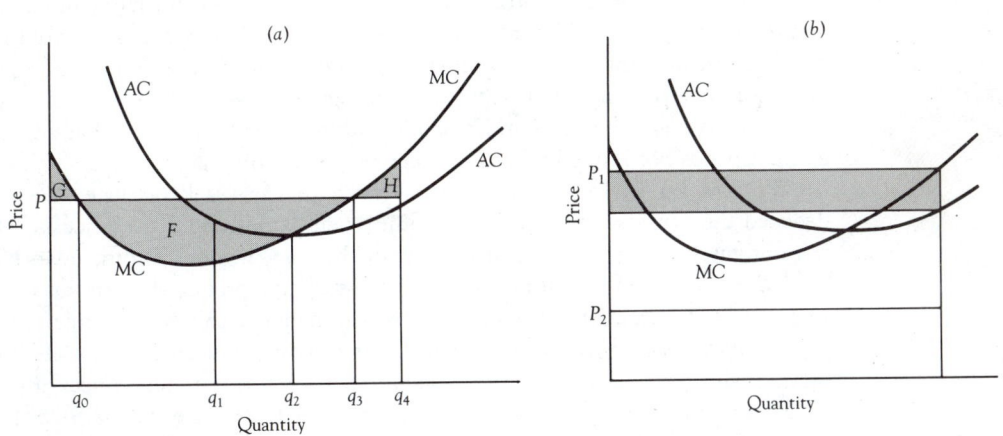

The effect of quantity on profit. If the firm produces q_3, where $MC = P$, profit is maximized. Expanding output to q_4 decreases profit by H; contracting output to q_0 decreases profit by F. Figure 9-7b shows another way of calculating profit—as quantity x (price − average cost).

average cost is total (including fixed) cost divided by quantity. And since profit is total revenue minus total cost, fixed cost also comes out of profit. So if we include the effect of fixed cost, profit on Figure 9-7a is $F - G - FC$.

Earlier I showed that the firm, if it produces at all, maximizes its profit by producing that quantity for which $MC = P$. It may have occurred to you, looking at Figure 9-7a, that there are *two* quantities (q_0 and q_3) for which $MC = P$. How does the firm decide which it should produce? The answer should be clear from the previous few paragraphs. If, in the region between the two points, the marginal cost curve is *below* the price line, then producing those units will increase profit—by area F on Figure 9-7a. So the firm is better off producing q_3 instead of q_0. If, in the region between the two points where marginal cost equals price, the marginal cost curve is *above* the price line, then the firm is losing money on those units and would be better off producing the lower quantity. As you should be able to see for yourself, this implies that the firm should produce a quantity at which the marginal cost curve crosses the price line *from below*—as it does at q_3 on Figure 9-7a.

Figure 9-7b shows another way of calculating profit—one which can be done from the figure without knowing the size of fixed cost. Average cost is, by definition, total cost divided by quantity. So total cost is average cost times quantity. Total revenue is price times quantity. So profit—total revenue minus total cost— is simply quantity times the difference between price (P_1) and average cost; it is shown as the shaded area on Figure 9-7b. That makes sense—price is what you get for each unit produced, and average cost is what it costs you to produce it— so price minus average cost is your per-unit profit. Multiply that by quantity, and you have total profit.

So profit is *negative* when price is below average cost; in that situation, the firm would do better by shutting down entirely, selling off all its facilities, and going out of business. If profit is negative for all quantities the firm could produce—if, in other words, the average cost curve is everywhere above the price line, as it would be if the price were P_2 on Figure 9-7b—the firm's optimal decision is to go out of business and produce nothing. Whether or not that situation exists depends both on the firm's cost curves and on the market price.

We now know, for any price, how much the firm will produce. We have deduced the firm's supply curve. The firm produces nothing if the price is below the minimum of average cost. If that is not the case, if there is some quantity of production for which the firm can make non-negative profits, the firm maximizes its profit by producing that quantity for which marginal cost equals price. So the firm's supply curve is the rising portion of its marginal cost curve above its intersection with average cost. Figure 9-8a shows a series of different prices, P_1, P_2, P_3, P_4, and for each, the quantity the firm chooses to produce. Figure 9-8b shows the resulting supply curve.

On Figure 9-8b, and on similar figures in Chapter 5 and later in this chapter, the horizontal section of the firm's supply curve is shown as a dashed line. This is to indicate that the supply curve does not really exist in that region; if price equals minimum average cost, the firm will produce either nothing at all or the quantity for which average cost is minimum—making a profit of zero in either case. It will not produce any intermediate quantity, since that would result in negative profit.

The analysis that we have just used to demonstrate the relation between the firm's marginal cost curve and its supply curve is the same that we used earlier to show that the individual's demand curve was equal to his marginal value curve. The only important difference is that we assumed marginal value always fell with quantity, while we expect marginal cost to first fall, then rise; the result is that the firm may have to produce over a range of output at which it is losing money on each additional unit (between zero and q_0 on Figure 9-7a, where marginal cost is greater than P) in order to reach a level of output where it is making money on additional units.

In this section, I have derived an important relationship linking the cost curves of the firm to its supply curve and to the amount of profit it makes. We will use these results repeatedly in this chapter and later in the book; you may want to go over the analysis again to be sure you understand it before continuing.

You may also find it useful to see how the analysis of the individual producer in Chapter 5 fits into this chapter as a special case—a one-person firm using a single input. The individual producer of Chapter 5 also had a supply curve that was equal to a marginal cost curve—the marginal cost to him of his own time. I explained the horizontal segment of a firm's supply curve by saying that below some price, the profit from producing is negative, so it is better not to produce. I explained the horizontal segment of the individual supply curve by the existence of a price for one good below which the producer is better off producing something else.

Figure 9-8

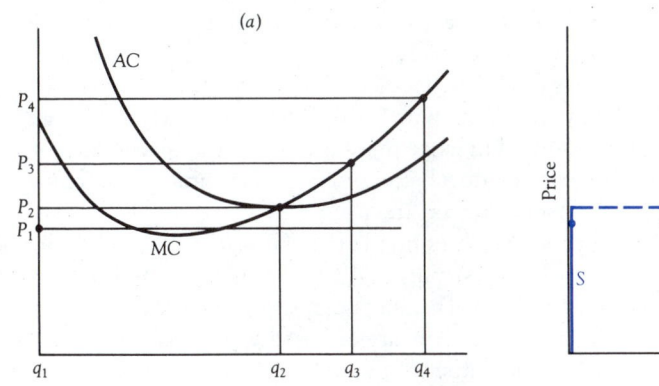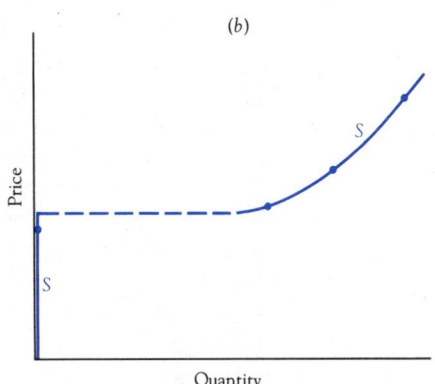

Deducing a supply curve from a marginal cost curve. Figure 9-8a shows, for each price, the profit-maximizing quantity. Figure 9-8b shows the resulting supply curve, S.

The two explanations seem different, but they are not. One cost of using your time to dig ditches is that you are not cooking meals at the same time. How great is that cost? It is equal to what you could make by cooking meals. If the hourly return from digging is less than the hourly return from cooking, then digging produces a negative profit—when the opportunity cost of not cooking is taken into account. In Chapter 5, it was convenient to think of the "cost of working" as the "disvalue of labor"—sore muscles, boredom, and the like. But that is only one example of a more general sort of cost. The cost of mowing lawns is whatever you give up in order to do so, whether that is the pleasure of lying in bed reading science fiction books or the income from washing dishes.

Industry Supply Curve: Closed Entry

We now know how to derive the supply curve of a single firm from its cost curves. The next step is to go from the supply curve of a firm to the supply curve of an industry made up of many firms. In doing so, we will encounter a number of complications. I will start with the simplest case and build up from there.

We begin with an industry made up of 10 identical firms. We assume that the number of firms is fixed by law; it is illegal for anyone to start a new one. Figure 9-9 shows the supply curve for a single firm, S_f, the supply curve for the industry, S_i, and the demand curve. S_i is simply S_f multiplied horizontally by 10—the number of firms. If, at a price P, a single firm produces a quantity q_f, then 10 firms will produce $10 \times q_f$. We are adding together, horizontally, 10 identical supply curves, just as we added demand curves in an earlier chapter. To find the market price, we simply look for the intersection of the supply curve and the demand curve, as in Chapter 7. It occurs at point E on Figure 9-9.

Figure 9-9 shows, in addition to the supply curves and demand curves, the average cost curves for the firm and the industry. The industry average cost curve is calculated in the same way as the industry supply curve; it is the horizontal sum of 10 of the corresponding firm curves. The average cost for each firm when the firm produces 100 units per year is $10. If each firm produces 100 units per year, then the output of 10 firms is 1,000 units per year, so $10 is the average cost when the industry is producing 1,000 units per year—as shown on the figure.

As we already know, profit per unit is the difference between price and average cost; hence profit is that difference times quantity—the shaded area on Figure 9-9. Since all 10 firms are identical, the profit of each firm is one tenth of the total profit—the dark shaded area on the figure.

A number of points are worth noting here. The first is that although price is independent of output from the standpoint of the firm, the same is not true from the standpoint of the industry. The output of any single firm is too small to significantly affect the price, so each firm takes the price as given and adjusts quantity accordingly. But the output of the industry as a whole does affect price. If all the firms increase output, price falls; if all the firms decrease output, price rises. In Chapter 10, we will see what happens if the firms act together to restrict output and drive up price. In this chapter, we assume that the number of firms is sufficiently large so that each individual firm merely concerns itself with its own

Figure 9-9

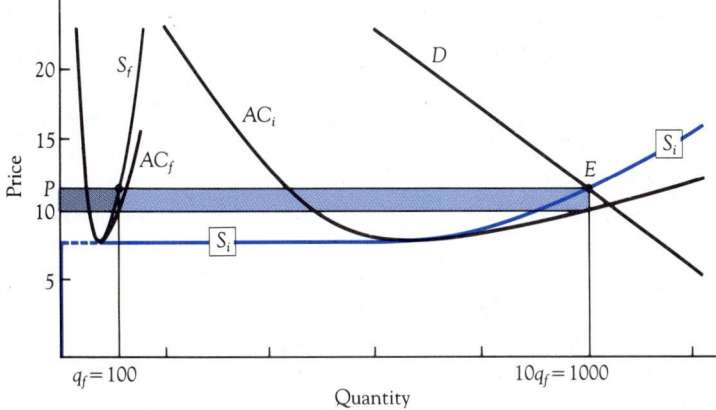

Deducing an industry supply curve from a firm supply curve in an industry with closed entry.   The industry has 10 identical firms. Its supply curve, S_i, is the horizontal sum of ten firms' supply curves, S_f. The figure assumes that the quantity of its inputs used by the industry has no effect on their price.

output and takes the behavior of the other firms as given. If there are only 10 firms, that assumption is a somewhat dubious one. I used 10 firms in my example because for much larger numbers, it becomes difficult to plot the firm supply curve and the industry supply curve on the same graph, as I did for Figure 9-9. You should really think of the analysis as applying to an industry with many more firms—hundreds or thousands of them. That is why, in drawing industry supply curves, I ignore the complications associated with small quantities of output— where there can be one firm producing, or two, but not one and a half.

    In deriving the firm's supply curve, we assumed that both the price at which it sold its output and the prices at which it bought its inputs were unaffected by the firm's decisions. While this is a reasonable assumption from the standpoint of one firm in the industry, it is less reasonable for an entire industry. If one farmer decides to double the amount of wheat he plants, he need not worry about the effect of that decision on the price of fertilizer or the wages of farm laborers; but if every farmer decides to double his planting of wheat, both fertilizer prices and farm wages are likely to rise.

    It may seem inconsistent to say that no firm affects the price of its inputs but that the industry, which is made up of all the firms, does. It is not. From the standpoint of a single firm in an industry containing many firms, the effect of its demand on the price of inputs may well be negligible; hence it can ignore that effect in calculating its supply curve. The same is not true for the industry as a whole. Each increase in the purchases of one firm causes a small increase in prices, which must be paid by all the other firms as well; this is what is called a *pecuniary externality* (an *externality* is a cost imposed by one firm or individual on another) and will be discussed in Chapter 17. The effect on one firm of the increased price of inputs due to the increase in that firm's consumption may be negligible, while the effect on all of the firms of the increased price of inputs due to the increased consumption of all of the firms is not.

Figure 9-9 takes no account of any such effect. It was drawn on the (unstated) assumption that the cost of the industry's inputs was unaffected by the amount of them that the industry bought—or, in other words, that the supply curve for the inputs is horizontal. This assumption is reasonable for some inputs to some industries—increased production of watches is not likely to have much effect on the price of steel, although steel is used in making watches—but not for all.

Figures 9-10a and 9-10b show how we can, if necessary, deal with this complication. Figure 9-10a shows supply curves for a firm, one of whose inputs (iron) becomes more expensive as the industry uses more of it. S_1, S_2, and S_3 are three different supply curves for the same firm, corresponding to three different prices of iron—$1/pound, $2/pound, and $3/pound. Figure 9-10b shows the supply curve for iron. QI_1 on Figure 9-10b is the quantity of iron produced if the price of iron is $1/pound, and similarly for QI_2 ($2/pound) and QI_3 ($3/pound). Q_1 on Figure 9-10a is the quantity of output which results in the industry buying QI_1 of input; Q_2 and Q_3 are related to QI_2 and QI_3 similarly.

S, the supply curve of the industry on Figure 9-10a, goes through three points marked A_1, A_2, and A_3. A_1 shows the price (P_1) at which the industry will supply quantity Q_1. It is the price which corresponds to quantity $Q_1/10$ on firm supply curve S_1. Similarly, A_2 is at quantity Q_2 and price P_2, where P_2 is the price at which a firm with supply curve S_2 produces quantity $Q_2/10$; A_3 has the same relation to Q_3, P_3, and S_3.

Each of the points A_1, A_2, and A_3 represents a possible price/quantity combination for the industry. In each case, at that quantity of output, the industry

Figure 9-10

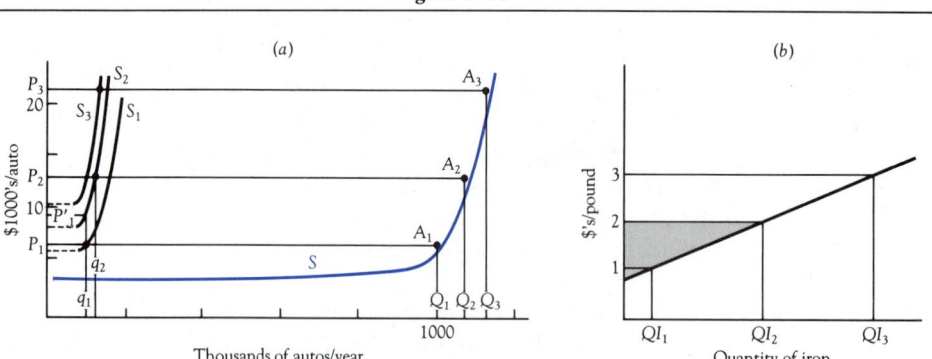

From the firm's supply curve to the industry's supply curve, taking account of effects on input prices. As in Figure 9-9, there are 10 identical firms, and no new firms can enter. S_1, S_2, and S_3 are the firms' supply curves corresponding to prices of $1, $2, and $3/pound for steel. As total industry output expands from Q_1 to Q_2 to Q_3, the price of steel rises, as shown on Figure 9-10b, moving the firms from S_1 to S_2 to S_3.

uses an amount of the input (QI_1, QI_2, QI_3) resulting in a price for the input ($1/pound, $2/pound, $3/pound) which results in a supply curve (S_1, S_2, S_3); the quantity produced by the industry (10 firms) is simply 10 times the quantity that a firm with that supply curve would produce at that price.

In comparing Figures 9-9 and 9-10a, there are two things you should notice. The first is that S_2 on Figure 9-10a, the supply curve for the firm when iron is at $2/pound, is the same as S_f on Figure 9-9. The second is that S in Figure 9-10a rises more steeply than S_i in Figure 9-9. To make this clear, I have shown both S and S_i together on Figure 9-11.

To see why S rises more steeply than S_i on Figure 9-11, we must go back to Figure 9-10a. When quantity falls from $q_2 = Q_2/10$ to $q_1 = Q_1/10$, price must fall first to P'_1, the price on S_2 corresponding to a quantity of q_1, then by an additional amount $P'_1 - P_1$ to get from S_2 to S_1. At the lower quantity (q_1), the industry uses less iron, the price of iron is therefore only $1/pound, and the firm's supply curve is lower—S_1 instead of S_2. Similarly, when quantity rises from q_2 to q_3, price must go up by enough to not only increase quantity on S_2 but also rise from S_2 to S_3. So price rises more rapidly as quantity is increased above Q_2 on S than it does on S_i, and it falls more steeply as quantity is decreased below Q_2. So S is steeper than S_i.

Why are S_1, S_2, and S_3 arranged in the way shown on Figure 9-10a? Because S_3 corresponds to a higher cost for the input than S_2. Similarly, S_2 is higher than S_1. The higher the cost of the input, the higher the marginal cost of producing the output, hence the higher the supply curve.

Figure 9-11

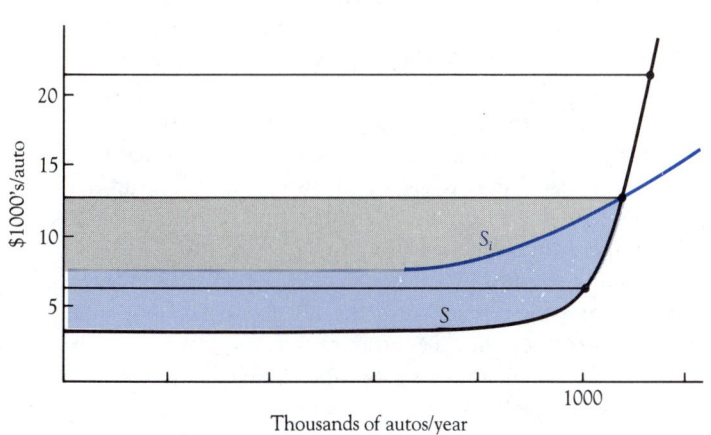

Industry supply curves with (S) and without (S_i) effects on input prices. The producer surplus calculated from S_i is equal to the summed producer surpluses of the 10 firms of Figure 9-10a. It is less than the producer surplus calculated from S; the difference represents producer surplus going to the steel industry of Figure 9-10b.

By introducing the possibility that the industry may have to pay a higher price for its inputs if it consumes more of them, I have considerably complicated the problem; I could have saved both myself and you a good deal of work by assuming the problem away, just as I assumed, for the purposes of this chapter, that variations in output by a single firm did not affect the prices at which it sold and bought. The reason I did not do so is that, in exchange for the additional complications of Figure 9-10a, we get two important results. One will be postponed to the next section; the other will be discussed here.

Back in Chapter 4, I proved that the consumer surplus calculated from a demand curve representing the total demand of many consumers was the same as the sum of the consumer surpluses for all the individual demand curves of the individual consumers and that the same was true for supply curves. This is true for Figure 9-9; the industry supply curve is simply the firm supply curve multiplied horizontally by 10, so the producer surplus (profit) of the industry at any price is 10 times the surplus of the firm. It does not, however, appear to be true for Figure 9-10a. If price is P_2, the firm's supply curve is S_2—which is identical to S_f on Figure 9-9, and hence implies the same amount of producer surplus. But the industry supply curve S is not the same as S_i on Figure 9-9. S and S_i intersect at point A_2 where price is P_2 and quantity is Q_2. Since S is steeper than S_i, the corresponding producer surplus at a price of P_2 (the entire shaded region on Figure 9-11) is larger than the producer surplus at the same price calculated from S_i (the lightly shaded region). If the producer surplus for S_i is 10 times that for S_f, the producer surplus for S must be more than 10 times that for S_2. But S_2 is the supply curve faced by a firm in the situation described by point A_2 (price of iron = $2/pound). There are 10 such firms. It appears that the producer surplus of the industry is greater than the producer surplus of the firms that make it up! What have we missed?

The answer is on Figure 9-10b. The firms shown on Figure 9-10a are not the only producers who benefit from their output—there are also the producers of iron. The higher the quantity produced on Figure 9-10a, the higher the quantity of iron used—and the price (on Figure 9-10b) at which it sells. If we had drawn the figure precisely and to scale, using actual production functions, the shaded area on Figure 9-10b, representing the producer surplus received by the producers of iron when the price of iron is $2/pound, would just make up the discrepancy between the total producer surplus calculated from S on Figure 9-10a and the producer surplus per firm calculated from S_2.

I have asserted this result: I have not proved it, nor will I in this book. Figures 9-9 through 9-11 and the discussion of the last few paragraphs should make the result seem plausible, since they demonstrate that the discrepancy exists and that it is the result of the same fact—a rising supply curve for iron—which is responsible for the existence of producer surplus on Figure 9-10b. But a plausibility argument is not a proof.

Free Entry and the Industry Supply Curve

So far, I have considered an industry with a fixed number of firms; in that context, the supply curve of the industry can be seen as simply the horizontal sum of the supply curves of the individual firms—with appropriate allowance for the way in which the firm supply curves shift if changes in the industry's output affect the price of its inputs. It is now time to drop the assumption that the number of firms in the industry is fixed and consider an ordinary competitive industry in which there is free entry; anyone who wishes may start a firm.

Now, when price increases, not all of the resulting increase in output need come from existing firms; some may come from new firms started to take advantage of the higher price. Hence the industry supply curve, which tells us how total output responds to changes in price, is not simply the firm supply curve multiplied by the number of firms.

The simplest way to derive an industry supply curve is to assume, as in the previous section, that existing firms all have the same production function and that there exist an unlimited number of "potential firms" each with the same production function as the existing firms. Just as at the beginning of the previous section, we will start by ignoring any effect that the actions of the industry may have on the price of its inputs.

In that situation, the industry supply curve is very simple. If existing firms are making positive profits—if their total revenue is larger than their total cost—it will pay new firms to come into existence. As new firms come into existence, supply expands, driving down the price. The process continues until profit is no longer positive. If, on the other hand, existing firms are making negative profits, then firms go out of business, reducing supply and driving price up—until profit is no longer negative. The equilibrium point is where profit is zero.

There is only one possible price—the price at which revenue exactly covers cost. If revenue exactly covers cost, then average cost must be equal to price. We know, from our analysis of the supply curve of the firm, that each firm is producing an output for which marginal cost equals price. So the equilibrium of the whole industry occurs where price, marginal cost, and average cost are all equal.

If marginal cost equals average cost, then, as we saw earlier in the chapter, average cost is at a minimum (or a maximum, a possibility we shall for the moment ignore). Hence the equilibrium of the industry has each firm producing at minimum average cost and selling its product for a price that just covers all costs. That implies that the supply curve for the industry is a horizontal line at price equal to minimum average cost, as shown in Figure 9-12a. Increases in demand increase the number of firms and the quantity of output, with price unaffected.

You may be puzzled by the assertion that new firms come into existence as soon as existing firms start making a profit; surely entrepreneurs require not merely some profit but enough to reimburse them for the time and trouble of starting a new firm. But profit is defined, by economists if not by accountants, as revenue minus cost, where cost *includes* the cost to the entrepreneur of his own "time and trouble." Hence if firms are making greater than zero profits, they are more than repaying their owners for the costs of starting them.

There is another way in which the ambiguity in the term "profit" can lead to confusion here; it is most easily illustrated in the case of a corporation, a company owned by its stockholders. For accounting purposes, the profit of such a firm is what is left after paying for labor, raw materials, and the interest on money borrowed by the firm; it is what the stockholders get in exchange for their investment. For economic purposes, however, the capital provided by the stockholders must also be considered an input, and its *opportunity cost*—what the stockholders could have gotten by investing the same money elsewhere—is one of the costs of production. The firm makes an *economic profit* only if its "profit" in the accounting sense is enough to more than just pay the stockholders for the use of their capital—to give them a return greater than the normal market return on the amount they invested in the firm. Such a firm is more attractive than alternative investments. So if firms in an industry are making positive economic profit, new firms enter that industry, driving the price down to the point where economic profit is again zero.

Two Roads to an Upward-Sloped Supply Curve

The supply curves that I described in Chapters 5 and 7 sloped up; the higher the price, the higher the output. The analysis of this chapter seems to imply a horizontal supply curve, with unlimited output available at one price, as shown in Figure 9-12a. What have we left out?

In discussing the supply curve of an industry with free entry, we have ignored the effect of increases in the size of the industry on the price of its inputs. It is now time to stop doing so. If the output of automobiles increases, so does the demand for steel, auto workers, and Detroit real estate. As the demand for these things increases, their price rises. As the price of the inputs increases, so does

Figure 9-12

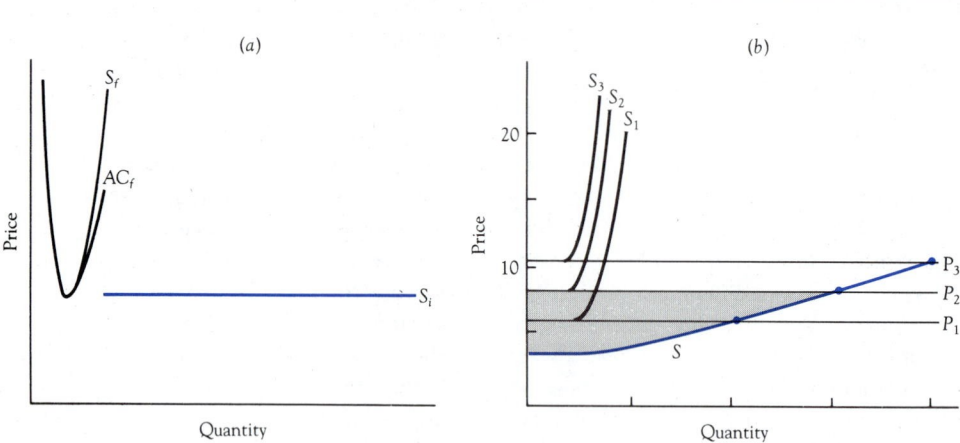

Deducing an industry's supply curve from a firm's supply curve in an industry with open entry. Figure 9-12a shows the case in which the industry's inputs are in perfectly elastic supply; Figure 9-12b shows the case where they are not.

average cost; the result is a rising supply curve. Figure 9-12b shows this; it corresponds to Figure 9-10a of the previous section.

What are the differences between the two situations—a competitive industry with open entry and a competitive industry with closed entry? One, which can be seen by comparing Figure 9-10a to Figure 9-12b, is in the relation between the firm supply curve and the industry supply curve. In Figure 9-12b, the individual firm is always at the bottom of its supply curve—receiving a price equal to average cost and making no economic profit. Increased price causes increased quantity not by sliding the firms up their supply curves but by pulling new firms into the market.

The other difference can be seen if we also look at Figure 9-12a. In the previous section, where we considered an industry with a fixed number of firms, the supply curve sloped up even before we took account of the effect of the industry on the prices of its inputs. In this section, it does not. In that section, the effect of a rising supply curve for the industry's inputs was to make a rising supply curve for its outputs rise more steeply than it otherwise would; in this section, it is to make a flat supply curve for the industry's outputs into a rising one.

In comparing the two sections, it is also worth noting the relevance of the earlier discussion of producer surplus to the situation discussed here. In a competitive industry with free entry, profit is competed down to zero, so the firms receive no producer surplus. But if the industry supply curve slopes up, the industry as a whole must have producer surplus—shown, for a price of P_2, as the shaded area on Figure 9-12b. The explanation is that all of the producer surplus passes through the firms to the suppliers of their inputs. If the suppliers are themselves competitive firms with free entry, it passes through them to their suppliers, until it eventually ends up in the hands of the ultimate suppliers—workers renting out their labor, landowners renting out their land, and so forth. This is a point that will become important in Chapter 13, where I discuss how incomes are determined by ownership of the factors of production—the ultimate inputs.

So far, I have explained upward-sloping supply curves, in the context of a competitive industry with free entry, as a result of upward-sloping supply curves for the industry's inputs. An alternative approach is to assume that some firms have access to "better" means of production than others, giving them better production functions. As the price rises, worse and worse firms are pulled into the market, with higher and higher minimum average costs. The price, at any level of production, must be high enough to cover the costs of the highest cost firm that is producing—the *marginal firm*—otherwise it will not produce. It must not be high enough to cover the costs of the next higher cost firm, the most efficient firm *not* producing—otherwise that firm would enter the market too. At a price at which marginal firms cover their costs, firms with lower costs than the marginal firms make net profits, unlike the zero profit firms of the earlier analysis. Figure 9-13 shows how such a situation can be graphed. At a price P, firm 1, with the lowest cost curves, makes positive profits, shown by the shaded area; firm 2 just covers its costs, and firm 3 has not yet come into existence.

Figure 9-13

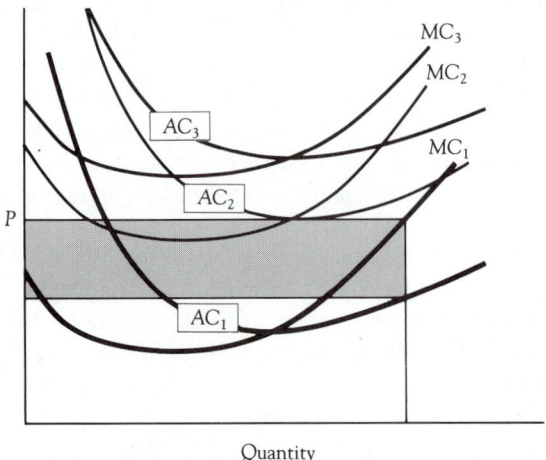

Quantity

An industry in which different firms have different cost curves.   Firm 1, with average cost AC_1 and marginal cost MC_1, is making positive profits. Firm 2 is the marginal firm and makes zero profit. Firm 3 does not exist; it is a potential firm which would come into existence only at a higher price.

These two ways of getting upward-sloping supply curves are really the same. The reason that input costs eventually rise with increasing demand for inputs is that there is not an unlimited supply of identical inputs. There are only so many skilled widget makers willing to work for \$8/hour. To get more, you must pay more, inducing those presently employed to work more hours and luring additional workers into the industry. The same applies to land, raw materials, and capital goods. The reason firms do not all have the same cost curves is that some possess "inputs" that others lack—a particularly skilled manager, an unusually good machine, a favorable location. It is the limited supply of those particular inputs which implies that increased production must use worse machines, less skillful managers, worse locations—or pay more in order to attract high-quality inputs away from wherever they are presently being used.

So long as the scarce inputs actually belong to the firm—consisting, for instance, of the talents of the firm's owner or real estate belonging to a corporation—the distinction between having a better production function and having scarce assets may not be very important. Seen in the one way, the firm receives positive profits from its operations and turns them over to its owners; seen in the other, its profits are zero, but its owners receive income on scarce resources which they rent to the firm. It is a more important distinction when the scarce asset belongs to the firm's landlord or one of its employees; when the relevant contracts are next renegotiated, the firm is likely to find that its positive profit was a purely short-run phenomenon.

Summing It Up

We have spent most of this chapter deriving the supply curve for an industry made up of many firms; the process has been sufficiently lengthy and contained enough complications and detours that you may well have lost track of just how we did it. This is a convenient place to recapitulate.

We start with a production function—a description of what quantity of output could be produced with any bundle of inputs. For any given set of input prices, we then calculate a total cost function by finding the cost of the least expensive bundle of inputs necessary to produce each level of output. From that total cost curve—total cost of production as a function of quantity produced—we calculate average cost and marginal cost curves. From those we calculate a supply curve for the firm; each firm maximizes its profit by producing that quantity for which marginal cost equals price—unless, at that quantity, price is still below average cost, in which case the firm produces nothing and exits the industry.

Once we have the supply curve for the firm, we are ready to find the supply curve for the industry. If the industry is closed—new firms are not permitted—the supply curve for the industry is simply the horizontal sum of the supply curves of the firms that make it up, with some possible complications due to the effect of the quantity that the industry produces on the price of its inputs. If the industry is open—new firms are free to enter—then in equilibrium, profit must be zero, since positive profit attracts firms into the industry, driving down the market price, and negative profit drives firms out, raising the market price. In the simplest case—an unlimited supply of identical firms with horizontal supply curves for their inputs—the result is a horizontal supply curve for the industry's output at a price equal to the minimum average cost of the firm. In the more complicated cases, the result is a rising supply curve. Price is still equal to minimum average cost—or if firms are not identical, it is between the minimum average cost of the highest cost firm that is producing and the minimum average cost of the lowest cost firm that is not.

Industry Equilibrium and Benevolent Dictation

The industry equilibrium we have just described—competitive equilibrium with free entry—has some interesting features. Suppose you were appointed dictator over the industry and told to produce the same output at the lowest possible cost. You would arrange things just as they are arranged in this solution—with each firm producing at minimum average cost.

From your standpoint, controlling the whole industry, there are really two marginal costs for increasing output, corresponding to two different margins on which output can increase. One is the margin of the number of firms—output can be increased by having more firms. The other is the margin of output per firm; output can be increased by having each firm produce more. Marginal cost is the same on both of these margins—and must be if goods are being produced at minimum total cost. This is precisely analogous to the argument which showed that the marginal utility per dollar produced by different goods being consumed must be the same if utility is being maximized—it is one more application of the equimarginal principle. I leave the proof as an exercise for you; it is essentially the same as the last two or three times.

Another interesting feature of the competitive equilibrium is that price equals marginal cost; this implies that the price of a widget to a consumer deciding whether to consume one more is equal to the cost of producing it. He will choose to consume it only if it is worth at least that much to him—in which case it is, in some sense, "worth producing it." This point will be discussed more precisely and in much more detail in Chapters 14 and 15.

Production and Exploitation

There is a sense in which nothing is produced. The laws of physics tell us that the sum total of mass and energy can be neither increased nor reduced. What we call "production" is the rearrangement of matter and energy from less useful to more useful (to us) forms.

It is sometimes said that only factories are really productive; middlemen (retailers and wholesalers) merely "move things about" while absorbing some of what others have produced. But all *anyone* does is to "move things about"—to rearrange from less to more useful. The "producer" rearranges iron ore and other inputs into automobiles; the retailer rearranges automobiles on a lot into automobiles paired up with particular customers. Both increase the value of what they work on and collect their income out of that increase.

It is often said that some participants in the economy "exploit" others—most commonly that employers "exploit" workers. This raises the question of what it means to "exploit" someone. Two different definitions are often used—simultaneously—in such discussions. The first is that I exploit you if I benefit by your existence and our association. In this sense, I hope to exploit my wife and she hopes to exploit me; hopefully we will both succeed. If that is what "exploitation" means, then it is the reason that humans are social animals and not, like cats, solitary ones.

The second definition is that I exploit you if I gain *and you lose* by our association. The connection between the two can be made either by claiming that the world is a "zero sum game" in which the only way one person can gain is at another person's expense, or by arguing that if I gain by our association, then you "deserve" to have the gain given to you; hence my refusal to give it to you "injures" you. The former argument is implausible. The second has a curious asymmetry to it. If I give you all the gain, you have now gained by our association and should obviously give it all back to me. It may be more sensible to keep the term "exploitation" out of economics and reserve it for political invective.

OPTIONAL SECTION

The Puzzle of the Firm

Our analysis so far has shown how individuals coordinate their action through the price system. This raises the question of why any other method is used. Why do firms exist? Why do we not observe an economy in which all producers are individuals, contracting with each other to buy and sell specific goods and services. Why do we observe instead firms, which buy people's time and then tell them what to do with it? Why is the capitalist beach made up of socialist grains of sand?

The simplest answer is that contracting can be costly. In Chapter 6, I described how bilateral monopoly (one buyer, one seller) can lead to costly bargaining as each party tries to get for himself as much as possible of the difference between the value of the good to the seller and to the buyer. While bilateral monopoly is in one sense rare, it is in another sense ubiquitous.

Consider a professor looking for a new job. There are, we will suppose, twenty universities as well suited to me as UCLA, and two hundred economists as suitable for UCLA to employ as I am. Suppose I accept a job at UCLA, move to Southern California, buy a house, and spend a year or two learning to know and work with my colleagues and discovering how to teach UCLA undergraduates (by slipping lecture cassettes into their Sony Walkmen). When I came to UCLA, my salary was (say) $20,000/year. Two years later, I am just as productive as expected and enjoy UCLA exactly as much as I expected to. But a problem arises.

The chairman of the department realizes that if I was willing to come for $20,000, even though I had to pay the costs of moving and adjusting, then I would probably stay even if he reduced my salary to $19,000—after all, there is no way I can get my moving expenses back by leaving. He calls me into his office to discuss the tight state of the department's budget.

I am glad to have a chance to talk to the chairman, for I too have been considering the situation. For my first two years, my productivity was reduced by the need to learn the ropes at my new job. If they were willing to offer me $20,000/year, it was probably because, although I was really worth only $15,000/year for the first two years, they expected me to be worth enough more than $20,000/year thereafter to make up for the initial loss. Now that I have an opportunity to talk to the chairman, I will explain that, after considering the difficulty of the work I am doing, I believe I am entitled to a substantial raise. After all, there is no way he can get back the money he has lost on me during the first two years.

What we have here is a situation which was initially competitive but became a bilateral monopoly (with potential bargaining costs) once the trading parties had made costly adjustments to each other. The obvious solution is long-term contracting. When I come to UCLA, it is with an agreement specifying my salary for some years into the future.

This solution is itself costly—it constrains us even if circumstances change so that the contract *should* be renegotiated. There is no easy way to distinguish renegotiation motivated by a change in circumstances from renegotiation designed to take advantage of the bilateral monopoly created by our adjustments to each other. We could try to make the salary contingent on relevant circumstances (cost of living, university budget, alternative job offers), but there will never be enough small print to cover all of them.

The firm is a particular sort of long-term contract, in which the workers agree to do what they are told (within certain limits) for a stated number of hours a day in exchange for a fixed payment. The central problem of the firm is summed up in the Latin phrase "qui custodes ipsos custodiet"—"Who will guard the guardians." Since the workers receive a fixed wage, their objective is to earn it in the most enjoyable way possible; this is not necessarily the same behavior that maximizes the firm's profits. It is necessary to hire supervisors to watch the workers and make sure they do their job. Who then is to watch the supervisors? Who is to watch him?

One answer is to have the top supervisor be the *residual claimant*—the person who receives the firm's net revenue (profit) as his income. He watches the supervisors below him, they watch the ones below them, and so on. The residual claimant does not have to be watched in order to make him act in the interest of the firm—his interest and the firm's interest are the same.

What I have described is a firm run by its owner. This is a common arrangement in our economy. It makes sense in a situation where the "worker" whom it is most difficult for anyone else to supervise is the top supervisor; since he is the residual claimant, he supervises himself. While it is a common arrangement, it is not a universal one; not all firms are managed by their owners. In some, the worker whom it is most difficult and important to supervise is not the top manager but some skilled worker on whose output the firm depends—an inventor, for instance, with a firm built around him to support his genius (Browning, Ruger, Dolby). It may make sense for him to be the residual claimant—the owner of the firm—and for the top manager to be an employee; that is how such firms are sometimes organized. In other firms, there may be a group of skilled workers who can most easily be supervised by each other. You then get a workers' cooperative, although not necessarily one that includes all of the workers. An example is a law partnership.

There is another solution to the problem of organizing a firm which is common in our society—a corporation, owned neither by its managers nor by its workers but by the stockholders who provide much of its capital, and controlled by the managers that those stockholders elect. Considering that solution brings us to some interesting problems—and a historical digression.

Even Homer Nods: Smith and the Corporation

Adam Smith, who in the eighteenth century produced the most influential economics book ever written, argued that corporations were almost hopelessly incompetent. With ownership widely dispersed, everybody's business is nobody's business; the managers can do what they like with the stockholders' money. Smith predicted that corporations would succeed only with government support, except in those areas which required large amounts of money and very little skill—such as banking and insurance.

Smith was wrong; even where they have no special support from government (save for the privilege of limited liability)—even when government imposes special taxes on them—corporations have successfully competed with owner-run firms and partnerships in a wide range of fields. His mistake was in failing to predict the benign effects of the take-over bid.

Imagine you know that a corporation is being badly run. You buy as much stock as possible—enough to let you take over the corporation and install competent managers. Earnings shoot up. The market value of your stock shoots up. You sell out and look for another badly managed firm. Such behavior is discouraged by securities regulation and vituperated by existing managements, for obvious reasons. It (and its threat, which helps keep managers honest) may be the reason for the success of the corporation in the modern world.

This raises an interesting idea. The same arguments which show that the corporation cannot work apply with still greater force to democratic government. In a presidential election, the individual voter has one chance in several million of deciding the outcome—so why should he spend valuable time and energy studying the candidates and the issues before he votes? Here again, everybody's business is nobody's business. The result is that most voters do not even know the names of many of the politicians who "represent" them.

Is there any reason why the solution to the problems of the corporation—the take-over bid—does not solve the problems of democratic government? Yes. The difference between the two cases is that your "share" in the U.S. is not transferable property—which may be why, if casual observation is to be trusted, democratic governments are worse run than most corporations.

Your share in the U.S. is not transferable property—but perhaps it could be. Imagine that it were. Each citizen owns one citizenship, which includes one vote. You may leave the country and sell your citizenship to someone who wants to live here. If the country is badly run, someone can buy up a vast number of citizenships, elect a competent government, and make a fortune reselling the citizenships at a higher price. The country need not be emptied while the operation is going on; the operator can always rent his citizenships out between the time he buys them and the time he sells them.

Production Function to Cost Curve via Calculus

At the beginning of this chapter, I described the production function of a firm producing clay pots and showed how it could be used to find the total cost curve. One problem with the procedure described there was that Table 9-1 showed only a few of the possible bundles of inputs. Looking over the alternative bundles shown on the table to find the least costly way of producing any level of output only guarantees that you end up with the best alternative among those shown; there may be other bundles, not shown on the table, which are even less costly. Another problem is that the table shows bundles for producing only a few of the many possible levels of output.

Both problems can be eliminated if we use calculus instead of trial and error. The production function, which is given at the bottom of Table 9-1, tells us how much output we can produce from any combination of inputs:

$$Q = L^{1/2}(K/100)^{1/4}R^{1/4}. \qquad \text{(Eqn. 1)}$$

Here Q is the quantity of output (number of pots), L the amount of labor, K the amount of capital, and R the amount of raw material (clay). Since according to Table 9-1, the price of labor is \$10/hour, the price of capital is .05/year (an interest rate of 5 percent), and the price of clay is \$4/pound, the cost of any bundle of labor, capital, and raw material is:

$$C = 10L + .05K + 4R. \qquad \text{(Eqn. 2)}$$

Our problem is to find the values of L, K, and R that minimize C for a given Q.

The first step is to use Equation 1 to eliminate one of the variables. Rearranging the equation, we have:

$$R = 100Q^4/L^2K. \qquad \text{(Eqn. 3)}$$

Substituting that into Equation 2 gives us:

$$C = 10L + .05K + 400Q^4/L^2K. \qquad \text{(Eqn. 4)}$$

Minimizing Equation 4 by varying K and L while holding Q constant gives us two first-order equations:

$$0 = dC/dL = 10 - 800Q^4/L^3K$$

and

$$0 = dC/dK = .05 - 400Q^4/L^2K^2.$$

Solving those, we have:

$$L^3K = 400Q^4/5 = 80Q^4 \qquad \text{(Eqn. 5)}$$

and

$$L^2K^2 = 40{,}000Q^4/5 = 8{,}000Q^4. \qquad \text{(Eqn. 6)}$$

Taking the square root of Equation 6 gives us:

$$LK = 200Q^2/5^{1/2}. \qquad \text{(Eqn. 7)}$$

Dividing Equation 5 by Equation 7 gives us:

$$L^2 = 2Q^2/5^{1/2}.$$

Solving for L, we have:

$$L = 2^{1/2}Q/5^{1/4}.$$

We can then plug that into Equation 7 and solve for K:

$$K = 20Q \times 2^{1/2}5^{3/4}.$$

We then find R by plugging K and L into Equation 3; the result is:

$$R = Q(5^{3/4})/2^{3/2}.$$

We now have L, K, and R as functions of Q. For any value of Q, they tell us how much of each input is included in the least-cost bundle that can be used to produce that quantity of output; mathematical purists may wish to check the second-order conditions to make sure we have minimized cost instead of maximizing it. Inserting the expressions for L, K, and R into Equation 2 gives us the total cost curve—the cost of producing any quantity of output in the least expensive possible way.

$$TC(Q) = 10Q \times 2^{1/2}/5^{1/4} + .05 \times 20Q \times 2^{1/2}5^{3/4} + 4Q \times 5^{3/4}/2^{3/2} =$$
$$Q \times (2^{1/2}/5^{1/4}) \times (10 + 4 + 4)$$

Bundles O, P, Q, and R on Table 9-1 show the results of solving for $Q = 1$, 2, 3, and 4; Figure 9-1 shows the total cost curve.

PROBLEMS

1. Figure 9-14 shows the average and marginal cost curves for a firm. At a price of \$6/widget, about how many widgets will the firm produce?
2. If additional firms like this are free to enter the market, what will the price of widgets eventually be?

Figure 9-14

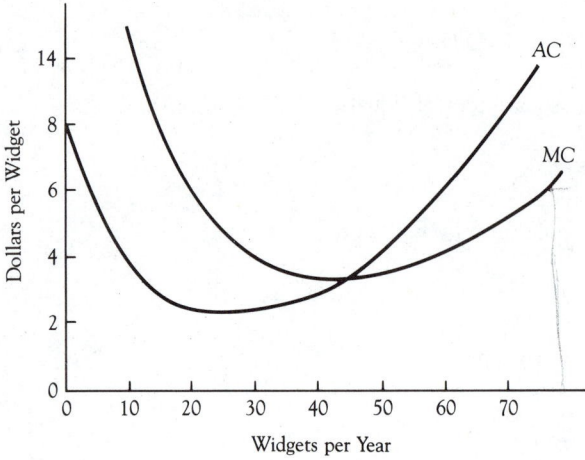

Cost curves for Problems 1 and 2.

3. Figure 9-15a shows a total cost curve (total cost of producing widgets as a function of quantity of widgets produced). Which of the curves shown in Figure 9-15b could be the corresponding marginal cost curve? Which could be the corresponding average cost curve? (The vertical axes of the figures are deliberately left unmarked; answering the question does not require that information.)

Figure 9-15

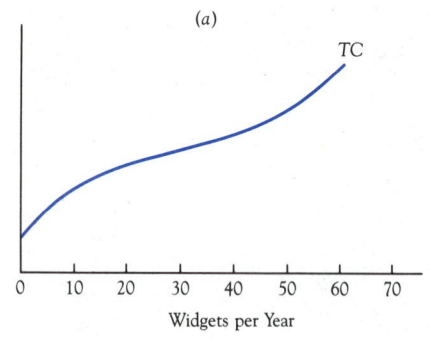

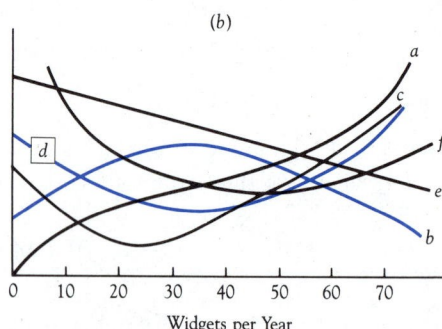

Cost curves for Problem 3.

4. Figure 9-16 shows several pairs of MC and AC curves; which are possible?
5. How does the relation between MC and AC tell you whether AC is at a maximum or a minimum?
6. Demonstrate that the firm always prefers the point where MC intersects P from below to the point where it intersects it from above. What does this imply about the situation where marginal cost crosses average cost at the maximum instead of the minimum of average cost?

Figure 9-16

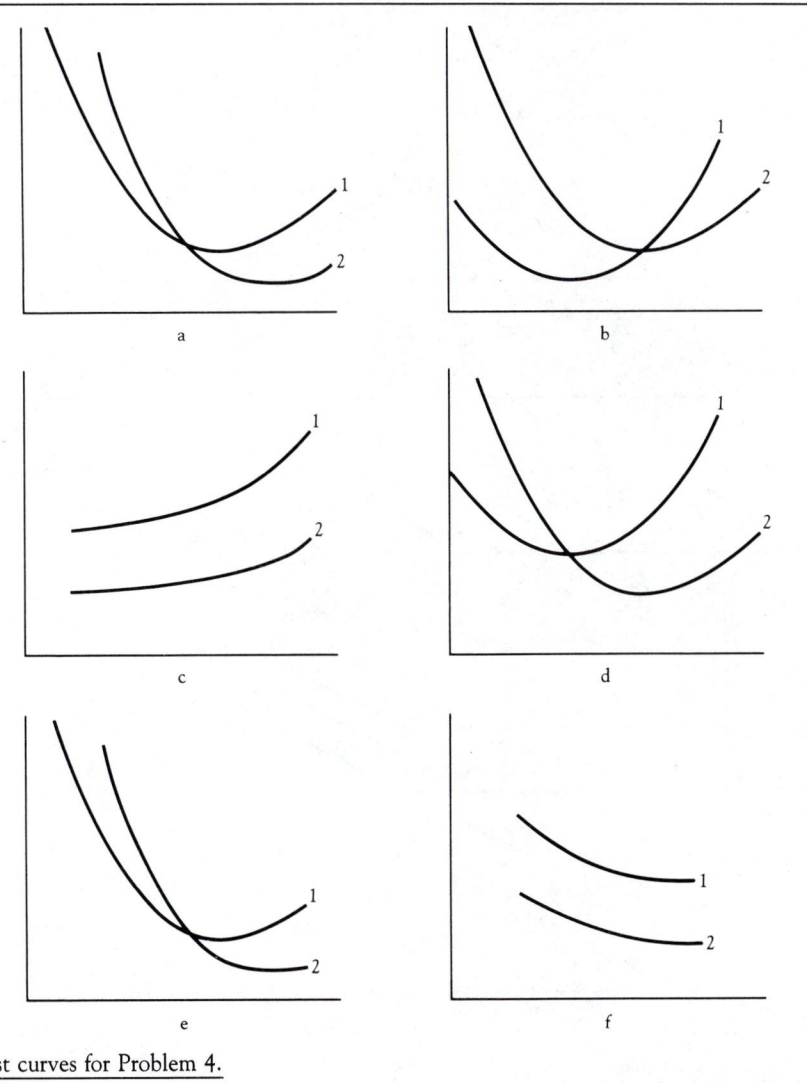

Cost curves for Problem 4.

7. In Figures 9-17a and 9-17b, marginal cost crosses price several times. At what quantity on each figure is profit maximized for P_1? P_2? How do you know?
8. Figure 9-18 shows the supply curves for three types of firms—type 1, type 2, and type 3. Assume there are 10 of each; no additional firms are allowed to enter the market. Draw the industry supply curve. Assume that all of the industry's inputs have horizontal supply curves; the amount purchased does not affect the price.
9. What are the essential differences between the analysis of production in this chapter and of consumption in Chapters 3 and 4?

Figure 9-17

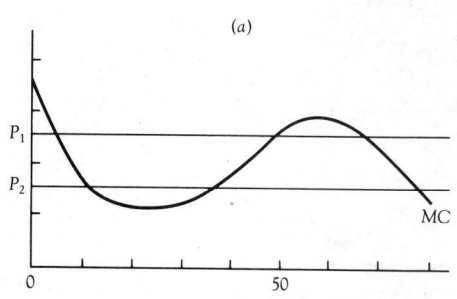 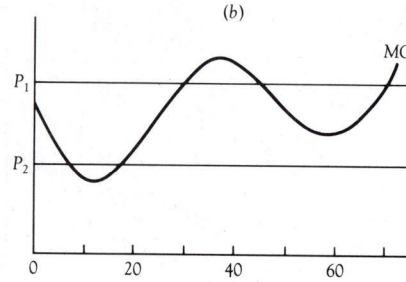

Marginal cost curves for Problem 7.

Figure 9-18

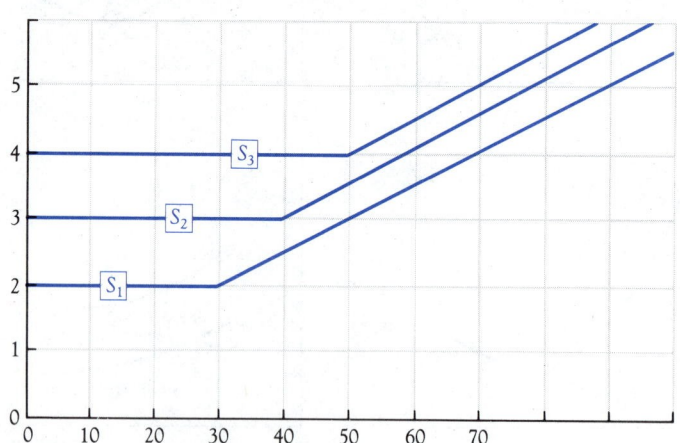

Supply curves for Problem 8.

10. Figure 9-19 shows the supply curve for a pencil firm and the producer surplus that the firm receives if the price at which it can sell pencils is $.10/pencil. As in several earlier figures, the supply curve is discontinuous; there is no price at which the firm chooses to produce more than zero and less than 10,000 pencils per week. The supply curve shows, for any price, the quantity the firm chooses to produce at that price, so in the range of quantity between 0 and 10,000, the supply curve does not exist.

Producer surplus is the area above the supply curve and below the price. In this case, between 0 and 10,000 pencils per week, there is no supply curve for it to be above. Nonetheless, here and earlier, the region representing producer surplus is drawn as if the supply curve had a horizontal section at the discontinuity—as if, in other words, the dashed line on the figure were really part of the supply curve.

Prove that this is the correct way of calculating producer surplus in this case. (This is a hard question.)

(Hint: You will want to use both the marginal cost and the average cost curves of the firm in your proof. Second Hint: What is producer surplus at a price of $.06/pencil? Why?)

Figure 9-19

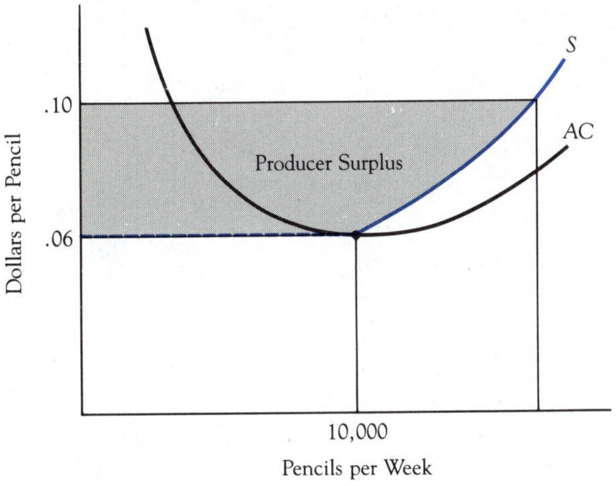

Supply curve and producer surplus for Problem 10.

11. Who or what do cats "exploit"? In which sense or senses of the word?

The following problems refer to the optional section:

12. The production function is the same as for Table 11-1; the price of labor is $5/hour, the price of capital is .04/year, and the price of clay is $6/pound. Find and graph the total cost curve.

13. Prices are the same as in Problem 12; the production function is:

$$Q = L^{1/3}K^{1/3}R^{1/3}.$$

Solve for L, K, R, and $TC(Q)$.

14. Your production function is as in Problem 13. You have decided to produce 100 pots; you have already bought 8 pounds of clay, so the only question is how much labor and capital to use. The wage rate is $10/hour, and the interest rate is 10 percent (i.e., capital costs you .10/year).

   a. Use calculus to find the optimal values of L and K.

   b. Solve the same problem using an isoquant-isoexpenditure diagram similar to Figure 9-2.

FOR FURTHER READING

Two interesting and original discussions of some of the questions raised in the optional section of the chapter are: Ronald Coase, "The Nature of the Firm," *Economica*, Vol. 4 (November, 1937), pp. 386-405, and Armen Alchian and Harold Demsetz, "Production, Information Costs, and Economic Organization," *American Economic Review*, Vol. 62 (December, 1972), pp. 777-795.

Chapter 10

Small-Numbers Problems:
Monopoly and All That

In everything I have done so far, except for parts of Chapter 6, I assumed that trade involved many individuals or firms on each side. In deciding how much to sell or buy, the effect of the decision on the market price could be ignored, since the amount bought or sold by a single firm or individual would have a negligible effect on the price. While the demand curve faced by an entire industry was downward sloping (the more they sold, the lower the price), the demand curve faced by a single firm was essentially horizontal; similarly the supply curve faced by a single consumer was essentially horizontal even though the overall supply curve was rising.

An example may make this clearer. If there were 100 identical firms in an industry, a doubling in the output of any single firm would cause total quantity supplied (by the industry) to increase by only one percent. The resulting fall in price would be even less than we would expect from applying a one percent increase in quantity to the demand curve, since as price falls, not only does quantity demanded increase, but quantity supplied (by the other 99 firms) also decreases. From the standpoint of the firm, the demand curve is almost perfectly elastic; changes in the quantity of output it produces have almost no effect on the price at which it can sell that output.

A firm in such a situation is sometimes described as a *price taker*. The firm takes the market price as given and assumes it can sell as much as it wants at that price. The firms described in Chapter 9 were price takers. The horizontal line which I drew at price in some of the figures of that chapter may be thought of as a (perfectly elastic) demand curve—the demand curve faced, not by the industry, but by the firm.

Not all industries consist of hundreds of firms. In this chapter, we will discuss situations where there are only a few firms in the industry, starting with the simple case of a *monopoly*—a firm that is the only seller of some particular good or service. In Part 1, we consider a monopoly that sells all of its output at the same price—a *single-price* monopoly. In Part 2, we consider a *discriminating* monopoly—a firm that is able to sell different units of its output at different prices. In Part 3, we discuss the different reasons why monopolies might exist. In Part

4, we consider *monopolistic competition*, a situation with elements of both monopoly and competition. Individual firms are price seekers, but additional firms are free to enter the industry—and do so as long as profit is positive. In Part 5, we expand the discussion to include other small-numbers cases—*oligopoly* (several—but not many—sellers), *oligopsony* (ditto buyers), and other still more complicated possibilities.

PART 1 · SINGLE-PRICE MONOPOLY

We start with a monopoly which finds that it must sell all of its output at the same price; the reasons why it must do so will be discussed later, when we consider the problems faced by firms that try to sell at different prices to different customers. Consider the widget firm whose situation is shown in Figure 10-1a. D is the total demand curve for widgets; since there is only one firm producing widgets, it is also the demand curve faced by that firm. MC is its marginal cost curve. The firm is producing at a quantity where $MC = P$, just as Chapter 9 says it should. Quantity is 20 widgets per month; price is $10/widget.

Suppose the firm reduces its output from 20 widgets to 19 widgets per month. Its production cost falls by about $9.50/month (the shaded area). Price rises to $11/widget. Before, it was making $200/month; now, it is making $209/month. Costs are down and revenue up, so its profit must have increased!

How can this be? Did we not prove in the previous chapter that profit was maximized at a quantity where $P = MC$? No. We proved that it was maximized at that quantity *for a price-taking firm*—a firm that could ignore the effect of its output on prices. If you go back to the relevant part of Chapter 9, you will see that we always took price as given.

The firm shown in Figure 10-1a is not a *price taker* but a *price searcher*. Rather than taking price as given and deciding how much to produce and sell at that price, it must decide how much to produce knowing that by doing so it simultaneously determines both price and quantity—the more it produces, the lower the price.

When a *price taker* increases his output by one unit, he gains or loses according to whether the revenue from the additional unit is more or less than the cost of producing it. The revenue from one unit is the price it sells for, P, and the cost of producing one more unit is MC. So he gains if $P > MC$ and loses if $P < MC$. As long as $P > MC$, his profit increases with each additional unit, so he keeps expanding his output until it reaches a level at which MC is equal to P, as described in Chapter 9.

For a *price searcher*, the situation is more complicated. When he increases his output by one unit, one of the effects is a small reduction in the market price. Since (by assumption) he sells all his widgets at the same price, this means that he gets a little less not only for the additional unit but also for each of the other units he is selling. His profit goes up by the price for which he sells the additional unit (P'), down by the cost of producing that unit (MC), and down by the quantity he was selling (Q) times the change in price ($P - P'$). The three terms are all shown on Figure 10-1b, for an increase in output from 20 widgets per

Figure 10-1

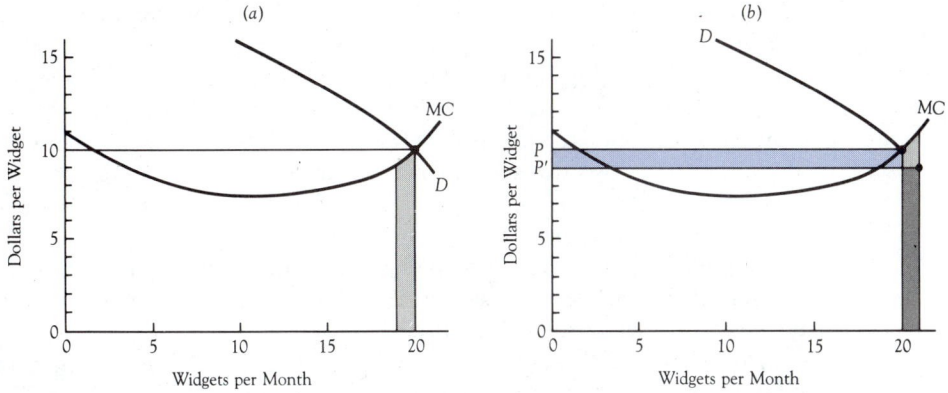

The effect of quantity on revenue and profit for a price searcher. Figure 10-1a shows the effect of reducing quantity from 20 to 19; Figure 10-1b shows the effect of increasing quantity from 20 to 21. On Figure 10-1b, the net reduction in revenue is the colored area; the reduction in profit is that plus the lightly shaded area.

month to 21. The increase in revenue—P' (times the additional number of units—1)—is shown darkly shaded. The decrease in revenue, $Q(P - P')$, is shown colored. The increased cost is the entire shaded area, light plus dark. The reduction in profit is the sum of the colored and the lightly shaded regions.

Students are often puzzled as to why the firm must reduce its price on the "previous" units just to sell an "additional" unit. The mistake they are making is to think of "previous" and "additional" as referring to an actual sequence of events taking place in the market. They are imagining that the firm *first* sells 20 units and *then* sells one more; why should the latter event affect the former? But we are describing a firm which is *either* going to sell 20 units per month for the next ten years *or* 21 units per month for the next ten years and is trying to decide which alternative will yield higher profits. If it chooses to sell 21 units, it must sell them at a price at which consumers are willing to buy that many—which means a lower price than if it sells only 20. "Previous" and "additional" describe the order in which we think about the alternatives, not the order in which things actually happen.

Marginal Revenue

To find out more exactly what the profit-maximizing quantity is for a single-price monopoly, we introduce a new concept—*marginal revenue*. Marginal revenue is defined as the increase in revenue per unit of increased quantity for very small changes in quantity, just as marginal cost was defined as the increase in cost per unit of increased quantity for very small changes in quantity. Students familiar with calculus may prefer to think of marginal revenue as the derivative of total revenue with regard to quantity, and marginal cost as the derivative of total cost with regard to quantity—calculus for the same thing.

If quantity is increased by one unit, revenue changes for two reasons. There is an increase in revenue of P' from selling one more unit, and there is a reduction in revenue of $Q(P - P')$. Here P is the price before the increase, P' the price after. The change in price due to one additional unit is small compared to the total price—but in calculating the change in profit, the total price is only multiplied by one unit, while the change in price is multiplied by Q units. Figure 10-2a shows the two terms for an increase in output from 20 units to 21 units and shows marginal revenue as a function of quantity over a range of output. The shaded vertical rectangle is the gain from selling the additional unit; the colored horizontal rectangle is the loss from selling the other units at a lower price. Note that marginal revenue is always *lower* than price—by the lost revenue on the previous units due to the fall in price.

On Figure 10-2a, the demand curve is a straight line. I drew it that way to illustrate a particularly simple way of finding a marginal revenue curve. It so happens that for a straight-line demand curve, marginal revenue is also a straight line, running from the vertical intercept of demand (the price at which quantity demanded is zero) to one half the horizontal intercept (half the quantity that would be demanded at a price of zero) as shown on the figure. This fact is of no significance at all for economics, since there is no reason to expect real-world demand curves to be straight lines, but it is very convenient for solving economics problems. Those of you familiar with calculus should be able to prove the result; it is quite easy. For those unfamiliar with calculus, it is almost the only thing in this book which you will find useful to learn without knowing why it is true; feel free to forget it as soon as the course is over.

Figure 10-2

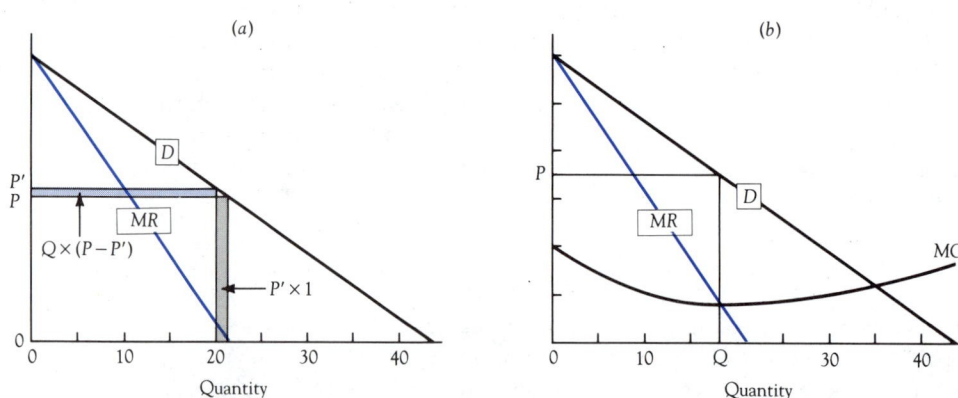

Using marginal revenue to find the profit-maximizing quantity. MR is the marginal revenue implied by the demand curve D. Figure 10-2a shows how MR could be calculated. Figure 10-2b shows the profit-maximizing quantity (Q)—where $MR = MC$. P is the price at which that quantity will sell.

Now that we have a marginal revenue curve, maximizing the monopolist's profit is simple. If marginal revenue is higher than marginal cost, he should increase his output—the additional revenue (even allowing for the effect of the fall in price) is greater than the additional cost. If marginal revenue is lower than marginal cost, he should decrease output. If he has the correct (i.e., profit-maximizing) output, marginal revenue will be equal to marginal cost. This solution is shown on Figure 10-2b.

Note that we are solving for quantity and then using the demand curve to find the price at which the quantity will be sold. A mistake which students often make in trying to solve this sort of problem is to confuse MR on the graph with P; they find quantity correctly at the intersection of MR and MC but then assume that the height of the point of intersection is the price. It is not; it is the marginal revenue, which as we have seen, is below the price for a price searcher. Marginal revenue, marginal cost, and price are all in the same units (money divided by quantity—dollars per pound, for example, or pennies per gram), and they are all functions of quantity, so they can be and are shown as different curves on the same figure—but that does not mean that they are the same thing.

Price Searcher vs Price Taker

The profit-maximizing rule for a price searcher—"produce that quantity for which marginal revenue equals marginal cost"—is also the correct rule for a price taker. Since the change in price with quantity for a price taker is zero (that is why he is a price taker), marginal revenue is equal to price; each additional unit he produces increases his revenue by the price he sells it for. Since for the price taker MR and P are the same, $MR = MC$ and $P = MC$ are for him the same thing. The price taker producing where price equals marginal cost is a special case of the price searcher producing where marginal revenue equals marginal cost.

In our analysis of price-taking firms in Chapter 9, one of our main objectives was to find supply curves—first the supply curve of a firm and then the supply curve of an industry made up of many firms. We cannot do the same thing here. We cannot find the supply curve of a price searcher because a price searcher does not *have* a supply curve.

A supply curve tells how much a firm or industry will produce as a function of the price it can get for its goods. But the amount a price taker produces does not only depend on the price it is getting; it also depends on the price it could get at other levels of output. Its output depends not just on a price—the height of the demand curve at one point—but on the shape of the whole demand curve.

To see this, compare Figures 10-3a and 10-3b, which show two different demand curves and the marginal revenue curves they imply. Both figures also show the same marginal cost curve. The market price that the firm chooses to charge is the same in both cases—P—but the quantity is different. This demonstrates that even if we know the cost curves of the firm and the price, we cannot predict the quantity. So the supply curve, which shows quantity supplied as a function of price, does not exist.

Figure 10-3

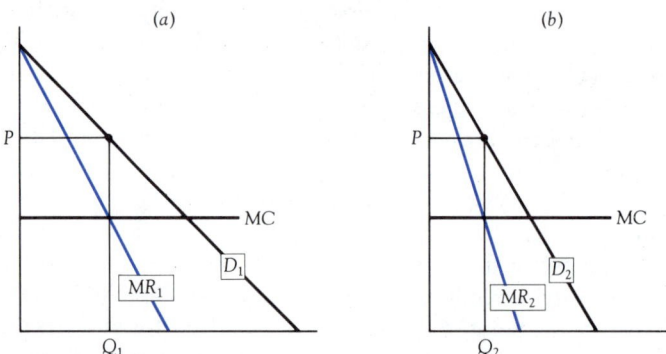

Two different demand curves which imply the same price but different quantities.

In deriving the supply curve of a firm from its cost curves in Chapter 9, the rule "produce a quantity for which MC = P" was only the first step. The second step was to observe that if profit was negative at that output, it could be increased by shutting down the firm and going out of business. This implies the additional rule "provided that at that quantity price is at least as high as average cost." That was why the supply curve was equal to the marginal cost curve only at and above its intersection with average cost.

The second rule applies to a monopoly as well; if the price at which the monopoly sells its products is less than its average cost, it would be better off going out of business. While the *marginal* revenue of a price searcher is different from that of a price taker, the *average* revenue is the same—price. If you are selling 1,000 apples at $.50 each, your total revenue is $500 and your average revenue (total divided by quantity) is $.50/apple—whether or not the amount you produce affects the price. So a different way of stating the rule is "Go out of business if average revenue is less than average cost."

The third step in deriving the supply curve for a price taker took us from the firm to the industry; as long as profit was positive, it would pay other firms to enter the industry. By doing so, they would drive down price and profit. The result was that in equilibrium, profit (revenue minus all costs) was zero.

In the case of a monopoly, the firm and the industry are the same; for one or another of several reasons discussed later in the chapter, no additional firms can enter. The argument for zero profit appears to vanish, leaving us with the possibility of "monopoly profit"—which will be discussed later, after we have looked at the different reasons why a monopoly might exist.

Elasticity or How Flat Is Flat?

In several chapters, especially this chapter and Chapter 9, I have found it useful to describe curves—supply curves, demand curves, cost curves—as more or less "flat." That is not an entirely adequate way of expressing the underlying idea; how flat a curve appears to be on a graph depends partly on how you choose to draw the vertical and horizontal scales. Figures 10-4a and 10-4b are graphs of exactly the same demand curve (for water); the difference is that the horizontal axis shows gallons per day in Figure 10-4a and gallons per week in Figure 10-4b. To check that the graphs are really the same, note that at a price of $.10/gallon, quantity demanded is 10 gallons per day (on Figure 10-4a) and 70 gallons per week (on Figure 10-4b). Yet the demand curve appears much flatter on Figure 10-4b than on Figure 10-4a. By changing the scale of the horizontal axis, we have, in effect, stretched the curve horizontally, making it look flatter.

The solution is to replace "flatness" with "elasticity." Elasticity was explained briefly in the previous chapter, but the idea was used there only in a qualitative way; "very flat" demand and supply curves were described as "very elastic," and "very steep" curves were described as "very inelastic." In discussing the behavior of a monopoly, we will require a somewhat more precise understanding of elasticity—as a quantitative, and not merely a qualitative, concept.

The definition of the elasticity of a demand (or supply) curve at some quantity Q (remember that how flat a curve is depends where on it you are) is the percentage change of quantity divided by the percentage change of price, calculated for a very small change. For those of you familiar with calculus, it is $dQ/dP \times P/Q$. The rest of you may think of it as the percentage change in quantity resulting from a one percent change in price, or as P/Q divided by the slope of the curve. Some economists include a minus sign in the definition of demand elasticity so as to make both supply and demand elasticity positive numbers (quantity demanded *decreases* when price increases, so the percentage change in quantity is negative); I will follow that convention.

So a highly elastic curve is one for which quantity changes a lot when price changes a little, whether the change is an increase or a decrease. A demand curve for which a price increase from $1.00 to $1.01 resulted in a decrease in quantity demanded from 100 widgets to 50 would be highly elastic; one for which a doubling of price caused only a one percent decrease in quantity demanded would be

Figure 10-4

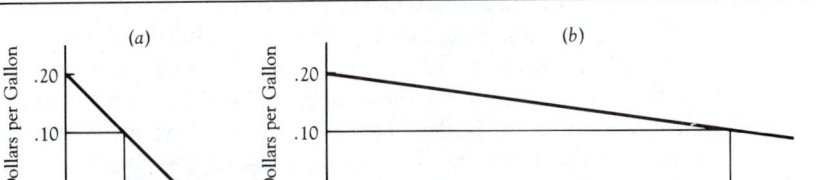

Two views of the same demand curve. Quantity is measured in gallons per day on Figure 10-4a and in gallons per week on Figure 10-4b. The same demand curve looks much flatter on Figure 10-4b than on Figure 10-4a.

highly inelastic. One way of remembering this is to think about how much quantity demanded (or supplied) "stretches" when price changes—if the curve is very elastic, it stretches a lot. A "unit elastic" curve is one for which a one percent change in price results in a one percent change in quantity—elasticity equals 1. A curve is called "elastic" if its elasticity is more than that and "inelastic" if it is less.

How flat a curve appears depends on how you draw it—changing the x axis from gallons per day to gallons per week flattens the curve considerably. This is not true of elasticity; if you change the units used to measure quantity by a factor of seven—as you do in going from gallons per day to gallons per week—both the quantity and the change in quantity are affected, but their ratio—the *percentage* change in quantity—remains the same. If a price drop of 1 percent causes you to increase your consumption of water by 10 percent, it does so whether consumption is measured in gallons per day or gallons per week. Elasticity is discussed further in the optional section of this chapter, where I show how to calculate it for various sorts of curves.

Using Elasticities

The concept of elasticity is useful in analyzing the behavior of a single-price monopoly. If elasticity is 1.0 at some point on a demand curve, that means that a 1 percent increase in price causes a 1 percent decrease in quantity. Since revenue is price times quantity, that means that where the demand curve is unit elastic, a small change in price or quantity has no effect on revenue—the effect on revenue of a higher (lower) price is just balanced by the effect of a lower (higher) quantity. Hence marginal revenue is zero. A similar argument shows that where elasticity is greater than 1.0 (the elastic region of the demand curve), marginal revenue is positive; where elasticity is less than 1.0, it is negative. The implications for a monopoly of the elasticity of its demand curve will be left as an exercise for the reader—in the form of problems at the end of this chapter.

PART 2 · DISCRIMINATORY PRICING

So far, we have assumed that the monopolist sells all of his output at the same price. To see why he might prefer not to do so, we start with the simple case of a monopolist with 1,000 customers, all identical. We can represent the total demand curve by the demand curve of a single individual, remembering that for the total, all quantities are 1,000 times larger. Figure 10-5 shows such a demand curve. The firm, following the prescription of Part 1, sells the customer 6 cookies per week at a price of $.70/cookie. At that quantity, marginal revenue equals marginal cost; for simplicity I have made marginal cost constant.

Looking at the figure, we—and the president of the cookie company—make the following observation. Additional cookies cost $.40 each to make. Up to a quantity of 12 cookies per week, additional cookies are worth more than $.40 each to the customer (remember that a demand curve for an individual is also his marginal value curve). It seems a pity to lose those additional sales—and the money that could be made on them.

Figure 10-5

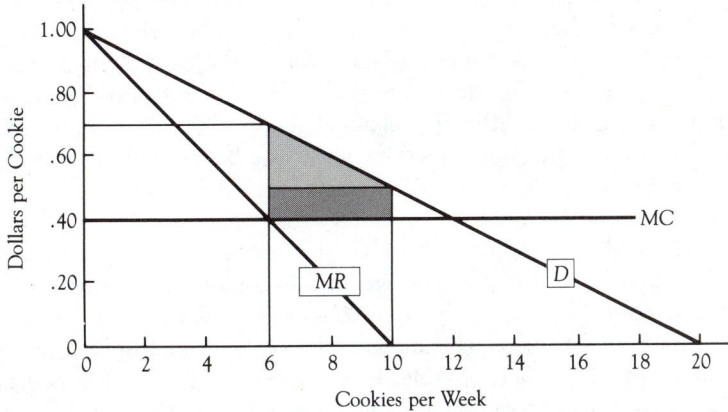

Discriminatory pricing in the cookie industry—first try. The profit-maximizing single price is $.70/cookie. The firm charges each customer that price for the first 6 cookies but sells additional cookies for $.50/cookie, increasing its profit by the darkly shaded area.

As long as the firm must sell all cookies at the same price, there is no solution to this dilemma; in order to sell the customer more cookies, the firm must lower its price, and that would decrease, not increase, its profit. The cookie president gets an idea.

As a special favor to our customers, and in order to celebrate the three-hundredth anniversary of the invention of the cookie, we are cutting our prices. For the first 6 cookies per week purchased by each customer, the old price of $.70 remains in effect, but additional cookies may be purchased for only $.50 each.

The result is shown on the figure. Each customer buys 10 cookies: 6 at $.70 each and 4 more at the reduced price of $.50. The customers are better off than before by the additional consumer surplus on the extra cookies (the lightly-shaded area); the cookie company is better off by the profit on the additional cookies (the darkly-shaded area). Since the additional 4 cookies cost $.40 each to produce and are sold for $.50, profit has increased by $.40/customer/week (4 cookies × $.10/cookie). With 1,000 customers, that comes to an additional $20,800/ year. The cookie president has reason to be proud of himself.

That is no reason to rest on his laurels. Figure 10-6a shows the more elaborate price schedule released for the next year. The first 6 cookies per week are still sold for $.70 each, but the rest are now on a sliding scale—$.65 for the seventh cookie, $.60 for the eighth, $.55 for the ninth, $.50 for the tenth, $.45 for the eleventh, and $.40 for the twelfth cookie. The increased profit (compared with the original single-price scheme) is again the darkly-shaded area on the figure; as you can see, it has grown.

At this point, the cookie president's daughter, who took this course last year and has just joined the firm, enters the discussion. "Why," she asks, "should our customers get so much out of our business? We are the ones doing all the work, yet they end up with a large surplus—the lightly-shaded area of Figure 10-6a. I don't mind losing the 6 little triangles—after all, they are entitled to a few crumbs—but surely we can do something about the big one." Figure 10-6b shows the pricing scheme she comes up with for the next year.

Figure 10-6b is very close to *perfect discriminatory pricing*—a set of prices which transfers all of the consumer surplus to the producer. Its imperfection—the "crumbs" referred to in the previous paragraph—comes from the problem of describing a discontinuous variable (3 cookies or 4 cookies but never 3.141432 cookies) with concepts, such as marginal value, more suited to continuous variables (water—or wine). It is possible, by setting the price schedule perfectly, to use such a set of prices to end up with all the surplus, crumbs included.

Figure 10-6

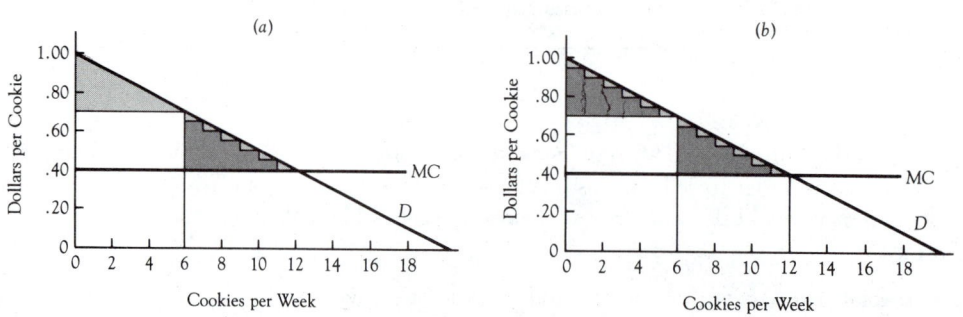

Discriminatory pricing in the cookie industry—improved versions. On Figure 10-6a, cookies are sold on a sliding scale starting at $.70/cookie. On Figure 10-6b, the price starts at $.95/cookie and is $.05 less for each additional cookie.

Two-Part Pricing

There is an easier way to do the same thing. The next year, the company announces a new and much simpler pricing policy. Cookies are no longer to be sold to the general public—only to members of the cookie club. Members can buy cookies at cost—$.40/cookie—and may buy as many as they wish at that price. The membership fee is $3.60/week. That, by a curious coincidence, is the total consumer surplus received by a consumer who is free to buy as many cookies as he wants at a price of $.40/cookie. This "two-part price" (membership plus per-cookie charge) first maximizes the sum of consumer-plus-producer surplus (by inducing the consumer to buy every cookie that is worth to him at least as much as it costs to produce) then transfers the entire consumer surplus to the producer.

Before I go on to more complicated cases, let us look a little more carefully at the result so far. The firm maximizes its profit by charging a price equal to marginal cost and an additional "membership fee" or "entrance price" equal to the entire consumer surplus. The effect of selling at MC is to maximize the sum of consumer and producer surplus; Figures 10-7a through 10-7c show that the sum for a price higher than MC (Figure 10-7a) or lower than MC (Figure 10-7c) is lower than for a price equal to MC (Figure 10-7b). Note that the colored area in Figure 10-7c is a *loss* due to selling below cost; it is larger than the increase in the lightly shaded area (membership fee) resulting from the lower price. The overall effect of reducing price below marginal cost is to reduce the firm's profits by the difference—the darkly shaded (and colored) triangle.

The conclusion can be simply stated. The effect of the entrance fee is to transfer the consumer surplus to the producer, giving him the sum of both surpluses—which he maximizes by setting price equal to marginal cost. If you think this sounds familiar, you are right. It is the same argument that was used at the end of Chapter 4 to show why movie theaters should sell popcorn at cost. For more on that subject, stay tuned. It is also the pattern of pricing often used by sellers of telephone services, electricity, and a variety of other goods and services.

Figure 10-7

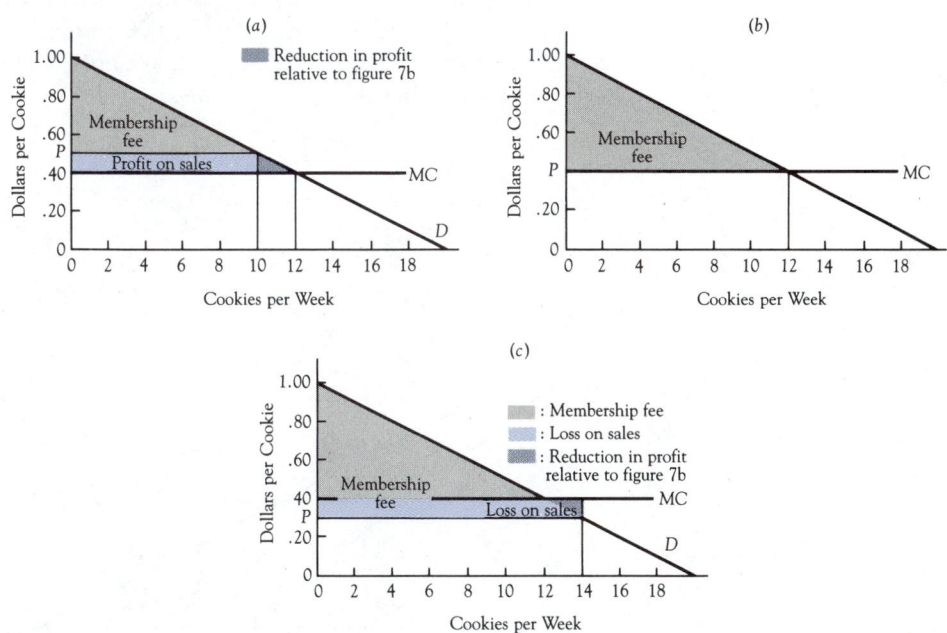

Two-part pricing—calculating the optimal price and membership fee. Figure 10-7b shows the pattern that maximizes the firm's profits; the price per cookie is equal to marginal cost, and the membership fee is equal to the consumer surplus at that price. Figures 10-7a and 10-7c show that a higher or lower price results in less profit.

So far, we have assumed that all customers are identical; under those circumstances, the seller may achieve something quite close to perfect discriminatory pricing, although there are some difficulties which we shall discuss later. I shall now complicate the problem by assuming that there are two different kinds of customer, each with his own demand curve. Type A customers have demand curve D_A on Figure 10-8, which is the same as the demand curve shown on Figures 10-5 through 10-7b; type B customers have demand curve D_B. There are 500 customers of each type.

The cookie president and his daughter have a problem. If they continue their previous two-part pricing system ($.40/cookie plus $3.60/week), customers of type A will continue to join the club and buy the cookies; but customers of type B, for whom the consumer surplus at $.40/cookie is only $2.40/week, will find that the cookie club costs more than it is worth and refuse to join. If, on the other hand, the membership fee is reduced to $2.40/week (the consumer surplus for type B consumers), the cookie company will "lose" $1.20/week that it could have gotten from the type A customers at the higher price.

The revenue from selling cookies just covers the cost of producing them (since the *per-cookie* price is just equal to cost), so whatever the membership price the firm decides to charge, profit will be equal to the revenue from selling membership in the cookie club. At the higher price, that is $3.60 from each of 500 type A customers; at the lower price, it is $2.40 from each of 1,000 customers (both type A and type B). Profit is maximized by charging the lower price—while regretting the consumer surplus left, unavoidably, in the hands of the type A customers.

Figure 10-8

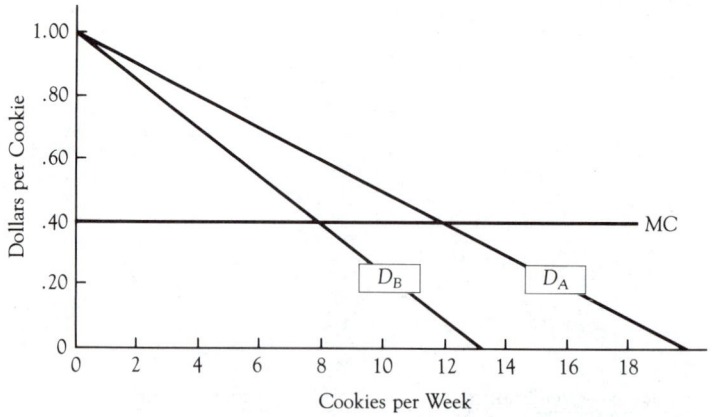

The case of nonidentical customers. D_A is the demand curve for type A customers; D_B is the demand curve for type B customers.

There are two ways in which the cookie president can try to improve on this result. One, which we will discuss later in this section, is to somehow figure out which customers are of which type and charge a higher membership fee to the type A customers—or rather, raise the membership fee to $3.60 and offer a "special low membership fee" to the type B customers. The other is to raise the per-cookie price.

The reason he might raise the price can be explained verbally as follows: "At any price, type A customers eat more cookies. Hence raising the price is an indirect way of charging them more than the type B customers. The total surplus is reduced, for the reasons shown in Figures 10-7a through 10-7c, but since I am no longer receiving the total surplus, that is no longer a conclusive argument against raising price. The increase in my share of the surplus may outweigh the reduction in the total."

The argument can be made rigorous with the use of graphs. I will limit myself to showing that there is a combination of higher price per cookie and lower membership fee which results in a higher profit in this particular case; this is shown on Figures 10-9a and 10-9b. Our previous solution (membership of $2.40) gave a profit of $2,400/week. The new solution is a price of $.50/cookie and a membership fee of $1.62. Revenue on memberships totals $1,620; profits on cookie sales ($.10/cookie times number sold) are $1/week on each type A customer and $.65/week on each type B customer. Total profit is $2,445/week—$45 more than with the previous solution.

This example demonstrates that in at least one case—the one I have just described—a monopoly can increase its profits by selling its product for more than marginal cost, even though it is in a position to charge a two-part price. The example does not demonstrate that it always, or even usually, pays a monopoly

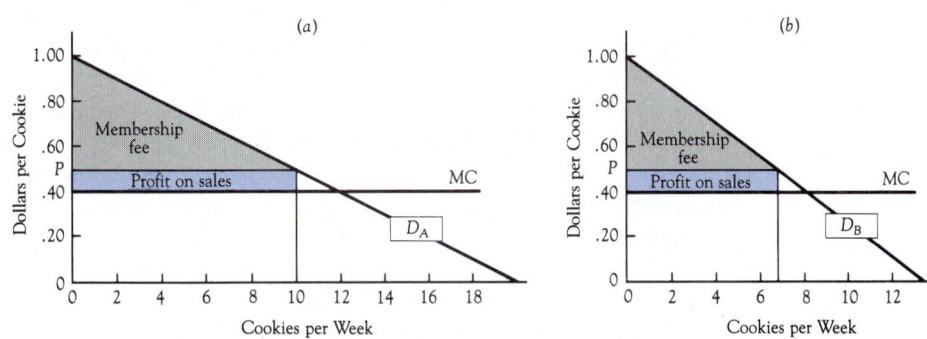

Figure 10-9

Price above marginal cost as a device for discriminatory pricing.   The firm is charging a price higher than MC as an indirect way of charging more to type A customers (Figure 10-9a) than to type B customers (Figure 10-9b). The resulting profit is higher than with $P = MC$.

to do so. Alfred Marshall, who put together modern economics about 100 years ago, warned in an appendix to his *Principles of Economics* of the danger of deducing general principles from specific examples; it is always possible that in choosing the particular example, you may, without realizing it, assume away one of the essential elements of the general problem. One should therefore, Marshall argued, base one's final conclusions not on examples but on proved theorems.

In this particular case, one can prove fairly easily what the circumstances are in which it pays the cookie company, or any monopoly whose customers have different demand curves, to raise its per-unit price above MC. Doing so in the case where the customers all have one or the other of two demand curves is one of the exercises at the end of this chapter; more ambitious students may wish to work out the general theorem for themselves.

We have finally found a possible solution to the popcorn puzzle. (I only kept you in suspense for eight chapters.) In my previous discussions, I assumed that the theater customers were all identical; if that assumption holds, so does the conclusion—that the theater should sell popcorn at marginal cost and make its profit on admission tickets. But if customers are not identical and if those who are willing to pay a high price for a ticket tend to be the same ones who buy a lot of popcorn, then the combination of cheap tickets and expensive popcorn may be an indirect way of charging a high admission price to those who are willing to pay it, without driving away those who are not.

Market Segmentation and Discriminatory Pricing

So far, most of the discriminatory pricing we have discussed was intended, in effect, to charge different prices to the same person for different units he consumed, thus taking advantage of the fact that the consumer has a higher marginal value for the first few units and will if necessary pay a higher price for them. This was done either by charging different prices for different units or by charging a two-part price—one price to buy anything and another for each unit bought. Only at the end of the previous section did we discuss attempts to discriminate between different customers, in the context of a monopolist who either knows exactly who has what demand curve and then prices accordingly or else uses a per-unit price higher than his marginal cost as an indirect way of discriminating between high-demand and low-demand customers.

An alternative approach for the cookie company—or any monopolist selling to a diverse group of customers—is to try to find some indirect way of determining which customers are willing to pay a higher or lower price and charging them accordingly. Discriminatory pricing of this sort is very common—so much so that some of us have gotten into the habit, whenever we see some pattern of behavior on the marketplace that does not seem to make sense, of trying to explain it in terms of price discrimination.

One familiar example is the policy of charging less for children than for adults at movie theaters. A child takes up just as much space as an adult—one seat— and may well impose higher costs, in noise and mess, on the theater and the other patrons. Why then do theaters often charge lower prices for children? The obvious answer is that children are (usually) poorer than adults; a price the theater can get adults to pay is likely to discourage children from coming—or parents with several children from bringing them.

A similar example is the "youth fare" which used to exist on airlines. It was a low fare for a standby ticket, offered only to those under a certain age. The lower fare reflected in part the advantage to the airlines of having standby passengers that could be used to fill empty seats, but that does not explain why it was only available to "youths." The obvious answer is that making the fare available to everyone might have resulted in a substantial number of customers "trading down"—buying a cheap standby ticket instead of an expensive regular one. Presumably the airlines thought that making it available to youths would result in their buying a cheap standby ticket on an airplane instead of taking the bus, driving, or hitching.

The same analysis that explains low fares for youths also explains special discounts for old people; they too are (often) poor. It also explains large price differences between "high-quality" and "low-quality" versions of the same product—hardcover books and paperbacks, first-class seats and tourist-class seats, and so on. The difference *may* merely reflect a difference in production cost—or it may be a device to extract as much consumer surplus as possible from those customers who are willing, if necessary, to pay a high price and are likely to prefer the "luxury" version of the product.

Another example of discriminatory pricing is the Book of the Month Club. A publisher who gives a special rate to a book club is getting customers most of whom would not otherwise have bought the book; since most of those who are willing to buy the book at the regular rate are not members of the club, he is only stealing a few sales from himself. Special "discount coupons" and "trading stamps" in grocery stores may be another example. Customers with a high value for their own time do not bother with such things—and pay a higher price.

A firm engaged in this sort of discriminatory pricing faces two practical problems. The first is the problem of distinguishing customers who will buy the good at a high price from those who will not. In the examples I have given, that is done indirectly—by age, taste, membership in a discount book club, or the like. A different way of solving this problem is said to be used by optometrists. When the customer asks how much a new pair of glasses will cost, the optometrist replies, "Forty dollars." If the customer does not flinch, he adds, "for the lenses." If the customer still does not flinch, he adds, "each." I use a similar technique in selling my services as a public speaker.

The second problem is preventing resale. It does no good to offer your product at a low price to poor customers if they then turn around and resell it to rich ones, thus depriving you of high price sales. This is why discriminatory pricing is so often observed with regard to goods that are "consumed on the premises"—transportation, movies, speeches, and the like. If GM sells cars at a high price to rich customers and at a low price to poor ones, Rockefeller can send his chauffeur to buy a car for him. There is little point in having the chauffeur take a trip for Rockefeller or see a movie for him.

The problem of controlling resale also exists with the form of discriminatory pricing discussed earlier in the context of identical customers—discriminating between what the customer is willing to pay for his first cookie and what he is willing to pay for his tenth. The problem occurs when a cookie club member buys 48 cookies per week, eats 12, and sells 36 to friends who have not paid for membership in the cookie club. That is why two-part (or more generally multipart) pricing is more practical with electricity or health spa services than with cookies.

The ability of a firm to engage in successful discriminatory pricing also depends on its being a price searcher—having some degree of what is sometimes called "monopoly power." In a market with many firms producing virtually identical products, price discrimination is impractical; if one firm tries to sell the product at an especially high price to rich customers (or customers who very much want the product), another firm will find it in its interest to lure those customers away with a lower price. Airlines do not wish to have their own customers trade down to a cheaper ticket—but Delta has no objection to getting a customer to give up a first-class ticket on Pan Am in order to buy a tourist ticket on Delta.

All of the cases I have described involve some element of monopoly. Youth fares existed at a time when airline fares were controlled by the Civil Aeronautics Board (CAB), a regulatory agency which provided government enforcement for a private cartel, keeping rates up and new firms out; they have since disappeared along with airline regulation. Copyright laws (and the economics of publishing) give each book publisher a monopoly—not of books, or even of a particular type of book, but at least of a particular book. The result is that publishers are price searchers; each knows that some customers are willing, if necessary, to pay a high price, while others will only buy the book if they can get it at a low price. Movie theaters have an element of monopoly, at least in those areas where there are few enough that a customer is rarely in a position to choose among several theaters showing the same film, all conveniently close.

This brings me to the question of why monopolies exist—which is the subject of the next part of the chapter.

PART 3 · WHY MONOPOLIES EXIST

Why do monopolies exist? Under what circumstances will there be only one firm in an industry? Why, if revenue is greater than cost, do not other firms choose to start producing the same product?

One answer may be that if they do, the monopolist will call the police. The original meaning of monopoly is a government grant of the exclusive right to produce something. Typically such monopolies were either sold by the government as a way of raising money or given to people that the government liked, such as the King's mistresses (or their relatives). Monopolies of this sort are still common. One obvious example is the Post Office—a monopoly which is not only protected by the government (the "private express statutes" make competition illegal) but also run and subsidized by it.

A second possibility is a "natural monopoly." This occurs when the shape of the firm's cost curve is such that a firm large enough to produce the total output of the industry can do so at a lower cost than could several smaller firms. Such a case is shown in Figure 10-10a. A firm producing q_1 at price P has positive profits (price is greater than average cost), but a firm producing $q_2 = q_1/2$ at the same price does not. If one large firm is formed and sells at P, smaller firms will not find it worth their while to enter the market.

Another case very similar to the natural monopoly is the "natural cartel." A cartel is a group of firms acting together as if they were a single monopoly. Cartels are most likely to occur in industries where *economies of scale* (advantages that allow large firms to produce more cheaply than small ones) are almost but not quite large enough to allow one giant firm to produce more cheaply than several somewhat smaller ones; such an industry is likely to consist of a few large firms. Figure 10-10b shows the sort of cost curves that might lead to a cartel; what is important is not simply the shape of the cost curves but their relation to the demand curve—the fact that minimum average cost occurs at a quantity which is a large fraction of total quantity demanded at price equal to minimum average cost. This guarantees that any firm producing less than (in this example) about one third of the industry's total production will have higher average costs than larger firms, and so be at a competitive disadvantage.

As long as the firms in a cartel cooperate with each other, the situation is essentially the same as with a natural monopoly. Some of the difficulties in maintaining such cooperation are discussed in the optional section of this chapter. One common solution is a government-enforced cartel, such as the U.S. airline industry prior to deregulation or the U.S. rail industry from the end of the nineteenth century to the present. Where government enforcement is available to keep prices up and new firms out, a cartel is possible even without the conditions

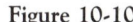

Figure 10-10

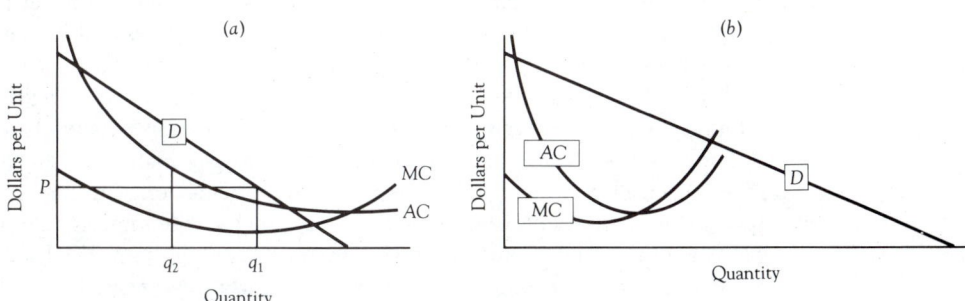

Cost curves for a natural monopoly (*a*) or natural cartel (*b*).   Figure 10-10*a* shows cost curves for which a large firm producing the entire amount demanded has a cost advantage over smaller firms. Figure 10-10*b* shows the case where a firm large enough to produce a large fraction of total industry output has lower costs than smaller firms.

for a "natural cartel." An example is the trucking industry, which would be highly competitive save for the intervention of the Interstate Commerce Commission (ICC).

Most people who think about "natural monopolies" imagine them as gigantic firms such as Bell Telephone or General Motors. It is widely believed that such firms, by taking advantage of mass production techniques, can produce more cheaply than any smaller firm; it has often been argued that, for this reason, free competition naturally leads to monopoly. As George Orwell put it, "The trouble with competitions is that somebody wins them."

This does not seem to be a correct description of the real world, at least at present. While there are advantages to mass production, in most industries a firm need not produce the entire world's output in order to take advantage of them. The steel industry, for example, produces in very large plants, but the largest firm (U.S. Steel) consists not of one gigantic steel mill but of over 100 large ones. A firm one percent of its size can operate one steel mill and take advantage of the same scale economies. The president of such a firm is closer to the worker pouring the steel by several layers of administration than is the president of U.S. Steel, which may be one reason that U.S. Steel has not, in recent decades, been one of the more successful firms in the industry.

Bell Telephone has, until recently, been a government-enforced monopoly—it was illegal for another firm to try to compete by offering local phone service in an area served by Bell, or for Bell to compete in an area served by General Telephone or one of the smaller companies. General Motors is not a monopoly even within the U.S., and such limited monopoly power as it does have in the U.S. market is largely a result of tariffs that restrict the ability of foreign auto producers to compete with it.

I am a more typical example of a natural monopoly than is General Motors. As a public speaker, I produce a product which is, I believe, significantly different from that produced by anyone else; if you want a certain sort of talk on certain sorts of subjects, you must buy it from me. The result is that I am a price searcher. Some groups are willing to pay a high price for my services, some a lower price, some would like me to speak but can offer nothing but expenses and dinner. If I sell my speeches at a fixed price, I must either price some of the customers out of the market (even though I might enjoy speaking to them, and so be willing to do so for free—at some levels of output, my marginal cost is negative) or else accept low fees from some groups that are willing to pay high ones. In fact, I engage in a considerable amount of discriminatory pricing, offering free or low-cost speeches to "especially worthy" (i.e., poor) groups. The same is true of my services as a writer; I have one outlet which pays a very high rate, but I recently wrote a column on something that interested me for a new magazine that paid nothing.

My monopoly over the production of certain kinds of speeches and articles is a far more common sort of natural monopoly than that of Bell or GM; it is due not to the huge scale of production but to the specialized nature of the product. Examples of similar monopolies would be the only grocery store in a small town or your favorite thriller writer. It is not only a more common sort of monopoly, it is also one much more important to those of you who expect to be in business. It is very unlikely that you will ever be the head of General Motors or U.S. Steel, and if you are, you may find that the monopoly power of those firms is very limited. It is much more likely that you will find yourself selling a specialized product in a particular geographical area, and so functioning as a price searcher facing a downward-sloped demand curve. It is even more likely that some of the firms you deal with will be in such a position. If so, the analysis of this chapter should help you understand why they sell their product in the way they do.

Artificial Monopoly

There is one more sort of monopoly worth discussing—the artificial monopoly. An *artificial monopoly* is a very large firm which has no advantage in production efficiency over smaller firms but nonetheless manages to drive all of its competitors out of business, remaining the sole producer in the industry. A typical example is the Standard Oil Trust—not the real Standard Oil Trust as it actually existed in the late nineteenth and early twentieth centuries but the Standard Oil Trust as it appears in many high school history books. In the optional section, I discuss that case along with the general problem of maintaining a monopoly position without either a natural monopoly or a government grant of monopoly power. My conclusion there is that the artificial monopoly is largely or entirely a work of fiction; it exists in history books and antitrust law but is and always has been rare or nonexistent in the real world, possibly because most of the tactics which it is supposed to use to maintain its monopoly position do not work.

Monopoly Profit

One important difference between an industry consisting of many firms and an industry consisting of one was mentioned earlier; in the former case, the equilibrium price is such as to make (economic) profit zero, since positive profits attract new firms and their output drives down the price. This is not the case for a monopoly industry. If it is a government-granted monopoly, new firms are forbidden by law; if it is a natural monopoly, there is only room for one firm.

The result is monopoly profit. If the government simply sells the right to be a monopoly to the highest bidder, the price should equal the full monopoly profit that the winner expects to make; if he had bid less, someone else would have outbid him. In this case, the monopoly firm makes no net profit, since its costs include what it paid to become a monopoly. What would have been monopoly profit all goes to the government. If instead of selling the monopoly privilege, the government gives it away, then the firm receives the monopoly profit—although "giving away" may really mean selling for something other than money paid to the government, whether the attentions of the King's mistress (old style) or discreet contributions to the re-election fund of the incumbent president (new style).

In the case of a natural monopoly, the situation is more complicated. Since the monopoly is not created by the government, there is no reason to expect the government to control who is the monopolist. Once a firm has the monopoly, it may be able to earn substantial monopoly profits without attracting competitors. A competitor would have to duplicate the initial firm's productive facilities, making the industry's capacity twice what it could sell at the price the existing monopoly was charging; the resulting price war might well hurt both firms, a possibility that may persuade the second firm not to try to enter the market.

This raises the question of how the first firm got its monopoly position in the first place. That question is discussed in Chapter 15, where it is shown that under at least some circumstances, the zero profit condition does apply to natural monopolies, with the monopoly profit being competed away in the process of obtaining it.

Monopsony

I began this chapter by dropping the assumption that individuals can sell *and buy* as much as they like without affecting the price. So far, I have discussed monopolies—individuals and firms which are the only sellers of some good or service. An individual or firm which is the only *buyer* of a good or service is called a *monopsony*. Just as a monopoly must consider how much its revenue from selling widgets increases when it sells one more widget, so a monopsony must consider how much its expenditure for widgets increases when it buys one more widget. A monopoly's marginal revenue is less than the price it sells its goods for, because in order to sell more, it must lower its price. A monopsony's "marginal expenditure" is *more* than the price it pays for each widget, because by buying more, it bids up the price—not only for the additional widget but for all other widgets it buys. In calculating its marginal cost, a monopsony must recognize that the cost of the additional inputs needed for additional production is not their price but the marginal expenditure they cost it. In maximizing its profit, a firm will generally use less of the input of which it has a monopsony (in order to hold down its price) and more of other inputs than if it were a price taker.

PART 4 · MONOPOLISTIC COMPETITION

In Chapter 9, we analyzed the behavior of a competitive industry with open entry; each individual firm was a price taker, and firms were free to enter or leave the industry. We concluded that each firm, if it produced at all, would produce a quantity for which marginal cost was equal to price and that firms would enter or leave the industry until economic profit was zero. We thus deduced the two conditions for competitive equilibrium—price equals marginal cost and profit equals zero. If profit is zero, then price is equal to average cost; so in competitive equilibrium, $P = MC = AC$. In Chapter 9, we also analyzed the situation of a competitive industry with closed entry. Since the firms were still price takers, the first condition, $P = MC$, still held; the zero profit condition did not.

So far in this chapter, we have been analyzing monopolies. A monopoly is a price searcher, not a price taker, and additional firms cannot enter its "industry," so neither condition can be expected to hold. We will now consider the interesting and important case of an industry made up of price-seeking firms but with open entry. The condition $P = MC$ does not hold, but the zero-profit condition does. The situation is called "monopolistic competition."

Figure 10-11 shows part of a long street with barbershops distributed along it. The customers of the barbershops live along the same street; they are evenly distributed with a density of 100 customers per block. Since all of the barbers are equally skilled (at both hair cutting and conversation), there are only two considerations determining which barbershop a customer goes to: how much it costs and how far it is from his home. The customers are all identical, all of them get their hair cut once a month, and all regard walking an extra block to a barbershop and back again as equivalent to $1; they are indifferent between going to a barber N blocks away and paying him a price P or going to a barber $N + 1$ blocks away and paying him $P - \$1$.

Consider the situation from the standpoint of barbershop B. His nearest competitors, A and C, both charge the same price for a haircut—$8. A is located 8 blocks west of B; C is located 8 blocks east of him. How does B decide what price to charge?

Figure 10-11

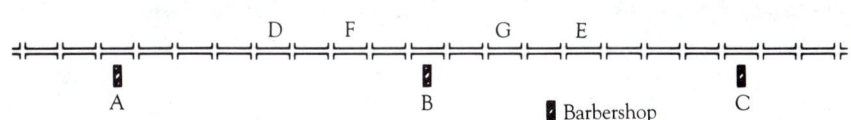

The street of barbers.   There is 1 barbershop every 8 blocks.

Suppose he also charges $8. In that case, the only difference among the barbershops, so far as the customers are concerned, is how close they are; each customer goes to whichever one is closer. Anyone living west of point D will go to barbershop A, anyone between D and E will go to B, and anyone east of E will go to C. From D to E is 8 blocks, and there are 100 customers living on each block, so barbershop B has 800 customers—and sells 800 haircuts a month.

Suppose barber B decides instead to charge a higher price—$12. A customer at point F is 2 blocks from B and 6 from A. Since a walk of a block is equivalent to him to a $1 price difference, the two barbershops are equally attractive to him; he can either walk 6 blocks and pay $8 or walk 2 blocks and pay $12. For any customer between F and B, B is the more attractive option; the shorter walk more than balances the higher price. The same is true for any customer between B and G. There are 4 blocks between F and G, so at the higher price, B has 400 customers.

Similar calculations can be done for any price between $16 (no customers) and zero; every time B raises his price by a dollar he loses 50 customers to A and

50 to C. Figure 10-12a shows the relation between the price B charges and the number of customers he has in the form of a demand curve. The figure also shows the corresponding marginal revenue curve and the barbershop's marginal cost curve; marginal cost is assumed constant at $4/haircut. Average cost is not yet relevant; it will be shown later.

Looking at Figure 10-12a and applying what we learned in Part 1 of this chapter, we conclude that the barber should produce that quantity for which marginal revenue equals marginal cost; he should provide 600 haircuts a month at a price of $10 each.

So far as barber B is concerned, we seem to have finished our analysis. We know that he maximizes his profit by charging $10/haircut. The only remaining question is whether, at that price, he more than covers his total cost; to answer that, we would have to know his average cost curve. If he covers total cost, he should stay in business and charge $10; if not, he should go out of business.

We are not done. So far, we have simply assumed that A and C charge $8/haircut. But they too wish to maximize their profits; they too can calculate their marginal revenue curves, intersect them with marginal cost, and pick price and quantity accordingly. If we assume that barbershops are spaced evenly along the street and that they all started out charging the same price, then A and C started in the same situation as B—and their calculations imply the same conclusion. They too raise their price to $10—and so does every other barbershop.

Figure 10-12

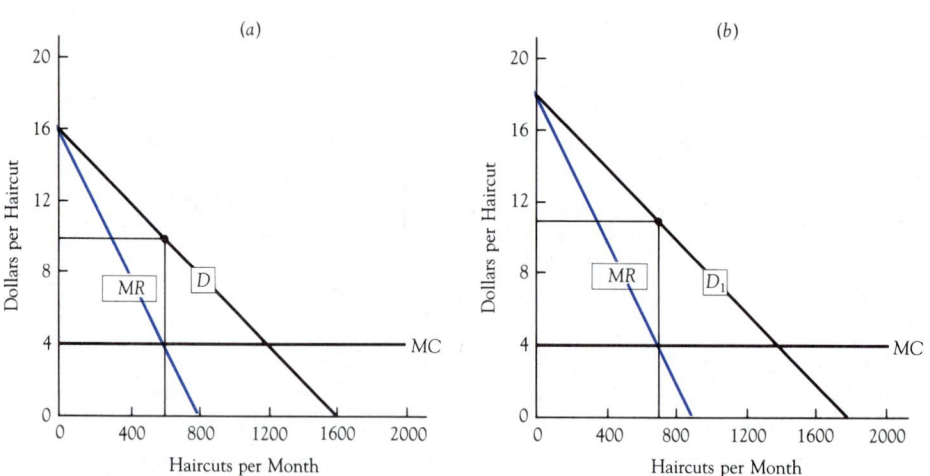

How to calculate the profit-maximizing price for a haircut.   Figure 10-12a shows the case where all other barbers charge $10; Figure 10-12b shows the case where they charge $11. In each case, we calculate the profit-maximizing price for one barber, holding constant the price charged by all other barbers.

We are still not done. Figure 10-12a was drawn on the assumption that shops A and C were charging $8; when they raise their prices, the demand curve faced by B shifts. Figure 10-12b shows the result; you should go over the discussion that led to Figure 10-12a in order to convince yourself that D_1 is the demand curve faced by B when A and C charge $10.

From Figure 10-12b, we conclude that if A and C are charging $10, B should charge neither $8 nor $10 but $11; at that price, he will sell 700 haircuts per month. But here again, we are not finished; we must also recalculate what A and C (and everyone else) should do. Having done so, and concluded that each of them should charge $11, we have again changed the conditions on which our figure was based; the demand curve faced by B shifts yet again when the other barbershops, having duplicated B's calculations, also raise their price from $10 to $11.

We have been here before; the street of barbers is beginning to look very much like the egg market of Chapter 7. Once again we are trying, unsuccessfully, to find the equilibrium of an interdependent system by changing one thing at a time. Every time we get the jelly nailed solidly to one part of the wall, we find that it has oozed away somewhere else.

Here, as there, we solve the problem by figuring out what the situation must look like when the equilibrium is finally reached. The analysis is more complicated than simply finding the intersection of a supply curve and a demand curve, so I shall start by sketching out the sequence of steps by which we find the equilibrium.

The Solution—A Verbal Sketch

The initial situation is a symmetrical one so far as the different barbershops are concerned, so we will assume that the solution is symmetrical as well—that in equilibrium, the barbershops are evenly spaced along the street and all charge the same price. This is an assumption about the solution, not about the problem. Individual barbers are free to locate wherever and charge whatever they like; we are simply looking for a solution in which they find it in their interest to be distributed evenly along the street and to each charge the same price. If we fail to find any such solution, we might have to drop the assumption. Even if we do find a symmetrical solution, there might still exist one or more asymmetrical solutions as well.

If, in equilibrium, the barbershops are evenly spaced and all charge the same price, then we can describe the equilibrium with two numbers—d, the distance between barbershops, and P, the price they all charge. Our problem is to find values of d and P which satisfy two requirements. The first is that if all the barbers charge a price P, no individual barber would be better off charging some other price. The second is that it does not pay anyone to start a new barbershop, or any old barbershop to go out of business. To meet the first condition, we use the profit-maximizing condition for a price searcher—marginal cost equals marginal revenue. To meet the second, we use the zero profit condition for an industry with open entry.

We start by finding, for any value of d, the equilibrium P. To do so, we first calculate the demand curve (and the corresponding marginal revenue curve) faced by barber B, given that the adjacent barbers charge a price P and are located a distance d away. We know that he will maximize his profit by charging P_b, the price corresponding to the quantity for which his marginal cost equals his marginal revenue. What that is will depend on the values of P and d. We then calculate, given d, what P must be such that $P_b = P$. In other words, we find a price such that if all the other barbers are charging that price, it pays barber B to charge it—and similarly for all other barbers. We call this price P^*. What it is will depend on d.

The second step is to find d. We do so by calculating, for each possible value of d, the corresponding P^*. From d and P^* plus the firm's marginal and average cost curves, we calculate the firm's profit. If it is positive, more firms will enter the industry. An increase in the number of barbershops will push them all closer together, reducing d. If profit is negative, firms will leave the industry, increasing d. So we look for the value of d that makes profit zero.

We now know what we are to do; it is time to do it. To deduce the solution, I will go through the argument once, briefly, using a trial and error approach, and then again, using algebra and geometry.

First Pass: Trial and Error

We start by assuming the density of barbershops shown on Figure 10-11; $d = 8$ blocks. For the first step in the argument, we hold the number and location of barbershops fixed; the only thing we are varying is the price. We assume that in equilibrium, all barbers charge the same price.

Step 1: Assume $d = 8$, Solve for P^*. If all barbers charge the same price, then each barber has the same number of customers; B, for example, has the 800 customers located between D and E. If when B is maximizing his profit, he has 800 customers, that must mean that at a quantity of 800, his marginal revenue is equal to his marginal cost. So in equilibrium, B's marginal revenue curve must run through point M on Figure 10-13: MR = MC = \$4/haircut; Q = 800 haircuts/month.

To find the marginal revenue curve, we need more than one point. We know from the relation between a straight line demand curve and the corresponding marginal revenue curve, which you were supposed to memorize earlier in this chapter, that the slope of the marginal revenue curve is just twice the slope of the demand curve. So if we can find the slope of the demand curve in equilibrium, we will know the slope of the marginal revenue curve. If we know the slope of the marginal revenue curve and one point on it (M), we can draw the curve; once we have drawn the marginal revenue curve, we can draw the corresponding demand curve. Once we know the demand curve (and quantity—800 in equilibrium), we also know the price.

Finding the slope of the demand curve is easy. As we saw earlier, every time B cuts his price by \$1, the region in which customers find him more attractive than A or C grows by half a block in each direction, so the number of customers

Figure 10-13

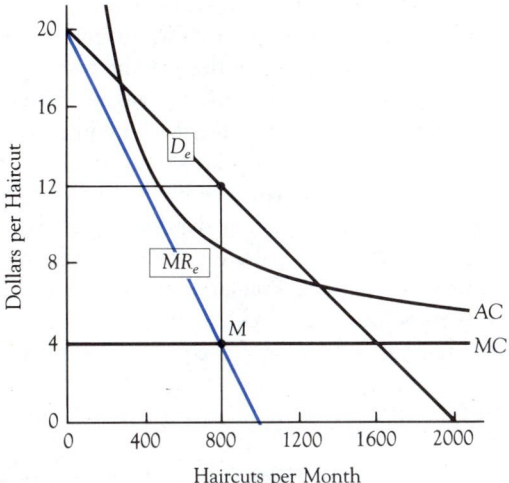

Haircuts per Month

Finding the equilibrium price if $d=8$. We pick an arbitrary density of barbershops and find the price such that, if all barbers charge that price, each is maximizing his profit. The solution, for 1 barbershop every 8 blocks, is a price of $12/haircut.

grows by 100; every \$.01 reduction in price increases quantity by 1 haircut per month. That means that the slope of the demand curve is $-\$1.00/(100$ haircuts per month). So the slope of the marginal revenue curve is $-\$2.00/(100$ haircuts per month). Drawing a curve with that slope through point M gives us MR_e on Figure 10-13; D_e is the corresponding demand curve. A quantity of 800 on D_e corresponds to a price of \$12/haircut. You should be able to check for yourself that D_e is the demand curve which B faces if A and C each charge \$12 for a haircut. We have found a consistent solution. If $d = 8$ blocks, $P^* = \$12$.

In finding the solution, we have also validated one of our assumptions—that there exists an equilibrium in which all barbers charge the same price. Given that A and C are each charging \$12, we have just demonstrated that B will do so as well; that is the profit-maximizing price on Figure 10-13. We do not know whether this is the only equilibrium; there might be others in which different barbers charge a variety of different prices. We do know that if each barber charges \$12, we have a stable equilibrium—stable in the sense that if one barber tried to charge a different price, his profits would go down, giving him an incentive to move his price back to \$12.

Step 2: Find the Equilibrium Value of d. So far, we have taken the number and location of the barbershops as given; all we have varied is the price. The solution shown on Figure 10-13 is thus very much like the solution of the competitive industry with closed entry in Chapter 9; each firm maximizes its profit, but the number of firms in the industry is fixed. Our next step is to allow the number of firms, as well as the price they charge, to vary, just as we did in analyzing a competitive industry with open entry.

Looking again at Figure 10-13, you will notice that it contains one curve that was not on the previous figure—average cost. With price equal to $12/haircut and quantity equal to 800 haircuts per month, average cost is only $8.50/haircut. Since price is above average cost, the firms are making positive profits; it pays additional firms to enter the industry. The number of barbershops increases. If we assume, somewhat unrealistically, that as new shops are built, the existing shops can adjust their locations so as to remain evenly distributed along the street, we can redo our calculations for a new, denser distribution of barbershops; if profits are still positive, we can let the distribution become still more dense and try again. Repeating our calculations for smaller values of d, we eventually find that when enough new barbershops have been built so there is one shop every 6 blocks, the price of a haircut is $10—and is equal to the average cost.

Second Pass: Algebra and Geometry

Let P be the price of a haircut in dollars, d the distance between adjacent barbershops in blocks, and Q the quantity of haircuts sold by barber B in hundreds of haircuts per month. Figure 10-14 shows the situation for an arbitrary P and d; $MC = 4$. Note that P is the price charged by all of the *other* barbers, hence the price that determines the demand curve faced by barber B; we are trying to find a value of P such that it will *also* be the price P_b that barber B finds it in his interest to charge.

Figure 10-14

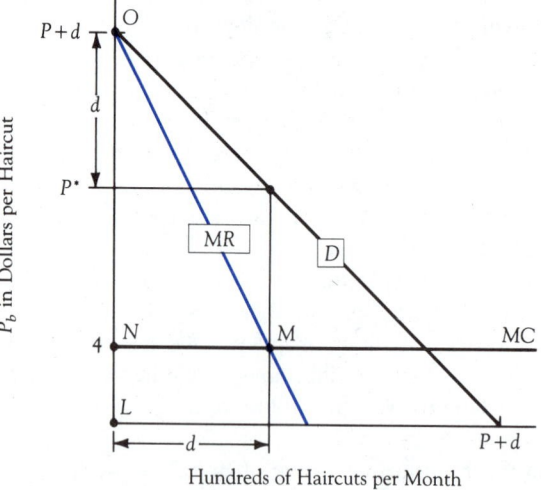

Finding the equilibrium price for an arbitrary value of d.

Step 1: Solve for P* as a Function of d. D intersects the vertical axis at a price $P_b = d + P$; if B charged that price, nobody would come—quantity demanded would be zero. D intersects the horizontal axis at $Q = d + P$; if B charged nothing, that is how many haircuts he would sell. As P_b increases, Q decreases at a rate of (100 haircuts/month) for every \$1/haircut change in price; D is a straight line with a slope of -1. So for any given values of d and P, we can draw the demand curve D and the marginal revenue curve MR.

We assume that in equilibrium, all barbershops charge the same price. If so, they divide the customers evenly among themselves; since there are $d \times 100$ customers per barbershop (d blocks per barbershop, 100 customers per block) and we are measuring Q in hundreds of haircuts per month, in equilibrium, $Q = d$, as shown on the figure. Since the slope of D is -1 and the slope of MR is -2 (see the figure or our previous discussion of the slopes), the distance from N to O must be twice the distance from N to M—which is d. So

$$NO = 2d$$

as shown. But

$$P + d = LO = LN + NO = 4 + 2d.$$

The value of P for which this is true is what we earlier called P^*, so

$$P^* = 4 + d.$$

Step 2: Solve for d. We now know, for any value of d, the equilibrium price P^*. Since in equilibrium, $Q = d$, we know that for any separation d, the equilibrium price (in dollars) equals the equilibrium quantity (in hundreds of haircuts per month) plus 4; $P^* = Q + 4$. Figure 10-15a shows that relation and the firm's average cost curve (from Figure 10-13). Their intersection—point E on Figure 10-15a—is the price/quantity pair which is consistent with both profit maximization by individual firms choosing their price *and* the zero profit condition (price equals average cost). The price of a haircut is \$10, and each barbershop gives 600 haircuts per month, so d is 6 blocks. The outcome is shown on Figure 10-15b, which corresponds to Figure 10-14 (plus the average cost curve), with P and d at their equilibrium values.

Instead of doing the last step graphically, we could have done it algebraically. One can calculate from the average cost curve on Figure 10-14 that the total cost curve is

$$TC = FC + Q \times MC = 36 + 4Q,$$

where TC is total cost in hundreds of dollars. Solving the zero profit condition:

$$TR = TC$$

gives us, for price equal to P^*,

$$TR = P^{*} \times Q = (Q + 4) \times Q = TC = 36 + 4Q$$

$$Q^{2} = 36$$

$$Q = 6; P^{*} = Q + 4 = 10,$$

which is the same answer that we got from Figure 10-15a.

We are now done. For any density of shops along the street of barbers, we have found the price that will be charged, given that each barbershop is maximizing its profit and all are charging the same price. Using that result, we have found the density at which economic profit is zero—barbershops exactly cover their costs. Under those conditions, the number of shops is in equilibrium; it does not pay anyone to start another one, and it does not pay existing shops to close down. We have solved the problem.

Figure 10-15

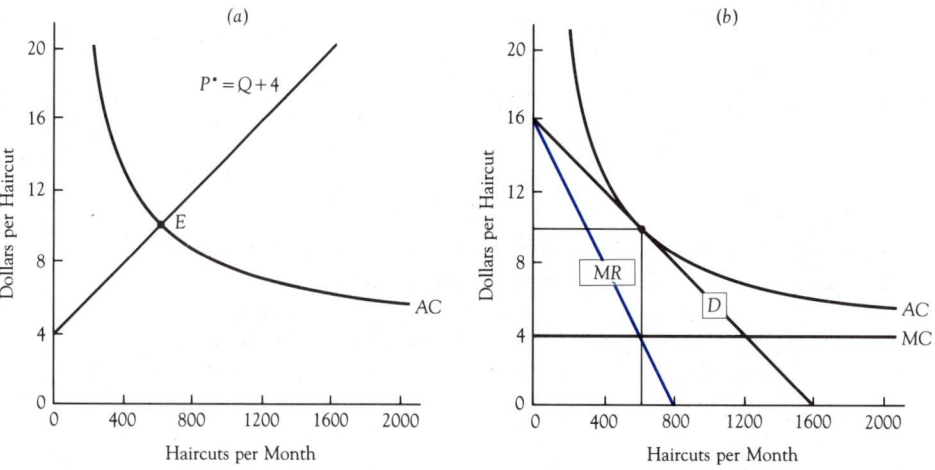

The solution—the equilibrium price of haircuts and density of barbershops. On Figure 10-15a, price equals average cost at point E, so that is the number of haircuts per month per barber for which profit equals zero. Figure 10-15b shows the corresponding demand curve, marginal revenue curve, and calculation of price.

Metastable Equilibrium?

There is one minor flaw in our solution to the barbershop problem. We have assumed throughout that barbershops space themselves evenly along the block. In the problem as given, there is no reason for them to do so; as you can check for yourself, barbershop B can move left or right along the street without changing the demand curve it faces. As long as it does not move past either A or C, it gains as many customers from the competitor it moves towards as it loses to the competitor it moves away from.

From B's standpoint, the situation is what I described in Chapter 7 as a *metastable equilibrium*. B has no reason to move and no reason not to; his situation is the same either way. If he does move, that will affect A and C; their responses will have further effects for the barbershops further along the street in both directions. If B decides to sit where we have put him—and everyone else does the same—we have a solution; if he does not, it is unclear just what will happen.

This ambiguity is due not to a mistake in our solution but to the particular way I set up the problem. It could be eliminated by adding an additional element—the customers' demand curve for haircuts. We have so far let the price charged affect which barber the customer goes to but not how often he has his hair cut; we have implicitly assumed that the demand curve for haircuts is perfectly inelastic.

When the barbershop is located exactly halfway between the other two shops, as shown in Figure 10-16a, the average distance from customer to barbershop is 3 blocks—one fourth the distance between A and C. If the barbershop moves away from the halfway point, the average distance increases; when shop B has moved all the way over to a point next to shop A, as shown in Figure 10-16b, the average distance from its customers is 6 blocks. As the average distance increases, so, for any price, does the average cost of a haircut to the customer—where the cost includes the walk as well as the price. The result, if the demand curve for haircuts is not perfectly inelastic, is to decrease quantity demanded. The firm will find that for any price it chooses to charge, it maximizes the number of haircuts it can sell by locating itself at the halfway point between the barbershops on either side of it. By adding a demand curve for haircuts, we have eliminated the one remaining flaw in our solution.

We have also changed the problem. If the demand curve faced by a single barbershop depends not only on the location and prices of its competitors but also on the distance its customers must walk, we must redraw Figures 10-12a

Figure 10-16

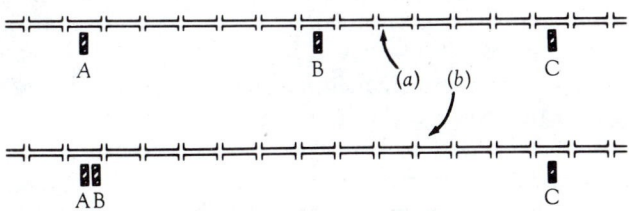

Possible arrangements of barbershops. With the perfectly inelastic demand for haircuts initially assumed, barbershop B does just as well in the position shown by Figure 10-16b as in the position shown by Figure 10-16a. If the demand curve is slightly inelastic, the barbershop does worse in Figure 10-16b, because the average distance its clients must walk is longer than in Figure 10-16a.

through 10-15*b*. That would make the problem considerably more complicated without altering its essential logic—which is why I did not do it that way in the first place. You may, if you wish, think of Figure 10-14 as showing an almost exact solution for customers whose demand curves are almost, but not quite, perfectly inelastic. Any elasticity in the demand curve, however slight, gives the barbershops an incentive to spread themselves evenly. If the elasticity is very small, it will produce only a tiny effect on the demand curve faced by the barbershop (D_e), so the solution shown in the figure will be almost, although not precisely, correct.

Are We Really Just Talking About Barbershops?

So far, we have discussed only one example of monopolistic competition—barbershops along a street. The same analysis applies to many other goods and services for which the geographic location of seller and buyer is important—goods and services that must be transported from the producer to the consumer and those, such as haircuts or movies, for which the consumer must be transported to the producer.

Any such industry is a case of monopolistic competition, provided that firms are free to enter and leave the industry and are sufficiently far apart so that each has, to a significant degree, a "captive market"—customers with regard to whom the firm has a competitive advantage over other firms. This may mean that the firm can deliver its wares to those customers at a lower cost than can its more distant competitors; or it may, as in the barbershop case, mean that it costs the customers less, in time or money, to go to one firm than to another. In such a situation, the firm finds that it is a price searcher—it can vary its price over a significant range, with higher prices reducing, but not entirely eliminating, the quantity it can sell.

Firms whose product is consumed on the premises have been mentioned before in this chapter. Because such firms are in a good position to prevent resale, they may also be in a good position to engage in discriminatory pricing. We could (but will not) examine the case of monopolistic competition with price discrimination; in doing so, we might produce a reasonably accurate description of movie theaters, lawyers and physicians in rural areas, private schools, and a number of other familiar enterprises.

There is another form of monopolistic competition which has nothing to do with geography or transport costs. Consider a market in which a number of firms produce similar, but not identical, products. An example might be the market for microcomputers. Any firm that wishes is free to enter, and many firms have done so. Their products, however, are not identical; some computers appeal more to people who have certain specific needs, certain tastes for computing "style," experience with particular computers or computer languages, or existing software that will only run on particular computers. Hence different microcomputers are not perfect substitutes for each other. As the price of one computer goes up, those customers who are least "locked into" that particular brand shift to something else, so quantity demanded falls. But over a considerable range of prices, the company can sell at least some computers to some customers—just as a barbershop can raise its price and still retain the customers who live next door to it.

If the manufacturers of all computers appear to be making positive profits, new firms will enter the industry; if existing firms appear to be making negative profits, some will exit the industry—just as with barbershops. If one type of computer appears to be making large positive profits, other manufacturers will introduce similar designs—just as high profits on one part of the street of barbers, due to an unusually high ratio of customers to barbershops on that part of the street, would give barbershops elsewhere on the street an incentive to move closer.

In early 1985, when I was doing the final revision of this chapter, Jack Tramiel, president of Atari, announced a new computer. The press dubbed it the "Jackintosh" because of its similarity to Apple's highly successful Macintosh computer. By the time you read this, you will probably know whether or not Tramiel put his new barbershop in the right place.

The situation of the computer manufacturers is very similar to the situation of the barbershops—and both can be analyzed as cases of monopolistic competition. The same is true for other industries where the products of one firm are close but not perfect substitutes for the products of another, where some customers prefer one "style" and some another, where manufacturers are free to alter the style of their product in response to profitable opportunities, and where firms are free to enter or leave the industry.

PART 5 · OTHER FORMS OF PRICE SEARCHING: THE HARD PROBLEMS

A market can have any number of buyers and any number of sellers. Most of my analysis so far has concentrated on the case of many buyers and many sellers; in this chapter, I have considered the cases of one seller and many buyers (monopoly) and one buyer and many sellers (monopsony). These are the easy cases, the ones for which economics gives relatively simple and straightforward solutions. The hard problems are the cases of oligopoly (several sellers and many buyers); oligopsony (several buyers and many sellers); bilateral monopoly (one buyer, one seller); bilateral oligopoly (several sellers, several buyers); one seller, several buyers (no name I know of); and one buyer, several sellers (ditto).

What all of these hard cases have in common is strategic behavior. In all of the analysis so far, except for the discussion of bilateral monopoly in Chapter 6, the individual or firm could decide what to do while taking what everyone else was doing as given. That is appropriate in a price taker's market; since my output is a negligible part of total output, it is not in the interest of any of my customers to say to me, "I want what you are selling at the price you are asking for it, but I will refuse to buy it, in order to force you to lower the price." If he tries that, I will sell it to someone else instead. It is also appropriate in the monopoly situation I have been discussing in this chapter, where there is one seller and many buyers—although selling my speeches, with one seller and a few buyers, approaches the case of bilateral monopoly.

But the assumption that we can ignore bargaining, strategic behavior, and the like is inappropriate in all of the hard cases. If there are several sellers and many buyers, everything a seller wants to know about the buyers' behavior is summed up in the demand curve; but a seller cannot use a supply curve to describe the behavior of the other sellers, since they do not have supply curves. Each has an incentive to try to persuade the others to keep their production down, in order that he can sell lots of output at a high price; each has an incentive to threaten that if the other producers expand their output, he will expand his. In the case of bilateral monopoly, the seller has an incentive to try to persuade the buyer to pay a high price by threatening not to sell at a low one, even if selling at the low price is better than not selling at all. For similar reasons, bargaining, threats, and the like are important elements in the other situations that do not consist of many people on one side and either one or many on the other.

Unfortunately, analyzing strategic bargaining is a hard problem. It is a subset of the more general problem of solving n-person games. *The Theory of Games and Economic Behavior* by Von Neumann and Morgenstern was an attempt to solve the general problem; it is a great book but an unsuccessful attempt. Economists since have spent a good deal of effort trying to understand such situations, with rather limited success. The subject will be discussed at somewhat more length in the optional section of this chapter.

PART 6 · APPLICATIONS

Disneyland

It is interesting to apply some of the ideas of this chapter (and others) to the problem faced by Disneyland in setting its pricing policies. Over the years, it has used various combinations of an entry fee plus per-ride charges. When I was last there, the per-ride charges were zero—the admission ticket provided unlimited rides. A few years earlier, when I was a visiting professor at the University of California at Irvine, the "hospitality package" that I received from the housing office included a card that permitted me to buy an unlimited ride ticket; at that time, I do not believe such cards were being sold to the general public, although they must have been very widely available.

How should Disney decide what combination of entry fee and per-ride ticket price to charge? To begin with, assume that all customers (and all rides) are identical. Figure 10-17 shows one customer's demand for rides. The horizontal axis shows the number of rides he buys as a function of the price he must pay for each ride.

Suppose Disneyland requires a ticket, costing $1, for each ride. The customer will choose to go on 5 rides, paying Disneyland $5. At a price of $.40, he would choose 8 rides and pay $3.20. At a price of $1.60, he would choose 2 rides and pay $3.20. At a price of $2, he would choose zero rides and pay nothing. What price should Disney charge?

The problem of choosing a ticket price appears to be the same as the problem of the price searcher trying to pick a price and quantity which was analyzed in

Part 1 of this chapter. If so, we know the solution; choose price so as to sell that number of rides for which marginal revenue is equal to marginal cost. If Disneyland's marginal cost is zero (it costs the same amount to run a ride whether or not anyone is on it), Disney should choose the price at which marginal revenue is zero and total revenue is at its maximum—$1/ride in this example.

That is the wrong answer. Disneyland need not limit itself to charging a price for the rides; it can and does also charge a price to come into the park. The more expensive the rides are, the less the amount people will be willing to pay to enter. What Disney wants to maximize is revenue from entry tickets plus revenue from ride tickets minus costs; it cannot do so by simply setting the price of the ride ticket so as to maximize revenue from ride tickets.

Figure 10-17

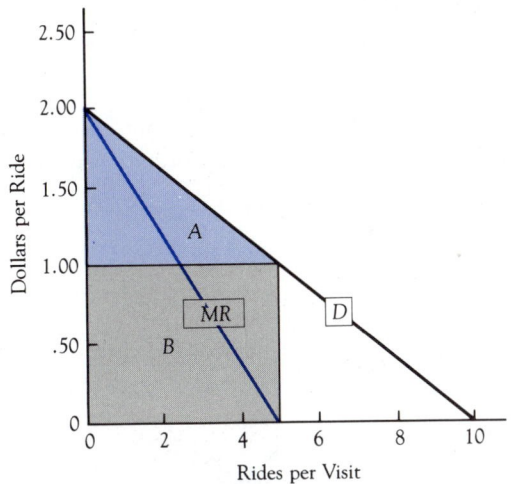

Demand for rides at Disneyland—the profit-maximizing price for a single-price monopoly. If the price for a ride is $1, which maximizes revenue from the rides, the consumer surplus, which is the amount that can be charged as an admission price, is area A.

To figure out what combination of prices Disneyland should charge, we need to know exactly how the price people will pay for admission is affected by the price they are charged for the rides. Fortunately, we do. Area A on Figure 10-17 is the consumer surplus received by a consumer who is free to buy as many rides as he wishes at $1/ride. Since his consumer surplus is defined as the value to him of being able to buy rides at that price, it is also the maximum that he will pay for the right to do so—which he gets by entering Disneyland. Hence area A is the highest entry fee Disneyland can charge if it charges $1 for each ride; at any higher fee, customers will stop coming.

Area *B* on the figure is the number of rides the customer takes (hence the number of ride tickets he buys) times the price of each ride ticket. So area *B* is the total revenue (from that customer) from ride tickets. Area *A* plus area *B* is Disney's total revenue from that customer—entry fee plus ride tickets. As you can easily see, the area is maximized if the ride price is zero, as shown in Figure 10-18*a*; the rides are free, and all the money is made on the entry fee.

I have assumed that the cost to Disney of having one more person go on the ride is zero. Suppose that is not true; suppose it costs $.20 more electricity to operate the ride with someone on it than with an empty seat. Figure 10-18*b* shows that situation, with price per ride set at $1. Area *A* is again consumer surplus (and maximum entry fee), but area *B* is now revenue from ride tickets minus the cost of those rides. Each ride the customer takes provides an extra $1 of income and an extra $.20 of cost, for a net gain of $.80. You should be able to satisfy yourself that the area *A* + *B* is now maximized by setting the price equal to $.20 per ride—the cost. The proof is the same one we have already seen twice—once in Chapter 4 for popcorn and once in this chapter for cookies.

There are at least two important complications we would have to add if we wanted to decide what the real Disneyland should do. One is that customers are not all identical; the admission price which one customer is more than willing to pay may be high enough to drive another customer away. If, on average, the customers who are willing to pay a high admission price are also the ones who go

Figure 10-18

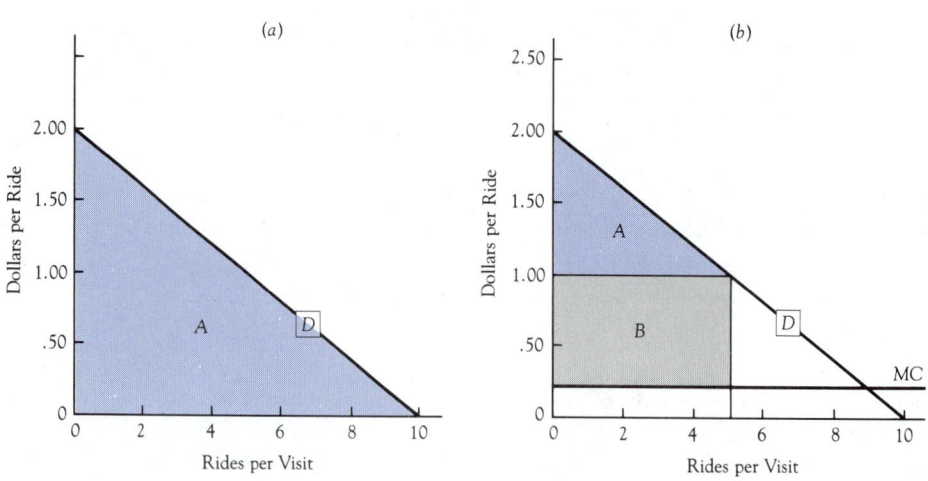

The profit-maximizing per-ride price with two-part pricing.   At a price of zero, the sum of admission price (*A*) and revenue from rides (*B* = 0 on Figure 10-18*a*) is maximized. If MC = 0 for the ride, as shown on Figure 10-18*a*, this is the profit-maximizing arrangement; if MC = .20, the profit-maximizing price is $.20/ride, as shown on Figure 10-18*b*.

on a lot of rides, then a high price for rides is an indirect way of charging a high total price (rides plus admission) to those who are willing to pay it; this greatly complicates the problem of choosing an optimum ticket price.

The second important complication is that some rides may be used to capacity. In this case, my decision to go on one more ride imposes a cost—even if it takes no more electricity to run the ride full than empty. Since the ride is already full, the cost of my going on it is that someone else does not. My decision to take the ride lengthens the line of people waiting for it, imposing costs on everyone else in the line and persuading someone else to take one fewer ride.

This appears to be a cost imposed on the customers, not on the park; why should Disney care how long the customers stand in line? The answer is that how long they have to stand in line to go on a ride is one of the things affecting how much they value visiting Disneyland, hence how much they will pay for the admission ticket. By going on one more ride, you impose a cost directly on the other customers and indirectly on Disney; Disney should take that cost into account in deciding what price to charge for the ride. It turns out that (assuming all customers are identical) the optimal price is the one which just reduces the line to zero. You may find it easier to figure out why that is true after you finish Chapter 16.

The Popcorn Problem

In the discussion of popcorn at the end of Chapter 4, I showed that if customers are identical, theaters should sell popcorn at cost. One explanation of what we observe is that they do—that the high price of popcorn (and candy and soda) reflects high costs. Since the theater is selling food for only twenty minutes or so every two hours, perhaps its operating costs are much higher than those of other sellers.

In this chapter's discussion of discriminatory pricing, I suggested an alternative explanation, based on the fact that customers are *not* identical. On average, the poor student who is just barely willing to pay $3 to see the movie will probably either do without expensive popcorn or smuggle in his own, while the affluent student (or the one trying to impress a new date) will be willing both to pay a high price and to buy a lot of popcorn. If so, then the combination of cheap tickets and expensive popcorn is a way of keeping the business of the poor student while making as much as possible out of the rich one.

How could one find out which explanation is right? Discriminatory pricing is only possible if the seller has a considerable degree of monopoly; in a competitive industry, if you try to charge a higher price to richer customers, some other firm will undercut you. In a small town, there may be only one movie theater; even if there are several, it is unlikely that more than one is showing a particular movie at a particular time. Each theater is then a monopoly (with regard to its particular movie) and can engage in discriminatory pricing by, among other things, charging above-cost prices for food. In a large city, the customers can choose among many theaters, several of which may be showing the same film. If the discriminatory pricing explanation is correct, we would expect the difference between the price of popcorn or candy in a movie theater and its price elsewhere to be larger in small towns than in big cities. If, on the other hand, the difference reflects a difference in cost, we would probably expect the opposite result, since both labor and real estate—the two things which contribute to the high cost of a food concession (inside a theater) which is only selling ten percent of the time—are generally more expensive in cities.

OPTIONAL SECTION

Calculating Elasticities

Figure 10-19a shows how elasticity varies with quantity along a straight line demand curve. The figure has two vertical axes; the one on the left shows price, the one on the right elasticity. The slope of a straight line is the same everywhere($-\frac{1}{2}$ for the demand curve shown on the figure) so $dQ/dP = 1/(dP/dQ) = 1/(-\frac{1}{2}) = -2$. Elasticity equals $-(P/Q)dQ/dP$; P/Q varies along the line. It is equal to infinity at the left end of D, where $P = 10$ and $Q = 0$; it is equal to zero at the right end, where $Q = 20$ and $P = 0$. Along the curve, elasticity varies as shown in Figure 10-19a. Points A, B, and C have been marked to allow you to check that the curve correctly shows the elasticity at those points.

Figure 10-19

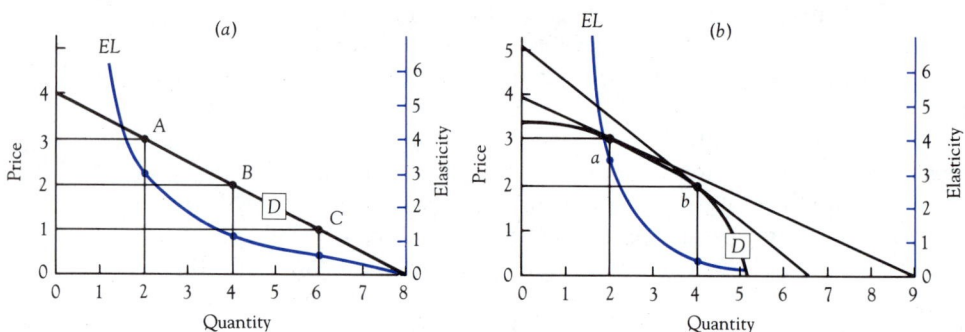

Calculating the elasticity of a demand curve.   Each curve shows demand and elasticity. Elasticity is calculated at three points on Figure 10-19a and two points on Figure 10-19b.

Figure 10-19b shows the same information for a demand curve that is not a straight line. Both dP/dQ—the slope—and P/Q vary along the line. This time I have marked two points—a and b—so that you can check my calculations. In each case, the slope—dP/dQ—is calculated by taking the slope of a line tangent to the curve at that point. Table 10-1 shows the calculations for Figures 10-19a and 10-19b. ΔP and ΔQ are the vertical and horizontal intercepts of the tangent; their ratio is its slope, which is equal to dP/dQ.

TABLE 10-1

Point	Q	P	ΔQ	ΔP	$\Delta Q/\Delta P$	$-(P/Q)\Delta Q/\Delta P$
A	2	3	8	-4	-2	3
B	4	2	8	-4	-2	1
C	6	1	8	-4	-2	$\frac{2}{3}$
a	2	3	9	-4	$-\frac{3}{4}$	$3\frac{3}{8}$
b	4	2	$6\frac{1}{2}$	-5	-1.3	.65

Figure 10-20 shows a simpler way of calculating elasticity. The triangles GED, HFE, and OFD are all similar. From the similarity of HFE and OFD, we have:

$$EF/EH = DF/OD.$$

Hence

$$EF = EH(DF/OD). \qquad \text{(Eqn. 1)}$$

From the similarity of GED and OFD, we have:

$$DE/GE = DF/OF.$$

Hence

$$DE = GE(DF/OF) \qquad \text{(Eqn. 2)}$$

Dividing Equation 1 by Equation 2, we have:

$$EF/DE = (EH/GE)(OF/OD). \qquad \text{(Eqn. 3)}$$

But, as you can see from the figure, $EH = P$, $GE = Q$, and OD/OF is minus the slope of the line DF. The slope of DF is equal to the slope of the demand curve at the point E—which is dP/dQ. So OF/OD is $-dQ/dP$, and Equation 3 becomes:

$$EF/DE = (P/Q)(-dQ/dP) = \text{elasticity of demand curve } D \text{ at point E.}$$

So one can calculate the elasticity of a demand curve by simply drawing the tangent and taking the ratio between EF (the distance from the point of tangency to the intersection with the quantity axis) and DE (the distance from the point of tangency to the intersection with the price axis). This gives us a simpler way of calculating the elasticity of a demand curve than the one shown on Table 10-1.

Figure 10-20

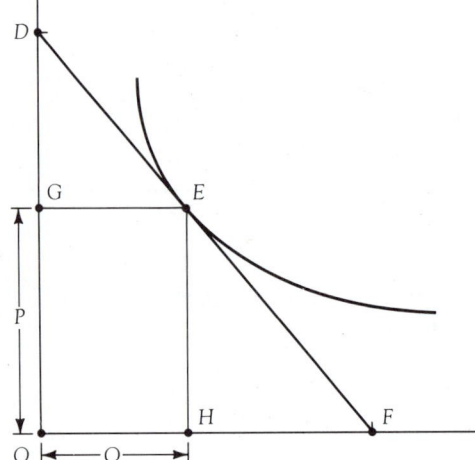

A simpler way of calculating elasticity.   The elasticity of the curve at point E is EF/DE.

Artificial Monopoly

Economies of scale are ways in which large firms can produce more cheaply than small ones; diseconomies of scale are the opposite. One important source of economies of scale is mass production; a firm which produces a million widgets per year can set up assembly lines, buy special widget-making machinery, and so forth. Another source may be economies of scale in administration; a large firm can afford to take advantage of specialization by having one executive specialize in advertising, one in personnel, and so on. Economies of scale are usually important only up to some maximum size; that is why a large firm, such as GM or U.S. Steel, does not consist of one gigantic factory, as it would if such a factory could produce at a substantially lower cost than several large factories.

An important source of diseconomies of scale, as mentioned earlier, is the problem of coordinating a large firm. The fundamental organizational problem of a firm is the conflict between the interests of the employees and the interests of the owners. The owners want to maximize profits. The employees, while they have no objection to profits, would prefer to take more leisure, work less hard, or benefit themselves in other ways, even if the result is less profit for the owners. This problem is "solved" by supervisors who watch the employees, give raises to those who work hard, and fire those who do not. The supervisors are themselves employees and must themselves be monitored by a higher level of supervisors. Since such monitoring is neither costless nor perfectly effective, every additional layer increases costs and reduces performance. The more layers there are, the more the employees find themselves pursuing, not the interest of the firm, but what they think the person above them thinks the person above him thinks is the interest of the firm. Seen from this standpoint, the ideal arrangement is the one-person firm; if its sole employee chooses to slack off, he, being also the owner of the firm, pays the cost in reduced profits.

When I was choosing a publisher for this book, I had offers from two firms, one substantially larger and more prestigious than the other. I ended up choosing the smaller and less prestigious firm, in large part because in dealing with it, I felt as though I was conversing with human beings—rather than being quoted to from a manual entitled *How to Deal With Aspiring Authors*. One reason for the difference may well have been that the people I dealt with at the smaller firm were a couple of layers closer to the top of their organization than were their opposite numbers at the larger firm.

If there were only diseconomies of scale, we would expect to see an economy of one-person firms, cooperating by trading goods and services with each other. Firms consisting of one person, one family, or a small number of individuals are common (writers, doctors, owners of small grocery stores), but so are much larger firms. It appears that diseconomies of scale are often balanced by economies of scale.

Consider an industry in which economies and diseconomies balance each other over a considerable range of production, giving the firm a cost function like that of Figure 10-21. Average cost is roughly constant over a large range of firm sizes, including a firm large enough to produce all of the output demanded at a price equal to average cost. It is widely believed that this is a common situation and one likely to lead to monopoly; the usual example is the Standard Oil Trust under John D. Rockefeller.

The argument goes as follows: I am Rockefeller and have somehow gotten control of 90 percent of the petroleum industry. My firm, Standard Oil, has immense revenues, from which it accumulates great wealth; its resources are far larger than the resources of any smaller oil company or even all of them put together. As long as other firms exist and compete with me, I can earn only the normal return on my capital and labor—economic profit equals zero. Any attempt

Figure 10-21

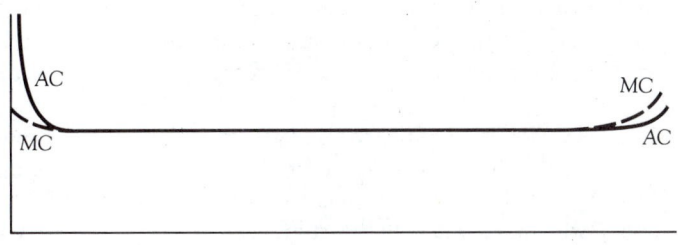

Quantity

A cost curve for an industry for which large and small firms have about the same average cost.

to push up prices will cause my competitors to increase their production and may also draw additional firms into the industry.

I therefore decide to drive out my competitors by cutting prices to below average cost. Both I and my competitors lose money; since I have more money to lose, they go under first. I now raise prices to a monopoly level, calculated as if I were a natural monopoly (marginal cost equals marginal revenue). If any new firm considers entering the market to take advantage of the high prices, I point out what happened to my previous competitors and threaten to repeat the performance if necessary.

This argument is an example of the careless use of verbal analysis. "Both I and my competitors are losing money . . ." sounds very much as though we are losing the same amount of money. We are not. If I am selling 90 percent of all petroleum, a particular competitor is selling 1 percent, and we both sell at the same price and have the same average cost, I lose $90 for every $1 he loses.

The situation is, from my standpoint, worse than that. By cutting prices, I have caused the quantity demanded to increase; if I want to keep the price down, I must increase my production—and losses—accordingly. So I must actually lose (say) $95 for every $1 my competitor loses. Worse still, my competitor, who is not trying to hold down the price, may be able to reduce his losses and increase mine by reducing his production, forcing me to sell still more oil at less than production cost, and so lose still more money. He may even be able to close down temporarily and wait until I tire of throwing my money away and permit the price to go back up. Even if he has some costs which he cannot escape without going permanently out of business, he may be able to reduce his total losses by temporarily closing his older refineries, running some plants half time, and failing to replace employees who move or retire. If so, for every $95 or $100 I lose, he loses (say) $.50.

But although I am bigger and richer than he is, I am not infinitely bigger and richer; I am 90 times as big and presumably about 90 times as rich. I am losing money more than 90 times as fast as he is; if I keep trying to drive him out by selling below cost, it is I, not he, who will go bankrupt first. Despite the widespread belief that Rockefeller maintained his position by selling oil below cost in order to drive competitors out of business ("predatory pricing"), a careful study of the record found no solid evidence that he had ever done so.

In one case, a Standard Oil official *threatened* to cut prices if a smaller firm, Cornplanter Oil, did not stop expanding and cutting into Standard's business. Here is the reply Cornplanter's manager gave, according to his own testimony:

> Well, I says, "Mr. Moffett, I am very glad you put it that way, because if it is up to you the only way you can get it (the business) is to cut the market (reduce prices), and if you cut the market I will cut you for 200 miles around, and I will make you sell the stuff," and I says, "I don't want a bigger picnic than that; sell it if you want to," and I bid him good day and left. That was the end of that.

> —quoted in John S. McGee, "Predatory Price Cutting: The Standard Oil (NJ) Case," *Journal of Law and Economics*, Vol.2 (October,1958), p.137.

In addition to predatory pricing, there are a variety of other tactics which have been suggested for a firm trying to get and maintain an artificial monopoly. One is for the firm to buy out all of its competitors; it has been argued that this, rather than predatory pricing, is how Rockefeller maintained his position. The problem is that if every time someone builds a new refinery, Rockefeller has to buy him out, starting refineries becomes a very profitable business, and Rockefeller ends up with more refineries than he has any use for.

It is hard to *prove* that none of these tactics can ever work. If, for instance, Rockefeller can convince potential customers that he is willing to lose an almost unlimited amount of money keeping them out, it is possible that no one will ever call his bluff—in which case it will cost him nothing. One can only say that the advantage in such a game seems to lie with the small firm, not the large, and that the bulk of the economic and historical evidence suggests that the artificial monopoly is mostly or entirely mythical.

One consequence of such myths may be to encourage monopoly. Selling below cost is a poor way of driving your competitors out of business but may be a good way for a new firm to persuade customers to try its products. Under present antitrust law, a firm which does so risks being accused by its competitors of unfair competition and forced to raise its price. Laws that make life hard for new firms— or old firms entering new markets—reduce competition and encourage monopoly, even if they are called antitrust laws.

Cartels

Consider the sort of case illustrated in Figure 10-10*b*, where minimum average cost occurs for a level of output equal to a sizable fraction of industry output. Since small firms will be unable to compete successfully with large ones, the industry will be made up of a small number of large firms. Such firms could choose to behave as if they were price takers, charging a price equal to marginal (and average) cost. If, instead, they all agree to reduce output and raise prices, they, like a natural monopoly, may be able to collect monopoly profits.

Such a cartel has some of the same problems as an artificial monopoly. Unless it can keep new firms from entering the industry, any successful attempt to raise prices is likely to attract competition. While it can try to drive competitors out by selling below cost, it faces the same difficulties as a monopolist; since the cartel has most of the output, it takes most of the losses.

A cartel also has some special difficulties of its own. Since price is above marginal cost, each member of the cartel would like to expand his output and sales at the expense of other members. There are two ways he can do so. First, he can pretend to maintain the cartel agreement while secretly cutting prices to at least some customers in order to increase his sales. Such behavior destroyed many of the attempts by railroad companies to organize cartels during the nineteenth century—sometimes within months of the cartel's formation.

Alternatively, he can withdraw from the cartel. The great weakness of a cartel is that it is better to be out than in. A firm which is not a member of the cartel is free to produce all it likes and sell it at or just below the cartel's price. The only reason for a firm to stay in the cartel and restrict its output is the fear that if it does not, the cartel will be weakened or destroyed and prices will fall. A large firm may well believe that if it leaves the cartel, the remaining firms will give up; the cartel will collapse and the price will fall back to its competitive level. But a (relatively) small firm may decide that its production increase is not enough to lower prices significantly; even if the cartel threatens to disband if the small firm refuses to keep its output down, it is unlikely to carry out the threat.

So in order for a cartel to keep its smaller members, it must permit them to produce virtually all they want, which is not much better than letting them leave. The reduction in output necessary to keep up the price, and the resulting reduction in profits, must be absorbed by the large firms. In the recent case of the OPEC oil cartel, it appears that the reduction of output has been mostly by Saudi Arabia and the United Arab Emirates. One consequence is that it is the Saudis who are the most reluctant to have OPEC raise its price, since it is they who will pay in reduced sales for any resulting reduction in the quantity demanded.

In discussing the problems a cartel faces, I have so far ignored the element of time. Production functions are usually much less elastic in the short run than in the long. If the price of oil rises sharply, it may be years before the additional investment (in exploration and drilling) generated by the opportunity to make high profits has much effect on the amount of oil being produced. The same is true for demand. In the short run, we can adjust to higher oil prices by taking fewer trips, driving more slowly, or lowering our thermostats. In the medium run, we can form carpools. In the long run, we can buy smaller and more fuel-efficient cars, live closer to our jobs, and build better insulated homes.

So even if a cartel can succeed in raising the price—and its profits—for a few years, in the long run, both the price and the cartel's sales are likely to fall as customers and potential competitors adjust to the cartel price. In the case of OPEC, the process of adjustment was somewhat delayed by the Iran-Iraq war—during which the combatants reduced each other's petroleum output by blowing up refineries, pipelines, and ports.

Government to the Rescue

. . . the high price for the crude oil resulted, as it had always done before and will always do so long as oil comes out of the ground, in increasing the production, and they got too much oil. We could not find a market for it . . . of course, any who were not in the association were undertaking to produce all they possibly could; and as to those who were in the association, many of them men of honor and high standing, the temptation was very great to get a little more oil than they had promised their associates or us would come. It seemed very difficult to prevent the oil coming at that price.

—John D. Rockefeller, discussing an unsuccessful attempt to cartelize the production of crude oil. Quoted in McGee, op.cit.

Rockefeller was too pessimistic; there is a way of keeping a high price from drawing more oil out of the ground. The solution is a monopoly in the original sense of the term—a grant by government of the exclusive right to produce.

Consider the airline industry. Until the recent deregulation, no airline could fly a route unless it had permission from the Civil Aeronautics Board. The CAB could permit the airlines to charge high prices while preventing new competitors from entering and driving those prices down. From the formation of the CAB (originally as the Civil Aeronautics Administration) in 1938 until the recent deregulation, no major scheduled interstate airline came into existence.

Even if the airlines, with the help of the government, were able to keep out new firms, what prevented one airline from cutting its fares to attract business from another? Again the answer was the CAB; until recently it was illegal for an airline to increase *or reduce* its fares without permission. The airline industry under regulation was a cartel created and enforced by the federal government, at considerable cost to the airlines' customers.

In order for a private cartel to work, the number of firms must be reasonably small; otherwise each small firm will correctly believe that an expansion in its output will increase its sales while having only a negligible effect on price. That is not true in the case of a governmentally enforced cartel. The government can provide protection against both the entry of outsiders and expanded output by those already in the industry, thus providing an industry of many small price-taking firms with monopoly profits—at the expense of its customers. That is precisely the situation discussed in Chapter 9—a competitive industry with closed entry.

One form which such arrangements often take is professional licensing. The government announces that in order to protect the public from incompetent physicians (morticians, beauticians, poodle groomers, egg graders, barbers, . . .), only those with a government-granted license may enter the profession. Typically the existing members of the profession are assumed to be competent and receive licenses more or less automatically. The political support for the introduction of such arrangements comes, almost invariably, not from the customers who are supposedly being hurt by incompetent practitioners but from the members of the profession. That is not as odd as it may seem; the licensing requirement makes entry to the profession more difficult, reducing supply and increasing the price for which those already in the profession can sell their services.

PROBLEMS

1. Economics is a competitive industry; my decision to become an economist or to teach one more course will not much affect the salary of economists. Economists as a group face a downward-sloping demand curve; the more there are, the less they can expect to get for their services. But each individual economist faces an almost perfectly horizontal demand curve; his decision to teach more courses, write more books, do more consulting, or whatever will have a very small effect on the price he receives for doing so.

   The argument does not apply to everything an economist does. This book, for example, may increase (or decrease!) your interest in becoming an economist; your decision to become an economist may affect the salary received by other economists—including me. How should that possibility affect my decision of how to write the book? If the book makes economics seem an attractive and interesting profession, what can you deduce about how many copies I expect to sell?

2. When I asked a realtor to find a house for me to buy, one of her first questions was, "How much do you want to spend?" This seems a rather odd question, since how much I want to spend, on houses or anything else, depends on what I can get for the money; even if I can buy a $200,000 house ($300,000 if enough of you buy this book), I might rather spend $100,000 if for that price I can get most of what I want. Why do you think the realtor puts the question this way? (Hint: Realtors are paid on commission; in most cities, they receive a fixed percentage of the value of the houses they sell.)

3. How should I answer the realtor in Problem 2? Should I tell her the maximum I am willing to spend for a house?

4. One can draw two different demand curves D_1 and D_2 such that a single-price monopoly would charge the same price whether faced by D_1 or D_2, but produce different quantities. One can also draw two curves D_3 and D_4 which result in the same quantity but different prices. Assuming that the producer has the MC curve of Figure 10-3a, draw demand curves D_1 - D_4 as described above.

5. Suppose a monopoly has no production cost. What can you say about the elasticity of demand at the profit-maximizing quantity? Can you give an example of a monopoly with no production cost? With marginal cost equal to zero? If so, do.

6. Suppose a monopoly has MC > 0. What can you say about the elasticity of demand at the profit-maximizing quantity? Prove your result.

7. Figures 10-22a, 10-22b, and 10-22c show demand curves, marginal cost curves, and average cost curves for three single-price monopoly firms. In each case, how much should the firm produce and at what price should it sell in order to maximize its profit?

Figure 10-22

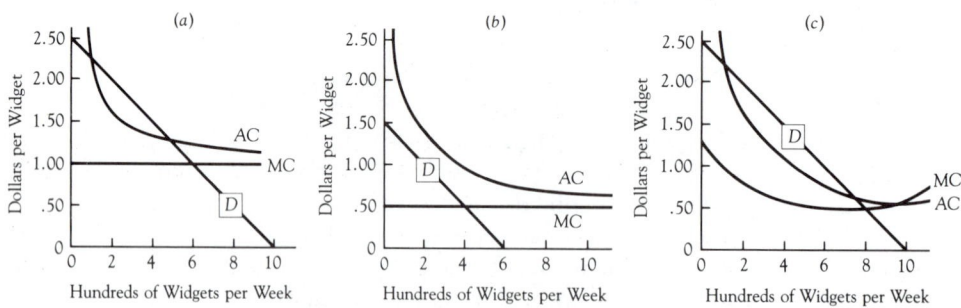

Demand and cost curves for Problems 7 and 8.

8. Suppose the firms in Problem 7 can engage in discriminatory pricing. Under what circumstances can they do so perfectly by using a "two-part price"? Assuming that they can do so, what should the two parts be for each firm—how large a per-unit charge and how large an admission charge? Assume that each firm has 100 customers.

9. Figures 10-23a and 10-23b show demand curves, marginal cost curves, and average cost curves for two monopolies. In the first case, there are 10 customers with demand curve D_A and 10 with D_B; in the second case, there are 10 type A and 5 type B customers. Note that average cost is shown as a function of total quantity produced, while each of the demand curves relates price to the quantity bought by a single customer.

   a. In each case, draw the total demand curve and find the profit-maximizing price, assuming the firm is a single-price monopoly.

   b. In each case, find the optimal two-part price (per-unit charge plus "membership fee" for the right to buy any units at all) *assuming the per-unit fee must equal marginal cost*.

   c. In each case, find some two-part price that yields a higher profit than you got in part (b).

   d. Is any general principle suggested by your answers to (c)? If so, prove it if possible. (This is a hard problem.)

Figure 10-23

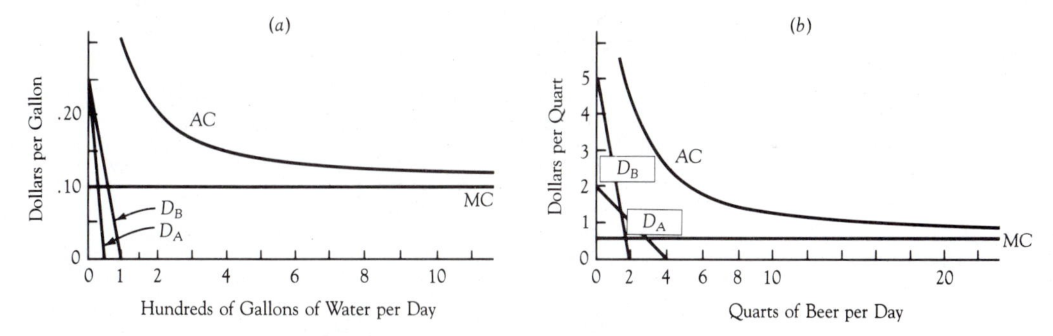

Demand and cost curves for Problem 9.

10. In an earlier chapter, I showed that a law requiring all landlords to guarantee their tenants 6 months' notice before evicting them either had no effect or injured both landlords and tenants. That argument assumed that landlords were price takers, so that price and quantity were determined at the intersection of the supply and demand curves. Suppose instead that the landlord is a monopolist; quantity produced is now at the intersection of marginal revenue and marginal cost, and price is the price at which that quantity is demanded. Show that the result still holds. You should assume a single-price monopoly, straight-line demand curve, constant marginal cost, and identical tenants.

The following problems refer to the optional section:

11. Figure 10-24 shows a demand curve; graph the elasticity as was done on Figures 10-19a and 10-19b. You may use whichever method of calculating it you prefer.

12. Figure 10-20 was used to derive a simple method for calculating the elasticity of a demand curve. What happens if you try to use the same method to calculate the elasticity of a supply curve? Can you use a similar argument to derive a similar method that works for a supply curve? If so, do.

Figure 10-24

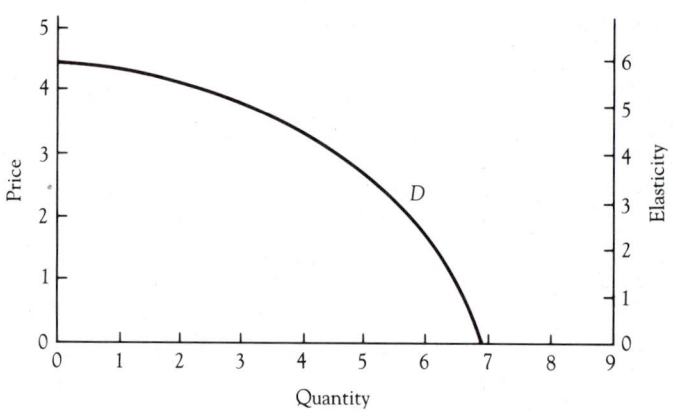

Demand curve for Problem 11.

FOR FURTHER READING

Students interested in a detailed, and original, discussion of monopoly and price discrimination may want to look at the classic discussion of the subject in A. C. Pigou, *The Economics of Welfare* (London: Macmillan, 1932), especially Chapters XIV-XVII. A more modern source would be George Stigler, *The Organization of Industry* (Chicago: University of Chicago Press, 1968).

For a discussion of strategic behavior, the original source is John Von Neumann and Oskar Morgenstern, *Theory of Games and Economic Behavior* (Princeton: Princeton University Press, 1944). A good modern summary is R. Duncan Luce and Howard Raiffa, *Games and Decisions: Introduction and Critical Survey* (New York: John Wiley & Sons, 1957).

An original set of essays on strategic problems is Thomas Schelling, *The Strategy of Conflict* (Cambridge: Harvard University Press, 1960).

I am not the first economist to think of applying economic theory to the Magic Kingdom. You may wish to read Walter Oi, "A Disneyland Dilemma: Two-Part Tariffs for a Mickey Mouse Monopoly," *Quarterly Journal of Economics*, Vol. 85 (February, 1971), pp. 77-96.

Chapter 11

Time...

In earlier chapters, I have ignored, so far as possible, two of the major complications of economics (and life)—time and uncertainty. While I have described production as occurring over time ("widgets per hour"), I have also assumed an unchanging world in which each hour is like the last. In relaxing those assumptions, I will first—in this chapter—describe how the picture must be changed to allow for a changing but still certain world, a world in which people never make mistakes, since they know exactly what is going to happen. In Chapter 12, I will then describe some of the effects of further changing the picture to describe the uncertain world in which we live.

TIME AND INTEREST RATES

The simplest way to introduce time into the picture is by recognizing that a good is *when* as well as *what*. An apple today and an apple tomorrow are two different goods—as any hungry child will tell you. Not only is there a price for apples today in terms of oranges today, there is also a price for apples today in terms of apples next year. If I trade 100 apples today for 110 next year, I am receiving an "apple interest rate" of 10 percent, since giving you goods now in exchange for goods in the future is the same thing as loaning you goods in exchange for the goods plus interest in the future. The interest rate (in apples for a one-year loan) is the price of apples today measured in apples a year from now (110/100 = 1.10) minus one. $1.10 - 1.00 = .10 = 10\%$.

The price of apples today in terms of apples a year from now—the rate at which apples today exchange for apples a year from now—is determined in the same way as other prices. If you want to consume fewer apples now and more in the future, you sell apples now in exchange for apples in the future, contributing to the supply of the former and the demand for the latter. If you want to consume now and pay later, you sell future apples in exchange for present ones, contributing to the supply of future apples and the demand for present apples. There is some price—some apple interest rate—at which quantity supplied (of current apples to be exchanged for future apples) equals quantity demanded (of current apples to be exchanged for future apples). That is the market interest rate.

262

Investing Apples

So far, I have assumed that all loans are "consumption loans"—people buy present apples with future apples (borrow) in order to eat the apples. Another reason is to plant them. Suppose you can take 10,000 apples, remove the seeds from some of them, and trade what is left for the labor of workers who will plant the seeds, water the baby apple trees when they come up, pull weeds, and eventually pick 11,000 apples from your new orchard. If you can do all this in a year (*very* fast-growing apple trees), you will "produce" 1,100 future apples using 1,000 present apples as input.

If the apple interest rate is below 10 percent, this is a profitable investment. You borrow 10,000 apples, plant them, pay back 10,000 plus interest a year from now, and have some left over. By doing so, you provide an additional demand for present apples and supply of future apples which must be included in the total demand and supply determining the apple interest rate. By buying present apples (borrowing apples now), "investing" them, and paying with future apples, you drive up the price of present apples in terms of future apples—the apple interest rate.

As long as the apple interest rate is below 10 percent, planting orchards is profitable. More and more orchards are planted. Each one increases the demand for present apples and the supply of future apples, driving the interest rate (the price of present apples measured in future apples) up. So if you, and everyone else, can convert 10 present apples into 11 future apples by planting an orchard, the apple interest rate cannot stay below 10 percent.

One way of producing future goods from present goods is by planting apple trees; another way is to put the present goods somewhere safe and wait. For goods without significant storage costs (gold bars—provided nobody knows you have them), you can produce one unit of the future good from one unit of the present good, so the interest rate for such goods cannot be less than zero. You would never give 10 ounces of gold in exchange for 9 a year from now, since you could always hide your 10 ounces and have 10 ounces a year from now. That is not true for perishable goods (tomatoes) or for goods that are expensive to store (gold bars—if everyone knows you have them). For such goods, negative interest rates are possible.

Apple Interest Rate = Orange Interest Rate

So far, I have talked only about apple interest rates, leaving open the possibility that there may be a different interest rate for every good. Whether this happens depends on what happens to relative prices (the price of apples now in terms of oranges now, for instance) over time. If the relative prices of all goods stay the same over time (so it always costs the same number of oranges to buy an apple, or a cookie, or a car, or anything else), then all goods must have the same interest rate. If the relative price of one good measured in another is changing, on the other hand, then the two goods will have different interest rates.

To see why this is true, imagine that the apple interest rate is 10 percent and that an apple always trades for two oranges. What is the orange interest rate?

Suppose you have 200 oranges now and want oranges a year from now. You trade your 200 oranges for 100 apples. You then trade your 100 apples today for 110 apples a year from now—in other words, you lend them out for a year at an apple interest rate of 10 percent. Finally, you trade 110 apples a year from now for 220 oranges. You have, indirectly, exchanged 200 present oranges for 220 future oranges.

The sequence of transactions is shown in Figure 11-1a. The solid arrows show the actual transactions, with the rates at which they occur in parentheses. The dashed arrow shows the overall effect with the corresponding rate in parentheses.

If you (and everyone else) can trade present oranges for future oranges indirectly at an interest rate of 10 percent (1 present orange for 1.1 future oranges), nobody will be willing to trade a present orange for less than 1.1 future oranges, so the orange interest rate cannot be *less* than 10 percent. If you reverse the arrows on Figure 11-1a and run the cycle backward (borrow 100 apples and trade them for 200 oranges, then pay the debt a year from now with 110 apples which you get by trading 220 oranges for them), you convert future oranges into present oranges at an interest rate of 10 percent (1.1 future oranges for 1 present orange). If you (and anyone else) can get present oranges in this way at a cost of 1.1 future oranges each, nobody will pay more than 1.1 future oranges for a present orange, so the orange interest rate cannot be *more* than 10 percent.

Since the orange interest rate cannot be more or less than 10 percent, it must be 10 percent. So the orange interest rate and the apple interest rate are the

Figure 11-1

(*a*)

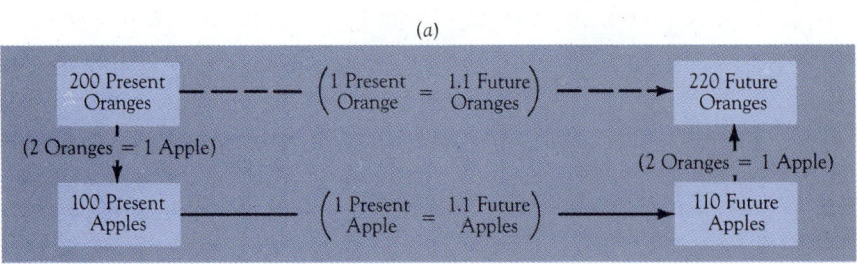

(*b*)

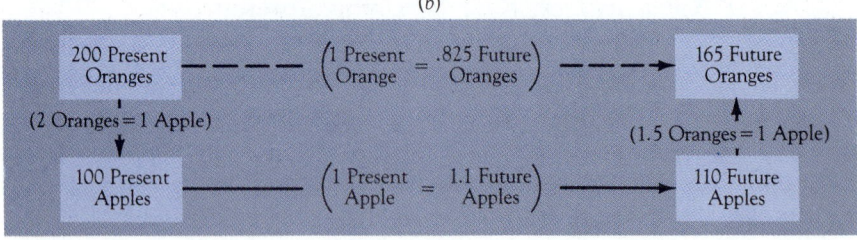

Arbitrage over time—converting present oranges into future oranges, using apples as intermediates. Solid arrows show actual transactions; dashed arrows show the net effect.

same. Precisely the same argument applies for any other goods. If the relative prices of any two goods stay the same over time, the goods must have the same interest rate; if the relative prices of all goods stay the same over time, all goods must have the same interest rate. This is what economists call the "real" interest rate, in contrast to the "nominal" interest rate—the rate at which you can exchange dollars today for dollars a year from now—which is the interest rate reported in the daily paper. The two are equal if, as we shall assume throughout this chapter, the price of goods measured in money is not changing—or, in other words, if the inflation rate is zero. The relation between real and nominal rates when the inflation rate is not zero will be discussed in Chapter 22.

Apple Interest Rate ≠ Orange Interest Rate

We now know what happens if relative prices stay the same over time. What happens if they do not? Suppose that the price of apples measured in oranges is falling; an apple buys 2 oranges today, but a year from now, 1 apple will exchange for only 1½ oranges. Running through the same example (present oranges to present apples to future apples to future oranges), you find that you have traded 200 present oranges for 165 future oranges, for an orange interest rate of about −17.5 percent. The cycle is shown on Figure 11-1b. Just as on Figure 11-1a, you can run through the cycle in either direction, lending or borrowing oranges at an interest rate of about −17.5 percent.

It may have occurred to you that this is not the first time you have seen this kind of argument. We used exactly the same procedure in Chapter 4 to show that if you knew the price of all goods in terms of one good, you could deduce the price of any good in terms of any other good. The process which we have illustrated here in Figures 11-1a and 11-1b was described there in a somewhat less complicated form; it is called *arbitrage*. All we have done here is to expand the argument to apply to goods that are labeled by *when* they are as well as by *what* they are.

PRESENT VALUES

You have 6 oranges, 3 apples, and an ice cream cone. If markets exist for oranges, apples, and cones, and if, as we generally assume, the costs of arranging to buy and sell goods are negligible, you can transform that bundle of goods into any other bundle with the same total price—by selling what you have and buying what you want. You are therefore indifferent among any two such bundles—not in the sense of being equally willing to consume each but in the sense of being able to transform one into the other by market transactions. So one useful way of "summing up" what you have is by calculating what it is worth; this makes it possible to compare (for purposes of buying and selling but not of consuming) very disparate bundles. I do not like diamonds and do like ice cream cones, but I would rather have a one-carat diamond than an ice cream cone—even Baskin-Robbins's Pralines and Cream. In this sense, $110 worth of anything is preferred to $100 worth of anything else.

The same method can be used to evaluate "bundles" across time. Suppose I am offered two employment contracts; one consists of $40,000/year for ten years, the other of $31,000 the first year and a $2,000 raise for each of the next nine. Each contract is a bundle of 10 different goods. The different goods are "money this year," "money next year," and so on. How can I compare them?

I can compare them by using the price of "money this year" in "money next year" (or "money two years from now" or . . .) to find a single market value for the bundle, just as I do for a bundle of different goods at the same time. Suppose the interest rate, at which I can either borrow or lend, is 10 percent. In that case, I can convert $1,000 this year into $1,100 next year (by lending) or $1,100 next year into $1,000 this year (by borrowing). In the first case, I lend out the $1,000 (losing the use of it now) and get $1,100 ($1,000 plus $100 in interest) a year from now; in the second case, I borrow $1,000 this year, and pay back the principal plus $100 in interest with the $1,100 I will have next year.

The *present value* of a series of payments is their total value measured in terms of money in a single year. Suppose, in the example I gave, I want the present value in year 1 of the series of payments associated with the first employment contract. Forty thousand dollars in year 1 is worth $40,000 in year 1, so the present value of the first term is easy. Forty thousand dollars in year 2 can be converted into $(1/1.1) \times \$40,000$ in year 1; if I borrowed that sum in year 1, I could exactly pay it off with my year 2 income. Forty thousand dollars in year 3 is equivalent to $(1/1.1) \times (1/1.1) \times \$40,000$ in year 1, and so on. The third column of Table 11-1 shows the present values of the payments in the first series. Adding them up we find that the present value of the first series of payments is $270,091. That is the sum I could borrow in year 1 and exactly pay off with the entire 10-year stream of payments.

TABLE 11-1

1 Year	2 Pay- ment(1)	3 Present Value(1)	4 Pay- ment(2)	5 Present Value(2)	6 Save	7 Accumulate
1	$40,000	$40,000	$31,000	$31,000	$9,000	$ 9,000
2	$40,000	$+\$40,000/1.1$	$33,000	$+\$33,000/(1.1)$	$7,000	$16,900
3	$40,000	$+\$40,000/(1.1)^2$	$35,000	$+\$35,000/(1.1)^2$	$5,000	$23,590
4	$40,000	$+\$40,000/(1.1)^3$	$37,000	$+\$37,000/(1.1)^3$	$3,000	$28,949
5	$40,000	$+\$40,000/(1.1)^4$	$39,000	$+\$37,000/(1.1)^4$	$1,000	$32,844
6	$40,000	$+\$40,000/(1.1)^5$	$41,000	$+\$37,000/(1.1)^5$	$-\$1,000$	$35,128
7	$40,000	$+\$40,000/(1.1)^6$	$43,000	$+\$37,000/(1.1)^6$	$-\$3,000$	$35,641
8	$40,000	$+\$40,000/(1.1)^7$	$45,000	$+\$37,000/(1.1)^7$	$-\$5,000$	$34,205
9	$40,000	$+\$40,000/(1.1)^8$	$47,000	$+\$37,000/(1.1)^8$	$-\$7,000$	$30,625
10	$40,000	$+\$40,000/(1.1)^9$	$49,000	$+\$49,000/(1.1)^9$	$-\$9,000$	$24,687
		$40,000 \times$		$259,621		$24,687
		$(1 + .909 + .909^2 + \ . \ . \ . + .909^9)$				
		$=\$40,000 \times (6.75)$				
		$= \$270,091$				

I can, in the same way, calculate the present value of the second series of payments (Table 11-1, column 5). It turns out that it is smaller. This implies that the first stream of income could, by appropriate borrowing and lending, be converted into the second with something left over. Hence the first stream of income is unambiguously preferable to the second, just as a bundle of goods worth $100 is unambiguously superior to a bundle worth $90, since one can sell the former, buy the latter, and have $10 left.

How would I convert the first stream of payments into the second? The answer is shown on columns 6 and 7 of the table. I would save (and lend out) $9,000 of my first year's salary (leaving me with $31,000 to spend, just as in the second stream), $7,000 of the second year's, $5,000 of the third, $3,000 of the fourth, $1,000 of the fifth. At that point I would have accumulated $25,000 plus interest. In the sixth year, I would pay myself $1,000 from my savings, in the seventh $3,000, and so on, for a total of $25,000. Column 7 of Table 11-1 shows, for each year, the accumulated savings, including interest. At the end, I would have had the same amount to spend each year as with the second employment contract—and I would have the accumulated interest of $24,687 left over.

Present value calculations provide a way of evaluating any project, employment contract, or the like that can be described as a stream of payments, positive (revenue) or negative (cost), through time. If the present value of a stream is positive, then it is worth having—if you do not have to give up something else, such as an alternative job with a higher positive present value, in order to get it. If it is negative, it is not worth having. If you must choose between two, the one with the higher present value is preferable.

Using the idea of opportunity cost introduced in an earlier chapter, we can reduce the previous paragraph to one simple sentence: "Choose any alternative that has a positive present value." If taking one job means not taking another, then not getting what you would have earned in the second job is the (opportunity) cost of taking the first and should be included in the present value calculation. If the result is still positive, then the present value of the income stream is higher for the first job than for the second, so you should take it.

One interesting present value is the present value of $1/year forever—which turns out to be $1 divided by the interest rate. To see why this is so, note that if you lend out $10 at 10 percent interest (10 equals 1/.10), you can collect $1/year forever—just collect the interest and keep reinvesting the $10. We shall use this fact shortly.

ECONOMICS IN A CHANGING WORLD

In the previous ten chapters, we have analyzed the economics of an unchanging world, where every year is exactly the same as the year before. In that context, a question such as "If we sell widgets, will we make a profit?" reduces to the question "Will we make a profit this year?" Since every year is the same, if you make a profit this year, you will make a profit every other year as well. In the real world, things are not so simple; a firm may wish to "take a loss" for several years in order to get profits in the future.

By using present values, we reduce the more complicated problem of choice in a changing world to the simpler problem that we have already solved. A firm trying to decide whether to produce widgets converts all of its future gains and losses into present values and adds them up. If the sum is positive (a net profit), it ought to produce; if the sum is negative (a net loss), it ought not to. Similar calculations can be made by a firm deciding how much to produce, what mix of inputs to use, and so forth. It compares the alternatives in terms of the present value of all gains and losses and chooses the one for which it is highest.

A firm is considering an investment (a factory, a piece of land, a research project) which will produce its return over a long period of time. Assume, for simplicity, that the investment lasts forever and produces the same return each year. If the present value of the annual profit made possible by the investment is greater than the cost of the investment, it is worth making; otherwise it is not.

The present value of a permanent income stream of X is X/r, where r is the interest rate, as I pointed out above. So if an investment of $1,000,000 yields a return of more than $(r) \times 1,000,000$, it is worth making. If, in other words, the investment pays more than the going interest rate, it is an attractive one.

The calculation is more complicated if you are investing in something that will eventually wear out; in that case, the investment must pay at least the interest rate plus its own replacement cost to be worth making. The corresponding present value calculation is to compare the present value of a series of payments ($X per year for as many years as the machine lasts) with the initial expense; if the present value of the payments is larger than the expense, the investment is worth making.

Redoing the previous ten chapters in these terms would make this a very long chapter indeed, so I will restrict myself to working out the logic of one particularly interesting case.

DEPLETABLE RESOURCES

Consider a depletable resource, say, petroleum. There is a certain amount of it in the ground; when it has all been pumped up, there will never be any more. Firms that own oil wells must decide how to allocate their production over time in order to maximize profits. What will be the result?

Assume, for simplicity, that it costs nothing to produce oil; if you own an oil well containing 1,000,000 barrels of oil, your problem is simply to decide when to sell how much. Further assume that the oil wells are owned by many firms, each of which has only a small fraction of the total, so that each firm is a price taker.

What the firm "takes" is not a single price but a pattern of prices over time—P_1 at the beginning of the first year, P_2 at the beginning of the second year, P_3 at the beginning of the third year, and so on. Since we are considering a world with change but no uncertainty, at the beginning of the first year everyone already knows what the entire pattern of prices over time is going to be.

Deducing the Pattern of Prices

Suppose that the market interest rate is 10 percent, the first year's price (P_1) is $10.00/barrel, and the second year's price (P_2) is $12.00/barrel. A firm that sells some of its oil at the beginning of the first year gets a present value (measured in year 1) of $10.00/barrel. A firm that sells oil a year later gets a present value (again measured in year 1 so that we can compare the two) of $12.00/ 1.1 = $10.91/barrel. Under those circumstances, all firms would prefer to sell their oil in the second year. If they hold money for a year, they get 10 percent; if they hold oil for a year, they get 20 percent.

But if no oil were offered for sale in the first year, the price would be much more than $10.00/barrel. The price structure I have just decribed—$10.00/barrel in year 1, $12.00/barrel in year 2, and an interest rate of 10 percent—is inconsistent with rational behavior. If it existed, it would make people behave in a way such that it could not exist.

The only way to avoid such inconsistencies is for the pattern of prices over time to be such that P_2 is exactly 1.1 times P_1, so that the present value a firm gets by selling a barrel of oil is the same whether it sells it in the first year or the second. If it sells it in the first year, it gets $10.00; if it sells it in the second, it gets $11.00. The same argument applies to all future years. The price of oil must go up, year by year, at the interest rate.

You may find this way of describing what "must" happen confusingly abstract. The alternative is to try to describe the process by which an equilibrium set of prices is reached. In doing so, we will ignore the fact that in the perfectly predictable world we are assuming, everyone knows everything in the first minute of the first year, so equilibrium establishes itself immediately.

Imagine, then, that firms are considering a pattern of oil sales which does not lead to the pattern of prices I have described (price rising at the interest rate). A firm notices that it does better by selling its oil in year 2 than it would by selling it in year 1 and investing the money. So the firm changes its plans, transferring any production it had planned to make in year 1 to year 2. The result is to drive down the price in year 2 and drive up the price in year 1, moving both prices towards the pattern I have described. If the present value of the year 2 price is still greater than the present value of the year 1 price, another firm changes its plans. The process continues until the year 2 price is equal to the year 1 price times $1 + r$. The same argument applies for the relation between the year 2 price and the year 3 price, the year 3 price and the year 4 price, and so on.

Deducing the Current Price

Suppose you knew the demand curve for petroleum, the total amount that now exists, and the interest rate. How would you calculate the price? The easiest way is to work backward. The intersection of the demand curve with the vertical axis tells you the highest price petroleum can sell for—the price it will sell for the day the last well goes dry. Call that price P_{max} and that year T_{dry}. A year earlier, in year $T_{dry} - 1$, the price must be lower by a factor of $1/(1 + r)$, two years earlier it must be lower by a factor of $1/(1 + r)^2$, and so forth.

How do we find the date of T_{dry}? Since we know the price of petroleum in year $T_{dry} - 1$ and the demand curve, we know how much was consumed that year. The same applies for year $T_{dry} - 2$ and for each earlier year. Add up consumption year by year, starting at T_{dry} (quantity demanded = 0) and working back. When the total quantity consumed adds up to the total that now exists, you have reached the present. Since you now know how many years separate the year that we run out of oil from the present year, you know when we will run out. The calculations are shown in Figure 11-2a, where price is calculated from the demand curve, and Figure 11-2b, where quantity is added up year by year. The figures assume an initial quantity of oil of a billion barrels.

Figure 11-2

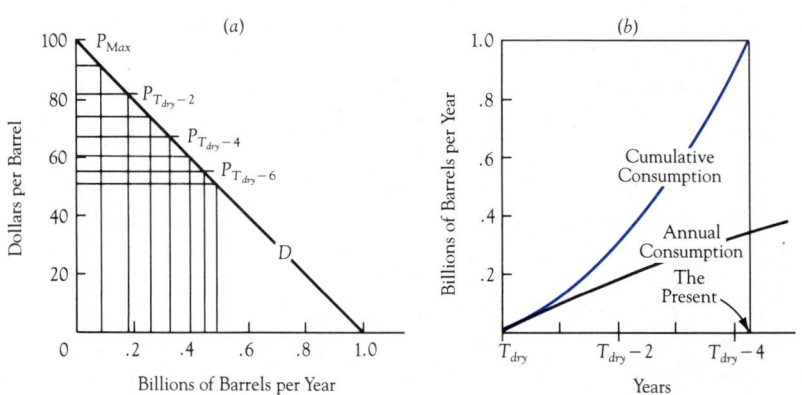

Calculating the price of a depletable resource by working backward from the date at which it is exhausted. T_{dry} is the year the last oil well runs dry. Working backward from T_{dry}, price falls at the interest rate, as shown on Figure 11-2a. Figure 11-2b shows annual and cumulative consumption; when cumulative consumption reaches the total amount now existing, we have reached the present.

As you may have realized, I have simplified the problem somewhat by assuming implicitly that everything happens at the beginning of each year, so that quantity consumed depends only on price at that instant. One could solve the problem a little more precisely by letting price rise and quantity demanded fall continuously through the year. Doing that would involve either using calculus or making the geometric calculations even more complicated than they are—which is why I did not do so.

In solving the problem, I assumed that the demand curve intersects the vertical axis—that there is some maximum price people will pay for petroleum. An alternative assumption is that as quantity goes to zero, price goes to infinity—people keep buying less and less petroleum at a higher and higher price per gallon. The calculation in that case is more complicated, since it involves an infinite sum (of smaller and smaller quantities of petroleum), but the logic of the problem is essentially the same.

Efficient Allocation Across Time

In discussing a competitive industry in Chapter 9, I pointed out that the structure of the industry was exactly that which would be chosen by a dictatorial administrator ordered to produce the same quantity at the lowest possible cost. A similar statement can be made about a competitive industry producing a depletable resource. The interest rate represents the rate at which goods this year can be converted into goods next year—as shown in the example of the apple orchard earlier in this chapter. The price of petroleum in any year is equal to its marginal value, for reasons explained back in Chapter 4. If the price of petroleum next year is less than $1 + r$ times the price this year (if, say, $P_1 = \$10.00$ and $P_2 = \$10.50$), that means that the marginal barrel this year goes to someone with a marginal value for it of $10 and the marginal barrel next year goes to someone with a marginal value of $10.50/barrel. By choosing to produce a barrel next year that we could have produced this year, we are in effect choosing a value of $10.50 next year instead of a value of $10 this year. But if the interest rate is 10 percent, someone who gives up $10 this year can convert it into $11 next year, so it is wasteful to give up $10 this year in exchange for only $10.50 next year. Following out this argument, a wise and benevolent administrator will allocate a depletable resource so as to make its price rise at the interest rate. As long as he does not do so, there is some way of reallocating production over time that produces a net gain.

This is only a sketch of an argument which cannot be made precisely until after the discussion of economic efficiency in Chapters 14 and 15. If you find the discussion of what a wise and benevolent administrator would do confusing, you may want to come back to it after reading those chapters.

Oil Prices and Insecure Property Rights

Before I leave the subject of depletable resources, several more points are worth making. The first is that the analysis I have given depends on the assumption that the owners of the resource have secure property rights—that they can confidently expect that petroleum they do not sell this year will still be theirs to sell next year.

Suppose that is not true; suppose, for example, that anyone who owns an oil well this year has a 10 percent chance of being expropriated next year. In that case, the same analysis implies that the price of petroleum will increase each year by a factor of $1.1 \times (1 + r)$. Owners of oil wells will sell petroleum next year instead of this year only if the price is enough higher to compensate them both for the interest they lose by not selling the oil until next year *and* for the chance that when next year arrives, the oil will no longer belong to them.

Most oil, at present, belongs to governments; most of those governments are at least somewhat unstable. The present rulers of Saudi Arabia, for example, would be foolish to base their plans on the assumption that they will still rule Saudi Arabia ten years from now—especially with the fate of the Shah of Iran still recent history. They should be, and doubtless are, aware that money in Switzerland is a more secure form of property than oil in Saudi Arabia.

The effects of insecure property rights are not limited to distant sheiks. The American government may be stable, but its economic policies are not; the imposition of special taxes (such as the "windfall profits tax") on oil companies is, in effect, a partial expropriation. If oil companies expect such taxes to increase, it is in their interest to produce oil now instead of saving it for the future—or, to put the conclusion more precisely, it is in their interest to produce more now and less in the future than they would if they did not expect such taxes to increase.

One implication of this argument is that the price of oil at present is too low! If most of it belongs to people with insecure property rights, they have an incentive to produce more now (driving the present price down) and less in the future (driving the future price up) than if property rights were secure. If, as I claim, the solution under secure property rights is in some sense optimal ("efficient" in the sense to be defined in Chapter 14), then insecure property rights create a less desirable outcome. Initially oil prices are "too low" and consumption "too high"; later prices are "too high" and consumption "too low." The allocation of the resource over time is inefficient; too much is consumed now and too little saved for later.

IS OIL A DEPLETABLE RESOURCE?

It may occur to some readers to ask whether the price of oil *has* been increasing at the interest rate over, say, the last fifty or a hundred years. The answer is no. From about 1930 to about 1970, the *real* price of oil—the price allowing for inflation—fell substantially. The OPEC boycott brought the real price most of the way back up to where it had been in 1930; events since have not yet brought it close to where it would be if it had been rising at the interest rate from 1930 to 1970.

There are at least three possible explanations for the apparent divergence between theory and fact. The first is that the economic theory of depletable resources is wrong. The second is that the theory is logically correct but that one of its assumptions—a predictable world—does not apply. If, for example, each year people overestimated future demands and/or underestimated future supplies, future prices would consistently turn out lower than expected and price would fail to rise over time at the interest rate. Economists are generally skeptical of such an explanation because it requires not merely mistakes but consistent mistakes; one would expect that after a decade or two of overestimating future oil prices, people would learn to do better—especially people who own oil wells.

The third, and most interesting, explanation of the observed pattern of prices is that oil is not a depletable resource! If this seems like an odd idea, consider that the world has been "about to run out of oil" for most of the past century; for most of that time, "proven reserves" have been equal to between ten and twenty years of production.

I started my analysis of a depletable resource by assuming that there were no production costs, so that the price of the resource was entirely due to the limited quantity. Suppose I had not made that assumption. How would the existence of production costs affect the conclusion?

Assume that production costs can be predicted with certainty. In that case, we can repeat our previous analysis, simply substituting "price minus production cost" for price. Price minus production cost is what the owner of an oil well ultimately gets by selling his oil. If it rises faster than the interest rate, all producers are better off holding their oil for future production; if it rises more slowly than the interest rate, all producers are better off selling everything immediately—or at least as fast as they can without raising production cost substantially in the process. In equilibrium, price minus production cost must rise at the interest rate—provided the owners of oil wells have secure property rights.

So one explanation of what has actually happened to oil prices is that most of the price is production cost—where that includes not only the cost of pumping the oil but also the cost of finding it. If production cost in that sense has been falling over time, then price could be falling as well—even if price, net of production cost, was rising.

In the previous discussion, we were considering a *pure depletable resource*—a resource whose price was entirely determined by its limited supply. Consider, at the other extreme, a resource of which only a limited amount exists but for which production costs are substantial and for which that "limited amount" is very large compared to the quantity demanded at a price sufficient to cover the cost of production. The amount is so large that even if the resource is sold at its production cost, technology, law, and political institutions will have changed beyond recognition before the supply is exhausted.

Under those circumstances, saving the good now in order to sell it when supplies run short is not a very attractive idea—before that happens, we may have stopped using it, or the owner may have been expropriated. Changes in its price over time will be almost entirely determined by changes in production cost. The good is, strictly speaking, depletable, but that fact has no significant effect on its price. The pattern of oil prices over the past ninety years or so suggests that that may well be how the market views petroleum.

If so, then the insecure property rights discussed earlier imply almost exactly the opposite of what they implied before. If the price of oil is determined by the cost of finding and producing it, then insecure property rights make the price of oil higher, not lower, than it would otherwise be. If someone who invests in finding and drilling an oil well has a 50 percent chance of having his well expropriated as soon as it starts producing, his return if he does keep the well must be at least twice his costs in order for him to be willing to make the investment. His return depends on the price he sells the oil for, so the price of oil will be higher in a world of insecure property rights. The same condition that makes the present price of a depletable resource (more precisely, a resource whose price is mostly due to its limited total quantity rather than to its cost of production) lower makes the present price of a resource whose price is mostly due to cost of production higher!

PRICE = VALUE THROUGH TIME AND SPACE

If an individual can buy apples for $0.50 apiece, he will adjust his consumption of apples until the marginal utility of an apple to him, the utility he gets from consuming one more apple, is the same as the marginal utility to him of $0.50—or, in other words, until the marginal value of an apple is $0.50. That is the argument by which we demonstrated, back in Chapter 4, that price equals marginal value—$P = MV$.

An interest rate is also a price. If the apple interest rate is 10 percent, the price of an apple this year is 1.1 apples next year. So I will adjust my consumption of apples in both years until the increased utility I get from consuming one more apple this year is the same as the increased utility I get from consuming 1.1 additional apples next year.

Impatience . . .

Why would an apple next year give me less utility than an apple this year? There are two major reasons. The first is impatience. Most of us, given the choice between the same pleasure now or in the future, would prefer to have it now. If so, then in comparing alternative patterns of pleasure over time—alternative utility streams—we will "discount utility" just as we discount income. If, in making a choice today, I am indifferent between receiving a "100-utile" pleasure now or a "105-utile" pleasure next year, I may be said to have an "internal discount rate" (for utility) of 5 percent.

My internal discount rate—my impatience—is a characteristic of my tastes; it describes my preferences between pleasures now and pleasures in the future, just as my utility function describes my preferences between apples and oranges. The market interest rate depends not merely on my tastes but on the tastes and productive abilities of everyone else as well. There is no particular reason why the two rates should be equal. Impatience may explain why the value to me of an apple now is greater than the value to me (now) of an apple a year from now, but it does not explain why the ratio of the two is exactly equal to the market interest rate.

. . . And Equilibrium

The equality between price and marginal value is not a characteristic of the consumer's tastes; it is a result of his rational behavior in deciding how much of what good to consume. This is true when the choice is between the same good at different times just as much as when it is between different goods at the same time. I will use Figure 11-3 to show how this works, in a world where the market interest rate is 10 percent, for a consumer whose internal discount rate is 0.

Suppose the consumer whose marginal utility curve is shown on Figure 11-3 consumed the same number of apples each year—say, 1,000 (he likes apples). The marginal utility of apples would be 10 utiles per apple, as shown on the figure. Since he consumes the same number of apples each year, he receives the same pleasure from consuming one more apple whichever year he consumes it. Since his internal discount rate is zero, he is indifferent between equal pleasures now and in the future. So he is indifferent between consuming an apple this year, next year, or in any future year.

The apple interest rate is assumed to be 10 percent, so he can trade 10 apples this year for 11 apples next year. Giving up 10 apples this year costs him about 100 utiles; consuming 11 more apples next year gives him about 110—the numbers are approximate because marginal utility will change a little over the range of quantities from 990 apples per year to 1,011 apples per year. He is indifferent between utiles this year and utiles next year, so losing 100 of the former and gaining 110 of the latter is a net gain. The consumer revises his consumption plans; instead of consuming 1,000 apples each year, he decides to consume 990 this year (point B on Figure 11-3) and 1,011 next year (point D).

Since he is now going to consume fewer apples in the first year than he had initially planned, their marginal utility will be higher. Since he is going to consume more apples in the second year, their marginal utility will be lower. As you can see from the figure, the marginal utility of apples in year 1 (990 apples per

Figure 11-3

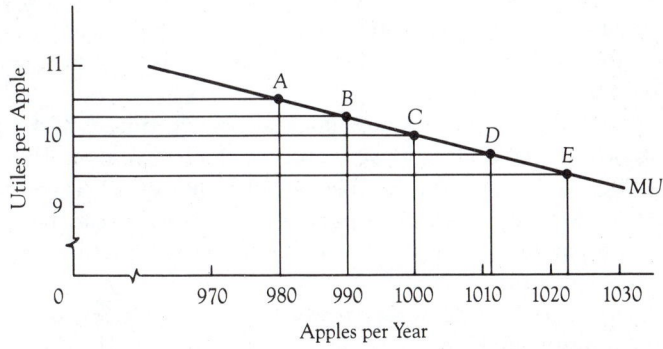

A consumer's marginal utility for apples. The consumer follows a pattern of consumption over time for which the present value (discounted at the discount rate for *utility*) of the marginal utility of an apple consumed next year equals $1/(1 + r)$ times the marginal utility of an apple consumed this year, where r is the apple interest rate. If the consumer's discount rate for utility equals the apple interest rate, he consumes the same number of apples each year (point C).

year) is about 10.25 utiles per apple; the marginal utility in year 2 (1,110 apples per year) is about 9.75 utiles per apple. Even with the revised plan, 11 apples next year are still worth more, in utiles, than 10 apples this year. So long as this is true—so long as the marginal utility of apples in year 1 is not at least 10 percent greater than in year 2—the consumer can improve his situation by revising his consumption plan and transferring consumption from year 1 to year 2. If the marginal utility of apples in year 2 were more than 10 percent greater than in year 1, he could improve his situation by revising in the opposite direction—transferring consumption from year 2 to year 1. He will achieve his optimal plan only when the amount he consumes in each year is such that the ratio of the marginal utility of apples in year 1 to the marginal utility of apples in year 2 is 1.1—equal to the price of apples in year 1 measured in apples in year 2. This, of course, is our old friend the equimarginal principle. The solution is shown on Figure 11-3 as points A (first year) and E (second year). The marginal utilities are about 10.5 and 9.5, so their ratio is about 1.1.

The analysis can easily be generalized to more than two years. We have shown that the ratio of marginal utilities between year 1 and year 2 must be 1.1. The same argument applies between year 2 and year 3, year 3 and year 4, and so forth. Consumption of apples rises, year by year, in such a way as to make the marginal utility of apples fall by 10 percent per year.

So far, we have done our calculations on the assumption that the consumer has an internal discount rate of zero—he is indifferent between identical pleasures now and in the future. Now let us consider a consumer who has an internal discount rate of 5 percent. He too will adjust his consumption plans until he is indifferent between an additional 10 apples this year and an additional 11 apples next year. Since he regards 10 utiles this year as equivalent to 10.5 next year, his optimal consumption plan will be one for which 11 apples next year produce 5 percent more utility (next year) than 10 apples this year produce (this year). His consumption for this year will be point B on Figure 11-3; his consumption for next year will be point D.

Finally, consider a consumer whose internal discount rate is 10 percent. His consumption will be point C this year and point C next year. Each year he consumes 1,000 apples and receives a marginal utility of 10 utiles per apple. Since he regards 10 utiles this year as equivalent to 11 next year, he can benefit neither by increasing his present consumption (10 apples more this year, 11 fewer next year) nor by decreasing it.

We have now answered the question which started this discussion. The marginal value of a future apple, measured in present apples, will be the same as the price of a future apple, measured in present apples; $MV = P$. Hence the *internal discount rate for apples* will be equal to the apple interest rate—and similarly, the internal discount rate for dollars will be equal to the dollar interest rate. The internal discount rate for apples is the sum of the internal discount rate for utility and the rate at which the marginal utility of apples declines with time. The rational consumer will adjust his consumption plans until that sum equals the apple interest rate.

PROBLEMS

1. One of my examples of goods that are inexpensive to store was "gold bars—provided nobody knows you have them." Why are gold bars expensive to store if people know you have them?
2. What does your answer to Problem 1 suggest might be one of the factors affecting interest rates?
3. What effect would each of the following have on interest rates?
   a. A new religion spreads which preaches the virtues of thrift; converts save their money for their old age.
   b. A new religion spreads which preaches that the end of the world is imminent.
   c. A social security system is established; people are taxed now and told that the money will be given back to them when they are old; they believe what they are told. The money collected is not invested but used to pay benefits to people who are presently old. (This is a hard problem.)
4. What effect will each of the following have on the apple interest rate? Assume that the supply curve for apples is upward sloping.
   a. A bad apple harvest this year.
   b. An expected bad apple harvest next year.
   c. A steady increase in the number of people who believe that an apple a day keeps the doctor away.
   d. A steady increase in medical costs, given that many people already believe that an apple a day keeps the doctor away.
5. According to the numbers at the bottom of Table 11-1, the first stream of income is worth $270,091, the second is worth $259,621, and their difference, the amount you would have if you received the first while simultaneously paying out the second, is $24,687. The numbers do not appear to add up. What is wrong? Show that the numbers are actually consistent.
6. You have a choice between two jobs. One of them pays you $20,000/year for 4 years, with the payment coming at the end of each year. The other pays you $19,000/year for 4 years, plus a "recruitment bonus" of $3,000 at the beginning of the first year. The market interest rate is 10 percent. Which job should you take?
7. You can build a factory for $1,000,000 which will permit you to manufacture 100,000 widgets per year at a cost of $1/widget (not counting the cost of the factory). The market interest rate is 10 percent.
   a. The factory will last forever; you do not expect the price of widgets to change. What is the *lowest* price for widgets at which the factory is worth building?
   b. The factory will last only three years. What is the lowest price for widgets at which the factory is worth building?
8. The government borrows money by selling at auction $1,000 bonds, payable in two years, with no interest payments. The market interest rate is 10 percent.

a. How much will the bonds sell for?

b. Even though the bonds do not "pay interest" (the buyer receives $1,000 when the bonds mature and nothing before that), buyers still end up receiving interest on their investment. Explain.

c. What interest rate are buyers of the bonds actually receiving on their investment? Explain.

d. What will happen if immediately after the bonds are sold, the market interest rate unexpectedly falls to 5 percent?

(Hint: The bonds must sell, both initially and after the change in interest rates, for a price at which the buyers are indifferent between buying them and investing their money at the market interest rate. If the selling price were higher than that, nobody would buy them; if it were lower, nobody would make any other investment.)

9. The following is a list of prices for wheat futures printed in February; the price for a wheat future is the price you pay now in exchange for delivery of wheat at some future date.

March	May	July	September	November	January
$2.00	$2.30	$1.20	$1.50	$1.80	$2.10

a. When is the new crop harvested? Explain.

b. About how much does it cost to store a bushel of wheat for a month? Explain.

For both parts you may, if you wish, assume that the interest rate is zero. (Note: This problem requires some original thinking by you; it has not been done anywhere in the chapter. The correct analysis is, however, very similar to the analysis of two different problems which are in the chapter.)

Chapter 12

...And Chance

I returned and saw under the sun, that the race is not to the swift, nor the battle to the strong, neither bread to the wise, nor yet riches to men of understanding, nor yet favour to men of skill; but time and chance happeneth to them all.

— *Ecclesiastes*

PART 1 · SUNK COSTS

So far, I have introduced time into the economy, but not uncertainty; everything always comes out as expected. The real world is not so simple. One of the consequences of uncertainty is the possibility of mistakes; another is the problem of what to do about them.

You see an advertisement for a shirt sale at a store 20 miles from your home. You were planning to buy some new shirts, and the prices are substantially lower than in your local clothing store; you decide the savings are enough to make it worth the trip. When you arrive, you discover that none of the shirts on sale are your size; the shirts that are your size cost only slightly less than in your local store. What should you do?

You should buy the shirts. The cost of driving to the store is a *sunk cost*— once incurred, it cannot be recovered. If you had known the prices before you left home, you would have concluded that it was not worth making the trip— but now that you have made it, you must pay for it whether or not you buy the shirts. Sunk costs are sunk costs.

There are two opposite mistakes one may make with regard to sunk costs. The first is to treat them as if they were not sunk—to refuse to buy the shirts because they are not inexpensive enough to justify the trip even though the trip has already been made. The second is to buy the shirts even when they are *more* expensive than in your local store, on the theory that you might as well get something for your trip. The something you are getting in this case is less than nothing. This is known as throwing good money after bad.

When, as a very small child, I quarrelled with my sister and then locked myself in my room, my father would come to the door and say, "Making a mistake and not admitting it is only hurting yourself twice." When I got a little older, he changed it to "Sunk costs are sunk costs."

In discussing firms' cost curves, one should distinguish between fixed costs and sunk costs—while the same costs are often both, they need not always be. *Fixed costs* are costs you must pay in order to produce anything—the limit of total cost as a function of quantity when quantity approaches zero. One could imagine a case where such costs were fixed but not sunk, either because the necessary equipment could be resold at its purchase price or because the equipment was rented and the rental could be terminated anytime the firm decided to stop producing.

The significance of sunk costs is that a firm will continue to produce even when revenue does not cover total cost, provided that it does cover non-sunk ("recoverable") costs, since non-sunk costs are all the firm can save by closing down. All costs, ultimately, are opportunity costs—the cost of doing one thing is not being able to do something else. Once a factory is built, the cost of continuing to run it does not include what was spent building it, since whatever you do, you will not get that back. It does include the cost of not selling it to someone else—which may be more or less than the cost of building it, depending on whether the value of such factories has gone up or down since it was built.

In deriving the supply curve of a competitive industry with open entry in Chapter 9, I assumed that the same cost curves possessed by one firm were available to an unlimited number of others. The conclusion was that firms would always produce at the minimum of average cost, where it crossed marginal cost. The reason was that if, at the quantity for which marginal cost equaled price (where profit is maximized for a price taker), price were above average cost, economic profit would be positive; it would pay other firms to enter the industry. They would do so until price was driven down to the point where it equaled both MC and AC, which occurs where they cross at the minimum of AC.

Does the relevant average cost include sunk costs? That depends on whether we are approaching the equilibrium from above or below, and in the latter case, on how long a time we consider. If prices start out above the equilibrium price, firms will only enter the industry as long as the price is above average cost *including* sunk cost—costs are not sunk until they are incurred, and the new firm starts out with the option of not incurring them. The equilibrium will be reached when price equals average total cost.

If we approach the equilibrium from below—if there are too many firms (perhaps because demand has recently fallen) and price is insufficient to cover even the average of non-sunk costs—firms will leave the market. They will continue to do so until price gets up to average non-sunk cost.

If the assets bought with the sunk costs (factories, say) wear out over time, then the number of factories will gradually decline and the price will gradually rise. Until it reaches average total cost, nobody will build any new factories. Eventually price will be equal to average total cost, just as it was when we reached the equilibrium from above, but it may take much longer to get there; it usually takes longer to wear out a factory than to build one.

In the next two sections, I will work through the logic of such situations in some detail while trying to show how it is related to the logic of a different sort of situation that was briefly discussed several chapters ago.

Upside, Downside, Cost Equals Price

In analyzing the industry supply curve in Chapter 9, I assumed an unlimited number of potential firms, all with the same cost curve; if existing firms make a profit, new firms come into existence until the profit is competed down to zero.

One objection to this which I discussed is that firms are not all identical. Some power companies own special pieces of real estate—Niagara Falls, for example—not available to their competitors. Some corporations are run by superb managers or possess the services of an inventive genius such as Browning or Kloss. Surely such fortunate firms can, as a result, produce their output at a lower cost than others—and can therefore make profits at a price at which it does not pay less fortunate firms to enter the industry.

But although firms which have, in this sense, low cost curves appear to make positive profits when less fortunate firms just barely cover their costs, that is an illusion. One should include in cost the cost of using the special assets (location, administrator, inventor, or whatever) that give that firm its advantage. The value of those assets is what the firm could sell them for or, in the case of human assets, what a competitor would pay to hire them away. One of the firm's (opportunity) costs of operating is not selling out and one of the costs to an inventor of running his own firm is not working for someone else's firm. If the possession of those special assets gives the firm an additional net revenue of, say, $100,000/year (forever—or almost), then the market value of those assets is the present value of that income stream. The interest on that present value is then the same $100,000/year. Since giving up that interest is one of the costs to the firm of staying in business, the firm should subtract it from revenue in calculating its economic profit.

Suppose, for example, that the firm is making an extra $100,000/year as a result of owning its special asset and that the interest rate is 10 percent. The present value of a permanent income stream of $100,000/year is $1,000,000, and the interest on $1,000,000 is $100,000. By using the asset this year, the firm gives up the opportunity to sell it and collect interest on the money it would get for it. We should include $100,000/year as an additional cost—foregone interest. Doing so reduces the profit of the firm to zero—the same as the profit of an ordinary firm. In one sense, this argument is circular; in another sense, it is not.

The same argument applies in the opposite direction to firms whose revenues fail to cover their sunk costs (firms whose revenues fail to cover their recoverable costs go out of business). Suppose a widget factory costs $1,000,000 to build and lasts forever; further suppose the interest rate is 10 percent, so that the factory must generate net revenue of $100,000/year to be worth building. At the time the factory is built, the price of widgets is $1.10/widget. The factory can produce 100,000 widgets per year at a cost (not including the cost of building the factory) of $.10/widget, so it is making $100,000/year—just enough to justify the cost of building it. Further suppose that the factory can be used for nothing but building widgets; its scrap value is zero.

Widget

FIMBRIATED GIDGET

The invention of the fimbriated gidget drastically reduces the demand for widgets. Widget prices fall from $1.10 to $0.20. At a price of $0.20, the firm is netting only $10,000/year on its $1,000,000 investment. So are all the other (identical) firms. Are they covering costs?

The factory is a sunk cost from the standpoint of the industry, but any individual firm can receive its value by selling it to another firm. How much will it sell for? Since it generates an income of $10,000/year and since at an interest rate of 10 percent an investment of $100,000 can generate the same income, the factory will sell for $100,000. Hence the cost of *not* selling it is $100,000—and the annual cost of not selling it is $10,000, the interest forgone. Ten thousand dollars is the firm's revenue net of costs before subtracting the cost of the factory, so net revenue after subtracting the cost of the factory—economic profit—is zero.

Again the argument is circular but not empty, since it tells us, among other things, what determines the price of a factory in a declining industry. In the case I have just described, the firm loses $900,000 the day the price of widgets drops, since that is the decrease in the value of their factory. Thereafter they just cover costs, as usual.

The assumptions used in this example, although useful for illustrating the particular argument, are not quite consistent with rational behavior. In the market equilibrium before the price drop, economic profit was zero. That is an appropriate assumption for the certain world of Chapters 1-10, but not for the uncertain world we are now discussing. If there is some possibility of prices falling, then firms will bear sunk costs only if the *average* return justifies the investment. Prices must be high enough so that the profit if they do not fall balances the loss if they do. The zero profit condition continues to apply, but only in an average sense—if the firms are lucky, they make money; if they are unlucky, they lose it. On average they break even. This point will be discussed at greater length later in the chapter.

Sunk Costs in the Shipping Industry

You may find it helpful to work through another example. Consider ships. Suppose that the total cost of building a ship is $10,000,000. For simplicity we assume that operating costs and the interest rate are both zero. Each ship lasts twenty years and can transport 10,000 tons of cargo each year from port A to port B. We assume, again for simplicity, that the ships all come back from B to A empty. It takes a year to build a ship. The demand curve for shipping cargo is shown in Figure 12-1a.

We start with our usual competitive equilibrium—price equals average cost. There are 100 ships and the cost for shipping cargo is $50/ton. Each ship makes $500,000 a year; at the end of twenty years, when the ship collapses into a pile of rust, it has just paid for itself. Every year five ships are built to replace the five that have worn out. If the price for shipping were any higher, it would pay to build more ships, since an investment of $10,000,000 would produce a return of more than $10,000,000; if it were lower, no ships would be built. The situation is shown in Figure 12-1a.

Figure 12-1b shows the effect of a sudden increase in the demand for shipping—from D to D'. In the short run, the supply of shipping is perfectly inelastic, since it takes a year to build a ship. The price shoots up to P_1, where the new demand curve intersects the (short-run) vertical supply curve.

Figure 12-1

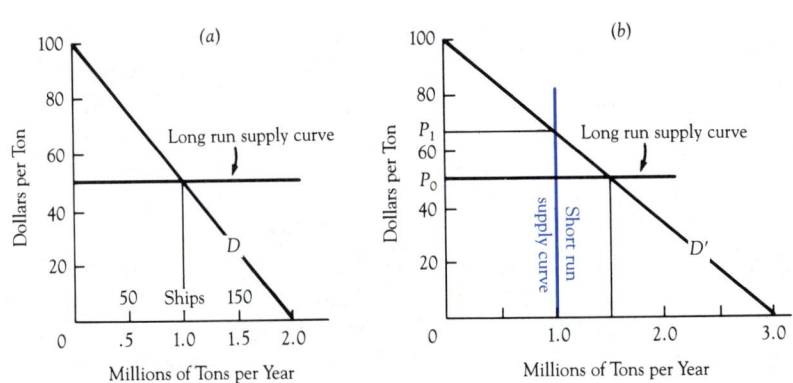

Supply and demand curves for shipping, showing the effect of an unanticipated increase in demand.   Figure 12-1a shows the situation before the increase and Figure 12-1b after. The horizontal axis shows both quantity of shipping carried each year and the equivalent number of ships. The short-run supply curve is vertical at the current number of ships (and amount of freight they carry). The long-run supply curve is horizontal at the cost of producing shipping (the annualized cost of building a ship divided by the number of tons it carries).

Shipyards immediately start building new ships. At the end of a year, the new ships are finished, and the price drops back down to the old level. Figure 12-2 shows the sequence of events in the form of a graph of price against time.

Looking again at Figure 12-1b, note that it has two supply curves—a vertical short-run supply curve and a horizontal long-run supply curve. No ships can be built in less than a year, so there is no way a high price can increase the supply of shipping in the short run. Since operating costs are, by assumption, zero, it pays shipowners to operate the ships however low the price; there is no way a low price can reduce the supply of shipping in the short run. So in the short run, quantity supplied is independent of price for any price between zero and infinity. Hence the short-run supply curve is vertical.

Figure 12-2

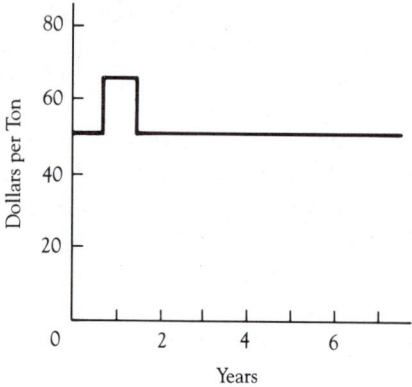

A possible pattern of freight rates over time.   At $T = 0$ there is an unexpected increase in demand, as shown on Figure 12-1b; price rises above its long-run equilibrium, then gradually falls back.

The situation in the long run is quite different. At any price where ships more than cover their construction cost, it pays to build ships; so in the long run, the industry will produce an unlimited quantity of shipping at any price above $P_0 = \$50$/ton. At any price below P_0, building a ship costs more than the ship is worth; so eventually—if you wait long enough for the existing ships to wear out—at any price below P_0, quantity supplied falls to zero. Hence the long-run supply curve is horizontal. It is worth noting that on the "up" side—building ships—the long run is a good deal shorter than on the "down" side.

Suppose that instead of the increase in demand shown in Figure 12-1b, there is instead a decrease in demand, from D to D'', as shown in Figure 12-3a. Price drops. Since (by assumption) there are no operating costs, ships continue to carry cargo as long as they get any price above zero. The price is at the point where the old (short-run) vertical supply curve intersects the new demand curve (A).

Building a ship is now unprofitable, since it will not, at the new price, repay its construction costs. No ships are built. Over the next five years, 25 ships wear out, bringing supply down to a point where the price is again $\$50$/ton (B). Figure 12-3b shows how the price and the number of ships change with time.

There is one thing wrong with this story. The initial equilibrium assumed that the price of shipping was going to stay the same over the lifetime of a ship—that was why ships were produced if, and only if, the return at current prices, multiplied by the lifetime of the ship, totaled at least the cost of production. The later developments assumed that the demand curve, and hence the price, could vary unpredictably.

If shipowners expect random changes in future demand, there will still be a freight price at which they are just willing to build ships, but there is no reason to expect it to be $\$50$/ton. If they believe that future decreases in demand will

Figure 12-3

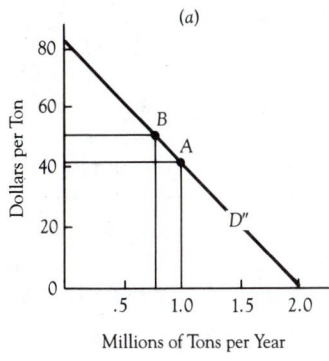

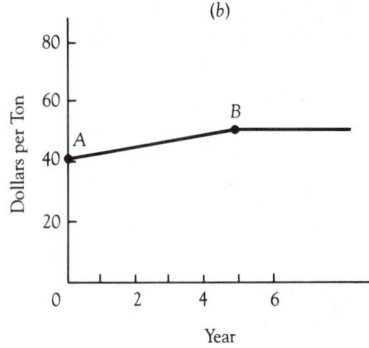

The effect of an unexpected decrease in demand for shipping.   Figure 12-3a shows the situation after the demand curve shifts. Figure 12-3b shows the resulting pattern of prices over time.

be at least as frequent and as large as future increases, the price at which they are just willing to build will be higher. Why? Because ships can be built quickly, so that the gain from an increase in demand is very short lived, but wear out slowly, so that the loss from a decrease in demand continues for a long time. Compare the short period of high prices in Figure 12-2 with the long period of low prices in Figure 12-3b. If the current price is high enough (P_e on Figure 12-4) so that any increase causes ships to be built, then an increase in demand will hold prices

Figure 12-4

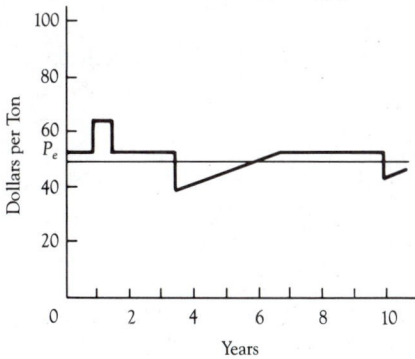

A possible pattern of freight rates over time.   Unlike Figure 12-2, this figure assumes that the producers expect unpredictable shifts in demand. The average return from selling shipping must be enough to just cover the costs of producing it.

above P_e for only a year. A decrease can keep prices below P_e for up to twenty years. If P_e were equal to $50/ton, the price at which ships exactly repay the cost of building them, the average price would be lower than that and ships, on average, would fail to recover their costs. So P_e must be above $50/ton.

This is, of course, the same point that I made earlier in describing the effect of sunk costs in the widget industry. In order to make the behavior of the shipowners rational, we must assume that they do not start building ships until the price is high enough so that the profits if demand does not fall make up for the losses if it does. The pattern of price over time in the industry then looks something like Figure 12-4.

How to Lie While Telling the Truth—
A True Story

Many years ago, while spending a summer in Washington as a congressional intern, I came across an interesting piece of economic analysis involving these principles. The congressman I was working for had introduced a bill which would have abolished a large part of the farm program, including price supports for feed grains (crops used to feed animals). Shortly thereafter the agriculture department released a "study" of the effects of abolishing those particular parts of the farm program. Their conclusion, as I remember, was that farm income would fall by $5 billion, while the government would save only $3 billion in reduced expenditure, so that there would be a net loss of $2 billion.

The agriculture department's calculations completely ignored the effect that the proposed changes would have on consumers—although the whole point of the price support program was (and is) to raise the price of farm products and hence of food. Using the agriculture department's figures, the proposed abolition would have saved consumers (as I remember) about $7 billion, producing a net gain of $5 billion. The agriculture department, which, of course, opposed the proposed changes, failed to mention that implication of its analysis.

Another part of the report asserted that the abolition of price supports on feed grains would drive down the price of the animals that consumed them. It went on to say that the price drop would first hit poultry producers, then producers of pork and lamb, and finally beef producers. All of this, to the best of my knowledge, is correct. The conclusion which appears to follow is that poultry producers will be injured a great deal by the abolition, lamb and pork producers somewhat less, and beef producers injured least of all. This is almost the precise opposite of the truth.

If you think about the situation for a moment, you should be able to see what is happening. Removing price supports on feed grains lowers the cost of production for poultry, pork, lamb, and beef—feed grains are probably the largest input for producing those foods. In the case of poultry, the flocks can be rapidly increased, so the poultry producers will receive an above-normal profit (cost of production has fallen, price of poultry has not) for only a short time. Once the flocks have increased, the price of chickens falls and the return to their producers goes back to normal. The herds of pigs and sheep take longer to increase, so their producers get above-normal returns for a longer period, and the beef producers get them for longer still. The situation is just like the situation of the shipowners when demand increases, except that there is a drop in production cost rather than an increase in the demand schedule. The agriculture department appeared to be saying that the beef producers would receive the least injury and the poultry producers the greatest injury from the proposed change; what they were actually saying was that the beef producers would receive the largest benefit and the poultry producers the smallest benefit.

PART 2 · LONG-RUN AND SHORT-RUN COSTS

So far, we have been analyzing the influence of uncertainty on prices by taking account of the effect of sunk costs on the behavior of profit-maximizing firms. A more technical description of what we are doing is that we are analyzing the effect of uncertainty in terms of "Marshallian quasi-rents"— "Marshallian" because this approach, along with much of the rest of modern economics, was invented by Alfred Marshall about a hundred years ago and "quasi-rents" because the return on sunk costs is in many ways similar to the rent on land. Both can be viewed as the result of a demand curve intersecting a perfectly inelastic supply curve— although in the case of sunk costs, the supply curve is inelastic only in the short run.

The more conventional way of analyzing these questions is in terms of short-run and long-run cost curves and the resulting short-run and long-run supply curves. I did not use that approach in Chapter 9, where supply curves were deduced from cost curves, and so far, I have not used it here. Why?

The reason I ignored the distinction between long-run and short-run costs in Chapter 9 was explained there; in the unchanging world we were analyzing, the distinction is meaningless. The reason I did not introduce the ideas of this chapter in that form is that the way in which I did introduce it provides a more general and more powerful way of analyzing the same questions. It is more general because it allows us to consider productive assets—such as ships and factories— with a variety of lifetimes and construction times, not merely the extreme (and arbitrary) classes of "short" and "long" lived. It is more powerful because it not only gives us the long-run and short-run supply curves but also shows what happens in between, both to the price of the productive assets and to the price of the goods they produce.

The simplest way to demonstrate all of this—and to prepare you for later courses which will assume you are familiar with the conventional approach—is to work out the short-run/long-run analysis as a special case of the approach we have been following. While doing so, we will also be able to examine some complications which have so far remained hidden behind the simplifying assumptions of our examples.

Factory Size and the Short-Run Supply Curve

We start with an industry. Since we used up our quota of widgets earlier in the chapter, we will make it the batten industry. Battens are produced in batten factories. A firm entering the industry—or a firm already in the industry that is replacing a worn-out factory—must choose what size factory to build. A small factory is inexpensive to build but expensive to operate—especially if you want to produce a large amount of output. Larger factories cost more to build and less to operate. A firm can only operate one factory at a time.

Figures 12-5 through 12-7 show the cost curves for three different factories. The first costs $1 million to build, the second costs $3 million, and the third costs $5 million. A factory has no scrap value, so the investment is a sunk cost. Each factory lasts ten years. The interest rate is zero, so the annual cost associated with each factory is one tenth the cost of building it. One could easily enough do the problem for a more realistic interest rate, but that would complicate the calculations without adding anything important.

Total cost, as you may remember from Chapter 9, is the sum of fixed cost— the cost of being able to produce anything at all, hence the limit of total cost as quantity approaches zero—and variable cost. The figures are drawn on the as-

Figure 12-5

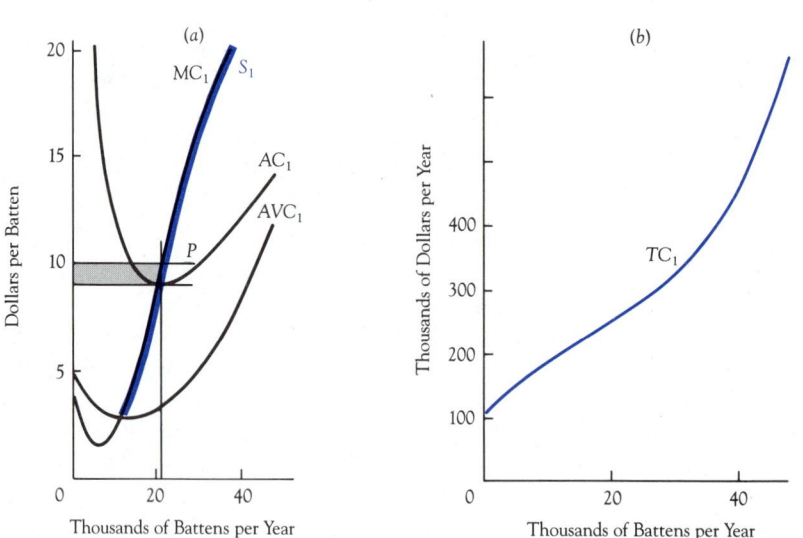

Cost curves and the resulting supply curve for a small batten factory. The factory costs $1,000,000 to build. Since it lasts for ten years, the annualized fixed cost (FC) is $100,000/year. The shaded area shows the profit at a price of $10/batten.

Figure 12-6

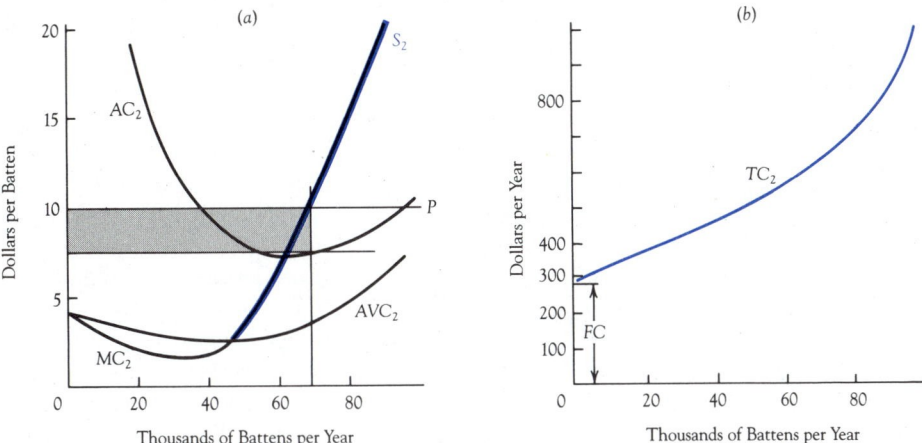

Cost curves and the resulting supply curve for a medium-sized batten factory. The factory costs $3,000,000 to build. Since it lasts for ten years, the annualized fixed cost (FC) is $300,000/year. The shaded area shows the profit at a price of $10/batten.

Figure 12-7

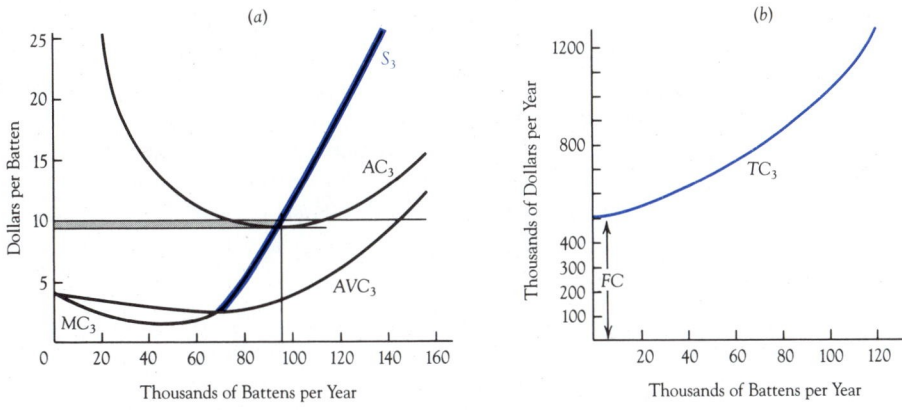

Cost curves and the resulting supply curve for a large batten factory. The factory costs $5,000,000 to build. Since it lasts for ten years, the annualized fixed cost (FC) is $500,000/year. The shaded area shows the profit at a price of $10/batten.

sumption that the only fixed cost in producing battens is the cost of building the factory; all other costs are variable. Since this implies that the fixed cost and the sunk cost are identical, so are *variable cost* (total cost minus fixed cost) and *recoverable cost* (total cost minus sunk cost). The figures show average variable cost (AVC); it might just as well have been labeled ARC for "average recoverable cost."

Each pair of figures shows four cost curves—total cost (TC), marginal cost (MC), average cost (AC), and average variable cost (AVC). Total cost includes the (annualized) cost of the factory; since that is assumed to be the only fixed cost, total cost at a quantity of zero is the annualized cost of the factory—$100,000/year on Figure 12-5b. Since average cost is defined as total cost over quantity, it too includes the cost of the factory. Average variable cost, on the other hand, does *not* include the cost of the factory, since that is fixed.

So far as marginal cost is concerned, it does not matter whether or not we include the cost of the factory. Marginal cost is the slope of total cost; adding a constant term to a function simply shifts it up without affecting its slope.

Suppose the batten firm has built the factory of Figure 12-5. The price of a batten is P; the firm must decide how many to produce each year. Just as in Chapter 9, the firm maximizes its profit by producing the quantity for which $MC = P$—provided that at that quantity, it is not losing money.

In Chapter 9, we could see whether the firm was making or losing money by comparing price to average cost; if average cost is greater than price, then profit is negative and the firm should go out of business. This time, however, we have two average costs—AC and AVC. Which should we use?

We should use AVC. The firm already has the factory; it is deciding whether or not to shut it down. If the firm shuts down the factory, it will not get back the money that was spent to build it—that is a sunk cost. What it will save is its variable cost. If the savings from shutting down the factory are greater than the loss from no longer having any battens to sell, then the factory should be shut down. Otherwise it should continue to operate. So as long as price is greater than average variable cost, the firm continues to operate the factory, producing the quantity for which marginal cost equals price. If price is lower than average cost, the factory is not paying back its cost of construction and should never have been built—but it is too late to do anything about that. Sunk costs are sunk costs.

The curves labeled S_1-S_3 on Figures 12-5 through 12-7 are the supply curves implied by the previous two paragraphs. Each S runs along the marginal cost curve, starting at its intersection with average variable cost. For any price lower than that, quantity supplied is zero.

The Long-Run Supply Curve

These are the *short-run* supply curves. They correctly describe the behavior of a firm which already owns a functioning factory. But in the long run, factories wear out and must be replaced. A firm that is about to build a factory is in a different situation, in two respects, from a firm that already has a factory. First, the cost of building the factory is not yet sunk—the firm has the alternative of not building and not producing. The firm will build only if it expects price to be above average cost—including in the average the cost of building the factory.

The second difference is that a firm about to build can choose which size of factory it prefers. Its choice will depend on what the price is. So the long-run supply curve must take account of the relation between the price of battens and the size of the factories in which they will be produced.

How do we find the long-run supply curve of a firm? We consider a firm which is about to build a factory and which believes that the price of battens will remain at its present level for at least the next ten years—the lifetime of the factory. The firm's long-run supply curve is then the relation between the quantity the firm chooses to produce and the price.

We solve the problem in two steps. First we figure out, for each size of factory, how many battens the firm will produce if it decides to build a factory of that size. Then we compare the resulting profits, in order to find out which factory the firm will choose to build. Once we know which factory the firm chooses to build and how much a firm with a factory of that size chooses to produce, we know quantity supplied—at that price. Repeat the calculation for all other prices and we have the firm's long-run supply curve.

Figures 12-5 through 12-7 show the calculations for a price of $10/batten. As we already know, if a firm produces at all, it maximizes its profit by producing a quantity for which $MC = P$. So for each size of factory, a firm that chose to build that factory would produce the quantity for which marginal cost was equal to price.

Having done so, what would the firm's profit be? Profit per unit is simply price minus average cost. The firm should include the cost of building the factory in deciding which factory to build, so the relevant average is average cost, not average variable cost. Total profit is profit per unit times number of units—the shaded rectangle in each figure. It is largest for Figure 12-6, so the firm builds a $3,000,000 factory and produces that quantity for which, in such a factory, price equals marginal cost.

Figure 12-8a shows the result of repeating the calculations for many different prices. As I have drawn the curves, the less expensive factories have a lower average cost for low levels of output and a higher average cost for high levels. The result is that as price (and quantity) increase, so does the optimal size of the factory. The long-run supply curve for the firm (Figure 12-8b) is then pieced together from portions of the short-run supply curves of Figures 12-5 through 12-7. In doing so, we limit ourselves to the part of each short-run supply curve above the corresponding average cost (AC not AVC)—in other words, the long-run supply curve for that size of factory. We end up with the long-run supply curve for a firm which is free to vary factory size as well as other inputs.

Looking at Figure 12-8b, we see that the smallest size of factory is irrelevant to the firm's supply curve, since there is no price of battens at which it would be worth building such a factory. If the market price is below P_0, none of the three sizes of factory can make enough money to justify the cost of building it, so the firm produces nothing. For prices between P_0 and P_1 on Figure 12-8b, the firm

Figure 12-8

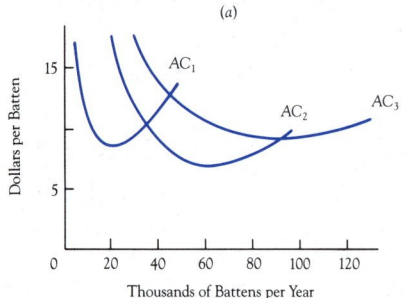
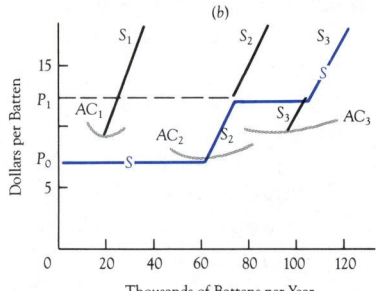

The short-run and long-run average cost curve and the long-run supply curve for a firm producing battens. AC and S are drawn on the assumption that there are only three possible factory sizes, corresponding to Figures 12-5, 12-6, and 12-7. For any price, the firm builds the factory which produces the largest profit at that price.

maximizes its profit by building a $3 million factory and producing the quantity for which the marginal cost (MC on Figure 12-6a) equals the price. For prices above P_1, it does better building a $5 million factory and producing along the MC curve of Figure 12-7a. So S is the firm's long-run supply curve.

An alternative way of deriving the long-run supply curve of the firm is to consider the factory itself as one more input in the production function. Just as in Chapter 9, one then calculates the lowest cost bundle of inputs for each level of output; the result tells you, for any quantity of output, how much it costs to produce and what inputs—including what size of factory—you should use. You then go on to calculate average cost (the same curve shown on Figure 12-8a), marginal cost, and the supply curve. Since we are considering the long-run supply curve, we are, temporarily, back in the unchanging world of Chapters 1-10.

Figure 12-9a shows what the firm's long-run average cost curve would be like if, instead of limiting the firm to only three sizes of factory, we allowed it to choose from a continuous range of factory sizes. The solid line on the figure is the resulting average cost curve; the gray lines are average cost curves for several different factory sizes, including those shown on Figures 12-5 through 12-7. Since for any quantity, the firm chooses that factory size which produces that quantity at the lowest possible cost, the average cost curve for a factory can never lie below the average cost curve for the firm. On the other hand, every point on the firm's average cost curve must also be on the average cost curve for some size of factory—the size the firm chooses to build if it expects to produce that quantity of output. The result is what you see on Figure 12-9a; the average cost curves for the different factory sizes lie above the firm's long-run average cost curve and are tangent to it.

One feature of figures such as 12-9a which some people find puzzling is that the point where a factory average cost curve touches the firm's long-run average cost curve is generally not at the minimum average cost for that size of factory.

AC_1, for example, touches AC not at point B, which is its minimum, but at point A, and similarly for all the others except AC_2. Mathematically, the reason for this is quite simple. AC_1 is tangent to AC at point A. At the point of tangency, the two curves have the same slope. Unless AC is at *its* minimum—as it is at point C, where it touches AC_2—its slope is not zero. Since the slope of AC is not zero at the point of tangency, neither is the slope of AC_1; hence AC_1 cannot be at its minimum. The same applies to all of the points of tangency except C.

As I have commented before, one can read through a proof without really understanding why the conclusion is correct; for some of you, the previous paragraph may be an example of that. Another way of putting the argument is to point out that while the firm which chooses to produce quantity Q_A could lower its average cost by expanding output to Q_B, it would then be producing a larger quantity; if it wished to produce that quantity, it could do so at an even lower average cost by using a bigger factory. B shows the minimum average cost for producing *in a $1 million factory*. It does not show the minimum average cost for producing a quantity Q_B; hence it does not show what the average cost would be for a firm that wished to produce that quantity and was free to build whatever size factory it preferred. Similarly, D is the minimum point on AC_3, but there is another (unlabeled) average cost curve lying below it, providing a lower cost way of producing Q_D—at point F.

Figure 12-9a showed the long-run average cost curve for a firm that could choose from a continuous range of factory sizes. Figure 12-9b also shows the long-run supply curve for such a firm. Every time the price went up a little, the optimal size of factory would shift up as well. The result would be the smooth supply curve of Figure 12-9b.

In Chapter 9, after finding the supply curve for a firm, we went on to find the supply curve for an industry made up of many such firms. We can do the same

Figure 12-9

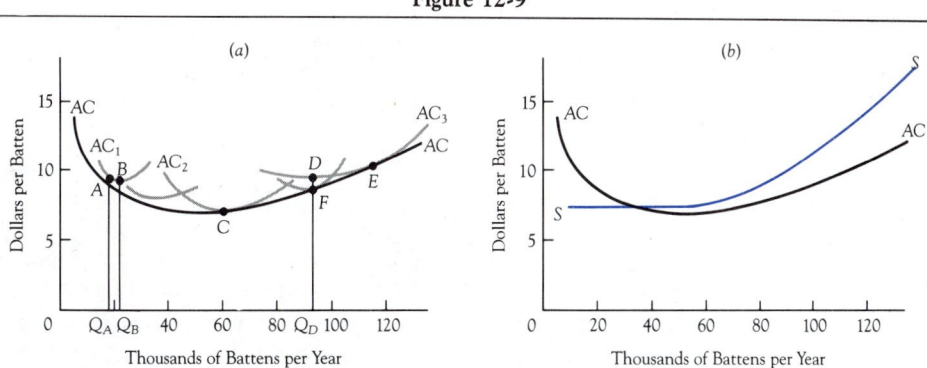

The long-run average cost curve and supply curve for a firm producing battens.　AC and S are drawn on the assumption that there is a continuous range of possible factory sizes. For any level of output desired, the firm builds the factory which produces that output at the lowest cost. For any price, it builds the factory which produces the largest profit at that price.

thing here. In the short run, the number of factories is fixed; there is not enough time to build more or for existing factories to wear out. So the short-run supply curve for the industry is simply the horizontal sum of the short-run supply curves for all the existing factories—just as in the case of the competitive industry with closed entry discussed in Chapter 9.

In the long run, the number of factories can vary; firms may build additional factories or fail to replace existing factories as they wear out. Unless there are barriers to entry, such as laws against building new factories, we are in the second case of Chapter 9—a competitive industry with free entry. If the inputs to the industry are in perfectly elastic supply so that their price does not depend on industry output, the industry's long-run supply curve is S on Figure 12-10—a horizontal line at price = marginal cost = minimum average cost. If the price of some of the inputs rises as the industry purchases more of them, the result is an upward-sloped supply curve, such as S'.

Figure 12-10

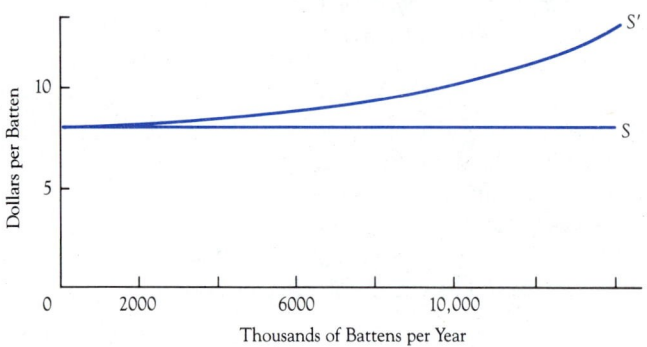

Two possible long-run supply curves for the batten industry.   S, which is horizontal at a price equal to minimum average cost, is drawn on the assumption that inputs are available in perfectly elastic supply. S' is drawn on the assumption that as quantity increases, input prices are bid up.

Part 1 vs Part 2—Two Approaches Compared

The short-run supply curve tells us how the firm will respond to changes in price over periods too short to make it worth changing the size of its factory; the long-run supply curve tells how the firm will respond to what it regards as permanent changes in price. We have now solved for both. In doing so, what have we learned that we did not already know?

The most important lesson is how to calculate the behavior of the firm over the short run. In all of the earlier examples of this chapter, the firms had simple all-or-none patterns of production. A widget factory either produced at capacity or shut down; a ship continued to carry a full load of freight as long as it got anything at all for doing so. We were, in effect, assuming the cost curves shown in Figures 12-11a and 12-11b—marginal cost constant up to some maximum level of production and infinite beyond that. We were also assuming that there was only one kind of factory and one kind of ship.

In analyzing the batten factory, we allowed for more realistic cost curves. By doing so, we saw how even in the short run, quantity supplied can vary continuously with price. We could have done the same thing in the earlier analysis; I chose not to. All-or-none production was a simplifying assumption used to avoid complications that were, at that point, inessential. The discussion of long-run and short-run supply curves was a convenient point at which to drop that simplification.

What are the disadvantages of the short-run/long-run approach? One of them is that it encourages students to confuse sunk costs and fixed costs. In the examples that are used, the two are generally the same, but there is no reason why they have to be—as was mentioned in Chapter 9.

In the batten industry, as I pointed out earlier, the curve labeled average variable cost could also have been labeled average recoverable cost, since the two are equal. I labeled it AVC in deference to convention; that is how you will generally see it in other textbooks. It would have been more correct to have labeled it ARC. It is the fact that the cost is recoverable, not the fact that it is variable, which is essential to the way in which the curve is related to the short-run supply curve. If we were considering a situation in which variable cost and recoverable cost were not the same, we could have simply drawn the ARC curve and forgotten about AVC.

One of the faults of the short-run/long-run approach is that it encourages confusion between fixed and sunk costs. One of its limitations is that it distinguished between only two kinds of costs—short run and long run. The more

Figure 12-11

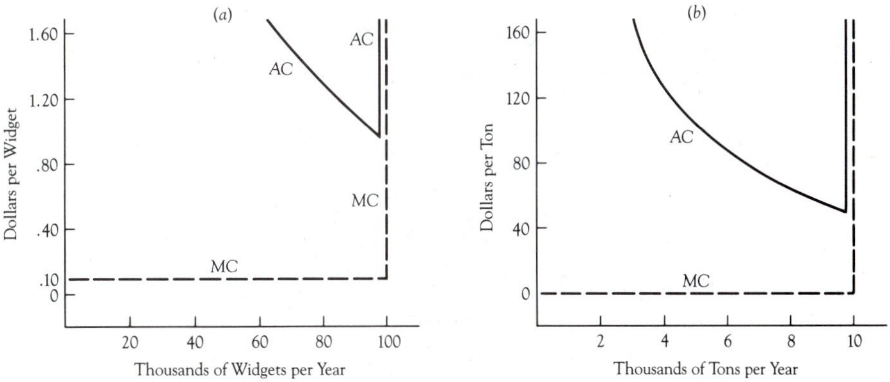

Cost curves for widgets and shipping. The figures show the cost curves for the widget (11a) and shipping (11b) industries discussed in Part I of the chapter.

general approach to sunk cost, which we developed earlier in the chapter, can be used to analyze a much broader range of situations, including ones in which there are several long-lived productive assets with different lifetimes.

A second limitation is that the short-run/long-run approach says nothing about what happens to price between the two periods—how it adjusts over time to unexpected changes in demand. If we know how many factories of what size exist, the short-run supply curve allows us to calculate price and quantity; whether or not we know how many factories exist, the long-run supply curve tells us what price and quantity must eventually be if the situation remains stable for long enough. But the approach does not explain how to calculate the path by which price and quantity move from the one value to the other—which is one of the things we did in analyzing the widget and shipping industries.

None of this means that the short-run/long-run approach is wrong. Both in using economics and in teaching it, one must balance the costs and benefits of different degrees of simplicity. The short-run/long-run approach described in this section has the advantages and the disadvantages of greater simplicity; it is easier to teach but tells us less of what we want to know than the approach used earlier in the chapter.

In one sense, the difference is entirely pedagogical. Once you understand either approach, you can develop the other out of it. Starting with short- and long-run cost curves, you could, with a little ingenuity, figure out how to analyze more complicated cases or how to trace the path of price and quantity over time. Starting with sunk costs, you can work out short-run and long-run cost curves as special cases—not only in the shipping industry of Figures 12-1a through 12-4 but in more complicated situations as well. By teaching the material in both ways, I hope I have allowed you to learn it in whichever way you found more natural. That is a benefit. Its cost is measured in additional pages of book and additional hours of time—mine in writing and yours in reading. The production of textbooks involves the same sort of trade-off between costs and benefits as does the production of anything—or any other action requiring choice.

PART 3 · SPECULATION

It is difficult to read either newspapers or history books without occasionally coming across the villainous speculators. Speculators, it sometimes seems, are responsible for all the problems of the world—famines, currency crises, high prices.

How Speculation Works

A speculator buys things when he thinks they are cheap and sells them when he thinks they are expensive. Imagine, for example, that you decide there is going to be a bad harvest this year. If you are right, the price of grain will go up. So you buy grain now, while it is still cheap. If you are right, the harvest is bad, the price of grain goes up, and you sell at a large profit.

There are several reasons why this particular way of making a profit gets so much bad press. For one thing, the speculator is, in this case at least, profiting by other people's bad fortune, making money from, in Kipling's phrase, "Man's belly pinch and need." Of course, the same might be said of farmers, who are usually considered good guys. For another, the speculator's purchase of grain tends to drive up the price, making it seem as if he is responsible for the scarcity.

But in order to make money, the speculator must sell as well as buy. If he buys when grain is plentiful, he does indeed tend to increase the price then; but if he sells when it is scarce (which is what he wants to do in order to make money), he increases the supply and decreases the price, precisely when the additional grain is most useful.

A different way of putting it is to say that the speculator, acting for his own selfish motives, does almost exactly what a benevolent despot would do. When he foresees a future scarcity of wheat, he induces consumers to use less wheat now. The speculator gets consumers to use less wheat now by buying it (before the consumers themselves realize the harvest is going to be bad), driving up the price; the higher price encourages consumers to consume less food (by slaughtering meat animals early, for example, to save their feed for human consumption), to import food from abroad, to produce other kinds of food (go fishing, dry fruit, . . .), and in other ways to prepare for the anticipated shortage. He then stores the wheat and distributes it (for a price) at the peak of the famine. Not only does he not cause famines, he prevents them.

More generally, speculators (in many things, not just food) tend, if successful, to smooth out price movements, buying goods when they are a little below their long-run price and selling them when they are a little above it, raising the price towards equilibrium in the one case and lowering it towards equilibrium in the other. They do what governmental "price stabilization" schemes claim to do—reduce short-run fluctuations in prices. In the process, they frequently interfere with such price stabilization schemes, most of which are run by producing countries and designed to "stabilize" prices as high as possible.

Cui Bono

Why indeed should we welcome you, Master Stormcrow? Lathspell I name you, Ill-news; and ill news is an ill guest they say.

— Grima to Gandalf in *The Two Towers* by J.R.R. Tolkien

At least part of the unpopularity of speculators and speculation may reflect the traditional hostility to bearers of bad news; speculators who drive prices up now in anticipation of a future bad harvest are conveying the fact of future scarcity and are forcing consumers to take account of it. Part also may be due to the difficulty of understanding just how speculation works. Whatever the reason, ideas kill, and the idea that speculators cause shortages must be one of the most lethal errors in history. If speculation is unpopular, it is also difficult, since the speculator depends for his profit on not having his stocks of grain seized by mob or government. In poor countries, which means almost everywhere through almost all of history, the alternative to speculation in food crops is periodic famine.

One reason people suspect speculators of causing price fluctuations is summarized in the Latin phrase *cui bono?*; a loose translation would be "Who benefits?" If the newspapers discover that a gubernatorial candidate has been receiving large campaign donations from a firm that made $10 million off state contracts last year, it is a fair guess that the information was fed to them by his opponent. If a coup occurs somewhere in the Third World and the winners immediately ally themselves with the Soviet Union (or the U.S.), we do not have to look at the new ruler's bank records to suspect that the takeover was subsidized by Moscow (or Washington).

While *cui bono* is a useful rule for understanding many things, it is not merely useless but positively deceptive for understanding price movements. The reason is simple. The people who benefit from an increase in the price of something are those who produce it, but by producing, they drive the price not up but down. The people who benefit by a price drop are those who buy and consume the good, but buying a good tends to increase its price, not lower it. The manufacturer of widgets may spend his evenings on his knees praying for the price of widgets to go up, but he spends his days behind a desk making it go down. Hence the belief that price changes are the work of those who benefit by them is usually an error and sometimes a dangerous one.

Speculators make money by correctly predicting price changes, especially those changes which are difficult to predict. It is natural enough to conclude, according to the principle of *cui bono*, that speculators cause price fluctuations.

The trouble with this argument is that in order to make money, a speculator must buy when prices are low and sell when they are high. Buying when prices are low raises low prices; selling when prices are high lowers high prices. Hence successful speculators decrease price fluctuations, just as successful widget makers decrease the price of widgets. Destabilizing speculators are, of course, a logical possibility; they can be recognized by the red ink in their ledgers. The Hunt brothers of Texas are a notable recent example. A few years ago, they lost several billion dollars in the process of driving the price of silver up to what turned out to be several times its long-run equilibrium level.

It is true, of course, that a speculator would like to "cause instability," supposing that he could do so without losing money; more precisely, he would like to make the prices of things he is going to sell go up before he sells them and of things he is going to buy go down before he buys them. He cannot do this by his market activities, but he can try to spread misleading rumors among other speculators; and no doubt, some speculators do so. His behavior in this respect is like that of a producer who advertises his product; he is trying to persuade people to buy what he wants to sell. The speculator faces an even more skeptical audience than the advertiser, since it is fairly obvious that if he really expected the good to go up, he would keep quiet and buy it himself. Hence the private generating of disinformation, while it undoubtedly occurs, is unlikely to be very effective.

I once heard a talk by an economist who had applied the relationship between stabilization and profitable speculation in reverse. The usual argument is that speculators, by trying to make a profit, provide the useful public service of stabilizing prices. The reverse argument involved not private speculators but central banks. Central banks buy and sell currencies, supposedly in order to "stabilize" exchange rates (an *exchange rate* is the price of one kind of money measured in another). They are widely suspected (by economists—and speculators) of trying to keep exchange rates not stable but above or below their market clearing levels.

If profitable speculation is stabilizing, one might expect successful stabilization of currencies to be profitable. If the banks are buying dollars when they are temporarily cheap and selling them when they are temporarily expensive, they should be both stabilizing the value of the dollar and making a profit. One implication of this argument is that the central banks are superfluous—if there are profits to be made by stabilizing currencies, speculators will be glad to volunteer for the job. A second implication is that we can judge the success of central banks by seeing whether they in fact make or lose money on their speculations. The conclusion of the speaker, who had studied precisely that question, was that they generally lost money.

CHOICE IN AN UNCERTAIN WORLD

In Chapters 1-10, we saw how markets work to determine prices and quantities in a certain and unchanging world. In Chapter 11, we learned how to deal with a world that was changing but certain. In such a world, any decision involves a predictable stream of costs and benefits—so much this year, so much next year, so much the year after. One simply converts each stream into its present value and compares the present values of costs and benefits, just as we earlier compared annual flows of costs and benefits.

The next step is to analyze individual choice in an *uncertain* world. Again our objective is to convert the problem we are dealing with into the easier problem we have already solved. To describe an uncertain world, we assume that each individual has a *probability distribution* over possible outcomes. He does not know what will happen but he knows, or believes he knows, what *might* happen and *how likely* it is to happen. His problem, given what he knows, is how to achieve his objectives as well as possible.

The Rational Gambler

Consider, for example, an individual betting on whether a coin will come up heads or tails. Assuming the coin is a fair one, half the time it will come up heads, and half the time it will come up tails. The gambler's problem is to decide what bets he should be willing to take.

The answer seems obvious—take any bets that offer a payoff of more than $1 for each $1 bet; refuse any that offer less. If someone offers to pay you $2 if the coin comes up heads, on condition that you pay him $1 if it comes up tails, then "on average" you gain by accepting the bet and should do so. If he offers you $.50 for the risk of $1, then on average you lose by accepting; you should refuse the bet.

In these examples, you are choosing between a certain outcome (decline the bet—and end up with as much money as you started with) and an uncertain outcome (accept the bet—end up with either more or less). A more general way of putting the rule is that in choosing among alternatives, you should choose the one that gives you the highest *expected return*, where the expected return is the sum of the returns associated with the different possible outcomes, each weighted by its probability. In the particular case where you are choosing between two alternatives, one of which consists of doing nothing, that implies that you should accept a bet if the expected return from doing so is positive and decline it if the expected return is negative.

Maximizing Expected Return. This is the correct answer in some situations but not in all. If you make a fifty-fifty bet many times, you are almost certain to win "about half the time"; a bet which "on average" benefits you is almost certain to give you a net gain in the long term. If, for instance, you flip a fair coin 1,000 times, there is only a very small chance that it will come up heads more than 600 times or less than 400. If you make $2 every time it comes up heads and lose $1 every time it comes up tails, you are almost certain, after 1,000 flips, to be at least $200 ahead.

The case of the gambler who expects to bet on the fall of a coin many times can easily be generalized to describe any game of chance. The rule for such a gambler is "Maximize expected return." Since we defined expected return as the sum, over all of the possible outcomes, of the return from each outcome times the probability of that outcome, we have:

$$<R> \equiv \Sigma p_i R_i. \qquad \text{(Eqn. 1)}$$

Here p_i is the probability of outcome number i occurring, R_i is the return from outcome number i, and $<R>$ is the expected return. Σ is the mathematical symbol for "sum"; in general:

$$\Sigma x_i = x_1 + x_2 + x_3 + . . .$$

with the sum being over as many different x_i's as there are values of i.

When you flip a coin, it must come up either heads or tails; more generally, any gamble ends up with some one of the alternative outcomes happening, so we have:

$$\Sigma p_i = 1. \qquad \text{(Eqn. 2)}$$

In the gamble described earlier, where the gambler loses a dollar on tails and gains two dollars on heads, we have:

$$p_1 = .5; R_1 = +\$2 \text{ (heads)}$$

$p_2 = .5; R_2 = -\$1$ (tails)

$$<R> = p_1 \times R_1 + p_2 \times R_2 = .5 \times (+\$2) + .5 \times (-\$1) = +\$.50.$$

Here p_1 and p_2, the probabilities of heads and tails respectively, are each equal to one half; your expected return is \$.50. If you play the game many times, you will on average make \$.50 each time you play. The expected return from taking the gamble is positive, so you should take it—provided you can repeat it many times. The same applies to any other gamble with a positive expected return. A gamble with an expected return of zero—you are on average equally well off whether or not you choose to take it—is called a "fair gamble."

We now know how a gambler who will take the same gamble many times should behave. In choosing among several gambles, he should take the one with highest expected return. In the particular case where he is accepting or declining bets, so that one of his alternatives is a certainty of no change, he should take any bet that is better than a fair gamble.

Maximizing Expected Utility. Suppose, however, that you are only playing the game once—and that the bet is not \$1 but \$50,000. If you lose, you are destitute—\$50,000 is all you have. If you win, you gain \$100,000. You may feel that a decline in your wealth from \$50,000 to zero hurts you more than an increase from \$50,000 to \$150,000 helps you. One could easily enough imagine situations in which losing \$50,000 resulted in your starving to death while gaining \$100,000 produced only a modest increase in your welfare.

Such a situation is an example of what we earlier called "declining marginal utility." The dollars that raise you from zero to \$50,000 are worth more per dollar than the additional dollars beyond \$50,000. That is precisely what we would expect from the discussion of Chapter 4. Dollars are used to buy goods; we expect goods to be worth less to you the more of them you have.

When you choose a profession, start a business, buy a house, or stake your life savings playing the commodity market, you are betting a large sum, and the bet is not one you will repeat enough times to be confident of getting an "average" return. How can we analyze rational behavior in such situations?

The answer to this question was provided by John Von Neumann, the mathematician whom I mentioned in an earlier chapter. He demonstrated that by combining the idea of "expected return" used in the mathematical theory of gambling (probability theory) with the idea of "utility" used in economics, it was possible to describe the behavior of individuals dealing with uncertain situations—whether or not the situations were repeated many times.

The fundamental idea is that instead of maximizing expected return in dollars, as in the case described above, individuals maximize expected return in utiles— expected utility. Each outcome i has a utility U_i. We define expected utility as:

$$<U> \equiv \Sigma p_i U_i. \hspace{3cm} \text{(Eqn. 3)}$$

Your utility depends on many things, of which the amount of money you have is only one. If we are considering alternatives which only differ with regard to the amount of money you end up with, we can write:

$$U_i = U(R_i).$$

Or, in other words, the utility you get from outcome i depends only on how much more (or less) money that outcome gives you. If utility increases linearly with income, as shown on Figure 12-12, we have:

$$U(R) = A + B \times R;$$

$$<U> = \Sigma p_i U_i = \Sigma p_i (A + BR_i) = A \Sigma p_i + B \Sigma p_i R_i = A + B<R>. \quad \text{(Eqn. 4)}$$

Comparing the left- and right-hand sides of Equation 4, we see that whatever decision maximizes $<R>$ also maximizes $<U>$. In this case—with a linear utility function—the individual maximizing his expected utility behaves like the gambler maximizing his expected return.

A Methodological Digression. In going from gambling games to utility graphs, we have changed somewhat the way in which we look at expected return. In the case of gambling, return was defined relative to your initial situation—positive if you gained and negative if you lost. That was a convenient way of looking at gambling because the gambler always has the alternative of refusing to bet and so ending up with a return of zero. But in an uncertain world, the individual does not usually have that alternative; sometimes—indeed almost always—he is choosing among alternatives all of which are uncertain. In that context, it is easier to define zero return as ending up with no money at all and to measure all other outcomes relative to that. We can then show the utility of any outcome on a graph such as Figure 12-12 as the utility of the income associated with that outcome. If you start with $10,000 and bet all of it at even odds on the flip of a coin—heads you win, tails you lose—then the utility to you of the outcome heads is the utility of $20,000. The utility to you of the outcome tails is the utility of zero dollars.

Figure 12-12

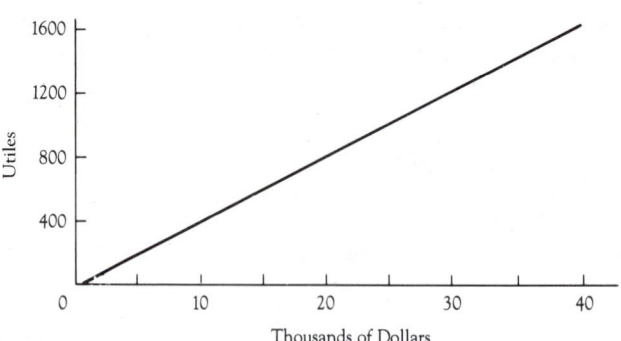

Total utility of income for a risk-neutral individual.

A second difficulty with Figure 12-12 is the ambiguity as to just what is being graphed on the horizontal axis—what is utility a function of? Is it income (dollars per year) or money (dollars)? Strictly speaking, utility is a flow (utiles per year) which depends on a flow of consumption (apples per year). The utility we get by consuming 100 apples, or whatever else we buy with our income, depends in part on the period of time over which we consume them.

If I were being precise, I would do all the analysis in terms of flows and compare alternatives by comparing the present values of those flows, in dollars or utiles. This would make the discussion a good deal more complicated without adding much to its content. It is easier to think of Figure 12-12, and similar figures, as describing either someone who starts with a fixed amount of money and is only going to live for a year, or, alternatively, someone with a portfolio of bonds yielding a fixed income who is considering gambles that will affect the size of his portfolio. The logic of the two situations is the same. In the one case, the figure graphs the utility flow from a year's expenditure; in the other case, it graphs the present value of the utility flow from spending the same amount every year forever. Both approaches allow us to analyze the implications of uncertainty while temporarily ignoring other complications of a changing world. To make the discussion simpler, I will talk as if we are considering the first case; that way I can talk in "dollars" and "utiles" instead of "dollars per year" and "utiles per year." The amount of money you have may still sometimes be described as your income—an income of x dollars/year for one year equals x dollars.

Risk Preference and the Utility Function
or
As I Was Saying When I So Rudely Interrupted Myself

Figure 12-12 showed utility as a linear function of income; Figure 12-13a shows a more plausible relation. This time, income has declining marginal utility. Total utility increases with income, but it increases more and more slowly as income gets higher and higher.

Suppose you presently have $20,000 and have an opportunity to bet $10,000 on the flip of a coin at even odds. If you win, you end up with $30,000; if you lose, you end up with $10,000.

In deciding whether to take the bet, you are choosing between two different "gambles." The first, the one you get if you do not take the bet, is a very simple gamble indeed—a certainty of ending up with $20,000. The second, the one you get if you do take the bet, is a little more complicated—a 0.5 chance of ending up with $10,000 and a 0.5 chance of ending up with $30,000. So for the first gamble, we have:

$$p_1 = 1; R_1 = \$20,000; U_1 = U(R_1) = U(\$20,000) = 1,000 \text{ utiles}$$

$$<U> = p_1 \times U_1 = 1,000 \text{ utiles.}$$

For the second gamble, we have:

$$p_1 = .5; R_1 = \$10,000; U_1 = U(R_1) = U(\$10,000) = 600 \text{ utiles}$$

$$p_2 = .5; R_2 = \$30,000; U_2 = U(R_2) = U(\$30,000) = 1,200 \text{ utiles}$$

$$<U> = p_1 \times U_1 + p_2 \times U_2 = .5 \times 600 \text{ utiles} + .5 \times 1,200 \text{ utiles} = 900 \text{ utiles.}$$

The individual takes the alternative with the higher expected utility; he declines the bet. In money terms, the two alternatives are equally attractive; they have the same expected return. In that sense, it is a fair bet. In utility terms, the first alternative is superior to the second. You should be able to convince yourself that as long as the utility function has the shape shown in Figure 12-13a, an individual will always prefer a certainty of $I to a gamble whose expected return is $I.

An individual who behaves in that way is "risk averse." A utility function that is almost straight, such as Figure 12-13b, represents an individual who is only slightly risk averse. Such an individual would decline a fair gamble but might accept one that was a little better than fair—bet $10 against $11 on the flip of a coin, for example. An individual who was extremely risk averse (Figure 12-13c)

Figure 12-13

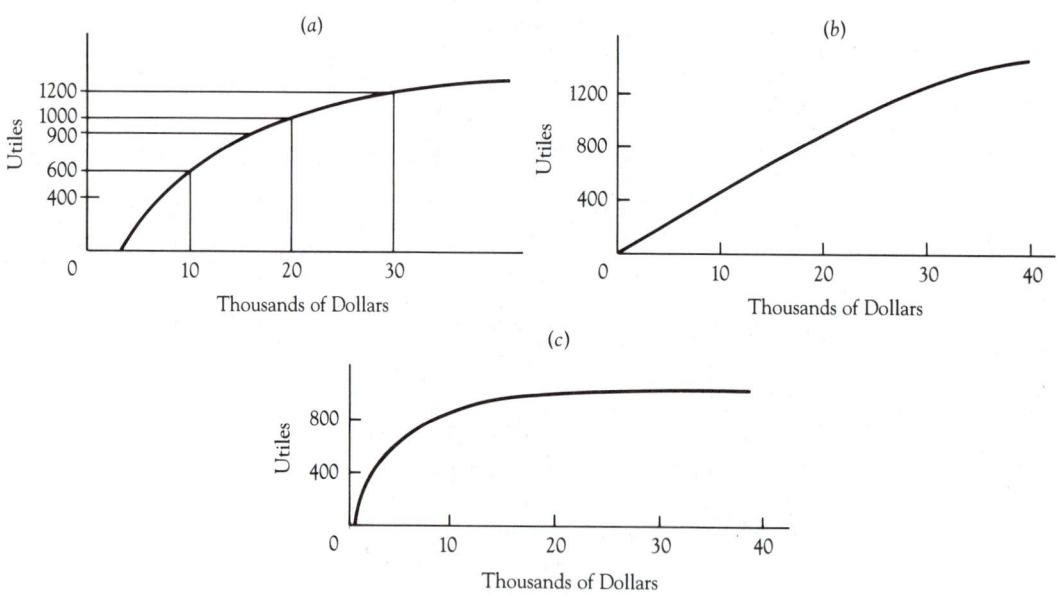

Total utility of income for a risk-averse individual.   Figure 12-13b corresponds to an individual who is only slightly risk averse; he will refuse a fair gamble but accept one that is slightly better than fair. Figure 12-13c corresponds to an individual who is very risk averse; he will accept a gamble only if it is much better than a fair gamble.

might still accept a gamble—but only one with a very high expected return, such as risking $1,000 on the flip of a coin to get $10,000.

Figure 12-14a shows the utility function of a *risk preferrer*. It exhibits increasing marginal utility. A risk preferrer would be willing to take a gamble which was slightly worse than fair—although he would still decline one with a sufficiently low expected return. An individual who is neither a risk preferrer nor a risk averter is called *risk neutral*. The corresponding utility function has already been shown—as Figure 12-12.

Consider an individual who requires a certain amount of money in order to buy enough food to stay alive. Increases in income below that point extend his life a little and so are of some value to him, but he still ends up starving to death. An increase in income that gives him enough to survive is worth a great deal to him. Once he is well past that point, additional income buys less important things, so marginal utility of income falls. The corresponding utility function is shown as Figure 12-14b; marginal utility first rises with increasing income, then falls.

Such an individual would be a risk preferrer if his initial income were at point A, below subsistence. He would be a risk averter if he were starting at point B. In the former case, he would, if necessary, risk $1,000 to get $500 at even odds. If he loses, he only starves a little faster; if he wins, he lives.

In discussing questions of this sort, it is important to realize that the degree to which someone exhibits risk preference or risk aversion depends on three different things—the shape of his utility function, his initial income, and the size of the bet he is considering. For small bets, we would expect everyone to be roughly risk neutral; the marginal utility of a dollar does not change very much between an income of $19,999 and an income of $20,001—which is the relevant consideration for someone with $20,000 who is considering a $1 bet.

The Simple Cases. The expected return from a gamble depends only on the odds and the payoffs; the expected utility depends also on the tastes of the gambler, as described by his utility function. So it is easier to predict the behavior of

Figure 12-14

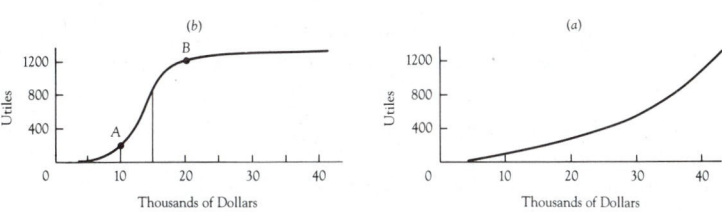

Total utility of income for a risk preferrer and for someone who is risk preferring for some incomes and risk averse for others. Figure 12-14b shows total utility of income for someone who requires about $1,500 to stay alive. Below that point, the marginal utility of income (the slope of total utility) increases with increasing income; above that point, it decreases.

someone maximizing his expected return than of someone maximizing expected utility. This raises an interesting question—under what circumstances are the two maximizations equivalent? When does someone maximize his utility by maximizing his expected return?

We saw one answer at the beginning of this section of the chapter. An individual who makes the same gamble many times can expect the results to average out. In the long run, the outcome is almost certain—he will get something very close to the expected value of the gamble times the number of times he takes it. Since his income at the end of the process is (almost) certain, all he has to do in order to maximize his expected utility is to make that income as large as possible—which he does by choosing the gamble with the highest expected return.

There are three other important situations in which maximizing expected utility turns out to be equivalent to maximizing expected return. One is when the individual is risk-neutral, as shown on Figure 12-12. A second is when the size of the prospective gains and losses is small compared to one's income. If we consider only small changes in income, we can treat the marginal utility of income as constant; if the marginal utility of income is constant, then changes in utility are simply proportional to changes in income, so whatever choice maximizes expected return also maximizes expected utility.

One can see the same thing geometrically. Figure 12-15 is a magnified version of part of Figure 12-13a. If we consider only a very small range of income—between \$20,000 and \$20,100, for instance—the utility function is almost straight. For a straight-line utility function, as I showed earlier, maximizing expected utility is equivalent to maximizing expected return. So if we are considering only small changes in income, we should act as if we were risk neutral.

Next consider the case of a corporation that is trying to maximize the market value of its stock—as the discussion of takeover bids in the optional section of Chapter 10 suggests that corporations tend to do. In an uncertain world, what management is really choosing each time it makes a decision is a probability distribution for future profits. When the future arrives and it becomes clear which of the possible outcomes has actually happened, the price of the stock will reflect what the profits actually are. So in choosing a probability distribution for future profits, management is also choosing a probability distribution for the future price of the stock.

How is the current market value of a stock related to the probability distribution of its future value? That is a complicated question—one which occupies a good deal of the theory of financial markets; if you are an economics major, you will probably encounter it again. The short, but not entirely correct, answer is that the current price of the stock is the expected value of the future price—the average over all possible futures weighted by the probability of each. The reason is that the buyer of stock is in the same position as the gambler discussed earlier; he can "average out" his risks by buying a little stock in each of a large number of companies. If he does, his actual return will be very close to his expected return. If the price of any particular stock were significantly lower than the expected value of its future price, investors would all want to buy some of it; if the price were higher than the expected value of its future price, they would all want

Figure 12-15

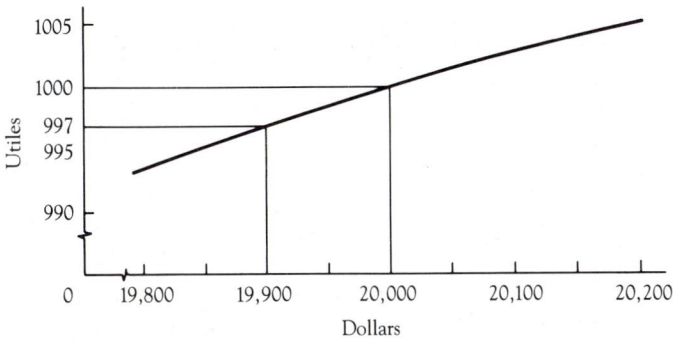

Magnified version of part of Figure 12-13a.   Although the total utility curve shown on Figure 12-13a is curved, corresponding to risk aversion, any small section of it appears almost straight. This corresponds to the fact that the marginal utility of income is almost constant over small ranges of income; hence individuals are almost risk neutral for small gambles.

to sell some. The resulting market pressures force the current price toward the expected value of future prices.

If, as suggested above, management wishes to maximize the present price of its stock, it must try to maximize the expected value of its future price. It does that by maximizing the expected value of future profits. So it acts like the gambler we started with; it maximizes expected returns.

This is true only if the firm is trying to maximize the value of its stock. The threat of takeover bids has some tendency to make it do so. It is not clear how strong that tendency is—how closely that threat constrains management. To the extent that management succeeds in pursuing its own goals rather than those of the stockholders, the conclusion no longer holds. If the firm takes a risk and goes bankrupt, the (present and future) income of the chief executive may fall dramatically. If so, he may well be unwilling to make a decision that has a 50 percent chance of leading to bankruptcy even if it also has a 50 percent chance of tripling the firm's value.

Insurance. The existence of individuals who are risk averse explains the existence of insurance. Suppose you have the utility function shown in Figure 12-13a. Your income is $20,000, but there is a small probability—.01—of some accident which would reduce it to $10,000. The insurance company offers to insure you against that accident for a price of $100. Whether or not the accident happens, you give them $100. If the accident happens, they give you back $10,000. You now have a choice between two gambles—buying or not buying insurance. If you buy the insurance then, whether or not the accident occurs, the outcome is the same—you have $20,000 minus the $100 you paid for the insurance (I assume the accident only affects your income). So for the first gamble, you have:

$$p_1 = 1; R_1 = \$19,900; <U> = p_1 \times U(R_1) = 997 \text{ utiles.}$$

If you do not buy the insurance, you have:

$$p_1 = .99; R_1 = \$20,000; U(R_1) = 1,000 \text{ utiles;}$$

$$p_2 = .01; R_2 = \$10,000; U(R_2) = 600 \text{ utiles;}$$

$$<U> = p_1 \times U(R_1) + p_2 \times U(R_2) = 990 \text{ utiles} + 6 \text{ utiles} = 996 \text{ utiles.}$$

You are better off with the insurance than without it, so you buy the insurance.

In the example as given, the expected return—measured in dollars—from buying the insurance was the same as the expected return from not buying it. Buying insurance was a fair gamble—you paid $100 in exchange for one chance in a hundred of receiving $10,000. The insurance company makes hundreds of thousands of such bets, so it will end up receiving, on average, almost exactly the expected return. If insurance is a fair gamble, the money coming in to buy insurance exactly balances the money going out to pay claims. The insurance company neither makes nor loses money; the client breaks even in money but gains in utility.

Insurance companies in the real world have expenses other than paying out claims—rent on their offices, commissions to their salespeople, and salaries for their administrators, claim investigators, adjusters, and lawyers. In order for an insurance company to cover all its expenses, the gamble it offers must be somewhat better than a fair one from its standpoint. If so, it is somewhat worse than fair from the standpoint of the company's clients.

The clients may still find that it is in their interest to accept the gamble and buy the insurance. If they are sufficiently risk averse, an insurance contract that lowers their expected return may still increase their expected utility. In the case discussed above, for example, it would still be worth buying the insurance even if the company charged $130 for it. It would not be worth buying at $140. You should be able to check those results for yourself by redoing the calculations that showed that the insurance was worth buying at $100.

Earlier I pointed out that with regard to risks that involve only small changes in income, everyone is (almost) risk neutral. One implication of this is that it is only worth insuring against large losses. Insurance is always worse than a fair gamble from the standpoint of the customer, since the insurance company has to make enough to cover its expenses. For small losses, the difference between the marginal utility of income before and after the loss is not large enough to convert a loss in expected return into a gain in expected utility.

The Lottery-Insurance Puzzle. Buying a ticket in a lottery is in a sense the opposite of buying insurance. When you buy insurance, you accept an "unfair" gamble—a gamble which results, on average, in your having less money than if you had not accepted it—in order to reduce uncertainty. When you buy a lottery ticket, you also accept an "unfair" gamble—on average, the lottery pays out less than it takes in—but this time, you do it in order to *increase* your uncertainty. If you are risk averse, it may make sense for you to buy insurance—but you should never buy lottery tickets. If you are a risk preferrer, it may make sense for you to buy a lottery ticket—but you should never buy insurance.

This brings us to a puzzle which has bothered economists for at least 200 years—the lottery-insurance paradox. In the real world, the same people sometimes buy both insurance and lottery tickets. More generally, some people both gamble when they know the odds are against them and buy insurance when they know the odds are against them. Can this be consistent with rational behavior?

There are at least two possible ways in which it can. One is illustrated on Figure 12-16. The individual with the utility function shown there is risk averse for one range of incomes and risk preferring for another, higher, range. If he starts at point A, in between the two regions, he may be interested in buying both insurance and lottery tickets. Insurance protects him against risks which move his income below A—where he is risk averse. Lottery tickets offer him the possibility (if he wins) of an income above A—where he is risk preferring.

This solution is logically possible, but it does not seem very plausible. Why should people have such peculiarly shaped utility functions, with the value to them of an additional dollar first falling with increasing income then rising again? And if they do, why should their incomes just happen to be near the border between the two regions?

Another explanation of the paradox is that in the real-world situation we observe, one of the conditions for our analysis does not hold. So far, we have been considering situations where the only important difference among the outcomes is money; the utility of each outcome depends only on the amount of money it leaves you with. It is not clear that this is true for the individuals who actually buy lottery tickets.

Figure 12-16

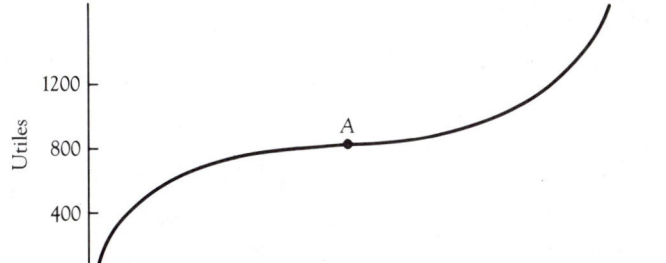

One solution to the lottery-insurance puzzle.   The total utility function shows declining marginal utility of income (risk aversion) to the left of point A and increasing marginal utility of income (risk preference) to the right. An individual at A may increase his expected utility by buying both insurance and lottery tickets.

Consider the lotteries you have yourself been offered—by *Reader's Digest* and similar enterprises. The price is the price of a stamp, the payoff—lavishly illustrated with glossy photographs—a (very small) chance of a new Cadillac, a Caribbean vacation, an income of $20,000 a year for life. My rough calculations—based on a guess of how many people respond to the lottery—suggest that the value of the prize multiplied by the chance of getting it comes to less than the cost of the stamp. The expected return is negative.

Why then do so many people enter? The explanation I find most plausible is that what they are getting for their stamp is not merely one chance in a million of a $40,000 car. They are also getting a certainty of being able to daydream about getting the car—or the vacation or the income—from the time they send in the envelope until the winners are announced. The daydream is made more satisfying by the knowledge that there is a chance, even if a slim one, that they will actually win the prize. The lottery is not only selling a gamble. It is also selling a dream—and at a very low price.

This explanation has the disadvantage of pushing such lotteries out of the area where economics can say much about them; we know a good deal about rational gambling but very little about the market for dreams. It has the advantage of explaining not only the existence of lotteries but some of their characteristics. If lotteries exist to provide people (a chance of) money, why do the prizes often take other forms; why not give the winner $40,000 and let him decide whether to buy a Cadillac with it? That would not only improve the prize from the standpoint of the winner but would also save the sponsors the cost of all those glossy photographs of the prizes.

But many people may find it easier to daydream about their winnings if the winnings take a concrete form—with pictures. So the sponsors (sometimes) make the prizes goods instead of money—and provide a wide variety of prizes to suit different tastes in daydreams. This seems to be especially true of "free" lotteries—ones where the price is a stamp and the sponsor pays for the prizes out of someone's advertising budget instead of out of ticket receipts. Lotteries which sell tickets and use (some of) the money for prizes seem more inclined to pay off in money—why I do not know.

Von Neumann Utility

Near the beginning of this section, I said that John Von Neumann was responsible for combining the ideas of utility and choice under uncertainty. So far, I have shown how the two ideas are combined but have said very little about exactly what Von Neumann (in conjunction with economist Oskar Morgenstern) contributed. You may reasonably have concluded that the great idea was simply to assert "People maximize expected utility" and keep talking—in the hope that nobody would ask "Why?"

What Von Neumann and Morgenstern actually did was both more difficult and more subtle than that. They proved that if you assume that individual choice under uncertainty meets a few simple consistency conditions, it is always possible to assign utilities to outcomes in such a way that the decisions people actually do make are the ones they would make if they were maximizing expected utility.

Von Neumann and Morgenstern started by considering that the individual was choosing among "lotteries." Each lottery is a collection of outcomes, each with a probability—a certain probability of one outcome, another probability for another, and so on, with all the probabilities together adding up to one. Just as, in considering ordinary utility functions, we assume that the individual can choose between any two bundles, so they assumed that given any two lotteries L and M, the individual either prefers L to M, prefers M to L, or is indifferent between them. They further assumed that preferences are *transitive*; if you prefer L to M and M to N, you must prefer L to N.

Another assumption was that in considering lotteries whose payoffs are themselves lotteries—probabilistic situations whose outcomes are themselves probabilistic situations—people combine probabilities in a "mathematically correct" fashion, by multiplying them. If someone is offered a ticket giving him a 50 percent chance of winning a lottery ticket, which in turn gives him a 50 percent chance of winning a prize, he regards that "compound lottery" as equivalent to a ticket giving a 25 percent chance of winning the same prize—and similarly for any other combination of probabilities.

The remaining two assumptions involve the continuity of preferences. One is that if I prefer outcome A to outcome B, I also prefer to B any lottery that gives me some probability of getting A and guarantees that if I do not get A, I will get B. The final assumption is that if I prefer outcome A to outcome B and outcome B to outcome C, then there is some "mix" of A and C—some lottery giving me a certainty of getting one or the other with some probability of each—which I consider equivalent to B. To put it in different words, this says that as I move from a certainty of A to a certainty of C via various mixtures of the two, my expected utility—probability of A times $U(A)$ plus probability of C times $U(C)$—changes continuously from $U(A)$ to $U(C)$. Since by assumption $U(A) > U(B) > U(C)$—that is what the "if" clause at the beginning of this paragraph says—as my utility moves continuously from $U(A)$ to $U(C)$, it must at some intermediate point be equal to $U(B)$.

All of these assumptions seem reasonable as part of a description of "rational" or "consistent" behavior under uncertainty. If an individual's behavior satisfies them, it is possible to define a *utility function*—a utility for every outcome—such that the choices he actually makes are the choices he would make if he were trying to maximize his expected utility. That is what Von Neumann and Morgenstern proved.

In the optional section of Chapter 3, I pointed out that utility as then defined contained a considerable element of arbitrariness; utility functions were supposed to describe behavior, but exactly the same behavior could be described by many different utility functions. All we could deduce from observing individuals' choices was that they preferred A to B—not by how much. Even the principle of declining marginal utility, to which I several times referred, is, strictly speaking, meaningless in that context; if you cannot measure the amount by which I prefer one alternative to another, then you cannot say whether the additional utility that I get when my income increases from \$9,000/year to \$10,000 is more or less than when it increases from \$10,000 to \$11,000. Declining marginal utility then has content only in the form of the declining marginal rate of substitution—a concept which, as I pointed out at the time, is closely related but not equivalent.

Once we accept the Von Neumann-Morgenstern definition of utility under uncertainty, that problem vanishes. The statement "I prefer outcome C to outcome B by twice as much as I prefer B to A" is equivalent to "I am indifferent between a certainty of B and a lottery that gives me a two-thirds chance of A and a one-third chance of C."

To see that the two statements are equivalent, we will work out the expected utilities for the two alternatives described in the second statement and show that the first statement implies that they are equal, as follows:

Let lottery 1 consist of a certainty of B, lottery 2 of a two-thirds chance of A and a one-third chance of C. We have for lottery 1:

$$p_1 = 1; U_1 = U(B); <U> = U(B).$$

We have for lottery 2:

$$p_1 = \tfrac{2}{3}; U_1 = U(A);$$

$$p_2 = \tfrac{1}{3}; U_2 = U(C);$$

$$<U> = p_1U_1 + p_2U_2 = \tfrac{2}{3}U(A) + \tfrac{1}{3}U(C).$$

Statement 1 tells us that:

$$U(C) - U(B) = 2 \times (U(B) - U(A)).$$

Rearranging this gives us:

$$U(C) + 2 \times U(A) = 3 \times U(B);$$

$$\tfrac{2}{3}U(A) + \tfrac{1}{3}U(C) = U(B). \tag{Eqn. 5}$$

The left-hand side of Equation 5 is the expected utility of lottery 2, and the right-hand side is the expected utility of lottery 1, so the expected utilities of the two alternatives are the same; the individual is indifferent between them.

We have now shown that statement 1 implies statement 2. We could equally well have started with statement 2 and worked backward to statement 1 (i.e., Equation 5). If each statement implies the other, then they are equivalent.

So using utility functions to describe choice among probabilistic alternatives makes the functions themselves considerably less arbitrary. In our earlier discussion of utility, the only meaningful statements were of the form "A has more utility to me than B" or, equivalently, "I prefer A to B." Now the statement

"Going from A to B increases my utility by twice as much as going from C to D" (or, equivalently, "I prefer A to B twice as much as I prefer C to D") has meaning as well. If we can make quantitative comparisons of utility differences, we can also make quantitative comparisons of marginal utilities, so the principle of declining marginal utility means something. We saw exactly what it meant a few pages ago; the statement "My marginal utility for income is declining" is equivalent to "I am risk averse." Similarly, the statement "my marginal utility for ice cream cones is declining" is equivalent to "I am risk averse if expected return is in ice cream cones rather than in dollars. I would not accept a gamble which consisted of a 50 percent chance of getting an ice cream cone and a 50 percent chance of losing one."

We have now eliminated much of the arbitrariness from utility functions, but not all of it. Nothing we have done tells us how big a utile is, so a change in scale is still possible. If I say that I prefer A to B by 10 utiles, B to C by 5, and C to D by 2, while you insist that the correct numbers are 20, 10, and 4, no possible observation of my behavior could prove one of us right and one wrong. We agree about the order of preferences; we agree about their relative intensity—all we disagree about is the size of the unit in which we are measuring them.

It is also true that nothing we have done tells us where the zero of the utility function is. If I claim that my utilities for outcomes A, B, and C are 0, 10, 30, while you claim they are -10, 0, and 20, there is again no way of settling the disagreement. We agree about the order; we agree about the differences—all we disagree about is which alternative has zero utility. So changes in the utility function which consist of adding the same amount to all utilities (changing the zero) or multiplying all utilities by the same number (changing the scale) or both do not really change the utility function. The numbers are different, but the behavior described is exactly the same. This means, for those of you who happen to be mathematicians, that utility functions are arbitrary with respect to linear transformations.

My own preference, in discussing utility, is to define zero as nonexistence or death; that, after all, is the one "outcome" in which one gets, so far as I know, neither pleasure nor pain. A friend and colleague once commented to me that she was not certain whether one's expected utility at birth was positive or negative—meaning that she was not sure whether, on net, life was worth living. I concluded that her life had been much harder than mine.

Where We Are Now

In the first ten chapters of this book, we used economics to understand how markets work in a certain and unchanging world. It may have occurred to you that doing so was a waste of time, since we live in a world which is uncertain and changing.

Looking back at what we have done in Chapters 11 and 12, you may now see why the book is organized in this way. In Chapter 11, we learned how to analyze choice in a changing (but certain) world using the same tools developed for an unchanging world—simply evaluate costs and benefits in terms of present values instead of annual flows. Now we have learned how to analyze choice in an uncertain world by again using the same tools; we merely evaluate costs and benefits by comparing the expected utilities of probabilistic outcomes instead of the utilities of certain outcomes. Combining the lessons of the two chapters in order to analyze choice in a world that is both changing and uncertain would be straightforward—evaluate choices in terms of the present value of expected utility.

What we have done is to first solve economics in a simple world and then show that the more complicated and realistic world can, for purposes of economic analysis, be reduced to the simple one. Introducing time and change does create some new problems, such as those associated with sunk costs. Yet it is still true that in learning to deal with the simple world of Chapters 1-10, we learned most of the basic ideas of economics, and that, in Chapters 11 and 12, we have taken a large step towards making those ideas applicable to the world we live in.

A Philosophical Digression

The concept of utility originated during the nineteenth century among thinkers interested in both philosophy and economics. It was proposed as a solution to the problem of "What should a society maximize?" The utilitarians asserted that a society should be designed to maximize the total utility of its members.

Their position has been heavily criticized over the years and is now in poor repute among philosophers. One of the major criticisms was that although we can, in principle, determine whether you prefer A to B by more than you prefer C to D, there seems to be no way of determing whether I prefer A to B by more than *you* prefer C to D. Hence there is no way of making "interpersonal comparisons of utility" in order to decide whether a change which benefits me (gives me A instead of B) and injures you (gives you D instead of C) increases or decreases total utility.

One possible reply to this criticism of utilitarianism goes as follows. Suppose we define utility in the sense of Von Neumann and Morgenstern and use it to evaluate some question such as "Should the U.S. abolish all tariffs?" It turns out that the utilitarian rule—"Maximize total utility"—is equivalent to another rule which some find intuitively more persuasive: "Choose that alternative you would prefer if you knew you were going to be one of the people affected but had no idea which."

Why are the two equivalent? If I have no idea who I am going to be, I presumably have an equal probability p of being each person; if there are N people involved, then $p = 1/N$. If we write the utility of person i as U_i, then the "lottery" that consists of a probability p of being each person has an expected utility:

$$<U> = \Sigma p_i U_i = \Sigma p U_i = p \Sigma U_i.$$

But ΣU_i is simply the total utility of the society, so whichever alternative maximizes total utility also maximizes $<U>$.

PROBLEMS

1. How should the developers of a new airliner take account of the plane's development costs in determining the price to charge airline companies? Should they suspend production if they cannot obtain a price that will cover development costs?

2. After reading this chapter, you are considering dropping this course. What costs should you take into account in deciding whether to do so? What costs that you should ignore in that decision should you have taken into account in deciding to take the course in the first place?

3. A new tropical disease permanently destroys the jute industry in Nigeria. The disease affects only jute plants, and only in Nigeria.

   a. What effect will this have on the world price of jute in the short run? The long run? Explain.

   b. Nigeria's other major crop is peanuts, of which it is the world's principal producer. The same land can be used to grow jute or peanuts, although some land is slightly better for one crop or the other. What will happen to the price of peanuts?

   c. Will the land on which peanuts are already being grown fall or rise in value?

   d. What will happen to the value of existing machines used for harvesting, shelling, roasting, packaging, and crushing peanuts? Why?

   e. How will the value in (d) change over time?

   (Note: This is supposed to be a hard question; it requires you to put together ideas from this and earlier chapters.)

4. It costs $100 to plant an apple tree, and the tree occupies land worth another $100. Once a tree is planted, it costs $10/year to take care of it; when the tree starts bearing apples, it takes an additional $10/year to harvest the apples. It takes two years from the time the tree is planted to the time it starts bearing; the tree bears ten bushels per year for the next two years, then dies. The market interest rate is 10 percent. The crop is harvested and sold at the end of the year; that is also when the cost of taking care of the tree for that year is paid. Dead trees are worth nothing.

   a. Assume a stable world in which the price of apples never changes and the same number of trees is planted each year. What is the price of a bushel of apples?

   b. What is the market price of a one-year-old apple tree (along with the land it occupies)? A two-year-old tree? A three-year-old tree? A four-year-old tree? In each case, give the price immediately *after* the tree has been harvested and the expenses of taking care of it have been paid.

   c. Figure 12-17 shows the demand curve D for apples. The situation is in equilibrium, as described in (a) above. As a result of the discovery that an apple a day does not keep the doctor away, there is a sudden and unexpected drop of the demand curve to D'. The drop occurs at the beginning of the year, just *after* the trees are planted. Show how the price of apples changes over the next six years, assuming that the demand curve never changes again and everyone knows it will never change again. Assume the interest rate is 0.

d. Do (c), assuming the interest rate is 10 percent.

(Parts (c) and (d) of this problem are very hard.)

Figure 12-17

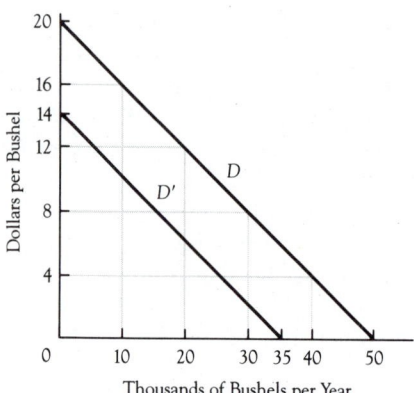

Problem 4—the demand curve for apples.   The curve shifts down from D to D'.

The following problems refer to the optional section:

5. You have $30,000; your utility function is shown by Figure 12-12. There is one chance in a hundred that your house will be struck by lightning, in which case it will cost $10,000 to repair it. What is the highest price you would be willing to pay, if necessary, for a lightning rod to protect your house?

6. Answer Problem 5 for the utility function of Figure 12-13a.

7. You have $30,000 and the utility function of Figure 12-13a. There is one chance in fifty that your house will burn down; it will cost $20,000 to replace it. What is the highest price you would, if necessary, pay to insure your house?

8. In answering Problem 7, you presumably assumed that if your house did burn down, you would replace it. Is that assumption appropriate? Discuss.

9. Figure 12-18 is identical to Figure 12-13a with the addition of a line connecting two points—A and E—on the utility function. I claim that point C, halfway between points A and E, represents the utility (vertical axis) and expected return (horizontal axis) of a fifty-fifty gamble between A ($10,000) and E ($30,000); the fact that C is below the graph of the utility functions

indicates that you prefer a certainty with the same expected return ($20,000) to such a gamble. Similarly, I claim that point B represents a gamble with a 75 percent chance of giving you A and a 25 percent chance of giving you E, and that point D represents a gamble with a 25 percent chance of A and a 75 percent chance of E.

Prove that these claims are true—that the vertical position of each point equals the expected utility of the corresponding gamble and that the horizontal position equals the expected return.

Figure 12-18

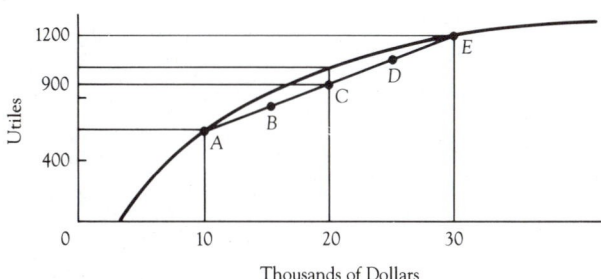

Problem 9—total utility of income for a risk-averse individual.

10. In the text, I asserted that declining marginal utility of income was equivalent to risk aversion and that increasing marginal utility of income was equivalent to risk preference. While I gave examples, I did not prove that the assertion was true in general. Use the result of Problem 9 to do so.

11. In discussing risk aversion, I have only considered alternatives that are measured in money. Suppose you are gambling in apples instead. Is it possible for someone to be a risk preferrer in terms of dollars and a risk averter in terms of apples? Vice versa? Does it depend on whether there is a market on which you can buy and sell apples?

FOR FURTHER READING

The original discussion of Von Neumann utility is in John Von Neumann and Oskar Morgenstern, *Theory of Games and Economic Behavior* (Princeton: Princeton University Press, 1944), Chapter 1. The book as a whole is devoted to inventing and explaining game theory; it is one of the major intellectual accomplishments of the twentieth century and, although in places mathematically difficult, well worth reading.

A classic discussion of the lottery-insurance paradox is Milton Friedman and Leonard J. Savage, "The Utility Analysis of Choices Involving Risk," *Journal of Political Economy*, Vol. 56, No. 4 (August, 1948), pp. 279-304.

For discussions of some of the philosophical issues associated with what, if anything, the good society would maximize, you may wish to look at two important books: Robert Nozick, *Anarchy, State and Utopia* (New York: Basic Books, Inc., 1974) and John Rawls, *A Theory of Justice* (Cambridge: Harvard University Press, 1971).

Chapter 13

The Distribution of Income
and the Factors of Production

PART 1 · THE DISTRIBUTION
OF INCOME

Three questions which are often asked of economists are: What is the distribution of income? What determines the distribution of income? Is it fair? In this part of the chapter, I will have a little to say about the first question and a good deal to say about the second. Whether what I say has anything to do with the third, you will have to decide for yourself.

Measuring the Distribution of Income

Curve G on Figure 13-1a is a graph of the cumulative income distribution for some imaginary society. The horizontal axis shows a percentage of the population, ranked by income; the vertical axis shows what percentage of national income goes to that part of the population. Point A on the figure shows that the bottom 25 percent of the population receives about 15 percent of national income; point B shows that the bottom 85 percent of the population receives about 80 percent of national income.

Curve H on Figure 13-1b is a similar graph for a society in which everyone has the same income. It is a straight line. Since everyone has the same income, the "bottom" 10 percent of the population has 10 percent of the income, the bottom 50 percent has 50 percent, and so on. Line G on Figure 13-1a, which shows an unequal distribution, must lie below line H on Figure 13-1b, since, for an unequal distribution, the bottom N percent of the population must have less than N percent of the income. Hence the shaded area in Figure 13-1a must be less than the shaded area in Figure 13-1b. To make this clearer, I have also shown H on Figure 13-1a.

319

The ratio of the shaded area on Figure 13-1a to the shaded area on Figure 13-1b, called the *Gini coefficient*, is a simple measure of how unequal the income distribution of Figure 13-1a is. The closer that ratio is to 1.0, the more nearly equal the income distribution. Various estimates of what the Gini coefficient is for the U.S. at present and how it has varied over time have been made.

One problem with most such estimates is that they measure current income rather than lifetime income. To see why this is a problem, imagine that we have a society in which everyone follows an identical career pattern. From ages 18 to 22, everyone is a student, earning $5,000/year at various part-time jobs. From 23 to 30, everyone has a job with a salary of $20,000/year. From 31 to 50, everyone makes $30,000/year; from 51 to 65, everyone makes $40,000/year and then retires on a pension of $15,000/year and lives to 77. Figure 13-1c shows the resulting income distribution, seen at a single instant. If you calculate a Gini coefficient from the figure, it is about .77.

This is a perfectly egalitarian society, since everyone's income follows the same pattern; but the income distribution appears far from equal on the graph, and the Gini coefficient is not equal to one, as it should be if all incomes are equal. The reason is that, at any one instant, some people are students, some are employees with varying degrees of experience, and some are retired. So if you look at a "cross section" of the society at a single instant, incomes appear quite

Figure 13-1

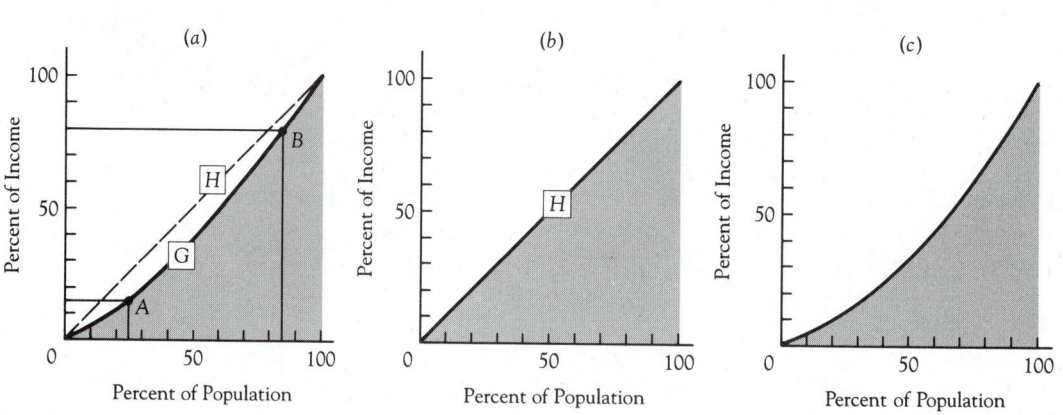

Cumulative income distributions.   Figure 13-1b shows the distribution for a population where everyone has the same income. The ratio of the shaded area on Figure 13-1a to the shaded area on Figure 13-1b is the Gini coefficient for the distribution shown on 1a. Figure 13-1c describes a population where lifetime incomes are all equal but current incomes are not.

unequal. Both the cumulative income distribution shown on Figure 13-1c and the corresponding Gini coefficient are the same as they would be if they described a society where one twelfth of the people had an income of $5,000/year, two tenths had $15,000/year, and so on—with everyone having the same income for his whole lifetime. The Gini coefficient as usually calculated tells us how unequal incomes are at one instant in time but does not distinguish between inequality due to different people being in different stages of their earning cycle and inequality due to some people being richer or more talented than others.

Most estimates of the income distribution are done in this way, which suggests that most estimates considerably overstate actual inequality. One study I saw which tried to allow for such effects concluded that they roughly doubled the difference between the estimated coefficient and 1.0, the coefficient for a perfectly equal society. If that result is correct, then if you consider lifetime income rather than income at one instant in time, the U.S. income distribution is about "half as unequal" as conventional estimates suggest.

A similar problem arises when one tries to figure out whether some particular program, such as social security, redistributes from the rich to the poor or from the poor to the rich. To see how the problem arises, we will start by considering a program that has no real redistributional effect; everyone gets back just what he paid in, plus accumulated interest (this is not the way the real social security system works). Since payments are made when you are employed and benefits received when you are retired, payments are made by someone with a higher income than the person who receives the benefits—not because the money is going from rich to poor but because it is going from you when you have a higher income to you in a later year when you have a lower income. If you look at a cross section of the population, it appears that social security redistributes from rich to poor—the people who are paying are richer than those receiving—even though, in this case, there is no redistribution at all.

It is not clear what the distributional effect of the real social security system is; it may actually redistribute from lower to higher income workers. The higher income worker typically starts working—and paying in—at an older age, which reduces his total payments, and lives longer, which increases his total benefits. Whether these effects are outweighed by other features of the system which provide relative advantages to the poor is not clear. What is clear is that a comparison of the incomes of those who in any particular year are receiving social security to the incomes of those who are paying for it always shows the system transferring from richer to poorer—and that that result tells us almost nothing about the real effect of the system on the distribution of income.

A third problem arises when we try to measure changes in the distribution of income over time. To do so, we require statistics on what incomes are and were. The obvious source for such statistics is the Internal Revenue Service (IRS). But IRS statistics tell us not what people earned but what they reported. Over the past 70 years, the rate at which income is taxed has increased enormously. The higher the tax rate, the higher the incentive for people with high incomes to make them appear lower than they are, at least when the IRS is looking. Hence

IRS figures almost certainly underestimate how well the rich are doing in recent decades as compared to the earlier part of the century.

The conclusion from all of this is that statements about the income distribution, about how it has changed over time and about how it is changed by particular government programs, should be viewed with considerable skepticism.

What Determines the Income Distribution?

You are a worker. What determines your salary? One answer is "the most you are worth to any employer." Another is "the least you are willing to work for." Both are true—for exactly the same reason that the price of a good is equal both to its value to the consumer and to its cost of production.

To Each According to His Product. Consider the president of a pants company, trying to decide how many workers to hire. Holding all of his other inputs constant, he calculates how many extra pairs of pants he produces for each extra worker he hires; the answer is five pairs per day. Five pairs of pants per day is the *marginal physical product* of a worker. This is the same marginal product discussed briefly in Chapter 9.

Suppose a pair of pants sells for $10. The *marginal revenue product* of a worker is then $50/day. If an employer hires one more worker, his output rises by five pairs of pants per day, he sells them for $10/pair, so his revenue increases by $50/day. Since marginal product is defined with all other inputs held constant, his cost rises by what he has to pay the extra worker. As long as the cost of hiring another worker is less than $50/day, he increases his profit by hiring him. As he hires more workers, their marginal product drops, due to the law of diminishing returns. He stops hiring when marginal revenue product equals the wage he must pay to get more workers. So a worker's wage equals what he produces—the value of the extra production from adding one more worker while keeping all other inputs fixed.

This is not a new argument; it is an old argument in a new application. The logic of the situation is the same that gave us demand curves from marginal value curves and supply curves from marginal cost curves. It applies not only to workers but to all inputs—as was pointed out in Chapter 9. As long as the producer can buy as much of an input as he likes at some price—as long, in other words, as he is a price taker on the market for his inputs—he will buy it up to the point where its marginal revenue product equals its price. Hence the prices received by the owners of all inputs to production—the wages of labor, the rent of land, the interest on capital—are equal to the marginal revenue products of those inputs. Since income ultimately comes from selling inputs, this appears to be an explanation of the income distribution.

To Each According to His Cost. That each factor receives its marginal revenue product is a true statement about the income distribution (provided we are only considering price takers—there are additional complications for price searchers), but it is not an explanation of the income distribution. One way of seeing that is to note that it is also true that each factor gets its marginal cost of production. A worker who can choose how many hours he wants to work will work up to the point where his wage equals the marginal value of his leisure—the cost, to him, of working an additional hour. Hence his wage is equal to what it costs him to work. Similarly, individuals will save (producing capital) up to the point at which the cost of giving up a little more present consumption in exchange for future consumption just balances what they gain by doing so—the interest rate. So the interest on capital is equal to the marginal cost of producing it.

One Explanation Too Many? We appear to have two explanations of the distribution of income—which some might consider one explanation too many. But neither is complete by itself. Labor receives its marginal product—but the marginal product of labor is determined in part by how much labor (and capital and land and . . .) is being used; the law of diminishing returns tells us that as we increase the amount of one input while holding the others constant, the marginal product of that input eventually starts to go down. Labor is paid its marginal cost of production—but that cost depends in part on how much labor is being sold; the law of declining marginal utility, applied to leisure, implies that the cost of working one more hour depends in part on how many hours you are working.

What we actually have is a description of equilibrium on the market for inputs—the same description we got some chapters earlier when we were considering the market for final goods. The full explanation of the income distribution is that the price of an input is equal to both its marginal cost of production and its marginal revenue product, and the quantity of the input sold and used is that quantity for which the marginal cost of production and the marginal revenue product are equal. (Marginal) cost equals price equals (marginal) value.

This conclusion is useful for seeing how various changes affect the distribution of income. Suppose the number of carpenters suddenly increases, due to the immigration of thousands of new carpenters from Mexico. Both before and after the change, carpenters receive their marginal revenue product. Both before and after, they receive a wage equal to the marginal value of the last hour of leisure they give up. But the wage after the migration is lower than the wage before. Since there are more carpenters, the marginal product of an individual carpenter is lower; with lower wages, the existing carpenters work fewer hours (assuming a normally shaped supply curve for their labor) and, when they are working fewer hours, have more leisure and value the marginal hour of leisure less. Alternatively, the existing carpenters may find that, at the lower wage, they are better off doing something else. In either case, the marginal cost to the worker of working an additional hour falls, either because the marginal hour is worked by one of the old carpenters who is now working fewer hours or because the old carpenters have abandoned the profession and the marginal hour is worked by one of the new immigrants.

In the short run, the additional carpenters are combined with the same quantity of other inputs—wood, hammers, saws—with the result that each additional carpenter produces considerably less than before. Over time, other inputs adjust.

But in the new equilibrium, carpenters are cheaper than before, so it pays to use more of them relative to other inputs—and when more of them are used, their marginal revenue product is lower.

Is It Just?

Once we know who owns inputs and how much each of the inputs gets, we also know the distribution of income. If I own 100 acres of land and land rents for $50/acre, I receive an income of $5,000/year from my land. If I also sell 2,000 hours per year of my own labor at $20/hour, I receive an income of $40,000/year from my labor. If these are the only inputs to production that I own, my total income is $45,000/year. We can in the same way calculate everyone else's income, giving us the distribution of income for the whole society.

One question often asked is, Is this distribution just? Supporters of the market system sometimes defend it by arguing that under the market, everyone "gets what he produces"—which seems fair. The wages of the laborer are equal to the market value of the additional output due to his labor, the interest received by the capitalist is equal to the value of the additional output due to the capital he has saved and invested, and so on. If the initial distribution of the ownership of inputs is just and if the principle "you are entitled to what you produce" is a legitimate one, it seems that the final distribution of income has been justified.

Even if you argue, as many would, that some inputs belong to the wrong people—for instance, that much of the land in the U.S. was unjustly stolen from the American Indians and should be given back—the argument still seems to justify a large part of the existing division of income. In a modern economy such as that of the U.S. at present, most income goes to human inputs—labor and the "human capital" embodied in learned skills—and most people would agree that a worker legitimately "owns" himself.

Another way in which one might try to justify the present distribution of income is by appealing to the second half of the market equality—price equals cost of production. If the idea "to each according to what he has sacrificed in order to produce" is appealing to you, you can argue that the capitalist "deserves" the interest he receives because it represents the cost to him of postponing his consumption—giving up consumption now in exchange for more consumption later—and that the worker "deserves" his salary because it just makes up to him for the leisure he had to give up in order to work.

If you are completely satisfied by either of these arguments, you have probably not entirely understood them. The product and the cost which equal price are *marginal* product and *marginal* cost. The worker's salary just compensates him for the last hour he works—but he gets the same salary for all the hours he works. The interest collected by the capitalist equals the value of the additional production made possible by the addition of his capital—but how great the marginal revenue product of capital is depends, in part, on how much labor, land, and other inputs are being used. Pure capital, all by itself, cannot produce much.

We are left with the problem of how to define a "fair" division of goods when the goods are produced not by any single person but by the combined efforts of many. While "payment according to marginal product" is a possible rule for division and one that describes a large part of what actually happens in a market economy, it is far from clear whether it is a "fair" rule, or even what "fairness" means in such a context. Fortunately, determining what is fair is one of the (few?) problems that is not part of economics.

What Hurts Whom?

So far, we have used our analysis of the distribution of income to try to determine whether it is just. The same analysis can also be used to help us answer a question of considerable interest to many of us—How do I find out whether some particular economic change helps or hurts me? The answer, put simply, is that an increase in the supply of an input I own drives down its price (and marginal revenue product) and so decreases my income. The same is true for an increase in the supply of an input that is a close substitute for an input I own. If I happen to own an oil well, I will regard someone else's discovery of a new field of natural gas—or a process for producing power by thermonuclear fusion—as bad news.

An increase in the supply of an input used with the input I own (a *complement in production*) has the opposite effect. As the relative amount of my input used in production declines, its marginal product increases (the principle of diminishing returns, applied in reverse). If I own an oil well, I will be in favor of the construction of new highways.

Economic changes can affect what I buy as well as what I sell. Increases in the supply of goods I buy, or of inputs used to produce goods I buy, lower the price of those goods and so tend to benefit me. Decreases in their supply tend to make me worse off, for the same reason.

This may help answer the practical question of what things I ought to be for or against in some cases, but not in very many. It is clear enough that if I am a (selfish) physician, I should be in favor of restrictive licensing laws which keep down the number of physicians, and that if I am a (selfish) patient, I should be against them. It is much less clear how I should view the effect on my welfare of government deficits, restrictions on immigration, laws controlling the use of land, or any of a myriad of other things which do not directly affect the supply of the particular inputs which I happen to own.

And for Our Next Act

You may by now have realized that economics involves a continual balancing act between unrealistic simplification and unworkable complication. Chapter 8 was a prime example of the latter; the attempt to fully describe even a simple economy involves a system of equations whose solution is well beyond the capacity of any existing computer.

In Part 2, I will swing us back in the other direction by showing how even a relatively complicated economy, such as the one we live in, can be viewed for some purposes as having only three inputs to production. This approach makes it possible to say something about how a particular person is affected by changes in the supply, demand, and price of goods that he neither buys nor sells.

PART 2 · THE FACTORS OF PRODUCTION

Consider apples. For most purposes, we talk about the "supply of apples," the "price of apples," and so on. But, strictly speaking, a Golden Delicious apple, a Jonathan apple, and a Granny Smith apple are three different things. Even more strictly speaking, two Jonathan apples are different things; one is a little prettier, a little sweeter, or whatever. Even if we considered two identical apples, they would still be in different places, and the location of a good is one of its important characteristics; oil companies spend large sums converting crude petroleum two miles down into (identical) crude petroleum in a tank above ground.

For some purposes, it is convenient to make very fine distinctions, for others it is not; one cost of fine distinctions is that they make analysis more complicated. It is more precise to treat Golden Delicious apples and Red Delicious apples as two different goods which happen to be close substitutes; it is simpler to treat them as the same good.

Treating goods as close substitutes has almost the same effect as treating them as the same good. If they are the same good, an increase in the price of one implies an exactly equal increase in the price of the other, since they must sell for the same price. If they are substitutes, an increase in the price of one leads to an increase in the demand for the other, and hence an increase in its price. If they are sufficiently close substitutes—and if one unit of one good substitutes for one unit of the other—then an increase in the price of one produces an almost equal increase in the price of the other. To say that two things are both units of the same good is equivalent to saying that they are perfect substitutes for each other, as one piece of paper is a perfect substitute for another even though the two pieces are not literally identical—they would look slightly different under a microscope.

One could make a simple picture complicated by viewing each apple as a different good. I am instead going to make a complicated picture simple by viewing many different things as "really" the same good. This is how it works.

How to Simplify the Problem

Consider three kinds of land—type A, type B, and type C. Suppose type A land is especially good for growing wheat, type C for growing soybeans, and type B good for both; for simplicity let an acre of A or B be equally good at producing wheat, and an acre of B or C equally good at producing soybeans. Further suppose supply and demand conditions are such that all the type A land is used for wheat, all the type C for soybeans, and some type B for each.

Under these circumstances, the price of all three grades of land must be the same. The price of an acre of type A land is the present value of the net revenue (revenue minus production costs) of producing wheat on it; so is the price of an acre of type B land being used to produce wheat. Since types A and B land are equally good at producing wheat, the two prices must be the same. The price of an acre of type C land is the present value of the net revenue from producing soybeans on it—so is the price of an acre of type B land that is used for producing soybeans.

But all type B land must have the same price, whatever it is used for. If it did not, if for instance land used to produce soybeans was worth more than identical land used to produce wheat, then land would shift out of wheat production and into soybean production, driving the price of soybeans down and the price of wheat up. This process would continue until either the land was equally valuable in both uses or all of the type B land was used for soybeans.

Suppose a flood wipes out 100 acres of type A land. The initial effect is to raise the market price of wheat and of land growing wheat. Some type B land is now shifted from soybeans to the (more profitable) wheat. The quantity of wheat supplied increases, driving the price of wheat part of the way back down toward what it was before the flood. The quantity of soybeans supplied decreases, since some land that had been producing soybeans is now producing wheat; the price of soybeans rises. When equilibrium is reestablished, the price of all three kinds of land is again the same. If it were not, more B land would shift from one crop to the other until it was. The final effect on the price of wheat, soybeans, and land is the same as if the flood had wiped out 100 acres of type C land or of type B land.

As long as we only consider changes in supply and demand (of land, wheat, and soybeans) which leave some type B land growing soybeans and some growing wheat, the situation is the same as if all the land were identical! We cannot directly replace type A land with type C land (or vice versa), but we can do so indirectly by replacing type A land with some type B land (converting it from soybeans to wheat) and replacing the type B land with type C land. Hence the price of all three kinds of land is the same, and all we need to know is the total supply of land. In analyzing this particular economy, we can reduce three different inputs—types A, B, and C land—into one.

This somewhat oversimplifies the situation which really exists with regard to land. There is a wide range of "types" of land (and crops); some land is very well-suited for one crop and very badly for many others, while some land can grow any of several crops. The qualitative result, however, still holds. For many purposes, we can think of land as a single good with a single price and quantity— not because all land is the same, or even because any piece of land is a good substitute for any other piece (it is not), but because there are always *some* pieces of land that are "on the margin" between being used for one purpose or another.

When the supply of land suited for one crop—say, corn—decreases, the price of that crop goes up. Land which, at the old price of corn, was used to grow some other crop that brought in a slightly higher income now generates more income by producing corn, so such land shifts out of other crops and into corn. By doing so, it transmits the decreased supply (and increased price) to the land used for what such "marginal" land was previously producing. A decrease in the supply of any one kind of land ultimately raises the price of all land, as does an increase in the demand for any one kind of land.

Land is not the only "good" that can be treated in this way. There are three traditional *factors of production*—land, labor, and capital. Each is really a group of goods which can substitute for each other sufficiently well to be treated, for many purposes, as a single good. In each case, what is essential is not that every unit can directly substitute for every other unit, but that there are always some marginal units which can shift from one use to another so as to transmit changes affecting one good in the group to all the others.

Most of the inputs to production can be classified as either land, labor, or capital, although not always in the way a non-economist might expect—a surgeon, for example, is mostly capital! So this approach allows us to view even a very complicated economy as if it had only three inputs to production. For analyzing short-run changes, the approach is not very useful—an increased demand for economists is unlikely to have much immediate effect on either the wages of ditchdiggers or the interest on bonds, although economists are a "mixture" of labor and capital, the wages of ditchdiggers are a measure of the price of labor, and the interest on bonds is a measure of the price of capital.

In the longer run, it is easier to transform one form of labor or capital into another. If the demand for economists increases, then more people will become economists—instead of ditchdiggers or politicial scientists or secretaries. Training additional economists will require that people—the economics students themselves, their parents, investors lending them money for their education, or the government—spend money now for a return in the future. So less money will be available to be spent now for a future return in other ways—to build factories, do research, or train people in other professions. Labor and capital are being shifted into producing economics and out of producing ditches, cars, and many other things.

In the short run, the economy is less flexible than in the long run, as has been pointed out before. In the short run, the only people who can do economics are economists; the only ways to produce more economics are by getting some economists presently producing economics to produce more of it, or by getting economists who are presently doing other things—writing textbooks, for example, or loafing on the French Riviera—to go back to doing economics. In the long run, the factors of production can be used to produce more economists, hence more economics—and similarly with anything else. So the factors of production are more useful for understanding what happens in the long term than for understanding what happens in the short term.

In the next few sections of the book, I will discuss the three traditional factors of production—labor, land, and capital—so that you can see what they are and how they differ from each other.

Labor

Workers combine in themselves two different factors of production—labor and human capital. To produce a steelworker, one requires both a person and training; the latter, like any other investment, involves consuming inputs now in exchange for future returns, so it is properly classified as a form of capital. The wages of a worker can then be divided into the return on "raw labor" and the return on the laborer's human capital.

People are not all identical; even before training, a 6-foot man can probably dig more ditches per day than a 5-foot woman. To some extent, one can deal with this by thinking of different people as containing different "amounts" of raw labor. The situation would be simple if the person who could dig twice as many ditches could also type twice as many pages and treat twice as many patients; you could then say that one person "contained" two units of labor and the other contained one. In the real world, it is more complicated.

One way of transforming one type of labor (secretaries) into another (ditch-diggers) is by having those few secretaries who are either 6-foot males or extraordinarily strong females switch jobs—or, if we consider long-term changes, having more of the people physically capable of being ditchdiggers become ditchdiggers and fewer of them become secretaries. That will not produce many ditchdiggers. A more indirect way is to convert secretaries into truck drivers and (other) truck drivers into ditchdiggers. Truck driving, despite its macho image, is a job that does not require a great deal of physical strength; it can be and often is done by women.

Suppose you are a potential secretary (currently doing something else) who is just as productive as the marginal secretary—the one who would become a truck driver if the wages of truck drivers went up a little (or the wages of secretaries went down a little). Suppose the marginal truck driver—the one who would become a ditchdigger if the wages of ditchdiggers went up a little—can dig twice as many ditches per day as the average ditchdigger. Two ditchdiggers retire. The wages of ditchdiggers rise slightly. The marginal truck driver becomes a ditchdigger, the marginal secretary becomes a truck driver, and you become a secretary. You have "substituted" for two ditchdiggers. You "contain" twice as much labor as the average ditchdigger—even if you cannot lift a shovel.

To the extent that we can regard labor as a single good, what can we say about its supply? There are two possible ways of looking at labor supply, both contained in Chapter 5. The first implies that the quantity of labor depends on the wage and that the supply curve may be backward-bending for some wage rates. The second implies that the supply of labor is perfectly inelastic—equal to 24 hours per day times the population.

Seen from this second standpoint, what appears to be the supply curve—the number of hours of labor offered for sale—is really the (inelastic) supply *minus* part of demand. If I offer to sell 8 hours of my own labor, I am really supplying 24 hours and buying 16 of them for my own use. Hence the supply of labor which appears on the market is really the total supply (fixed) minus the demand for non-market uses—labor spent in leisure, household production (cooking meals), investment in human capital (what you are doing at this very moment), and so on. While this may seem an unnecessarily odd way of looking at the labor market, it will prove useful for seeing in what way the supply of labor is or is not different from the supply of land or capital.

In the short run, the total supply of labor is fixed; neglecting differences among workers, it is equal to the population times 24 hours per day. But in the long run, the population can change. The originators of modern economics— Adam Smith at the end of the eighteenth century, Thomas Malthus and David Ricardo at the beginning of the nineteenth—made this fact a central part of their analysis. They believed that the higher the wages of labor were, the more willing the mass of the population would be to have children—and the higher the growth rate of the population.

If everyone were poor, the cost of having a child would be giving up things that potential parents valued highly—such as food or clothing for themselves. So most people would marry late and, once married, try to avoid having children. The result would be a low birth rate, a decline in the quantity of labor relative to the other two factors of production, and an increase in wages.

If, on the other hand, wages were high, people would be more willing to have children. The result would be an increase in population and a decline of wages. Hence, the classical economists argued, there was an *equilibrium wage*—the wage at which the population just maintained itself. Wages above that increased the population, pushing the wage rate back down; wages below that decreased the population, pushing the wage rate back up.

Reaching the equilibrium might take awhile. An economy in which the stock of capital was growing could maintain wages for an extended period of time above their equilibrium level, with population and capital growing together. But the limited supply of land, combined with the principle of diminishing returns, would eventually bring growth to a standstill and wages back to their long-run equilibrium level. This was the so-called *iron law of wages*. One conclusion which Ricardo drew from this was that it would be a good thing if the poor acquired expensive tastes. They would then require a higher standard of living before they would be willing to bear the cost of having children, so the equilibrium wage would be higher.

Modern economics has tended to abandon such discussions and limit itself to considering an economy with a given population. One reason may be that wages have risen enormously, and fairly continuously, from Ricardo's day to ours, suggesting that there is no long-term equilibrium wage. Very recently, with rising concern about overpopulation and limited resources, there has been some revival of interest in economic theories which include changes in population as one of the variables to be explained and taken account of.

Land

I started my discussion of the factors of production by showing how different types of land could be treated as if they were all the same good. For simplicity I set my assumptions up so that an acre of each kind of land was equivalent to an acre of each other kind. I could as easily have assumed that one acre of type A land produced the same return as two acres of type B land used for growing wheat, and that one acre of type B land used for growing soybeans produced as much as two acres of type C land. In that case, the price of an acre of A land would have been twice the price of an acre of B land and four times the price of an acre of C land. We would then think of A land as containing four units of land per acre, B as containing two, and C as containing one. We could then analyze land as if it were all the same—with the total quantity of land equal to the amount of type C land plus twice the amount of type B land plus four times the amount of type A land. This is much like the situation discussed earlier with regard to labor; types A, B, and C land correspond to secretaries, truck drivers, and ditchdiggers, respectively, in the earlier example.

There are a certain number of square miles on the surface of the earth; the number has not changed significantly in the past hundred thousand years, and, short of some massive redesign of the planet, it will not change significicantly in the next hundred thousand. Hence if we consider only "raw land" and classify investments that increase its productivity (fertilizing, draining, clearing) as capital, the supply of land, unlike the supply of most other things we have discussed, is almost perfectly inelastic.

If the supply of land is perfectly inelastic, the supply curve for land is vertical, which implies that a tax on land, whether "paid" by owner or renter, is entirely borne by the owner, with none of it passed on to the renter. It also implies that a tax on land generates no excess burden—as you showed (I hope) in your answer to Problems 9 and 10 of Chapter 7. Both results are shown on Figure 13-2,

Figure 13-2

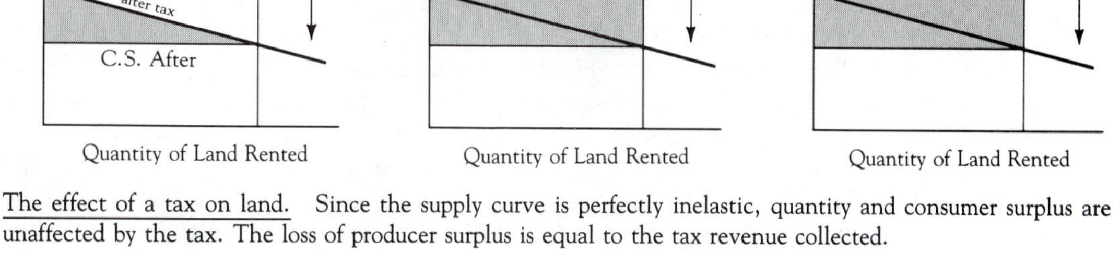

The effect of a tax on land. Since the supply curve is perfectly inelastic, quantity and consumer surplus are unaffected by the tax. The loss of producer surplus is equal to the tax revenue collected.

where the tax is "paid" by the consumers. I drew it that way because a tax "paid" by the producer shifts the vertical supply curve vertically, which is difficult to show; the shifted curve would be identical to the unshifted one.

These facts have sometimes been used to argue that land is the ideal thing to tax—there is no excess burden, and all of the tax is borne by the landowners. One difficulty with this proposal is that in order to tax something, you must measure it. "Raw land" may be in perfectly inelastic supply, but the land we actually use—to live on, grow our food on, build our roads on—is not. It is a combination of raw land and other resources—labor used to clear the land, capital invested in improving it, and so on. One measure of the difference between "land in use" and "raw land" is the fact that only about one tenth of the land area of the earth is under cultivation—and the amount used for houses, roads, and the like is even less.

If you tax the market value of land, you discourage people from increasing the value of raw land by using capital and labor to improve it; the supply curve for improved land is by no means perfectly inelastic. So in order to impose the so-called *single tax* (a tax on the value of unimproved land, proposed as a substitute for all other taxes), you first have to find some way of estimating what the land would have been worth without any improvements—which is difficult.

Rent and Quasi-Rent

Because land is the standard example of a good in perfectly inelastic supply and because payment for the use of land is called *rent*, the term *rent* has come to be used in economics in two different ways. One is to mean payment for the use of something, as distinguished from payment for ownership (*price*). In this sense, one buys cars from GM but rents them from Avis. The other is to mean payment for the use of something in fixed (i.e., perfectly inelastic) supply.

In this second sense, rent can be applied to many things other than land. Scarce human talents—the abilities of an inventive genius or the combination of good coordination and very long legs—can be thought of as valuable resources in fixed supply and without close substitutes; hence the wages of Thomas Edison or Wilt Chamberlain may be analyzed as a sort of rent. Rent in this sense is a price that allocates the use of something among consumers but does not "tell" producers how much to produce, since the good is not being produced. The opposite case is payment for something with a horizontal supply curve—in that case, payment is simply equal to cost of production.

The shape of a supply curve depends on how much time producers have to adjust their output. In the very short run, practically everything is in fixed supply. In the longer run, many things are; and in the very long run, practically nothing is. One may even argue that if certain talents produce high incomes, the possessors of those talents will be rich and have lots of children, thus increasing the supply of those talents, or that a sufficiently high rent on land will encourage the exploration and development of other planets, thus increasing the quantity of land. So the economic analysis developed to explain the rent on land may be inapplicable to anything—even land—in the (very) long run. But it can be used to explain the behavior of many prices in the (sufficiently) short run—which may be a day for fresh fish and thirty years for houses.

In the previous chapter, I discussed goods whose cost of construction was a sunk cost, such as ships or factories. As long as the price shipowners get for carrying freight is high enough so that their ships are worth something and not high enough to make it worth building more ships, the supply of ships is perfectly inelastic. The number of ships does not change with price, although it does gradually shrink as ships wear out. The same is true for prices at which it is worth building more ships—if we limit ourselves to times too short to build them. So the returns on ships can be thought of as a sort of rent—called a quasi-rent—provided we limit ourselves to a sufficiently short-term analysis. That is just what we did in Chapter 12.

Capital

The third factor of production is capital. The meanings of labor and of land (more generally, unproduced natural resources) seem fairly obvious; the meaning of capital is not. Does producing capital mean saving? Building factories? Investing your savings? What is capital—what does it look like?

One (good) answer is that using capital means using inputs now to produce outputs later. The more dollar-years required (number of dollars of inputs times number of years until the outputs appear—a slight oversimplification but good enough for our purposes), the more the "amount" of capital used. Capital is productive because it is (often) possible to produce more output if you are willing to wait than if you are not—to spend a week chipping out a flint axe and then use the axe to cut down lots of trees instead of spending two days scraping through a tree with a chunk of unshaped flint, or to make machines to make machines to make machines to make cars instead of simply making cars. Capital is expensive because people usually prefer consumption now to consumption in the future and must be paid to give up the former in exchange for the latter. *Capital goods* are the physical objects (factories, machines, apple trees) produced by inputs now and used to produce outputs in the future.

Describing capital as a single good is both less and more legitimate than is a similar simplification for land or labor. It is less legitimate because once capital goods are built, they are not very flexible; there is no way an automobile factory can produce steel or a milling machine grow grain. In the case of labor and land, we argued that one variety could substitute for another through a chain of intermediates—from secretary to ditchdigger in the one case, from wheat to soybeans in the other. Finding a chain to connect a steel mill to a drainage canal, or an invention (capital in the form of valuable knowledge produced by research) to a tractor, would be more difficult.

But treating all capital as one good is more legitimate than treating all labor or all land as one if we consider capital before it is invested. A steel mill cannot be converted into a drainage canal—but an investor can decide whether he will use his savings to pay workers to build the one or the other. So the anticipated return on all investments—the interest rate—must be the same. If investors expected to make more by investing a dollar in building a steel mill than by investing a dollar in digging a drainage canal, capital would shift into steel; the increased supply of steel would drive down the price of steel and the return on investments in steel mills. The reduced supply of capital in canal building would, similarly, increase the return on investments in canals. Investors would continue to shift their capital out of the one use and into the other until the returns on the two were the same.

A reduction in the supply of steel mills—the destruction of a hundred mills by a war or an earthquake, say—will drive up the price of steel, increase the return on investments in steel mills, attract capital that would otherwise have gone elsewhere into the steel industry, and so drive up the general interest rate. Thus in the long run, there is a single quantity of capital and a single price (more precisely, rent) on capital—the interest rate. All capital is the same—before it is invested.

After it is invested, capital takes many forms. One of the most important is one that non-economists rarely think of as capital—human capital. A medical student who invests $90,000 and six years in becoming a surgeon is bearing costs now in return for benefits in the future, just as he would be if he had invested his time and money in building a factory instead. If the salary of surgeons were not high enough to make investing in himself at least as attractive as investing in something else, he would have invested in physical capital instead. So the salary of a surgeon should be considered, in part, the wages of labor, in part, the "rent" on certain scarce human talents, and, in part, interest on his human capital.

There is one important respect in which human capital differs from other forms of capital. If you have an idea for building a profitable factory but not enough money of your own to pay for it, you can raise more money either by letting other investors be part-owners of the factory or by borrowing, putting up the factory itself as your security. Your ability to invest in your own human capital is much more limited. You cannot sell shares of yourself because that would violate the laws against slavery—you cannot put yourself up as collateral for the same reason. You can borrow money to pay for your training—but after the money is spent, you may, if you wish, declare bankruptcy. Your creditors have no way of repossessing the training that you bought with their money.

In a market economy, investments in physical capital that can be expected to yield more than the normal market return will always be made. The same is not true for investments in human capital. They will be made only if the human in question (or his parents or someone else who values his future welfare or trusts him to pay back loans) can provide the necessary capital. In that respect, the market for human capital is an imperfect one.

The source of the imperfection was discussed in Chapter 11—insecure property rights. In Chapter 11, the property rights of owners of oil were insecure because of the possibility of expropriation—one consequence was to discourage investment in finding oil and drilling oil wells. Here the property rights of lenders are insecure because of the possibility of bankruptcy; the result is to discourage investment in (someone else's) human capital. The existence of this imperfection provides, on the one hand, an argument for government provision (or guarantees) of loans for education, and on the other hand, an argument for relaxing the prohibition against (self-chosen) slavery—to the extent of limiting the ability of people who borrow for their education to declare bankruptcy.

The Factors—Similarities and Differences

We have now looked at all three of the factors of production—labor, land, and capital. How are they similar? How are they different?

One respect in which some factors differ from each other and some do not is in the degree to which each is property. Land and physical capital are entirely property; they may be bought, sold, transferred, lent. Labor and human capital are property of a very limited sort, at least in our society. They may be rented out, but the contract can almost always be canceled at the will of the owner—the worker can always quit. Neither labor nor human capital can be sold, and neither can be used as collateral, since there is no way the lender can collect.

A second difference is in supply. Land is in absolutely fixed supply. Labor is also in fixed supply, if we include an individual's demand for his own labor as part of demand rather than as something affecting supply. The quantity of labor changes over time due to changes in population; but since the "producers" of new labor (parents) do not own it and cannot sell it, it is not clear whether or not an increase in the price of labor will increase the supply, even in the long run. The quantity of capital changes as a result of saving; individuals who consume less than their income have the remainder available to invest. The higher the interest rate, the more you get next year in exchange for what you save this year, so we would expect the supply of new capital to increase with the interest rate—although for capital, as for labor, a backward-bending supply curve is not logically impossible.

We have now finished our sketch of the three factors of production. In ending, it is worth noting that there are some inputs to the productive process which do not fit comfortably into our categories. Two examples would be unproduced raw materials—iron ore, for instance—and special human abilities. Both "behave like" land, in the sense of being in fixed supply. But neither "is" land, since neither is a close substitute for the other things that are contained in the collection of related goods called land.

PART 3 · APPLICATIONS

In Part 1 of this chapter, I showed how the distribution of income was determined and discussed how I might decide whether or not some particular change was in my interest by how it affected my share in the distribution. The conclusion was that I could expect to benefit by any change that raised the price of the productive inputs that I owned and from which I got my living or lowered the price of the goods I consumed; I could expect to lose from any change that lowered the price of the inputs I owned or raised the price of the goods I consumed.

The problem, as I pointed out at the time, is that many potential changes whose effects I might want to know cannot be evaluated in this way. They have no direct effect on the particular inputs I own and sell or the particular goods I consume, and the net consequence of their numerous indirect effects is hard to judge. The factors of production were introduced as a solution to this problem; when all inputs have been simplified down to three, it may be possible to judge both how some change affects each of the three factors and how a change in the prices of the factors affects my welfare.

That is what we will be doing in Part 3. We will consider three different public policy issues—immigration restrictions, limitations on foreign investment in poor countries, and governmental controls on land use. In each case, the question we are primarily interested in is not whether the policy is good or bad but who gains and who loses. In each case, we will try to answer that question by looking at the effect of the policy on the factors of production.

Immigration

We can combine Parts 1 and 2 of this chapter in order to analyze a number of interesting questions; we will start with the effect of increased immigration on the welfare of the present inhabitants of the U.S. Prior to the 1920s, the U.S. followed a general policy of unrestricted immigration, although there were some restrictions on immigration of Orientals. The result was a flood of immigrants which at its peak exceeded a million a year. Suppose we went back to unrestricted immigration. Who would benefit and who would lose?

Immigrants have, on average, less human and physical capital than the present inhabitants of the U.S.; they are less skilled and poorer. So one result of increased immigration would be an increase in the ratio of labor to capital in the U.S. Immigrants bring labor and some capital but no land, so another result would be to decrease the ratio of land to both labor and capital. Hence increased immigration would decrease the price of labor and increase the price of land; the effect on the price of capital is ambiguous, since it becomes scarcer relative to labor and less scarce relative to land. My guess is that since the additional immigrants who would come in under a policy of unrestricted immigration would bring very little capital with them—rich immigrants can come in under present laws—the return on capital would increase.

The net result would probably be to injure the most unskilled American workers. It might well benefit many or even most other workers, since what they are selling is not pure labor but a mixture containing a large amount of human capital. People who were net buyers of land would be injured by the increased price of land; people who were net sellers of land would be benefited. Net lenders would be benefited if the return on capital (the interest rate) increased; net borrowers would be injured.

Can we say anything about the overall effect on those presently living in the U.S.? Yes—but to do so, we must bring in arguments from a previous chapter. One way of looking at immigration restrictions is as barriers to trade; they prevent an American consumer from buying the labor of a Mexican worker—by preventing the worker from coming to where the labor is wanted. The same comparative advantage arguments which were discussed in Chapter 6 and will be discussed again in Chapter 18 apply here as well. Since there is a net gain to trade, the abolition of immigration restrictions will produce a net benefit for present Americans, although some will be worse off—just as the abolition of tariffs produces a net benefit, although American auto workers (and GM stockholders) may be injured. These net benefits are, of course, in addition to the (very large) benefits to the new immigrants which would motivate them to come.

A more precise discussion of what we mean by "net benefits" would carry us into the next chapter—which is about just such questions. A more rigorous explanation of why open immigration produces net benefits would carry us beyond the limits of this course. There are, however, two more points worth making before we finish with the question of immigration.

So far in my discussion of immigration, I have assumed a private property society in which the only way to get income is to sell labor or other inputs. In fact there are at least two other ways—from government (in the form of welfare, unemployment payments, and the like) and by private violation of property rights (theft and robbery). To the extent that new immigrants support themselves in those ways, they impose costs on the present inhabitants without providing corresponding benefits; in such a situation, the demonstration that new immigrants provide net benefits no longer holds.

It is unclear what, if any, connection there is between that argument and the abandonment of open immigration by the U.S. It is tempting to argue that immigration restrictions were one of the consequences of the welfare state. As long as it was clear that poor immigrants would have to support themselves, they were welcome; once they acquired the right to live off the taxes of those already here, they were not. The argument neatly links two of the major changes of the first half of this century—and does so in a way that fits nicely with my own ideological prejudices.

Unfortunately for the argument, immigration restrictions were imposed in the early 1920s, and the major increase in the size and responsibility of government occurred during the New Deal—about a decade later. At most one might conjecture that both resulted from the same changing view of the role of the state.

Whether or not there was any historical connection between the rise of the welfare state in the U.S. and the end of unrestricted immigration, it seems clear that present objections to immigrants often involve the fear that as soon as they arrive, they will go on welfare. It is much less clear that that fear is justified; a good deal of evidence seems to suggest that new immigrants are more likely to start working their way up the income ladder—in response to the opportunity to earn what are, from the standpoint of many of them, phenomenally high wages.

My final comment on free immigration concerns its distributional effects. Opponents of immigration argue that it "hurts the poor and helps the rich," since the obvious losers are unskilled American workers. If we limit our discussion to those presently living here, they are probably right. But the big gainers from immigration would be the immigrants—most of whom are very much poorer than the American poor. From a national standpoint, free immigration hurts the poor; from an international standpoint, it helps them. By world standards, the American poor are, if not rich, at least comfortably well off.

Economic Imperialism

The term "economic imperialism" has at least two meanings. It is applied by some economists to the use of the economic approach to explain what are traditionally considered "non-economic" questions. We are "imperialists" attacking the intellectual territory presently held by political scientists, sociologists, psychologists, and the like. Much more commonly, it is used by Marxists to describe—and attack—foreign investment in "developing" (i.e., poor) nations. The implication of the term is that such investment is only a subtler equivalent of military imperialism—a way by which capitalists in rich and powerful countries control and exploit the inhabitants of poor and weak countries.

There is one interesting feature of such "economic imperialism" which seems to have escaped the notice of most of those who use the term. Developing countries are generally labor rich and capital poor; developed countries are, relatively, capital rich and labor poor. One result is that in developing countries, the return on labor is low and the return on capital is high—wages are low and profits high. That is why they are attractive to foreign investors.

To the extent that foreign investment occurs, it raises the amount of capital in the country—driving wages up and profits down. The effect is exactly analogous to the effect of free migration. If people move from labor-rich countries to labor-poor ones, they drive wages down and rents and profits up in the countries they go to, while having the opposite effect in the countries they come from. If capital moves from capital-rich countries to capital-poor ones, it drives profits down and wages up in the countries it goes to and has the opposite effect in the countries it comes from.

The people who attack "economic imperialism" generally regard themselves as champions of the poor and oppressed. To the extent that they succeed in preventing foreign investment in poor countries, they are benefiting the capitalists of those countries by holding up profits and injuring the workers by holding down wages. It would be interesting to know how much of the clamor against foreign investment in such countries is due to Marxist ideologues who do not understand this and how much is financed by local capitalists who do.

I should warn you that in the last few paragraphs I have used the term *profit* in the conventional sense of the return to capital, that being the way it is usually used in such discussions. A better term would be *interest*. That way, one avoids confusing profit in the sense of the return on capital with profit in the sense of economic profit—revenue minus all costs, *including* the cost of capital.

Land-Use Restrictions

In the U.S. and in similar societies elsewhere, there are often extensive limitations on how property owners can use their land. Many of these limitations can be defended in terms of *externalities*—a subject that will be discussed in Chapter 17. Whether or not the restrictions are justified, it is interesting to analyze their distributional effects.

Suppose the English government requires (as it does) that "greenbelts" be established around major cities—areas surrounding the urban center within which dense populations are prohibited. The result is to reduce the total amount of residential land available in such cities. The result of that is to increase rents. A law which is defended as a way of protecting urban beauty against greedy developers has as one of its effects raising the income of urban landlords at the expense of their tenants. It would be interesting to analyze the sources of support for imposing and maintaining greenbelt legislation, in order to see how much comes from the residents whose environment the legislation claims to protect and how much from the landlords whose income it increases.

PART 4 · WAGE DIFFERENTIALS

So far, we have been using the ideas of Parts 1 and 2 of this chapter to determine who is injured or benefited by various policies. The same ideas can also be used to answer another question: What determines the different wages in different professions?

We begin with the observation from Part 2 that in equilibrium all sorts of labor are in some sense the same, as are all sorts of capital and land. If so, then one would expect that all jobs would receive the same pay. Obviously this is not so. Why?

Disequilibrium

The first answer is that we may not be in long-run equilibrium. Equilibrium is created and maintained by the fact that when one profession is more attractive than another, people tend to leave the less attractive profession and enter the more attractive one; similarly, new workers coming onto the market choose those professions that they expect to be most attractive. As workers enter the attractive professions, they drive down their wages; as workers leave the unattractive ones, the wages in those professions rise. The process stops only when all professions are equally attractive.

All of this takes time. An individual who has spent considerable time and money training himself for one profession will switch to another only if the return is not only larger but enough larger to justify the cost of the move. This is less of a problem for new workers coming onto the market, since they have not yet made the investment—but it may take a long time before the reduced inflow of new workers has much effect on the total number in the profession. So if an unexpected reduction in the demand for some particular type of labor pushes wages in that field below their long-run equilibrium level, it may be years before they come all the way back up. Similarly, an unexpected increase in demand for some particular sort of labor may keep wages above the normal level for some time, especially if the profession is one that requires lengthy training.

Differing Abilities

A second answer is that differing wages may reflect differing abilities. If, for example, intelligence is useful in practically any field and if nuclear physicists are, on average, more intelligent than grocery store clerks, then they will also have higher wages. The individual nuclear physicist may, in this case, earn no more than he would if he were a clerk—but the same man who is an average physicist, earning an average physicist's salary, would be an above-average clerk, earning an above-average clerk's salary. This is the case I described earlier as one person "containing more labor" than another. One hour of the intelligent worker's time may be equivalent to two hours of the average worker's time.

If this were the whole story, there is no obvious reason why nuclear physicists would be more intelligent than clerks—the intelligent individual would get the same return in either profession. In fact, of course, intelligence—and other abilities—are more useful in some fields than in others. Being seven feet tall is very useful if you are a basketball player; if you are a college professor, it merely means that you bump your head a lot.

Differences in such specialized abilities may not matter very much if the abilities are in sufficiently large supply. If 10 percent of the population consisted of men who were seven feet tall and well coordinated, basketball players would not get unusually high salaries—there would be too many tall clerks, tall professors, and tall ditchdiggers willing to enter the profession if they did. Similarly, whether the talents that make a good salesman bring high salaries to their possessors depends on both the supply of and demand for those talents. If equilibrium is reached only when all of the people who have those talents, plus some of those who do not have them, are salesmen, then the return to selling must be high enough to make it a reasonably attractive profession even to those who are not unusually talented at it—and a very attractive profession to those who are. If, on the other hand, in equilibrium all of the salesmen are talented and only some of those with the appropriate talents are salesmen, then talented salesmen will receive only a normal return for their efforts.

We are now discussing what I earlier described as rents on scarce human abilities. If, to take an extreme case, only people who are over seven feet tall can play basketball, and if the demand for basketball players at a price equal to the wage in other professions is higher than the total number of people over seven feet tall, then the wages of basketball players can never be driven down to the ordinary wage rate. Nobody can move from other professions to basketball because everybody over seven feet tall is already playing basketball. Just as in the earlier discussion of land, the price is determined by the point where the demand curve intersects a perfectly inelastic supply curve.

Usually, the situation is not quite that extreme. There are people who could play basketball and do not; but they are, on average, shorter (or worse coordinated or in some other way less suited for basketball) than the people who do play. In equilibrium the wage is such that the marginal basketball player—the individual just balanced between choosing to play basketball and choosing to do something else—finds both alternatives equally attractive. If the average player is considerably better than the marginal one, he will also receive a higher salary. The same argument can be worked through for any profession in which the individual's productivity depends on his possession of rare characteristics or abilities.

Equal Net Advantage

We have now discussed two reasons why different professions might not, on net, be equally attractive—disequilibrium and differential abilities. There remains the possibility that even if neither of those factors is important—even if all professions are equally attractive—they may still be attractive in different ways.

Consider a group of professions. We assume that none of them requires any special human abilities; indeed, to make the situation even simpler, we assume that all individuals start with the same abilities. We also assume that the economy is in equilibrium; there have been no unexpected changes in the demand for different sorts of labor, so everyone is getting about the wage he expected to get when he chose his field.

Even in this situation, we may observe wide variations in the wages received by people in different professions. What is equal in equilibrium is the *net advantage* in each field, not the wage. If, for example, a particular profession, such as economics, is much more fun than other professions, it will also pay less. If it did not—if its wages were the same as those in less enjoyable fields—then *on net* it would be more attractive. People who were leading dull lives as ditchdiggers, sociologists, or lawyers would pour into the field, driving down the wage.

The argument applies not only to professions that are more fun but also to professions that have other non-pecuniary advantages. If, for example, many people want to be film or rock stars, not because the job is fun but because they like the idea of being watched by adoring multitudes, that will tend to drive down the wages of those professions. The same argument also works in reverse, for professions which have non-pecuniary disadvantages. That is why it costs more to hire people to drive trucks loaded with dynamite than trucks loaded with dirt.

A second factor which makes wages unequal even when net advantage is equal is the difference in the cost of entering different professions. Becoming a checkout clerk requires almost no training; becoming an actuary requires years of study. If both professions earned the same wages, few people would become actuaries. In equilibrium the wage of the actuary must be enough higher to repay the time and expense invested in learning the job. Since the cost of training occurs at the beginning of his career and the return occurs later, the actuary must receive enough extra income to pay not only the cost of his training but also the interest on his investment in himself. If he did not, he would be better off investing his money in something other than himself and becoming a clerk instead.

There is one more element that should be taken into account in explaining wage differentials—uncertainty. In some professions, the wage is fairly predictable; in others it is not. Movie stars make very large incomes, but the only actress I ever knew personally supported herself largely by temporary secretarial work. In a profession where most people are failures, at least from a financial standpoint, it is not surprising that the few successes do very well. An individual entering such a profession is, in effect, buying a ticket in a lottery—one chance of making several hundred thousand dollars a year, nine hundred and ninety-nine chances of barely scraping by on an occasional acting job supplemented by part-time work and unemployment compensation, and a few chances of something in between the two extremes. My impression is that the *average* wage of actors and actresses is very low and that the willingness of men and women to enter the profession reflects either unrealistic optimism, large non-pecuniary returns from doing what they really want to do, or both.

PROBLEMS

1. Why is a backward-bending supply curve more plausible for "labor" considered as a factor of production than for any particular kind of labor (table making) or the product of such labor?
2. The supply of labor can be seen in two ways—in one it is perfectly inelastic; in the other it is not. The supply of "raw land" was described as perfectly inelastic. Is there a way of looking at the supply of "raw land," analogous to the "other way" of looking at the supply of labor, which gives it a non-vertical supply curve? If so, can it be backward bending? If it is, does that mean that land is an inferior or a normal good? Discuss.
3. There are several examples of the equimarginal principle buried in the chapter; find and briefly describe them.
4. Suppose you wanted to calculate the Gini coefficient properly; further suppose you had complete information about everyone's income from birth to death. Exactly how would you solve the problem (confusion of changing income over time with changing income across people) discussed at the beginning of this chapter? (Hint: Use a concept from Chapter 11.)
5. My wife is a geologist employed by an oil company. We spend less than one percent of our joint income for gasoline and several percent more for heating (gas) and power. Do you think we are better or worse off if the price of oil goes up? Would your answer be very much different if we had oil heat? If she was a geologist employed by a university? Discuss.

6. What alternative professions would you seriously consider entering if their wage, relative to the wage you expect in the profession you plan to follow, rose by 10 percent? By 50 percent? What alternative professions would you have seriously considered if before you started training for this one, their wages had been 10 percent higher than they were? What if they had been 50 percent higher?

7. Suppose we say that two professions are "linked" if there is at least one person in each who would have been in the other if the wage had been 10 percent higher. How many steps does it take to link your profession to the profession of a ditchdigger? A professional athlete? A hit man? A brain surgeon? A homemaker? Describe plausible chains in each case.

   (Example: The chain economist-lawyer-politician links me to a politician and has two links. Some economists are people who might well have become lawyers instead—and would have if the wages of lawyers were a little higher. Some lawyers are people who might well have become politicians instead—and would have if the "wages" of politicians were a little higher.)

8. Explain briefly why Problems 6 and 7 are in this chapter.

9. There are some people who very much want to be actors and will enter the profession even if they receive barely enough to live on. Discuss, as precisely as possible, under what circumstances actors *will* make barely enough to live on, and under what circumstances they will make about the same wages as people in other fields. You may wish to simplify the problem by ignoring the probabilistic element—assume all actors make the same amount. You may find it useful to consider the effect on wages of different possible supply and demand curves for actors.

10. We described the additional salary received by someone who possesses scarce human talents as a sort of rent. What similar term might be used to describe the additional salary received by someone in a profession where wages are temporarily above their long-run equilibrium? Discuss. (Hint: See Chapter 12.)

11. What we have described as rent on human abilities might also be called producer surplus. Draw supply-demand diagrams to illustrate the discussions of basketball players in the text and of actors in Problem 9, showing both the case where they do and the case where they do not receive unusually high or low wages.

FOR FURTHER READING

The classic discussion of the economics of wage differentials was published in 1776. It can be found in Chapter X, Book I, of Adam Smith, *An Inquiry into the Nature and Causes of the Wealth of Nations* (New York: Oxford University Press, 1976). The book is still well worth reading.

Students interested in a much more advanced treatment of one of the subjects raised in this chapter may want to look at Gary Becker, *Human Capital: A Theoretical and Empirical Analysis* (2nd ed; New York: Columbia University Press, 1975).

The most famous supporter of the idea of taxing the site value of land stated his argument in Henry George, *Progress and Poverty* (New York: Robert Schalkenbach Foundation, 1984).

Judging Outcomes

Chapter 14

Economic Efficiency

POSITIVE VS NORMATIVE

Positive statements are statements about what is; *normative* statements are statements about what ought to be. Economics is a positive science. An economist who says (correctly or incorrectly) that a one-dollar increase in the minimum wage will increase the unemployment rate half a percentage point is expressing his professional opinion. If he goes on to say, "Therefore we should not increase the minimum wage," his statement is no longer only about economics. In order to reach a "should" conclusion, he must combine opinions about what is, which are part of economics, with *values*, opinions about what ought to be, which are not.

Of course, one of the main reasons people learn what is, is in order to decide what ought to be. Economists have values just as everyone else does. Those values affect both their decision to become economists instead of ditchdiggers or political scientists and the questions they choose to study. But the values themselves, and the conclusions which require them, are not part of economics.

Economists frequently use terms, such as "efficient," which sound very much like "ought" words. Once one has proved that something leads to "greater efficiency," it hardly seems worth asking whether it is desirable. Such terms, however, have a precise positive meaning, and it is quite easy to think of reasons why "efficiency" in the economist's sense might not always be desirable.

My own interpretation of why we use such terms is as follows. People keep coming to economists and asking them what to do. "Should we have a tariff?" "Should we expand the money supply?" The economist answers, "Should? I don't know anything about 'should.' If you have a tariff, such and such will happen; if you expand the money supply, . . ." The people who ask the questions say, "We don't want to know all that. On net, are the results good or bad?" The economist finally answers as follows:

346

As an economist, I have no expertise in good and bad. I can, however, set up a "criterion of goodness" called *efficiency*, which has the following characteristics. First, it has a fairly close resemblance to what I suspect you mean by "good." Second, it is so designed that in many cases I can figure out, by economics, whether some particular proposal (such as a tariff) is an improvement in terms of my criterion. Third, I cannot think of any alternative criterion closer to what I suspect you mean that also has the second characteristic.

One could object that the economist, defining efficiency according to what questions he can answer rather than what questions he is being asked, is like the drunk looking for his wallet under the streetlight because the light is better there than where he lost it. The reply is that an imperfect criterion of desirability is better than none.

The point of this story is to show how it is that economists claim to be positive scientists yet frequently use normative-sounding words. Three of these words are "improvement," "superior," and "efficient". They are used in a number of different ways in economics, and it is easy to confuse them.

IMPROVEMENT AND EFFICIENT

While the terms "improvement," "superior," and "efficient" are used in a number of different ways in different contexts—we shall discuss five ways in this chapter—the three words always have the same relation to each other. An *improvement* is a change—in what is being produced, in how it is produced, in who gets it, or whatever—which is in some way desirable. Situation B is *superior* to situation A if going from A to B is an improvement. A situation is *efficient* (in some particular respect) if it cannot be improved—if, in other words, there is no possible situation that is superior to it.

One simple example is production efficiency. An improvement in production means using the same inputs to produce more of one output without producing less of another (*output improvement*), or producing the same outputs using less of one input and no more of any other (*input improvement*). As long as both inputs and outputs are goods, an improvement in this sense is obviously desirable; it means you have more of one desirable thing without giving up anything else. An output process is *production efficient* (sometimes called *X-efficient*) if there is no way of changing it that produces an output or input improvement. It is *output efficient* if there is no change that produces an output improvement, and it is *input efficient* if there is no change that produces an input improvement. Input efficiency usually implies output efficiency, and vice versa.

Output improvements and output efficiency provide a way of evaluating different outcomes which does not depend on our knowing the relative value of the different goods to the consumer. As long as we know that both are goods, it follows that a change which gives him more of one without less of the other is an improvement. This, as we will see shortly, is analogous to a rule that allows us to evaluate changes affecting several people without having to compare the relative importance of a gain to one and a loss to another.

In discussing changes that involve one person getting more of one good and less of another, we can judge whether they are, on net, improvements by using indifference curves (or a utility function) to determine whether the consumer ends up better or worse off. Analyzing the relation between output improvement, output efficiency, and net improvements in this situation may help us later when we analyze a similar set of relationships in the much more difficult situation where we are trading off not goods against goods but one person's welfare against another's.

Figure 14-1a shows a production possibility set for producing two goods, X and Y, using a fixed quantity of inputs; every point in the shaded region represents a possible output bundle. The curve F is the frontier of the set; for any point in the set which is not on F (such as A), there is some point on the frontier (B) which represents an improvement; in the case illustrated, B represents more of both X and Y than A. The points on the frontier are all output efficient; starting at B, the only way to produce more X is by producing less Y, as at C, and the only way to produce more Y is by producing less X, as at D.

This is the first time I have talked about the idea of production efficiency, but not the first time I have used it. From Chapter 3 on, I have been drawing figures with possibility sets and frontiers. A budget line, for example, is the frontier of a possibility set—the set of bundles it is possible to purchase with a given income. In indifference curve analysis, we only consider points on the budget line, not points below it, even though points below it are also possible—we could always throw away part of our income. Figure 14-1b shows this—the shaded area is the *consumption possibility set*; the line B is the *consumption possibility frontier*, alias the budget line.

Figure 14-1

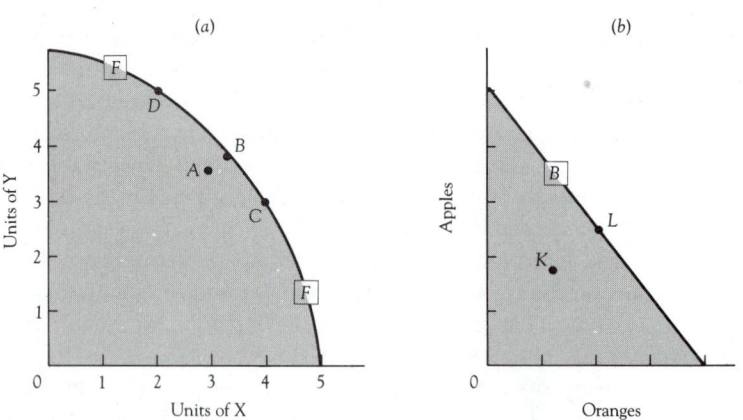

Possibility sets and frontiers. Figure 14-1a shows a production possibility set; F is its frontier. Figure 14-1b shows the set of alternative bundles available to a consumer; the budget line B is its frontier.

But since insatiability implies that there is always something we want more of, we would never choose to throw away part of our income. Any point on the interior of the possibility set is dominated by a point on the frontier representing a bundle with more of both goods. Point K on Figure 14-1b is dominated by point L just as A is dominated by B on Figure 14-1a. So if we are looking for the best bundle, we need only consider points on the frontier.

Similar considerations explain why, in diagrams such as Figures 5-9a and 5-9b of Chapter 5, we only considered output bundles on the frontier of the production possibility set (the number of lawns that could be mowed and meals cooked or ditches dug and sonnets composed with a given amount of labor). If you are going to work that number of hours, you might as well get as much output as possible—not spend some of the time walking around in circles instead of either mowing lawns or cooking meals.

So long as we only consider output efficiency, there is no way of choosing between points B, C, and D on Figure 14-1a, all of which are output efficient. To do that, we must introduce preferences. Figure 14-2a is Figure 14-1a with the addition of a set of indifference curves. If I am producing X and Y in order to consume them myself and the indifference curves represent my preferences among the different bundles of goods I can produce, I can use the indifference curves to compare different efficient points. Point D, for example, is on a higher indifference curve than point C; I would rather consume 5 units of Y and 2 of X (point D) than 3 units of Y and 4 of X (point C).

A *utility improvement* is a change that increases my utility—moves me to a higher indifference curve. A situation is *utility efficient* if no further such improvements are possible. On the diagram, point E is the only point in the production possibility set that is utility efficient.

The fact that one point is output efficient and another is not does not mean that the first point is either output or utility superior to the second. On the diagram, point C is output efficient and point A is not—but A is on a higher indifference curve than C! A is inefficient because B is superior to it (more of both X and Y). B is also on a higher utility curve than A; it must be, since X and Y are both goods. C is efficient not because it is output superior to A (it is not—C has more X but less Y; hence neither is output superior to the other) but because nothing is output superior to it. Since C is not output superior to A, there is no reason why it cannot be utility inferior to it—and in fact it is. If someone argued that "You should produce at C instead of at A, since C is efficient and A is not," his argument would sound plausible but be wrong.

On first reading, the previous paragraph may seem both confusing and irrelevant. The reason it is there is that the same point is important in understanding the use (and misuse) of another and very important form of improvement and efficiency—Pareto efficiency—which I shall describe later in the chapter. The relevant concept—that the fact that A is not efficient and C is does not imply that C is an improvement on A or that C is in some other sense better than A—is easier to understand in the context of output efficiency than in the context of Pareto efficiency, so I advise you to try to understand it at this point.

Figure 14-2

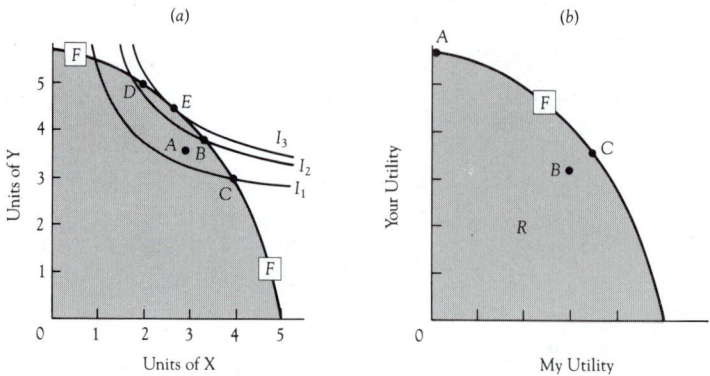

Efficient and inefficient outcomes.   On Figure 14-2*a*, the alternatives are different output bundles to be consumed by an individual whose tastes are shown by the indifference curves; on Figure 14-2*b*, they are different allocations of goods (and hence utility) to two individuals. In each case, points on the frontier are efficient, and points not on the frontier are not, but the former are not necessarily superior to the latter.

SUMMING UTILITIES: THE PROBLEM

The fundamental problem in defining what economic changes are "on net" improvements is the problem of comparing the welfare of different people. If some change results in my having two more chocolate cookies and one less glass of Tab, there is a straightforward sense in which that is or is not an improvement; I do or do not prefer the new set of goods to the old (utility improvement). But what if the change results in my having two more cookies and *your* having one less glass of Tab? It is an improvement from my standpoint, but not from yours.

The usual solution to this problem is to base the definition of efficiency on the idea of a *Pareto improvement* (named after the Italian economist Vilfredo Pareto)—defined as a change that benefits one person and injures nobody. A system is then defined as *Pareto efficient* if there is no way it can be changed to produce a Pareto improvement. The problem with this approach is that it leaves you with no way of evaluating changes that are not Pareto improvements; the attempt to get around that problem while retaining the Paretian approach leads to serious problems, which I will discuss later.

One reason why so many examples in earlier chapters involved identical producers and identical consumers was that I wanted to avoid the problem of balancing a loss to one person against a gain to another. If everyone is identical, any change which is in any sense an improvement must be a Pareto improvement—if it benefits anyone, it must benefit everyone. Early in the book, with the discussion of efficiency still many chapters in the future, that was very convenient.

Output efficiency is analogous to Pareto efficiency, with different people's utilities in the latter case corresponding to outputs of different goods in the former. A situation is Pareto efficient if there is no way of changing it that benefits one person and harms nobody—increases someone's utility without decreasing anyone else's. A situation is output efficient if there is no way of changing it which increases one output without decreasing some other output. Figure 14-2b shows the similarity; the axes are my utility and your utility, the region R consists of all possible combinations, and the frontier of that region, the curve F, consists of all the Pareto-efficient combinations.

In the case of output, we have a common measure by which to compare various points on the boundary—the utility of the individual consuming the output. This lets us compare two alternative output bundles neither of which is unambiguously superior (i.e., more of one good and at least as much of the other) to the other. The important difference between Figure 14-2b and Figure 14-2a is the absence of indifference curves on 14-2b. The problem in comparing outcomes that affect several people is that there is no obvious way of comparing two different outcomes, one of which "produces" more utility for me and less for you than the other.

Some economists have tried to deal with such problems by imagining that there exists a social equivalent of the individual utility function (called a *social welfare function*). A social welfare function would give the "welfare" of the whole society as a function of the utilities of individuals, just as the utility function gives the welfare of the individual as a function of the quantities of goods he consumes. If we knew the social welfare function for the two-person society shown on Figure 14-2b, we could draw a set of "social indifference curves" on Figure 14-2b, just as we drew individual indifference curves on Figure 14-2a.

If we assume there is a social welfare function, we can analyze the outcome of different economic arrangements in terms of social preferences without actually knowing what the social preferences are—just as we have analyzed situations involving individual preferences without knowing what any particular real-world individual's preferences actually are. Some of the difficulties with this approach are discussed in the optional section of this chapter.

PARETIAN AND MARSHALLIAN EFFICIENCY

Another way of approaching the problem is to claim that although we have no way of deciding which of two Pareto-efficient outcomes is preferable, at least we should prefer efficient outcomes to inefficient ones. This argument is often made and sounds reasonable enough, but it runs into the difficulty that I discussed earlier in the context of output efficiency. While we may all agree that a Pareto improvement is an unambiguously good thing, it does not follow that a situation that is Pareto efficient is superior to one which is not.

Consider a world of two people, you and me, and two goods, cookies and Tabs (twenty of each). The situation is shown on Figure 14-2b; the axes are not Tabs and cookies but my utility (which depends on how many of the Tabs and cookies I have) and your utility (which depends on how many you have). One possible situation (A on Figure 14-2b) is for me to have all the cookies and all the Tabs. That is Pareto efficient; the only way to change it is to give you some of what I have, which makes me worse off, and hence is not a Pareto improvement. Another possible situation (B) is for each of us to have ten cookies and ten Tabs. That may be inefficient; if I like cookies more, relative to Tabs, than you do, trading one of my Tabs for one of your cookies might make us both better off (move us to C). The first situation is (Pareto) efficient and the second is not, yet it seems odd for me to say that the first situation is better than the second and expect you to agree with me.

The problem is that situation B is inefficient not because changing from B to A is a Pareto improvement (it is not) but because changing from B to a third alternative, C (I have nine Tabs and eleven cookies, you have eleven Tabs and nine cookies), is; it is hard to see what that has to do with A being better than B.

As this suggests, there are serious difficulties with the Paretian solution to the problem of evaluating different outcomes. They are sufficiently serious to make me prefer a different solution, due to the British economist Alfred Marshall; while he did not use the term "efficiency," his way of defining an improvement is an alternative to Pareto's, and I shall use the same terms for both. In most practical applications, the two definitions turn out to be equivalent, for reasons that I shall explain in the next section; but Marshall's definition makes it clearer what "improvement" means and in what ways it is only an approximate representation of what most of us mean by describing some economic change as "a good thing," "desirable," or the like. I have introduced the Paretian definition here because it is what most economics textbooks use; you will certainly encounter it if you study more economics.

To understand Marshall's definition of an improvement, we consider a change (the abolition of tariffs, a new tax, rent control, . . .) that affects many people, making some worse off and others better off. In principle we could "price" all of the gains and losses—we could ask each person who was against the change how much money he would have to be given so that on net the money plus the (undesirable) effect of the change would leave him exactly as well off as before. Similarly we could ask each gainer what would be the largest amount he would pay to get that gain, if he had to. We could, assuming everyone was telling us the truth, sum all of the gains and losses, reduced in this way to a common measure. If the sum was a net gain, we would say that the change was a (Marshallian) improvement. If we had a situation where no further (Marshallian) improvement was possible, we would describe it as efficient.

This definition does not correspond perfectly to our intuition about when a change is good (or makes people "on average, happier") for at least two reasons. First, we are accepting each person's evaluation of how much something is worth to him; the value of heroin to the addict has the same status as the value of insulin to the diabetic. Second, by comparing values according to their money equivalent, we ignore differences in the utility of money to different people. If you were told that a certain change benefited a millionaire by an amount equivalent for him to $10 and injured a poor man by an amount equivalent for him to

$9, you would suspect that in some meaningful sense $10 was "worth less" to the millionaire than $9 to the poor man and therefore that "net human happiness" had gone down rather than up. "Efficiency" or "Marshallian improvement" are intended as workable approximations of our intuitions about "good"; even if we could make the intuitions clear enough to construct a better approximation, it would still be less useful unless we had some way of figuring out what changes increased or decreased it.

How do we find out what changes produce net benefits in Marshall's sense? Do we actually ask everyone affected how much he values his benefits or gains? No. The answer to how do we do it is that we have been doing it, without saying so, through most of the book. Consumer (or producer) surplus is the benefit to a consumer (or producer) of a particular economic arrangement (one in which he can buy or sell at a particular price) measured in dollars according to his own values.

Several chapters back, I showed that the area under a summed demand curve was equal to the sum of the areas under the individual demand curves. So when we measure consumer surplus as the area under a demand curve representing the summed demands of many consumers, we are summing benefits—measured in dollars—to many different people. If we argue that some change in economic arrangements results in an increase in the sum of consumer and producer surplus, as we shall be doing repeatedly in the next few chapters, we are arguing that it is an improvement in the Marshallian sense.

One way of describing what we, and Marshall, are doing is to say that the essential problem we face is how to add different people's utilities together in order to decide whether an increase in utility to one person does or does not compensate for a decrease to another. Marshall's solution is to add utilities as if everyone had the same utility for a dollar. The advantage of that way of doing it is that since we commonly observe people's values by seeing how much they are willing to pay for something, a definition that measures values in money terms is more easily applied in practice than would be some other definition.

Alfred Marshall was aware of the obvious argument against treating people as if they all had the same value for a dollar—the fact that they do not. His reply was that while that was a legitimate objection if we were considering a change that benefited one rich man and injured one poor man, it was less relevant to the usual case of a change that benefited and injured large and diverse groups of people—all consumers and all producers of automobiles, all the inhabitants of London and all the inhabitants of Birmingham, or the like. In such cases, individual differences could be expected to cancel out, so that the change which improved matters in Marshall's terms probably also "made things better" in some more general sense.

There is another respect in which Marshall's definition of improvement is useful, although it is one that might not have appealed to Marshall. If a situation is inefficient, that means that there is some possible change in it which produces net (dollar) benefits. If so, that suggests that a sufficiently ingenious entrepreneur might be able to organize that change, paying those who lose by it for their cooperation, being paid by those who gain, and pocketing the difference. If, to take a trivial example, you conclude that there would be a net improvement, in

Marshall's sense of the term, from converting the empty lot on the corner into a McDonald's restaurant, one conclusion you may reach is that the present situation is inefficient. Another is that you could make money by buying the lot and reselling it to McDonald's.

MARSHALL, MONEY, AND REVEALED PREFERENCE

There are several ways in which it is easy to misinterpret the idea of a Marshall improvement. One is by concluding that since net benefits are in dollars, "Economics really is just about money." Dollars are not what the improvement is but only what it is measured in. If the price of apples falls from $10 apiece to $.10 apiece and your consumption rises from zero to 10/week, you have $1/week less money to spend on other things, but you are *better off* by the consumer surplus on 10 apples per week—the difference between what they cost and what they are worth to you. Money is a convenient common unit for measuring value; that does not mean money itself is the only, or even the most important, thing valued. The definition of a Marshall improvement does not even require that money exist; all values could have been stated in apples, water, or any other tradable commodity. As long as the price of apples is the same for all consumers, anything that is a net improvement measured in apples must also be a net improvement measured in money. If, for instance, apples cost $.50, a gain measured in apples is simply twice as large a number as the same gain measured in dollars—just as a distance measured in feet is three times the same distance measured in yards.

A second mistake is to take too literally the idea of "asking" everyone affected how much he has gained or lost. Basing our judgments on people's statements would violate the principle of revealed preference, which tells us that values are measured by actions, not words. That is how we measure them when analyzing what is or is not a Marshall improvement. Consumer surplus, for example, is calculated from a demand curve, which is a graph of how much people *do buy* at any price—not how much they say they think they should buy.

If we decided on economic policy by asking people how much they valued things, and if their answers affected what happened, they would have an incentive to lie. If I really value a change (say, the imposition of a tariff) at $100, I might as well claim to value it at $1,000. That will increase the chance that the change will occur, and in any case I do not actually have to pay anything for it. That is why, in defining a Marshall improvement, I added the phrase "assuming everyone was telling us the truth." What they were supposed to be telling the truth about was what they would do—how much they would give, if necessary, in order to get the result they preferred.

MARSHALL DISGUISED AS PARETO

The conventional approach to economic efficiency defines a situation as (Pareto) efficient if no Pareto improvements are possible in it. At first glance, that definition appears very different from the one I have borrowed from Marshall, which compares losses and benefits using the (somewhat arbitrary) measure of dollars and defines a situation as efficient if no net improvement can be made in it. The Paretian approach appears to avoid any such comparison by restricting itself to the unobjectionable statement that a change which confers only benefits and no injuries is an improvement. The problem comes when one tries to apply this definition of efficiency to the real world.

Consider the example of tariffs. The abolition of tariffs on automobiles would make auto workers and stockholders in American car companies worse off. Buyers of cars and producers of export goods would be better off. It can be shown that under plausible simplifying assumptions, there exists a set of payments from the second group to the first which, combined with the abolition of tariffs, would leave everyone better off. The payments by members of the second group would be less than their gain from the abolition; the receipts by members of the first group would be more than their losses from abolition.

This is equivalent to showing, as I shall do in Chapter 18, that the dollar gains to the members of the second group total more than the dollar losses to the members of the first group—that the abolition of tariffs is an improvement in Marshall's sense of the term. If I gain by $20 and you lose by $10, it follows both that there is a net (Marshallian) improvement and that if I paid you $15 the payment plus the change would leave us both better off (by $5 each), making it a Pareto improvement. So a Marshall improvement plus an appropriate set of transfers is a Pareto improvement; and any change which, with appropriate transfers, can be converted into a Pareto improvement must be a Marshall improvement.

The abolition of auto tariffs by itself, however, is not a Pareto improvement; auto workers and stockholders are worse off. How then can Pareto efficiency be used to judge whether the abolition of tariffs would be a good thing? By the following magic trick.

The abolition of tariffs plus appropriate payments from the gainers to the losers would be a Pareto improvement. Actually arranging the payments is probably impossible, since there is no practical way of discovering exactly who gains or loses by how much. Since the situation with tariffs could be Pareto-improved (by abolition plus compensation), it is not efficient. The situation without tariffs cannot be Pareto-improved (I have not proved this; assume it is true). Hence abolition of tariffs moves us from an inefficient to an efficient situation. Hence it is an improvement.

If you believe that, I have done a bad job of explaining, earlier in this chapter, why a movement from an inefficient to an efficient situation need not be an improvement—a point made once in the context of output efficiency and again in the context of Pareto efficiency. A world without tariffs (and without compensation) is efficient, and a world with tariffs is not; but it does not follow that going from the latter to the former is an improvement. The situation with the tariff is being condemned not because it is Pareto inferior to the situation without the tariff but because it is Pareto inferior to yet a third situation—abolition of the tariff plus compensating payments.

Half of the trick is in confusing "going from a Pareto-inefficient to a Pareto-efficient outcome" with "making a Pareto improvement." The other half is in the word "possible." Imagine that someone asserted that tariffs are inefficient because there is a possible change—abolition plus compensating payments—which would be a Pareto improvement. If arranging the payments is impossible (or costly enough to wipe out the net gain), then the Pareto improvement is really not possible; hence the initial situation is not really Pareto inefficient. The concept of Pareto improvement, and the associated definition of efficiency, can be applied to judge many real-world situations inefficient if you assume that compensating payments can be made costlessly (i.e., with no cost other than the payments themselves). Without this assumption (which is usually not made explicit), the Paretian approach is of much more limited usefulness.

One way to get out of this trap while retaining the trappings of the Paretian approach is to describe the abolition of the automobile tariff (without compensation) as a *potential Pareto improvement* or *Kaldor improvement*, meaning that it has the potential to be a Pareto improvement if combined with appropriate transfers. This, as I pointed out above, is equivalent to saying that it is an improvement in Marshall's sense.

I prefer to use the Marshallian approach, which makes the interpersonal comparison (via dollar value) explicit, instead of hiding it in the "could be made but isn't" compensating payment. To go back to the example given earlier, a change which benefits a millionaire by $10 and costs a pauper $9 is a "potential Pareto improvement," since if combined with a payment of $9.50 from the millionaire to the pauper, it would benefit both. If the payment is not made, however, the change is not an actual Pareto improvement. The "potential Paretian" approach reaches the same conclusion as the Marshallian approach and has the same faults; it simply conceals them better. That is why I prefer Marshall. From here on, whenever I describe something as an improvement or an economic improvement, I am using the term in Marshall's sense unless I specifically say that I am not.

It is worth noting that although a Marshall improvement is usually not a Pareto improvement, the adoption of a general policy of "Wherever possible, make Marshall improvements" may come very close to being a Pareto improvement. In one case, the Marshall improvement benefits me by $3 and hurts you by $2; in another it helps you by $6 and hurts me by $4; in another . . . Add up all the effects and, unless one individual or group is consistently on the losing side, everyone, or almost everyone, is likely to benefit. That is one of the arguments for such a policy and one of the reasons to believe that economic arrangements which are Marshall efficient are desirable.

EFFICIENCY AND THE BUREAUCRAT-GOD

In describing some economic arrangement as efficient or inefficient, we are comparing it to "possible" alternatives. This raises a difficult question: What does "possible" mean? One could argue that only that which exists is possible—in order to get anything else, some part of reality must be different from what it is.

But one purpose of the concept of efficiency is to help us decide how to act—how to change reality to something different than it now is. So any practical application of the idea of efficiency must focus on some particular sorts of changes. What sorts of changes are and should be implicit in the way we use the term?

One could argue that however well organized the economy may be, it is still inefficient. A change such as the invention of cheap thermonuclear power or a medical treatment to prevent aging would be an unambiguous improvement—and surely some such change is possible. That might be a relevant observation—if this were a book on medicine or nuclear physics. Since it is a book on economics, the sorts of changes we are concerned with involve using the present state of knowledge (embodied for our purposes in production functions—ways of converting inputs to outputs) but changing how much is produced and consumed by whom.

One way of putting this that I have found useful is in terms of a *bureaucrat-god*. A bureaucrat-god knows everyone's preferences and production functions and has unlimited power to tell people what to do, reallocate goods, and the like. He does not have the power to make gold out of lead or produce new inventions. He is benevolent; his sole aim is to maximize welfare in Marshall's sense.

An economic arrangement is efficient if it cannot be improved by a bureaucrat-god. The reason we care whether an arrangement is efficient is that if it is, there is no point in trying to improve it. If it is not efficient, there still may be no practical way of improving it—since we do not actually have any bureaucrat-gods available—but it is at least worth looking for one.

At this point, it may occur to you that while efficiency as I have defined it is an upper bound on how well an economy can be organized, it is not a very useful benchmark for evaluating real societies. Real societies are run not by omniscient and benevolent gods but by humans; however rational they may be, both their knowledge and their objectives are mostly limited to things and people that directly concern them. How can we hope, out of such pieces, to assemble a system that works as well as it would if it were run by a bureaucrat-god? Is it not as inappropriate to use "efficiency" in judging the performance of human institutions as it would be to judge the performance of race cars by comparing their speed to *its* theoretical upper bound—the speed of light?

The surprising answer is no. As we will see in Chapter 15, it is possible for institutions that we have already described—institutions not too different from those around us in the real world—to produce an efficient outcome. That is one of the most surprising—and useful—implications of economic theory.

WARNING

While the way in which this textbook teaches economics is somewhat unconventional, the contents—what is taught—are not very different from what many other economists believe and teach. This chapter is the major exception. While Alfred Marshall was, in other respects, a much more important figure in the history of economics than Vilfredo Pareto, Marshall's solution to the problem of deciding what is or is not an improvement has largely disappeared from modern economics; virtually all elementary texts teach the Paretian approach. Both the

Marshallian approach and the Paretian, as it is commonly applied, have the same implications for what is or is not efficient; what differs is the justification given for the conclusions that both imply.

I am by no means the only contemporary economist who feels uncomfortable with the Paretian approach, but I may be the first to put that discomfort, and the Marshallian solution, into a textbook. In that respect, this chapter is either "on the frontier" or "out of the mainstream," according to whether one does or does not agree with it.

OPTIONAL SECTION

SOCIAL WELFARE AND THE ARROW IMPOSSIBILITY THEOREM

Earlier in this chapter, I mentioned that one "solution" to the problem of evaluating outcomes that affect different people is to assume that there exists a *social welfare function*—a procedure for ranking such outcomes—without actually specifying what it is. This is somewhat like the way we handle individual preferences; we assume a utility function that allows the individual to rank alternatives that affect him, although we have no way of knowing exactly what that function is.

But in the case of the utility function, although we cannot predict it, we can observe it by observing what choices the individual actually makes. There seems to be no equivalent way to observe the social welfare function, since there is no obvious sense in which "societies" make choices. We could try to describe a particular set of political institutions in this way, substituting "the outcome of the political process" for "what the individual chooses." But while this might be a useful way of analyzing what those institutions *will* do, it tells us nothing about what they *should* do—unless we are willing to assume that the two are identical. This leaves the social welfare function as an abstract way of thinking about the question, with no way of either deducing what it should be or observing what it is.

Even as an abstract way of thinking about the problem, the social welfare function has problems; not only is it an unobservable abstraction, it may well be a logically inconsistent one. To explain what I mean by that, I will start by showing how we can eliminate a particular "candidate" for a social welfare function—majority rule. I shall then tell you about a similar and much stronger result that eliminates a broad range of possible social welfare functions.

A social welfare function is supposed to be a way of ranking "social alternatives," outcomes that affect more than one person; it is intended to be the equivalent, for a group, of an individual's utility function. There are two different ways in which one could imagine constructing a social welfare function. One is to base social preferences on individual preferences, so that what the society "prefers" depends, perhaps in some complicated way, on what all of the individuals prefer. The other is to have some external standard—what is good according to correct philosophy, in the mind of God, or the like. Economists, knowing very little about either the mind of God or correct philosophy, are reluctant to try the second alternative, so they have usually assumed that social preferences are built on individual preferences.

One advantage of defining social preferences in terms of individual preferences is that individual preferences express themselves in individual actions. Perhaps if we could set up the right set of social institutions, the choices made by all the individual members of society would somehow combine to produce the "socially preferred" outcome for the society. That, in a way, is the idea of democracy: Let each individual vote for what he prefers and hope that the outcome will be good for the society. Seen in this way, "majority rule" is a possible social welfare function. For each pair of alternatives, find out which one more people like and label that the "socially preferred" choice.

One problem with this was pointed out several centuries ago by Condorcet, a French mathematician. Majority vote does not produce a consistent set of preferences. Consider Table 14-1, which shows the individual preferences of three individuals among three outcomes. Individual 1 prefers outcome A to outcome B and outcome B to outcome C; Individual 2 prefers B to C and C to A; Individual 3 prefers C to A and A to B. Suppose we consider a society made up of only these three people and try to decide which outcome is "socially preferred" under majority rule. In a vote between A and B, A wins two to one, since Individuals 1 and 3 prefer it. In a vote between B and C, B wins two to one, since 1 and 2 prefer it. It appears that we have a social ranking; A is preferred to B and B to C.

Table 14-1

| Ranking | Individual | | |
	1	2	3
First	A	B	C
Second	B	C	A
Third	C	A	B

If A is preferred to B and B to C, then A must also be preferred to C. But it is not. If we take a vote between A and C, Individual 1 votes for A, but both 2 and 3 vote for C—so C wins. We have a system of "preference" in which A is preferred to B, B to C, and C to A! This is what mathematicians call an *intransitive ordering*; obviously it does not produce a consistent definition of what is "socially preferred."

This *Condorcet Voting Paradox* eliminates majority rule as a possible definition of social welfare. A similar and much more general result by Kenneth Arrow, called the *Arrow Impossibility Theorem*, eliminates practically everything else. Arrow made a few plausible assumptions about what a social welfare function must be like and then proved that no possible procedure for going from individual preferences to "social preferences" could satisfy all of them.

What are the assumptions? One is nondictatorship; the social welfare function cannot simply consist of picking one individual and saying that whatever he prefers is socially preferred. Another has the long name *independence of irrelevant alternatives*. What it says is that if the social welfare function, applied to individuals with a particular set of individual preferences, leads to the conclusion that alternative A is preferred to alternative B, then a change in preferences which does not affect anyone's preferences between A and B cannot change the social preference between A and B. Another is that social preferences are positively related to individual preferences; if some set of individual preferences lead A to be preferred to B, a change in the preference of one of the individuals from preferring B to preferring A cannot make the social preference change in the other direction. The society cannot switch to preferring B as the result of an individual switching to preferring A. Finally the social welfare function must lead to a consistent set of preferences; if A is preferred to B and B to C, then A must be preferred to C.

What Arrow proved was that no rule for going from individual preferences to group preferences could be consistent with all of those assumptions.

Economics Joke #2: *A physicist, a chemist, and an economist were shipwrecked on a desert island. After a while, a case of canned beans drifted to shore; the three began discussing how they could open the cans. The chemist (a physical chemist) suggested that if they started a fire and put a can of beans on it, he could calculate at what point the resulting pressure would burst the can. The physicist said that he could then calculate the trajectory the beans would take as they spouted out of the burst can, and he put a clean palm leaf down for them to land on. "That's too much trouble," the economist said. "Assume we have a can opener."* (That is a joke about the social welfare function.)

The Arrow Impossibility Theorem does not quite prove that a social welfare function is logically impossible. For one thing, the theorem only applies to social preferences based on individual preferences; a social welfare function which says, "Socially preferred means what God wants" or "What a philosopher can prove that we all ought to want," is not eliminated by the theorem. Furthermore it applies to social welfare functions based only on preferences, not to those based on utility functions. The only form in which utility functions are observable is as preferences; we can observe that you prefer a cookie to a Tab (because given the choice, you take the cookie), but we cannot observe by how much you prefer it. Even the Von Neumann version of utility discussed in the optional section of Chapter 12, while allowing quantitative statements about my preferences, does not allow quantitative comparisons between my preferences and yours.

If, in deciding what was socially preferred, we could use not only the fact that I preferred A to B but also that I preferred A to B by seven utiles and B to C by two, while you preferred B to A by one utile and C to B by three, the theorem would no longer hold. In this case, the obvious social welfare function would be total utility: Add up everyone's utility for each outcome, and use the sum as your social welfare function. This rule for defining what is desirable, called *utilitarianism* by philosophers, played an important role in the development of economics (and philosophy). Alfred Marshall, for instance, was a utilitarian who proposed what I have called "Marshallian efficiency" as an approximate rule for maximizing the (unobservable) total utility.

As I mentioned in the optional section of Chapter 12, there are a number of problems with utilitarianism that have caused its popularity with both economists and philosophers to decline over the past century or so. One is the problem of interpersonal comparison of utility; how, in principle, could one ever decide that "I prefer an apple to a pear by more than you prefer a Tab to a cookie"? Marshall "solves" this problem, as I mentioned earlier, by simply assuming that everyone receives the same utility from having one more dollar to spend, so that we can "sum" utilities by finding how many dollars the alternative is worth to everyone and then adding. If an apple is worth fifty cents more to me than a pear and a Tab is worth a dollar more to you than a cookie, then an outcome in which I get a pear and you get a Tab is "better" than one in which I get an apple and you get a cookie. Marshall's assumption is false but, for reasons discussed earlier, may still be useful.

AMBIGUITIES IN THE CONCEPT OF IMPROVEMENT

For most purposes, improvement in Marshall's sense provides an adequate working rule for applying our rather vague ideas of what is or is not a "net improvement," but there are situations in which it can lead to apparently inconsistent results. Imagine a society of two people, you and me. There is one good in this society that is immensely valuable—a life-extension pill that doubles the life expectancy of whichever one of us takes it. There are also other goods. Suppose we want to use Marshall's approach to decide which of us should have the pill.

If I have the pill, there is no sum you could offer me which would make me willing to give it up; the pill plus the goods I already have are worth more to me than all of the other goods (mine plus yours) without the pill. The maximum you would be willing to offer me for the pill is less than all of your goods, since there is no advantage to you in taking the pill and then starving to death. So the dollar value of the pill to me (the amount I would have to be paid to give it up) is greater than its dollar value to you (the amount you would pay to get it). Leaving me with the pill is then, by Marshall's criterion, the preferred outcome; more precisely, taking the pill away from me is not an improvement.

But suppose we start with you having the pill. Following exactly the same argument, we find that leaving you with the pill is the preferred outcome! The problem is that since the pill is immensely valuable to both of us, whoever has it is, in effect, much wealthier than if he did not. He is wealthier not because he has more money but because he already has the most important thing that he would want money to buy—the pill. Since he is wealthier, the utility of money to him is less. So the money value of anything to him—what he would be willing to pay to get other goods or what he would have to be paid to give up the pill— is higher than it would be if he did not start out owning the pill. Since we are measuring utility by how much money (or goods) someone is willing to give to get something or willing to accept in exchange for giving something up, we get different results according to who we assume starts off with the pill.

Most applications of Marshall's definition of improvement do not involve this problem. If, for example, we consider the desirability of tariffs, it probably does not matter whether we start by assuming that tariffs exist and ask how people would be affected by abolishing them (measuring the amount of gains and injuries by their dollar equivalents) or start by assuming they do not exist and ask how people would be affected by imposing them. One reason it would not matter is that most of the gains and losses are themselves monetary; the dollar value to you of a $1 increase in your income is the same however rich you are. Another reason is that even if some of the gains and losses were non-monetary, the abolition (or institution) of tariffs would have a relatively small effect on most people's income, hence a small effect on the monetary equivalent to them of some non-monetary value.

This sort of problem is not limited to the Marshallian approach. Under the strict Pareto definition (an improvement means a Pareto improvement—someone is benefited and no one is hurt), most alternatives are incomparable; not only is there no way of deciding who should get the life-extension pill, there is no way of deciding whether tariffs should be abolished. As long as one person is worse off by the abolition, it is not a Pareto improvement. Under the "potential Pareto" criterion (a change is an improvement if there is some set of transfers from gainers to losers which, combined with the change, results in a Pareto improvement), one gets exactly the same problems as with Marshall's criterion.

PROBLEMS

1. In Figure 14-3a, the production possibility set for a worker working eight hours per day is shown as the shaded area R. Which labeled points are output efficient? Which labeled points are output superior to point A?
2. In Figure 14-3b, the shaded area R shows possible outcomes in terms of the resulting divisions of income between two people, John and Lisa; nobody else

Figure 14-3

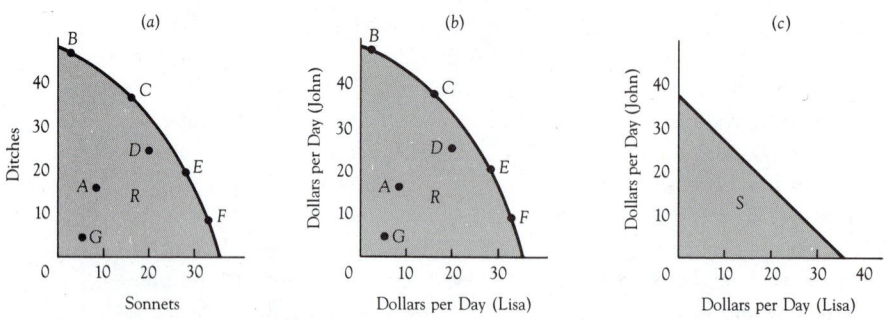

Opportunity sets for Problems 1-3.

exists. Which labeled points are Pareto efficient? Which are Marshall efficient? Which are Pareto superior to point A? Which are Marshall superior to point A? Which are "potentially Pareto superior" to point A?

3. Figure 14-3c is similar to Figure 14-3b. What do you think is the significance of the difference between the shapes of R in Figure 14-3b and S in Figure 14-3c? (Warning: This question requires original thought.)

4. In this chapter, I gave one example of a Marshall improvement that many people would consider undesirable—a change that benefited a rich man by $10 and injured a poor man by $9. Give at least two examples of Marshall improvements that many people (including people not themselves affected) would consider undesirable, where the reason for the conflict between the Marshall criterion and "desirability" does not depend on differences in income or wealth among the people affected. (Warning: This question requires original thought.)

5. The government passes a law which imposes a tax of $.10/pound on artichokes; the money is used to give everyone $5 for Christmas. Assume that people are not all identical. Is the law a Pareto improvement? A Marshall improvement? Would its abolition be a Pareto improvement? A Marshall improvement? Explain.

6. Do Problem 5 on the assumption that people *are* all identical.

7. In Problem 5, the tax was on artichokes. Is there anything the government could have taxed instead which would have changed your answer to Problem 5? To Problem 6? Discuss.

8. The government passes a law which imposes a $.10/pound tax on artichokes; the supply and demand curves are shown in Figure 14-4. The money is used to finance research on thermonuclear power. Each dollar spent on such research produces two dollars worth of benefits. Answer as in Problem 5. (Warning: This problem requires you to put together ideas from at least two different chapters.)

Figure 14-4

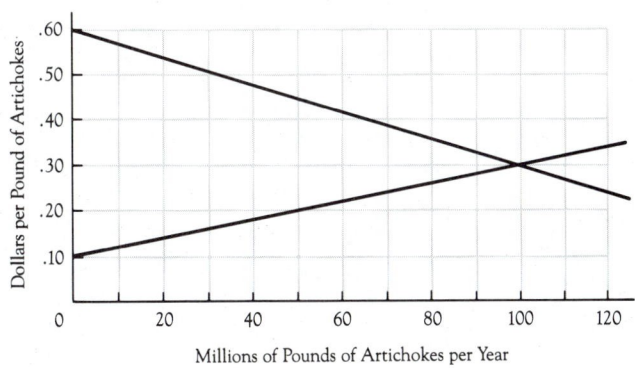

Supply and demand for artichokes—Problem 8.

9. The situation is as in Problem 8, except that you can vary the level of tax. How would you find the (Marshall) efficient level? Approximately what is it? (Warning: This is a hard problem. A verbal explanation requires original thought. A numerical answer may require either more mathematics than some of you have or a good deal of trial and error.)

FOR FURTHER READING

The ideas I have described as "Marshall improvement" and "Marshall efficiency" are more commonly referred to in economics as the *Hicks/Kaldor* criterion. For the original, interesting, and readable discussion of those ideas, you may want to look at Alfred Marshall, *Principles of Economics*, (8th. ed.; London: Macmillan, 1920), Chapter VI.

Some other important papers on the Hicks/Kaldor criterion include: Nicholas Kaldor, "A Note on Tariffs and the Terms of Trade," *Economica* (November, 1940; John R. Hicks, "The Foundations of Welfare Economics," *Economic Journal* (December, 1939); and Tibor Scitovsky, "A Note on Welfare Propositions in Economics," *Review of Economic Studies* (November, 1941).

The Arrow Impossibility Theorem is proved in Kenneth Arrow, *Social Choice and Individual Values*, (2nd ed.; New Haven, CT: Yale University Press, 1970).

Chapter 15

What Is Efficient?

In Chapter 14, I explained the idea of Marshall efficiency and suggested that it could be used as a benchmark for evaluating different economic arrangements. In this chapter, we do so, starting with the competitive industry of Chapters 3-9 and then going on to the single-price and discriminating monopolies of Chapter 10. The objective in each case is to prove either that the outcome is efficient or that it is not. To prove that it *is* efficient, I must show that it cannot be improved by a bureaucrat-god. If it *is not* efficient, I will prove its inefficiency by showing how a bureaucrat-god could improve it. That may also give us some idea of why it is inefficient, and hence of how, in the real world, the inefficient institutions might be improved.

A COMPETITIVE INDUSTRY

We assume an industry made up of many identical price-taking firms. The industry sells its output to consumers at a price P; it buys its inputs from the owners of the factors of production—workers, landlords, capitalists. All those involved—firms, consumers, owners—are price takers.

An efficient outcome is, by definition, one that cannot be improved by a bureaucrat-god. We will therefore consider the ways in which a bureaucrat-god might change the outcome produced by the market; if we can show that no possible change is a Marshall improvement, then the original equilibrium must have been efficient.

There are three ways in which the market outcome could be changed. The bureaucrat-god could have the same quantity of the good produced in the same way, while changing its allocation—who gets it. He could produce the same quantity and allocate it to the same people, while changing how it is produced. Finally, he could change the quantity.

We begin by considering a change in allocation, quantity held constant. Initially, since the good is sold at a price P, everyone who values it at P gets it; everyone who does not value it at (at least) P does not. Figures 15-1a and 15-1b

show the marginal value curves of two consumers, Uno and Duo; each is buying that quantity (Q_1, Q_2) for which his marginal value is equal to P. Any change of allocation must involve reducing the quantity consumed by one consumer and increasing the quantity consumed by another. Figures 15-1a and 15-1b show the effect of transferring one unit from Uno to Duo. The value Uno gets from his consumption is the area under his demand curve; his consumer surplus is that minus what he pays.

If we change the allocation without changing any of the associated payments, Uno is worse off by area A_1, and Duo is better off by area A_2; as you can see from the figure, A_1 must be larger than A_2. To prove this mathematically, note

Figure 15-1

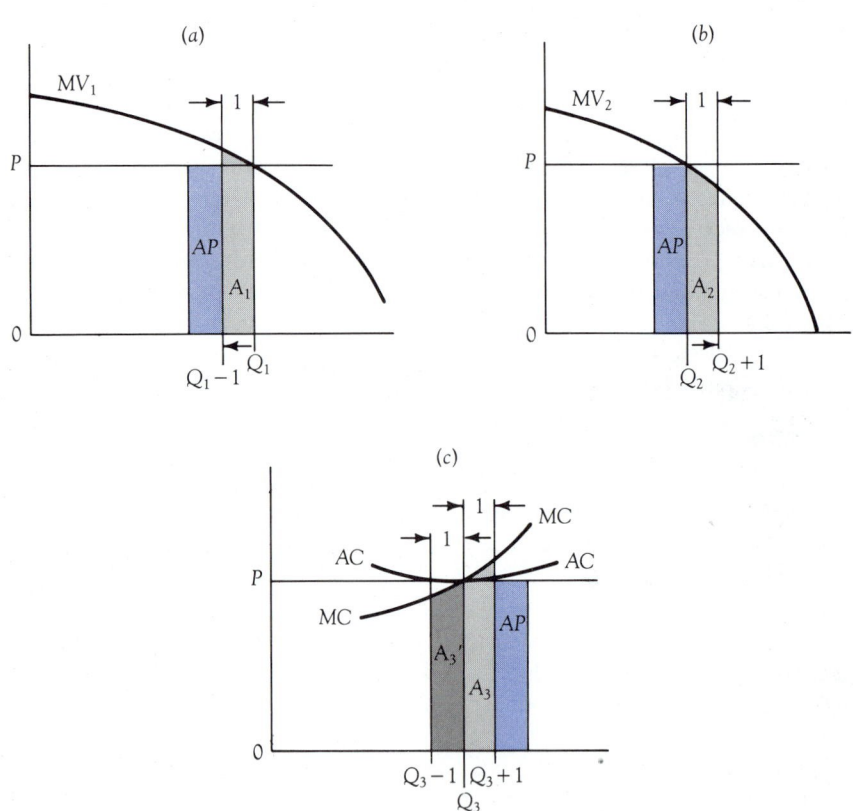

Effects of changing the quantity or allocation of output by one unit. Figures 15-1a and 15-1b show the effects of transferring one unit of output from Uno (1a) to Duo (1b). Figure 15-1c shows the increased (decreased) cost to a firm of producing one more (less) unit of output.

that since the marginal value curve MV_1 is above P to the left of Q_1, and the marginal value curve MV_2 is below P to the right of Q_2, A_1 must be greater than a rectangle P high and one unit wide (AP), and A_2 must be less than that same rectangle; so $A_1 > A_2$. P is a height on the graph ("$/unit"), while A_1 and A_2 are areas ("$"), so we had to convert P into the area $P \times 1$ unit in order to compare it to the areas A_1 and A_2. You should be able to satisfy yourself that the same relation holds however large the transfer and whatever the shape of the MV curves. Hence the transfer is a Marshall worsening; the only people affected are Uno and Duo, and the gain to Duo (A_2) is less than the loss to Uno (A_1).

The same argument can be made verbally. Before the transfer, everyone is consuming up to the point where $MV = P$. A transfer from Uno to Duo takes away from Uno units that were worth at least P to him, since at a price P he chose to buy them. It gives to Duo units that are worth less than P to him, since at a price of P he chose not to buy them. Each unit transferred is worth more to the person who loses it (Uno) than to the person who gets it (Duo); hence the change is a worsening.

I am measuring value, as usual, by the amount an individual is willing to give up to get something. Some of you may respond that when we take steak from a rich man who is willing to pay $4/pound for it and give it to a poor man who is willing to pay only $3, that is "really" an improvement, since something worth $3 to the poor man is more important than something worth $4 to the rich man. That is one of the objections to the Marshall criterion discussed in Chapter 14. What it is really saying is that we should maximize total utility rather than total value. But utility cannot be observed and value can. Hence we can describe (and perhaps construct) institutions that maximize total value but not ones that maximize total utility; the former may be regarded as a workable means for approximating the latter.

We have now seen that no reallocation of the existing quantity of output can be a Marshall improvement. The allocation produced by selling the good to all comers at the price at which quantity demanded equals quantity supplied allocates units of the good to those who most value them; any reallocation must transfer from someone who values the units of the good he is losing at more than its price to someone who values the units he is losing at less. The conclusion holds not only for the quantity of output produced by a competitive industry but for *any* quantity of output; however much is produced, selling it at the price at which that quantity is demanded is the efficient way to allocate it. The next question is whether a bureaucrat-god could produce an improvement by changing the way in which the (fixed) quantity of output is produced; after that, we will consider whether he can produce an improvement by changing that quantity.

There are two ways in which the cost to an industry of producing a given quantity of output might be lowered. One is for each firm to produce the same output as before at a lower cost; the other is to change the division of output among firms. But in the initial situation, each firm is already producing its output in the least costly way. Any reduction in cost would have increased the firm's profits; hence the firm would have made the reduction itself. As you may remember from Chapter 9, a firm gets its total cost curve from its production function by finding, for each level of output, the least expensive way of producing it. So there is no way the bureaucrat-god can reduce the cost to the firm of producing a given quantity of output.

What about reallocating production among firms—closing down one firm and having each of the others produce a little more or creating a new firm and having each firm produce a little less? Neither of these changes can decrease cost. In equilibrium, as you may remember from Chapter 9, the firms in a price-taking industry are producing at the minimum of their average cost curves—at Q_3 on Figure 15-1c. Since the firms are producing at minimum average cost, any change in output per firm must raise average cost, not lower it. Here again, just as in the case of allocation, the result is not limited to the particular price and quantity actually produced. If the demand curve shifted out, increasing price and quantity, the new quantity would again be produced in the least costly way.

We now know that no change in how output is produced or in how it is allocated can be an improvement. In at least these two dimensions, the competitive industry is efficient in the strong sense discussed in Chapter 14; no change that a bureaucrat-god could impose can be an improvement. The one remaining possibility for improvement is a change in the quantity produced.

To see why this also cannot be an improvement, consider Figures 15-1b and 15-1c. Figure 15-1b shows the marginal value curve of a consumer; Figure 15-1c shows the marginal cost curve of a producer. He is producing a quantity Q_3 for which $P = MC = $ Minimum AC. If the producer increases his output to $Q_3 + 1$, the additional cost will be the area A_3. If the additional unit goes to Duo, it will increase his consumption to $Q_2 + 1$; the value to him of the additional consumption is area A_2. As you can see from the figure, A_3 is greater than AP, and A_2 is less than AP; hence $A_3 > A_2$. It follows that the change is a worsening; the gain to the consumer from the additional output is less than the cost of producing it.

The same argument applies if we decrease output instead of increasing it; this time, look at Figures 15-1a and 15-1c. The reduction in output by the firm saves it area $A_3' < AP$, and the loss in consumption to Uno costs him area $A_1 > AP$; hence there is again a net loss.

What if, instead of increasing output by having one firm produce an additional unit, we increase it by adding one more firm (producing Q_3 units) to the industry? The cost of each unit of additional output is now only AP—P per unit times one unit. But since the value per unit to the consumer of the additional units is *less than* P each, the net result is still a worsening. The same is true if instead of adding a firm and increasing output by Q_3, we close down a firm and decrease output by Q_3.

The argument can be put verbally as well as graphically. In competitive equilibrium, the price of the good is just equal to the cost of producing a little more or less; $P = MC$. But since, in competitive equilibrium, consumers buy the good up to the point where its marginal value to them is P, any reduction costs the consumers more than P per unit, and any increase benefits them by less; hence any reduction in output saves the firms less than it costs the consumers, while any increase costs the firms more than it saves the consumers. In competitive equilibrium, consumers are consuming up to the point where each unit is worth exactly its cost of production; any further increase involves producing units that cost more to produce than they are worth to the consumers. Any reduction means failing to produce units that are worth more to the producers than they cost to produce.

So far, we have only considered changing one variable at a time—allocation, production, or quantity. Could the bureaucrat-god perhaps create a Marshall improvement by changing two or three variables at once? No. We proved that the market allocation rule (sell at the price at which consumers want to buy exactly the amount produced) is the efficient way to allocate *any* quantity of output and that the way in which a competitive industry produces is the efficient way to produce *any* quantity of output. So whatever the quantity produced, the allocation and production should be done in the way they would be done by a competitive industry. That leaves only one variable—quantity—and we just proved that if output is produced and allocated in that way, the efficient quantity is the quantity a competitive industry chooses to produce.

We are done. We have shown that no change in the outcome produced by an industry of competitive, price-taking firms can be a Marshall improvement. The outcome of a competitive market is efficient.

Filling In Details

In presenting the proof that the outcome of a competitive market is efficient, I have deliberately ignored a number of details in order to make it easier for you to see the whole pattern without being distracted by a series of lengthy digressions. I will now go back and fill in the missing points. Two of them are missing pieces of the proof; one is an explanation of something about the proof that you may have found confusing.

Dollar Cost, Value Cost. In demonstrating that the outcome of a competitive market could not be improved, I showed that no change in how the industry produces the output can lower the cost of production. This is not quite the same thing as showing that no change can be a Marshall improvement. A change in cost of production, after all, is merely a change in the number of dollars paid by the firms to the owners of the inputs. What is the connection between showing that a change raises the number of dollars paid ("raises cost") and showing that it is a Marshall worsening ("net loss of value")?

That connection comes from Chapter 4, where we saw that the price of an input (labor in that case) was equal to the cost to the individual of producing it. The marginal disvalue of labor (aka "the marginal value of leisure") was equal to the wage rate. If a producer changes his production process by using an extra hour of labor, the price he must pay for that labor, its "cost in dollars," is also the cost to the worker of working the extra hour, its "cost in value." By paying the worker his wage, the firm transfers the cost to itself; the worker is neither better nor worse off as a result of working the extra hour (and being paid for it), and the firm is worse off by the amount it has paid. The same analysis applies if the firm uses an hour less of labor—the money saved by the firm is just equal to the value to the worker of the extra leisure he gets. The analysis also applies to the other factors of production, as described in Chapter 13.

The analysis also applies to inputs for which the alternative to consumption by the firm is consumption by individual consumers—apples which can either be turned into apple sauce or eaten as apples. Each consumer consumes a quantity of apples for which the marginal value of the last apple is just equal to its price, so if he eats one less apple (because the firm has bought it to make apple sauce), the loss of value to him is the same as the dollar cost to the firm. The situation with regard to apples is the same as with regard to labor—if the firm buys an hour of my leisure, I reduce my consumption of leisure by an hour; the cost of doing so is my marginal value of leisure, which in equilibrium equals the price of leisure—my wage. The same is true with apples if we substitute "apples" for "leisure" and "price of apples" for "wage."

This implies that the total cost to the firm of any method of production—any set of inputs—is equal to the sum of the disvalues involved in producing (or not consuming) those inputs. So a change which lowers (dollar) cost also lowers the total "value cost" of producing the goods—the disvalues of producing the inputs—and a change which increases dollar cost also increases the total disvalues. It follows that a change which raises total cost as measured by firms and changes nothing else must also be a Marshall worsening.

One possibility I have not yet considered is that if the industry uses an additional unit of input, it might get it by bidding it away from some other industry. If the steel industry chooses to use more labor, that may mean not that workers have less leisure but that some workers move from producing autos to producing steel.

What is the cost to the auto industry of losing a worker? It is the worker's marginal revenue product—the increase in output, measured in dollars, from employing him. That, as I showed in Chapter 13, is equal to his wage. His wage is what the steel industry must pay to get him. So the cost in dollars to the firm hiring the input is again the same as the cost in value elsewhere; this time, the loss of value takes the form of lost output in another industry rather than of lost leisure to the worker.

The same argument applies to the other factors of production as well. A firm that increases its use of land, by building one-story factories instead of three-story ones, does not impose any cost on the land—land does not, like labor, consume its own leisure. It does impose a cost on whoever else is, as a result, not able to use the land. That cost is equal to the rent the firm must pay for the land. A similar analysis holds for a firm that increases its consumption of capital at the expense of other firms.

I have now shown that cost of production as measured by the firms in dollars they spend is the same as the total loss of value from their use of their inputs. Since the competitive industry produces its output at the minimum cost in dollars, it also produces it at the minimum cost in value. So any change in how it produces that quantity of output (everything else held fixed) must be a Marshall worsening.

Shuffling Money. One element in my proof of the efficiency of a competitive equilibrium that may have confused you is the way in which many of the arguments seemed to ignore money payments. I described the cost of an extra hour of labor as its marginal disvalue to the worker, but I then went on to say that the worker was no worse off, since he was paid for his time. I calculated costs and benefits to consumers Uno and Duo by looking at the area under their MV curves, rather than by looking at their consumer surplus—the area under the curve and above price. I described the cost to a firm of producing an extra unit as MC, while ignoring the income it got from selling that unit.

All of these (possibly puzzling) features of the proof have the same explanation. A transfer of money from one person to another is neutral in terms of the Marshall criterion—neither a gain nor a worsening. One person gains by a dollar; another person loses by a dollar. The only way we can produce improvements or worsenings is by changing what happens with goods—how they are produced, how much of them is produced, who gets them. Hence in calculating net gains or losses, in order to discover whether something is a Marshall improvement or a worsening, we do not have to worry about flows of money.

In discussing the effect of reallocating goods to consumers, for example, I assumed that Uno and Duo continued to pay the same amount of money to the producer as before; the bureaucrat-god simply took one unit of the good from Uno and gave it to Duo. Since there was no transfer of money involved, Uno lost by the value of the good to him, and Duo gained by its value to him.

I could just as easily have assumed that the bureaucrat-god took a unit of the good from Uno and gave it to Duo while at the same time taking P dollars from Duo and giving them to Uno; that would correspond to ordering Uno to buy one fewer good and ordering Duo to buy one more, both at the price P. In that case, Uno would have lost his consumer surplus on one unit (area B_1 on Figure 15-2a) while Duo gained his (negative) consumer surplus on one unit (he *loses* area B_2 on Figure 15-2b). He loses because he is buying units for more than they are worth to him, and hence is worse off than if he did not have to buy them. As you should be able to see from the figures, the net loss if we do it this way, $B_1 + B_2$, is the same as $A_1 - A_2$ on Figures 15-1a and 15-1b, which was the loss when there was no transfer of money. A_1 is $AP + B_1$, and A_2 is $AP - B_2$; so AP, the amount of money transferred, cancels, giving us $A_1 - A_2 = B_1 + B_2$.

Similarly for the other cases that may seem puzzling. If a worker is ordered to work another hour and is not paid for it, his cost is equal to his MV of labor. If he is paid for the hour, the cost is transferred to whoever pays him. Net cost is unaffected—we are simply shuffling money.

The same rule of ignoring money payments because they have no effect on what is or is not a Marshall improvement takes care of another problem with my proof that some readers may have spotted. If a firm decides to increase its consumption of labor, one effect is that a worker works an additional hour. Another effect is that wages rise a little—that is why the worker increases the number of hours he chooses to work. That small increase in wages can be ignored by the

Figure 15-2

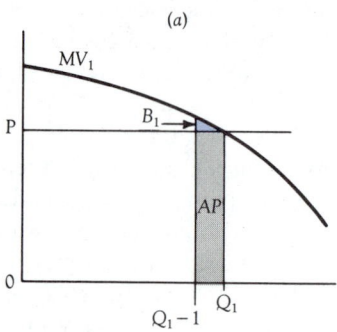
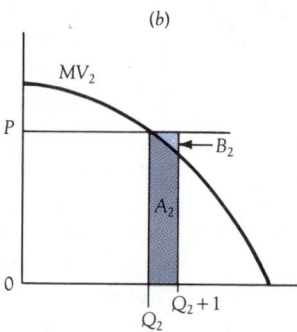

Effect of ordering Uno to buy one unit less and Duo one unit more. AP is the amount spent for one unit; B_1 is the consumer surplus loss to Uno and B_2 the consumer surplus loss to Duo as a result of the change.

firm, since as a price-taker, it finds the effects of its actions on the prices of the things it buys to be negligible. But for the industry as a whole, or the economy as a whole, that small increase in the wage rate must be multiplied by all of the hours worked by all workers—and the result may not be negligible. Should I not take that into account in calculating the costs and benefits that result from increasing the firm's input of labor by one unit?

The answer is no. The increase in wages is a transfer between the sellers and the buyers of labor. Each dollar that one person loses, someone else gets. There is no net gain or loss, hence no effect on whether the change is or is not a Marshall improvement. Such "pecuniary externalities" will be discussed in Chapter 17.

One problem in giving a proof of this sort is that I must present calculus arguments in verbal and graphical form. Strictly speaking, much of the analysis should be put in terms of infinitely small changes—working an extra second rather than an extra hour or consuming one millionth of an apple more or less. Since any large change can be broken up into an infinite number of infinitely small changes, a proof showing that each small change makes things worse also implies that large changes do so. Putting things that way is a good deal harder in a verbal argument than in a mathematical one—but the failure to limit ourselves to infinitesimal changes occasionally introduces errors or confusions into the argument.

It would be possible to give a precise verbal statement of the proof that a competitive equilibrium is efficient, but it would make the proof considerably more difficult than it already is. The proof as given is, I think, sufficiently precise to give you a clear understanding of why the result is true. Readers who feel comfortable with calculus may find it of interest to try to translate the proof into that more precise language.

Competitive Layer Cake. So far, I have described an economy in which there is only a single layer of firms between the ultimate producers and the ultimate consumers. Most real economies are more complicated than that. Many of the outputs of firms—steel ingots, typewriters, railroad transport—are inputs of other firms. While this makes the situation harder to describe, it does not change its essential logic, nor does it invalidate our conclusion that a competitive equilibrium is efficient.

To see why, we will start one layer up from the bottom. Consider a good produced by an industry that buys all its inputs from their original owners (workers, landowners, owners of capital) but produces as output a good that is used by another firm. The price at which it sells that good equals its marginal cost of production; as we have shown, this is the same as the ultimate cost to those who give up the inputs used in producing it. So when a firm one layer further up uses that good in its production process, the price it must pay for the good is equal to the disvalues involved in producing the good, just as it would be if the good were one of the factors of production instead of something produced by another firm. So our proof of the efficiency of competitive equilibrium applies to the second layer of industry too. We can repeat the argument for as many layers as necessary, thus showing that the whole competitive layer cake is efficient.

A number of other simplifications also went into our argument. One, which has hardly been mentioned so far, is the assumption that each firm produces only one kind of good. Dropping that would make things considerably more complicated and would introduce an interesting set of puzzles involving *joint products* (things produced together, such as wool and mutton, or two metals refined from the same ore), quality variations among goods, and the like, many of which you may encounter in more advanced texts. It would not change the result.

What about introducing the complications of time and uncertainty that were discussed in Chapters 11 and 12? As I explained there, the effect of time in a certain world can be taken into account by doing all calculations using present values of future flows—of revenue, cost, and value. Having done so, we could reproduce the proof we have just gone through and so demonstrate that a competitive equilibrium was efficient in a changing (but perfectly predictable) world.

Efficiency in an uncertain world is a more complicated issue, for two reasons. The first is that, in evaluating outcomes in an uncertain world, we must be careful to specify just what the bureaucrat-god is assumed to know—what sort of "perfect" economy we are using as our benchmark. If the bureaucrat-god knows the future, and the real participants in the market do not, he can easily improve on their performance. It seems more reasonable to assume that the bureaucrat-god, like the bureaucrats who enforce regulations in the real world, has no better a crystal ball than the rest of us. Given that assumption, the efficiency proof holds in an uncertain world as well as in a certain one.

There is another sort of problem introduced by uncertainty, which takes us beyond the bounds of this chapter. So far, we have ignored *transactions costs*, the costs of negotiating contracts, arranging to buy and sell goods, and the like; the only exception was the discussion of bilateral monopoly in Chapter 6. In order to get an efficient outcome in an uncertain world, one must assume that firms can buy and sell a very complicated set of goods—there must be a complete set of markets for *conditional contracts*. An example of a conditional contract would be my agreement to give you 100 gallons of water next year if the price of grain was above $2/bushel and rainfall in Iowa was less than 14 inches.

Such conditional contracts are useful in an uncertain world—you may be an Iowa farmer who only wants the water if both of those conditions hold. But the assumption that there are markets for all of the conditional contracts one can imagine and that on all of those markets transaction costs are negligible is implausible. It is far more implausible than the assumption that in a certain world, where we know what is going to happen next year, there are markets for all goods and that transaction costs on those markets are negligible. Here, as elsewhere, the introduction of transaction costs may invalidate proofs of the efficiency of a competitive equilibrium—or other arrangements. Inefficiencies connected with transaction costs will be discussed at somewhat greater length in Chapter 17.

Competitive Efficiency—Summing Up

At the end of Chapter 14, I raised the question of whether efficiency might be an unreasonable standard for judging real-world economies. You are now in a position to see to what degree that is or is not true. I have shown you how a set of institutions—competitive markets—can generate an efficient outcome, in the full sense in which the term *efficient* is used in Chapter 14—an outcome which cannot be improved by a bureaucrat-god. I have also, I hope, given you some feeling for why that is only an approximation, although not a wildly unreasonable one, of a real economy.

Throughout the argument, I have assumed that everyone concerned—firms, owners of the factors of production, and consumers—is a price taker. If even a single participant in the market is not, then somewhere in the chain of argument, a link fails and we can no longer prove efficiency.

As you may suspect from the amount of space I have spent on this discussion and the number of different things from different chapters that have fed into it, the efficiency of a competitive market is an important result. Insofar as one is interested in using economics to improve the well-being of mankind, it is probably the most important single result of economic theory. While we cannot expect any real-world economy to fit the requirements of the proof precisely, many economies, or at least many parts of many economies, come close enough to make us suspect that they are very close to being efficient. Where the assumptions necessary to prove efficiency break down, as in the case of the price-searching firms discussed in Chapter 10, understanding why the failure of the assumption leads to a failure of the proof is the obvious starting point for anyone who wishes to figure out how the situation could be improved.

MONOPOLY

So far, we have been analyzing the efficiency of the outcome of a *competitive industry*—an industry in which all the participants are price takers. We will now go on to analyze the efficiency of the outcome of an industry containing a price searcher—a *monopolistic industry*. Just as in Chapter 10, we will start with a single-price monopoly and then go on to more complicated cases.

One of the difficulties in teaching (and learning) economics is that many students start out believing they already know it. The subject is the world we all live in, and many of the words are ones whose meaning everyone already knows. It is easy to forget that a term such as "efficient" or "competitive," when used in economics, is a technical term with a meaning quite different from the same term used in ordinary conversation.

One of my favorite examples of this problem is the sentence "Monopoly is inefficient." The natural response of a student hearing or reading that sentence is, "Of course; I already knew that. Monopolists are rich and lazy; they have no competitors to put pressure on them, so they run their firms badly."

As you will see shortly, rich and lazy monopolists running their firms badly have nothing at all to do with what an economist means when he says that monopoly is inefficient. Indeed, in the sense in which "efficient" is used in ordinary conversation, economic theory suggests that monopolies should be just as efficient as competitive firms. It is only in the very different sense of "efficient" discussed in the previous chapter that we have reasons to expect at least some kinds of monopolies to be inefficient—not because the monopolist runs his firm badly but because he runs it well.

Single-Price Monopoly

Consider the firm whose marginal cost, marginal revenue, and average cost are shown in Figure 15-3, along with the demand curve for its product. It costs the firm $1,000 to produce any widgets at all and $10/widget for each additional widget it produces, so its fixed cost is $1,000/year and its marginal cost is $10/widget. Since the firm has a positive fixed cost and a constant marginal cost, average cost is lower the more the firm produces; the more widgets it is divided among, the lower the fixed cost per widget. The result is a natural monopoly; the larger the firm, the lower its average cost.

Is this efficient? Our proof of the efficiency of a competitive industry involved three parts—efficient allocation of output, efficient production of output, and efficient quantity of output. So far as allocation is concerned, the proof applies to the single-price monopoly as well; it, like a competitive industry, sells its goods at a price P at which quantity demanded equals quantity produced. Any reallocation of the existing quantity of output must transfer a good from someone to whom it is worth at least its price to someone to whom it is not; hence it must be a Marshall worsening.

The proof also holds with regard to production efficiency. If the firm could produce the same quantity of output at a lower cost, it would, since a reduction in cost would increase profits. Nor can the cost of production be lowered by a change in the number of firms. Since we are starting out with only one firm, any reduction means that there are no firms at all, hence no output. Since the firm is a natural monopoly, any increase in the number of firms must raise average cost. So the monopoly industry is efficient both in how it allocates its output and in how it produces it.

Figure 15-3

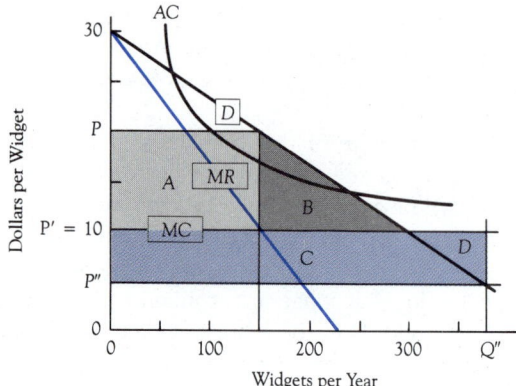

Widgets per Year

The profit-maximizing price (P) and the efficient price (P') for a single-price monopoly. Lowering the price from P to P' lowers the monopoly's profit by A but increases consumer surplus by A + B for a net gain of B. A further reduction to P'' would cost the monopoly C + D and benefit consumers by C, for a net loss of D.

What about the quantity it chooses to produce? The firm charges a price P at which MC = MR, since that maximizes its profit. If it lowered its price to P' = MC = $10/widget, its profit on the 150 widgets per year that it had been selling for a price P would decline by the area A, since it would be selling those widgets for a price of only P'. At a price of P', it would also be producing and selling an additional 150 widgets per year, for a total of 300; but it would neither make nor lose money on those additional widgets, since they would each cost $10 to produce (MC) and would each be sold for $10.

The drop in price would benefit consumers by area A plus area B—the increase in their surplus. Area A is the savings on the widgets they would have bought at the old price; area B is the consumer surplus on the additional widgets. Since the change benefits the consumers by more than it costs the producer, the decrease in price from P to P' is, on net, an improvement.

Would lowering the price even further improve things even more? No. A further price change to P'' = $5/widget, as shown in Figure 15-3, would cost the producer an amount equal to the area of the entire colored rectangle C + D = Q'' × (P' − P'') and benefit consumers by the colored area C; there would be a net loss equal to the area D. You should be able to convince yourself that at any price above or below P' = MC, net benefit is less than at P'. Hence the efficient arrangement is for the monopoly to charge a price equal to marginal cost.

The same argument can be made verbally without using the figure. As long as price is above marginal cost, there are people who value an additional widget at more than it would cost to produce it; producing that additional widget and giving it to such a person produces a net benefit. If the price were below marginal cost, some people would be consuming widgets who valued them at less than their cost of production; reducing the production and the consumption of such a person by one widget would produce a net benefit. So we get an efficient outcome only with price equal to marginal cost. This is the same rule that defines the efficient price for a competitive industry.

But while price equal to marginal cost maximizes net benefit, it does not maximize the monopoly's profit; if the monopoly shown on Figure 15-3 sold at $10/widget (MC), it would just cover its variable cost and lose $1,000/year of fixed cost. It prefers to charge price P, corresponding to a quantity for which marginal cost equals marginal revenue, instead of $P' = MC$. So a single-price monopoly (we are not yet considering the possibility of discriminatory pricing) will charge an inefficiently high price—not because the monopolist does not know how to maximize his profit, but because he does.

A competitive firm, on the other hand, charges a price equal to marginal cost; the same argument shows that that is the efficient arrangement. It would seem to follow that there is an efficiency gain to breaking up a single monopoly firm into many small firms.

A glance at Figure 15-3 should convince you that that is wrong; if the firm is broken up into ten smaller firms, average cost will be much higher and the price will go up instead of down. Not only that, but the situation will be unstable. Since average cost falls as output increases, one of the firms will expand, driving (or buying) out the others. We will then be back to where we started, with a single monopoly firm.

What the demonstration does imply is that if the cost curves are consistent with competition, as in Figures 15-4a and 15-4b, a competitive industry results in a greater net benefit than a monopoly. This is an argument not against natural monopolies but against government-enforced monopolies (or cartels) in naturally competitive industries, such as trucking. In Figure 15-4a, the costs for a large firm (producing Q_2) and a group of small firms (producing Q_1 each) are the same, so the loss due to a government-enforced monopoly is the loss of the area B—the consumer surplus on the goods that would be produced if the industry were competitive and sold at marginal cost but are not produced when it is a monopoly. In Figure 15-4b, the large firm actually has larger costs than the small; so there is the additional loss of the area B', equal to the difference in average cost between five small firms and one large one times the monopoly output.

The same analysis also demonstrates the undesirability of artificial monopoly and so provides an argument in favor of government antitrust measures designed to discourage it. I argued in the optional section of Chapter 10 that attempts to establish artificial monopolies—monopolies formed and maintained in industries where a monopoly firm has no advantage in production costs over a somewhat smaller firm—are unlikely to succeed. If that conclusion is correct, there is no need for antitrust laws to prevent them; if it is wrong, the argument for the inefficiency of monopoly is an argument for antitrust.

Figure 15-4

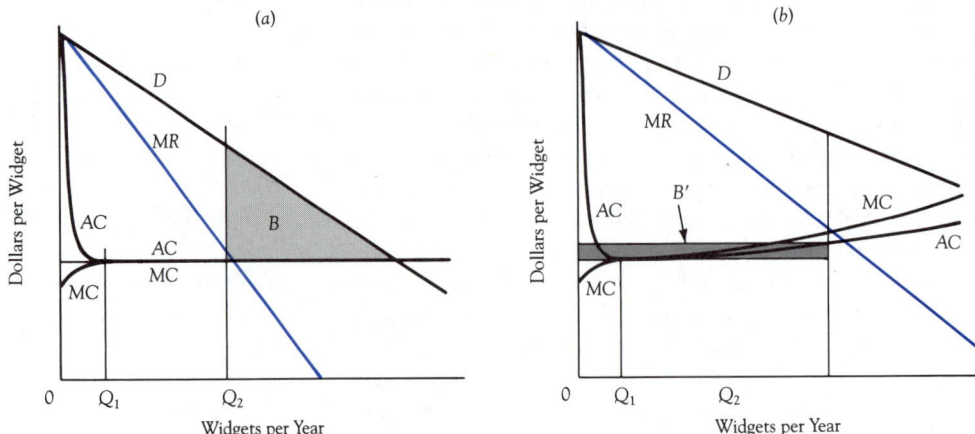

Efficiency gains from breaking up an "unnatural" monopoly.   Figure 15-4a shows the case where a large firm has the same average cost as a small firm; B is the gain from increased output when the industry becomes competitive. Figure 15-4b shows the case where cost is larger for a larger firm; breaking up the monopoly then also reduces production cost by B'.

What about the hard case—the natural monopoly illustrated in Figure 15-3? The government could pass a law requiring the firm to sell at a price equal to marginal cost—but the firm would respond by going out of business, since, at that price, it is losing money.

One solution is for the government either to regulate the monopoly or to run it, charging a price equal to marginal cost and making up any net loss out of tax revenues. This leads to a number of additional problems.

Regulation and the Second Efficiency Condition. In the previous section, I demonstrated one efficiency condition for a monopoly—that price equals marginal cost. That condition determines how much a monopoly should produce, since price (and the demand curve) determines quantity. There is a second efficiency condition which determines whether the monopoly should produce anything at all. Figure 15-5a shows cost curves and a demand curve for a firm whose fixed cost is so great that average cost is always above the demand curve—which means that it cannot make a positive profit at any price. Whatever level of output it chooses, its average cost of production is higher than the price it can sell that output at. Such a firm will never come into existence, or if it does (due to an error), it will go out of business after its owners recognize the situation.

Should such a firm come into existence? Will net benefit be higher if it exists? That depends. If it produces a quantity Q at price $P = MC$, as shown on Figure 15-5b, the firm will lose its fixed cost (the colored area B on Figure 15-5b), while its customers will gain their consumer surplus—the shaded area A. If the consumer surplus is larger than the fixed cost, there is a net benefit (although the firm still loses money); if the consumer surplus is less than the fixed cost, there is a net loss. Our first efficiency condition was "Price equals marginal cost"; our second is "Produce only if, at the quantity for which price equals marginal cost, consumer surplus plus profit is positive" or, in other words, consumer surplus is larger than the loss to the firm, if any.

Looking at a graph such as Figure 15-5b, how can one tell whether the loss to the firm is more or less than the gain to its customers? We know that if the firm exists, it should produce quantity Q. If it does, consumer surplus will be the shaded area A. On average, the firm makes $P - AC$ on each of Q units; since P is less than AC, it is losing the colored area B. If A is larger than B, the firm is producing a net benefit. If B is larger than A, it produces a net loss; abolishing it would be a Marshall improvement.

A private, profit-maximizing monopoly will only produce when profit is positive (or zero), in which case profit *plus* consumer surplus must be positive. So it will never produce when, according to the second efficiency condition, it should not. It may, however, fail to produce when it should—if profit is negative but the loss to the firm is less than the gain to its customers. In addition, as pointed out above, such a firm will not meet the first efficiency condition, since it will set marginal revenue equal to marginal cost instead of price equal to marginal cost.

Can a government-owned or government-regulated monopoly do better? It is not obvious that it can. There are two sorts of problems that it faces. First, there are problems associated with getting the regulatory agency to do what it "should" do. There is no obvious reason to expect the commissioners of a regulatory agency, or the official in charge of a government monopoly, to have any more

Figure 15-5

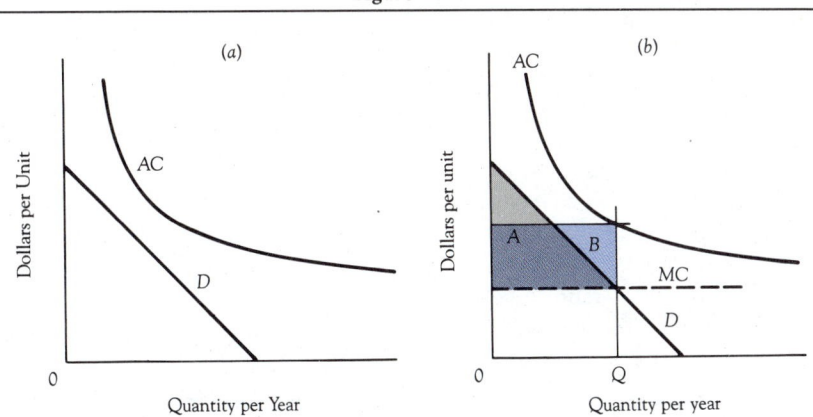

A natural monopoly that cannot cover its costs. Since for any quantity of output, AC is above the price that quantity sells for, a single-price monopoly cannot cover its costs. If such a monopoly operates and sells at $P = MC$, A is the resulting gain to its customers and B the resulting loss to the monopoly firm.

interest in maximizing net benefit than the owner of a private monopoly. Regulators may well find it in *their* interest to regulate a monopoly in some way other than that recommended by economists. They might choose to allow the monopoly to make large profits in exchange for political contributions to the incumbent administration or future high-paying jobs for the regulators, or they might force the monopoly to provide service at a price far below marginal cost, in order to buy popularity with consumer-voters at the expense of the monopoly firm's stockholders. Similarly, an official running a government monopoly such as the U.S. Post Office is presumably trying to maximize some combination of private benefit to himself and political benefit to the administration of which he is a part; it is not obvious that he does either by maximizing net benefit to producers and consumers.

Government regulation or ownership of monopolies is what economics textbooks have traditionally offered as the cure for the efficiency problems of private monopoly. What is wrong with this traditional analysis is that it treats the owners and managers of a private monopoly as part of the economic system, acting to achieve their own objectives, but treats government officials as if they were benevolent bureaucrat-gods, standing outside the system. There seems no good reason for such an asymmetrical treatment of the two alternatives. In Chapter 18, we will see the results of including goverment within our analysis, applying the same assumptions to the participants in the political market as to the participants in the ordinary market.

Suppose, however, that the regulators do have the best of intentions; their only objective is to maximize net benefits by forcing the firm to follow the prescription of the two efficiency conditions—sell at marginal price, provided that at that price, net benefit is positive. They will find it difficult to do so.

In order to keep the regulated firm in business, someone, presumably the government, has to make up the firm's losses—the difference between what it costs the firm to produce its output and what it is allowed to sell it for. If the government simply provides a subsidy equal to the difference between the regulated firm's revenue and its costs, the management of the firm has no incentive to keep down costs—especially the cost of things that can be used to make the life of management easier. If, instead, the regulatory agency estimates what marginal cost and average cost ought to be and offers the firm a fixed subsidy to cover the difference (while ordering it to sell at marginal cost), the firm has an incentive to try to misrepresent its cost function so as to make average cost appear as high as possible. This will either permit the firm to charge a price higher than the true marginal cost (if it makes marginal cost appear larger than it is) or get the firm a larger subsidy (by making the difference between average cost and marginal cost appear larger than it is). The regulators must come very close to running the firm themselves if they are to guarantee both that price equals marginal cost and that the total cost for producing whatever level of output can be sold at that price is as low as possible.

Suppose we assume these problems away too—specifically, we assume not only that the regulatory commission is trying to maximize net benefit but also that it knows the firm's cost curves. Even under these rather implausible assumptions, there is still a problem with the conventional regulatory solution to natural monopoly.

The problem is the second efficiency condition. The combination of marginal cost pricing plus a subsidy to cover the resulting loss will permit a monopoly to stay in business even if it does not meet the second efficiency condition—even if its costs are larger than the value to its customers of what it produces. In order for the regulatory agency to subsidize only those monopolies that should stay in business, it must know not only the cost curves of the firm but also the demand curve for its output, so that it can calculate what consumer surplus will be if the firm sells at marginal cost. If the consumer surplus is less than the required subsidy, the firm should be allowed to go out of business. But all the agency can observe directly is one point on the demand curve—quantity demanded at a price equal to marginal cost. That point gives very little information about consumer surplus; through the same point, one can draw two demand curves (D_1 and D_2 on Figure 15-6), one of which yields almost no consumer surplus at a price equal to marginal cost and one of which, at the same price, yields a very large consumer surplus.

Can the regulatory agency determine the demand curve by asking the monopoly's potential customers how much they would buy at each price? Not if the customers are rational. However much the customers say they would pay, if the monopoly produces, they will only be charged marginal cost. It is in their interest to have the monopoly produce, since the customers receive all of the benefit and pay only a small part of the taxes for the subsidy; so it is also in their interest to lie about how much it is worth to them, exaggerating the figure in order to induce the agency to subsidize the monopoly.

Figure 15-6

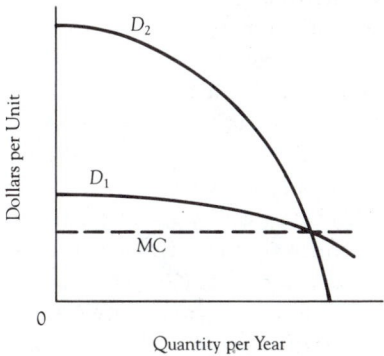

Two different demand curves which result in the same quantity demanded at $P = MC$.

It seems as though even a benevolent and well-informed regulatory agency faces a nearly insuperable problem in deciding which monopolies should be subsidized in order to keep them in business. It could be argued that the same information problem exists for an unregulated single-price monopoly. Consider, for instance, the case of an unregulated railroad deciding whether to build a new rail line, and contrast it to the case of a regulatory agency deciding whether to subsidize the construction of a new rail line. The regulatory agency wants to maximize total value; the unregulated monopoly wants to maximize its profit. Each, in order to achieve its goal, must first estimate demand and then decide whether the rail line should be built; hence each must estimate demand before it can measure demand directly.

There is one important difference between the two cases. The unregulated monopoly discovers, after the line is built, whether its decision was correct; there either is or is not some price at which the monopoly can make a profit on the new line, and it soon learns which. Since it can recognize success and failure, it can continually improve whatever techniques it uses to estimate demand; crudely speaking, if it builds a line and loses money, it can fire the market researchers who told it to build the line. The regulatory commission has no comparable test; even after the line is built, the commission never learns whether the line was worth building, since all the commission observes is quantity demanded at price equal to marginal cost.

Nationalized Monopoly. It is sometimes suggested that the government, instead of regulating natural monopolies, should nationalize them and run them itself "for the public good." This solves one of the problems of regulated monopoly. The regulatory agency no longer has to duplicate the work of management in order to get the information necessary to regulate; now the agency *is* the management of the firm. It does not solve the incentive problem; it is by no means obvious that the interests of the managers of a nationalized firm, or of the politicians who appoint them, are the same as the interests of the population as a whole. Nor does it solve the problem of satisfying the second efficiency condition.

There is at least one important respect in which both regulation and nationalization may be worse than unregulated single-price monopoly. So far in this chapter, I have described natural monopoly as if it were an all-or-nothing matter. In fact, there are many intermediate points between perfect competition and natural monopoly, and the location of a particular industry along that continuum may change. In the case of an unregulated natural monopoly, if conditions change so that it becomes possible for smaller firms to enter the industry successfully, they will do so; the monopoly will gradually break down. If the industry is regulated or nationalized, the regulatory agency or the nationalized industry may use the force of law to control or prevent new competitors, thus converting the industry into a government-enforced monopoly. An example is the regulation of the trucking industry by the Interstate Commerce Commission. In the absence of regulation, the trucking industry would be highly competitive, since large firms have no important advantage in production cost over small ones. The ICC, however, has regulated—and to a considerable degree cartelized—the trucking industry in order to protect its original regulatees, the railroads.

Discriminatory Monopoly: The Solution?

So far, we have only considered single-price monopolies; we will now shift to the opposite extreme and consider a perfectly discriminating monopoly. Since it can sell at different prices to different customers, or sell to a single customer at a range of prices, it always pays the monopoly to produce and sell to any customer whose value for the product is higher than the marginal cost of production. So it sells the same amount, to the same people, as if it were selling at marginal cost.

The difference is that what would be consumer surplus for the single-price monopoly selling at marginal cost becomes revenue for the perfectly discriminating monopoly. Since the monopoly is collecting the sum of producer and consumer surplus, it is in the monopoly's interest to maximize that sum; hence a perfectly discriminating monopoly satisfies both the first and second efficiency conditions! The information needed to satisfy the second efficiency condition—the shape of the demand curve—is part of the information which a firm needs in order to be a perfectly discriminating monopoly. And unlike the regulatory commission, the firm, having made an estimate of the shape of the demand curve, tests it by its pricing scheme. If, for example, the firm uses two-part pricing (per widget plus entry fee), an overestimate of consumer surplus will result in too high an entry fee and no customers.

This result holds only for a perfectly discriminating monopoly. Imperfect price discrimination not only fails to produce an efficient outcome; in some situations, it produces a worse outcome than single-price monopoly.

Rent Seeking

The arguments I have given so far suggest that perfectly discriminating monopoly, insofar as it is feasible, is the ideal solution to the problem of "natural monopoly." It is ideal in that it maximizes total value, although it does so in a way that gives all the net value resulting from the monopoly's activities to the monopoly instead of leaving some of it with the customers. If we look at this situation from a point of view sufficiently broad to give the same weight to the interests of the stockholders of the monopoly firm as to those of its customers, the only defects to this solution seem to be the considerable difficulties in actually running a perfectly discriminating monopoly.

There is another and more profound difficulty with this solution. A perfectly discriminating monopolist, or even an ordinary single-price monopolist, receives profits above and beyond the normal return on capital. Firms therefore compete to become monopolists. If we consider such competition as itself an ordinary profit-maximizing economic activity, we expect that a firm will be willing to spend, in the attempt to become the monopolist, anything up to the full value of the expected profits. Insofar as this expenditure does not produce anything for anyone (aside from getting that firm, instead of another firm, the monopoly), it is sheer waste. If the firm consumes the full value of the monopoly in the process of getting it, and if, as in the case of perfectly discriminating monopoly, that value is the entire value to all concerned from the existence of the industry (consumer plus producer surplus), then the private perfectly discriminating monopoly, rather than being the best possible solution to the problem of natural monopoly, is the worst. The industry generates no net value to anyone.

This point can be clarified by an example. Suppose there is a certain valley into which a rail line could be built. Further suppose that whoever builds the rail line first will have a monopoly; it will never pay to build a second rail line into the valley. To simplify the discussion, we assume that the interest rate is zero, so we can ignore complications associated with discounting receipts and expenditures to a common date. Assume that if the rail line is built in 1900, the total profit that the railroad will eventually collect will be $20 million. If the railroad is built before 1900, it will lose a million dollars a year until 1900, because until then, not enough people will live in the valley for their business to support the cost of building and maintaining the rail line. Lastly, suppose that all of these facts are widely known in 1870.

I, knowing these facts, propose to build the railroad in 1900. I am forestalled by someone who plans to build in 1899; $19 million is better than nothing, which is what he will get if he waits for me to build first. He is forestalled by someone willing to build still earlier. The railroad is built in 1880—and the builder receives nothing above the normal return on his capital for building it.

This phenomenon—the dissipation of above-market returns in the process of competing to get them—has recently become known as *rent seeking*. It is a new and somewhat complicated subject; the results are not always as perverse as in this example. One can, for instance, add the additional assumption that there exists a strip of land which controls the only potential rail access to the valley. In this case, the $20 million profit, instead of being dissipated by building the railroad early, goes to the person who owns that strip of land and auctions it off to the highest bidder; perfect discriminatory pricing is again the perfect solution to the problem of natural monopoly.

The Problem

The great mistake in most discussions of the problem of natural monopoly is the assumption that the problem is monopoly. The problem is a particular kind of production function—one for which marginal cost remains below average cost, and average cost therefore continues to fall, up to a level of output equal to the total amount of the good produced and sold. A single-price private unregulated monopoly is one (imperfect) solution to the problem posed by such a cost curve. It is imperfect because although it is efficient in the sense of producing a given quantity of output at the lowest possible cost, it is inefficient in both the quantity it produces (too low) and its decision of whether to produce at all (sometimes it will not when it should). Regulated private monopoly is another imperfect solution, one which may do better than unregulated private monopoly with regard to quantity but worse with regard to least-cost production, and which is less likely to disappear when and if the problem disappears. Government-run monopoly is yet another imperfect solution, with many of the same problems. Perfectly discriminating monopoly, to the extent it is possible, is an elegant solution which avoids the defects of the other solutions only to introduce a potentially worse defect in the form of rent seeking.

OPTIONAL SECTION

Production Efficiency—Firm vs Industry

Whatever quantity of output a firm chooses to produce, any reduction in cost of production results in a corresponding increase in profit. So both a profit-maximizing competitive firm and a profit-maximizing monopoly are production efficient. The only firm we discussed which might not be production efficient was the regulated monopoly receiving a subsidy; if the government is willing to cover its costs, it has no incentive to minimize them.

Even if all the firms in an industry are production efficient, the industry may not be. In proving the efficiency of a competitive industry, I used the fact that each firm produces the quantity of output for which average cost is minimum. If that were not true, there would be some way of reorganizing the industry to give the same output at lower cost. If the quantity were too low for minimum average cost, the number of firms could be reduced and the output of each increased; if quantity were too high, the number of firms could be increased and output per firm decreased.

This is a point which I first made back in Chapter 9, when I showed that the size of the firms in a competitive industry was exactly what it would be if the industry had been designed by an omniscient and benevolent bureaucrat trying to produce the output at the lowest possible cost. That discussion was intended as a preview of the concepts of this chapter.

What about an industry made up of price-searching firms? In the case of a monopoly, the industry *is* the firm; if the firm is production efficient, so is the industry. But as I pointed out in Chapter 10, there are industry structures intermediate between perfect competition and monopoly. Consider the situation shown in Figures 15-7a and 15-7b. There are two firms in the industry; they are not, as in most of my examples, identical. Firm 1 has a high average and marginal cost and can only produce a small amount of output; when Q rises above 10, cost shoots up. Firm 2 has lower cost curves and can produce, at low cost, much greater quantities.

Assume the firms act independently. If the price is below P_1, firm 1 produces no output at all; for higher prices, it produces about 10 widgets per year. Firm 2 has two possible strategies. It can charge a price just below P_1 and sell Q_1 (equal to total demand, since firm 1 produces nothing at that price), or it can charge price P_2, which maximizes its profit for demand curve D', i.e., D minus the output of firm 1. For the curves of Figure 15-7b, the second strategy is the more profitable.

Figure 15-7

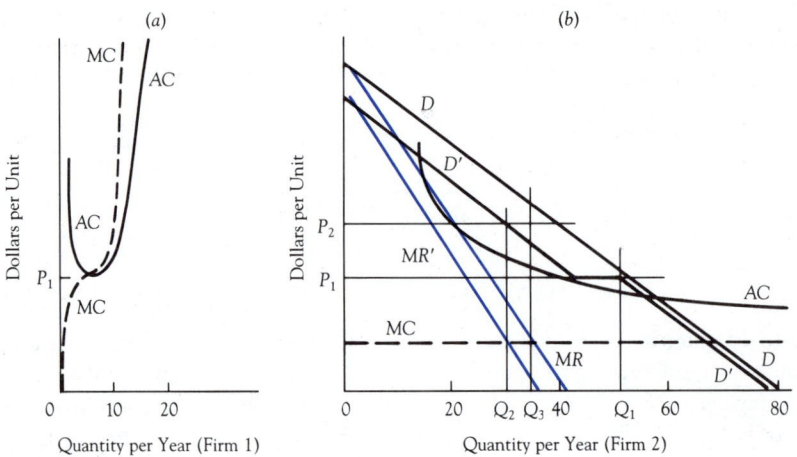

A two-firm industry.   The figures show a small firm (7a) and a large firm (7b) in the same industry. D is industry demand; D', the demand curve faced by the large firm, is D minus the quantity supplied by the small firm. The large firm maximizes its profit by producing a quantity Q_2; if the small firm did not exist, the large firm would produce Q_3.

The industry is now producing a quantity $Q_2 + 10$, with Q_2 produced by firm 2 and 10 by firm 1. The same output could be produced by firm 2 alone; since each additional unit costs firm 2 its marginal cost, 10 additional units would cost 10 times that. Those 10 units are at present costing the first firm 10 times its average cost. Since MC for firm 2 is much lower than AC for firm 1, total cost would be less if firm 2 produced the units that firm 1 is producing. It would be possible to produce the same output at a lower cost; hence the industry is not production efficient.

One conclusion which might be drawn from this argument is that if a firm is a natural monopoly, such as firm 2 in the example, competition should be made illegal. Otherwise, smaller and less efficient firms may find it in their interest to produce part of the industry's output—at a higher cost than the large firm could produce it. The large firm could drive such competitors out, since it can make money at a price at which they cannot; but by lowering its price to do so, it forfeits part of its monopoly profit. Unless it has some way of *keeping* them out, it may do better to charge a high price and let them have some of the business.

This is a correct argument, so far as it goes, but not, I think, a correct conclusion. The problem is that if natural monopolies are allowed to keep out competitors by force of law, they will be not only natural but permanent; even if technological change makes real competition possible, it will remain illegal.

Another important problem with the argument is that while I have shown that an industry consisting of just firm 2 is production efficient, while an industry with both firms producing is not, that does not necessarily imply that the former is superior to the latter. Firm 2 alone produces its output at a lower cost than both firms together, but it also produces less total output, as can be seen from the figure. Q_3, the output the large firm would choose if the small firm were forbidden to produce, is less than $Q_2 + 10$, the combined output of the two firms. The gain from producing at lower cost must be balanced against the reduced consumer surplus from the higher price and lower total output.

Patents and Efficiency

In several places in the text, you have been told that a single-price monopoly is inefficient; since it sells at a price above marginal cost, there will be some customers willing to pay more than the cost of production who do not get the good. If the monopoly lowered its price to MC and increased production accordingly, there would be a transfer from it to its present customers plus a net gain on the increased production.

This is true for the monopoly resulting from a patent or copyright, just as for other monopolies. The owner of a patent or copyright charges a licensing fee to the producer for each unit he produces; this raises the price above the true marginal cost, since part of the cost the producer pays on each unit is simply a transfer to the inventor. The *marginal* cost of the inventor's contribution is zero— it costs no more to invent something of which a million will be manufactured than something of which one will be manufactured. Hence patents result in the same sort of inefficiency as other monopolies.

Just as with other monopolies, one way of eliminating this inefficiency is discriminatory pricing. Assume that is not practical. Before condemning patents and arguing that all license fees should be set to zero, you should remember that there are two efficiency conditions to consider. One is the optimal quantity of a good to produce if it is produced at all; the other is whether it should be produced. If license fees are zero, which is the appropriate marginal cost, inventors have no incentive to invent (except to the extent that they can keep the invention secret or take advantage of having it first). This is one of the problems with government regulation of monopoly: If the monopoly must charge MC, it does not pay it to operate at all; and if the government solves the problem by offering to pay the fixed cost (or the inventor's salary), government has the problem of deciding which goods are worth producing or which inventions are worth trying to invent.

PROBLEMS

1. Figures 15-8a through 15-8c show average cost, marginal cost, and demand curves for three industries. Answer the following questions for each figure.
   a. If the industry is a single-price monopoly, will it choose to exist?
   b. If it is a perfectly discriminating monopoly, will it choose to exist?
   c. Should it exist (in the sense of Marshall)?

Figure 15-8

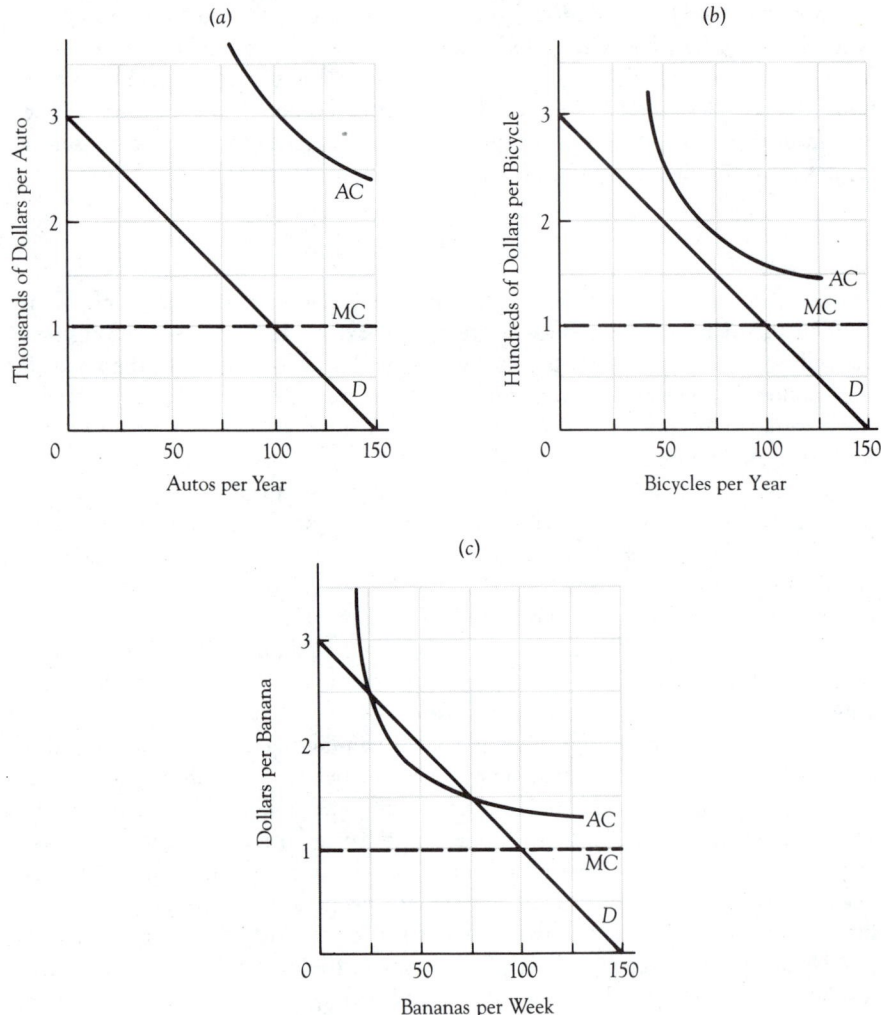

Three monopoly firms—Problem 2.

d. Suppose the government auctions off the right to be the single firm in the industry. How much will it get if the firm is to be a single-price monopoly? A perfectly discriminating monopoly? You may assume that the interest rate is 10 percent and that the curves shown are expected to remain the same forever.

2. In each of the cases shown on Figures 15-8a through 15-8c, how large is the net loss (to consumers, producers, and government) if the firm operates as a private, profit-maximizing, single-price monopoly (or, if it cannot cover its

costs, goes out of business) instead of following the rule for efficient production suggested in this chapter?

By "net loss" here, I mean "The number of dollars per year which, divided in some way between producers and consumers, could leave them exactly as well off with the private monopoly as they would be without the extra money but with an efficient monopoly." Note that one way of dividing $100 between me and you is to give me $200 and take $100 from you; $200 + (-$100) = $100.

3. Much of the land of the U.S. became private property through homesteading. Whoever first claimed the land and worked it for a fixed number of years owned it. As the frontier moved west, any particular piece of land was first not worth farming (costs higher than benefits), then just worth farming, and then more than worth farming (benefits higher than costs). Under the homesteading law, at which point in this process would settlers start to farm the land? What can you say about the efficiency of this way of turning over the land to private ownership? Compare it to the alternative of auctioning off the land and using the income to reduce taxes.

The following problems refer to the optional section:

4. On Figure 15-7b, MR' is only shown for quantities from 0 to about 35. Draw it for the entire range of quantity from 0 to 70.
5. In the situation illustrated by Figures 15-7a and 15-7b, exactly how would you find out whether closing down firm 1 and allowing firm 2 to produce at its profit-maximizing level of output would be a net improvement or a net worsening? You may want to show your answer on a sketch of Figure 15-7b.
6. Do you think that this book was sold to you at a price equal to the marginal cost of producing it? If not, would you be better or worse off if there were a law requiring publishers to sell books at marginal cost? Discuss.

FOR FURTHER READING

Two interesting articles on rent seeking are: Gordon Tullock, "The Welfare Costs of Tariffs, Monopolies and Theft," *Western Economic Journal*, Vol.5 (June,1967), pp. 224-232 and Terry Anderson and P. J. Hill, "Privatizing the Commons: An Improvement?" *Southern Economic Journal*, Vol.50, No.2 (October,1983), pp.438-450. (April,1975), pp.173-179.

Chapter 16

Market Interference

PRICE CONTROL

So far, we have analyzed markets in which price is free to move to the point at which quantity supplied equals quantity demanded. That may not be true if the government imposes a legal maximum or minimum price, or both. If the price control is binding—meaning that the supply/demand equilibrium price is above the maximum or below the minimum permitted—we have a new situation.

You cannot consume something that nobody produces, so even under price control, quantity consumed and quantity produced must be the same (except in the short run, when you can consume stocks of the good accumulated in the past). If at the controlled price, the quantity consumers wish to consume is greater than the quantity producers wish to produce, some mechanism other than price must allocate the limited supply.

In Chapter 2, I briefly discussed one such situation—price control on gasoline. I shall now redo that argument more precisely, using some of what you have learned since.

The Gasoline Paradox

Figure 16-1 shows demand and supply curves for gasoline; they intersect at a price of $1/gallon and a quantity of 20 billion gallons per year. The government imposes price control on gasoline; the maximum price is $.80/gallon. At that price, producers only want to pump, refine, and sell 17 billion gallons per year, but consumers want to buy 26 billion. Consumers cannot, for very long, use 9 billion gallons per year more than is being produced; gas stations rapidly run out of gasoline. When they do so, the cost of gasoline goes up, even though its price does not.

How? One way of making sure you get as much as you want of the limited supply is by getting up early in the morning and arriving at the station shortly after the tank truck leaves. If everyone tries to do that, the result is a long line. Having to wait in line raises the cost of gasoline to the consumer, adding a cost in time to the cost he is already paying in money.

Figure 16-1

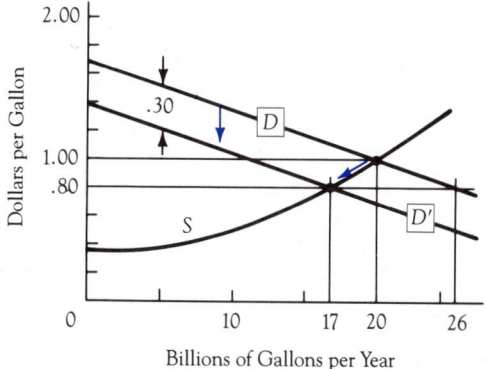

The effect of price control on gasoline. Price control at $.80/gallon produces a shortage; quantity demanded is larger than quantity supplied. Lines grow until their cost shifts demand down to D'. Consumers are paying $.20/gallon less in money and $.30/gallon more in time.

Increased costs due to the price control will come in other forms as well. One example is uncertainty—you can never be sure of getting gas when you want it. Every time you take a long trip, you risk being stranded in Podunk. Another additional cost (in time) is making more frequent visits to the gas station in order to be sure your tank is always full. Another may be bribes to the station owner. In at least one case during the gasoline shortage created by the price control of the early seventies, a prominent figure bought his own gas station in order to be sure he and his friends would get gas.

It does not matter, for the present argument, exactly what form the additional cost takes, although it is convenient to think of it, as in the discussion of Chapter 2, in terms of waiting in lines. All we need in order to analyze the effect of price control is the assumption that the additional cost is proportional to the amount of gasoline used (the more you use, the more times you have to wait in line to fill your tank) and is the same for all users. Given those assumptions, we can analyze the effect of price control, using techniques that we developed in Chapter 7 to analyze the effect of taxes.

If I must pay $.80 in money plus $.30 in waiting time and other inconveniences for each gallon of gasoline I buy, I will buy the same amount as I would if the price were $1.10/gallon ($.80 + $.30). The additional cost is equivalent to a $.30/gallon tax on consumers; like such a tax, it shifts the demand curve down by $.30, as shown on Figure 16-1.

Thirty cents is not a number picked at random. As you can see on the figure, a $.30 shift in the demand curve is just enough to make quantity demanded equal quantity supplied at the controlled price. If the cost (of lines and other inconveniences) to the consumers was less than $.30, quantity demanded would still be more than quantity supplied. The attempts of individuals to compete against each other for the limited supply would drive the cost up further; in the simple example, lines would grow longer.

So far, I have assumed that the additional nonpecuniary costs (costs that do not take the form of money payments) imposed on the consumer as a result of price control neither harm nor benefit the producer. This may not always be true; lines, for example, may allow the gas station to pump the same quantity of gas in less time, lowering labor costs and allowing the owner to shut up the station and go home halfway through the day. If so, the reduction in operating cost will shift the supply curve down at the same time that the increase in cost to the consumer shifts the demand curve down; producers will produce the same quantity at a lower price if they receive nonpecuniary benefits as well.

There are two possibilities in such a situation. One is that the increase in cost to the consumer is greater than the benefit to the producer. In that case (shown in Figure 16-2a), the results are qualitatively the same as in the case shown in Figure 16-1, where there is no effect on the producer at all; the consumer is, on net, worse off as a result of the price control. The other possibility is that the gain to the producer is greater than the loss to the consumer. That possibility is shown in Figure 16-2b. The reduction in pecuniary costs (price) is larger than the increase in nonpecuniary costs, so the consumer is better off as a result of the price control.

In that situation, however, the initial "without price control" equilibrium shown in the figures would not be stable. If the saving to gas stations of having long lines is greater than the cost to customers, station owners will find they can increase their profit by lowering their price, reducing their labor force, and letting lines grow. That is exactly what some discount stores do.

Figure 16-2

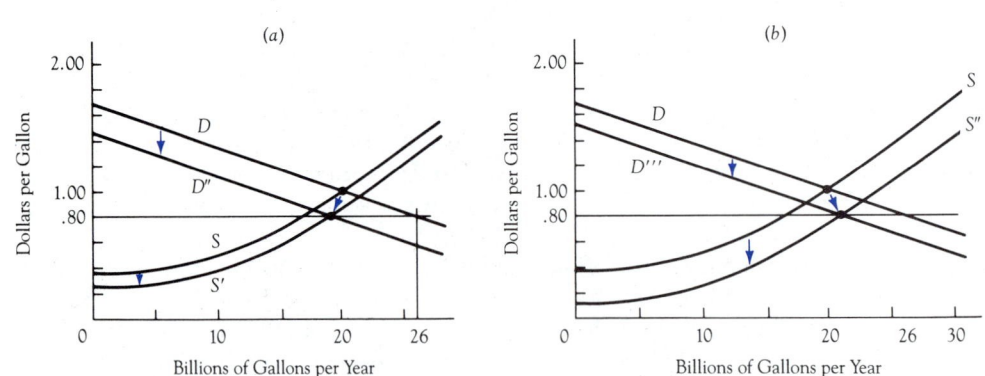

The effect of price control on gasoline—more complicated cases. Price control produces a shortage which produces lines. The lines reduce the per-gallon operating costs of gas stations and so shift the supply curve by less (Figure 16-2a) or more (Figure 16-2b) than the cost they impose on customers.

If the station owners know their business, there is no change they could make and have not made which would produce benefits to the firm larger than the resulting cost to the customer. If there were such a change, then making it— while at the same time cutting prices to compensate the consumers—would increase profits, since the reduction in price would be less than the reduction in the firm's costs. So it would already have been made.

Since rational profit-maximizing firms will already have made any changes of the sort shown on Figure 16-2b, any additional changes produced by price control either have no effect on the operating costs of the producers, as shown on Figure 16-1, or lower them by less than they increase cost to the consumers, as shown on Figure 16-2a, or raise the producers' costs—a possibility not shown on the figures.

If you think you have seen this argument before, you are right. The analysis of price control in this chapter is very similar to the analysis of legal restrictions on rental contracts in Chapter 7. There the government was setting one nonpecuniary term in the agreement between buyer and seller (the amount of notice the landlord had to give before evicting the tenant), and the result was to change the pecuniary part of the contract (the rent). Here the government sets the pecuniary terms of the contract (the price of gasoline), and the result is to change a nonpecuniary dimension of what is sold. In each case, the result is the same; if the intervention has any effect, it is to make both buyer and seller worse off.

The startling thing about this analysis is that price control at a below-market price has not only, as one might expect, injured the producers, it has also raised the cost of gasoline to the consumers—by $.10 in the initial example. This result does not depend on the details of the diagram; as long as the supply curve slopes up, price plus nonpecuniary cost with price control must be more than price without, although the amount of the increase depends on the relative slopes of the supply and demand curves. In Figure 16-1, the supply curve is twice as steep as the demand curve. Since price determines how much is produced, it is the height of the supply curve at the equilibrium quantity; since cost—pecuniary plus nonpecuniary—determines how much consumers want, it is the height of the demand curve at the equilibrium quantity. As you move left on the figure, the demand curve rises $.50 for every $1.00 the supply curve falls, so the increase in total cost due to price control is half the reduction in price.

The analysis *does* depend on my assumption that the additional cost is, like a tax, a per-gallon cost. Another way of putting this is that the increase in the marginal cost of gasoline to the consumer is assumed to be the same as the increase in the average cost. Usually when we discuss costs to consumers, we are talking about prices; the price of a gallon of gasoline is both the marginal cost to you of buying one more gallon of gasoline and the average cost of all the gasoline you buy. That may not always be the case for nonpecuniary costs.

Rationing

To see why this is important, consider a system of gasoline rationing. The price of gasoline is set at $.80/gallon, and each year everyone receives ration tickets allowing him to buy 85 percent of what his annual consumption of gasoline was before price control. Anyone who tries to buy more than his ration is shot. *Average cost* for buying rationed gas is now only $.80/gallon, but *marginal cost* beyond the rationed amount is very high—your life for the first pint. People buy until marginal cost equals marginal benefit—which happens at a quantity equal to what they have ration tickets for, since at that point, marginal cost abruptly increases. The situation, for one consumer, is shown in Figure 16-3. The analysis (consumer buys up to that point at which marginal cost equals marginal value) was first done in Chapter 4; the only change is that marginal cost of gasoline to the consumer is no longer independent of quantity and no longer necessarily equal to price.

Figure 16-3

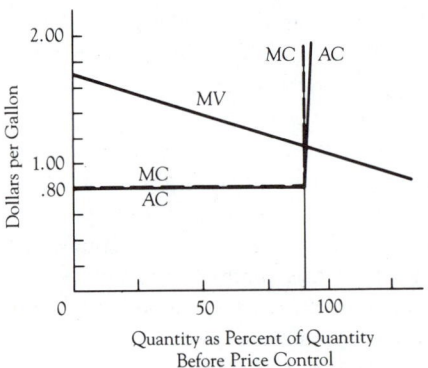

The cost of gasoline under rationing. The consumer can purchase at the controlled price 85 percent of what he consumed before price control; additional purchases are illegal.

Once we allow the marginal cost of gasoline to the consumer (which determines how much he buys) to differ from the average cost (which determines how much he pays for it), our proof that price control must injure the consumer is no longer valid. That does not mean that price control plus rationing will necessarily benefit the consumer. He gets gasoline at a lower price, but he also gets less gasoline. He is better off if the colored area A in Figure 16-4 (consumer surplus after price control plus rationing) is greater than the shaded area B (consumer surplus without price control), and he is worse off if it is less.

In more complicated real-world cases, one should also take account of the cost of running and enforcing a rationing scheme and adjusting it to a changing world. During the period of price control and gasoline shortage in the seventies, gasoline was not rationed to individuals but was rationed to regions, on the basis of past consumption; the Department of Energy, in effect, decided how much went where. It has been argued that part of the shortage was caused by the resulting misallocation; the formula used did not take proper account of population movements which were altering the relative demands of different areas of the country.

Figure 16-4

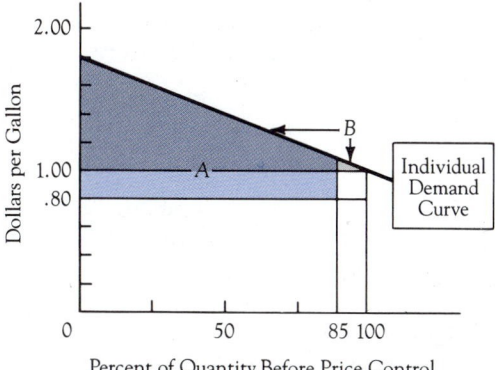

Percent of Quantity Before Price Control

Gains and losses to the consumer due to price control with rationing. Consumer surplus is B before price control and A after; the consumer is better off if B > A, worse off if B < A.

Gasoline price control—and gasoline shortages—are for the moment only memories, but other forms of price control are still with us. One of the most common, rent control, provides an interesting case for discussing the distinction between *allocational* and *distributional* effects.

DISTRIBUTION VS ALLOCATION

Economists find it useful to distinguish two sorts of issues, to which they have given the confusingly similar names of "allocation" and "distribution." "Allocation" is the allocation of goods to people (I get a car with manual transmission, you get a car with automatic transmission, he gets a bicycle—who gets what) or of particular inputs to producing particular outputs (make it this way instead of that way). "Distribution" is the distribution of real income, including both pecuniary and nonpecuniary benefits (who gets how much). Non-economists tend to think of all issues as distributional ("If cars are sold on the market, then rich people get them and poor people do not; if we have private schools, then rich people get better educations"). Economists tend to think of all issues as allocational ("Consider two people with the same income but different tastes. Let cars and education both be sold. One person buys a car and no education; one buys education and no car").

Economists tend to focus on allocational issues not because distribution is unimportant but because they have less to say about it. Allocational changes typically do—or at least can—benefit (or harm) everyone, so we can evaluate them without worrying about how to balance gains to one person against losses to someone else. Distributional changes are just the opposite. Pure redistribution (I lose a dollar, you gain a dollar, there are no other effects) is neither a gain nor a loss in Marshall's sense. Efficiency is unaffected, and efficiency is the least unsatisfactory criterion we have for judging what is or is not an improvement.

Rent Control

One example of the distinction between allocation and distribution and of the difficulty in changing one without affecting the other is rent control. Suppose the city government of Santa Monica decides to impose rent control and sets the maximum rent for each apartment below what its market level would be. The obvious effect is distributional—landlords are worse off and tenants are better off. The less obvious effect is allocational. At the controlled rent, demand for apartments is higher than supply (since at the market rent, they were equal!). If you are occupying a rented apartment, you have a good deal; but if you want to rent an apartment, you have a problem.

Normally, as families change, they move. A young couple has children and moves from a four-room to a six-room apartment; an older couple moves from a six-room to a four-room apartment after the children leave home. But suppose that, under rent control, the older couple has a six-room apartment for (say) $600/month; controlled four-room apartments rent for $400, and at that price, the couple would be happy to move, since the additional rooms are no longer worth $200 to them. But since quantity demanded at the controlled price is larger than quantity supplied, there are no four-room apartments for rent in Santa Monica. Uncontrolled four-room apartments outside of Santa Monica rent for $600. The couple stays in the six-room apartment even though it has two rooms more than they want.

The same problem exists for people who would normally move from a four-room apartment in one part of town to an apartment the same size but in a different location—perhaps because they have changed where they work. If rent control remains in effect for a long time, where people live becomes determined more and more by where they used to live and less and less by where (size and location of apartment) it is now appropriate for them to live. This is an allocational problem—it makes some people worse off without making other people better off.

There is a simple solution. Allow tenants to sublet their apartments—for whatever rent they can get. There will now be two rents for any apartment—the controlled rent ($600 for a six-room apartment in the example we have been discussing) and the rent that a sublessee would pay the original tenant ($800, say) which is what the market rent would have been in the absence of rent control. The cost to an elderly couple of remaining in their six-room apartment is not $600 but $800—if they moved out, they would not only save $600 in rent for themselves, they would also make an additional $200 by continuing to pay rent at $600 and subletting to someone else at $800. Hence they are willing to pay (say) $600 to someone who will sublet a four-room apartment to them, just as (if there were no rent control) they would have been willing to move from an $800 apartment (six rooms) to a $600 apartment (four rooms).

What the combination of rent control plus uncontrolled subletting has done is to permit a free market in apartments while giving the original tenant part ownership of the apartment which he occupied when rent control was imposed. In effect, the tenants of the six-room apartment are quarter owners; if they choose to sublet, they receive $800; three fourths of that goes to the landlord as rent and one fourth they keep. This appears to be a way of producing a *distributional* effect (which may be "desirable" for political or other reasons) without any undesirable *allocational* effects.

There are several problems with this. The first is that landlords have almost no incentive to maintain their apartments. In an uncontrolled market, it pays the landlord to make any repairs or improvements which are worth more to the tenant than they cost; he can expect to get the money back in increased rent. Under rent control, all that matters to the landlord is that the apartment be in sufficiently good shape to command the controlled rent. If (as in the example) that is three fourths of the market rent, he can let the apartment deteriorate to three fourths of its previous market value at no cost to himself. The fall in its market rent will all be paid for by his original tenants. If they live in the apartment themselves, they will pay by living in a deteriorated apartment; if they sublet it to someone else, the deterioration will lower the difference between the rent they pay the owner and the rent they receive from the sublessee.

When rent control has been in effect for a while, apartments start to deteriorate; this results in laws (if they do not already exist) specifying how landlords must maintain apartments. A system of uncontrolled rents in which the landlord was led by his own interest to make those repairs and improvements which were worth making has been replaced by a system of rent control in which uniform standards are set and enforced in order to make landlords do things that it is no longer in their interest to do voluntarily.

An allocational problem also arises with regard to new construction. Rent control means, in effect, that part of the value of a new apartment building is automatically given to the first set of tenants; they get to rent the apartment from the landlord at the controlled price and to the sublessees at an uncontrolled price. That discourages construction. The obvious solution is to make rent control apply only to buildings that already exist and exempt new construction.

But the same forces which made it politically profitable to impose rent control on existing housing this year (while promising not to control new housing) can be expected to make it profitable, five years hence, to impose rent control on the buildings built during that interval—while promising to leave future construction uncontrolled. Unless the politician not only promises that new housing will not be controlled but also finds some convincing way of committing himself, forcing himself to keep the promise in the future whether or not he still wants to, builders may not believe his promise—and not build. Even if the politician can bind *himself*, that may merely mean that, five years hence, he will be defeated by another politician running on a platform of controlling the "unfairly" uncontrolled new buildings.

Price Control: A Summary Schema

Figure 16-5 shows demand and supply curves for a good whose price is controlled; P_c is the controlled price. To avoid having to shift lines around on the figure, we use a trick introduced in Chapter 7, when we were analyzing the effect of taxes. The supply curve shows quantity produced as a function of price received by the producer; the demand curve shows quantity consumed as a function of cost—price plus nonpecuniary costs—to the consumer.

We begin with price control and no rationing. Lines (or other nonpecuniary costs) grow until they are large enough to reduce quantity demanded to quantity supplied. The nonpecuniary costs are shown on the graph as the difference between price received by the producer and cost paid by the consumer—C_{np} on Figure 16-5. The net loss as a result of price control is area B (loss of consumer and producer surplus on goods no longer produced) plus area A (nonpecuniary costs per unit—time waiting in lines and the like—multiplied by the number of units consumed) plus any costs of administering and enforcing the controls.

We now add a rationing system such as that shown in Figure 16-3. Each consumer receives a fixed number of ration tickets, proportional to his previous year's consumption. In order to buy one unit of the good, say one gallon of gasoline, he must pay one ration ticket plus the controlled price of the good.

Under this system, the lines disappear, so the nonpecuniary cost A is eliminated, but new costs are introduced due to the misallocation produced by the rationing system. If, for example, I have just moved from the suburbs to the city, my ration of gas—my previous year's consumption times the ratio of current production to last year's production—is as much as I want at P_c. If the price were any higher, I would not use my full ration. You, on the other hand, have just

Figure 16-5

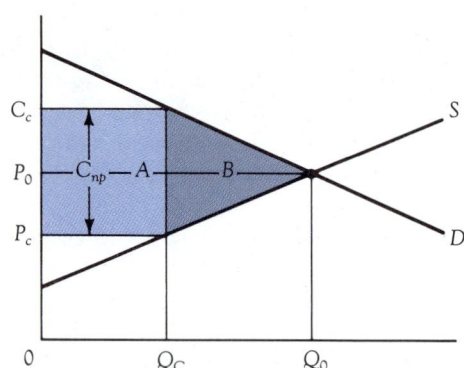

Costs associated with price control. B is a net loss of surplus due to reduced quantity produced and consumed. A is the non-pecuniary cost if there is no rationing. It is the total market value of ration tickets if there is rationing with transferable tickets.

moved from the city to the suburbs and are desperate for gas. Since your allocation—that same fixed fraction of your previous year's consumption—is far less than you want, you would gladly pay several times the controlled price to get additional gallons. Since I am consuming gas which is worth more to you than to me, we have an inefficient allocation. Figure 16-5 shows total demand as a function of price; in order to show the effects of inefficient allocation among consumers, we would need to know their individual demand curves and allocations. There is no way to tell from Figure 16-5 how large the resulting loss is; it depends on how accurately the rationing scheme fits the actual demands of the consumers. Net loss due to rationing is now area B plus an unknown additional loss due to such misallocation, plus the costs of running and enforcing the rationing system.

There is an easy way to eliminate the misallocation; make the ration tickets marketable. If you want gasoline more than I do, I sell you some of my ration. Under such a system, ration tickets have a market price; at that price, anyone can buy or sell as many as he wishes. Just as for any other good, the price of the ticket will be that price at which quantity supplied equals quantity demanded. The cost of buying gasoline is then the price of gasoline plus the price of a ration ticket. This is obviously true for consumers who use more than their ration and must buy additional tickets—if they want another gallon of gasoline, they must buy both the gasoline and the ration ticket. It is equally true for consumers who use some of their ration tickets and sell the rest. By consuming a gallon of gasoline from their own ration, they give up the opportunity to *sell* a ration ticket. The cost to them of consuming the gallon is then its price, P_c, plus the price they could have gotten for the ration ticket they used in buying it.

We know that the quantity of gasoline supplied is Q_c. The cost to the consumer at which that quantity is demanded is C_c on Figure 16-5. Since the cost to the consumer is the price of the gasoline plus the price of the ration ticket, it follows that the price of the ration ticket is C_{np}—what the nonpecuniary cost would have been without rationing. The price of the ration ticket is serving exactly the same function that the cost of waiting in line served before—reducing the quantity of gasoline that consumers demand to the quantity producers supply. The area A is now equal to the market value of the ration tickets—the number of tickets times the value of one ticket. The net cost is the area B plus any costs of administering and enforcing the rationing.

Aside from administrative costs, the system is precisely equivalent to a tax of C_{np} imposed on producers, with the revenue from the tax distributed to consumers in proportion to their previous year's consumption—the same way that the ration tickets are distributed. In both cases, the price received by the producers, the controlled price in the one case or the market price net of tax in the other, is P_c. In both cases, the cost to the consumers of a gallon of gas is C_c. In the one case, consumers get ration tickets with a market value of C_{np} dollars each; in the other case, they get an equivalent amount of money.

Why is it that rationing systems usually do not permit individuals to buy and sell ration tickets? Perhaps because that would make the effect of price control plus rationing more obvious—and harder to defend. It is fairly easy to argue that, as a matter of justice, national hardships should be borne by everyone—that if there is "not enough" gasoline, everyone should be allowed to have as much gas as he "needs" and no more—and that the gasoline companies should not be allowed to "profit from the hardship of others." That is a (favorable) description of price control plus a simple rationing system. It is much harder to argue for the peculiar system of taxes and subsidies described in the previous paragraph—which is equivalent to a rationing system after it is improved by making the ration tickets transferable. Yet it is hard to see how one can argue against making ration tickets transferable, since that change benefits everyone—buyers (who get additional tickets for less than they are worth to them) and sellers (who give up tickets for more than they are worth to them).

Can one "improve" rationing even further in order to eliminate the lost surplus B? Perhaps. The solution is to "ration" production as well as consumption. Producers must sell a quantity Q_c at the controlled price; any additional production sells at the market price to anyone who wants it (no tickets required). Since the quantity producers produce depends on the marginal revenue from an additional unit, which is now equal to the market price (i.e., the controlled price plus the ticket price), output expands up to Q_0, the old uncontrolled output. Ticket price drops to P_0 (the original uncontrolled price) minus P_c. The system has become a pure transfer of producer surplus to the consumers—very much like the tranfer of consumer surplus to the producer under perfect discriminatory pricing. The details of who actually pays are complicated and depend on how the "production ration" is divided up among producers and how new producers are treated.

During oil price control, the U.S. government attempted just this sort of a system. "Old oil," meaning oil produced by conventional methods from wells that were already producing, was controlled at a low price. "New oil"—oil from new wells, or additional oil produced from old wells in expensive ways, or imported oil—was uncontrolled (the system was actually somewhat more complicated; this is only a rough sketch). Of course, all consumers (refiners) wanted to buy cheap old oil instead of expensive new oil, so the government rationed the old oil. The rationing rule used was that refiners got allocations of old oil proportional to the total amount of oil they refined. So for each barrel of uncontrolled foreign oil the refiner used, he was entitled to buy a certain amount of cheap, price-controlled domestic oil. These allocations were transferable ration tickets like those discussed above, and were valuable. The government was, in effect, paying refiners to import foreign oil, with the payments coming out of the revenue of the domestic (old) oil producers—a peculiar way of reducing America's dependence on foreign oil.

So far, I have considered the distinction between distributional and allocational effects of government decisions in the context of price (specifically rent) control; the same distinction is relevant to other issues. Just as in the case of rent control, the non-economist is likely to perceive the issue as purely distributional, the economist as mostly allocational.

Liability Rules

One example of this is the issue of who should be liable for injuries due to defective products. Consider two liability rules: caveat emptor and caveat venditor. *Caveat emptor* (Latin for "let the buyer beware") means that the seller or producer is not responsible for defects in his product; *caveat venditor* ("let the seller beware") means that he is. One's first instinct is to suppose that if the law changes from caveat emptor to caveat venditor, consumers gain (and producers lose) the amount the producers have to pay the consumers to compensate them for defective products. But this conclusion depends on a hidden assumption—that the change in the law will not affect the price at which the goods are sold. That is most unlikely; the new legal rule raises the cost to the producer (when he sells the good, he becomes liable to pay if it is defective) and the value of the good to the consumer. Both the supply curve and the demand curve shift up, so the price must rise.

One's next guess might be that there is no effect at all—the consumers, on average, pay in higher prices just as much as they receive for defective products. This is closer but still not quite right. If the producer is liable for defective products, that gives him an incentive to make the product better. If the consumer is liable, that gives him an incentive to treat the products more gently and to take more precautions to minimize the cost of accidents—wearing safety glasses while using power tools, for instance.

To the extent that the consumer knows how good products are before he buys them, the first incentive is unnecessary—even if the producer is not liable, he will still try to avoid defects in order to make consumers willing to buy his product. Just as in similar cases discussed earlier, the producer will find it in his interest to make any improvements in quality which are worth more to the consumers than they cost him to make, since he can more than cover the additional costs with the increased price the consumers will be willing to pay for the improved product. But to the extent that the cost to consumers of evaluating the products they buy is high enough so that they choose to buy in partial ignorance, the incentive provided by caveat venditor may serve a useful purpose.

This seems to imply that the rule should be caveat emptor where the main danger is from careless use by the consumer or where the consumer can readily inform himself of the quality of the good. It seems to imply that the rule should be caveat venditor where the consumer cannot readily judge quality and the best way to avoid problems is for the producer to produce better goods.

A still better solution is the combination of either caveat emptor or caveat venditor with freedom of contract. Suppose the rule is caveat emptor, and further suppose that consumers would much prefer to buy under a rule of caveat venditor, even at a price that compensated the producers for the cost of that rule. In that case, producers will find that selling their product with a guarantee (at a higher price) is more profitable than selling it without a guarantee. In effect, the producer who offers a guarantee is converting the rule for his product into caveat venditor—he is voluntarily making himself liable for product defects.

Suppose instead that the rule is initially caveat venditor. The consumer can, if he wishes, convert it to caveat emptor in exchange for a lower price—by signing a waiver in which he agrees not to sue. One area where such waivers could make a very large difference is in medical malpractice. Given how high the costs of malpractice suits and malpractice insurance are, a doctor might offer a much lower charge to a patient who signed an agreement not to sue—or even an agreement only to sue in case of gross negligence. Under present law, unfortunately, such a waiver is unenforceable; the patient can sign it before the operation then "change his mind" and sue anyway.

PROTECTING CONSUMERS FROM THEMSELVES

Legal restrictions on price are usually defended as ways of protecting consumers from producers. Restrictions on what you can buy or whom you can hire are defended as ways of protecting the consumer from his own ignorance. How many of us, it may reasonably be asked, are competent to judge how good a doctor, or a drug, is?

In evaluating such arguments, it is useful to distinguish between licensing and certifying, or equivalently between government control of what can be sold and government control of labeling. If doctors are licensed, then an unlicensed doctor can be jailed for practicing medicine. If doctors are merely certified, then an uncertified doctor can practice. He cannot legally claim to be certified, but it is up to the customer to decide whether to accept the judgment of the governmental body that certifies doctors. The customer might decide that even though certified doctors are better, he prefers the uncertified doctor because of the doctor's lower price, greater availability, ability to speak the customer's language, or some other compensating advantage. Similarly, one could imagine a system in which drugs which are now illegal or require a prescription could be freely bought but would have to have a prominent label saying: "In the opinion of the Surgeon General, this drug should be used only when prescribed by a physician."

Certifying seems to satisfy the requirement of protecting customers from their own ignorance—unless what one wishes to protect the customers from is their "ignorance" of how wise and benevolent the government that does the certifying is. Those who argue for licensing instead of certifying must either argue that even with information, people cannot be trusted to act in their own best interest or else that the interest being served is not that of the customer. An example of the first sort of argument would be the assertion that people are not willing to spend as much money on their health as they should. It is my impression that such claims are usually made by people who have more money to spend than do those whom they are criticizing.

An example of the second sort of argument for regulation—that we are regulating someone for someone else's benefit—is the justification commonly given for compulsory vaccination designed to prevent the spread of contagious disease. Vaccinating me against smallpox not only protects me from the disease, it also protects the people who might catch it from me. Similarly, it is often argued that illegal drugs (or pornography, or dangerous ideas) should be prohibited because they indirectly injure people other than those who choose to consume them.

While some government regulations, such as compulsory vaccination, may make sense as attempts to force consumers to act in the general interest, many more seem designed to serve very narrow private interests. The obvious example is the use of licensing to keep the number of people in a profession down and their salaries up—a reason that is rarely stated in public argument but seems the most plausible explanation for the severe licensing requirements imposed, in many states, upon barbers, egg graders, yacht salesmen, librarians, and a host of other "professionals."

ALLOCATION, DISTRIBUTION, AND THE EFFECTS OF INTERVENTION IN THE MARKET

In discussing gasoline price control, I assumed that all consumers were affected alike by the nonpecuniary costs resulting from a below-market price. A more realistic description would allow for the difference between the cost of waiting in line to a busy professional and the cost to a student who can (if he wishes) study while he waits. The nonpecuniary cost must still be high enough to drive quantity demanded down to quantity supplied, but it does so by imposing low costs on some customers (and reducing the quantity they demand only slightly) and high costs on others. The "average" effect is to injure all consumers of gasoline (the increase in nonpecuniary costs is greater than the decrease in price), but there may be many individual exceptions.

Similarly, under rent control, tenants who start with rent-controlled apartments are benefited at the expense of landlords, at least until and unless the apartments are allowed to deteriorate substantially; those who move into the area later, or wish to move from one apartment to another, are injured. There is an obvious distributional transfer from landlords to tenants and a less obvious allocational loss—due to misallocation of people to apartments, inefficient levels of construction and maintainance of apartments, and the like.

The same is also true of the change from one liability rule to another. The particular consumer who is injured by an exploding coke bottle may be better off under a rule of caveat venditor—but the consumers who are not injured must still pay a higher price because the legal rule raises the producer's cost, the value of the product to the consumer, and hence the supply curve, the demand curve, and the equilibrium price. So they are worse off as a result of caveat venditor. As in the case of gasoline price control, consumers and producers, on average, are worse off as a result of the rule—or of a rule imposing caveat emptor. Both would (on average) be benefited by freedom of contract.

What these examples suggest is that the effect of market interference is almost the opposite of what one might at first think. One would expect the effect to be mostly distributional, with price control, rent control, or caveat venditor benefiting buyers at the expense of sellers. In fact, it is mostly allocational; the restrictions have as their main effect a less efficient allocation of resources, a smaller pie to be divided up. Such distributional effects as do occur are (except in the rent control case) mostly among consumers (and among producers) rather than between producers and consumers.

Why is it that rent control, unlike price control of gasoline, has substantial distributional effects? There are two reasons. One is that the supply of housing is, in the short run, very inelastic; landlords do not start tearing down apartment buildings when rents fall by 10 percent. Hence the short-run effect of rent control on the supply of housing is small compared to the effect of gasoline price control on the supply of gasoline.

The other reason is that the tenant who has an apartment when rent control is imposed is like the purchaser of gasoline under a rationing system—he can consume a certain amount of housing (i.e., use the apartment he is presently renting) at the controlled price; the higher price that reduces quantity demanded to quantity supplied affects him only when he wants to move to another apartment. In the short run, rent control is accompanied by a built-in system of rationing—allocate each apartment to the tenant presently living in it. In the very long run, the case of rent control is essentially the same as the case of price control on gasoline—but the short run is long enough so that many individuals benefit for a period of years and sometimes decades, which may explain why it is more popular than most other forms of price control.

DISTRIBUTION VS ALLOCATION: THE PROGRESSIVE INCOME TAX

In discussing rationing, we found it useful to distinguish between costs which were, like prices, proportional to the amount purchased and costs which were not. In discussing taxes in Chapter 7, I assumed that the tax you paid on something was proportional to the amount of it you bought or sold. That is true of almost all sales taxes, but it is not true of income taxes in the U.S. at present.

Under a *graduated income tax*, the tax you pay is not proportional to the amount of income you receive. Your income is divided into brackets, each with a different tax rate. In a *progressive* system, the higher the bracket, the higher the rate. In a *regressive* system, the higher the bracket, the lower the rate. While "progressive" sounds as though it means something good and "regressive" something bad, the terms are simply descriptions of two sorts of graduated taxes—one in which rates rise ("progress") with income and one in which they fall ("regress").

The graduated income tax system of the U.S. at present is progressive. To simplify the discussion, I will consider a progressive system with a simpler set of brackets and tax rates than we actually have. The first bracket will be from 0 to $10,000/year, the second from $10,000/year to $20,000/year, and so forth. You pay one rate (in our example, zero) on income in the first bracket, a higher rate (10 percent) on income in the second, a still higher rate (20 percent) on income in the third, and so on.

So if your income is below $10,000/year, you pay no tax; if it is between $10,000/year and $20,000/year, you pay 10 percent of any income above $10,000/year. If you make $25,000/year, you pay 10 percent of your income in the second bracket (.10 × $10,000/year = $1,000/year) plus 20 percent of your income in the third bracket (.20 × $5,000/year = $1,000/year), for a total tax of $2,000/year.

An alternative system of taxation which has been widely discussed is a flat-rate tax. In its purest form, this would mean that everyone would pay a fixed percentage of his income. In considering the effect of shifting from one system to the other, we will discuss first allocational and then distributional effects.

Allocation

One way of eliminating distributional effects in order to focus on allocational ones is to analyze a situation in which everyone is identical. Suppose, to start with, that everyone has an income of $25,000/year. Under the graduated tax, everyone is paying $2,000/year, which is 8 percent of his income. So we will start by considering what would happen if the graduated system were replaced by a flat rate of 8 percent. Will people be better or worse off?

If your answer is "They are paying the same amount in taxes as before, so the change has no effect," you have not yet finished learning to think like an economist. Once people have adjusted to the new tax system, they will be paying more taxes than before—and they will be better off!

Just as the sales taxes analyzed in Chapter 7 affected the amount producers sold and consumers bought, so an income tax affects the amount of their leisure that workers choose to sell. Suppose the wage rate is $10/hour. Under the graduated system, an individual who chooses to sell more leisure—or in other words, to work more hours—receives only $8 for each extra hour worked; the other $2 goes to the IRS. An individual who sells less leisure—works fewer hours—loses only $8 for each hour less he works. We showed in Chapter 5 that a rational individual chooses to work a number of hours such that the marginal value of his leisure (alias the marginal disvalue of labor) is equal to the wage he receives for working. So each individual works up to the point where the marginal disvalue of one more hour (the marginal value of leisure) is $8/hour.

Under the new flat-rate tax system, the marginal (and average) tax rate is only 8 percent. An individual who works an extra hour at $10/hour receives $9.20 of extra income; an individual who works an hour less is $9.20 poorer. After the tax law changes, workers increase the amount they work (increase the amount of their leisure that they sell, decrease the amount they consume themselves) until the marginal value of leisure rises to $9.20/hour. They are working more hours, receiving more income, paying more in taxes, and are better off.

They are making more because they are working more hours. They are paying more in taxes because 8 percent was the flat rate which would have yielded the same amount as the previous system of rates if incomes had stayed the same. Incomes have risen, so 8 percent of the new income is more than the amount produced by the old system. They are better off not simply because they have more money—that must be balanced against the additional hours they are working—but because each person has chosen an outcome, a bundle of a certain amount of income plus a certain amount of leisure, which he prefers to what he had before.

How do I know that? Under the new system, each individual could choose to work the same number of hours as before and pay the same tax—that, after all, is how the tax rate was calculated. That he does not choose to do so demonstrates that he now has an alternative he prefers. To put the argument more formally, the old optimal bundle is still in his new choice set; the fact that it is no longer optimal means that the new choice set contains a bundle he prefers to it.

If we now readjust the tax rate (down) so that everyone ends up paying the same tax as under the graduated system ($2,000/year), people are even better off. The flat-rate system now yields government the same revenue while giving every taxpayer an outcome (7 percent, say) which he prefers to the outcome under a flat rate of 8 percent—which he preferred to the old system. The change is not only a Marshall improvement, it is even (under our assumption that everyone is identical) a Pareto improvement.

Some Complications

In proving this result—that a flat rate tax is unambiguously superior to a progressive graduated tax if all taxpayers are identical—I have skipped over a number of complications. The most important is the effect of the change in the tax law on the wage rate. Unless the demand for labor is perfectly elastic, one effect of an increased supply of labor (everyone is working more hours because of the change in the tax law) will be a fall in the wage rate. A full analysis of the effects of the change would have to take this into account, just as the analysis of the effect of taxes in Chapter 7 included the resulting change in price.

Including that effect would not change the essential result, however; it would simply transform some of the gain from producer surplus (going to the sellers of labor) to consumer surplus (going to the buyers). If everyone is identical, everyone ends up with an equal share of consumer and producer surplus. The analysis would be a little more complicated, but the net effect would still be a gain.

A further complication is the fact that selling leisure is not the only way of getting income; there are other factors of production. The same argument would apply to them as well. An income tax reduces the landowner's incentive to rent out his land, since if he "consumes" it himself (lives on it), he will get his return in an untaxed form, just as the worker avoids taxes by consuming his leisure instead of selling it. The effect is larger the higher the tax rate. In the same way, an income tax reduces the individual's incentive to save (and loan out his savings—rent out capital—in order to get income).

One could imagine a variety of other complications as well. So far as I know, none would alter the result. The essential logic of the situation is quite simple. In deciding whether to earn an additional dollar of income, the relevant consideration is how much of that dollar the income earner will be able to keep, so it is the marginal tax rate—the rate paid on each additional dollar of income—that determines how much the taxpayer chooses to earn. Under a progressive graduated system, the marginal rate must be higher than the average rate, hence higher than the flat rate that would yield the same revenue from the same income. From the standpoint of efficiency, the optimal rate is zero, since at a tax rate of zero, the individual sells his leisure (or anything else) if and only if its value to the buyer is greater than its value to him—which is the efficient outcome. The flat-rate system has a lower marginal rate, hence is closer to the efficient arrangement, than a progressive system with the same average rate. Since a lower marginal rate means higher income, the flat rate can actually be below the average of the graduated system and still yield the same tax revenue, making it still more attractive.

The principle here is exactly the same as in the solution to the Hero problem of Chapter 1. The Hero, as you may remember, is being pursued by 40 bad guys and has only 10 arrows. The solution is to shoot the bad guy in front. Then shoot the bad guy in front. Then shoot the bad guy in front. Then the bad guys start competing to see who can run slowest.

What we have here, just as with the graduated tax (and the ideal rationing system discussed earlier in the chapter) is a discrepancy between an *average* cost and a *marginal* cost. On average, the Hero can only kill a fourth of his pursuers. But on the *margin*, the margin of who runs fastest, he can kill all of them—until he runs out of arrows. No one is willing to face a certainty of death just to give the survivors the pleasure of killing the Hero. So once he has made it clear what he is doing, they all decline the honor of running in front.

That is also, as you may remember from Chapter 1, how Jarl Sigurd lost the battle of Clontarf—he ran out of men who were willing to carry the banner and accept a certainty of being killed. It is also how you impose a very large penalty for consuming gasoline without actually punishing anyone; if everyone believes he will be shot for exceeding his ration, nobody exceeds it and nobody is ever shot.

Distribution

As long as we limit ourselves to a world of identical individuals, the case against a progressive tax system is overwhelming. The argument *for* such a tax system is a distributional one—it is a way of imposing higher tax rates on individuals with higher incomes. In discussing efficiency, I pointed out that most people believe a dollar is worth more to a poor man than to a rich man. If so, a tax system that shifts more of the tax burden onto the rich may produce net benefits—in utility although not in dollars—even if, because of the allocational problems I have just discussed, the rich man is (say) two dollars worse off for each one-dollar benefit to the poor man.

The declining marginal utility of income provides one reason why some people might wish to benefit the poor at the expense of the rich, even if there are efficiency costs to doing so. There are others. In Chapter 13, we discussed, but did not resolve, the question of whether the distribution of income produced by the market is in some sense just. For those who decide that it is not, one possible conclusion is that no inequality in income is justified and that the tax system should be designed to equalize incomes for reasons not of utility but of justice.

Whatever the reason, if one wishes to make the after-tax income distribution more equal than the before-tax distribution, a progressive graduated tax is an obvious—if costly—way to do it. It is not, however, entirely clear whether the tax system that presently exists in the U.S. has that effect. In analyzing the allocational effects of the two systems, I asserted, and to some degree demonstrated, that complicating the system did not change the essential result. It is less clear whether the same is true of the distributional effects.

It is easier to hide some kinds of income than others. If you are the employee of a large firm and your salary is your entire income, what you report to the IRS is probably very close to what you actually make. If you are self-employed, the opportunities for converting your consumption into "business expenses" for tax purposes—or even concealing income entirely—are much greater. If your income is from capital, you may not be able to conceal it; but you can, at some cost, convert it into capital gains, which are taxed at a lower rate. Or you can convert your capital into state and municipal securities—which pay a lower interest rate than other investments but are tax exempt.

These complications, and others both legal and economic, imply that the actual tax system redistributes in many different directions. While there may be some tendency for richer people to pay more than poorer, thus making the income distribution more equal, there is also a tendency for people with identical incomes to pay very different amounts of tax, thus making the after-tax distribution less equal. Determining what really happens is difficult. The main source of statistics on incomes and taxes is the IRS, and what one is interested in is, in large part, the income that is not reported to the IRS.

Conclusions

Even if the system did, on net, make the income distribution more equal, that would not necessarily mean that the poor would be better off. A more equal distribution would mean a larger share of the pie for the poor; but the allocational costs discussed earlier imply that under a progressive system, the pie as a whole is smaller. It is hard to know what the net effect actually is.

The most fundamental mistake in popular discussions of the issue is the assumption that what is good for the rich is *necessarily* bad for the poor, and vice versa. That way of looking at it is an example of the non-economist's tendency to assume that all issues are distributional. To take a simple counterexample, consider a rich man who is in a 50 percent bracket, earns $200,000/year, and (legally or illegally) conceals most of it—at a cost (to himself) of 45 cents on the dollar. He is behaving rationally—it is worth paying 45 percent to avoid paying 50 percent. If the tax rate falls to 40 percent, he finds it is no longer worth the cost of concealing his income; the rich man is better off, and the IRS collects more money.

The classic example of this phenomenon is due not to Arthur Laffer—who recently popularized it under the name of the "Laffer Curve"—but to Adam Smith. His example was an import duty—a tariff—so high that everything that came in was smuggled. If the duty were lowered to the point where it was no longer worth the cost of smuggling, both consumers and tax collectors would be better off.

PROBLEMS

1. In discussing the effect of price control on the cost of gasoline to the consumer, I mentioned but did not graph the case where the longer lines *increased* the producer's cost (his lot is so crowded that he cannot, as he used to, rent out parking spaces to people shopping in the neighborhood). Draw a figure similar to Figures 16-1 and 16-2a showing the effect of price control in that case.

2. Demonstrate that the rents for subletting (with rent control) will be the same as the market rent would have been without rent control. What simplifying assumption must you make? (This is a hard question. The simplifying assumption has something to do with income effects.)

3. In my final discussion of price control, I discussed a series of alternatives starting with simple price control, going on to price control plus rationing, going on to price control plus rationing plus tranferable ration tickets, and ending with all that plus uncontrolled prices for additional output. The examples I used involved oil and gasoline. In the case of rent control, what would correspond to each of those arrangements?

4. In Chapter 10, I said that Disneyland should charge a per-ride price just high enough to reduce the line at each ride to about zero. Explain why this is true. You will want to combine the analysis of Chapter 10 with the analysis of this chapter. (This is a hard problem.)

5. Under the system of oil price control, a refinery's allocation of cheap "old oil" was proportional to the total amount of oil it refined. This amounted, in effect, to a subsidy on both imported oil and "new" (uncontrolled) domestic oil. The subsidy on imported oil would tend to increase imports; the subsidy on new domestic oil would tend to increase domestic output and hence to decrease imports. Is there any way of telling what the net effect on imports would be? Explain. (Hint: There is a simple, but not necessarily obvious, answer.)

6. I demonstrated that in a world of identical individuals, a flat rate tax was superior to a progressive graduated tax. Is the flat rate tax the most efficient way of collecting a given amount of revenue in such a world, or is there another alternative that is even better? Discuss.

7. I claimed that the increased income as a result of lowering the marginal tax rate represented a net improvement. Suppose one could somehow impose a negative tax rate—on the margin, for every dollar you earn, the government gives you $.20. Putting aside, for a moment, the problem of where the government gets the money, would the resulting increase in the number of hours people worked represent an improvement or a worsening? Explain your answer.

8. Combine your answers to Problems 6 and 7 to describe a tax system which, in a world where everyone is identical, would result in everyone paying a negative marginal rate. Is this better or worse than whatever system you described in answering Problem 6? Discuss.

9. Repeat my analysis of the allocational effect of moving from a progressive to a flat rate system, using supply and demand curves for labor. (This is a hard problem.)

10. Repeat the analysis using indifference curve diagrams to show the choice between leisure and income, as in Chapter 5. (This is a hard problem.)

11. I demonstrated that, in a world where everyone is identical, moving from a graduated to a flat rate system is an improvement. Does the conclusion depend on the supply curve for labor not being backward bending? (This is a very tricky question; my editor, who has a Ph.D. in economics, got it wrong.)

Chapter 17

Market Failures

TRANSACTION COSTS: BARTER, MARRIAGE, AND MONEY

So far, I have always assumed that if there is a possibility for a trade—if I am willing to sell something at a price at which you are willing to buy it—the trade occurs. I have ignored both the problems of finding a trading partner and negotiating a trade and the associated *transaction costs*.

Barter vs Money

The simplest form of trade is barter; I trade goods that I have and you want for goods that you have and I want. This raises a problem. I must find a trading partner who has what I want *and* wants what I have—what economists call a "double coincidence of wants." In a simple society in which there are only a few goods being traded, this may not be a serious problem; but in a complicated society such as ours, it is. If I want to buy a car, I first look in the classified ads to find someone who is selling the kind of car I want, then call him up and ask him if he wants to be taught economics in exchange for his car. This drastically reduces the number of potential trading partners.

The solution is the development of money—some good which almost everyone is willing to accept in exchange. Money usually starts out as some kind of a good (gold, cloth, cattle—the word *pecuniary* comes from the Latin word for cattle) valued for its own uses; people are willing to accept it even if they do not intend to consume it, because they know they can later exchange it for something else. Since the good is widely accepted, it is useful to everybody (as a means of exchange); hence it becomes still more widely accepted. In a money economy, I find one person who wants what I have, sell it to him, and then use the money to buy what I want from someone else.

The advantage of money is obvious; the disadvantage is that you cannot eat it or wear it (exception—wadmal, wool cloth used as money in medieval Iceland). If markets are "thin"—if there are few people buying or selling—the individual who chooses to hold a stock of money may find that he cannot easily exchange it for what he needs when he needs it.

Thin markets cause two different problems for someone who wants to buy or sell. The first is that there may be nobody who wants what he is selling today or is selling what he wants to buy; the mere process of locating a trading partner may be expensive and time consuming. The second is that if he does find a trading partner, he becomes part of a bilateral monopoly—one buyer, one seller. Bilateral monopoly, for reasons discussed in an earlier chapter, can lead to substantial transaction costs—time and energy spent haggling over the price, and deals that do not get made because of a breakdown in bargaining.

In a society in which markets are thin and the number of traded commodities is small enough so that the double coincidence problem is not too serious, individuals may find it more convenient to hold wealth for trading in the form of goods rather than money. This was probably the situation in early medieval Europe. Coins existed and were used in exchange; but barter was, for several centuries, more common.

A Market We All Know and Love

In order to understand the difficulties of barter, it is useful to consider the large-scale barter market of which you are all part—the marriage/dating/sex market. The reason this is a barter market is that if I am going with or married to you, you are necessarily going with or married to me. Hence I must find a woman whom I want and who wants me—the double coincidence of wants. Sex can, of course, occur as a money rather than a barter transaction, but that is inefficient compared to "normal" (i.e., barter) sex. A transaction that would produce benefits for both parties if they were properly matched is producing benefits for only one and is producing costs for the other—which the party who benefits must pay for. Suppose a bureaucrat-god rearranged that particular market outcome so that all of the former prostitutes were with men they *wanted* to be with and all the surplus customers were paired with women who wanted a husband or lover if only they could find the right man (and for whom that particular surplus customer was the right man). Surely the result would be a very large net benefit.

We observe, in this market, large search costs, long search times, lots of frustrated and/or lonely people of both sexes—in other words, a market where traders have a hard time getting together, due largely to the high transaction costs of barter.

PUBLIC GOODS AND EXTERNALITIES

In Chapter 1, I pointed out that even if every individual in a group behaves rationally, the result may be undesirable—for every individual. This happens when one person's actions impose costs or benefits on others. The examples I gave in Chapter 1 involved students cutting across the lawn and fighters running away in battle, shooting their weapons without aiming them, or not shooting at all. In such situations, the rationality of the individual does not imply that the group acts as if it were rational.

The rest of this chapter will be devoted to a discussion of situations of this sort. I will start with a number of specific examples, and then go on to explain the two general categories under which such problems are usually classed in economics—public goods and externalities.

Good for Each May Not Be Good for All: Some Examples

I will give four examples of conflicts between the individual rationality of the members of a group and their welfare. Two—the first and the last—are situations which should be familiar to every reader over the age of 17. A third is a widely discussed public policy issue with which I hope that most of you have had no personal experience. The remaining example—The Prisoner's Dilemma—is an imaginary case popular with economists and game theorists; many people who are neither find the analysis disturbingly counterintuitive.

To Vote or Not to Vote? In deciding whether to vote in the next election, one should consider both costs and benefits. The costs are fairly obvious—a certain amount of time standing in line and additional time spent studying issues and candidates in order to decide how to vote. The benefits are of two sorts—benefits *of* voting and benefits *produced by* voting. An example of the first sort might be your feeling of having done your civic duty or your pleasure at voting against a candidate you particularly dislike.

The second sort of benefit comes from the effect of your vote on the outcome of the election. In evaluating such benefits, you should consider two questions—how important it is that the right candidate win and how likely it is that your vote will affect the outcome. In most large elections, the probability that your vote will affect the outcome is very small; in a presidential election, it is well under one in a million. Unless getting the right person elected is immensely valuable to you—so valuable that you are willing to bear the costs of voting in exchange for one chance in a million of influencing the outcome—the effect of your vote on the election is not a good reason for voting unless you expect the election to be extraordinarily close. If you vote anyway—because you enjoy voting or because you believe that good citizens vote or because you like being part of a history-making event reported on nationwide television—the effect of your vote on the election is not likely to be enough of an incentive to make you go to much trouble to be sure you are voting for the best candidate.

The usual response to arguments of this sort is either "You are saying people should be selfish" or "What if everyone did that?" The answer to the first is that I have not assumed that you are selfish in any conventional sense of the word. I assume you are concerned with costs and benefits, but I include as a benefit the achieving of any "unselfish" objectives you happen to have. Obviously individuals have objectives that are not selfish in any narrow sense—they value the welfare of their children, their friends, and (to a lesser degree) people they do not even know. One reason you might put a high value on electing the right candidate is the belief that doing so will benefit not only yourself but hundreds of millions of other people. If you were so altruistic as to give the same weight to the welfare of every other person as to your own, then the benefit of electing the right candidate would be hundreds of millions of times as great as the direct benefit to you. That might be a sufficient reason to spend an hour or two voting, even if you realized that all you were buying was one chance in a million of influencing the outcome of the election. Casual observation suggests that few people are that altruistic.

The question "What if everybody acted like that?" can be answered in two ways. The first is to point out that if enough people refrained from voting, the remaining voters would each have a substantial chance of influencing the outcome of the election, and it would then pay them to vote. The equilibrium would be a situation in which the (say) ten thousand most concerned citizens voted.

The second answer to the question "What if everybody acted like that?" is to point out that the question implicitly assumes that true beliefs must have desirable consequences—and hence that beliefs with undesirable consequences must be false. There is no reason why this must always be so. Perhaps it is true both that "Sensible people will not vote" and that if everyone acts on that principle the consequences will be bad. If so, it might be wise for me not to tell you that sensible people do not vote, but that does not make it untrue. A statement may be both true and dangerous. The previous sentence is such a statement—since it provides ammunition for those who wish to argue against free speech.

The apparent paradox—that if everyone correctly perceives how to act in his own interest and does so, everyone may be worse off as a result—comes from the fact that different people have different objectives. Suppose there are a hundred of us, each of whom can individually choose action A or action B. Action A gives me $10 and costs the rest of you a total of $20—similarly for everyone else. As long as we are acting separately, it is in the interest of each of us to take action A—and the result is that we are all worse off than if we had all taken action B. The problem is that I only control what action I take—and I am better off taking A than B. I am worse off because you took A, and you are worse off because I took A; but what I control is my action, not yours, and similarly for you. This, of course, is the problem we encountered long ago in the discussion of why soldiers run away.

The Prisoner's Dilemma. A simple and striking example of such a situation is the "prisoner's dilemma." Two men are arrested and charged with jointly committing a crime. They are put in separate cells. The D.A. goes to the first and makes the following offer:

> If you confess to the crime and agree to testify against your accomplice, and if he refuses to confess, I will let you off with a token fine of $100. If you stay silent and he confesses, I will certainly get a conviction and will impose the maximum possible fine of $1,000. If both of you confess, I will impose a fine of $600 on each of you. If you both stay silent, I may not get a conviction, but I can force you to spend $200 each on lawyer's fees in order to get off. I am going to make exactly the same offer to your fellow criminal.

In analyzing the prisoner's decision, we assume that the D.A. is telling the truth and that the costs he has listed are the only costs relevant to the decision;

obviously if a prisoner believes he will be murdered if he testifies, that will change the situation. The choices available to the two prisoners are shown in Table 17-1; in each box, the upper number is the cost of that outcome to the first prisoner, and the lower number is the cost to the second prisoner. In considering what he should do, the first prisoner reasons as follows:

If my accomplice stays silent and I stay silent, it will cost me $200; if he stays silent and I confess, it will cost me $100. So if I expect him to stay silent, I am better off confessing.

If he confesses and I stay silent, it will cost me $1,000; if I confess, it will cost only $600. So if I expect him to confess, I should confess too.

Whatever I expect my accomplice to do, I am better off confessing. Therefore I will confess.

Table 17-1

| | | First Prisoner's Choices | |
		Confess	Not Confess
Second Prisoner's Choices	Confess	$600 $600	$1,000 $100
	Not Confess	$100 $1,000	$200 $200

The other prisoner reasons in exactly the same way. Both prisoners confess, and each receives a $600 fine. If both had remained silent, each would have paid $200. They are worse off than if they had both stayed silent, yet each has acted rationally. If this situation makes you uncomfortable, you have plenty of company.

Plea Bargaining: A Real-World Prisoner's Dilemma. A *plea bargain* is an arrangement by which a prosecutor, instead of trying a defendant on a charge of, say, first-degree murder, allows the defendant to plead guilty to a lesser charge, such as second-degree murder or manslaughter. It is widely criticized as a way of letting criminals off lightly. In fact, it is likely that the existence of plea bargaining results in criminals being punished, on average, more severely rather than less. If plea bargaining were abolished—as some people suggest it should be—it is likely that average sentences would become lighter, not heavier.

How can this be? Surely the criminal will only plead guilty to the lesser charge if doing so is in his interest—which means that a certain conviction on the less serious charge is preferable, for him, to whatever he believes the chance is of being convicted on the more serious charge. True. But the chance of a conviction depends on what resources, of money and time, the prosecution spends on that particular case—which in turn depends on how many other cases had to go to trial and how many were settled by plea bargaining.

Suppose there are 100 cases per year, and the district attorney has a budget of $100,000. He can only spend $1,000 on each case, with the result that 90 percent of the criminals get acquitted. With plea bargaining, the D.A. concentrates his resources on the 10 criminals who refuse to accept the bargain he offers. He spends $10,000 prosecuting each of them and gets a conviction rate of 50 percent. As a result, each criminal deciding whether to accept the D.A.'s offer knows that if he refuses, he has about a 50 percent chance of being convicted—so he accepts any offer that he prefers to a 50 percent chance of conviction. On average, all the criminals, both the ones who accept the bargain and the ones who do not, are worse off—more severely punished—than if the D.A. prosecuted all of them on the more severe charge and convicted one in ten. Each individual criminal benefits by accepting the D.A.'s offer—but by doing so, he frees resources that the D.A. can then use against another criminal, raising the average conviction rate. The higher conviction rate makes criminals willing to accept worse bargains (i.e., ones implying more severe punishment). All of the criminals would be better off if none of them accepted the D.A.'s offer, but each is better off accepting. This is the prisoner's dilemma in real life.

Why Traffic Jams. This is a situation in which each individual takes the action that is in his individual interest; they are all, as a result, worse off than if they had acted differently. A more familiar example of such a situation occurs twice a day, five days a week, about two blocks from where I used to live. The time is rush hour; the scene is the intersection of Wilshire Boulevard and Westwood Avenue in Los Angeles, said to be the busiest intersection in the world. As the light on Wilshire goes green, ten lanes of traffic surge forward. As it turns yellow, a last few cars try to make it across. Since Wilshire is packed with cars, they fail and end up in the intersection, blocking the cars on Westwood, which now have a green light. Gradually the cars in the intersection make it across, allowing the traffic on Westwood to surge forward—just as the light changes, trapping another batch of cars in the intersection.

If drivers on both streets refrained from entering the intersection until there was clearly enough room for them on the far side, the jam would not occur. Traffic would flow faster, and they would all get where they are going sooner. Yet each individual driver is behaving rationally. My aggressive driving on Wilshire benefits me (I may make it across before the light changes, and at worst I will get far enough into the intersection not to be blocked by cars going the other way at the next stage of the jam) and harms drivers on Westwood. Your aggressive driving on Westwood benefits you and harms drivers (possibly including me) on Wilshire. The harm is much larger than the benefit, so on net we are all worse off. But I receive all of the benefit and none of the harm from the particular decision that I control. I am correctly choosing the action that best achieves my objectives—but if we each made a mistake and drove less aggressively, we would all be better off.

My point—in this and the previous examples—is not that rationality implies selfishness. That is a parody of economics. Drivers may value other people's time as well as (although probably not as much as) their own. In Chapter 20, we will discuss the economics of *altruism*—the behavior of people who value the happiness of other people. If drivers value the welfare of other drivers, rationality may prevent the jam instead of causing it.

The point—which to some readers may seem paradoxical—is that rational behavior by every individual in a group may sometimes lead to an outcome that is undesirable in terms of precisely the same objectives (getting home earlier in this case or getting a light sentence or surviving a battle in some of the other cases we have discussed) that each individual's rational behavior is correctly calculated to achieve. Such situations generally involve what economists call "public goods" or "externalities," two concepts which we will now discuss.

Public Goods

There are a number of different, closely related definitions of a *public good*. I prefer to define it as "a good such that, if it is produced at all, the producer cannot control who gets it." The public good *problem* arises because the producer of a public good cannot, like the producer of an ordinary ("private") good, tell the consumer that he can only have it if he pays for it; the consumer knows that if it is produced at all, the producer has no control over who gets it.

One example of a public good is a radio broadcast; if it is made at all, anyone who owns a radio and lives in the right area can receive it. This example demonstrates several important things about public goods. The first is that whether or not a good is public depends on the nature of the good. It is not that the producer *should* not control who gets it but that he *cannot*; or, at least, he can control who gets it, if at all, only at a prohibitively high cost (hiring detectives to creep around people's houses and arrest them if they are listening to the broadcast without having paid for it). While the "publicness" of a good may be affected by the legal system (whether it is legal to listen to a broadcast without the broadcaster's permission), it is mostly just a fact of nature; even if it were legal to forbid "unauthorized" listening, the law would be prohibitively expensive to enforce.

A second important thing to note about a public good is that it is *not* defined as a good produced by the government. In this country, radio broadcasts are mostly private; they are still public goods. Many of the things government does produce, such as mail delivery, are private goods; the government can and does refuse to deliver your letter if it does not have a stamp on it. The fact that a good is public presents a problem to a private producer—the problem of how to get paid for producing it—but the problem is not necessarily an insoluble one, as the example of a radio broadcast illustrates.

Private Production of Public Goods. There are a number of ways in which the problem of producing public goods privately may be solved. One, which works best if the size of the "public"—the group of people who will receive the good if it is produced—is small, is a unanimous contract. The producer gets all the members of the public together, tells them how much he wants each to pay toward the cost of producing the good, and announces that unless each agrees to chip in if everyone else does, the good will not be produced.

Assume that they believe him. Consider the logic of the situation from the standpoint of a single member of the group deciding whether he should agree to chip in. He argues as follows:

Either someone else is going to refuse, in which case the deal falls through, I get my money back, and my agreement costs me nothing, or else everyone else is going to agree. If everyone else agrees and I refuse, I do not have to pay for the public good, but I also do not get it. So as long as the good is worth more to me than my share of the cost, I ought to agree.

The same argument applies to everyone, so if the public good is worth more to the consumers than it costs to produce, the entrepreneur should be able to divide up the cost among the "public" in such a way that each individual finds it in his interest to agree.

One difficulty with this is that if the public is large, it may be hard to organize a unanimous contract. A solution is to find a "privileged minority"—a subgroup of the public that is small enough so that its members can form their own unanimous contract and that receives enough benefit from the public good so that its members can be persuaded to bear the whole cost. When I mow my front lawn, I am acting as a privileged minority (of one); the mowed lawn makes the neighborhood more attractive, benefiting everyone, but I receive enough of the benefit to be willing to pay the whole cost.

Consider how this might work in the case of one of the largest public goods in our society and one of the most difficult to produce privately—national defense. Imagine that the inhabitants of Hawaii believe that there is a 10 percent chance of a nuclear strike against their island next year. If the strike occurs, the island will be wiped out. The inhabitants can flee the island before the attack, so the cost will be distributed roughly in proportion to the value of the land they own. Table 17-2 is an (entirely imaginary) listing of how land ownership is divided on the island and how much each owner would pay, if necessary, to prevent the attack.

Table 17-2

Landowner	Value of Land	Value of Defense
Dole Pineapple	$500,000,000	$50,000,000
Hilton Hotels	$400,000,000	$40,000,000
United Fruit Co.	$300,000,000	$30,000,000
Maxwell House Coffee	$250,000,000	$25,000,000
Howard Johnson's	**$200,000,000**	**$10,000,000**
Everyone Else	$900,000,000	$90,000,000

Suppose an entrepreneur comes up with a system for defending Hawaii from nuclear attack at a cost of $100 million. He goes to Dole, Hilton, United Fruit, and Maxwell House and tells them that if they pay him $110 million, he will defend the island. Since the value of the defense is more than that and since there are only a few firms that have to agree, they raise the money.

In this case, the story has a happy ending. Suppose, however, that the total cost of the defense were $149 million. In that case, it is still worth having—the top five landowners alone value it at more than its cost—but it will be very hard to get. If the entrepreneur asks the Big 5 to each put up the same proportion of the value of their land (just under 10 percent), Howard Johnson will refuse. Unfortunately for Hawaii, the Howard Johnson firm is run by an optimist who believes the chance of an attack is only 5 percent and therefore is willing to pay only 5 percent of his land value to protect against the attack.

If the information on Table 17-2 were a matter of public knowledge, agreement could still be reached, with Howard Johnson contributing at half the rate (as a fraction of land value) of the other four. The problem is that the other contributors are likely to view Howard Johnson's "optimism" as a bargaining ploy—a way to get them to bear more than their share of the cost. If there is no simple rule for dividing up the cost of defense, agreement on who pays what may well be impossible.

The larger the number of people whose agreement is needed and the less obvious it is how much each values what he is getting, the harder it will be to get agreement. If the public good is cheap—if defense costs only $40 million— the problem is soluble; the entrepreneur can either leave Howard Johnson out of the contract or else charge *everyone* 5 percent of land value and still raise enough money. But if the cost of the public good is a large fraction of the benefit it produces and if the benefit is spread among many people, raising the money is a serious and perhaps insoluble problem.

In the example discussed, the concentration of land ownership in Hawaii greatly simplified the situation. The Big 5 were a privileged minority; they received a large fraction of the total benefit, so the entrepreneur could, with luck, raise the money he needed from them while ignoring the large number of small holders. The term "privileged minority," which is commonly used in this way, has always struck me as somewhat strange, since the minority has the "privilege" of paying for what all the other members of the public get.

Arranging contracts of the sort I have been describing is one solution to the problem of producing a public good. Another solution is to convert the public good temporarily into a private good. Suppose the public good is flood control; building a dam will reduce floods in the valley below, increasing the value of farm land there. One way to pay for the dam is for the entrepreneur to buy up as much as possible of the land in the valley (or buy options on the land at its current price), build the dam, then sell the land back (or sell the options back to the owners). Since the new flood protection makes the land worth more than when he bought it, he should be able to get a higher price than he paid, for either the land or the options.

Another ingenious solution, which would never have occurred to me if I had not seen it in operation, is to combine two public goods and give away the package. The first public good has a positive cost of production and a positive value to the customer; the second has a negative cost of production and a negative value to the customer. The package has zero or negative cost of production and positive value to the consumer. This is how radio and television broadcasts are produced; the first good is the program and the second the commercial. Commercials have a negative cost of production, from the standpoint of the broadcaster, since he gets paid by the sponsor to broadcast them. Since there is generally no convenient way to listen to the program without hearing the commercials, the listener must choose to accept or reject a "package deal"— program plus commercial. If the net value of the package is positive to him, he will accept it. If the net cost (cost of operating the station minus payment from the sponsor) is negative, or in other words if advertising revenues more than cover operating expenses, the broadcaster can and will stay in business.

An interesting example of the public good problem, and several interesting solutions, occur in the computer industry. A $500 computer program can be copied onto a $5 floppy disk. Programs can be protected against copying, but this is inconvenient for the user, who would like at least one backup copy in case his original gets damaged and may also find it convenient to copy several of the programs he has purchased onto one disk. Even if programs are protected, someone with a reasonable amount of expertise can frequently "break" the protection—figure out how to copy them. There are even programs on the market designed to copy copy-protected programs. In one case, a program capable of copying other copy-protected programs is copy-protected against itself; a second company sells a program to copy *it*!

If you cannot effectively copy-protect a program, then selling it to one person means, in effect, giving it to everyone. The program is then a public good and figuring out how to make money producing it is a public good problem. Firms that produce and sell software have come up with a number of ingenious solutions. One of them is "bundling." You sell a computer along with a bundle of programs designed to run on that particular computer; in effect you charge for the programs in the price of the computer. Anyone can copy the programs—but to use them, he has to buy the computer.

Another kind of "bundling" also used to solve the problem is to sell a package consisting of a program plus service—a voice on the other end of a telephone to answer questions about how to make the program work. The seller keeps track of who bought the program and only gives help to registered owners. One computer magazine spoofing this approach described an imaginary company (Kitchen Table Incorporated) that produced a program (DrossDos) designed to be easily copied (the instruction manual was only legible after it was xeroxed). They sold three copies, a million were "pirated" (illegally copied)—then they sold each of the million pirates the information on how to fix the program so it would work.

As these examples suggest, there are a variety of ways in which public goods can be privately produced. Each of these may succeed, under some circumstances, in producing some quantity of a public good. None of them can be expected to lead to an efficient level of production in the strong sense in which we have been using the term—an outcome so good that it could not be improved by a bureaucrat-god. Typically, the private producer of a public good succeeds in collecting only part of the additional value of each unit of the good produced. He produces up to the point where what he gets for an additional unit (an additional hour of broadcasting, or an additional dollar spent making the program better) is equal to what it costs him. That is a lower level of output than the efficient point where marginal cost equals marginal value to the consumer.

To see more clearly the sense in which private production of public goods is inefficient, consider some of our examples. In the Hawaiian defense case, Hawaii was worth defending as long as the cost was less than $245 million, since that was the total value of the defense to all the inhabitants put together. If the cost of the defense happened to be only $40 million, private arrangements might produce it, which is the efficient outcome. If the cost were $235 million, it is unlikely that the defense would be produced; since it still costs less than its value, a bureaucrat-god who ordered Hawaii defended would be producing a net benefit. So if the cost of defending Hawaii is $235 million, private production results in an inefficient outcome. Hawaii is worth defending—and is undefended. So the private production of public goods is inefficient in the sense of sometimes leading to an inefficient outcome—failing to produce a good that is worth producing.

So far, we have assumed that there are only two possible "amounts" of defense—none or enough. Whether or not that is plausible in the case of defense, the equivalent assumption is obviously wrong for radio broadcasts or computer programs; in each case, the manufacturer decides how much he will spend and what quality of product he will produce. The efficient outcome is one in which he makes all quality improvements that are worth more to the consumers than they cost him to make. But from his standpoint, improvements are worth making only if they increase his revenue by at least as much as they cost. Since he will generally be able to collect only part of the value he produces, there will generally be improvements worth making that he does not find it in his interest to make, so here again the outcome could be improved by a bureaucrat-god. The good may be produced, but it is generally underproduced—an increase in quality, number of hours of broadcasting, or some other dimension above the level the producer finds it in his interest to produce would result in net benefits. Hence private production of public goods is generally inefficient in the technical sense in which I have been using the word.

Public Production of Public Goods. One common solution to this problem is to have the government produce the good and pay for it out of taxes. This may or may not be an improvement on imperfect private production. The problem is that the mechanism by which we "control" the government and try to make it act in our interest—voting—itself involves the private production of a public good. As I pointed out earlier in this chapter, when you spend time and energy deciding which candidate best serves the general interest and then voting accordingly, most of the benefit of your expenditure goes to other people. You are producing a public good—a vote for the better candidate. That is a very hard public good to produce privately, since the public is a very large one—the whole population of the country. Hence it is underproduced—very much underproduced. The underproduction of that public good means that people do not find it in their interest to spend much effort deciding who is the best candidate—which in turn means that democracy does not work very well, so we cannot rely on the government to act in our interest.

If we cannot rely on the government to act in our interest, we cannot rely on it to produce the efficient quantity of public goods. Just as with a government agency regulating a natural monopoly, the administrators controlling the public production of a public good may find that their own private interest, or the political interest of the administration that appointed them, does not lead them to maximize economic welfare.

Even if the government wishes to produce the "right" amount of a public good, it faces problems similar to the problems of regulators trying to satisfy the second efficiency condition. In order to decide how much to produce, the government must know how much potential consumers value the good. In an ordinary market, the producer measures the demand curve by offering his product at some price and seeing how many he sells. The producer of a public good cannot do that, since he cannot control who gets the good, so the government must find some indirect way of estimating demand. Individuals who want the public good have an incentive, if asked, to overstate how much they want it—which means that a public opinion poll may produce a very poor estimate of demand.

In dealing with the public good problem, just as in dealing with the closely related problem of natural monopoly, we are faced with a choice among different imperfect ways of solving the problem, some private and some governmental. None of the alternatives can be expected to generate an optimal result. As I pointed out earlier, the fact that something is inefficient means that it could be improved by a bureaucrat-god. That does not necessarily mean that it can be improved by us, since we do not have any bureaucrat-gods available.

As you may have realized by now, public good problems of one sort or another are very common—indeed many common problems, both "public" and private, can be viewed as public good problems. One example is the problem of getting anything accomplished in a meeting. Most of us like attention; when we are in a meeting and happen to have the floor, we take the opportunity not only to say what we have to say about the issue on hand but also to show how clever, witty, and wise we are. This imposes a cost on other people (unless we really are witty and wise); if there are sixty people in the room, every minute I speak costs a person-hour of listener time. Brevity, in this case, is a public good—and hence underproduced.

At the beginning of this section, I mentioned that different economists use slightly different definitions of a public good. The definition I have used emphasizes "non-excludability"—the inability of the producer to control which consumers get the good. The other characteristic usually associated with a public good is that one person's use does not reduce the amount available for someone else. A different way of stating this is to say that the marginal cost of producing the good is zero on the margin of "how many people get it," although there may still be a cost to producing more on the margin of "how good it is" (consider television broadcasts). Something which is a public good in only this sense (it has zero marginal cost, but the producer can control who gets it) is simply a natural monopoly with MC = 0. Since the problems associated with natural monopoly have already been discussed, I prefer to concentrate on the inability of the producer to control who consumes the good, which seems to me to be the essential characteristic of public goods responsible for the special problems associated with them.

Externalities

The long-winded speaker is underproducing the public good of brevity. Another, and equivalent, way of describing the situation is to say that he is overproducing his speech. The problem can be described either as underproduction due to the public good problem or as overproduction due to the existence of an externality.

An *externality* is a cost or benefit that my action imposes on you. Familiar examples—in addition to the cost of listening to me talk too long in a meeting—are pollution (a negative externality—a cost) and scientific progress as a result of theoretical research (a positive externality—a benefit). Externalities are all around us—when I paint my house or mow my lawn, I confer positive externalities on my neighbors; when you smoke in a restaurant or play loud music in the dorm at 1:00 a.m., you confer negative externalities on yours.

The problem with externalities is that you, rationally enough, do not take them into account in deciding whether or not to smoke or play the music; hence you may do so even when the total cost (including the cost to your neighbors) is greater than the total benefit, so that there would be a net gain if you stopped. Similarly, I may fail to mow my lawn this week because the total benefit *to me* is less than the cost, even though the total benefit (including the benefit to my neighbors) is more.

As you can see by these examples, "externalities" and "public goods" are really different ways of describing the same problems. A positive externality is a public good; a negative externality is a "negative" public good and refraining from producing it is a positive public good. In some cases, it may be easier to look at the problem one way, in some cases the other—but it is the same problem.

Efficient Pollution and How to Get It: The Public Solution. The "textbook" solution to externalities is to impose the cost on, or give the benefit to, the producer. If I am benefiting others by scientific research, subsidize me; if I am polluting the air, charge me an "effluent fee" of so many dollars per cubic foot of pollution emitted, corresponding to the costs that my pollution imposes on others. I will continue to pollute only if the net value of what I am doing is more than the damage done—in which case, pollution is efficient.

"Pollution" is a loaded word. To be in favor of pollution sounds like being in favor of evil; the phrase "an efficient level of pollution," lifted from a book like this one, would be fine ammunition for a speech on the inhumanity of economics—and economists.

If you find the idea that some amount of pollution is desirable a shocking one, consider that carbon dioxide is commonly regarded as a pollutant, and the only way you can stop producing it is to stop breathing. This is an extreme case, but it makes an important point—that the real issue is whether, in any particular case, the costs of pollution are greater than the costs of not polluting.

While there is, in this sense, an efficient level of pollution, it is not clear how to get that level. The problem with using effluent fees to control externalities is the same as the problem with government provision of public goods; it depends on the government finding it in its interest to act in the interest of the public and knowing how to do so. Just as in previous cases, "knowing how" includes somehow estimating the value of something to people by some method other than offering it at a price and seeing whether they take it. The result of the governmental solution may be better or worse than the alternatives of either accepting the overproduction of negative externalities and the underproduction of positive ones, or dealing with the problem in some imperfect private way.

Private Solutions. How might one control externalities privately? One (real-world) solution is a proprietary community. A developer builds a housing development and sells the houses with the requirement that the buyer must join the neighborhood association. The neighborhood association either takes care of lawns, painting, and other things that affect the general appearance of the community or requires the owners to do so. A friend of mine who lived in such a community could not change the color of his front door without his neighbors' permission. This sounds rather like government coercion masquerading as a private contract, but there are two important differences. It is in the private interest of the developer to set up the best possible rules, in order to maximize the price for which he can sell the houses. And nobody is forced to purchase a house and membership from that developer; if the package is not more attractive than any alternative, the customer can and will go elsewhere.

Another solution that is in one sense governmental and in another sense private is the definition and enforcement of property rights in whatever is affected by the externality. An example is the case of British trout streams. Trout streams in Britain are private property. Each stream is owned by someone—frequently the local fishing club. An industrial polluter dumping effluent into such a stream is guilty of trespass, just as if he dumped it on someone's lawn. If he believes the stream is more valuable as a place to dump his effluent than as a trout stream, it is up to him to buy it. If he believes (and the fishing club does not) that his effluent will not hurt the trout, he can buy the stream and then—if he is right—rent the fishing rights back to the previous owners.

As this example suggests, what is or is not an externality depends in part on how property rights are defined. When I produce an automobile, I am producing something of value to you—it is not an externality because I can control whether you get it and will refuse to give it to you unless you pay me for it. Some externality problems arise because property rights are not defined when they should be—fertilizing land or planting wheat would be an externality if land were not private property. Other problems arise because there is no way of defining property rights that does not lead to externalities in one direction or another. If I have to get your permission to play my stereo when you want to sleep, I can no longer impose an externality on you—but your decision to go to sleep when I want to play my stereo imposes an externality on me! If only two people are involved, they may be able to work out an efficient arrangement by mutual negotiation—but air pollution in Los Angeles affects several million people. For reasons I have already discussed, the costs of arranging to produce a public good privately become larger the larger the size of the public.

One way of looking at this is to say that all public good/externality problems are really transaction cost problems. If bargaining were costless, then the problems leading to inefficiency could always be solved—as long as there was some change which would produce net benefits, someone could put together a deal that would divide up the gain in such a way as to benefit all concerned. This argument has a name—it is called the *Coase Theorem*. Looked at in this way, the interesting question is always "What are the transaction costs that prevent the efficient outcome from being reached?"

Pecuniary Externalities

Suppose something I do imposes both positive and negative externalities, and by some coincidence they are exactly equal. I will, as always, treat the external costs and benefits as if they were zero—and in this case, I will be right; the *net* effect will be zero. Since on net all of the costs and benefits due to my actions are borne by me, I will make the "right" decision as to whether or not to do it. If it produces net benefits to me, I will do it; if not, I will not.

One would think it an unlikely coincidence for positive and negative externalities to precisely cancel; but there is an important situation, called a "pecuniary externality," in which that is exactly what happens. Whenever I decide to produce more or less of some good, to enter or leave some profession, to change my consumption pattern, or in almost any other way to alter my market behavior, one result is to slightly shift some supply or demand curve and so to change some price; this affects all other buyers and sellers of the good whose price has changed. In a competitive market, the change in price due to one person's actions is tiny— but in calculating the size of the effect, one must multiply the small change in price by the large quantity of goods for which the price has changed—the entire market. When, for example, I decide to become the million and first physician, the effect of my decision in driving down the wages of each existing physician is tiny, but it must be multiplied by a million physicians. The product is not necessarily negligible.

It appears that there can be no economic action without important externalities. But these are precisely the sort of externality that can be ignored. When price falls by a penny, what is lost by a seller is gained by a buyer; the loss to the physicians is a gain to their patients. The result is what is called a "pecuniary externality" or "transfer externality." My decision to buy or sell more or less has an effect on others, but it imposes neither *net* costs nor *net* benefits, so I can ignore it in deciding what to do without producing an inefficient outcome as a result.

Because of the problem of stating a "calculus argument" in English, the proof I have just given that such changes in price are only pecuniary externalities and can be ignored was slightly oversimplified. A change in price typically results in both a transfer and a change in quantity; the latter causes changes in total consumer and producer surplus which are not simply transfers. We may, however, ignore such changes in surplus when considering a competitive market. The reason can be seen by looking at Figure 17-1, which shows the effect on consumer surplus of a small increase in price. The transfer (the loss of consumer surplus that will be matched by an increase in producer surplus) equals the change in price times the total quantity being sold—the area of the colored rectangle A in Figure 17-1. The net change in consumer surplus is the area of the triangle B whose height is the change in price and whose base is the change in quantity. Since the change in quantity is approximately proportional to the change in price (for small changes), the area B becomes negligible compared to the area A as the change in price becomes very small. In a competitive market, the effect on price of any individual buyer or seller is small; that is the definition of a competitive

Figure 17-1

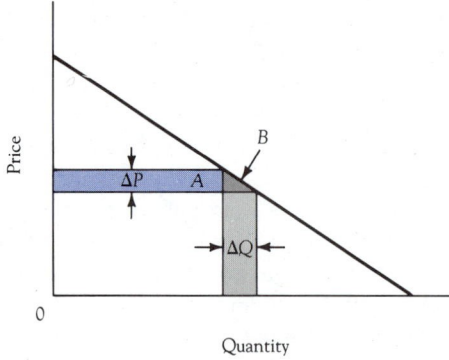

The effect on consumer surplus of a small increase in price. A is a transfer from consumers to producers; B is a net loss of surplus. As ΔP becomes very small, so does the ratio of B to A.

market. So in a competitive market, the effect of my action on prices results in only a pecuniary externality and may be ignored in calculations of the net effect on producer and consumer surplus.

Information as a Public Good

One cost associated with buying goods is the cost of acquiring information about what to buy. This may be one reason firms are as large as they are; brand names represent a sort of informational capital. There may be a better deal available from an unknown producer, but the cost of determining that it is a better deal may be greater than the savings. Not only do you know that the brand name product has been of good quality in the past, you also believe that the producer has an incentive to maintain the quality so as not to destroy the value of his brand name.

Why do we rely on brand names instead of buying information about the quality of goods from someone who specializes in producing such information? To some extent, we do buy information—by reading *Consumer Reports*, *Car and Driver*, or *Handgun Tests* and by taking economics courses. Yet much of the information we use we produce for ourselves—probably a much larger fraction than of most other things we consume. Since we do not have the time to become experts on everything we buy, we end up depending on brand names and other indirect (and very imperfect) ways of evaluating quality.

Why do we find we have to produce so much information for ourselves? Why is information a particularly hard good to produce and sell on the market?

The problem is that it is hard to protect the property rights of a producer of information. If I sell you a car, you can resell it only by giving up its use yourself. If I sell you a fact, you can both use that fact and make it available to all your friends and neighbors. This makes it difficult for those who produce facts to collect the value of what they produce; it is the same problem that I earlier discussed in the case of computer programs—which can be thought of as a kind of information. Information is in large part a public good; because it is a public good, it is underproduced.

One of the solutions to this problem, in our society, is the existence of large brand name retailers, such as Sears. Sears does not produce what it sells, but it does select it. You may buy any particular product only once every year or two, which makes it hard to judge which producer is best. But you buy something from Sears much more often, so it is easier for you to judge that Sears (or one of its competitors) "on average" gives you good value for your money. Sears is then in the business of learning which brands of the products it buys represent good value for the money and selling them to you under its brand name, thus implicitly selling you the information. By not telling you who really makes the product, it prevents you from reselling the information—to a friend who would then buy the same brand at a discount store. All you can tell your friend is to buy from Sears—which is fine with Sears.

Religious Radio: An Application of Public Good Theory

Whenever I spend much time listening to a variety of stations on the radio, I am struck by how many of them are religious. One could take this as evidence that America is a very religious country—except that the popularity of religion on the airwaves does not seem to be matched elsewhere. If I go to a newsstand or a bookstore, I see relatively few religious newspapers, magazines, or books—far fewer, as a percentage of the total, than for radio programs.

There is a simple explanation for this discrepancy. Publishers can control who gets their publications; broadcasters cannot control who listens to their broadcasts. So broadcasters, unlike publishers, are producing a public good and depend on some solution to the problem of producing a public good privately in order to stay in business.

Commercials are one solution to that problem; religion is another. The people who listen to religious broadcasters presumably believe in the religion. For most of them, that means that they believe in the existence of a god who rewards virtue and punishes vice. If, as many radio preachers claim, donating money to their programs is a virtuous act, then the program is no longer, for those listeners, a pure public good. The preacher may not know which listeners help pay for the show and which do not, but God knows. One of the benefits produced by the program is an increased chance of a heavenly reward; you are more likely to get that benefit if you pay for it. Thus religion provides a solution to the public-good problem.

Nothing in the analysis depends on whether the particular religion is or is not true; what matters is only that the listeners believe it is true and act accordingly. The result is that religious broadcasters have an advantage over secular broadcasters. Both produce programs that their listeners value, but the religious broadcaster is better able to get the listener to pay for them. The religious publisher has no corresponding advantage over the secular publisher. So religion is more common on the air than in print.

PROBLEMS

1. Describe two public good problems that you have confronted in the past year and discuss how they might be dealt with; you should not use any that are discussed in the chapter.
2. He: "I love you."
   She: "I love you too."
   What do economists call this fortunate situation?
3. In ordinary markets, supply and demand are balanced by price. Given that our customs prohibit, in most social contexts, cash payments as part of a date (or a marriage), what sorts of "prices" balance those markets in the U.S. at present? If supply and demand on the dating/sex/marriage market are not balanced (i.e., quantity supplied is not equal to quantity demanded—more men want to go out or have sex or get married than women, or vice versa), what mechanisms ration out the insufficient supply (i.e., decide which men get women, or vice versa)? What prices balance supply and demand for similar markets in other countries or have done so at other times?
4. How would the style of dating and marriage change if a war substantially reduced the ratio of men to women? How would it change if a lot of men migrated to the U.S., substantially raising the ratio of men to women?
5. "Heterosexual men are traditionally hostile to homosexual men. If they correctly considered their own interests, their attitude would be just the opposite." Discuss.
6. Does polygyny make women better or worse off? Discuss. Does it make some women better off and some women worse off? What about polyandry (one wife having several husbands)?
7. In the chapter, I explained the prevalence of barter during the early part of the Middle Ages as a response to circumstances in which money was not very useful; people used bread or cattle instead of coins because, although bread and cattle were not as convenient for buying things with, they were much more useful if nothing you wanted was for sale.

   An alternative explanation (by historians, not economists) is that Western Europe had an "unbalanced" trade, importing goods and exporting gold and silver, so that after a while there was "not enough" money for the economy to function.

   Figure 17-2 shows a (hypothetical) demand curve for gold money in medieval Europe; the price of money is shown in apples per ounce of gold. What

Figure 17-2

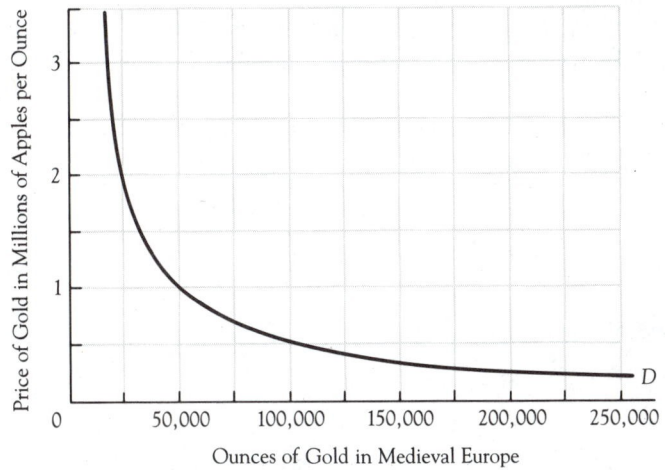

A hypothetical demand curve for gold in medieval Europe—Problem 7.

would happen if the total amount of gold in Europe declined from 100,000 ounces to 50,000 ounces? In what sense would there be "just as much" gold money after the change as before? Assuming that the demand curve has the shape shown, sketch an argument to refute the historians' explanation of what happened.

(Hint: You may find it useful to consider what would happen if every dollar bill in America suddenly twinned—turned into two dollar bills—along with corresponding increases in tens, twenties, checking accounts, and so on.)

8. A tape recorder can copy a recording of a concert onto a cassette just as a computer can copy a program onto a disk. Why is the problem of "pirating" (making copies without paying royalties) less serious in the case of tapes than in the case of programs?

9. In my experience, FM radio is less religious than AM; you may wish to check that conclusion for yourself. Can you suggest any reasons why? (I am not sure I know the answer to this one.)

10. Last year Bryan and Brian occupied separate apartments; each consumed 400 gallons per month of hot water. This year they are sharing a larger apartment. To their surprise, they find they are consuming 1,000 gallons per month. Explain.

11. " . . . another reason to contribute to our fund-raising campaign is self-interest. The money you give us will improve the quality and reputation of the University, raising the value of your degree. If each alumnus gave $100 . . ." (extract from a fund-raising letter). What is wrong with this argument? Why is it unlikely to succeed?

FOR FURTHER READING

An interesting discussion of barter in the Middle Ages is found, along with a number of other interesting discussions, in Carlo M. Cipolla, *Money, Prices, and Civilization in the Mediterranean World* (Staten Island, N.Y.: Gordian Press, 1967).

The Coase Theorem first appeared in Ronald Coase, "The Problem of Social Cost," *Journal of Law and Economics*, Vol. 3 (1960), pp. 1-44.

Section V

Applications — Conventional and Un

Chapter 18

The Political Marketplace

The purpose of this chapter is to use some of the ideas developed in previous chapters to understand the behavior of political institutions. It contains three parts. The first is an analysis of the effects of tariffs—in particular, the question of whether imposing a tariff is a Marshall improvement or a Marshall worsening. The second is a sketch of two variants of "public choice theory"—the economic analysis of government—intended in part to explain the inconsistency between the sorts of tariffs that economists can defend as efficient and the sorts that exist. The third part uses the concept of "rent seeking," introduced in Chapter 15 in a different context, to analyze the cost of government activity.

TARIFFS

Chapter 5 introduced the principle of comparative advantage and showed why such standard arguments for tariffs as "The Japanese can produce everything cheaper than we can" or "Tariffs protect American jobs" are wrong. Showing that particular arguments for tariffs are wrong is not the same thing as showing that tariffs are undesirable. In that chapter, trade was discussed mainly as one individual trading with another; in that context, there was a range of possible prices at which both parties could benefit from the exchange. Since at that point in the book, we had not yet seen how market prices were determined, we could not then analyze trade in terms of a market with many buyers, many sellers, and a single market price. Now we can.

In order to show that tariffs are undesirable, we would have to show not only that both sides can gain by trade but also that the particular prices and quantities which will occur under free trade are preferable to the result of any tariff. Whether we can do this depends both on what we assume about international markets and on whose interests we take into account in judging one arrangement superior to another—only the interests of Americans or the interests of both Americans and the people we trade with.

In the first section of this part of the chapter, I will prove that *if America as a whole is a price taker in international markets*, then American tariffs are undesirable even if we take into account only the interests of Americans—or, in other words, that the abolition of American tariffs would produce net benefits for Americans. The result will be proved once graphically and once verbally. In both cases, I will assume, for simplicity, that the U.S. imports one good (autos) and exports one good (wheat); the proof could be generalized to apply to any number of goods. I will also assume that both the American wheat industry and the American auto industry are competitive and that neither produces significant externalities. I will ignore transportation costs.

In the next section, I will show several exceptions to the general rule that tariffs are undesirable; in each case, the exception depends on dropping one of the assumptions used in the proof. Some of the exceptions are cases where tariffs may be desirable if we consider only the interests of Americans but not if we include the effect on foreigners; others are cases where the imposition of a particular tariff is a Marshall improvement even when we count the effects on everyone.

Having answered the question of what tariffs we *should* have, I will then, in the second part of the chapter, take up the question of what tariffs we *do* have—and why.

Why Tariffs Are Undesirable

I will start by listing the assumptions used in the proof. We assume only one good is imported (autos) and one good is exported (wheat). We assume that America is a price taker in international markets; in other words, changes in our production of wheat and consumption of autos are not sufficient to change the rate at which autos exchange for wheat abroad. The wheat and auto industries in the U.S. are price-taking industries with no substantial externalities.

The Geometric Proof. Figure 18-1 shows the supply curve for American production of automobiles and the demand curve for American consumption of automobiles, both before and after the imposition of a tariff. P_A is the market price before the tariff, P_A' after the tariff. Q_A is the quantity of imported cars before the tariff, Q_A' after. Figure 18-2 shows the corresponding curves, prices, and quantities for wheat.

The first thing that should strike you about Figure 18-1 is that at neither P_A nor P_A' is quantity supplied equal to quantity demanded. This is because the U.S. imports autos; quantity demanded (with or without a tariff) is equal to quantity supplied (by the U.S. auto industry) plus imports. Similarly, in Figure 18-2, I assume that the U.S. exports wheat. Quantity produced (by U.S. farmers) equals quantity demanded (by U.S. consumers) plus exports.

The next question that might occur to you concerns Figure 18-2. The tariff is on autos; why should it affect the price of wheat? The answer is that wheat is what we are sending foreigners in exchange for the autos they are sending us. If, because of the tariff, fewer dollars go abroad to buy foreign cars, then foreigners will have fewer dollars with which to buy American wheat. Foreign demand for American wheat falls; the price of wheat in America drops. This effect is shown on Figure 18-2.

Figure 18-1

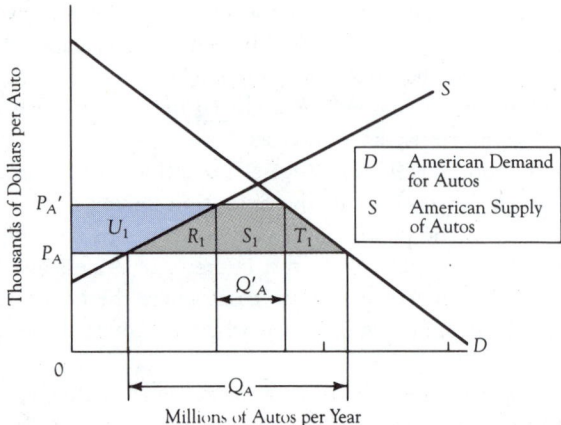

The effect on the domestic auto market of a tariff on autos. D and S are the domestic demand and supply curves for autos. Q_A is the rate at which autos are being imported before the tariff is imposed, Q'_A the rate after. P_A is the U.S. price of autos before, P'_A the price after.

Figure 18-2

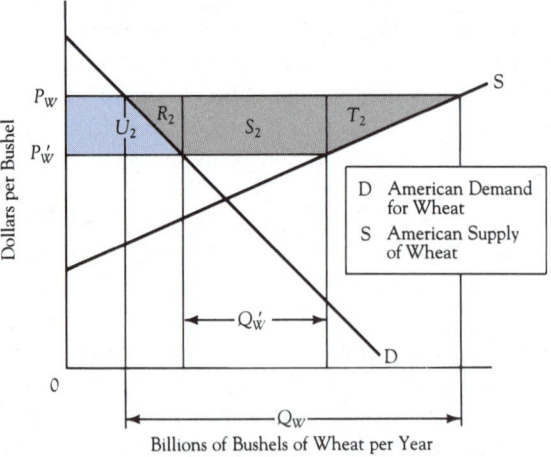

The effect on the domestic wheat market of a tariff on autos. D and S are the domestic demand and supply curves for wheat. Q_W is the rate at which wheat is being exported before the tariff is imposed, Q'_W the rate after. P_W is the U.S. price of wheat before, P'_W after.

The colored area U_1 on Figure 18-1 is the increase in (American) producer surplus as a result of the tariff; U_1 plus the shaded area $R_1 + S_1 + T_1$ is the reduction in (American) consumer surplus. The shaded area is the net loss (to Americans) of surplus on autos as a result of the tariff. Similarly, on Figure 18-2, U_2 is the gain in (American) consumer surplus as a result of the fall in the price of wheat produced by the tariff on automobiles, and $U_2 + R_2 + S_2 + T_2$ is the loss of (American) producer surplus. The shaded area $R_2 + S_2 + T_2$ is the net loss (to Americans) of surplus on wheat as an indirect result of the tariff on autos.

There is one more term to be considered in calculating the net effect of the tariff on Americans—the money actually collected by the tariff. If the tariff is \$$t$/ auto, the government collects t dollars on each of Q_A' autos imported each year, so its revenue from the tariff is $t \times Q_A'$. If that is larger than the sum of the two shaded areas, then the tariff produces net gains and is a Marshall improvement; if it is smaller, then the tariff is a Marshall worsening, and its abolition would be a Marshall improvement. What I am going to show is that the area $S_1 + S_2$ is equal to $t \times Q_A'$, the revenue collected by the tariff. Since $S_1 + S_2$ is only part of the cost of the tariff, that will imply that the total cost is larger than the revenue collected, and hence that the tariff produces net costs rather than net benefits.

I will use two relations implicit in the situation I have described. The first is that since America is assumed to be a price taker in international markets, the tariff does not affect the relative prices of autos and wheat outside the U.S. Before the tariff, the price ratio is P_A/P_W. After the tariff, the price of wheat abroad (in dollars) is P_W', the price of autos abroad is $P_A' - t$, so the price ratio is $(P_A' - t)/P_W'$.

How do I know that the world price of autos is $P_A' - t$? P_A' is the price of autos in the U.S. In order to get foreign autos into the U.S., you must pay their world price plus the tariff t; the price in the U.S. is P_A', so the world price must be $P_A' - t$.

Since the price ratio outside the U.S. is the same before and after the tariff, it follows that:

$$P_A/P_W = (P_A' - t)/P_W'. \tag{Eqn. 1}$$

Autos are, by assumption, our only import and wheat our only export, so the total number of dollars foreigners get for the cars they sell *to* us must equal the number of dollars they spend for the wheat they buy *from* us. Using prices and quantities after the tariff is imposed, this gives us:

$$P_W' \times Q_W' = \$\text{'s spent on wheat by foreigners} = \$\text{'s received for cars by}$$
$$\text{foreigners} = (P_A' - t)Q_A'. \tag{Eqn. 2}$$

(We spend P_A' on each car, but since t goes to the government to pay the tariff, only $P_A' - t$ goes to foreigners).

Finally, from Figures 18-1 and 18-2, we have:

$$S_1 + S_2 = (P'_A - P_A)Q'_A + (P_W - P'_W)Q'_W. \qquad \text{(Eqn. 3)}$$

Equations 1 and 2 imply that:

$$Q'_W = Q'_A(P'_A - t)/P'_W = Q'_A(P_A/P_W).$$

Substituting this into Equation 3 gives us:

$$S_1 + S_2 = Q'_A(P'_A - P_A) + Q'_A(P_A/P_W)(P_W - P'_W) =$$

$$Q'_A\{P'_A - P_A + (P_A/P_W)(P_W - P'_W)\} =$$

$$Q'_A\{P'_A - P_A + P_A - P'_W(P_A/P_W)\}.$$

If we cancel out $-P_A + P_A$ and use Equation 1 to replace P_A/P_W with $(P'_A - t)/P'_W$, we get:

$$S_1 + S_2 = Q'_A\{P'_A - P'_W(P'_A - t)/P'_W\} =$$

$$Q'_A(P'_A - P'_A + t) = Q'_A \times t.$$

$$\text{(Eqn. 4)}$$

Since $S_1 + S_2$ is only part of the net loss to American consumers and producers caused by the tariff and $Q'_A \times t$ is all of the revenue collected by the tariff, net loss is larger than revenue; the imposition of the tariff is a Marshall worsening and its abolition would be a Marshall improvement. This assumes that $R_1 + R_2 + T_1 + T_2 > 0$. If all the triangles were equal to 0 (if, for instance, all of the supply curves were perfectly inelastic—which seems implausible), then the tariff would produce net benefits of zero. The general result is that the tariff cannot make things better and is almost certain to make them worse.

The Verbal Proof. I have now proved my result—that if the U.S. is a price taker in international markets and American firms are price takers in domestic markets, American tariffs result in a net injury to Americans—mathematically. Next I will prove it again in another language—English.

From the standpoint of the U.S., foreign trade is a technology for turning wheat into autos at the rate P_A/P_W. We proved in Chapter 15 that a competitive industry (without externalities) is efficient. Hence the result of the competitive industry for turning wheat into autos is efficient. A tariff alters that result, taxing the conversion of wheat into autos and so reducing the quantity of wheat used and autos produced. That change could be made by a bureaucrat-god. A bureaucrat-god cannot improve an outcome that is already efficient—that is the definition of "efficient." Hence a tariff cannot be a Marshall improvement. Since it alters a situation that is already efficient, it is almost certain to be a Marshall worsening.

Capital in Action. There are two things I would like you to notice about what we have done so far in this chapter. The first is that our proofs are themselves examples of the use of capital in production. We have spent the previous 17 chapters accumulating intellectual capital—learning a complicated set of ideas, many of which must, at times, have seemed entirely useless. Using that capital, we have now, with a few pages of high school geometry and algebra plus a paragraph of reasoning, proved one of the more important practical results of economic theory—twice.

The second thing I would like you to notice is the contrast between the two proofs, a contrast typical of the differences between the two languages we used. The advantage of the verbal proof is that it helps us to intuit *why* tariffs are undesirable—provided we have previously learned to intuit why a competitive industry is efficient. Trade is simply a technology for converting exports into imports; a competitive industry uses that technology up to the point where the benefit of one more unit of imports is balanced by the cost of producing the exports that must be exchanged for it. A tariff adds an additional cost of production; the industry reduces its output, depriving some consumers of imported goods which they valued at more than their cost but less than their cost plus the tariff. The tariff is simply a tax on a particular way of producing things; the net loss is the resulting excess burden, just as with any other tax. It is zero only if either the demand or supply curve is vertical, in which case the tax does not affect quantity produced and consumed.

Does this conclusion depend on assuming that the U.S. is a price taker in international markets? For the mathematical proof, the answer is yes; that is how we got Equation 1, which was used twice in the proof. In the verbal proof, however, I said nothing at all about whether the U.S. *as a whole* was a price taker; all I assumed was that the export and import industries were price takers within the U.S. (and hence efficient). That is not at all the same thing. If U.S. agriculture consists of a million small farms, each farmer is a price taker; but if the U.S. produces 90 percent of the world's wheat, the U.S. as a whole is not—changes in how much wheat we export will affect world prices.

In fact, the verbal proof does depend on the U.S. being a price taker, but the reason is a somewhat subtle one. If the U.S. is not a price taker, then the quantity of wheat exported (and autos imported) affects the price ratio abroad, which means that it affects the rate at which we can convert wheat into autos. From the standpoint of the U.S., that is an externality; when I buy autos abroad, I drive up their price (and drive down the price of the wheat I use to pay for them), making it more expensive for *you* to buy autos abroad. If we think of trade as a way of converting wheat into autos, this is like a situation where my increased production of widgets somehow makes your widget factory less productive—which would be an externality. We know from Chapter 17 that a competitive industry with externalities does not generally produce an efficient outcome. So if the U. S. is a price searcher, the initial situation (without a tariff) is not efficient, and it is possible that a tariff may improve it.

From the standpoint of the world as a whole, the "externality" in question is a pecuniary externality, so it may be ignored; if my purchases of automobiles drive up the world price, that is a loss to the other buyers but a gain to the sellers. But if the buyers are Americans, the sellers are foreigners, and we consider only the interests of Americans, there is a net externality—we count the loss and ignore the gain. Hence if the U.S. is a price searcher in international markets, the outcome without tariffs is efficient if all interests are considered but inefficient if only American interests are.

The Exceptions—"Good" Tariffs

Three important assumptions went into the proof that tariffs were undesirable: that the U.S. was a price taker in international markets, that American import and export industries were price takers within the U.S., and that they had no important externalities. We will discuss the results of dropping two of them.

America as a Monopolist. Suppose the U.S. is not a price taker in international markets; suppose, for example, that we have a monopoly on wheat. Individual farmers are still price takers, so they produce up to the point where $MC = P$. All of the farmers taken together, however, would do better if they acted like a monopoly or a cartel, restricting their production and driving up price to the point where $MR = MC$. The government can produce that result by imposing an export tax—a sort of backwards tariff—on wheat. The export tax drives up the price of wheat abroad; Americans as a whole (including the government collecting the tax) gain just as they would if the farmers had gotten together and raised their price. The same result can also be produced by a tax on imports—an ordinary tariff. Importing and exporting are two sides of the same transaction—trading wheat for cars—so it does not matter at which point you impose the tax. It follows that if we are price searchers in international markets, a tariff may produce net benefits for us.

The same argument applies if we are price searchers as consumers of automobiles—monopsonists. In that case, a tariff on automobiles drives up their price in the U.S., lowers U.S. consumption, and so drives down the price of automobiles abroad. Since the U.S. is a net importer, we benefit by the lower price.

What happens in both of these cases is that without a tariff, individual Americans function as price takers in international markets even though America as a whole has some monopoly power. The tariff, in effect, creates a monopoly (or monopsony) out of a multitude of small firms. The result is a net gain at the expense of our trading partners. When we drive the international price of autos down (by imposing a tariff that decreases our consumption) or the international price of wheat up (by imposing an export tax on wheat), we benefit, since we are sellers of wheat and buyers of autos. Our trading partners lose, since they are buyers of wheat and sellers of autos. Just as in the (single-price) monopolies discussed earlier, the result is a net loss but a gain for the monopolist. Such a tariff is a Marshall improvement if we consider only gains and costs to Americans; it is a Marshall worsening if we include gains and losses to foreigners.

Protecting Infant Industries. A tariff designed to create monopoly profits for the nation that imposes it is one example of an "efficient" tariff, provided that we ignore the effect on foreigners. A second example, and one often used by supporters of tariffs, is a tariff to protect an "infant industry." This can, under some assumptions, result in an improvement even if we include the effects on foreigners.

Assume the U.S. has the potential to produce tin and export it but does not yet have a tin industry. A company which tries to start a tin foundry in the U.S. will have a hard time of it—American workers do not know how to work with tin, American railroads have no experience shipping tin and no special freight cars designed to carry it, and American coal mines have no experience at producing the particular kinds of coal needed to refine tin from tin ore. Until all those problems are solved, American tin will be more costly than imported tin. If only the tin industry could get established, it would be profitable, but nobody wants to be first. One solution is for the government to put a temporary tariff on imported tin and remove it once the "infant industry" is "large enough to compete."

One problem with the argument as stated is that if the tin industry is going to be profitable in the long run, tin companies should be willing to accept losses in the first few years, treating them as an investment to be paid back out of later profits. If companies are not willing to do that, perhaps the profits are not large enough, or certain enough, to make the losses worth taking.

To get around this argument, one must assume that the process of development occurs within the industry but outside the firm. No firm can do it by itself, but if they all do it together, workers will become skilled in working tin, subsidiary industries will grow up to support tin manufacture, and so on. Another way of putting this is that there are large positive externalities produced by the first few firms in an industry; while they are losing money producing tin, they are also producing a body of skills and knowledge in their employees and suppliers which will lower the costs of future producers.

If this is true, then since the initial firms do not include the (external) benefits they produce for others in calculating the value of what they produce, they may never start production—unless they are subsidized by a tariff that raises the cost of imported tin. This is the argument for an infant industry tariff. We have dropped the assumption that the firms in the industry have no important externalities; the result is that a tariff may be desirable—in other words, imposing it may be a Marshall improvement. In this case, unlike the previous one, a tariff may be desirable even if we take into account the interests of everyone concerned. If the U.S. has the potential to produce tin less expensively than it can be imported, the gains to the U.S. producers and their customers will ultimately outweigh the losses to foreign producers.

Should vs Will. So far, I have shown that tariffs are usually undesirable but that there are exceptions—situations where tariffs are desirable, at least from the standpoint of the countries that impose them. Is that why the U.S., and most other countries, have tariffs? Apparently not. The tariffs we observe in the real world have little resemblance to the ones that can be defended as economically desirable. It is not infant industries that get protection but senile industries— American auto and steel producers, for example. Why?

To answer that question, we need to understand not what laws *should* exist but what laws *will* exist. We need, in other words, an economic theory of politics. The branch of economics which deals with such questions is called *public choice theory*, presumably because it explains "public choices," while ordinary economics deals with "private choices." The name is somewhat deceptive, however, since what makes public choice theory part of economics is that it analyzes the behavior of political institutions as the outcome of the choices of rational individuals, each seeking his own objectives. It is a theory of the behavior of political institutions that results from private choices on the political marketplace.

In the next section, I will sketch one version of public choice theory; after doing so, we will see how that theory can be used to explain the observed pattern of tariffs. One of the questions we will be interested in is whether the political system can be expected, like the competitive market of Chapter 15, to generate efficient results. If so, we would expect the tariffs actually observed in the real world to correspond fairly closely to the "good" tariffs discussed above.

If, on the other hand, the political market—like the private market with monopoly, externalities, or public goods—produces inefficient outcomes, then there is no strong reason to expect the tariffs that economists observe to correspond to those they recommend. The problem is then to predict the outcomes of the political market—to show which particular industries will or will not get tariff protection. We can then compare the predictions of the theory with what we actually observe, in order to test the theory and perhaps, if its predictions turn out to be correct, understand the reasons for the outcomes we observe.

PUBLIC CHOICE: ECONOMIC ANALYSIS OF THE POLITICAL MARKET

Public choice theory is simply economics applied to a market with peculiar property rights. Just as in the economic analysis of an ordinary market, individuals are assumed to pursue their separate objectives rationally; just as in that analysis, one may first make and later drop simplifying assumptions such as perfect information or zero transaction costs. The property rights on the public market, however, are different from those on the private market; they include the right of individuals to vote for representatives, of representatives to make laws, of government officials to enforce the laws, of judges to interpret them, and so on.

Ordinary economics is greatly simplified if we treat firms as imaginary individuals trying to maximize their profits; in this way, we reduce "General Motors" from several hundred thousand individuals to one. There is some cost to the simplification, since it ignores the conflicts of interest within the firm among managers, employees, and stockholders. So far, no alternative simplification seems to work as well. So economists continue to analyze an economy of profit-maximizing firms, except when the particular problem being considered hinges on intra-firm interactions—for instance, in the theory of the firm, of which the optional section of Chapter 9 provides a brief sample.

One of the ways in which different public choice theories differ from each other is in what they take to be the equivalent of the firm on the political market and what it is assumed to maximize. For the moment, I shall consider the "entrepreneurs" on the political market to be elected politicians and limit my discussion to the market for legislation. This is a simplification of the political market and only one of several possible simplifications—two others will be discussed in later sections—but it provides a convenient way of sketching the theory.

The Market for Legislation

Consider, then, the market for legislation. Individuals perceive that they will be benefited or harmed by various laws. They offer payments to politicians for supporting some laws and opposing others. The payments may take the form of promises to vote, of cash payments to be used to finance future election campaigns, or of (concealed) contributions to the politician's income. The politician is seeking to maximize his long-run income (plus nonpecuniary benefits, one of which may be "national welfare"), subject to the constraint that he can only sell legislation for as long as he can keep getting reelected.

Is It Efficient? To see whether we can expect the outcome of this market to be efficient, let us consider a simple example. A legislator proposes a bill which inefficiently transfers income from one interest group to another; it imposes costs of $10 each on a thousand individuals (total cost $10,000) and grants benefits of $500 each to ten individuals (total benefit $5,000). What will be "bid" for and against the law?

The total cost to the "losers" is $10,000, but the maximum amount they will be willing to offer to a politician to oppose the law is very much less than that. Why? Because of the public good problem. Any individual who contributes to a campaign fund to defeat the bill is providing a public good for all the members of the group. The same arguments used in Chapter 17 to show that public goods are underproduced apply here. The larger the "public," the lower the fraction of the value of the good that can be raised to pay for it.

The benefit provided to the "winners" is also a public good, but it goes to a much smaller public—ten individuals instead of a thousand. A smaller public can more easily organize, perhaps through conditional contracts ("I will contribute if and only if you do"), to fund a public good. Even though the benefit to the small group is smaller than the cost to the large one, the amount the small group is able to offer politicians to support the bill will be more than the amount the large group will offer to oppose it.

The effect is reinforced by a second consideration—information costs. Assume that information about the effect of legislation on any individual can be obtained, but only at some cost in time and money. For the individual who suspects that the bill may injure him by $10, it is not worth obtaining the information, unless it is very inexpensive. His possible loss is small and so is the effect on the probability that the bill will pass of any actions he is likely to take. The member of the "dispersed" interest chooses (rationally) to be worse informed than the member of the "concentrated" interest.

If we abandon the particular example and consider the extreme case of an American presidential election, the argument becomes even clearer. Suppose we believe that the election result is about equally likely to be a 5 million vote victory for one candidate, a 5 million vote victory for the other, or any point in between. The probability that the election will be a tie, hence that one additional vote can decide it, is then one in 10 million. So the return to an individual who figures out who is the "right" candidate and votes accordingly, instead of voting at random (or not voting at all), is an increase by one chance in 10 million of the probability that the right candidate will be elected. Unless the voter has an extraordinarily high value for electing the right candidate, it is not worth paying very much in order to increase the probability of that outcome by one in 10 million; hence he does not bear the information costs necessary to decide for whom he "should" vote. This is an example of "rational ignorance"; it is rational to be ignorant if the cost of information is greater than its value.

Let us now return to the case of a proposed bill which injures a thousand individuals by $10 each and benefits ten by $500 each. We see that the interests of the smaller group are much more heavily weighted on the political market than those of the larger. This is true both because the smaller group can more easily overcome the public good problem of raising money to buy legislation with and because individuals in a small group with a large benefit per individual have more of an incentive to bear the information costs necessary to determine what political actions it is in their interest to take.

What Does Concentration Mean? So far, I have discussed only one characteristic of a group—its size. It is useful to think of the terms "concentrated" and "dispersed" as useful shorthand for the whole set of characteristics that determine how easily a group can fund a public good; the number of individuals in the group is only one of those characteristics.

Consider, for example, a tariff on automobiles. It benefits hundreds of thousands of people—stockholders in auto companies, auto workers, property owners in Detroit, and so forth. But General Motors, Ford, Chrysler, American Motors, and the UAW are organizations which already exist to serve the interests of large parts of that large group of people. For many purposes, one can consider all of the stockholders and most of the workers as "being" five individuals—a group small enough to organize effectively. The beneficiaries of auto tariffs are a much more "concentrated" interest than a mere count of their numbers would suggest— which may explain why such tariffs exist, even though the costs they impose on consumers of automobiles and American producers of export goods, both dispersed interests, are larger than the benefits to the producers of automobiles.

The reason the public good problem leads to inefficiency in ordinary private markets is that the amount which a group can raise to "buy" a public good benefiting that group is less than the total value of the good to the members of the group; hence some public goods which are worth more than it would cost to produce them fail to get produced, which is inefficient. The reason it leads to inefficiency in public markets is that both costs and benefits are only "fractionally represented" on the market, due to the public good problem—and if the weights are different, as they almost always will be, laws which impose net costs may be passed and laws which impose net benefits may not be. This again is inefficient.

Predictions. What predictions can we make on the basis of this simple model of individuals and interest groups bidding for legislation? One is that observed legislation will tend to benefit concentrated interest groups at the expense of dispersed interest groups—where "concentrated" and "dispersed" describe the bundle of characteristics that determine how large a fraction of the benefit that the members of the interest group would receive from legislation can be raised by the group to "buy" the legislation.

A second prediction is that although the system may frequently generate inefficient outcomes, nonetheless more efficient outcomes will be preferred to less efficient—all other things being equal. Consider, for instance, a politician choosing among different ways of subsidizing a particular concentrated interest at the expense of a particular dispersed interest. One scheme will provide the beneficiaries with $1 million and cost the victims $10 million; an alternative will provide $1 million and cost $5 million. The amount spent to oppose him will be less in the second case than in the first, so he prefers it; he is choosing a transfer with an "overhead" of 80 percent ($.20 return for every dollar of cost) over one with an overhead of 90 percent. The same argument applies if both schemes cost the victims the same amount —say $10 million—but one provides $1 million to the beneficiaries and one provides $2 million. The larger the benefit, the larger the amount he can get paid, in one form or another, by the beneficiaries.

So far, we have two rules for transfers. They go from dispersed interests to concentrated interests, and they are made as efficiently as possible, all other things being equal. This raises an obvious problem in explaining the real world— why do we ever observe inefficient transfers, such as tariffs? Why do not politicians always prefer to simply tax the proposed victims and turn the receipts over to the proposed beneficiaries, thus reducing transfer costs to the unavoidable minimum—the administrative cost of collecting the tax and paying out the benefits, and the associated excess burden?

One answer is that there is a third prediction implicit in our model. Politicians will prefer transfers for which the information cost of figuring out what is really happening is as high as possible for the victims and as low as possible for the beneficiaries; if the cost is the same for both victims and beneficiaries, high information costs will generally be preferred to low ones.

The first half of this is obvious—the harder it is for the victims to know they are victims, the less they will spend trying to prevent the legislation; and the easier it is for the beneficiaries to know they are beneficiaries, the more they will spend supporting it. The second half—the general preference for high information costs—follows from the fact that beneficiaries are generally more concentrated than victims. As I pointed out earlier, it is easier for a concentrated interest to overcome the problems associated with information costs. So if information costs are high, it is likely that the beneficiaries will still pay them—and support the legislation—while the victims will fail to pay them and so fail to oppose it.

The preference for high information costs helps to explain the existence of inefficient forms of transfer. Given the choice, the sponsors of legislation designed to benefit some people at the expense of others would prefer to disguise it as something else. A bill to tax consumers and give the money to GM, Ford, Chrysler, American Motors, and the UAW membership is likely to encounter more opposition than an auto tariff designed to do the same thing—because the auto tariff can be (and is) defended as a way of "protecting American jobs from the Japanese."

We now have three predictions about the outcome of political markets: They favor concentrated interests, they prefer more efficient to less efficient transfers, and they prefer transfers disguised as something else. How do these fit what we observe?

Tariffs in the Real World. One very common observation about real-world tariffs is they tend to go, not to infant industries, but to senile ones. In part, this is what we would expect from our discussion of concentrated versus dispersed interests. The American steel industry is a powerful concentrated interest; potential infant industries which do not now exist but could be created by an appropriate tariff are not. Hence it is the old industries that get the protection.

This explains why infant industries do not get tariffs, but it does not explain which industries do get them. If, as seems to be the case, tariffs tend to go to declining industries, a satisfactory theory should explain why. The discussion of sunk costs in Chapter 12, combined with the prediction that politicians will prefer transfers that give the highest possible ratio of benefit to cost, all other things being equal, can do so.

Suppose a tariff is imposed on imports that compete with a growing, competitive, domestic industry. Before the tariff, price was equal to average cost, so economic profit was zero. The tariff reduces the supply of imports, so prices and the industry's output rise. But once enough new (domestic) firms have entered the industry to reestablish equilibrium, average cost is again equal to price—profit is again zero. There is no gain to the industry, hence no reason for it to reward the politicians who imposed the tariff, save during the adjustment period.

If some of the inputs used by the industry are in fixed supply, such as certain types of land, their value will be bid up; their owners may be willing to offer part of the increase to get the tariff passed and maintained. If the inputs instead have a highly elastic supply curve, or if their ownership is divided among many individuals, no one of whom finds it worth his while to try to work for a tariff (because of the public good nature of lobbying), then only transitional profits are available to reward the supporters of the tariff.

Consider next the case of a tariff on a declining industry. In such an industry, there is usually an important resource in fixed supply—factories which produce enough revenue to be worth keeping but not enough to be worth building. The ownership of that resource is as concentrated as the industry is. The tariff increases domestic demand by raising the cost of the competing imported goods and hence increases the present value of the factories. In this case, unlike the case of a growing industry, a large part of what the consumers lose in higher prices the producers receive in increased wealth; their earnings rise, and so does the market value of the factories necessary to get those earnings.

The cost of a tariff is still larger than the benefits—but the cost is spread among many consumers, and the benefits are concentrated on a few producers. Since the benefits to the industry are much larger in the case of a declining industry than in the case of a growing one, declining industries will be willing to work much harder to get tariffs. It is not surprising that they are generally more successful. The result is a pattern of tariffs almost exactly opposite to the pattern that could be justified as efficient.

The same analysis explains why tariffs on agricultural products are common—not so much in the U.S., which is a net exporter of farm products, as in the common market countries, which are net importers. In the case of a tariff on farm products, the relevant fixed resource is land; increased demand for domestic crops drives up its price. Just as in the case of a declining industry, the producers get a large fraction, although not all, of what the consumers lose—if the fraction is large enough, and if the producers are sufficiently concentrated and well organized in comparison to the consumers, the result may be a tariff.

Another way of looking at this argument is in terms of excess burden. In analyzing the effects of a tax in Chapter 7, we saw that a highly inelastic demand or supply curve resulted in low excess burden. The supply curve for land, or for old factories that are worth keeping but not worth building, is highly inelastic, as discussed in Chapters 12 and 13. So the excess burden produced by a tariff on agriculture or the products of a declining industry—the difference between the cost to the consumers and the benefit to the producers (and the government that collects the tariff)—is lower than for most other tariffs. The lower the excess burden, the more likely it is that the beneficiaries, being more concentrated than the victims, will succeed in outbidding them on the political market.

This situation is a good deal more complicated than the one analyzed in Chapter 7, since the tax is not on a good but on a particular way of producing a good—producing autos out of wheat (or, in the case of our European and Japanese trading partners, wheat out of autos) via trade. The simple tax of Chapter 7 injured both consumers and producers; the only beneficiary was the government that collected the tax. This more complicated tax harms producers who produce in the way that is being taxed and benefits producers who produce in other ways—Americans who build cars instead of growing them or Europeans who grow wheat instead of building it.

Alternative Approaches

So far, my discussion of public choice theory has focused on the market for legislation in a way which appears to downplay the arrangements by which we are taught, in high school civics classes, that our society is run—democratic elections. My reasons for doing so are in large part implicit in the discussion. Information costs make it difficult for voters to know which politicians are really acting in their interest, and the public good problem means that it is rarely in the interest of voters to pay the costs and buy the information necessary to recognize and support "good" politicians.

This is one approach to public choice theory, but not the only one. There are other approaches, some of which choose to ignore such problems and analyze a democratic government in terms of the outcome of a system of majority voting among voters who correctly perceive their own interests and the positions of the candidates. The following is an example, applied to a recent election.

Hotelling and Hayden. You are planning to build a store on the block shown in Figure 18-3. After you build your store, your competitor will build his. The customers are evenly distributed along the block; each customer always goes to the nearer store. Where do you build?

One wrong answer is shown in Figure 18-3a; your store is A, and your competitor's store is B. By locating his store as shown, he gets all of the customers to his right. He maximizes the number of customers he gets by building next to you,

Figure 18-3

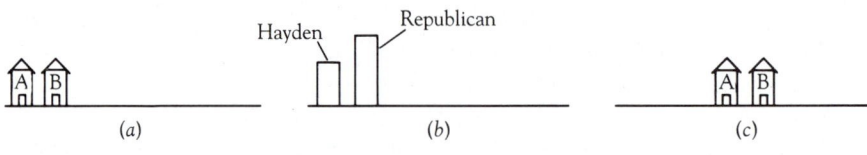

The Hotelling Theorem applied to stores and to politicians.

on the side toward the center of the block. Your correct strategy is to build in the center, as shown on Figure 18-3c, forcing him to build on one side or the other. You each get about 50 percent of the market.

A few years ago, while teaching one of the courses out of which this textbook developed, I was reminded of this simple but elegant argument (originated by Harold Hotelling) by the campaign advertisements of Tom Hayden and his Republican opponent. Hayden was running a very left-wing campaign for the California legislature from a district including the city of Santa Monica—sometimes referred to by those unhappy with its politics as the People's Republic of Santa Monica. His opponent appeared to be taking very left-wing stands for a Republican—support of rent control, opposition to offshore drilling, and the like. The obvious interpretation is shown in Figure 18-3b, which is merely 18-3a relabeled. With Hayden far to the left on the political spectrum, his opponent maximizes his votes by being almost equally far left. Voters to his right have nowhere to go.

The same analysis explains the tendency of the American political system to nominate two similar candidates, both near the political center. That corresponds quite nicely to the prediction shown on Figure 18-3c. The fact that presidential candidates are not always at the center, like the fact that Hayden ran (and won) on a noncentrist platform, may be a result of additional complexities in the system. For one thing, issues cannot be perfectly represented as a one-dimensional left-right spectrum. For another, political support is not limited to voting; a voter near one end of the spectrum may be willing to vote for a candidate he perceives as only a little less bad than his opponent, but be reluctant to donate time or money to his campaign.

Hotelling's argument, as applied to politics, is called the *median voter* model of public choice. The idea is that on any issue for which positions line up in a one-dimensional pattern, such as the issue of how large government spending should be, the outcome will always represent the desires of the median voter. Any position on one side of that favored by the median voter (such as a proposal to spend slightly more money on some project than he wishes spent) will be defeated by a coalition consisting of the median voter and everyone on the other side of him (those who want to spend less than he does)—just over 50 percent of the votes. So will a position on the other side of him. So the median voter gets exactly what he wants.

Here again, the conclusion depends on issues having an unambiguous one-dimensional ordering, and on all the voters correctly perceiving their own interests and voting accordingly. In a more realistic model, the results become much more ambiguous. If, for example, the issue is income redistribution, the voter with the median income might be defeated by a coalition of the two extremes—rich and poor voting to tax the middle class for their joint benefit. That coalition could in turn be defeated by a coalition between the middle and the poor (or the rich), that by still another coalition, and so on without end. A full discussion of such issues would require a chapter on game theory and strategic behavior—which I do not intend to write, at least for this edition.

The Revenue-Maximizing Bureau. As a final example of the diversity of public choice theories, consider William Niskanen's theory of bureaucracy. In his analysis, the essential actor is the government bureau—the U.S. Department of Defense, the Water and Sewer Department of the City of New Orleans, or any other organized body of bureaucrats with a common interest. The objective of each bureau is to maximize its budget, in order to maximize the power and income of its members.

Since bureaus cannot generally impose their own taxes, they must get money from a legislature—which can. They do so by offering the legislature a selection of price/output packages—each consisting of a certain amount of output (defense, water and sewers, schooling, or whatever) to be produced with a budget of a specified size. Since, in Niskanen's model, bureaus know their own cost functions but legislatures do not, the bureau can and does lie to the legislature about the cost of alternative levels of output. Its objective is to get the largest possible appropriation; to do that, it understates the amount it could produce with lower budgets, in order to make those packages less attractive in comparison to the (high budget) package it is trying to sell the legislature. The strategy of the revenue-maximizing bureau turns out to be very similar to the strategy of the monopolist with perfect price discrimination. Each is trying to offer the "customer" a package that he will just barely accept, in order to transfer as much of the resulting gain as possible to the producer.

Obviously, this model too has its problems. For one thing, it is not clear that bureaucrats would want to maximize their budgets even if they could do so. If in order to get the maximum budget, the bureau must promise the legislature—and produce—a large output, it might be better off with a slightly smaller budget and a much smaller set of obligations. If less has to be produced, more money will be available to be spent on the salaries (and other perquisites) of the bureaucrats.

RENT SEEKING AND THE COST OF GOVERNMENT

In Chapter 15, I introduced the idea of rent seeking in order to explain why perfect discriminatory monopoly might, under some circumstances, be the worst rather than the best way of organizing an industry. The term "rent seeking" and the associated set of ideas were actually introduced to economics in a context more appropriate to this chapter. The analysis goes as follows.

Friedman's Second Law: How Not to Give Things Away

A government has valuable favors to give out—import permits, licenses, or the like. They take the form of pieces of paper giving the recipient permission to do something. Each piece of paper is worth a million dollars; a potential recipient would, if necessary, pay up to that amount to get it. A thousand such pieces of paper are to be given out.

If you are giving away something worth a million dollars, there will be no shortage of claimants. Some way must be found to choose among them. Suppose, to begin with, that the permits are supposed to be given out to those firms that will use them "in the public interest." The society is a democratic one; government officials try to give the permits to the firms which the voting public prefers.

Firms can and do act to influence the public's perceptions. If your firm wants a permit and does not expect to get it, it may be worth spending some money on improving your public image—perhaps by producing advertisements telling the general public how important your product is to the national welfare, how many jobs depend on you, and how crucial it is that you get the permit.

How much will you be willing to spend on such advertising? If it makes the difference between getting and not getting the permit, anything up to the value of the permit—$1,000,000. Initially, perhaps, you can get away with less. But when other firms observe that your $100,000 ad campaign is going to result in your getting one of the permits and their not getting one, they start their own ad campaigns—budgeted at $200,000. You reevaluate the situation and increase your budget. They do the same.

As long as, on average, an expenditure of less than $1,000,000 on advertising gets a government favor worth $1,000,000, there will always be more firms willing to enter the game. By doing so, they either raise the amount that must be spent or lower the probability of success. Equilibrium is reached when each firm, on average, spends as much to get the permit as the permit is worth. If the firms that spend more are certain to get the permits, the result is that 1,000 firms spend $1,000,000 each. If the situation is more uncertain, there may be 2,000 firms spending $500,000 each and each ending up with a 50 percent chance of success.

From one standpoint, the result is unsurprising; in equilibrium, marginal cost (as usual) equals marginal value. From another, it is very surprising indeed—the government is giving out, for free, a billion dollars worth of special favors, and the recipients are ending up with nothing—the full value of the favors is used up in getting them. I sometimes describe this conclusion as Friedman's Second Law: "The government cannot give anything away."

I have assumed that potential recipients of the permits can influence their chances by using advertising to improve their public image. The result does not depend on that particular assumption. One can imagine a variety of other ways in which potential recipients might influence the result, including political donations to the party in power and direct bribery of the officials allocating the permits. The logic of the situation remains the same—the firms spend as much getting the favors as the favors are worth.

This argument was originally made, and the term *rent seeking* introduced to economics, in an article by Anne Krueger. The particular case she was discussing was the giving out of import permits in developing countries. Such countries frequently try to maintain an "official" exchange rate for their currency higher than the market rate and use import permits to ration the resulting "shortage" of foreign currency. If a native of (say) India earns dollars by selling goods abroad, he is supposed to turn them over to the government at the official rate—which means that he gets fewer rupees for his dollars than they are worth on the market.

Indians who are given import permits by the government are allowed to convert rupees into dollars at the official rate, in order to use the dollars to buy goods abroad and import them into the country. Since the official rate gives them more dollars than their rupees are actually worth on the market, such permits are worth a great deal of money. Krueger estimated that the market value of the permits given out by the governments of Turkey and India, and hence the amount wasted on rent-seeking activity, was about 5 to 10 percent of their national income.

Rent seeking is not limited to developing countries. In analyzing the market for legislation, I concentrated on the outcome of that market without discussing its costs. If special interests "buy" legislation from politicians, that increases the value of being a (successful) politician, which in turn increases the amount spent on getting and keeping political office. This brings us to an interesting puzzle.

The Cost of Elections

It is common, especially around election times, to read articles lamenting how much is spent on campaigning. What surprises me is how *little* appears to be spent on political campaigns, considering the size of the prize competed for. In a presidential year, total expenditure by both parties on the presidential race and all congressional races is on the order of a hundred or two hundred million dollars; the prize is control of the federal government for several years—during which that government will spend several trillion dollars.

One explanation for the disproportion between the prize and what is spent to get it is the public good problem faced by even a relatively concentrated interest group. If a group can only raise, for political contributions, 10 percent of the value to its members of what it is buying, then the ability to deliver a dollar's worth of benefits is worth only $.10 to the politician delivering it. A second explanation is the inefficiency of even relatively efficient transfers; a government expenditure of $10 million on behalf of some interest group may provide them with only a million dollars worth of benefits. The difference between cost and benefit represents, in effect, the cost of hiding the transfer; a more direct and less inefficient arrangement would also be more obvious to the victims, hence less politically attractive. Combining the two effects would mean that a politician controlling $10 million in expenditure would end up with only $100,000 in campaign contributions or bribes.

A final explanation is that much of the cost of "buying" a political office never appears in records of campaign expenditure—not even in the politician's private records. It consists of promises of a share of the loot—or, to use less biased language, political commitments given to individuals and groups in exchange for their support.

PROBLEMS

1. Whenever you go to your favorite restaurant for dinner, you find that you must wait in line for half an hour. Suppose the restaurant raised its price, reducing the waiting time to five minutes. Would you be better off? Worse off? The same? What about the owner of the restaurant? Discuss. (Hint: This problem involves rent seeking.)

2. Considering your answer to Problem 1, why do restaurants in the situation described not raise their price? Discuss. (I am not sure I know the answer to this one.)

3. A popular rock group is giving a concert. At a price of $20/ticket, the number of tickets sold would be equal to the number of seats available. The group announces that since it does not wish to exploit its fans, tickets will be sold for $10 on a first come-first served basis, starting a week from now. Discuss.

4. The government of India is giving out $10 billion worth of import permits. In order to be fair, they announce that every firm in India which applies will get one permit; the size of the permit (i.e., how many rupees the firm is allowed to change into dollars, which determines how much the permit is worth) will be decided by dividing the number of dollars available by the number of firms that apply. (Note: The value of a permit and the number of dollars it entitles you to buy are not the same. You may assume for this problem that a permit allowing you to buy $10 at the official exchange rate is worth $5; the government is allocating $20 billion of foreign exchange and "selling" it for half what it is really worth to holders of import permits.)

   Discuss the effect of this policy. What form will rent seeking take?

5. Discuss the rickshaw surplus of Chapter 7 in terms of rent seeking.

6. Describe how Europeans and Japanese "build" wheat.

7. It is commonly said that we need auto tariffs to protect the jobs of American auto workers. Have we ignored this argument in our analysis of the net cost of tariffs? If not, where in our calculations did we include the value to the workers of the jobs they will lose if tariffs are abolished? Explain.

8. When a tariff is imposed on some particular import good, the beneficiaries are the domestic producers that the imported good competes with. The victims include not only consumers of that good but also producers of the export goods that would have been exported in exchange for the imports. There is no particular reason to expect the typical export industry to be any less concentrated than the typical import-competing industry. Nonetheless, exporters, like consumers, are a dispersed interest. Explain.

FOR FURTHER READING

✶ The original article on rent seeking is Anne Krueger, "The Political Economy of the Rent-seeking Society," *American Economic Review*, Vol. 64 (June, 1974), pp. 291-303.

My original discussion of "Friedman's Second Law" (not under that name) is in David Friedman, *The Machinery of Freedom: Guide to a Radical Capitalism* (New York: Harper & Row, 1971), Chapter 38.

Other sources for public choice theory are: James Buchanan and Gordon Tullock, *The Calculus of Consent* (Ann Arbor, Mich.: University of Michigan Press, 1962); Anthony Downs, *An Economic Theory of Democracy* (New York: Harper & Row, 1957); William Niskanen, *Bureaucracy and Representative Government* (Chicago: Aldine-Atherton, 1971); and Mancur Olson, *The Logic of Collective Action* (Cambridge, Mass.: Harvard University Press, 1965).

✶ A discussion of the market for legislation similar to that in this chapter appears in Gary Becker, "A Theory of Competition Among Pressure Groups for Political Influence," *Quarterly Journal of Economics*, Vol. 98 (1983), pp. 371-400.

Hotelling's original contribution is in Harold Hotelling, "Stability in Competition," *Economic Journal*, Vol. 39, No. 1 (March, 1929), pp. 41-57.

Chapter 19

The Economics of Law and Law Breaking

This chapter consists of four parts. The first two take the existing legal structure as given, using economics first to understand criminal activity and suggest ways of defending against it and then to analyze the net costs of crime and in the process to suggest why certain things should be illegal.

The remaining two parts of the chapter take the existing system of laws and law enforcement as an object of study rather than as a framework within which to study crime. The third part sketches the analysis of what the punishment for crimes ought to be and how hard we should try to apprehend criminals—how much we should spend and what fraction of the criminals we should catch. The final part discusses the advantages and disadvantages of two alternative systems for catching and convicting offenders—public, as in our present criminal law, and private, as in our present civil law.

PART 1 · THE ECONOMICS OF CRIME

By "the economics of crime," I do not mean "the effect of crime on the GNP" or "why poverty causes crime." "Economics" means the same thing here that it meant in Chapter 1 and has meant throughout the text—a particular way of understanding human behavior. The economic approach to analyzing crime starts from the assumption that a burglar burgles for the same reason I teach economics—because he finds it a more attractive profession than any other. It draws the obvious conclusion that if one wishes to reduce burglary—whether one is a legislator or a homeowner—one does so by raising the costs of the burglar's profession or reducing its benefits.

Many years ago, I had a disagreement with a friend concerning a practical element of life in New York City; our argument illustrates in a small way the difference between the economic and the non-economic approach to crime and criminals. I was at the time living in a somewhat hazardous part of Manhattan. When I found it necessary to go out at night, I was in the habit of carrying with me a four-foot walking stick. My friend argued that I was making a dangerous mistake; potential muggers would feel challenged and swarm all over me. I felt, on the contrary, that muggers, like other profit-maximizing businessmen, would prefer to obtain their income at the lowest possible cost. By carrying a stick, I was not only raising the cost I could inflict on them if I chose to resist, I was also announcing my intention of resisting; they would rationally choose easier prey.

I never got mugged, which is some evidence that my view of the matter was correct. More evidence comes from observing who the people are who do get mugged. If muggers are out to prove their machismo, they ought to pick on football players; there is not much glory in mugging little old ladies. If muggers are rational businessmen seeking to obtain revenue at the lowest possible cost, on the other hand, mugging little old ladies makes a lot of sense. Little old ladies—and other relatively defenseless people—get mugged. Football players do not. It is said that someone once asked Willie Sutton why he robbed banks. "That's where the money is" was his (rational) reply.

The same analysis which helped me decide what to take with me on my evening strolls around Manhattan's Upper West Side can also be used in analyzing a question that often comes up in discussions of gun control. Opponents argue that gun control, by disarming potential victims, makes it more difficult for them to protect themselves from criminals. Supporters reply that criminals are more likely to know how to use guns than victims; hence in any armed confrontation, the odds are with the criminal. This is probably true, but it is almost entirely irrelevant to the argument.

Suppose one little old lady in ten carries a gun. Suppose that one in ten of those, if attacked by a mugger, will succeed in killing the mugger instead of being killed by him—or shooting herself in the foot. On average, the mugger is much more likely to win the encounter than the little old lady. But—also on average—every hundred muggings produce one dead mugger. At those odds, mugging is a very unattractive profession—not many little old ladies carry enough money in their purses to justify one chance in a hundred of being killed getting it. The number of muggers—and muggings—declines drastically, not because all of the muggers have been killed but because they have, rationally, sought safer professions.

When, as children, we first learn about the different sorts of animals, we are likely to imagine them arranged in a strict hierarchy, with the stronger and more ferocious ones preying on everything below them. That is not how it works. A lion could, no doubt, be fairly confident of defeating a jaguar, or a wolf of killing a fox. But a lion that made a habit of preying on jaguars would not survive very long. While any particular jaguar would probably lose the fight, there would be some small chance of the lion getting killed in the process and a larger chance of his getting injured. That is too high a price for one dinner. That is why lions prey on zebras instead. In just the same way, a potential victim does not have to be more deadly than the criminal, just deadly enough so that the cost to the criminal is a little greater than the benefit.

This does not, of course, prove that gun control is a bad thing; while I have rebutted one argument, there are many others, both pro and con. It does illustrate an important general principle. In analyzing conflict, whether between two animals, criminal and victim, competing firms, or warring nations, our natural tendency is to imagine an all-out battle in which all that matters is victory or defeat. That is rarely if ever the case. In the conflict between the mugger and the little old lady, the mugger, on average, wins. But the cost of the conflict—one chance in a hundred of being killed—is high enough so that the mugger prefers to avoid it. In this case, as in many others, the problem faced by the potential victim is not how to defeat the aggressor but only how to make aggression unprofitable.

Economics Joke #3: An economist and a businessman were walking in the woods when they encountered a hungry bear. The economist turned to run. "That just goes to show how ridiculous you economists are with your assumptions," said the businessman. "You're assuming you can outrun the bear." "Wrong!" replied the economist. "I'm only assuming that I can outrun you."

Economics of the Spaceways

There is a nice fictional illustration of this point in a science fiction story by Poul Anderson. The setting is a far future in which interstellar travel and trade are common. There is a potentially profitable trade route connecting two groups of stars. Unfortunately the route runs through the territory of a nasty little interstellar empire. The nasty little empire ("Borthu") has the unpleasant habit of seizing passing starships, confiscating their cargo, and brainwashing their crews; the crew is then added to Borthu's fleet, which is critically short of trained manpower.

Borthu is a nasty *little* empire; the trading corporations could, if they chose, get together, build warships, and defeat it. But doing so would cost more than all of the profits to be made on the trade route. They could also arm their trading ships—but the cost of building and manning an armed ship would more than wipe out the profit the ship would generate. They *can* win—but, being rational profit maximizers, they won't.

The problem is solved by Nicholas Van Rijn, the head of one of the trading corporations—after he has first persuaded his competitors to agree to pay a fraction of their profits on the route to whoever solves the problem. The solution is to arm one ship in four, reducing the profit but not eliminating it. Warships carry larger crews than merchant ships. Three times out of four, the empire attacks a trading ship, capturing it and its four-man crew. One time out of four, the trading ship is armed; the empire loses a warship and its twenty-man crew. Every four attacks cost the empire, on net, eight crewmen. Piracy is no longer profitable, so it stops.

The logic of the problem, and the solution, is nicely summed up in Van Rijn's reply to one of his colleagues, who suggests that they should fight a war with the empire, even if it costs more than the trade is worth to them.

Revenge and destruction are un-Christian thoughts. Also, they will not pay very well, since it is hard to sell anything to a corpse. The problem is to find some means within our resources to make it *unprofitable* for Borthu to raid us. Not being stupid heads, they will then stop raiding and we can maybe later do business.

— "Margin of Profit," in *Un-man and Other Novellas* by Poul Anderson

Superthief

I recently came across another discussion of the economics of crime and crime prevention in a book on the subject written from the inside—in several senses. The title was *Secrets of a Superthief* (by Jack Maclean). The author, according to both his own account and the journalist who wrote the introduction, was a spectacularly successful burglar, specializing in high-income neighborhoods. As he tells it, he ran a class act—when a house contained nothing he thought worth stealing, he would pile up the rejected booty on the kitchen table and steal the control panel from the burglar alarm. His general policy was to reset burglar alarms on his way out, to make sure no less discriminating thief broke in and messed up the house.

Eventually Superthief made a small professional error and found himself taking an unplanned vacation, courtesy of the state of Florida. Being an energetic fellow, he spent his time behind bars polling fellow inmates on their techniques and opinions and writing a book on how not to get burgled. One of Superthief's principal insights is the same as Van Rijn's—the essential objective in any conflict is neither to defeat your enemy nor to make it impossible for him to defeat you but merely to make it no longer in his interest to do whatever it is that you object to.

In giving advice to potential victims, Superthief argues that making it impossible for a burglar to get into your house is usually not an option; few doors will stand up to a determined burglar properly equipped. Even if the burglar cannot open or force the lock, take off the hinges, or break down the door, there is always the alternative of either going through a wall or sawing out the bars protecting a window. The function of strong doors and locks is not to make burglary impossible but to make it more expensive, by increasing the skill and equipment needed by the burglar as well as the chance that he will be detected before finishing the job.

A less expensive and possibly more effective way of raising the cost and lowering the benefit of burglary is to use what Superthief calls "mind games." Figure 19-1 shows my version of one of his suggested tricks—in the form of a note taped to my back door. Both Mrs. Jones and Rommel are wholly imaginary. A potential burglar may suspect that, but he has no way of being sure. Exterminators are common enough in this part of the country, the reference to the "back rooms" is vague enough to make it uncertain just where he can go without breathing insecticide, and Rommel, presumably a German shepherd or Doberman pinscher (can you imagine a poodle named Rommel?), is in the room which, according to

Figure 19-1

> Mrs. Jones —
>
> The exterminators came and we have not aired the house yet, so stay out of the back rooms.
>   Mr. Friedman
>
> P.S. Rommel is in the bedroom.

A fictitious note to a fictitious cleaning lady.

Superthief, burglars consider most worth robbing. Superthief's version of the note referred to pet rattlesnakes loose in the house—a better story than mine but one less likely to be believed.

Superthief gives many other examples of simple and inexpensive mind games—such as leaving a large dog-feeding dish or a jumbo-sized rubber bone lying around the backyard. He suggests using warning stickers referring to imaginary alarm systems—imaginary not only in that you do not have them but that nobody else has them either. A competent burglar may know how to deal with all the varieties of burglar alarm that really exist, but how can he know how to deal with one that you made up while designing the sticker? Figure 19-2a is a sample of my own devising.

Figure 19-2b shows another of my precautions—a solution to a problem which Superthief does not discuss. One of the rooms in the back part of my house contains some things which a thief might well find worth stealing; for that reason,

Figure 19-2

> Warning
> This House Protected by a
> Laser Alarm System
>
> Active and Passive Defenses
> Occupant Assumes no Liability
> for Injuries to Intruders
>
> Lasalarm Inc.   Cupertino, CA

> Dangerous Chemicals
> Keep Out
> This means you, Patri

Low-cost burglar repellents.

I have equipped it with its own deadbolt lock. This raises a problem. A rational thief will assume that I am a rational victim and deduce that if I have a lock on that door, it is probably because I have things worth stealing behind it. My solution is the sign shown in Figure 19-2b. It is intended to suggest an alternative explanation for the lock—dangerous chemicals in the room and a curious child in the house. The solution is original with me, but I believe Superthief would approve.

Illegal Markets

"(On earth they) even have laws for private matters such as contracts. Really. If a man's word isn't any good, who would contract with him? Doesn't he have reputation?"

— Manny in *The Moon is a Harsh Mistress* by Robert Heinlein

So far, we have been using the economic analysis of crime to figure out how, on an individual level, to deal with it; the discussion is in that sense practical as well as theoretical. Before ending the section and going on to analyze questions of law and law enforcement, we will first use economic analysis to explore an equally interesting but less immediately useful question—the structure of illegal markets.

We are used to thinking of markets as public, socially accepted institutions such as the stock market, the wheat market, or a supermarket; one important feature of such markets is that the agreements to buy and sell made in them can usually be enforced, if necessary, in the courts. But the concept of a market is much broader than that. There are markets for political influence in the Soviet Union—and in Washington. There are markets for illegal drugs and stolen goods. There are markets for sex, both legal (see Chapter 20) and illegal. The enforceability of contracts by public courts may be useful for the working of markets, but it is certainly not essential.

Economics applies to illegal markets as well as to legal ones. When one input to production is eliminated, substitutes become more valuable; if contracts cannot be enforced in the courts, alternative ways of getting people to abide by their contracts become more important. We would expect substitutes for the service provided by the court system to be important elements of illegal markets. One substitute is reputation. The traditional definition of an honest politician is one who stays bought. Another and more violent substitute for the courts will be discussed a little later.

Another characteristic of illegal markets is that the handling of information is more costly than in legal markets; the same information about your employees that you want in order to decide on your future dealings with them is also useful to a prosecutor deciding on his future dealings with you. This is one of the reasons that I (and others) regard "organized crime" or the "Mafia" as mythical, at least as they are commonly portrayed. A "General Motors of Crime" makes little sense. In order to run such a firm, someone at the top has to know what people at the bottom are doing, in order to (among other things) decide whether they are earning their pay. Passing such information up many levels of hierarchy would be hazardous in the extreme. It seems more likely that crime is mostly done by individuals or small firms and that "organized crime" is analogous, not to a giant corporation, but to something more like a chamber of commerce or better business bureau for the criminal market.

Such an interpretation flies in the face of what we are usually told, in newspapers and congressional hearings alike. Before you reject it on that basis, it is worth considering how credible the sources of information for the newspapers and the committees are and whether their incentives are geared to generating accurate research or exciting stories. Newspapers want to sell copies and politicians want to get reelected; announcing that organized crime is *not* a major threat seems a poor way of doing either. The sources of information are either law enforcement officials who want to prove that they need more money and power to "fight organized crime" or criminals testifying in exchange for immunity—with an obvious incentive to say whatever their captors wish to hear. It is interesting, in reading such accounts, to compare descriptions of the power and importance of the Mafia with descriptions of how the witnesses actually ran their criminal enterprises; the latter generally portray the witnesses as independent entrepreneurs, not employees of some criminal superfirm.

Academic studies of the criminal market involve certain difficulties not present in most other fields of research. Nonetheless, such studies have occasionally been done, and there is at least some scholarly evidence that seems to support my conclusions. For example, a study of illegal gambling in New York, based on records produced by police wiretapping, found that bookies were small independent operators and that numbers operators were somewhat larger but also competitive. Neither bookies nor numbers operators seemed to have much ability to use violence against their competitors; they even had difficulty enforcing the profit-sharing agreements they had with the subcontractors who brought in their customers.

My own conjecture is that what the Mafia really is, at least in part, is a substitute for the court system; its function is to legitimize the use of force. To see how that might work, imagine that you are engaged in some criminal enterprise and one of your associates pockets your share of the take. Your obvious response is to have him killed—murder is one of the products sold on the market you are operating in. The problem with that is that if people who work with you get killed and it becomes known that you are responsible, other participants in the illegal marketplace will become reluctant to do business with you.

The solution is to go to some organization with a reputation, within the criminal market, for fairness. You present the evidence of your partner's guilt, invite him to defend himself, and then ask the "court" to rule that he is the guilty party. If it does so—and he refuses to pay you appropriate damages—you hire someone to kill him; since everyone now knows that he was in the wrong, the only people afraid to do business with you will be those planning to swindle you.

That, I suspect, is the function, or one of the functions, that the Mafia and similar organizations serve on the criminal market. This is a conjecture about "organized crime," not something I can prove; but it is not, so far as I know, an implausible one. If it is correct, then the arrangements of the criminal market are, in that respect, very similar to the legal institutions of one historical society that I have studied—and will describe in the last part of this chapter.

PART 2 · THE COST OF CRIME

So far, I have taken the legal structure as given and used economics to analyze the behavior of criminals. The next step is to use economics to analyze the cost imposed by crime. The objective in doing so is in part to show why, from the perspective of economics, certain things should be illegal, and in part to show how the analysis of the market for crime can be fitted into the general framework of economics. Here and in the remaining parts of this chapter, we will continue to assume that the participants in the criminal marketplace—criminals, victims, and law enforcers—are rational, correctly choosing the means to achieve their differing objectives.

What Is Wrong With Robbery Anyway?

We take it for granted that certain activities, such as robbery, theft, and murder, are bad things that ought to be prevented. From the standpoint of economic efficiency, it is not immediately obvious why. Theft appears to be merely a transfer; I lose $100 and the thief gains $100. From the standpoint of efficiency, that appears to be a wash—costs measured in dollars just balance benefits in dollars. If so, what is wrong with theft or robbery?

If that were all that happened, theft would indeed be neutral from the standpont of efficiency, neither an improvement nor a worsening. It is not. Robbery is not costless; the thief must spend money, time, and effort buying tools, "casing" the house, breaking in, and so forth. How much time and effort? To answer that question, we do not have to find any actual thieves and interrogate them. Economic theory tells us what the cost will be—at least for the marginal thief. In equilibrium on the thieves' market just as on other competitive markets, marginal cost equals average cost equals price. So the marginal thief has no gain to balance the cost he imposes on his victim; the average thief has a gain, but it is less than the amount stolen, hence less than the cost. The analysis goes as follows:

Suppose that anyone who wished to become a thief could steal $100 at a net cost, including operating expenses, value of time, and risk of being caught, of only $50. Revenue is greater than cost, so economic profit is positive; firms enter the industry. If stealing pays higher "wages" than alternative occupations, people will leave those occupations to become thieves.

As more people become thieves, the return from theft falls. Many of the most valuable and easily stolen objects have already been stolen. Every diamond necklace has three jewel thieves pursuing it. A thief breaks into a house only to discover that Superthief has stolen all the more valuable jewelry—and reset the alarm. Just as in other industries, increased output drives down the return—although not for quite the same reason. The "price" that a thief gets for his work—the amount he can steal for each hour of his own time that he spends stealing—falls.

How far does it fall? As long as stealing yields a higher return than alternative occupations, people will leave those occupations to become thieves. Equilibrium is reached when, for the marginal thief, his new profession is only infinitesimally better than his old—and for the next person who considers becoming a thief and decides not to, it is infinitesimally worse. In equilibrium, the marginal thief is giving up a job which paid him, say, $6/hour in order to make, after subtracting expenses of his new profession such as lawyer's fees and occasional unpaid vacations, $6.01/hour.

So in equilibrium, theft is not a transfer at all. The marginal thief who steals $100 spends about $100 in time and money to do so. His costs and his return almost exactly cancel—leaving the cost to the victim as a net loss. The transaction is not a wash but a Marshall worsening of about $100.

So far, I have discussed only the marginal thief. What about the individual who is exceptionally talented at stealing or exceptionally bad at alternative professions, so that being a thief is more attractive to him, relative to other professions, than to the individual who just barely decided to become a thief? His situation is like that of the firm with a particularly good production function, discussed in Chapter 9; at a "price" at which marginal firms just cover their cost, the "inframarginal" firm, or thief, makes a profit. When he steals $100, he does so at a cost of only $50, leaving him $50 ahead. Since the victim ends up $100 behind, the result is still a Marshall worsening, although not by as much as in the case of the marginal thief.

So far, we have the following result. If all thieves are marginal thieves—if, in other words, there is not much variation among potential thieves in their comparative advantage for thievery—the net cost of theft, including costs and benefits to both thieves and victims, is about equal to the amount stolen. If thieves vary widely, the net cost is still positive, but less than the amount stolen.

There are two directions we can go from here in analyzing the cost of theft. One is to make the analysis more realistic by including some costs which so far have been omitted—the costs of defense against theft. These would include both private costs—locks, burglar alarms, security guards, and the like—and the public costs of police, courts, and prisons. I have not actually done such calculations; my guess is that such costs are much larger than the net gains of theft to the "inframarginal" thieves, making the total cost of theft more, not less, than the total value of all goods stolen.

The other thing we can do at this point is to see how the analysis of theft fits into the general structure of economic theory. We will start by converting the verbal analysis of "marginal" and "inframarginal" thieves into a conventional supply and demand diagram. We will go on to show that the undesirability of theft can be seen as merely a special case of something we already know—indeed of two different things we already know.

Figures 19-3*a* through 19-3*d* are supply and demand diagrams for theft. The horizontal axis shows hours spent stealing. The vertical axis shows dollars stolen per hour—the "price" that thieves receive for each hour of stealing "produced." The supply curve S, like any other supply curve, shows how much will be produced at any price—how the number of hours spent stealing depends on the number of dollars per hour that can be stolen. The demand curve D shows how the "price" varies with the amount stolen. As the number of hours spent stealing increases, the return per hour falls, so D slopes down—as a demand curve should.

By using hours spent stealing as my measure of "quantity," I have implicitly assumed that the difference among thieves is in how much it costs them to spend an hour stealing, not in how much they can steal in an hour. Such differing costs reflect differences among the thieves in their taste for leisure, their earning opportunities in alternative employments, and their estimate of how likely they are to be caught.

Figure 19-3

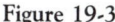

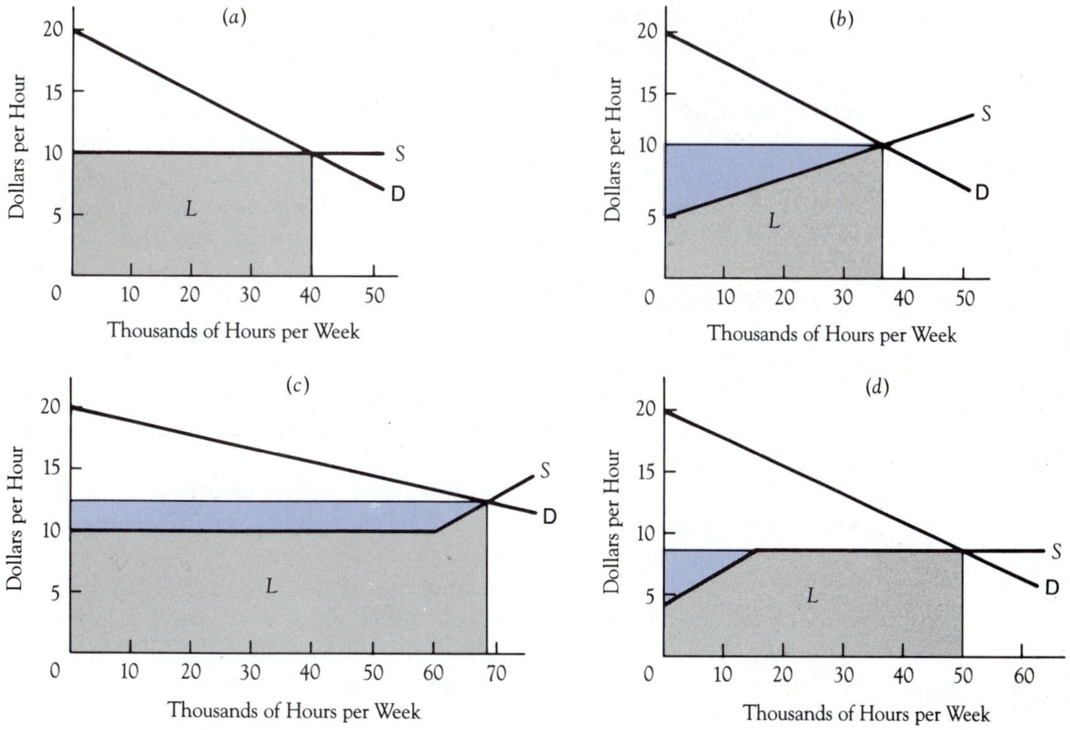

The market for theft. On each figure, the shaded area *L* shows the net loss due to theft—the loss to the victims minus the producer surplus (colored) received by the thieves.

I could, if I wished, take account of differing abilities to steal by defining my unit as some kind of "standard hour"—where an hour spent by an incompetent thief counts as half a standard hour, and an hour spent by Superthief counts as ten. That would make the analysis a little more complicated without changing anything essential—which is why I am not doing it that way.

The curves labeled S on Figures 19-3a through 19-3d are conventional supply curves, but D is not exactly a demand curve, although it serves much the same function in our analysis. An ordinary demand curve describes voluntary transactions. If at \$.25 apiece, I choose to buy 10 cookies, that tells us not only something about the market for cookies but also something about the value of cookies to me—that my marginal value for cookies is \$.25/cookie at a quantity of 10 cookies. The fact that you can "sell me" 5 hours of theft for \$10/hour—spend 5 hours stealing \$50 from me—tells us something about the market for theft but does not imply that I like being stolen from, since the transaction is not a voluntary one. D in Figures 19-3a through 19-3d does describe quantity as a function of price but is not, like a real demand curve, equal to a marginal value curve.

When we derived the concepts of consumer and producer surplus in Chapters 4 and 5, the relation between demand and supply curves and the corresponding marginal value and marginal cost curves was an essential part of the argument. Here that relation holds for S but not for D. So in Figures 19-3a through 19-3d, the area above S and below P is producer surplus, just as with an ordinary supply and demand diagram; but the area below D and above P is *not* consumer surplus.

Figure 19-3a shows a situation where the supply curve for theft is perfectly elastic; all thieves, actual and potential, are identical; hence all are marginal. Since S is horizontal, there is no producer surplus. The total amount stolen equals the number of hours spent stealing times the amount stolen per hour—the area of the shaded rectangle L. Since the victims lose L and the criminals gain nothing, L is also the net loss—the total cost of theft.

Figure 19-3b shows a situation in which thieves are no longer identical. The loss to the victims is the same rectangle as before, but now, part of that loss is a gain to the thieves—shown as the colored area on the figure. The net loss L—the shaded area under the supply curve—is equal to the loss to the victims minus the gain to the thieves.

Figure 19-3c shows a situation in which the supply curve is perfectly elastic over a range of quantity and then bends up; it could be the same S shown on Figure 19-3a, combined with a higher D. This corresponds to a situation in which there are a number of (equally) talented thieves, but not enough to drive the return to the point where only talented thieves find it worth stealing. Since the return from theft is high enough to pull in additional, less talented thieves, the talented thieves must be making a positive economic profit—or, if you prefer, receiving a rent on their scarce ability.

Figure 19-3d is similar to Figure 19-3c, but has the elastic part of the supply curve at the opposite end. This time we have a few talented thieves with varying levels of talent—Superthief and his ilk—who would be willing to steal even for a very low return. There are not enough of them to drive the return from theft down to the return at which only Superthieves find it worth stealing. In equilibrium the Superthieves are making positive profits; the ordinary thieves—plentiful and identical to each other—are not.

Supply and demand curves are one way of looking at the market for theft and analyzing its costs. Another way is to consider the cost of theft as one more example of the inefficiency of rent seeking. Rent seeking occurs when individuals or firms compete to get some valuable asset; their competition involves spending resources in a way which produces nothing but improves the chance that they, rather than someone else, will get what they are competing for. Typically the result is that the value of what is competed for is dissipated in the competition; the winners, on average, spend the full value of what they win in the process of winning it.

The market for theft can be seen as a case of rent seeking among the thieves; they compete to steal the same objects. From this standpoint, it is not pure rent seeking; increased efforts by one thief may result in merely redistributing the booty—getting him something that someone else would otherwise have stolen— but they may also result in stealing something that otherwise would not have been stolen at all. From the standpoint of the thieves, although not of the society as a whole, this is a productive expenditure since it increases the total take.

A more interesting way of looking at theft is as a case of rent seeking among thieves *and victims*. Both want the same objects—all of which, initially, belong to the victims. Seen from this standpoint, expenditures by each individual thief are pure rent seeking—either they result in his getting the loot instead of some other thief or they result in his getting the loot instead of its owner keeping it. From this standpoint, defensive expenditures by the victims are also pure rent seeking—the function of a burglar alarm is to make sure that the property remains in the hands of its original owner.

What we have really been doing is showing the advantage of a system of secure property rights. If property rights are insecure, some individuals have an incentive to spend resources trying to get property transferred to them, while some have an incentive to spend resources keeping property from being transferred away from them. That is true whether the transfer is done by private theft or government taxation. Some of the inefficiencies we have just been discussing for the former case are known as excess burden in the latter; they were discussed at some length in Chapter 7. Not earning taxable income or not buying taxed goods are (costly) ways of defending yourself against taxation, just as installing a burglar alarm is a (costly) way of protecting against theft. Other inefficiencies on the political marketplace are classified as costs of lobbying. Making campaign donations to a candidate who promises to provide special benefits to you and your friends is an expenditure on transferring property in your direction almost precisely analogous to a burglar's expenditure on tools.

Yet another way of looking at theft—or rent seeking in general—is as a special case of the inefficiency of markets with externalities. If I spend $10,000 producing a car and in the process produce some air pollution, my measure of the cost of producing the car is too low by the amount of damage done by the pollution. The result is inefficient—not because air pollution is evil but because it is not, like other costs, included in my calculation of whether and at what price to produce. If the industry is competitive, everyone to whom a car is worth at least $10,000 gets one. If the air pollution does $5,000 worth of damage, then the real production cost is $15,000; anyone who values the car at more than $10,000 but less than $15,000 is getting something that is worth less to him than it costs to produce.

Theft is an extreme case of this—the external cost, imposed on the victim, is the entire value of what is stolen. The thief steals up to the point where the (marginal) value to him of what he steals is equal to the (marginal) cost to him of stealing it; since he ignores the cost to the victim, equilibrium occurs at a point where marginal cost to all concerned is much larger than marginal benefit. Because in this special case, external cost is equal to value, not only some but all of the "units produced" cost more than they are worth.

We have now used economics to analyze the market for theft. In doing so, we took the system for preventing theft—police and punishments—as a given, one of the elements determining the cost to the thief of stealing. The next step is to use our analysis to say something about how that system should work—what should be illegal, what the nature and amount of the penalty should be, and how much we should be willing to spend on catching and convicting thieves. All of those can be viewed as simply issues of economic efficiency. While you may not believe that that is all they are, you should find the attempt to analyze them from that standpoint an instructive exercise.

Efficient Crimes and the Efficient Level of Crime

In discussing the market for theft, I used the word *value* to describe both the value of what was stolen to the victim and its value to the criminal, without distinguishing between them. If what is stolen is money, gold, bearer bonds, or other "liquid" commodities—things that can be easily bought and sold at about the same price—that is a reasonable way of using the word. In other cases, it is not.

I have spent 20 hours searching art galleries to find a painting I particularly like and then bought it for $100. Replacing it will require a similar effort and a similar expenditure, so a thief who steals it injures me by considerably more than $100. The thief himself will be lucky to get $50 for it; even if he finds the right gallery and the right buyer—one who does not recognize the painting and does recognize its quality—he will get what the gallery pays for paintings, not what it gets for them.

In such a situation, the value to the thief of what he steals is much less than its value to the victim. That is why in many societies, including our own, there are well-established procedures by which thieves sell things back to their owners. Kidnappers are an extreme example of this. They steal something—a person—whose only value to them is what they can get by selling it back to (representatives of) its "owner."

This divergence between value to victim and value to thief suggests another way of looking at the inefficiency of theft. If you have something that is worth more to me than to you, I have no need to steal it; I can buy it from you. Goods which, if theft were impossible, would not be bought, but which would be stolen if theft were possible, must be worth more to their present owner than to the potential thief. Hence the additional "transfers" which become possible as a result of theft are inefficient ones—transfers of a good to someone who values it less than its present owner. That is why I asserted, earlier, that the efficient level of theft was zero.

There are exceptions—what we may call "efficient crimes." Suppose, for example, that you are lost in the woods and starving. You come upon an empty, locked cabin. You break in, feed yourself, and use the telephone to summon help. Almost certainly, the value to you of using the cabin was greater than the cost you imposed on its owner; you will probably be glad to replace both his food and his lock. Your "crime" transferred a resource—temporary control of the cabin—to someone to whom it was worth more than its value to the initial owner. You could only do it by a crime—you could not buy the use of the cabin—because the owner was not there to sell it to you.

This is one example of an efficient crime, a crime which is a net Marshall improvement. A less exotic example is speeding when you are in a hurry. We have speed limits, at least in part, because driving fast increases the chance of an accident. That is a cost but not an infinite one; there are times when getting somewhere quickly is sufficiently important to justify doing so at 80 miles per hour. One way of dealing with such situations is for the law to make it illegal to drive faster than 70 miles per hour except when there is an important reason to do so. The problem with such a law is that it may be difficult or impossible for a court to judge whether your reason was really good enough to justify an exception. An alternative solution is for the law to impose a penalty large enough so that only those who really have a good reason to drive faster will find it worth breaking the law and paying the penalty. Speeding is then always a crime—but if the punishment is correctly calculated, it is a crime that occurs when and only when it is efficient.

Seen in this way, a speeding law serves essentially the same function as the emission fee discussed in Chapter 17. If air polluters must pay an emission fee equal to the damage done by the pollution, they will choose to pollute—and pay—only when the value of what is being produced is greater than the cost, including the cost of the pollution. Similarly, if driving fast imposes costs on other drivers, we can use speeding tickets to force drivers to include those costs in their decision of whether to speed.

The analysis so far suggests a simple rule for setting punishments: The amount of the punishment should equal the damage done by the crime. That way, only efficient crimes will be committed—crimes for which the value to the criminal is greater than the amount of damage done.

There are two things wrong with that rule. The first is that criminals are not always caught. If a criminal faces a 10 percent chance of being caught and convicted, he will discount the punishment accordingly in calculating the cost to himself of committing the crime. Roughly speaking, the punishment should then be 10 times the damage done by the crime in order to assure that only efficient crimes—crimes for which the gain to the criminal is greater than the cost to the victim—occur.

This suggests that the right rule is something like "The punishment times the probability that the perpetrator will be caught and convicted should be equal to the damage done by the crime." A more precise statement would also have to allow for the criminal's attitude toward risk, as discussed in the optional section of Chapter 12; if the criminal is risk averse, one chance in ten of losing $100 may from his standpoint be more than equivalent to a certainty of losing $10.

This raises an interesting problem. The enforcement system can choose among many different combinations of probability and punishment; the same deterrence may be provided by a certainty of a $1,000 fine, a 50 percent probability of a $2,000 fine, a 10 percent chance of a $10,000 fine, or any of a variety of other alternatives, including some in which the punishment is not a fine but imprisonment or execution. How should it decide which to use?

The answer is the same as the answer to a similar problem many chapters back—the problem of choosing the mix of inputs for producing an output. Just as in Chapter 9, the first step is to pick a level of output and find the least costly way of producing it. In our present situation, the output is deterrence; it is produced by imposing a cost on the criminal. Pick a cost—a fine of, say, $100 imposed with certainty on anyone who commits the crime. Consider all the combinations of (lower) probabilities and (higher) punishments which the criminal considers equivalent to a certainty of paying $100—and which will therefore have the same effect in discouraging him from committing the crime. For each combination, calculate the cost of catching that fraction of the criminals and imposing that punishment on each. Find the combination for which that cost is lowest. Now pick another level of cost and repeat the calculation. When you are finished, you will have a total cost curve for deterrence and you will know, for any level of deterrence, what combination of probability and punishment should be used to produce it.

Two sorts of costs go into the calculations I have just described—enforcement costs and punishment costs. The nature of enforcement costs is fairly clear—they represent the expense of paying police, running the courts, and the like. But what are punishment costs?

Consider a fine. The convicted criminal pays $1,000; the court system collects $1,000. The money may be used to pay the expenses of operating the court system, given to victims of crime, or in some other way transferred, directly or indirectly, to someone other than the criminal. The criminal loses $1,000, and other people—victims of crime or taxpayers who would otherwise have had to pay the expenses of the court system—gain about $1,000, so the net cost is about zero.

Suppose that instead of fining the criminal, we execute him. The cost to him is his life; there is no corresponding gain to the rest of us. His life is also the amount of the punishment, so the cost of the punishment and the amount of punishment are the same.

Finally, suppose we neither fine him nor execute him but simply lock him up. The cost to him is the value of his time and freedom. He loses that, but we do not get it; not only do we get nothing from him, we also must pay the cost of running the prison. The cost of the punishment—the cost to him plus the cost to us—is greater than the amount of the punishment.

As a rule, it is easier to collect small fines than large ones, since criminals are more likely to be able to pay them. So, as a general rule, punishment cost increases with the size of punishment. Enforcement cost, on the other hand, is larger the larger the percentage of criminals you are trying to catch. As we move from small punishments imposed with high probability to large punishments imposed with small probability, we are trading off a decrease in enforcement cost against an increase in punishment cost; somewhere between one extreme (catching 100 percent of the criminals and making them give back what they stole) and the other (catching only one criminal and boiling him in oil), there is likely to be an optimal combination.

The first problem with our simple rule—punishment equal to damage done—was that it ignored the probabilistic nature of the punishment. The second problem is that it ignores the costs of catching and punishing criminals. To see why this matters, consider the following situation.

There is a crime which does $10 worth of damage each time it is committed. If there is no punishment at all, 100 crimes per year will be committed, so the total damage will be $1,000/year; the net cost, including the benefits to the criminals and assuming the victims spend nothing on protecting themselves, will be between zero and $1,000.

The police force would like to impose an expected punishment of $10 on the criminals, as suggested by our previous discussion. The least expensive way to do this turns out to be catching one tenth of the criminals and fining them $100 each. Unfortunately, the cost of doing so is $2,000/year. The "efficient" level of punishment involves spending $2,000/year to eliminate a cost of less than $1,000! Obviously, that is the wrong answer; in the situation as described, the least bad solution is to put up with 100 crimes a year.

As this suggests, the full analysis of what should be a crime, what percentage of the criminals should be caught, and what should be done to them is moderately complicated. The answer depends on the supply curve (for amount of crime as a function of the cost imposed by the enforcement system on the criminal—not the S of Figures 19-3a through 19-3d, although the two are related); on the damage done by the crime; and on the cost functions for producing apprehensions, convictions, and punishment. In principle, we now know how to solve the problem—just as, in principle, we know how to calculate how much a firm should and will produce and how, or what, prices and quantities will be in a competitive equilibrium.

How do you calculate the efficient solution for the "problem" of preventing crime? Start by writing a cost function that includes costs and benefits to everyone affected. Next assume criminals and victims will choose values for the variables they control—amount of crime and amount of private defense against crime—that maximize their own welfare. Finally, find values for the remaining variables—percentage of criminals convicted, nature and amount of punishment—that maximize net benefits.

Private or Public Enforcement of Law?

When we talk about law enforcement, we usually mean law enforcement by police officers. Actually, in our present system, much of law enforcement is private. If someone breaks your arm, you call the police; but if he breaks a window or a contract, you call a lawyer. In the one case, law is enforced by government employees who gather evidence, present it to the court, collect the fine, and run the prison or close the switch on the electric chair. In the other case, law is enforced by a private individual, working for pay or a share of the settlement; he is responsible for gathering evidence and presenting it to the court, and he and his employer, the injured party, receive the "fine" paid by the convicted offender.

In our system, the division between public and private enforcement roughly corresponds to the division between criminal and civil law. Criminal law involves police, district attorneys, and sentences for criminals; civil law involves private detectives, private attorneys, and damages paid by defendants to plaintiffs. The form is in many ways different, but the substance is similar. In both cases, it is alleged that someone has done something he should not have and in both something undesirable happens to the convicted defendant—whether we call it punishment or paying damages.

This raises some interesting questions about our system. Is there something natural about the present division into "public" and "private" enforcement? What are the advantages and disadvantages of the two systems? Could we have a system in which all law enforcement was public, so that a businessman who failed to deliver goods on time would be arrested, indicted, and jailed? Could we have a system in which all enforcement was private, so that a murderer would be sued for damages by the heirs of his victim?

Whether our present system is in some sense natural or optimal or efficient is a subject of dispute among economists involved in the economic analysis of law. My own belief is that it is not; some of my colleagues believe that it is. What is clear is that different divisions between private and public enforcement are possible and have existed in other societies and at other times. They include some in which enforcement was entirely private; killing someone resulted in a lawsuit instead of an arrest.

Whether or not we have the correct mix of private and public enforcement, it is clear that both systems have advantages and disadvantages. One of the inherent disadvantages of public enforcement is illustrated by the following immoral tale.

You are a police officer. You have got the goods on me. You have collected sufficient evidence to arrest and convict me; the resulting punishment would be equivalent, to me, to a $20,000 fine. Perhaps the punishment *is* a $20,000 fine; perhaps it is a period of imprisonment which I would pay $20,000 to avoid. For the purposes of the story, we will assume the former.

Arresting me will improve your professional reputation, slightly increasing your chances of future promotion. That is worth $5,000 to you in increased future income. Seen from the viewpoint of *Dragnet*, the rest of the story is clear; you arrest me and I am convicted. Seen from the viewpoint of this book, the result is equally clear. You have something—the collected evidence against me—which is worth $5,000 to you and $20,000 to me. Somewhere between $5,000 and $20,000, there ought to exist a transaction in our mutual benefit. I pay you $10,000, and you burn the evidence.

So far as you and I are concerned, that is an eminently satisfactory outcome, but it is not a very effective way of enforcing the law. In this respect, the public enforcement system is not "incentive compatible." The system requires you to do something—arrest me—in order for it to work, and the system makes it in your interest to do something else. The system, of course, can and will try to control the problem—for example, by punishing police officers who are caught accepting bribes. But the fact that it must devote some of its limited resources to catching police officers instead of catching criminals is itself a defect.

Another way to solve the problem is to pay you, not a wage, but the value of the fines collected from the criminals you convict. Under such a system, you lose $20,000 when you burn the evidence, so $20,000 is the lowest bribe you will accept. Since $20,000 is also the cost to me of being convicted, there is little point in my offering you that much to let me off—save perhaps as a way of saving the time and expense of standing trial. If I do bribe you, no damage has been done; I have still paid $20,000 and you have still received it. We have merely eliminated the middleman.

This may sound like an odd and corrupt system, but it is the way in which civil law is presently enforced. The enforcing is done by a lawyer, acting as the agent of the victim; the "punishment" is paid by the defendant to the victim. What we call bribery in criminal law is called an out-of-court settlement in civil law. The only addition to my scheme needed in order to make it correspond exactly to ordinary civil law is to make the claim against the criminal start out being the property of his victim; the "police officer"—who in this system is a private entrepreneur rather than a government employee—buys the claim from the victim before hunting down the criminal.

Elements of such a system for enforcing criminal law existed in the U.S. in the last century, as shown by the "Wanted Dead or Alive: $200 Reward" posters familiar in films and books about the Wild West. The policemen of that system were called bounty hunters. A complete system of private enforcement existed in Iceland in the early Middle Ages. Not only was killing treated as a civil offense, but the enforcement of court verdicts, including the job of hunting down convicted defendants who refused to pay and were consequently declared outlaws, was left to the plaintiffs and their friends. Odd as it may seem, the system appears to have worked fairly well; the society of which it was a part was one of the most interesting and in some ways one of the most attractive then existing. It was the source of the original *sagas*—historical novels and histories written in the thirteenth and fourteenth centuries and in many cases still in print today, in English translations. Their quality and quantity put it, in terms of literary output per capita, in the same class as Periclean Athens or Elizabethan England.

Private enforcement has one great advantage over public enforcement; the enforcers are working in their own interest, not that of the "public," so they have a private incentive to do the job. It also has some problems. One of them is that many criminals are "judgment-proof"; they lack the assets necessary to pay any large fine. A public enforcement system can punish such criminals by imprisoning (or, in extreme cases, executing) them, but it is not immediately obvious how a private enforcer can make a profit that way. One cannot, it is said, get blood from a turnip, and while a pound of flesh may add drama to a Shakespearean play, its market value is near zero. If a private enforcer cannot make money out of catching criminals, he has no incentive to do so, just as there is no incentive in our civil system to sue someone, however guilty, if he obviously cannot pay damages.

There are other problems with private enforcement. In criminal law, unlike civil law, one usually does not start out knowing who the guilty party is. As a result, one may have only a small probability of catching him. This creates a number of complications for a system which uses private enforcement to try to implement the "solution" described earlier in this chapter—to impose the optimal level of fines with optimal probability.

In analyzing the choice between private and public enforcement, as in discussing the problem of optimal punishment earlier, we get into complications that cannot be adequately dealt with in this book; so I will leave unresolved the question of whether our system of enforcement should be more private or less so. At the end of this chapter, I list some articles and books, including several of mine; readers who wish to pursue the issues raised in this chapter may find them of interest.

I have not given final answers to many questions in this part of the chapter, nor have I "solved" many problems. What I hope I have done, here and in the previous parts, is to convince you that economic analysis can be used to evaluate such fundamental issues as what the laws should be, what the penalties should be for breaking them, and how those penalties should be enforced. The economic analysis of law is an important part of what some of us like to call "economic imperialism"—the use of economics to analyze what have traditionally been considered "non-economic" questions—and, as you may have guessed, one which I have found particularly interesting.

PROBLEMS

1. In discussing the efficient level of crime, I pointed out that my earlier analysis failed to distinguish between the value of what was stolen to the victim and its value to the thief. How could we correct that omission? Which value would be used in deriving the "price" on the vertical axis of Figures 19-3a through 19-3d? Explain. (This is a hard problem.)
2. Throughout the chapter, I have ignored the possiblity that some people might abstain from stealing because they thought it was immoral. How could we include that possiblity in the analysis? Would it change any of the results? Discuss.
3. It is sometimes said that "Crime does not pay." Discuss the truth or falsity of this from the standpoint of various parts of this chapter.

4. There is a way to make theft forever impossible—perhaps by adding a "guilt drug" to the water supply which would make anyone who steals anything after taking the drug feel intolerably guilty. Would all, some, or none of those who are presently thieves be in favor of doing this? Suppose that adding the drug requires the unanimous consent of everyone in the society. Under what circumstances, if any, would everyone agree to it?

5. In Chapter 17, I discussed problems associated with "software piracy"—the unauthorized copying of computer programs. As the name suggests, this can be regarded as a form of theft; indeed, I once shocked one of my colleagues by suggesting that his possession of disks full of pirated software made him the moral equivalent of a burglar. Suppose there is some way of making such software piracy impossible. Should none, some, or all of those who presently use pirated software be in favor of the change? Discuss.

6. "We can always lower the cost of our criminal justice system by catching half as many criminals as before and punishing them twice as harshly; the system will be just as effective as before at deterring crime and we will not need to hire as many police officers." Discuss.

7. I defined "efficient crimes" as crimes that were Marshall improvements. What do you think I mean, in one of the headings of this chapter, by the "efficient level of crime." (Hint: I do not mean the level at which only efficient crimes occur.)

8. In this chapter, I have argued that certain things should be illegal on grounds of economic efficiency. If this is our criterion, what things that are presently illegal should not be? Should they be illegal on other grounds? If so, why? Discuss.

9. "One reason someone may appear on Figures 19-3a through 19-3d as a 'good thief' is that he is good at stealing; another is that he is bad at everything else." Discuss. What principle from a much earlier chapter does this point illustrate.

10. In our verbal analysis of the market for theft shown in Figures 19-3a through 19-3d, we are really talking about cost on two different "margins." One is the margin of how many hours an individual thief "works." The other is the margin of how many people are thieves. Quantity of theft can be increased or decreased on either margin. State, as precisely as possible, the implications of our usual result for a competitive industry with free entry (price = marginal cost = average cost) in this case, distinguishing where necessary between the two margins, and among thieves of differing abilities.

FOR FURTHER READING

My analysis of private enforcement is in "Efficient Institutions for the Private Enforcement of Law," *Journal of Legal Studies* (1984), which also contains references to earlier work on the subject by others, not all of whom agree with me. *The Machinery of Freedom*, cited in the previous chapter, contains a nontechnical discussion of how a fully private system of courts, police, and laws might work.

My earlier article, "Private Creation and Enforcement of Law—A Historical Case," *Journal of Legal Studies* (March, 1979), describes the working of the Icelandic system, as does the book by Jesse Byock (a historian, not an economist), listed below. My "Reflections on Optimal Punishment Or: Should the Rich Pay Higher Fines?" in Richard Zerbe (ed.), *Research in Law and Economics*, Vol. 3 (1981) contains a detailed analysis of optimal punishment.

Other works of interest include Jesse Byock, *Feud in the Icelandic Saga* (Berkeley: University of California Press, 1982); Norval Morris and Gordon Hawkins, *The Honest Politician's Guide to Crime Control* (Boston: Little, Brown & Co., 1977); Richard Posner, *Economic Analysis of Law* (Chicago: University of Chicago Press, 1972); and Gordon Tullock, *The Logic of the Law* (New York: Basic Books, 1971).

Chapter 20

The Economics of Love and Marriage

This chapter consists of two parts. The first discusses the economics of marriage; it starts with an analysis of the marriage market and goes on to consider what marriage is and why it exists. The second part of the chapter is devoted to the economics of *altruism*—the analysis of rational behavior by an individual who values the welfare of another. It demonstrates that altruism, which one might think of as "outside of economics," actually fits neatly into economic theory. The result is not merely to accommodate the theory to an important feature of the real world but also to use economics to derive some surprising results about the consequences of altruism.

THE ECONOMICS OF MARRIAGE

We start our discussion of marriage by taking marriage itself as a given. We assume that some people want to marry other people and that they prefer some potential partners to others. We also assume that although marriage partners, potential and actual, may put considerable value on each other's welfare—a phenomenon to be analyzed in the second part of the chapter—there is still room for some conflict of interest between them. There is therefore also room for some bargaining over the terms, implicit or explicit, of the marriage.

To add interest to the discussion, I will focus on a particular policy issue. In our society, only *monogamous* marriages are permitted—one husband, one wife. In various other societies, *polygynous* marriages (one husband, two or more wives) and *polyandrous* marriages (one wife, two or more husbands) have also been legal. What would the effect of legalizing polygyny or polyandry be on the welfare of men? On the welfare of women? On the net welfare of all concerned?

In order to answer this question, we require a formal model of the marriage market. I will work out the implications of two different ones. The first is designed to make the marriage market appear very similar to the markets with which we are by now familiar; the second is designed to emphasize two of the respects in which it differs from such markets.

One element common to both models is the assumption that women and men belong to themselves—that the marriage partners are the only ones whose consent is required in order for the marriage to take place. This is appropriate if we are considering marriage in the U.S. or some similar society, since in such societies, adults do, in that sense, belong to themselves. It is less appropriate if we are comparing the institutions of our society to those of others. In many past societies (and some present ones), unmarried women were to some degree the "property" of the male head of their household; his consent was required in order for them to be married, and it was he who collected the "bride price," if any. Economic analysis is as applicable to such a society as it is to ours, but the results must be modified to take account of the different property rights; gains which in our society would go to the bride may in such a society go to her father instead. Similar modifications would apply in the less common case where sons, as well as or instead of daughters, were the property of their families.

Model 1: A Market With Prices

In many societies, marriage is commonly accompanied by payments—bride price paid by the groom or his family to the family of the bride, dowry provided by the bride's family to the new couple, and so on. While explicit payments of this sort are not a part of our marriage institutions—unless you count expenditures on the wedding and the wedding gifts—one may argue that a marriage still contains an *implicit* price. When two people get married, they do so with some general understanding of the terms they are committing themselves to—how free a hand each will have with the common funds, what duties each is expected to perform, and so on. One may think of the terms of this understanding as corresponding to a price and serving the same function as an explicit price in other markets.

Imagine, for example, that a plague kills off many young women of marriageable age. After the plague is over, young women find it easy and young men difficult to get married. One result we would expect is a shifting of the "price" associated with marriage—men will find that they are implicitly bidding against each other for wives, and the terms of the bidding may include the willingness of the men to accept marriage terms pleasing to the women. This is particularly likely in a society in which divorce is relatively easy, so that each partner can enforce the terms of the contract by threatening to dissolve it and find someone else. If, in a society where women are scarce, the man who promised before the wedding to do everything his wife wanted proves less accommodating afterward, some other man will be willing to take his place. Similarly, if some war greatly reduced the population of marriageable men, we would expect to find the terms of the marriage contract swinging toward the men's side.

For our first model, then, we will think of the marriage market as an ordinary market with a price. There exists some "standard marriage contract." Any other contract can be viewed as a standard contract plus or minus a certain number of dollars paid by the husband to the wife; plus represents a contract more favorable to the wife than the standard, while minus represents one less favorable. Supply and demand behave just as they do on any other market. The quantity supplied of wives—the number of women willing to marry—will be higher, and the quantity demanded lower, the higher the price. The model is entirely symmetrical, as we will see on Figures 20-1a and 20-1b; we can just as easily speak of the quantity demanded and quantity supplied of husbands. As long as all marriages are monogamous, the number of husbands supplied and the number of wives demanded are the same, since a man seeking to become a husband is a man seeking to

Figure 20-1

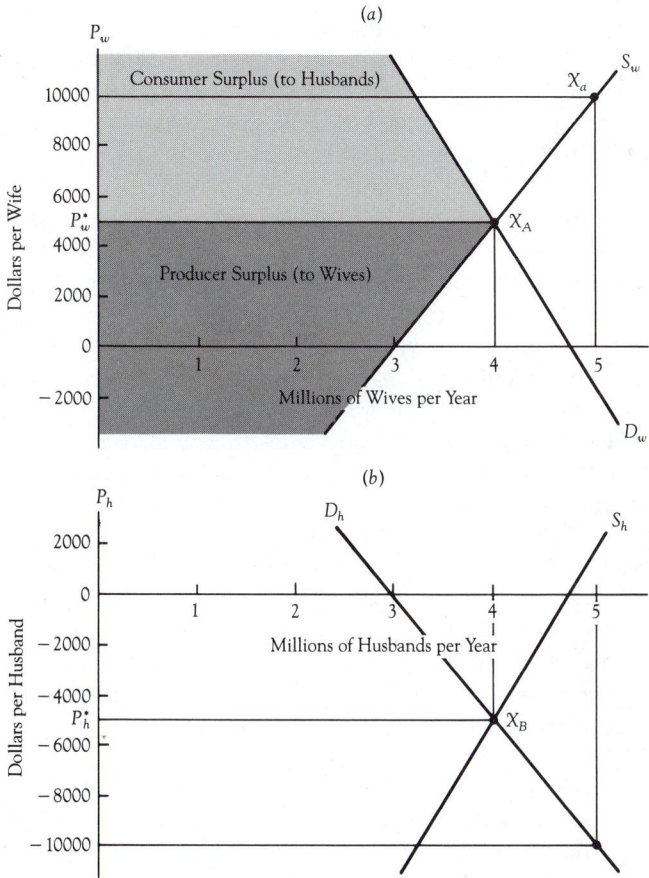

The monogamous marriage market. Figure 20-1a is drawn from the standpoint of a potential husband, who sees the market as a market for wives. Figure 20-1b is drawn from the standpoint of a potential wife, who sees it as a market for husbands. P_w is "price of a wife," defined as the terms of the actual marriage contract relative to the terms of some arbitrary standard contract. P_h is the "price of a husband," defined similarly relative to the same standard contract. P_w is positive (and P_h negative) if the terms of the actual contract are more favorable to the wife than the terms of the standard contract.

obtain a wife, just as, on a barter market, someone who offers to trade wine for beer is both supplying wine and demanding beer. Similarly, the number of wives supplied is the same as the number of husbands demanded.

Omissions. Before using this model to analyze the consequences of polygyny and polyandry, several additional points should be made. We have so far ignored quality differences in potential husbands and wives—the fact that some people are more desirable marriage partners than others. We can, if we wish, include this in our model by including it in what we mean by a "standard" contract. We would then define a "standard contract" (price = 0) for marrying an unusually desirable woman as one in which the woman received specially favorable terms to balance the advantages the husband received from having a particularly desirable wife. Perhaps the husband would have to agree to wash all of the dishes. Seen from this standpoint, attractiveness is simply one element of the initial wealth of an individual. A man or a woman who has good looks or a pleasant disposition is wealthier—has a greater command over the desirable things of life—than someone who has not, just as someone who has inherited a million dollars is wealthier than someone who has not.

We would still be failing to take account of another important feature of marriage—not everyone has the same tastes. The woman I recognized as a one in ten thousand catch was not even being pursued by anyone else, with the result that I married her on quite reasonable terms—I did not even have to agree to wash all of the dishes. Some of the women that my friends married, on the other hand, I would not have chosen on any terms they could have offered. Yet my friends obviously preferred them, not only to remaining bachelors but to trying to lure my intended away from me.

This feature of the marriage market is not, of course, unique to it. We would observe the same thing in the market for houses or the market for jobs—indeed in most markets where both the good and the purchaser are very inhomogeneous, so that the problem is not merely the allocation of limited quantities but the proper matching of buyer and bought. One of the implications of such situations—high transaction costs—was mentioned in the discussion of barter in Chapter 17. Another will come up in the discussion of unemployment in Chapter 22.

I think it would be possible to take account of this feature of the marriage market without substantially altering the results of our analysis, although I cannot be sure, since I have not actually tried. It would, however, make the model too complicated for our present purposes. We will therefore ignore complications associated with varying quality of potential mates until we come to the second model and ignore complications associated with differing tastes throughout this chapter.

The Effect of Legalizing Polygyny and Polyandry. Figures 20-1a and 20-1b show the same marriage market seen from two sides. In Figure 20-1a, S_w is the supply curve for wives, D_w the demand curve for wives; in Figure 20-1b, S_h is the supply curve for husbands, D_h the demand curve for husbands. In Figure 20-1a, P_w is a price (positive or negative) paid by husbands to wives—the "price of a wife." Similarly, in Figure 20-1b, P_h is a price paid by wives to husbands—the price of a husband. Both figures convey the same information; S_w is identical to D_h except for the differing definitions of price. For $P_w = +\$10,000/\text{wife}$, $S_w = 5,000,000$ wives per year (point X_a); for $P_h = -\$10,000/\text{husband}$, $D_h = 5,000,000$ husbands per year (point X_b). A price of $10,000 paid by a husband to a wife is the same thing as a price of $-\$10,000$ paid by a wife to a husband. Both prices—$P_w = +\$10,000$ and $P_h = -\$10,000$—represent the same contract, one which is equivalent to a standard contract plus a $10,000 payment by the husband to the wife. At this price, the quantity of wives supplied is greater than the quantity of wives demanded (or, equivalently, the quantity of husbands demanded is greater than the quantity supplied), so it is not the equilibrium price.

P_w^* on Figure 20-1a is the equilibrium value of P_w, the value for which quantity of wives supplied equals quantity demanded. $P_h^* = -P_w^*$ is similarly the equilibrium value of P_h on Figure 20-1b. On the particular marriage market shown by the figures, the equilibrium price of a bride is $5,000; in order to get married, a man must offer marriage terms that are $5,000 "more favorable to the wife" than the "standard" marriage contract relative to which P_w is defined.

Skip Figure 20-2 for the moment; we will get back to it. Figure 20-3a shows what happens if polygyny is legalized; Figure 20-3b shows what happens if polyandry is legalized (with polygyny still illegal). Figure 20-3a corresponds to Figure 20-1a, Figure 20-3b to Figure 20-1b. On Figures 20-3a and 20-3b, as on Figures 20-1a and 20-1b, equilibrium occurs where quantity supplied equals quantity demanded.

The essential thing to notice about the figures is that P_w^* is higher on Figure 20-3a than on Figure 20-1, and $P_h^{*\prime}$ is higher on Figure 20-3b than on Figure 20-1. The result is exactly the opposite of what one might expect; polygyny benefits women and polyandry benefits men!

Figure 20-2

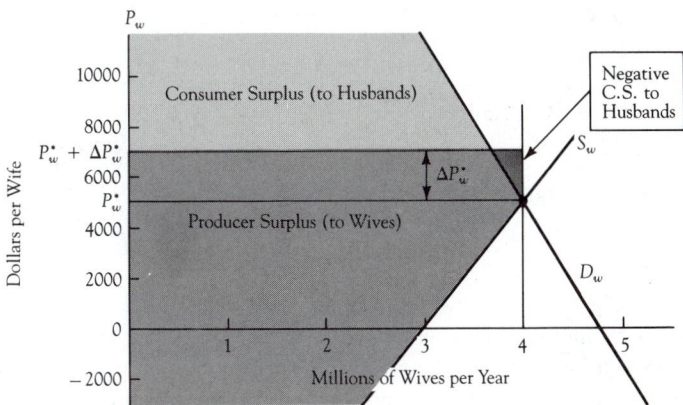

The monogamous marriage market with P_w set at its level under polygyny.   The situation is the same as in Figure 20-1a, except that every husband pays every wife ΔP_w^*—the amount by which the price of a wife would increase if polygyny were legalized.

Figure 20-3

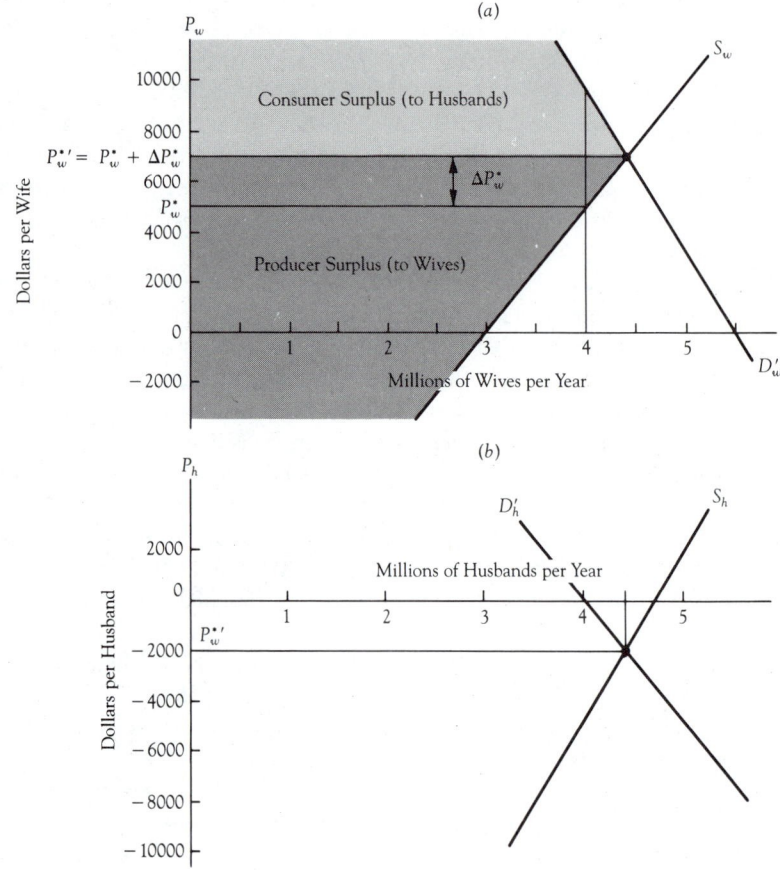

<u>Polygamous marriage markets.</u> Figure 20-3*a* shows the market for wives (Figure 20-1*a*) after the legalization of polygyny; Figure 20-3*b* shows the market for husbands (Figure 20-1*b*) after the legalization of polyandry. In each case, the supply curve remains the same, the demand curve shifts out, and the equilibrium price rises.

Why? On Figure 20-3*a*, the supply curve for wives is the same as on Figure 20-1*a*. The legalization of polygyny does nothing to increase or reduce the number of wives willing to accept any particular marriage contract. Of course, a woman willing to accept a monogamous marriage may be unwilling to share the same husband with another wife, but that is already taken into account in the definition of P_w. Since P_w was defined relative to a standard contract—one of whose features, in Figure 20-1*a*, was monogamy—a bigamist who "offers" a price $P_w = 0$ for a wife must be offering her terms sufficiently favorable to balance the cost to her of having to share him with another wife, so that on net, what he offers is equivalent to a standard contract. The same applies at all other values of P_w; we define the price corresponding to any particular bigamous marriage contract as the price earlier assigned to that monogamous contract which potential wives consider equivalent to it.

We can now see why the equilibrium price in Figure 20-3a is higher than in Figure 20-1a. Suppose it were not; suppose the two prices were equal. Quantity supplied on Figure 20-3a would then be the same as on Figure 20-1a, but quantity demanded would be higher. Legalizing polygyny will hardly make a man who before wanted one wife decide that (at the same price) he now wants none, but it will allow some who before wanted one to marry two instead—even if they must offer terms at which potential wives are willing to accept half a husband apiece. So when polygyny becomes legal, quantity demanded at any price rises—the demand curve shifts out from D_w to D_w'. At the old equilibrium price (P_w^*), quantity demanded is now higher than quantity supplied. So the price must rise; the new equilibrium price ($P_w^{*\prime}$) must be higher than the old. Since price is defined in such a way that an increased price means a contract more favorable to the wife, this means that women are better off.

What about men? Those who end up with only one wife are worse off, since they must offer her more favorable terms than before. They are worse off by $\Delta P_w^* \equiv P_w^{*\prime} - P_w^*$, the increase in the "price" they must pay for a wife. Those who end up with two (or more) wives may or may not be better off. The fact that someone chooses to marry two wives shows that he prefers "buying" two wives at a price of $P_w^{*\prime}$ each to "buying" one at that price; it does not tell us whether he prefers two at $P_w^{*\prime}$ to one at P_w^*.

Is the change a Marshall improvement or a Marshall worsening? It is a Marshall improvement. To see this, imagine that we go from Figure 20-1a to Figure 20-3a via Figure 20-2. Figure 20-2 is Figure 20-1a plus a transfer of ΔP_w^* from every husband to every wife. Going from Figure 20-1a to Figure 20-2 is a pure transfer; wives gain what husbands lose. The next step, from Figure 20-2 to Figure 20-3a, is a Marshall improvement; husbands with one wife are unaffected, and husbands with more than one wife, or women who at the old price did not choose to marry but at the new price do, are better off. A pure transfer plus a Marshall improvement adds up to a Marshall improvement.

Figure 20-3b shows the effect of legalizing polyandry. The logic is exactly the same as for polygyny, with the roles of women and men reversed. Since some women now "buy" two (or more) husbands, the demand curve for husbands shifts out. At the old price for husbands, demand is greater than supply, so the price rises. Women marrying only one husband must compete against the polyandrous women to get him, hence must offer better terms than before. Men are better off, monogamous women are worse off, and polyandrous women may be better or worse off. The net effect is a Marshall improvement.

To many readers, the conclusion may seem extraordinary—how can women possibly be made better off by polygyny and men by polyandry? That reaction reflects what I described in Chapter 2 as naive price theory. Naive price theory is the "theory" that prices do not change. If polygyny were introduced and nothing else changed, then it seems likely that women would be worse off—except for those who prefer to share the burden of putting up with a husband. But when polygyny is introduced, something else does change—the demand curve for wives shifts up, and so does the price for wives implicit in the marriage contract. Those wives who end up with one husband get him on more favorable terms—he must bid more for a wife because of the competition of his polygynous rivals. Those who accept polygynous marriages do so because the "price" they are offered is sufficient to at least balance, for them, the disadvantage of sharing a husband.

Another reason why you may regard the result as implausible is that in many historical societies, including some of the polygynous ones, women did not belong to themselves. In such a situation, a woman's father, or whoever else was in a position to control whom she married, could have ended up receiving a large part of the "price" implicit in the marriage contract. If so, the demonstration that women are benefited by the legalization of polygyny no longer holds. That is why, at the beginning of the discussion, I explicitly assumed a society in which men and women belonged to themselves.

The result would seem less paradoxical if we substituted cars and car buyers for wives and husbands (or husbands and wives). Suppose there were a law forbidding anyone to own more than one car. It seems obvious enough that the abolition of that law would increase the demand for cars. Sellers of cars would be better off. Buyers who did not take advantage of the new opportunity—those who bought only one car—would be worse off, since they would have to pay a higher price. Buyers who bought more than one car would be better off than if they bought only one car at the new price (otherwise that is what they would have done) but not necessarily better off than if they bought one car at the old price, an option no longer open to them.

One thing which you may find confusing in all this is the time sequence. Am I describing a situation in which, after polygyny becomes legal, some men divorce one wife to marry two others, and some women insist on renegotiating their marriage contracts? No. What I am doing is comparing two alternative futures, one with polygyny (or polyandry) and one without. The man who would have married one wife if polygyny had remained illegal either marries one wife on different terms if polygyny is legal or marries two (or more) wives.

Most discussions of whether changes are or are not improvements compare hypothetical futures in this way, whether or not they say so. When you decide that your house will be warmer with a new furnace than with your old clunker, you are making a prediction about the furnace, not the weather. If the new furnace is installed in November, you do not necessarily expect that the new furnace will keep the house warmer in December than the old one did in September, but only that the new one will keep you warmer in December than the old one would have. Similarly in the discussion of marriage, when I say that introducing polygyny makes wives better off, I do not mean that it makes those married before the change better off—they already have a husband and a marriage contract. I mean that it makes those who get married after the change better off than they would have been if the change had not occurred.

The Second Model

So far, we have modeled the marriage market in a way designed to make it as similar as possible to more conventional markets. The next step is to switch to an entirely different model—one that some of you may find more realistic.

We start by assuming that there is no way marriage partners can offer prices to each other, implicit or explicit. One reason might be the difficulty of enforcing such contracts, especially in a society where divorce is difficult. The obvious strategy in such a situation, when seeking a mate, is "Promise anything but don't wash the dishes." Actual cash payments between the mates, as a substitute for more or less favorable marriage terms, might be either illegal or impractical. The latter would be the case if, after the marriage, all property were held in common; there is little point in bribing someone with what will belong to him or her after the marriage anyway.

In such a society, the marriage market is a market without a price. The absence of a price does not eliminate the fundamental problem of scarcity; it just means that some other means of allocating the scarce supply of desirable mates (of both sexes) must be found.

We will now explicitly include one of the features which we earlier pushed into the background—the varying quality of mates. We suppose that all of the potential mates of each sex can be arranged in a hierarchy ranging from "most desirable" to "least desirable" and that everyone agrees on who belongs where in the hierarchy.

We now have a very simple rationing mechanism. The most desirable woman has her pick of mates, so she accepts the most desirable man; he, having his pick of mates, is only interested in her. The second most desirable woman would gladly accept the most desirable man, but he is already taken, so she settles for the second most desirable man. The process continues until all the members of whichever gender is less plentiful on the marriage market have been paired up, leaving the least desirable members of the other gender unmarried.

Suppose we now permit polygyny in this society. The most attractive woman can no longer be certain of marrying the most attractive man. He may prefer two less attractive women—and they may each prefer half of him to all of a less attractive man. If fewer men than women want to get married, some women may be choosing half of a husband over the alternative of no husband at all.

The result is no longer an unambiguous improvement from the standpoint of women, as it was in the first model. Some women at the top of the hierarchy find themselves with less attractive men than before. Neither is it an unambiguous worsening; some women who were previously unmarried may now have (half of) a husband, while others may get half of a man instead of all of a dolt.

It may or may not be an unambiguous improvement for the men. Some men benefit by getting two wives instead of one. In addition, every time a man near the top of the hierarchy settles for two (lower quality) women instead of one (high quality) one, he opens up a rung on the ladder—the men below him move up a step and end up with more desirable wives than they could have before. Figure 20-4 shows such a change; A, B, C, . . . are the men, in order of desirability, while 1, 2, 3, . . . are the women. When *B* chooses 7 and 8 instead of 2, whom he would have married in a monogamous society, *C-G* all find themselves with more attractive wives as a result.

How can the change injure men? A man is worse off if someone above him marries two wives, both higher in the women's hierarchy than the woman he was going to marry. In that case, the change eliminates one step above him on the men's ladder and two steps on the women's, pushing his relative position down a step; he must be content with a woman one step below the one he could have gotten if monogamy were the rule. In Figure 20-4, that is what happens to *H* and everyone below him.

Just as in the first model, the argument can be repeated for the case of polyandry, with essentially the same results. When polyandry becomes legal, some men near the top of the hierarchy almost certainly lose; some near the bottom—in particular those, if any, who could not find a wife before—gain. Women may all gain, or those at the top may gain at the expense of those at the bottom.

Figure 20-4

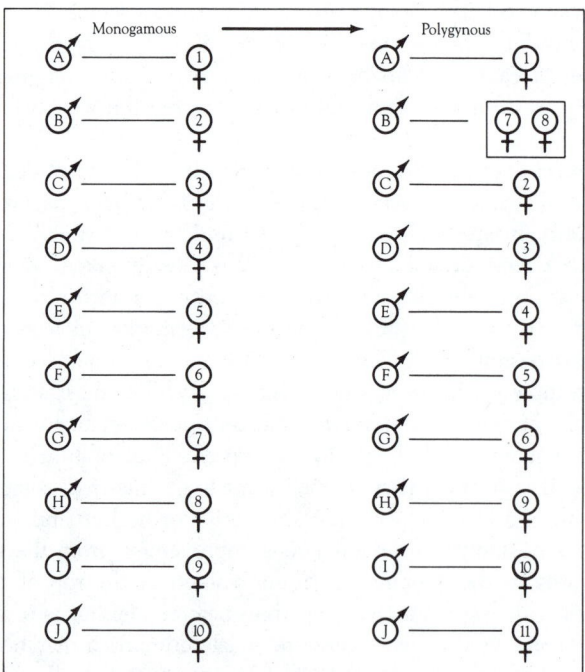

The effect of polygyny in a marriage market without prices. Both men and women are ranked (A,B,C, . . . ; 1,2,3 . . .) according to their attractiveness as marriage partners. If polygyny is illegal, A marries 1, B marries 2, etc. If it is legal, A marries 1, B marries 7 and 8, C marries 2, etc.

Markets With and Without Price—Some General Comments

Whenever it is suggested that something should be provided on the market instead of produced and allocated by government, one of the objections made is that such a proposal only benefits the rich, since if something is sold, "The rich get it all." The outcome of the marriage market I have just described—a market without price—is much more like that stereotype than is the outcome of an ordinary market with a price. On an ordinary market, differences in income are one of the factors determining who gets what, but not the only one. An individual who particularly values something—car, clothes, books—may end up with more of it than a competitor with higher income but different tastes. And the outcome is not all or nothing; the individual who spends more money gets, not all of the good, but an amount proportioned to what he is willing to spend.

On the marriage market without price, on the other hand, it does not matter how much a man wants an intelligent and beautiful wife and how many other things he is willing to give up to get her; if there is anyone above him on the hierarchy who also wants her, he has no chance. "Wealth"—not in money but in whatever makes for an attractive mate—is the sole determinant of who gets what. And the competition, for any particular mate, is all-or-nothing; if you have half the attractiveness of your competitor, the result is not that you get a third of what you want and he gets two thirds but that he gets all of it.

The situation is still worse for those at the bottom of the ladder—the least attractive members of whichever gender has more people wanting to get married. On an ordinary market, at least in a reasonably prosperous society such as ours, the poorest people do not get as much food as the richest, but they do get fed. Their equivalents on the marriage market do not get married, however much they may wish to.

Money, Beauty, and Folk Songs

The Brown Girl she has house and lands, fair Ellender she has none.

— No. 73 of *The English and Scottish Popular Ballads* collected by Francis James Child

At the end of this chapter, there is a brief discussion of the "anti-money" bias of our culture—the attitude that regards money transactions, especially in a social context, as somehow base or corrupt. Those who do not believe that such a bias exists may find it instructive to reread the earlier parts of this chapter or explain them to their friends and examine their own and their friends' reaction to describing marriage as buying a wife or husband.

One aspect of this which is particularly relevant to our two models of the marriage market—with and without price—is a motif frequently seen in folk songs. A young man must choose between two women, one beautiful and one rich. Almost invariably he chooses the rich one. The result is tragedy; at least two and often all three of the parties end up dead. The lesson is clear: Marry the beautiful woman.

It is always assumed in such songs that marrying a woman for her money is bad, but marrying her for her beauty is fine. It is not entirely clear why. True, the Brown Girl (dark complexioned, hence less attractive than "Fair" Ellender) does not "deserve" her (parents') wealth; hence one could argue that she does not deserve to get Lord Thomas. But no more does Fair Ellender deserve her beauty. All either of them has done is to pick the right parents, the one for wealth and the other for looks. Why then is it good and noble for Lord Thomas to reject wealth for beauty and base and wicked for him to reject beauty for wealth?

One answer may be that the plot depends on something which I earlier assumed away. In the world of folk songs—and in many, perhaps most, human societies—the bride and groom are not the only ones whose interests are involved in their marriage, nor are they the only ones with some control over it. Both sets of parents are involved as well. What may really be going on in "Lord Thomas and Fair Ellender"—and other songs with the same plot line—is a conflict of interest between the groom and his family. If Lord Thomas marries Fair Ellender, he will be the only one to benefit by her beauty; if he marries the Brown Girl, his parents may reasonably hope to get their hands on some of her wealth. Perhaps they are counting on it to support them in their old age. It is Lord Thomas's mother who persuades him to marry the Brown Girl.

If that is what is going on, it is clear enough which side of the generation gap the singer is on. Or, more precisely, which side he believes his audience is on.

What and Why Is Marriage?

(Miss Manners) also asks that you not bore her with explaining the comparative quality of marital and nonmarital relationships, especially when using the term "honesty" or asking the nonsensical question of what difference a piece of paper makes. Miss Manners has a safe-deposit box full of papers that make a difference.

— *Miss Manners' Guide to Excruciatingly Correct Behavior* by Judith Martin

So far in our discussion of the marriage market, we have taken it for granted that marriage exists and that many people want to get married. We will now turn from examining the market to examining the institution. Our first questions are "What is marriage" and "Why does it exist?"

Marriage as a Firm. One way of looking at marriage is as a rather odd sort of package deal, an exchange in which the two parties agree to share income, housing, sexual favors, and a collection of productive activities such as cooking meals (for themselves), cleaning house, washing dishes, and rearing children. Seen from this standpoint, the motivation for marriage is, in part, the existence of economies of scale in production—it is easier to cook one meal for two people than two meals each for one person—and, in part, the advantages of division of labor. A marriage is simply a particular kind of two-person firm.

But a firm is not the only way of taking advantage of division of labor—there is the alternative of the market. Most of us take advantage of the comparative advantage of the butcher, the baker, and the brewer; but we do not have to marry them to get our dinner. The wife in a traditional marriage may have a comparative advantage over the husband in cooking, and the husband might have a comparative advantage over the wife in carpentry. But outside of the household, there are surely better cooks and better carpenters than either of them. Why does the couple limit itself to division of labor within the household?

The Reasons for Household Production. Few couples do; most of us obtain much of what we want by buying it on the open market. The typical family does, however, rely on "household production" for a considerable range of what it consumes—most meals, most domestic cleaning, much child care and education, and so on. Why are not these things too purchased on the market?

One reason is the existence of transaction costs. If you are going to build a house, it is worth hiring a carpenter. If you are simply fixing a few loose shingles, the time and trouble of finding a good carpenter, negotiating mutually satisfactory terms, and making sure he does the job may more than wipe out the carpenter's comparative advantage. The carpenter may be better at fixing the shingles than I am, but I am the one who gets wet if the roof leaks, so I have an incentive to do a good job even if nobody is watching me. And I have no incentive to waste time and energy haggling with myself over the price.

A second reason may be specialization—not in a particular product but in a particular set of customers. The cook at the restaurant my wife and I would go to if we spent less time cooking and more time earning money to pay for going to restaurants is probably better at cooking than we are. But the restaurant cook is worse than we are at cooking *for us*. We, after all, are specialists in what we like. This may be still more true for some other forms of household production.

We now have at least a partial explanation for the existence of marriage as a firm. A second element worth investigating is the fact that marriage, in most societies, is a very long-term contract. Why?

Marriage and the Costs of Bilateral Monopoly. The answer was given back in Chapter 6, in the discussion of bilateral monopoly. Before I went to work at UCLA, both I and the economics department were participating in a large and moderately competitive market; once I had accepted the job and spent a year or two learning to do it, we were both to some degree locked into a bilateral monopoly. Both they and I had borne substantial costs associated with training me for that particular job and equipping the department to deal with that particular professor.

Marriage is a more extreme version of the same situation. Individuals choose their mates on a large and competitive market—however much they may protest that there could never have been anyone else. But once they are married, they rapidly acquire what in other contexts is known as *firm-specific capital*. If they decide to end the contract and find other partners, they incur very large costs which they would have avoided if they had chosen the right partners to start with. Their specialized knowledge of how to live with each other becomes worthless. One, at least, must leave a familiar and accustomed home. Their circle of friends will probably be divided between them. Worst of all, the new mate, whatever his or her advantages, is not the other parent of their children.

As I explained in Chapter 6, one problem with acquiring firm-specific capital is that it creates a large bargaining range between the two parties. Each may be tempted, in trying to get things his way, to take advantage of the fact that the other is locked into the relation and will choose to leave it only if things get very much worse. There is no way of entirely eliminating such problems, in marriage or in other contexts, but long-term contracting, explicit or implicit, is a common way of reducing them.

Enforcement Problems. The marriage contract involves two different elements, one a good deal more enforceable than the other. The agreement to remain married "till death do us part" is to a considerable degree enforceable; in many societies, although not ours at present, getting out of one marriage and into another is a difficult and expensive undertaking. Henry VIII, as you will remember, had to change the religion of an entire country in order to cancel his long-term contract with Catherine of Aragon.

But preventing the parties to a contract from backing out of it entirely does not solve the problem unless the contract specifies the precise obligations of each party—and does so in a way that can be enforced. Marriage without divorce can result in an even larger bargaining range than marriage with divorce, since one party can threaten to make the other's life so unpleasant that divorce would be an improvement. Whether the threat is a believable one may depend on the cost of carrying it out. If both parties know that when the argument is over they are still going to be married to each other, that may give them an incentive to avoid extreme strategies.

This suggests that the ideal solution would be a long-term contract which completely specifies the obligations of both parties. Before the contract is signed, there is no marriage, hence no bilateral monopoly, hence not much of a bargaining range. After the contract is signed, on the other hand, there is nothing left to bargain about.

To a considerable extent, marriage is supposed to be such a contract. It is, in principle, possible for a husband or wife to claim that the other is not living up to his or her responsibility—for a wife to sue a husband for failing to support her, for example. The problem is, first, that one can never write a contract detailed enough to specify all the relevant terms and, second, that even if one could, it would be almost impossible to enforce it. Here, as with price control, the individual who is legally obliged to provide a specified product at a specified price can generally avoid the obligation by lowering quality. So far as I know, nobody has ever successfully sued his or her spouse for cooking—or making love—badly. So a considerable amount of bargaining room remains, and is used, even in marriages in traditional societies.

Love and Marriage. So far in this chapter, I have said nothing about love, which is widely believed to have some connection with marriage. One reason is that love, under the name of altruism, is the subject of the second part of this chapter. A second reason is my suspicion that the emphasis on love, and in particular on romantic love, as the chief element in marriage is a peculiarity of our culture that should not be given too much weight in a general discussion.

Nonetheless, we are still left with the question of why particular elements are included in the package deal we call marriage. It may seem odd to ask why we marry someone we love, instead of marrying someone whose tastes agree with and whose skills complement our own and then conducting our respective love lives on the side, but it is a legitimate question.

There are two answers. The first is that love is associated with sex, for reasons which can be explained (by *sociobiology*—economics applied to genes instead of people) but will not be here, and sex with having children. Parents much prefer rearing their own children to rearing other people's, and much of child rearing is most conveniently done in the home of the rearer; so it is convenient, to say the least, if a child's parents are married—to each other.

The second answer is that love serves to reduce, although not necessarily to eliminate, the conflicts of interest that lead to costly bargaining. If I love my wife, her happiness is one of the main things determining mine; we therefore have a common interest in making her happy. If she also loves me, we also have a common interest in making me happy. Unless our love is so precisely calculated that our objectives are identical, there is still room for conflict, in either direction; if we love each other too much, my attempts to benefit her at my expense will clash with her attempts to benefit me at her expense. Conflict is reduced but not in general eliminated.

A more precise discussion of the logic of such situations will have to wait for the second part of the chapter, where I work out in some detail the situations in which altruism does or does not lead altruist and beneficiary to have identical objectives.

The Decline and Fall of American Marriage. Now that we have at least a sketch of an economic theory of marriage, we might as well do something with it. One obvious thing to do is to explain the decline of marriage in the U.S. (and some similar societies) over the course of this century. Why has marriage become less common and why has the effective term of the contract become so much shorter?

The simple answer is that the amount of time spent in household production has declined drastically, and with it the amount of firm-specific capital acquired by the partners, especially the wife. Earlier I remarked that it was not necessary, in order to get dinner, to marry one's butcher, baker, and brewer. In fact, a few hundred years ago, it was not uncommon for a man to be married to his baker and brewer and a woman to her butcher—all three of those professions were to a considerable extent carried out within the household, especially in rural areas. Dorothy Sayers, in one of her essays, suggests that men who complain about women stealing "men's jobs" should be asked whether they wish to return to women all the industries which used to be conducted by housewives and have now moved onto the market, such as brewing, preserving food, weaving cloth, and making clothes.

One factor reducing the amount of household production has been the increase in specialization over the past few centuries. Bacon, clothing, jams, and many other things are now mass-produced instead of being made at home. A second factor has been the mechanization of much of what remains. Clothes and dishes are still washed at home, but a good deal of the work is really done by the firms that make the washing machines. A third factor has been the enormous decrease in infant mortality. It used to be necessary for a woman to produce children practically nonstop in order to be fairly sure of having two or three survive to adulthood, with the result that bearing and rearing children was virtually a full-time job. In a modern society, a couple that wants two children produces two children.

The result of all three changes has been to greatly reduce the amount of work done by an average housewife. Thus, being a housewife is no longer a full-time profession, save in certain unusual cases—families that want a lot of children, couples going "back to the land," and the like. But household production in general and child rearing in particular are the source of a large part of the "specialized capital" associated with marriage. If husband and wife each spend 80 percent of the day working at a job and 20 percent taking care of the household and if they have no young children, the costs of divorce are not all that great. Even for a somewhat more traditional family, with the husband working full time and the wife dividing her time between work, housekeeping, and rearing one or two children, the costs of divorce are much lower than they were a few generations ago.

Divorce is not all costs—there are benefits too; otherwise nobody would ever get divorced. If the benefits remain unchanged and the costs are reduced, the number of cases in which at least one partner finds that the benefits are greater than the costs will increase. Judging by the divorce rate, it has. Seen from this standpoint, the increase is neither inherently good nor inherently bad, neither evidence of increased freedom nor a consequence of declining moral standards. It is merely a rational adjustment to a changing world.

It is good insofar as it reflects, and accommodates, an increase in the range of choice available to individuals. We could choose to live in eighteenth century households, tanning our own leather and brewing our own beer. Some people do—you can read about their lives in *Mother Earth News* every month. The fact that most do not is evidence that, for most of us, the costs of living that kind of life instead of our present one are larger than the benefits.

The increased divorce rate, and the general difficulties with modern marriage, are bad things only to the extent that they reflect the failure of our institutions and expectations to adjust completely to new circumstances. The terms on which two people can live a happy and productive life together are not so simple that each couple can invent them independently in a few hours. The division of labor has a place in building institutions as well as houses. In a relatively static society, we can observe successful arrangements—patterns that have worked in the past and will probably work in the future. In a rapidly changing society, it is more difficult to figure out what kind of a contract we should or should not agree to and what kind of a marriage—or alternative arrangement—we should or should not choose. Hence there are likely to be more mistakes. Here as in most other areas, economic theory is more useful for describing the equilibrium than for describing the process by which we move from one equilibrium to another.

THE ECONOMICS OF ALTRUISM

A common argument against economics is the claim that economists either assume or advocate selfishness, whereas people in the real world should and do care
for others. There is some truth to this charge, but not very much. Economists do
assume that people have their own objectives and act to achieve them, but, as I
have pointed out several times, there is no reason why those objectives must be
selfish; economists can and do assume that one of the things some people value
is the welfare of other people.

Geometric Version

Someone who values the welfare of someone else is called an *altruist*. It is possible
to use economics to analyze the rational behavior of an altruist and of the person
whose welfare he cares about, and in the process to derive some surprising results.

Figure 20-5*a* shows the indifference curves of an altruist A, who is concerned
with his own consumption, C_A, shown on the vertical axis, and the consumption
of a beneficiary B, C_B, shown on the horizontal axis. Both C_A and C_B are goods
for A, so his indifference curves slope down and to the right; both exhibit declining marginal utility, so the curves are convex toward the origin. In drawing the
figure, I have assumed that both C_A and C_B are normal goods; as his income rises,
he chooses to consume more of both. That assumption will be retained throughout the discussion.

A has an income I_A and B an income I_B. If A gives nothing to B, each will
consume his own income, putting them at point X ($C_A = I_A$, $C_B = I_B$). But A
can, if he wishes, transfer part of his income to B, reducing his own consumption
and increasing B's. As he does so, he moves down the line L. The slope of L is

Figure 20-5

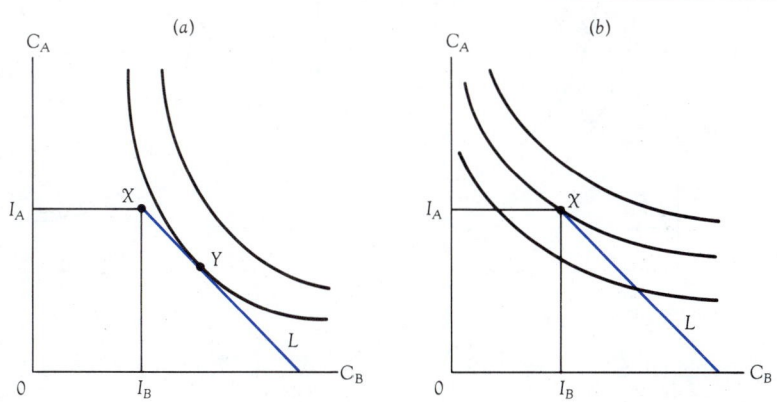

Budget line/indifference curve diagram for an altruist. By choosing how much of his
income (I_A) to give to the beneficiary, the altruist is choosing a point on the budget line
L. Figure 20-5*a* shows an interior solution at Y; Figure 20-5*b* shows a corner solution at X.

−1; when A gives B a dollar, A's consumption goes down by a dollar and B's goes up by a dollar. A will continue to make transfers until he reaches point Y, where an indifference curve is tangent to L. This is, from his standpoint, the optimal point on L, just as the point where an ordinary budget line is tangent to an indifference curve was the optimal point for an ordinary consumer in Chapter 3—it is the most desirable point available to him.

Figure 20-5a shows a situation in which the altruist chooses to make transfers to the beneficiary. Figure 20-5b is similar, except that the altruist's preferred point is X, where he starts out; any transfer will move him to a lower indifference curve. In this case, he makes no transfers. The altruist consumes his entire income (I_A), and the "beneficiary" consumes his entire income (I_B).

Figures 20-5a and 20-5b are almost exactly like the budget line-indifference curve diagrams we constructed in Chapter 3. A is "buying" two goods, C_A and C_B, with a "total income" of $I_A + I_B$. The only difference is that since the altruist can make transfers to B but cannot force B to make transfers to him, the line stops at X; there is no way he can choose a bundle higher and further to the left than that. In effect, the altruist is deciding how to divide the total income, $I_A + I_B$, between himself and the beneficiary, subject to the condition that the beneficiary has to end up with at least I_B.

Figure 20-6a shows the effect of two possible changes in the situation. The solid line *df* (case 1) is the result of a change that decreases I_A by \$10; the dashed line *cf* (case 2) is the result of a change that instead decreases I_B by \$10. The two

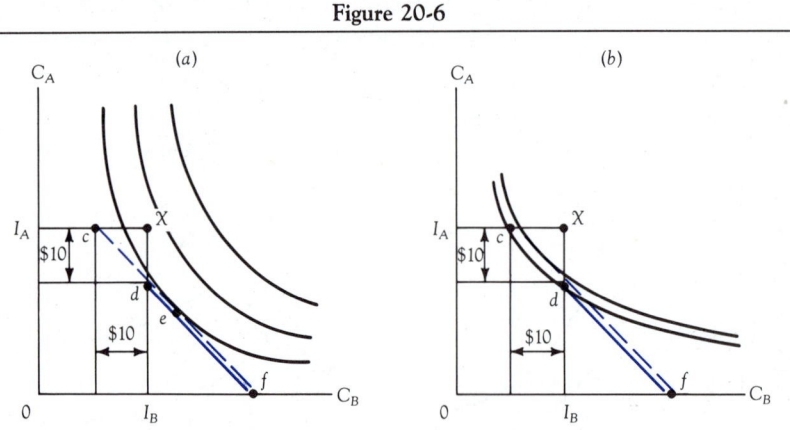

Figure 20-6

The effect on an altruist's situation of a change in the combined income of altruist and beneficiary. In each case, the solid line shows the effect of a \$10 reduction in the altruist's income, and the dashed line shows the result of a \$10 reduction in the beneficiary's income. In Figure 20-6a, where the optimum is an interior solution, it is the same for both cases; in Figure 20-6b, one of the optima is a corner solution (no transfer) and is not the same as the other.

lines are identical except that the dashed line goes a little farther up and to the left. In the figure as I have drawn it, the optimal point chosen by the altruist (*e*) is the same in both cases.

As you should be able to see from the figures, this is not an accident. The two lines, one representing the situation where the altruist loses $10 and the other the situation where the beneficiary does, are the same except for the section *cd*, which exists only for the dashed line. So unless the altruist's optimal point is on *cd*, it must be the same for both cases. If the optimal point is on *cd*, as shown on Figure 20-6*b*, then in case 1, where the altruist loses the money, his new optimum is at *d*. This is a corner solution—the altruist chooses not to transfer anything, so each ends up consuming all of his own income.

Verbal Version

The analysis can be put in words as well as in figures. The altruist, in deciding how much of his income to give to the beneficiary, is dividing the combined income of the two ($I_A + I_B$) between them, subject to the condition that the beneficiary cannot end up with less than he starts with (I_B). The altruist can choose to give the beneficiary nothing (in which case, the final distribution is I_A to the altruist and I_B to the beneficiary), or everything (0 to the altruist, $I_A + I_B$ to the beneficiary), or anything in between. A $10 decrease in either the altruist's or the beneficiary's income means that there is now $10 less to be divided. The only difference between the situation where the decrease is in the altruist's income (case 1) and the situation where it is in the beneficiary's (case 2) is that in the former case, the least the beneficiary can end up with is I_B, his original income, and in the latter, the least he can end up with is $I_B - 10$, his new, lower, income. If the altruist's preferred division involves the beneficiary consuming more than I_B, as it does in Figure 20-6*a*, the constraint does not matter; even if he could create a division in which the beneficiary consumed less than I_B, as he can in case 2, he would not choose to. So the outcomes of case 1 and case 2 are the same, as shown on Figure 20-6*a*.

This means that as long as we only consider situations in which the altruist chooses to make some transfer (unlike Figure 20-5*b* and case 1 on Figure 20-6*b*, where he does not), changes in the combined income of altruist and beneficiary have the same effect on the consumption of both, whether they change the altruist's income or the beneficiary's income. The beneficiary, if he understands this analysis, will find it in his interest to pay as much attention to maintaining the income of the altruist as to maintaining his own. In this respect, the beneficiary ends up acting rather as though he too were an altruist—even though he is actually indifferent to the altruist's welfare.

I have stated the argument in terms of income and consumption, since that makes it simple enough to draw on a piece of two-dimensional paper. The same argument can be made in a more general form in which the utility of both altruist and beneficiary depends on many things; an altruist is then defined as someone whose utility depends, among other things, on the utility of someone else (the beneficiary). The result is, as in the simpler case, that the utility of the beneficiary depends on the circumstances of both himself and the altruist. In situations similar to those illustrated in Figure 20-6a, where all the alternatives involve the altruist making some transfer, the beneficiary finds it in his interest to pay as much attention to the welfare of the altruist as to his own.

More precisely, it is in the interest of the beneficiary to take any action which produces net gains to himself plus the altruist, in exactly the same sense in which we discussed net gains in the context of Marshall efficiency. Any change which is a Marshall improvement will also be an improvement for the beneficiary—if we include in our calculations the effect of the change on the amount that the altruist chooses to transfer. A change which benefits the altruist by $5 and hurts the beneficiary by $3 will also result in the altruist increasing his transfer to the beneficiary by at least $3 and less than $5; a change which injures the altruist by $5 and benefits the beneficiary by $3 will result in a reduction of the transfer by something between $3 and $5. I have proved this result graphically in the simple two-dimensional case where all changes are in money; the proof in the more general case (where the loss might be a broken arm, a broken window, or even a broken heart) is similar but more complicated.

Your response to this result may be that it is not surprising; if the beneficiary hurts the altruist, the altruist "punishes" him by reducing the transfer, so the beneficiary finds it in his interest not to offend his patron. That is not what is happening. Nothing in the argument I gave, or the more general argument whose results I described, depends on the altruist knowing that the beneficiary is responsible for the change. Exactly the same thing will happen in the case of a change produced by some third party, or by nature. If the change is a Marshall improvement, both beneficiary and altruist end up better off after the change—and the resulting change in the amount the altruist chooses to transfer. If it is a worsening, both end up worse off.

You can see that result in Figure 20-6a, where the equilibrium position depends only on the combined income $I_A + I_B$, not on the individual incomes. That remains true as long as, both before and after the change, the altruist chooses to make some transfer to the beneficiary. Figures 20-5b and 20-6b show situations where that is not true; two of the equilibria on those figures are corner solutions with zero transfer. Since in such situations, $C_A = I_A$ and $C_B = I_B$, the division of consumption depends on I_A and I_B, not just on their sum.

The Rotten Kid Theorem

Consider a situation with one altruist ("parent") and two beneficiaries ("kids"). One of them is a rotten kid who would enjoy kicking his little sister. It is possible to show, using the sort of argument I have already described, that if the dollar value to the rotten kid of kicking his sister (the number of dollars worth of consumption he would, if necessary, give up in order to do so) is less than the dollar cost to the sister of being kicked, the rotten kid is better off not kicking her. After the parent has adjusted his expenditure on the kids to take account of the increased utility of the kid and the decreased utility of the kicked sister, the rotten kid will have lost more than he has gained. Here again, the argument does not depend on the parent observing the kick but only on his observing how happy the two kids are.

This result—that a rotten kid, properly allowing for the effects of parental altruism, will find it in his self-interest to kick his sister only if it is "efficient" to do so—is known as the *Rotten Kid Theorem*. There is a sense in which the altruist in such a situation functions, unintentionally, as a stand-in for the bureaucrat-god—at least as far as the tiny society made up of altruist and beneficiaries is concerned. Because of the altruist's peculiar utility function—one which contains the beneficiaries' utilities among its arguments—both altruist and beneficiaries find it in their private interest to maximize Marshall efficiency, to make all decisions according to whether the net effect on altruist and beneficiaries is or is not a Marshall improvement.

Altruism and Evolution

What, if anything, is this analysis of altruism useful for, other than entertainment? Gary Becker, the economist whose ideas I have been describing, has used them to try to resolve one of the principal puzzles of sociobiology—the existence of altruism. If, as the theory of evolution seems to imply, animals (including ourselves) have been selected by evolution for our ability to serve our own reproductive interest (roughly speaking, to act in such a way as to have as many descendants as possible), those who sacrifice their interest for the interest of others should have been selected out. Yet altruism seems to occur among a variety of species, possibly including our own.

One explanation is that altruism toward kin (most obviously toward my children, but the argument turns out to apply to siblings and other relatives as well) is not really altruism from the point of view of evolution; I am serving my reproductive interest by keeping my children alive so that they can have children. This still leaves altruism toward non-kin as a puzzle to be explained. Becker's argument is that altruism generates cooperative behavior via the mechanism described above and so benefits the altruist as well as the recipient, by giving each recipient an incentive to behave "efficiently" vis-à-vis the entire group—including the altruist. A group containing an altruist will therefore be more successful than one which does not contain an altruist; it will have more surviving descendants, and its genes, including the genes for altruism, will become increasingly common.

One problem with this argument is that at the same time that the altruist is promoting the reproductive success of his group vis-à-vis other groups, he is also sacrificing his own reproductive success vis-à-vis other members of his group. He is, after all, transferring resources of some sort from himself to them. If Becker's analysis is correct, genes for altruism should be becoming less frequent over time within groups containing one or more altruists, but the genes of such groups should be becoming more frequent over time; only if the second process at least balances the first will altruism survive.

Fair Ellender and the Rotten Kid

In the first part of this chapter, I asked why marrying for beauty is generally considered better than marrying for money. We now have a possible answer. It is widely believed that beauty is, and wealth is not, one of the things that makes men fall in love with women. Our analysis of altruism suggests that people will work together much more easily if one of them is an altruist with regard to the other, since it is then in the interest of both altruist and beneficiary to maximize their joint welfare. Lord Thomas is in love with Fair Ellender and is not in love with the Brown Girl, as he informs her immediately after the wedding—with the result that the Brown Girl stabs Fair Ellender, Lord Thomas kills the Brown Girl, and Lord Thomas then commits suicide, thus ending the song and presumably teaching his parents a lesson. If we are willing to identify "being in love" with "altruism," perhaps the moral of the song is correct. If you marry the beautiful woman, you get not only beauty but also the advantage of being part of an efficient household—coordinated by your own altruism.

Of course, it only works one way; we have no reason to believe that Fair Ellender's beauty makes her any more likely to act altruistically toward Lord Thomas. But that is not a serious objection; we know, from the Rotten Kid Theorem, that one altruist in a family is enough.

A more serious objection is that it is not clear how close the relationship is between "being in love" and altruism; Fair Ellender's response to being jilted by the man she was "in love" with was to dress up in her finest ("every village she came through, they thought she was some queen") and go spoil her ex-boyfriend's wedding. "Being in love" seems to describe a mix of emotions, some of them far from altruistic. To what extent the elements in the mix associated with physical beauty involve altruism, and, if they do, whether they are likely to survive the first six months of marriage, is at least an open question.

Gift vs Money

Why do people ever give gifts in any form other than money? If, as we normally assume, each individual knows his own interest, surely he is better off getting money and buying what he wants instead of getting what the donor decides to buy for him.

There are two obvious reasons to give gifts instead of cash. The first is that the donor may believe the recipient's objectives are different from his own. I may give you a scholarship not because I like you but because I want there to be more educated people in the society or more smart high school students going to my alma mater. I give you the money, but only on condition that you spend it on buying schooling from a particular school.

Another example is the food stamp program. The idea is not merely to help poor people, but to get them to buy more food. This leads to another question: Why do we care what the poor people spend the money on? If they feel clothing or shelter is more important than food, why not let them make that choice? One answer to that question is that the program is largely supported by politicians from food-producing states.

The food stamp program is probably not very successful in forcing people to spend what they are given on food, since it is difficult to prevent recipients from selling unused food stamps—or food bought with food stamps—to nonrecipients. As long as resale is easy and the total amount people (including nonrecipients who can buy food stamps from recipients) want to spend on food is larger than the face value of all the food stamps given out, the food stamp program is virtually equivalent to a cash grant. Those who get more food stamps than they wish to use sell them at slightly below their face value and use the money to buy what they want.

A second reason for giving restricted gifts is paternalism. If you believe that you know better than the recipient what is good for him, you will naturally want to control how he spends your money. The obvious example is the case of parents dealing with children. A second reason to give food stamps instead of money may be the belief that some of the poor should spend money on food but, if given a choice, will spend it on whiskey instead.

It is not entirely obvious that paternalism is a sensible policy even for children. When I was quite small, my family traveled, by train, from Chicago to Portland, Oregon, to visit grandparents. The trip took three days and two nights. My father offered me and my sister the choice of either having sleeping berths or sitting up and being given the money that the berths would cost. We took the money.

This brings us back to the question of why we give gifts instead of cash—to our friends and even our parents on Christmas, birthdays, and the like. Even if paternalism is appropriate toward one's children, it hardly seems an appropriate attitude toward one's parents. A possible answer is that, in this particular small matter, we do think we know their interest better than they do—we are giving, say, a book we have read and are sure they will like. I doubt that this is a sufficient explanation—considering how often we give people gifts we have no special reason to think they will like. I suspect that the correct answer is somehow connected with the hostility to money, especially in personal interactions, which seems typical of our society. Consider, for example, the number of men who would think it entirely proper to take a woman to an expensive restaurant in the hope of return benefits later in the evening, but would never dream of offering her money for the same objective.

Such an explanation leads to a further problem—explaining why our society is hostile to the use of money, especially in personal relations. As an economist, I would like to find an economic explanation even for "anti-economic" behavior.

Suspension of Disbelief

Some of my more courageous readers may at this point be about ready to ask whether I expect them to take this chapter seriously. Do I really believe that love and marriage can be analyzed with the abstract logic of economics? Do I really believe that a 7-year-old boy, in deciding whether or not to kick his little sister, works out a cost-benefit calculation based on economic theory that is fully understood by almost no one without a Ph.D. in economics?

The answer is "yes, but." I do believe that the analysis of this chapter is *useful* in understanding love, marriage, and children as they exist in the real world. I do not believe that the analysis is *sufficient* to understand them, without also knowing a good deal about what it is like to be human, to love, to be a child, to be a parent. Nor do I believe that if theory clashes with what we observe in the real world, it is the real world that must back down; I am not willing to say, in the words of a famous German philosopher confronted with evidence contrary to his theories, "So much the worse for the facts."

Economics is one way of understanding the real world. It depends, in virtually all practical applications, on using an approximate picture of the real world, one which retains the essential features while eliminating inessential elements whose inclusion would make the analysis intolerably complicated. Making such approximations correctly is a matter of judgment; one way of finding out whether you have done so is by seeing how well the predictions of the theory fit what you actually observe. It is most unlikely that they will fit perfectly, since the world you observe is not identical to the simplified picture of it that you have analyzed. But an approximate theory is still better than no theory at all.

All that being said, it is also true that for some of us, the creation of economic theory, especially economic theory of things that everyone else regards as "outside of economics," is an entertaining game and even, perhaps, a form of art. As long as that is all it is, the theory is properly judged by artistic criteria—elegance and consistency. It is only when we stop sketching out theories for fun and start testing them against the real world that economics becomes a science as well as an art and its analysis useful as well as entertaining.

PROBLEMS

1. In analyzing the first model of marriage, I drew a supply curve for wives, S_w. An increase in the "price" that potential husbands offered for wives resulted in an increased quantity of wives supplied, since improved marriage terms made more women willing to marry.

   Suppose we were considering a society in which the price went to the bride's parents instead of the bride. Discuss how and why the supply of wives would depend on the price, in both the short and long run.

2. In analyzing the effects of polygamy and polyandry, Figure 20-3a was based on Figure 20-1a and Figure 20-3b on Figure 20-1b. Why do you think I did it that way? What complications would have arisen if I had used a figure similar to 20-1b for analyzing the effects of polygamy and a figure similar to 20-1a for polyandry? You may find it instructive to try doing it that way. Pay careful attention to what you mean by the "supply" of husbands and wives.

3. In analyzing the effects of polygamy, I claimed that the polygamists themselves—the men who ended up with more than one wife—might be worse off as a result of the legalization of polygamy. How can that be—if they are worse off, why do they not simply decide to marry only one wife? Discuss.

4. It is said that there exists a traditional society in which every year there is a "bride market." It takes the form of an auction, starting with the most desirable bride. The money paid by suitors for the desirable brides is collected. When the auctioneer gets to a bride nobody wants to pay to marry, the price goes negative—he starts offering a payment to potential suitors, paid out of the money collected. As the brides get less desirable, the payments get larger. The auction continues until all of the young women of the appropriate age have been auctioned off.

Discuss the workability and the implications of this system. What would be the effect of legalizing polygamy? Polyandry?

5. In the case of the second model of the marriage market, discuss how the welfare implications for men and for women of the introduction of polygamy or polyandry are affected by whether the market starts with a surplus of men or a surplus of women.

6. Can you suggest reasons for the hostility to money, especially in social contexts, discussed in the chapter? Ideally the reasons should involve the sort of economic analysis of "social institutions" that we have just been doing.

7. In analyzing marriage in the first part of this chapter, I treated implicit prices and contracts as if they were identical to the explicit prices and contracts that we see on ordinary markets. To what extent is that legitimate; to what extent is it not? You may want to think of an implicit contract as embodied in, and enforced by, a set of social expectations about marriage—what a good wife or husband does or is.

8. In discussing the nature of marriage, I presented reasons why both love and sex are normally part of the "package"—along with cooking, housecleaning, child rearing, and a variety of other services. This does not seem to have been true of French upper-class society in the nineteenth century, at least as depicted by French novelists. One has the impression that every well-to-do husband had a mistress and every wife a lover.

Discuss possible reasons why marriage may have taken the form it did in that society. In general, what relation would you expect to observe between stability of marriage and income. Does this correspond to what actually happens, in that society and others?

9. Throughout the analysis of altruism, I assumed not only that the beneficiary's utility was a good for the altruist but that it was a normal good. Suppose it is instead an inferior good. How would the conclusions of the analysis be changed? How would the beneficiary find it in his interest to behave?

10. Suppose that the utility of one person is a *bad* for another. How might one describe this situation? What results would you expect?

11. Suppose we concede that my sister and I correctly perceived our own interest when we chose money over berths for our train trip. What reasons can you suggest, in terms of the analysis of this book, why letting us make the choice might nonetheless not have lead to the efficient outcome?

12. An individual receives \$200/month of income plus \$100/month of food stamps. Food stamps can be resold (illegally) at 90 cents on the dollar. Draw

an indifference curve-budget line diagram showing the consumption bundles (food vs expenditure on all other consumption) available to that individual. Assume that there are no restrictions on how much of the payment for food may be made with food stamps.

13. For the situation of Problem 12, draw three sets of indifference curves—one for which the individual will choose to sell some food stamps, one for which the individual spends all of the food stamps and only the food stamps for food, and one for which the individual spends all of the food stamps plus some money for food.

FOR FURTHER READING

An excellent introduction to sociobiology—the study of the behavior of animals, including humans, on the assumption that it has been "designed" by evolution to maximize the reproductive success of the individual's genes—is Richard Dawkins, *The Selfish Gene* (New York: Oxford University Press, 1976).

For a more advanced discussion of the economics of marriage (and other things), I recommend Gary Becker, *A Treatise on the Family* (Cambridge: Harvard University Press, 1981).

A less theoretical and more practical guide to (among other things) courtship and marriage is Judith Martin, *Miss Manners' Guide to Excruciatingly Correct Behavior* (New York: Atheneum Publishers, 1982).

Finally, for a witty and intelligent discussion of the differences between men and women, first written some sixty years ago and well designed to equally infuriate all parties to the issue, I recommend H. L. Mencken, *In Defense of Women* (New York: Octagon Books, 1976).

Chapter 21

The Economics of Heating

At the beginning of this book, I defined economics as that way of understanding human behavior based on the assumption of rationality—that individuals have objectives and tend to choose the correct way to achieve them—and gave several simple examples. It may have occurred to you that if that is all economics is, economics is really nothing more than a straightforward application of common sense. It may have occurred to you since to wonder why it is necessary to load common sense with so heavy a burden of technical analysis—marginal cost curves, externalities, firm and industry equilibrium, and the like.

Using "common sense" to deduce the implications of rational behavior is not as simple as it might seem. So far, our techniques have been applied mostly to "textbook problems"—hypothetical shipping industries, trade between Mr. *A* and Ms. *B*, and the like. In this chapter, I will apply some of those same tools to a set of real-world problems with which you are familiar—home heating. In the first part of the chapter, I demonstrate that two commonly observed features of "heating behavior"—decisions by homeowners concerning how warm to keep their homes—which seem inconsistent with "common sense" are actually implied, in a fairly simple way, by economic analysis. In the second part of the chapter, I will derive the profit-maximizing rule by which the owner of an apartment building should decide how warm to keep the apartments.

The purpose of this chapter is not so much to teach you how to heat your house, or even how to make money heating apartments, as it is to demonstrate that with the economics you now know, it is possible to derive surprising, interesting, and useful results about the real world.

THE PHYSICS OF HEATING

Before analyzing the economics of home heating, it is necessary first to say a little about the physics. Heat tends to flow from hot objects to cold ones. If the inside of your house is at 70° and the outside temperature is 0°, heat flows from the inside through the walls to the outside. In order to maintain the house at 70°, the heating system must put heat into the house as fast as it flows out—just as, in order to maintain the water level in a leaky tub, you must pour water in the top as fast as it comes out the bottom. The cost of maintaining a house at some particular interior temperature, given the external temperature, is simply the price of heat times the rate at which the house loses heat under those conditions.

There are three processes by which heat is transmitted from the inside to the outside of a house—or, more generally, from any object to any colder object. They are called conduction, convection, and radiation. The first, *conduction*, is, for our purposes, both the most important and the easiest to analyze; so in this chapter, I shall ignore the other two and discuss home heating as if conduction were the only way in which heat could be lost. Those students who are familiar with the physics of heat transmission may find it interesting to see to what degree the results can be generalized to include one or both of the others.

The physics of conduction is very simple. The rate at which heat flows through an insulating barrier—a wall, for example—is proportional to the temperature difference between the two sides of the barrier ($T_i - T_o$ in Figure 21-1a). The formula is:

$$H = \text{Heat Flow} = C \times (T_i - T_o). \tag{Eqn. 1}$$

C depends in part on how good an insulator the barrier is. If the wall is well insulated, then C is small—only a little heat flows through it, even with a substantial temperature difference. If the wall is poorly insulated, C is large. C also depends on the dimensions of the barrier—the more area there is for heat to flow through, the greater the heat flow. Thus for the house shown in Figure 21-1b, C depends both on how well it is insulated and on its size and shape.

The cost of heating a house is the price of heat times the rate at which heat must be put into the house to make up for the heat flowing out through the walls. Hence:

$$TC_h = P_h \times H = P_h \times C \times (T_i - T_o), \tag{Eqn. 2}$$

Figure 21-1

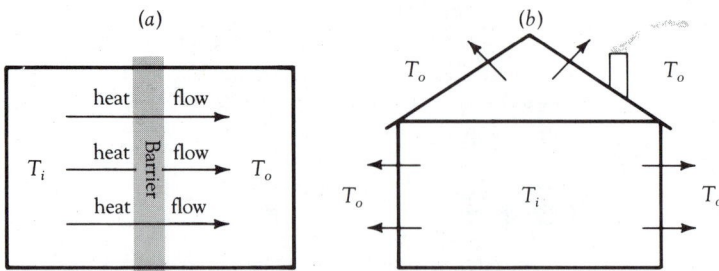

Heat flow. Heat flows from a warmer object at a temperature of T_i to a cooler object at a temperature of T_o through an insulating barrier. The rate of flow is proportional to $T_i - T_o$; the proportionality constant depends on the barrier.

where P_h is the price of heat and TC_h is the total cost of heating. TC_h is a rate, measured in dollars per day, just as H is a rate of heat flow, measured in BTU's per day. The price of heat depends on the cost of fuel oil, coal, electricity, or whatever input is used to heat the house and on the efficiency of the furnace, fireplace, or whatever is used to transform that input into heat.

Figure 21-2 shows the implications of Equation 2 for several different houses. The total cost of heating each house is shown as a function of the internal temperature—the thermostat setting. TC_1, TC_2, and TC_3 correspond to identical houses with different external temperatures—0° for TC_1, 30° for TC_2, 60° for TC_3. TC_4 shows total cost for a better insulated house and TC_5 for a worse insulated house, both with an external temperature of 0°. Since this chapter is concerned only with heating and not with air conditioning, the figure does not show any cost for internal temperatures lower than the external temperature.

As you can see by looking at Equation 2, the slope of the total cost curve is simply $C \times P_h$; every time T_i goes up 1°, TC_h goes up by $C \times P_h$. TC_1, TC_2, and TC_3 represent identical houses; the values of C and P_h are the same, so all three lines have the same slope. TC_4 is the total cost of heating a better insulated house, so its slope is less—the better insulated the house, the less additional heat required for each additional degree of internal temperature. TC_5 is the total cost of heating a worse insulated house, so its slope is steeper than the slopes of TC_1, TC_2, and TC_3.

The difference among TC_1, TC_2, and TC_3 is not the house but its environment. TC_1, TC_2, and TC_3 correspond to three different external temperatures—three different climates, or the same climate at three different times of the year.

Figure 21-2

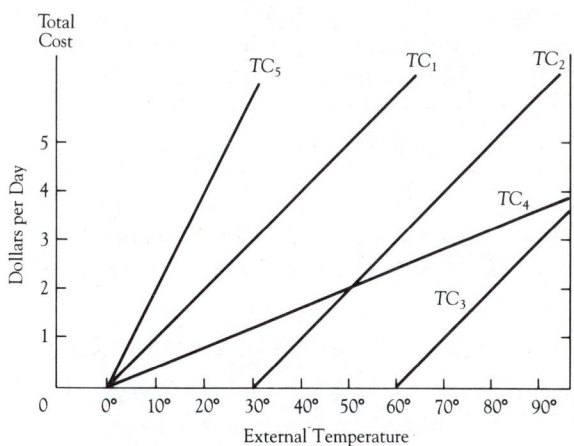

Total cost of heating various houses as a function of their internal temperature.   1, 2, and 3 are identical houses with different outside temperatures; 4 is a better insulated house and 5 a worse insulated one, each with the same outside temperature as House 1 (0°).

Looking at Equation 2, you can see that when $T_i = T_o$, TC_h is zero; it requires no heating to keep the temperature inside the house equal to the temperature outside. So TC_1, which shows total heating cost for a house with an external temperature of $0°$, is zero for an internal temperature of $0°$. TC_4 and TC_5 represent houses with the same external temperature as TC_1, so they are zero at the same internal temperature; all three lines intersect the horizontal axis at $T_i = 0°$. Similarly, TC_2 is zero at $T_i = 30°$ and TC_3 at $T_i = 60°$.

We are now finished with the physics of heating. We have learned two essential facts. The first is that maintaining a house at a constant temperature requires that heat be put in as fast as it flows out. The second is that the rate at which heat flows out is proportional to the temperature difference between inside and outside, with the constant of proportionality (C) depending on characteristics of the house such as size and insulation. The implications of those facts are shown in Equations 1 and 2 and Figure 21-2. With that, plus some economics, we are equipped to understand why people heat their houses as they do.

PART 1 · COLD HOUSES IN WARM CLIMATES: A PARADOX OF RATIONAL HEATING

A native of Chicago who spends a winter in Los Angeles or Canberra is likely to find the houses uncomfortably cold and to express surprise that the natives are too stingy to heat their houses properly even though it would cost very little to do so. An Angelino wintering in Chicago or the Northeast is likely to have the opposite reaction; why, he wonders, do the inhabitants of such ferocious climates spend a fortune on overheating?

The pattern suggested by such casual observation—an inverse relation between external and internal temperature—seems inconsistent with both common sense and economic rationality. Home heating is more expensive in Chicago than in Los Angeles, so we would expect people to buy less of it, not more. If the opposite is observed—if houses are kept warmer in Chicago than in Los Angeles—that would seem to be evidence of irrational behavior.

Appearances are deceiving. Not only is the observed pattern consistent with rationality, it is implied by it. The "common sense" intuition in the opposite direction depends on a common economic error—the confusion among different sorts of costs. *Total* heating cost, for any internal temperature, is higher in Chicago than in Los Angeles, but *marginal* heating cost is lower.

Step 1: Identical Houses in Different Climates

To see why this is true, we start by considering two identical houses in December. One is in Los Angeles, where the temperature outside is $60°$; the other is in Chicago, where it is $0°$. The houses are occupied by identical people, with identical tastes for internal temperature. Those tastes can be described by a marginal value curve, showing the value to the occupant of each additional degree of internal temperature. If, for instance, the occupant would be willing to give a maximum of \$.15/day in order to have his house at $61°$ instead of $60°$, then his marginal value for internal temperature is about $.15/degree-day between 60° and 61°. If he would be willing to give only $.05/day to have the house at 71° instead of 70°, then at that part of the curve, his marginal value for internal temperature is only $.05/degree-day.

Figures 21-3a and 21-3b show marginal value curves for two identical individuals, one in Los Angeles and one in Chicago. Since they are identical, their marginal value curves are the same; in each case, the occupant's favorite temperature—the temperature he would choose if the cost of temperature were zero—is 75.5°, where the MV curve intersects the horizontal axis. At temperatures below that, the occupant is willing to pay for more heat; at temperatures above, for less.

Figure 21-3

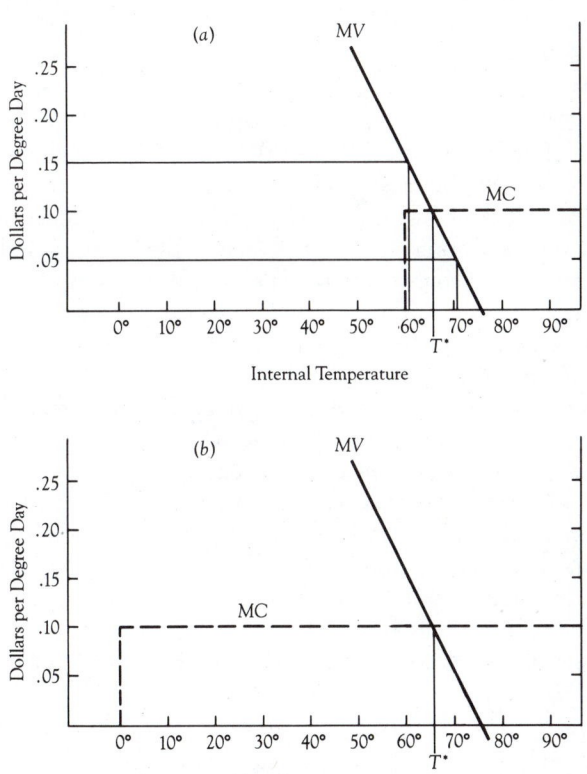

The marginal cost and marginal value of internal temperature for identical houses in Los Angeles (Figure 21-3a) and Chicago (Figure 21-3b). In each case, the occupant sets the thermostat to T^*, where marginal cost equals marginal value. For internal temperatures above the external temperature, marginal cost is the same for both houses, so T^* is the same in both cities.

Figures 21-3a and 21-3b also show the marginal cost curves faced by occupants in Los Angeles and Chicago. They are not identical. In Los Angeles the outside temperature is 60°; in Chicago it is 0°. Marginal cost, as you will remember from earlier chapters, is simply the slope of total cost. The total cost curves for the two houses are shown on Figure 21-2; TC_1 is the cost of heating the house in Chicago (outside temperature of 0°) and TC_3 the cost of heating an identical house in Los Angeles. As I pointed out earlier, TC_1 and TC_3, although they are different lines, have the same slope. The total cost of heating a house to, say, 70° is much higher when the external temperature is 0° than when it is 60°; but marginal cost, the cost of keeping the house at 70° instead of 69°, or 71° instead ot 70°, is not.

How can the marginal costs be the same when the total costs are not? The marginal costs are identical only for the upper part of their range. The inhabitant of Chicago and the inhabitant of Los Angeles pay the same amount for the additional cost of having a house at 69° instead of 68°, but the inhabitant of Los Angeles need pay nothing to have his house at 60°, while the inhabitant of Chicago pays for every degree above 0°.

Faced with the situation shown in Figure 21-3a, how does a rational occupant behave? He heats his house to that temperature for which $MC = MV$ (T^* on Figure 21-3a). If the house were colder than that, each additional degree by which he increased the thermostat setting would be worth more to him than it cost—$MV > MC$. If the house were hotter than that, each reduction of 1° would save him more on his heating bill than the value of the temperature he was giving up. We have seen this argument before. The individual's demand curve for internal temperature is the same as his marginal value curve for internal temperature, for exactly the same reason that the demand curve was the same as the marginal value curve in Chapter 4.

If you compare Figures 21-3a and 21-3b, you see that for temperatures above 60°, the MC curves are the same. Thus, as you can see from the figures, the optimal temperatures (T^*) chosen by the occupants of the two houses are also the same. As long as we are considering internal temperatures which are higher than the external temperature in both cities—as long, in other words, as both occupants heat their houses—identical houses with identical occupants will be heated to the same temperature in both Los Angeles and Chicago. The total cost of heating is much higher in Chicago, but the marginal cost is not—and it is the equality between marginal cost and marginal value that determines the optimal temperature.

Step 2: Designing a House—The Optimal Amount of Insulation

So far, we have been considering identical houses in Los Angeles and Chicago. But houses in those two cities are not identical—not, at least, if their builders are rational. We have been analyzing the decision of where to set the thermostat; the next step is to analyze the decision of how to build the house.

One of the decisions made in designing a house is how much insulation to put in it. Insulation costs money. A rational builder who expects to live in the house himself will insulate it up to the point where the additional cost of one more inch of insulation is just equal to the resulting benefit in reduced heating bills. So will a rational builder who intends to sell the house; the lower the future heating bills are expected to be, the higher the price a rational customer is willing to pay for the house. This is an example of a point first made in Chapter 7; it is in the interest of a producer to make a quality improvement in his product that costs him less than the improvement is worth to the customer who buys the product.

Looking at Equation 2, you can see that, for any particular interior and exterior temperature, the total cost of heating is proportional to C. If you add together a series of costs, each of which is proportional to C, the sum is also proportional to C. So, for any pattern of future internal and external temperatures, the present value of the total of all future heating bills is proportional to C. If, to simplify the mathematics, we ignore discounting (i.e., assume the interest rate is zero), the total cost of all future heating is simply the average value of $T_i - T_o$ times P_h times C times the total number of years for which the house will be heated.

The lower the external temperature, the higher the cost of heating; the higher the cost of heating, the greater the savings from insulation. So the lower T_o is, the greater the savings from reducing C by adding more insulation. Since the cost of insulation is presumably about the same in Los Angeles and Chicago, and outside temperatures are, on average, much lower in Chicago, the rational builder will use more insulation in Chicago than in Los Angeles. Figure 21-4 shows a graphic analysis of the situation. The curve MC (the marginal cost of insulation,

Figure 21-4

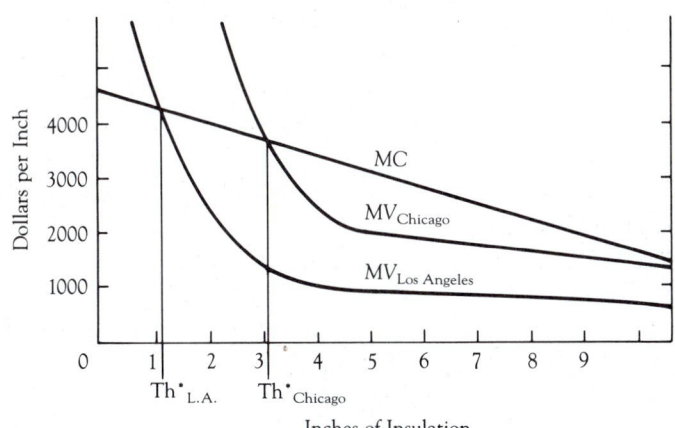

Marginal cost and marginal value of insulation in Chicago and Los Angeles. Marginal cost is the same in both cities; marginal value is higher in Chicago because the average temperature is lower there. Hence the optimal thickness of insulation, Th^*, is greater in Chicago.

not, as before, of temperature) is the same in both cities; MV, the savings in heating bills due to each additional inch of insulation, is higher in the colder city. Th^* is the optimal thickness of insulation. This time, the result of economics and common sense is the same; houses are built with more insulation in Chicago than in Los Angeles.

Figure 21-5 shows the final step of the argument. Since houses in Chicago are better insulated, the slope of the TC curve is lower; the curve representing the house in Chicago (on Figure 21-2) is TC_4 rather than TC_1. The marginal cost of heating does not depend on external temperature, but it does depend on how well insulated the house is; since houses in Chicago are better insulated than houses in Los Angeles, the marginal cost of internal temperature is less. It follows that the optimal internal temperature is higher. Looking at Figure 21-5, you can see that $MC_{Chicago}$ intersects MV at a higher temperature than does $MC_{L.A.}$; $T^*_{Chicago}$ is greater than $T^*_{L.A.}$. Houses in Chicago are warmer in winter than houses in Los Angeles.

Figure 21-5

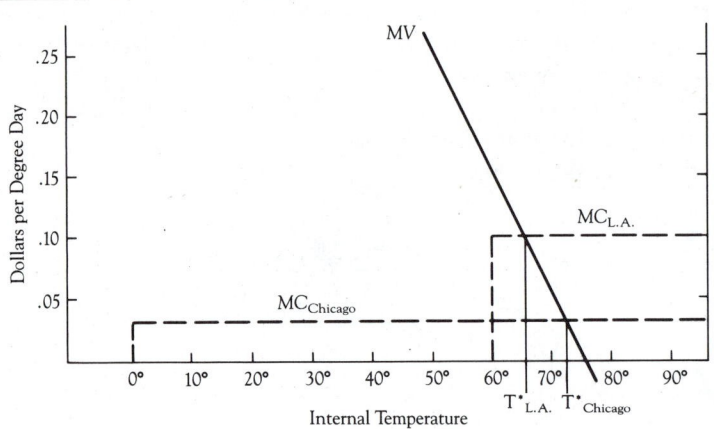

Marginal cost and marginal value of internal temperature for optimally insulated houses in Chicago and Los Angeles.   The house in Chicago is better insulated; hence MC is lower and T^* is higher than for the house in Los Angeles.

Free Bonus: Why We Don't Juggle the Thermostat All Winter

Exactly the same analysis explains a second paradox of rational heating. Just as it is more expensive to heat a house in Chicago than in Los Angeles, so it is more expensive to heat a house in Chicago in December than in September. The same intuition which suggests that houses in Chicago should be kept colder than houses in Los Angeles—because heating them "is more expensive"—also suggests that houses in Chicago should be kept colder in winter than in fall.

Here again, economics and "common sense" give different answers—not because economics is irrational but because "common sense" has not thought the question through carefully enough. Figures 21-3a and 21-3b were originally drawn to show two identical houses in different places at the same time; the figures could just as easily show the same house in the same place at different times. The cost of keeping a particular house in Chicago at 70° instead of at 69°—the marginal cost of internal temperature—is the same whether the temperature outside is 60° or 0°. So the optimal internal temperature is also the same. The rational decision is to keep the thermostat at the same setting throughout the heating season—which is what, in my experience, most people do.

Some Complications

So far, I have discussed the problem on the assumption that people in Los Angeles and Chicago are identical. That corresponds to the way my observations were made; when I visit in Los Angeles, I visit the same sort of people, in terms of income and tastes, as I visit in Chicago. When I lived in Los Angeles, I was the same person as when I was living in Chicago.

It might be argued, however, that there is one large and relevant difference between people in Chicago and people in Los Angeles—their heating bills. Similar people with similar incomes will have different amounts left after paying for heating in the two cities. Does this not mean that people in Chicago are, in effect, poorer, hence value money more (higher marginal utility of income), hence have a lower MV curve—since the MV curve measures the value for temperature in terms of money?

Not necessarily. If similar people, with similar skills and tastes, were better off in Los Angeles than in Chicago, one would expect people living in Chicago to move west. As they did so, the decreasing population would drive down property values in Chicago while the increasing population drove up property values in Los Angeles—making Chicago a more attractive place to live in than before, and Los Angeles less attractive. *In equilibrium*—equilibrium, this time, of population distribution—the two cities must on net be equally attractive. If they were not, it would be in the interest of some people to move—which would mean that we were not yet in equilibrium.

You should by now be getting a feel for the complication and fascination of this sort of analysis. Equilibrium sounds like a simple idea when we are merely crossing two lines on a graph. But individuals and markets in the real world are in equilibrium, or tending toward equilibrium, in many different dimensions—marginal cost and marginal value are being equated simultaneously on many different margins. In solving the problem of home heating, we have used three simultaneous equilibria, resulting from rational behavior with regard to three different choices—thermostat setting, insulation, and where to live.

There is one interesting case in which the argument from migratory equilibrium does not hold. Suppose fuel costs rise sharply and unexpectedly—as they did after the Arab oil boycott. The result is to increase the relative advantage of Los Angeles over Chicago—since fuel is more expensive, the difference in the total cost of heating in the two cities is higher than before. People begin moving west. Property values in Chicago (and Boston and Cleveland and . . .) go down. The newspapers start talking about a land boom in the "Sunbelt."

But most of the property, or at least most of the residential real estate, in Chicago belongs to people who live in Chicago. Suppose I am such a person; I live in Chicago in a house I own. So far as my incentive to move is concerned, the fall in housing costs fulfills exactly the same function for me as for a tenant renting an apartment. If I move to Los Angeles, I must sell my present house at a low price and buy a house in Los Angeles at a high price—which is a reason for me not to move, just as having to give up a low-rent apartment in Chicago and move into a high-rent apartment in Los Angeles is a reason for a tenant not to move. But so far as my welfare is concerned, the effect is quite different. The low rent in Chicago, after fuel prices have just risen, compensates tenants for their increased heating costs. But the fall in the market value of my house is no compensation for higher heating bills if I own the house.

The fact that heating is expensive in Chicago does not make people in Chicago poor, but the fact that it has just become unexpectedly more expensive does. As people move out, the value of assets that cannot move—houses, in my example, but also firms with a local reputation, employees with experience working in a particular local job (firm-specific human capital), and the like—goes down. Most of those assets belong to people in Chicago, so people in Chicago are, on average, worse off than before. When people are poorer, they buy less of most things—including heat. The increased cost of heating drives down thermostats in both Los Angeles and Chicago, but in Chicago the substitution effect of a higher marginal cost of heating is reinforced by a substantial income effect. Houses in the Midwest and the Northeast were very cold in the winter of 1971-2.

PART 2 · HOW TO MAKE MONEY BY SUBSIDIZING TENANTS: AN EXERCISE IN APPLIED EXTERNALITIES

You are a landlord; you own a building containing two apartments, both of which you rent out. How should you decide how warm to keep the apartments?

Before answering this question, we should first ask why (aside from legal requirements) you want to heat the building at all. The answer is that if you do not, no one will rent your apartments. This suggests a further question—exactly how is the amount you can get for your apartments affected by how warm you keep them?

Suppose that other landlords offer apartments just like yours, heated to a temperature of 68°, for $200/month. The rental market is competitive; if you too heat your apartment to 68°, you can get all the tenants you like at $200/month, and none at any higher rent.

Tenants value apartments for many different characteristics—including their temperature. Just as in Part 1 of this chapter, a tenant's taste for internal temperature may be represented by a marginal value curve. The total value to him of increasing the temperature from 68° to 73° is the sum of the marginal values for each little increase in temperature along that range—the area B under the MV curve between 68° and 73°, as shown on Figure 21-6. The analysis is just like the analysis that originally gave us consumer surplus. Since, at this point in the discussion, the landlord is paying for the heat, the difference in surplus to the tenant between a temperature of 68° and of 73° is the full area under the curve, not just the area between MV and P.

But if a change in temperature, as from 68° to 73°, changes the total value the tenant receives from the apartment, it also changes the maximum rent he is willing to pay. The area under a marginal value curve between one quantity and another shows the difference in what a consumer is willing to pay for the different quantities, as we saw first in the explanation of consumer surplus in Chapter 4 and later in the analysis of two-part pricing in Chapter 10. So, a tenant who was willing to pay $200/month for an apartment heated to 68° should be equally willing to pay $200/month + B for the same apartment heated to 73°—or $200 − A for the apartment heated to 63°.

Figure 21-6

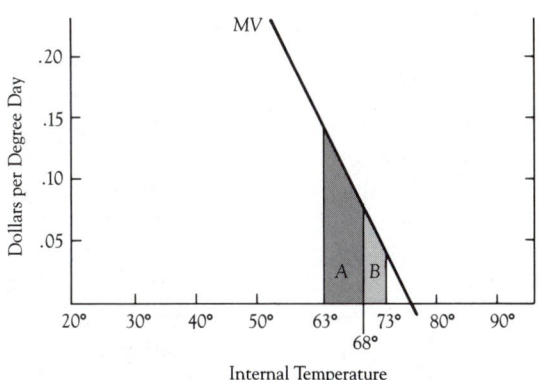

The effect on rent of changes in the internal temperature of an apartment. MV shows the marginal value of temperature to the tenant. A is the decrease in the maximum rent he will be willing to pay if temperature is at 63° instead of 68°; B is the increase if it is at 73° instead of 68°.

Finding the Profit-Maximizing Temperature

You, the landlord, now have a choice. You can offer better heated apartments than your competitors do and charge higher rents; you can offer cooler apartments and charge lower rents. The change in the rent you can collect (i.e., the highest rent at which you will be able to find tenants) will be equal to the change in consumer surplus on Figure 21-6. You maximize your profit by raising the temperature of the apartment as long as the resulting increase in surplus, and hence rent, at least balances the increased cost of heating. Here, just as in the Disneyland case discussed in Chapter 10, what starts as consumer surplus (on rides in Disneyland, on temperature in your apartment building) ends up as revenue to the producer (entry price in Disneyland, rent on the apartment).

Identical Tenants, Identical Apartments. Assume that all tenants are identical; each has the MV curve shown in Figure 21-6. Further assume that the marginal cost of internal temperature is P ($= C \times P_h$ in the first part of the chapter). I call it P because it is the "price" you pay for each degree of intenal temperature that you "buy" for your tenants.

With these assumptions, the solution to the problem of heating a building with two identical apartments is simple. Since each 1° increase in temperature benefits each tenant by MV, the total benefit from each 1° increase—which you can collect in higher rents—is $2 \times MV$. Heat the building to the temperature T^*, at which $2 \times MV = P$. The analysis should by now be familiar. At any lower temperature, $2 \times MV > P$, so an increase in temperature increases total surplus, and hence rent, by more than it increases heating cost. So if the temperature is less than T^*, it is in your interest to increase it; you will be able to raise the rent by more than the increase in your heating bill and still find tenants. At any temperature above T^*, $2 \times MV < P$, so a *decrease* in temperature decreases total surplus, and hence rent, by less than it decreases heating cost. If the temperature is higher than T^*, it is in your interest to lower the temperature; the savings on your heating bill will more than compensate you for the reduction in the rent you can get for the apartments. If the temperature is lower than T^*, it pays to raise it; if it is higher than T^*, it pays to lower it. So the optimal temperature, from your standpoint, is T^*.

Identical Apartments, Different Tenants. To make the problem more interesting, I now drop one of the simplifying assumptions—the assumption that both tenants have the same tastes for temperature (identical MV curves). The situation is now shown by Figure 21-7, where MV_1 represents the tastes of Tenant 1, and MV_2 the tastes of Tenant 2. The total marginal value of internal temperature is $MV_1 + MV_2$; that is the amount by which the value of the apartments to your tenants, and hence the rent you can charge without losing them, increases for each degree by which you increase the temperature of the building. To find the optimal (i.e., profit-maximizing) temperature, you merely find the intersection of $MV_1 + MV_2$ with P, as shown on Figure 21-7.

This is the correct answer *if you assume that both apartments must be at the same temperature.* Suppose, however, that you can separately control the temperatures of the two apartments. If the apartments are identical, as in the building shown in Figure 21-8, then the cost of heating each apartment is simply $P/2$ per degree. Heat can only be lost through the external walls; since each apartment has half the external walls of the whole building, the heat loss to the outside from holding Apartment 1 at a temperature T_1 is simply half what the heat loss would be from holding the whole building at that temperature.

I specified the heat loss *to the outside.* If T_1 is higher than T_2 (as shown in Figure 21-8), heat will also flow through the wall between the apartments; the rate at which you must put heat into Apartment 1 in order to maintain it at T_1 is then more than half what would be needed to hold the whole building at T_1. But that additional heat loss from Apartment 1 costs you nothing; every dollar spent to replace heat that flows through the interior wall is a dollar less spent

Figure 21-7

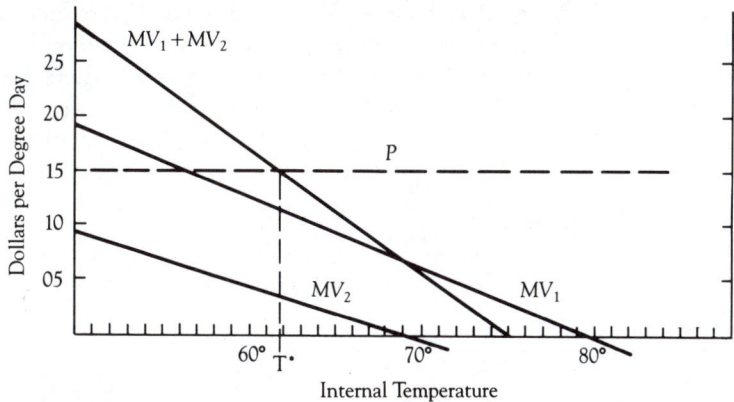

Finding the optimal internal temperature for a building with two tenants. The two apartments are identical; the tenants are not. The landlord maximizes his profit by heating the apartment to a temperature at which P, the cost of internal temperature, equals $MV_1 + MV_2$, the total marginal value of temperature to the tenants.

Figure 21-8

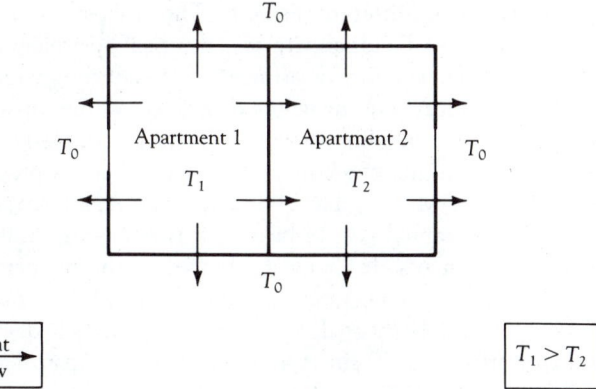

A building with two identical apartments. T_1 is the internal temperature of Apartment 1, T_2 is the internal temperature of Apartment 2, and T_o is the temperature outside the building. Heat flows from both apartments to the outside and from the warmer apartment (1) to the cooler (2).

heating Apartment 2. Hence the net cost to the landlord of each extra degree of interior temperature in Apartment 1 (or 2) is only the cost of the heat lost to the outside—$P/2$.

The cost to the landlord of each degree of temperature in Apartment 1 is $P/2$; the benefit is MV_1, received by the tenant but transmitted, in the form of higher rent, to the landlord. Profit is maximized at a temperature T_1^* where $MV_1 = P/2$. Similarly, for the second apartment, profit is maximized at T_2^*, with $MV_2 = P/2$. The solution is shown on Figure 21-9; profit is increased, relative to the result shown in Figure 21-7, by the colored areas.

Figure 21-9

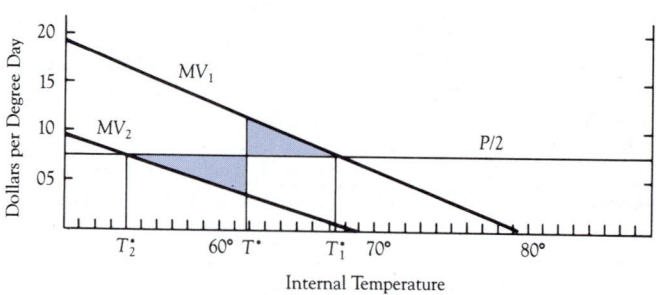

The gain from heating identical apartments to different temperatures. Each apartment is heated to the temperature at which the marginal value of internal temperature equals its marginal cost $(P/2)$. The colored areas show the gain relative to the solution shown on Figure 21-7.

Different Apartments, Different Tenants. The problem has been solved in a particularly simple case—a building with two identical apartments. The solution can easily be generalized. For each apartment, calculate the marginal cost of internal temperature, ignoring any heat loss that goes to other apartments. If, for the single-story apartment building shown in Figure 21-10, we ignore heat losses through the roof and ceiling, the cost for each apartment is proportional to its exterior wall area, as shown in Table 21-1. Note that Apartment 3 has no exterior walls; hence the marginal cost of heating it is zero—any heat lost goes into one of the other apartments. It should be heated to the temperature at which marginal value of internal temperature is zero. Figure 21-11a, page 514, shows how the building should be heated: P_1 is the price of each degree of internal temperature in Apartment 1, P_2 in Apartment 2, P_3 in Apartment 3; T_1 is the optimal temperature for Apartment 1, T_2 for Apartment 2, T_3 for Apartment 3. For more realistic three-dimensional cases, in which heat can be lost in any direction, the calculation of the marginal cost of heating each apartment is more complicated. But once the marginal cost has been calculated—by a physicist or a building engineer, not an economist—the profit-maximizing temperature is found in the same way.

Table 21-1

Apartment	External Wall (feet)	Internal Wall (feet)	Price of Internal Temperature ($/day)
1	40	20	.08
2	70	51	.14
3	0	54	0.

We are not yet done. So far, I have assumed that you have perfect knowledge both about the rent tenants are willing to pay and about their taste for temperature, as shown by their MV curves. The first half of the assumption is realistic enough in a competitive market; you can determine the highest price anyone is willing to pay for an apartment by posting a high rent and gradually lowering it until you get a tenant. Determining your tenant's taste for heat is a more difficult problem. I will therefore drop the second half of the assumption. From here on, we will assume that whatever temperature you heat the apartment to, you will always collect the highest rent your tenant is willing to pay, but that you know nothing at all about his taste for temperature.

Figure 21-10

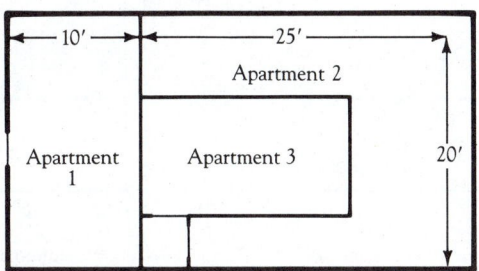

A building with three apartments, all different.

Getting the Tenant to Choose the Profit-Maximizing Temperature

Even if you do not know the tenant's taste for temperature, he does. To use that knowledge, you install a thermostat in each apartment and let the tenant set it to whatever temperature he prefers. What happens?

Two Wrong Answers. One possibility is shown in Figure 21-11b. Here the tenant sets the interior temperature while the landlord continues to pay the heating bill. The tenant of Apartment 1 sets his thermostat to T_a, the point for which the marginal value of temperature to him reaches zero; since he is not paying for internal temperature, he consumes it as long as it has any value at all. This is inefficient (and unprofitable) compared to the optimal solution (T_1) shown in Figure 21-11a, since some of the temperature the tenant consumes is worth less

Figure 21-11

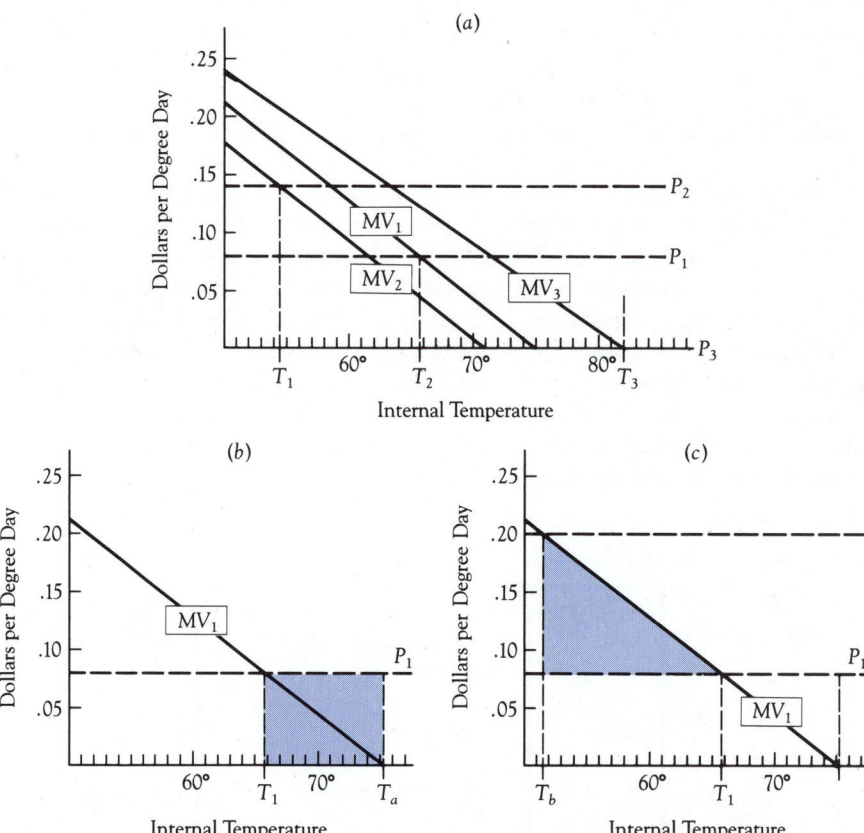

Alternative heating arrangements for the apartments of Figure 21-10. Figure 21-11*a* shows the optimal solution, assuming that the landlord knows the *MV* curves of the tenants. Figure 21-11*b* shows the result, for Apartment 1, if the tenant sets his own thermostat and the landlord pays for the heat. Figure 21-11*c* shows the result if the tenant sets his own thermostat and pays for the heat. The colored areas on 11*b* and 11*c* show the loss in profit to the landlord relative to 11*a*.

to the tenant than it costs the landlord to produce. The loss of profit on Apartment 1, relative to the solution shown in Figure 21-11*a*, is shown as the colored area on Figure 21-11*b*. It is the difference between the value to the tenant of the additional temperature between T_1 and T_a (the shaded area) and its cost to the landlord, $P_1 \times (T_a - T_1)$.

A second possibility is shown in Figure 21-11*c*. Here the tenant not only sets the thermostat, he also pays the bills. Each apartment is heated by its own electric heater, and the cost is part of the tenant's electric bill. The figure shows the result for Apartment 1.

This result is also inefficient—and unprofitable—compared to the solution shown in Figure 21-11a. In Figure 21-11b, the apartment is too hot, since the tenant sets the thermostat as if heat were free. In Figure 21-11c, it is too cold. The cost to the tenant of raising the temperature of his apartment is equal to the cost of the additional flow of heat necessary to maintain the higher temperature. When he turns up his thermostat, the result is to increase not only the heat loss to the outside but also the heat loss to the other apartments; since internal walls are usually less well insulated than external walls, the increased heat loss to the other apartments may be several times as great as the increased heat loss to the outside. In drawing Figure 21-11c, I have assumed that C_i, the constant describing heat conduction from the apartment to other apartments, is three times as great as C_o, the corresponding constant for heat loss to the outside world.

In order to simplify the next few paragraphs, I will define $\tilde{C}_i \equiv C_i \times$ (area of internal walls) and $\tilde{C}_o \equiv C_o \times$ (area of external walls). For Apartment 1, $\tilde{C}_i = 1.5 \times \tilde{C}_o$. Obviously, $\tilde{C}_i$ and $\tilde{C}_o$ will vary from one apartment to another, but since we will for the most part be discussing only Apartment 1, this will not matter.

Remember that here, just as in the first part of this chapter, what determines the choice of temperature is not total cost but marginal cost. If the apartment is at 70°, the adjacent apartments at 65°, and the outside world at 0°, total heat loss to the outside will be much larger than total heat loss to the other apartments. But if the internal temperature is increased by 1°, heat loss to the outside goes up by 1° × $\tilde{C}_o$, heat loss to the inside goes up by 1° × $\tilde{C}_i$; so the *marginal* heat loss to the other apartments is 1.5 times the marginal heat loss to the outside. The total cost of maintaining the apartment at 70° consists largely of the cost of replacing heat lost to the outside, but 60 percent of the marginal cost—the cost of heating it to 71° instead of 70°—comes from the increase in the amount of heat lost to the other apartments.

This is true *even if the other apartments are hotter, not colder, than the apartment we are considering*. Heat flow is proportional to the temperature difference between the two sides of the wall, as shown in Equation 1. If Apartment 1 is at 70° and the adjacent apartments are at 75°, heat is flowing from them into Apartment 1. If the temperature of Apartment 1 goes up to 71°, the heat flowing into it decreases—by 1° × $\tilde{C}_i$. A decrease in the amount of heat you are getting—for free—from the neighboring apartments increases your heating bill, just as an increase in the heat you are losing to the neighboring apartments would. Whether the adjacent apartments are warmer than Apartment 1, cooler, or some warmer and some cooler, each degree by which the tenant of Apartment 1 raises his thermostat costs him $P_h \times (\tilde{C}_i + \tilde{C}_o)$ in additional electricity. That is the price, to him, of temperature; he maximizes his consumer surplus by choosing the temperature, T_b, for which $MV = P_h \times (\tilde{C}_i + \tilde{C}_o)$.

With the values of C_i and C_o which I have assumed, the cost that tenant 1 pays to raise the temperature of his apartment is about two and one half times the cost to the landlord; out of each five BTU's he puts into raising the temperature of his apartment, three flow through the interior wall and end up lowering his neighbors' heating bills. That ultimately benefits the landlord; the lower the heating bills for his apartments, the more rent people will be willing to pay for them. From the standpoint of the tenant, the marginal cost of raising the temperature of Apartment 1 by $1°$ is $P_h \times (\tilde{C}_i + \tilde{C}_o)$; from the standpoint of the landlord, it is only $P_h \times \tilde{C}_o$.

The Right Answer. How does the landlord produce the result shown on Figure 21-11a without knowing MV, the tenant's marginal value curve for temperature? By letting the tenant set the thermostat and then subsidizing his heating bill. Of every $5 spent on heating Apartment 1, the landlord pays $3 and the tenant $2. From the standpoint of the tenant, the cost of interior temperature is now $P_h \times (\tilde{C}_i + \tilde{C}_o)/2.5 = P_h \times \tilde{C}_o = P_1$. He maximizes his consumer surplus (from buying temperature) at T_1.

At this point, you may be feeling somewhat confused about the contract between landlord and tenant. If the rent is a function of the tenant's surplus, which in turn depends on the temperature he sets his thermostat at, should he not take that as well as his heating bill into account in deciding what temperature to keep his apartment at? The answer is no. The tenant is renting the apartment for a fixed rent, say $200/month. Given that he is doing so, he sets his thermostat at whatever temperature maximizes his surplus from buying temperature—T_a if the landlord pays the heating bill, T_b if the tenant pays it, T_1 if it is split in the way I have described.

What determines the rent? The amount that other, similar, potential tenants are willing to pay. What determines that? Among other things, the surplus they would receive, if they rented the apartment, from buying temperature on whatever terms the landlord is offering it at. So the rent includes the surplus a tenant can get. If one tenant chooses to buy less (or more) temperature than the "optimal" level under the arrangements of Figures 21-11a, 21-11b, or 21-11c, he finds that the apartment, which was just worth renting if he bought the optimal amount of temperature, is now no longer worth renting; either he readjusts his thermostat or he gives up the apartment to another tenant.

It is up to the landlord to determine on what terms he should sell temperature (and housing) so as to maximize his total profit—rent minus his expenditure on heating (and other operating expenses irrelevant to this discussion). What I have shown is that the rule which maximizes his profit is to sell temperature "at cost." The logic of the situation is the same as the logic of perfect discriminatory pricing (Chapter 10), discussed there in terms of cookies and Disneyland. What is special in this case is that the cost of internal temperature to the tenant, if he provides it himself, is greater than the cost to the landlord; so the landlord "sells temperature at cost" by subsidizing the tenant's heating bill.

Externalities

So far, I have discussed the problem as an exercise in perfect discriminatory pricing. There is another, and equally valid, way of looking at the same problem and deriving the same result—in terms of externalities.

We start by ignoring the landlord and considering the situation of Figure 21-11c (tenant pays his own heating bill) from the standpoint of the tenant. He is deciding on the temperature of his apartment by rationally balancing cost and benefit; he increases the temperature up to the point where an additional degree is worth just what it costs him (T_b). Why is this unsatisfactory?

It is unsatisfactory because every time he raises his thermostat, he provides positive externalities to his neighbors—the warmer his apartment is, the more heat flows from it into theirs (or the less from theirs into it), hence the lower their heating bill. As I explained in Chapter 17, a good with positive externalities (a mowed lawn, a handsome skyscraper, basic research) is underproduced. The producer produces only up to the point where *his* marginal benefit is equal to the marginal cost of production, rather than up to the point where the total marginal benefit, including the external benefit received by other people, equals marginal cost. That is precisely the outcome shown on Figure 21-11a. Temperature of Apartment 1 is underproduced; T_b is less than T_1.

The "textbook solution" to the underproduction of goods with positive externalities is to subsidize them, paying the producer an amount equal to the external benefit. His gain from each unit produced is then equal to internal gain (his value for consuming it, or the price for which he can sell it) plus external gain; so he produces up to the point where total marginal benefit, external plus internal, equals marginal cost. That is precisely the result shown in Figure 21-11b. The tenant of Apartment 1 is receiving a subsidy of $P_h \times \tilde{C}_i$ for each degree of temperature he produces. $P_h \times \tilde{C}_i$ is just equal to the value of the increased heat flow to the other apartment resulting from a 1° increase in the temperature of Apartment 1.

We have gotten to the same place by two quite different routes. The first argument derived the optimal rule from the behavior of a landlord trying to maximize his profit; the second derived the same rule from the policy that leads to the efficient level of production of a good that generates positive externalities. Why are the results the same?

The answer has been given already, back in Chapter 15. Under conditions of perfect discriminatory pricing, all of the benefits from the good in question end up in the pocket of the seller. Hence the arrangements which maximize net benefit (are Marshall efficient) also maximize his profit, and vice versa.

There is one important difference between this chapter and the previous discussions of discriminatory pricing. In all the previous cases, the discriminatory pricing was done by a monopolist. In this case, the landlord is a "monopolist" only in the sense of having a monopoly over the heating of his own apartment building; otherwise the rental market is assumed to be perfectly competitive. The consumer surplus which the landlord "pockets" is the surplus due to the tenant renting that particular apartment rather than some other apartment. It is positive only if the landlord has some advantage over his competitors—perhaps because he has read this chapter and instituted the "subsidy" it describes.

The demonstration in this chapter that a landlord will find it in his interest to produce an efficient level of heat is really a special case of the demonstration, in Chapter 7, that landlords will find it in their interest to make all improvements, and only those improvements, which are worth at least as much to the tenant as they cost the landlord. Just as in that case, the landlord gets an above-market return from making such improvements only if, for some reason, his competitors do not make them. If everyone sees, and follows, the logic of this chapter, the competitive housing industry, like other competitive industries with open entry, finds that the maximum profit it can make is zero. The gains produced by the improvement are then divided between the owners of the inputs to the housing industry—urban land, for instance—and its consumers.

Efficiency Gains: Doing Good by Doing Well

If my analysis is correct, a landlord who followed the policy I describe would increase his profit—the additional rent he received would more than repay the cost of the subsidy. If so, others would imitate him; the ultimate result would be a rental industry in which such subsidies were common practice, at least for those buildings for which it was practical to separately control and separately bill the heating of different apartments. If, as I have argued, the result would be a Marshall improvement, where would the improved efficiency come from?

It would come in two ways. The first, and more obvious, is the efficiency gain shown in my figures. Buildings in which the previous rule was to heat all apartments to the same temperature (Figure 21-7) would save by eliminating the overheating of apartments occupied by tenants with a low MV for temperature and the underheating of those occupied by tenants with a high MV for temperature. They would also gain by increasing the temperature of apartments that were inexpensive to heat, such as Apartment 3 on Figure 21-10, and lowering the temperature of apartments that were expensive to heat. Buildings in which the previous rule was "tenant controls, landlord pays" (Figure 21-11b) would eliminate the resultant overheating; those where the rule was "tenant controls and pays" (Figure 21-11c) would eliminate underheating. In each case, temperatures would rise if the value of the additional temperature was worth more than its cost and fall if it was worth less; both changes represent net gains.

There would be another efficiency gain as well. Consider Apartment 3 in Figure 21-10. Since it is entirely interior to the building, it costs nothing to heat it; any heat that flows out of it flows into another apartment (I fudged the numbers a little by ignoring heat loss through the door). Under the system I have described, the landlord would pay the entire heating bill for Apartment 3.

Given that he did so, its relative attractiveness would be greater for a tenant who wanted an unusually warm apartment, so it would probably be rented by such a tenant. Apartment 2, on the other hand, which has an unusually large amount of external wall, would be expensive to heat and would receive a low subsidy; it would be relatively more attractive to tenants who intended to keep their apartment cool.

The overall result would be a more efficient allocation of tenants to apartments, with those tenants who liked warm apartments tending to end up in apartments which were inexpensive to heat—at higher rents, of course—and those who liked cool apartments ending up in those that were expensive to heat. This is a second, and less obvious, efficiency gain resulting from the arrangements I have described.

Description, Prescription, and
Hats for Economists

It may have occurred to you that in this second part of the chapter, I am not describing but prescribing. So far as I know, heating subsidies are not normal practice in apartment buildings, not even in buildings where it is practical for each tenant to control, and pay for, his own heat. If so, that is evidence either that my analysis is wrong or that the market is, in this instance, failing to produce the efficient—and profit-maximizing—outcome.

I argued in Chapter 1 that economists assume rationality not because it is true but because it is useful; people are, in part, rational, and it is their rationality that provides the predictable element in their behavior. This implies that irrationality is not very useful, since it is unpredictable, but not that it does not exist. Perhaps the absence of heating subsidies is the result of irrationality on the part of either landlords or tenants.

It is a dangerous policy for an economist to explain divergences between the predictions of his analysis and his observations of the real world as instances of irrationality. Such divergences may, after all, be evidence that the economic analysis is mistaken; if we automatically shrug them off as "irrational," we are abandoning our best tool for spotting our own mistakes. It is a particularly dangerous policy, given that economists, like other people, are reluctant to believe that they have made a mistake.

On the other hand, if all of us, economists and economic actors alike, assume that whatever is currently being done must be correct, then we will never discover better ways of running our businesses or our lives. This suggests that every economist should wear two hats. As an economist, he should assume that all observed behavior is rational and treat any divergence between what his analysis predicts and what he observes as evidence that the analysis is wrong. As a participant in the economy—an economic actor—he should assume that it is up to him to figure out what is rational in order to decide what to do. Economic theory, which consists largely of figuring out how a rational individual would act, is a useful tool in doing so. If, as in the second part of this chapter, his conclusion is that there is a better way of running a business than the way it is being run, he should regard that not as an anomaly but as a profit opportunity.

Economics Joke #4: *A professor of economics and a graduate student were walking down the street. "Look," the student said, "there is a $10 bill on the sidewalk." "Nonsense," the professor replied. "If there had been a $10 bill on the sidewalk, someone would have picked it up."* (This is an example of the application, and limitation, of the assumption of rationality.)

The argument for this sort of "double vision" was brought home to me some years ago when I was a member of the board of directors of a company that ran health spas. It was common practice in the health spa industry (and nonprofit equivalents, such as YMCA's and country clubs) for firms to sell their services in the form of memberships—long-term, nonrefundable contracts. The Federal

Trade Commission was trying to force the industry to instead offer the customers short-term contracts, which the customers could cancel if they found that they did not like the product.

In the course of their campaign, the FTC produced a piece of economic analysis which appeared to demonstrate that the introduction of cancelable contracts would lead to a net efficiency gain—a Marshall improvement. Although the article did not say so, its analysis also implied that a spa which offered such contracts—and charged the customers a higher price for the more desirable product—would increase its profits. The author missed that conclusion because he assumed that the new contract would be sold for the same price as the old, even though the option of withdrawing from the spa and getting a refund would make the new contract a more attractive product. He was guilty of what I described in Chapter 2 as "naive price theory"—assuming prices do not change when there is a good reason why they should.

I found myself in an odd position. As an economist, my assumption was that the firms in the industry knew how to maximize their profits and did so; the problem was to explain why the present policy—long-term, nonrefundable contracts—was correct. As a member of the board of directors of one such firm, it was my business to help figure out how the firm could maximize its profits—which was hardly consistent with assuming it was already doing so.

My response, as an economist, was to write an article providing a plausible, although not necessarily correct, justification for the way the industry was selling its product. My response as a member of the board was to try to persuade management to experiment with refundable contracts. I failed; management, like its opponents in the FTC—and possibly for the same reasons—was persuaded that the present policy maximized its profits. A year or two later, the firm was partly taken over by a very successful group of health spa companies—one of whose innovations was offering short-term contracts.

PROBLEMS

1. Throughout the chapter, I have ignored air conditioning.
   a. Redraw Figure 21-2 on the assumption that using air conditioning to take heat out of a house costs the same amount per BTU as using a heating system to put heat into a house.
   b. If we included the effect of air conditioning, would the conclusion of Part 1 of the chapter—that houses in warmer climates are kept cooler in winter than houses in colder climates—be affected? Discuss.
2. In analyzing how you should heat your apartment building, I assumed that your competitors were charging $200/month for similar apartments and heating them to 68°. If I change one or both of those numbers, will the result be to change the rent you should charge, the temperature you should heat the apartments to, both, or neither? Explain.
3. Assume that all tenants have the marginal value curve for temperature shown by Figure 21-6. Your apartment building has two identical apartments; heating

costs are the same as on Figure 21-7. In each of the following cases, what rent should you charge and how warm should you keep the apartments?

a. Your competitors charge $200/month for similar apartments heated to 68°.

b. Your competitors charge $180/month for similar apartments heated to 63°.

c. Your competitors charge $200/month for similar apartments heated to 73°.

4. I have told you the conclusion of the FTC's analysis of nonrefundable membership contracts for health spas; I have not explained how the conclusion was reached. You know enough economics to do the problem yourself—to show why long-term, nonrefundable contracts are inefficient. Do so. You may make the argument verbal, graphical, or both, as you prefer. (This is a hard problem.)

5. What rate of subsidy should the landlord offer to the tenants of Apartments 2 and 3?

6. Suppose that with electric heating, it is practical for each tenant to control and pay for his own heating; with gas heating, it is not. Tenants have the MV curves shown in Figure 21-11a; the cost of electric heat is shown in Table 21-1. How cheap would gas heating have to be in order for the landlord to prefer gas heating and a uniform temperature to electric heating with subsidies? Assume the landlord knows the demand curves of his tenants. Express your answer as a ratio between the cost, per unit of heat, of gas heating and of electric heating. (This is a hard problem.)

7. How often does one find a $10 bill lying on the sidewalk? (Hint: The answer is given, for several analogous cases, in the optional section of Chapter 1.)

Chapter 22

Inflation and Unemployment

An adequate discussion of the nature, causes, and cures of inflation and unemployment requires not a chapter but a book. My purpose here is to show how the ideas developed in this book would provide the groundwork for that one. I start, in Part 1, by explaining what inflation is, why it occurs, and what its consequences are. Part 2 discusses the nature and causes of unemployment. Part 3 will combine elements of Parts 1 and 2 with ideas from earlier chapters in order to suggest reasons why governments often follow policies that lead to inflation.

PART 1 · INFLATION

The prices we have discussed so far are relative prices—the price of oranges measured in apples, of houses measured in cookies, and the like. If we are talking about relative prices, it makes no sense to say that "prices in general" are going up. If the price of oranges measured in apples is going up, the price of apples measured in oranges must be going down, since one is the inverse of the other. If a house used to cost a million cookies and now costs two million, the price of houses measured in cookies has doubled—but the price of cookies measured in houses has fallen in half, from one millionth of a house per cookie to one two-millionth.

People who complain about inflation and say that "All prices are going up" are talking about *money prices*—prices of goods measured in money. During an inflation, the prices of goods measured in other goods may go up, down, or stay the same—but the money prices of most goods are going up.

If the prices of one or two goods, measured in money, go up, the reason may be some special circumstance affecting those goods—a bad apple harvest or a fire that has burned down half the houses in a city. If the money prices of almost all goods are going up, it is far more likely that the cause involves, not the goods, but the money in which their prices are all being measured. One way of describing such a situation is to say that the prices of apples, oranges, houses, cookies, and many other things are going up. A simpler way is to say that the price of money is going down. If apples used to cost $.50 and now cost $1, then the price of a dollar has fallen—from two apples to one. During an inflation, the price of goods is rising in terms of one of the things in which it can be measured—money. The price of money is falling in terms of almost all the things in which it can be measured.

In this part of the chapter, we shall first see what determines the price of money—the amount of other goods you must give up to get a dollar. We shall then go on to look at the causes of inflation and some of its consequences.

For the purposes of this chapter, I shall assume that only one kind of money exists—*currency*, the green paper that most of us use to buy things—and that it is produced by the government. That is a simplification of the actual monetary system of the U.S. at present, since other things, such as deposits in checking accounts and money market funds, serve much the same function as currency, and not all of them are controlled by the government. The situation becomes still more complicated if we go beyond our own society. In other times and other places, there have been many different kinds of money, including some over which government had little or no control.

The Price of Money

The price of money is determined, like the price of everything else, by supply and demand. The supply is the amount of currency in circulation; the government can increase the supply of money by printing more of it or decrease the supply by collecting more money than it spends and burning the excess.

Note that in economic language, the "supply of money" is the amount of money in circulation, not the rate at which new money is being produced. If no new money is printed (and none wears out), the supply of money is constant, but not zero. If each year, the government prints one dollar for every ten in circulation, the supply of money increases at 10 percent per year.

What about the demand for money? That too is an amount of money, not a number of dollars per year. Spending a dollar removes it from your pocket, but it does not use it up; someone else gets it. Your demand for money is not the amount you spend but the amount you hold. The total demand for money is the total amount that all of us together hold.

Why do we hold money at all? If I arranged my life so that income and expenditure exactly matched, I would have no need to hold money; as soon as a dollar came in for something I had sold, it would go out again for something I bought. This is not the way I (or you) actually live. It is more convenient to arrange income and expenditure separately in the short run, sometimes taking in more than we spend and sometimes spending more than we take in. When we take in more than we spend, our cash balances go up; when we spend more than we take in, they go back down again. Thus my cash balance functions as a sort of shock absorber.

Demand is not a number but a relationship—quantity demanded as a function of price. The quantity of money demanded—the number of dollars you choose to hold—actually depends on two different prices. First, it depends on the price of money; the higher the price of money—the more it can buy—the less you choose to hold, since the more a dollar can buy, the fewer dollars you require to buy things with. Second, the amount of money you hold depends on the cost of *holding* money.

Suppose I choose to hold, on average, a cash balance of $100. What I gain is flexibility in arranging my income and expenditures. What I lose is the interest I would have collected if, instead of holding $100 as currency, I had lent it out and collected interest on it. So the cost of *holding* money is the *money interest rate*—also called the *nominal interest rate*. The higher that interest rate—the more I could get for each dollar I lent out—the more expensive it is for me to hold currency, hence the less I shall choose to hold.

The distinction between the price of money and the cost of holding money— what we might also describe as the *rent* on money—is crucial to understanding how the general price level is determined, and confusion between the two is at the root of many of the more common economic mistakes. The *price* of money is what you must give up to get money—the higher the general price level (the amount of money you must give up to get something else), the lower the price of money. The *cost* of holding money—more precisely, the cost of holding money measured in money, the number of dollars per year you give up for each dollar you hold—is the nominal interest rate.

There is one important respect in which the demand for money differs from the demand for almost anything else. Since money is used to buy goods, the usefulness to you of a particular bundle of money depends not on how many dollars it contains but on how much it will buy; if all (money) prices doubled, two dollars after the change would be precisely as useful as one dollar before. Hence your demand is not really for a particular amount of money but for a particular amount of *purchasing power*. What you want is a certain *real* cash balance, not a certain *nominal* cash balance.

The Equilibrium Level of Prices

This unusual characteristic of the demand for money turns out to be very useful in understanding how the price of money changes with changes in supply or demand. Suppose demand and supply for currency are initially in equilibrium. The number of dollars individuals want to hold is equal to the total number of dollars available to be held; quantity demanded equals quantity supplied. Suddenly the government decides to double the money supply; the new dollars are printed up and distributed to the populace as a "free gift." What happens?

Everyone has twice as much money as before. Since, before the change, people were already holding as much currency as they wanted to, they now find themselves with more currency than they want to hold. The obvious solution is to spend more than they take in, thus reducing their cash balances and converting the surplus into useful goods.

Oddly enough, this obvious solution cannot work. While each of us individually can reduce his cash balance by spending more than he takes in—buying more than he sells—all of us together cannot. If I buy something, I am buying it from someone else—who is selling it. If I get rid of my surplus currency by giving it to you in exchange for goods, my cash balance falls, but yours rises.

What is even odder is that although we cannot reduce our *nominal* cash balances—the number of dollars we hold—the attempt to do so does reduce our *real* cash balances. Since we are all trying to buy more than we sell, on net the quantity of goods demanded is greater than the quantity supplied. If quantity demanded is greater than quantity supplied, price rises. The rise in prices of goods (measured in money) corresponds to a fall in the value of money (measured in goods). We have just as many dollars as before, but they are worth less. The process continues until real cash balances are down to their desired level. Everyone has twice as many dollars as before and every dollar buys half as much as before; prices have doubled, and nothing else has changed.

Another way of understanding the same process is to think of all markets as money markets. If you are selling goods for money, you are also buying money with goods; if you are buying goods with money, you are also selling money for goods. If actual cash balances are larger than desired cash balances, that means that the supply of money is larger than the demand, so the price of money falls. It continues falling until actual and desired cash balances are equal. In nominal terms, the fall in the price of money raises desired cash balances until they equal actual cash balances. In real terms, the fall in the price of money lowers actual cash balances until they equal desired cash balances.

I have just described how equilibrium is established on the market for money—how quantity supplied and quantity demanded are made equal. In doing so, I have also shown how the general level of (money) prices is determined. The equilibrium price level is that level at which the real value of the existing supply of money is equal to the total desired real cash balances of the population. If prices are higher than that, then individuals are holding less cash (in terms of what it will buy) than they wish. They attempt to increase their cash balances by buying less than they sell; in the process, they drive prices down toward their equilibrium level. If prices are below their equilibrium, the same process works in reverse to drive them back up. This description of how the general price level is determined and how it changes is a somewhat simplified one, mostly because I have not discussed what happens while the system is adjusting and have ignored interactions between prices and interest rates; but it is essentially correct, and it will be sufficient for the purposes of this chapter.

Inflation—The Changing Price of Money

Suppose we observe that prices are rising. Since rising prices of goods (in money) correspond to a falling price of money (in goods), rising prices mean that either the supply of money is increasing or the demand for money is decreasing.

A change in prices could be the result of a change in either supply or demand, but, in practice, almost all rapid changes in the price of money (and hence the general level of money prices) are due to changes in supply. A change in the demand for money means that individuals are choosing, on average, to hold larger or smaller cash balances than before—perhaps because of a change in their income, the pattern or predictability of their expenditures, or some other feature of their lives affecting how much money they wish to hold. Such real changes, affecting not merely one individual but the average of a large society, rarely occur very fast; it would be unusual, for instance, if the real income of a society grew by more than 10 percent in a year. Changes in supply can occur much more rapidly. In a paper-money system like ours, the government can double the supply of money in a few days, simply by printing a lot of large-denomination bills—and some governments have done so.

Changes in demand can, of course, produce substantial changes in the price level, given enough time. An example is the gradual fall in prices during the final decades of the nineteenth century. Money at the time was not paper but gold; it could not be printed, and not very much of it was being mined. The economies of the countries that used gold as money were growing, and so was the number of such countries. Demand rose faster than supply, so the price of money rose—and the prices of goods fell. The process was eventually ended by the discovery of the South African gold fields and the invention of new technologies for extracting gold from lower grade ores.

Such *deflations*—periods of falling prices—are much rarer than *inflations*—changes in the opposite direction. An inflation occurs when the supply of money increases faster than the demand, causing prices to rise. In the U.S., inflation rates of 10 percent or more a year ("double digit inflation") have occurred several times in recent years. In many other countries, inflation rates of 20, 50, or 100 percent per year are common.

Consequences of Inflation

The consequences of inflation depend on the degree to which it is anticipated. If everyone in the society knows how prices have been changing, are changing, and are going to change in the future, then everyone can allow for the changing value of the dollar over time in setting future prices, making contracts for future payments, and so on. Under such circumstances, inflation is a nuisance, but not much more. If, on the other hand, individuals incorrectly anticipate inflation—failing to expect inflation that does occur, expecting inflation that does not occur, or correctly predicting inflation but incorrectly predicting the rate—the results are much more serious. We shall first consider the less serious case of fully anticipated inflation, then go on to consider the problems of unanticipated or incorrectly anticipated inflation.

Anticipated Inflation. Suppose I am lending you money, in a world of constant 10 percent inflation. The interest rate at which I lend it to you will depend on my (and everyone else's) supply of loans and your (and everyone else's) demand for loans, as we saw back in Chapter 11. Both you and I know that when you pay the money back, a year from now, each dollar will buy 10 percent less than it does now. What I ultimately consume is not money but goods. What determines the amount I am willing to lend is how much present consumption I must give up by lending you the money instead of spending it myself and how much I shall be able to buy with the money you will pay me back a year later. So my supply of loans is a function not of the nominal interest rate, the interest rate measured in money, but of the real interest rate, the interest rate measured in goods. Similarly, and for the same reason, your demand for loans depends on the real, not the nominal, interest rate.

I would be equally willing to lend (and you to borrow) at a nominal interest rate of 10 percent in a world of 10 percent per year inflation, 20 percent in a world of 20 percent inflation, or zero percent in a world of zero percent inflation; in each case, the real interest rate is zero, since the money paid back buys the same amount of goods as the money lent. Similarly, nominal interest rates of 25, 20, or 15 percent in a world of 10 percent inflation correspond to real interest rates of 15, 10, and 5 percent—and to nominal rates of 15, 10, and 5 percent in a world of no inflation. The nominal interest rate simply equals the real interest rate plus the inflation rate. Both the supply of loans and the demand for loans depend on the real interest rate, so two economies which are identical except for their inflation rates will have the same real interest rates. Nominal interest rates will be different, with the difference just making up for the different inflation rates.

In the case of loans, high nominal interest rates compensate lenders for the effects of anticipated inflation. The same sort of thing happens with other contracts. Just as in the case of loans, the individuals concerned are ultimately interested in goods, not money; so the supply and demand curves that determine prices are functions of the real, not the nominal, amount of future payments. If you hire me on a five-year contract in an inflationary world, both you and I know that the dollars you pay me will be worth less and less each year. If the *real* terms we are willing to agree on are, say, $20,000/year for the next five years, we can and will implement them with an agreement for you to pay me $20,000 this year, $22,000 next year, and so on. Similarly, for other contracts that involve payments over time, the number of dollars adjusts to compensate for the anticipated change in their value.

This analysis suggests that the main cost of *anticipated* inflation is the time and trouble of taking account of it in arranging our lives. If, as in most of this book, we ignore such transaction costs, then anticipated inflation would seem to have no important effects.

Unanticipated Inflation. So far, we have been considering fully anticipated inflation; everyone—lenders and borrowers, employers and employees—knows what is happening and what will happen to prices over time. We shall now drop that assumption and consider the effects of unanticipated inflation. We start with the simple case where everyone expects an inflation rate of zero.

We live in a world where prices have been, and are expected to be, stable. I lend you $1,000 at an interest rate of 5 percent. During the next year, to our surprise, prices rise 6 percent. At the end of the year, you pay me back $1,050 —and I find that it will buy less than the $1,000 I lent you. The loan we thought we were making was at a real and nominal rate of 5 percent; it turned out to be at a nominal rate of 5 percent but a real rate of -1 percent.

As you can see by this example, an unexpected inflation revises the real terms of loans against creditors and in favor of debtors. The same is true if we expect inflation—but less inflation than we get. If we had both anticipated a 5 percent inflation, we would have agreed to a nominal interest rate of 10 percent. The result, if the actual inflation rate turned out to be 10 percent, would have been a real interest rate of zero instead of the 5 percent you thought you were paying and I thought I was getting.

Unanticipated inflation has a similar effect on other contracts. Suppose I have agreed to work for you for the next five years for $20,000/year, in the belief that prices will be stable. I am wrong; prices rise—and my real income falls—at 10 percent per year. I have gotten a worse deal than I thought—and you have gotten a better one. In this case, it is the employer who gains by inflation and the employee who loses. The same thing would be true if our original agreement made allowance for inflation, but the inflation rate turned out to be higher than we expected. Exactly the opposite would happen if we *overestimated* future inflation; the increase in nominal wages built into my employment contract would more than compensate me for the inflation that actually occurred.

The effects of unanticipated or misanticipated inflation on debtors, creditors, employers and employees are all special cases of a more general principle: Inflation injures individuals with net nominal assets and benefits individuals with net nominal liabilities.

What do I mean by "net nominal assets"? My house is a *real* asset; it continues to provide me with the same services, whatever happens to the general price level. A pension of $10,000/year is a *nominal* asset; since I am receiving a fixed number of dollars, the real value of my pension—what it can buy—goes up or down with the value of money.

When I lend you $1,000 at 5 percent, I acquire a nominal asset—a claim against you for $1,050, payable a year from now. You acquire a nominal liability—your obligation to pay that amount a year from now. If the inflation rate rises unexpectedly, the real value of my asset falls, and so does the real value of your liability—which is bad for me and good for you. Similarly, if I agree to work for you for five years at $20,000/year, I acquire a nominal asset—$20,000/year for five years. You acquire a nominal liability—the obligation to pay $20,000/year for five years.

An individual may have both nominal assets and nominal liabilities—an employment contract which pays him a fixed number of dollars in the future and a mortgage that requires him to pay a fixed number of dollars in the future. If his nominal liabilities are larger than his nominal assets, then *on net* he has nominal liabilities; if the assets are larger, he has net nominal assets. The comparison is simple if the assets and liabilities all come due in the same year. Otherwise things become more complicated. The same individual may be benefited by one pattern of future inflation—with most of the inflation occuring after he collects on his assets and before he must pay on his liabilities—and injured by a different pattern of inflation.

So the general principle is that inflation injures those who have, on net, nominal assets, and benefits those who have, on net, nominal liabilities. *Deflation*—a fall in prices—benefits those who have net nominal assets and injures those who have net nominal liabilities.

In separating the effects of inflation or deflation from the effects of *unanticipated* inflation or deflation, there is a somewhat subtle distinction that must be made. In one sense, inflation injures a creditor whether or not it is anticipated; the higher the inflation rate, the less the value of the dollars paid back to him. Once the loan is made, the higher the inflation rate turns out to be, the worse off the creditor is and the better off the debtor. But creditors are not worse off in a world of (fully anticipated) 10 percent inflation than in a world of (fully anticipated) 0 percent inflation; the higher nominal interest rate in the inflationary world just compensates them for the lower value of the money they get back.

A slightly different way of putting this is to point out that in a world of fully anticipated inflation, creditors only lend money (and debtors only borrow it) if they are better off making (or taking) the loan than not doing so. In a world of incorrectly anticipated inflation, the contract is, in effect, revised after it has been made; so the lender (or borrower) may discover that the deal he actually made, unlike the deal he thought he made, is worse than no deal at all.

Uncertain Inflation. So far, we have considered unpredicted inflation in a situation in which people think they know what is happening to prices and turn out to be wrong. A more realistic situation would be one in which everyone knows that he does not know what the inflation rate is going to be. Every long-term nominal contract is then a gamble. If you borrow or lend, accept a job or offer one, you are agreeing to a contract whose real terms depend on what the inflation rate turns out to be. To some extent, one can compensate for this by designing contracts whose terms depend on what happens to the price level; but the result is still to increase considerably the cost, complication, and uncertainty of doing business.

PART 2 · UNEMPLOYMENT

In analyzing markets, including the market for labor, we have almost always assumed that price adjusts until quantity demanded equals quantity supplied. If your only source of economic information is this book, that may seem like an adequate description of how the economy works. If you also read newspapers, watch television, or listen to radio, you may have wondered how, if quantity of labor demanded is equal to quantity supplied, there can be several million people unemployed.

Kinds of Unemployment

The first step in answering that question is to look at what is meant by "unemployment." The unemployment figure reported in the newspapers is an estimate of the number of people who, if asked whether they are looking for a job and do not have one, would answer yes; the figure is calculated by asking that question of some small fraction of the population, and, from their answers, estimating what the result would be of asking everyone. Unemployment is usually given in the form of the *unemployment rate*—the number of people unemployed as a percentage of the total labor force.

Different reasons why someone might answer yes to that question correspond to different sorts of unemployment. Some of them involve an inequality between quantity of labor supplied and quantity demanded; others do not.

Search Unemployment. You have just resigned—or been fired—from a job as an engineer with a salary of $40,000/year. You could, if you wished, walk into the neighborhood restaurant and offer to wash dishes; by doing so, you might make as much as a quarter of your old income. You decide instead to look for another job as an engineer.

After a few days spent reading the want ads, you locate a possible job. It requires a long commute and pays only $30,000. You keep looking. After another two weeks, you find a better job, one that pays $40,000 and is located reasonably close to where you live. You go in for an interview and are offered the job. You spend a few more days looking around in the hopes of finding something better, then accept.

You spent about three weeks between jobs. During how much of that time were you unemployed? In one sense, all of it; in another sense, none.

At any time during those weeks, you would, if asked, have said that you wanted a job and did not have one; so from the standpoint of the Bureau of Labor Statistics, you were counted as unemployed. But during all of that time, you could have had a job—as a dishwasher—if you had wanted one. The reason you did not work as a dishwasher was that you had a better job. You were employed, by yourself, at the job of looking for a job. You obviously preferred that to the alternative of being a dishwasher—as shown by your choice.

Such "search unemployment" makes up a substantial fraction of reported unemployment. In a market where goods are not identical, such as the housing market, the marriage market, or the labor market, searching is a productive activity. If your search finds you a job close to home instead of one on the other side of the city, a job utilizing all of your skills instead of half of them, or a job working with people you enjoy working with, you have produced something of considerable value while "unemployed."

In the case of search unemployment, the individual who says that he is looking for a job is telling the truth. What is deceptive about calling that "unemployment" is the implication that the supply of labor is greater than the demand. Search unemployment is a normal and desirable feature of the labor market. One could reduce or even eliminate it—by announcing that anyone who was unemployed for more than a week would be shot, for example, or by making it illegal for anyone to quit or be fired unless he already had another job. But the result of such a law would be to make the situation worse, not better, by eliminating a productive activity—spending time producing information necessary to choose the right job.

Fictitious Unemployment. Another source of measured unemployment consists of people who find it in their interest to say they are looking for a job when they are not. A condition for receiving welfare, for many although not all recipients, is that the recipient be looking for a job. Presumably some of the people receiving such welfare would rather be unemployed (or employed covertly) and receive welfare than be employed, at the sort of job they could get, and not receive welfare. If you do not want a job, it is easy enough not to find one. So some reported unemployment consists of people who are pretending to look for a job, would accept a job if a sufficiently attractive one were offered to them, but prefer unemployment to the sort of job that will be offered to them. One study estimated that changes in federal welfare rules which made "looking for work" a prerequisite for welfare produced an increase in the measured unemployment rate of between one and two percentage points. If that result is correct, it suggests that unemployment of this sort may be responsible for about one fourth of total measured unemployment.

Involuntary Unemployment. Consider someone so unproductive that he is worth nothing to any employer. He could get a job only by agreeing to work for nothing or less than nothing. So far as a supply and demand diagram is concerned, the quantity of his labor supplied is equal to the quantity demanded, just as we would expect. Unfortunately, the equilibrium price is zero.

This is an extreme case, but it demonstrates the sense in which even the most involuntary unemployment may be "voluntary" so far as the logic of economics is concerned. In terms of the ordinary meaning of words, someone who can only get a job by agreeing to work for nothing is involuntarily unemployed. Yet it seems odd to say that the market is not working merely because an equilibrium price turns out to be zero.

Individuals who want to work but have an equilibrium wage of zero are probably rare, but there is a similar—and even more involuntary—type of unemployment which is quite common. Under current minimum wage laws, it is illegal, in most fields, for someone to work for less than the minimum wage. If for some kinds of labor—unskilled teenagers, for example—the wage that equates quantity supplied and quantity demanded is below the minimum, then at the minimum wage, the quantity of such labor supplied is greater than the quantity demanded. The excess workers—people who are willing to work for the minimum wage and might be willing to work for less but cannot get jobs at the lowest wage that it is legal for employers to pay them—show up in the statistics as unemployed. Minimum wages produce a surplus of labor, just as maximum rents produce a shortage of housing.

Disequilibrium Unemployment. So far, all but one of the sorts of unemployment I have discussed have been consistent with equilibrium on the labor market. The exception is unemployment due to minimum wage laws; in that case, the market cannot reach the equilibrium price because the equilibrium price, for some types of labor, is illegal.

There remains one further category—unemployment due to disequilibrium. Throughout this book, I have limited my discussion of disequilibrium to the demonstration that moving a market out of equilibrium creates forces tending to move it back. Such forces do not operate instantaneously. In a changing and unpredictable society, prices at any instant may be above their equilibrium level, with excess supply tending to push them back down; or they may be below their equilibrium level, with excess demand tending to push them back up. Disequilibrium is particularly likely, and particularly long lived, in markets for inhomogeneous goods, such as labor or spouses. If all units of a good are identical—ounces of pure silver, for example—it is relatively easy to observe price, quantity supplied, and quantity demanded, and adjust accordingly. With a million different "qualities" of labor (and jobs and spouses), the informational problem associated with finding the equilibrium price is far harder. It is harder still when what is being sold is not a day's consumption of the good but a contract for the next several years—as is frequently the case on those markets. In that case, the equilibrium price must take account not only of supply and demand conditions today, but of estimated supply and demand conditions over the entire period of the contract. This is made more difficult by something we discussed earlier in the chapter—the effect of uncertain inflation on long-term contracting.

Unemployment and Inflation

In arguing that "search unemployment" is a desirable activity, I implicitly assumed that the individual had an accurate idea of what sort of jobs were available and would therefore choose to search only if the return was, in some average sense, at least as great as the cost. Suppose this is not true. Suppose the worker has somehow been fooled into thinking that if he only looks a little longer, he can get a job paying $40,000/year, when in fact there are no such jobs available. He may waste months looking for a nonexistent job before he realizes his mistake.

One possible source of such errors is unanticipated or misanticipated inflation. Consider the effect of an unexpected drop in the inflation rate. Prices have been rising at 10 percent per year for many years; most people expect them to continue doing so. For some reason, the government, which has been producing the inflation with a corresponding increase in the money supply, decides to turn off the printing presses.

Everyone has gotten used to the old level of inflation; in buying or selling goods, in taking jobs or hiring workers, the universal assumption is that a dollar will be worth 10 percent less next year than this year. Initially, after the government stops printing money, things continue as before; producers increase the prices of their goods and workers increase their wage expectations at the usual 10 percent per year.

The number of dollars available to buy those goods and hire those workers, however, is not increasing. Producers find that at the prices they are charging, they cannot sell as much as they have produced; they reduce their prices. Eventually, when everyone has gotten the message, prices fall back to where they were when the government stopped increasing the money supply.

Some people get the message faster than others. Producers are selling their goods every day; they quickly discover that their prices are too high and change them. The individual worker looks for a new job only once every several years, so it takes workers much longer to recognize the change and adjust their expectations. In the meantime, workers expect wages above the actual equilibrium wage—the wage at which supply and demand for labor are equal. Seen from the standpoint of the employer, the real wage at which he can get workers has gone up, so he hires fewer workers. Seen from the standpoint of the worker, he is engaging in search based on an overly optimistic picture of what can be found, so he keeps searching long beyond the point where additional search is worth what it costs.

In the situation I have described, incorrect search leads to an undesirably high level of unemployment. It can also lead to an undesirably low level. Consider the case discussed earlier in the chapter, where prices have been stable for a long time and suddenly begin to rise. A worker has just quit a $30,000 job in the (correct) belief that he is worth at least $40,000 elsewhere. The next day, he accepts a job that will pay him $40,000/year for the next five years. What he does not know—and his employer does—is that the inflation rate has risen from zero to 10 percent. In real terms, he is being offered $40,000 this year, $36,364 next year, and $33,058 the year after. If he had known that, he would have kept on looking.

In this case, the unexpected onset of inflation has reduced the unemployment rate, but it has done so in a way that makes the newly employed people worse off; they have been tricked into accepting a worse job than they could have gotten by looking a little longer. Employers, on the other hand, are better off. Since the amount of labor supplied is based not on what the workers are really getting (adjusted for inflation) but on what they think they are getting, the supply curve for labor has shifted out and the equilibrium real wage has fallen. Profits rise. Eventually the workers realize what is happening, the supply curve for labor shifts back, and profits go back to their normal level; but during the adjustment period, the employers are better off and the workers worse off as a result of the workers' mistake.

PART 3 · WHY INFLATION HAPPENS: A PUBLIC CHOICE PERSPECTIVE

I have given a simple—some may think oversimple—explanation of inflation: Inflation occurs because the government expands the supply of money. This raises an obvious question. All politicians—including the ones who get elected—are against inflation, as one can easily discover by listening to their speeches. If all they have to do to stop it is to stop printing money, why do they not do so? Why does inflation ever occur; and if it does start, why is it not immediately stopped?

There are two possible answers. One is that inflation is a mistake; the politicians controlling monetary policy, in the U.S. and elsewhere, do not recognize the connection between the amount of money they print and the value of that money.

This is, to put it mildly, implausible. Our understanding of inflation goes back at least as far as David Hume, who correctly analyzed the causes of inflation more than 200 years ago. While the details of the relation between the money supply, the price level, and other economic variables are complicated, there is an enormous body of evidence, from many different societies at many different times, showing that a large increase in the money supply almost inevitably results in a large increase in prices, and a large increase in prices almost never occurs without a large increase in the money supply. It is hard to believe that if it were in the interest of politicians to know what causes inflation and to use that knowledge in order to prevent it, they would not yet have managed to do so.

The second and more plausible explanation is that politicians frequently find that inflation benefits them. Their behavior, in campaigning against inflation but not doing anything about it when elected, is then entirely rational. They campaign against inflation because they want the support of voters who are opposed to it. They act for inflation because they benefit from some of its consequences. They trust to the rational ignorance of the voters to conceal the inconsistency between words and deeds.

This brings us to the question of why it may often be in the interest of politicians to create or maintain inflation. There are at least two reasons. The first and simplest is that government itself is often a major beneficiary of inflation. The second and more complicated is that (unanticipated) increases in the inflation rate tend to have benefits that are immediate and visible and costs that are delayed and invisible, while (unanticipated) decreases tend to have visible and immediate costs and invisible and delayed benefits. Because of the public good nature of voting, discussed in Chapter 18, costs and benefits that are visible and immediate are much more important, politically speaking, than ones that are not. So it is often in the interest of politicians to increase the inflation rate and against their interest to decrease it.

Government as a Beneficiary of Inflation

In my earlier discussion of inflation, I pointed out that it benefits debtors, or, more generally, people with net nominal liabilities, and injures creditors, or, more generally, people with net nominal assets. Governments, as a rule, have lots of nominal liabilities and few nominal assets; hence they are among the largest beneficiaries of inflation.

One very large nominal liability of the present government of the U.S. is the national debt. It owes its creditors—the owners of government bonds—a fixed number of dollars. If all prices double, the real value of what it owes falls in half. This is what has happened over the past several decades. The reason why the national debt, in real terms, was lower in 1980 than in 1945 despite the almost uninterrupted deficits of the intervening years is that much of the debt had been inflated away.

Of course, if the government keeps inflating, it will eventually find that in order to borrow money, it must offer higher nominal interest rates to compensate lenders for what they expect to lose through inflation. At that point, if investors correctly anticipate future inflation, the government no longer gains by inflation. Like any other creditor, the government succeeds in getting below-market real interest rates only if inflation is unanticipated.

The government still has an incentive to continue inflating, even in this situation. If it does not, inflation will be below what lenders anticipated, and it will find itself paying a higher real interest rate than either the government or its creditors expected; it will be, in effect, compensating lenders for inflation that is not occurring.

A second large liability of the government is its obligation to make future payments—social security, veterans' benefits, and the like. This is only in part a nominal liability. To the extent that cost-of-living adjustments are built into such obligations, what the government owes is a real, rather than a nominal, quantity—an amount of purchasing power rather than a number of dollars.

Inflation as a Source of Revenue. Inflation not only reduces the real value of the liabilities of the governments of the U.S. and similar countries but may also increase their real income. Under a graduated tax system, the higher your nominal income, the higher the percentage of that income that you must pay as taxes. If all prices and all incomes double, your real income before taxes is the same as before, but your tax rate is higher; so the real value of the taxes the government collects from you is higher. This phenomenon, often described as "bracket creep" (inflation makes your income "creep" into higher brackets), means that inflation produces an automatic tax increase. Politicians, as a general rule, like to be able to spend more money but do not like to be associated with raising taxes, since expenditures are popular with voters and taxes are not. Inflation provides the (political) benefit without the (political) cost.

At present, this particular device for invisible tax increases no longer exists in the U.S. Changes in the tax law passed in 1981 and coming into effect in 1985 provided for *indexing*—the automatic adjustment of tax brackets to take account of inflation. Whether that reform will remain in effect or be eventually reversed by congressional action remains to be seen.

Bracket creep is not the only way in which government revenue is increased by inflation. When the money supply is increased by the printing of additional currency, someone gets the new money. If the government prints the new money, the government gets it. Printing money is a way by which a government can generate revenue without any visible tax.

Deficit Spending and Inflation. It is often claimed that deficit spending is a major cause of inflation. The usual arguments for this conclusion are wrong; if the government spends more than it takes in and borrows the difference, the effect is to increase the supply of government bonds, not the supply of money. Of course, a government could, and some governments do, finance a deficit by printing money instead of borrowing it; but in that case, it is the money creation, not the deficit, that is producing the inflation.

There is a different sense, however, in which deficit spending may well be linked to inflation. Deficit spending increases the national debt. The larger the national debt, the larger the benefit the government receives from inflation. So although deficit spending does not cause inflation, it does increase the benefit of inflation to the politicians currently in power and so increases the probability that they will follow inflationary policies.

How to Fool All of the People Some of the Time. In discussing the relation between inflation and unemployment, I showed how an unanticipated increase in the inflation rate results, in the short term, in an increase in profits and a decrease in the unemployment rate. The increased profits are paid for by a decrease in real wages—but at the beginning of the inflation, that is not yet obvious to the workers. The decrease in unemployment represents a net loss, not a net gain, to the newly employed workers, since they are accepting jobs that they would have rejected if they had understood the real as well as the nominal terms of what they were being offered. But since they do not yet know that, they believe they are better off. Employers are happy about their high profits, workers are happy about their low unemployment rate; everyone is (apparently) better off. If it happens to be an election year, the incumbent president is reelected by a landslide.

After a while, people adjust. Unemployment goes back up; profits go back down. Prices rise steadily. The incumbent administration blames the inflation on the unreasonable wage demands of the unions (when giving speeches to the Chamber of Commerce) or the attempt of corporations to extort "obscene profits" from consumers (when giving speeches to the AFL-CIO). After a while, another election comes around. The government buys new printing presses and increases the rate of expansion of the money supply from 10 percent to 20. Profits rise. Unemployment falls. The incumbent administration's ticket is reelected in a landslide. Prices are now rising at 20 percent per year. The administration blames the inflation on OPEC.

While this strategy may work for a while, it has some long-run problems. The effects of inflation on profits and unemployment depend on its being unanticipated. The more experience people have with high and rising inflation rates, the harder they are to fool, hence the greater the increase necessary to produce the effect. High and unpredictable inflation rates produce undesirable and politically unpopular effects. At some point, the administration—or its opponents—may conclude that it is politically desirable to stop increasing the inflation rate, and perhaps even to decrease it.

Doing so can be and generally is politically costly. If people expect the inflation rate to remain at 20 percent per year and the money supply expands at a rate of only 10 percent, actual inflation will be lower than anticipated inflation. If people expect the inflation rate to continue to rise, from 20 percent to 30 percent, then even keeping the rate at 20 percent will make actual inflation lower than anticipated inflation. In either case, the result is the opposite of what happened earlier when actual inflation was higher than anticipated inflation. Profits fall; unemployment rises. The fall of profits is associated with a rise in real wages, but since workers are not yet aware of the change in the inflation rate, they do not know they are better off. The politicians who cut the inflation rate lose the next election.

This suggests the possibility of a *political business cycle*. The administration starts inflating a few months before election day, thus getting itself elected, and stops after the votes are all cast, thus reestablishing expectations of stable prices— to be taken advantage of with another inflation just before the next election. If the president controlled the process, we would get a four-year business cycle; if the congress controlled it, a two-year cycle.

While this provides an elegant explanation for variations in inflation and unemployment rates, it does not appear to be a correct one; statistical studies so far have not found any clear relation between the pattern of elections and the business cycle. What does seem clear is that actions taken by the government have substantial effects on the inflation and unemployment rates and that those rates, in turn, affect how people vote. The resulting connection between policy and votes provides an incentive influencing the policies that incumbent politicians follow, and one that may explain much of what they do.

Two Warnings

Before ending the chapter, I should warn you of two things. The first is that, in my experience, economics students have a tendency to confuse the inflation rate and the interest rate. The best way to avoid doing so is to analyze everything in real rather than nominal terms, thus eliminating money and the price of money from the analysis. That is what I did in Chapter 11, where I first introduced interest rates. One can then go from results in real terms to results in nominal terms by converting all prices and flows of money from "constant dollars" (purchasing power) to "current dollars" and all interest rates from "real interest rates" to "nominal interest rates."

The second warning is that this chapter is a short and sketchy explanation of a difficult and complicated set of ideas and relationships. I believe the sketch is in essence an accurate one, although some competent economists might disagree, but it is in any case only a sketch. If you want a clearer understanding of the causes and nature of inflation and unemployment, and the relation between both and government policy, you should take a course or read a book on what used to be called monetary theory and is now more often described as "macroeconomics." The purpose of this chapter is not to replace such a book but to show you that the study of macroeconomics can and should be based on price theory—usually called, with more symmetry than sense, "microeconomics." This is, in two senses, a micro macro chapter.

OPTIONAL SECTION

PRICE INDICES

Relative prices continually change as a result of shifts in demand and supply curves; so during an inflation, money prices increase at different rates for different goods. There may even be goods whose money price falls while most prices are rising—computers and calculators in the 1970s, for example.

So far, I have said nothing about how we define the inflation rate when the money prices of different goods are going up at different rates. The obvious solution is to use a *price index*—an average of the prices of many different goods. In calculating such an average, we need some way of deciding how much weight each good should have. It does not make much sense to say that if the prices of pins and thumbtacks have gone down 10 percent and the prices of food and housing have gone up 10 percent, "on average" prices have stayed the same.

One obvious solution to this problem, and one that is often used, is to define the general level of prices as a weighted average, using the quantity of each item consumed in a year as the weight. Such a price index measures the money cost of buying the entire bundle of goods and services consumed in a year. It is usually expressed relative to some base year. Suppose the base year is 1980. If the price index for 1981 is 1.10, that means that the entire bundle of goods and services consumed in a year cost 10 percent more in 1981 than in 1980.

This raises a further problem—which year's consumption do we use for our weights? Do we compare what the consumption of 1980 would have cost at the prices of 1981 to what it did cost at the prices of 1980, or do we compare what the consumption of 1981 cost at the prices of 1981 to what it would have cost at the prices of 1980? Since the relative amount of different goods consumed will be different in different years, the two methods of computing the price index can be expected to give at least slightly different results.

In actually calculating price indices, both methods have been used. The *Laspeyres* index is calculated using quantities in the first year, the *Paasche* index using quantities in the second year. If we define the "true" percentage increase in prices between Year 1 and Year 2 as that percentage increase in income that would exactly compensate the consumer for the change in prices from Year 1 to Year 2, it is possible to show that the Laspeyres index overstates the increase in price and the Paasche understates it. If the Laspeyres index goes up 10 percent from Year 1 to Year 2, then a consumer whose income also went up 10 percent would be better off in Year 2 than in Year 1—he would be able to buy a bundle of goods which he preferred to what he bought in Year 1. If the Paasche index went up 10 percent, a consumer whose income went up 10 percent would be worse off in the second year. Proving these results will be left as an exercise for the reader—in the form of Problems 11 and 12.

PROBLEMS

1. Throughout this chapter, I have used "inflation" to mean "an increasing level of prices." Some economists prefer to use "inflation" to mean "an increase in the supply of money." Usually a situation is either an inflation in both senses or in neither. Describe some possible exceptions—situations where the money supply is going up and prices are not, or prices are going up and the money supply is not.

2. In discussing the benefits government receives from inflation, I said that by printing money, the government can collect revenue without any *visible* tax. Precisely what is the *invisible* tax associated with money creation? Who pays it? (Hint: Consider a situation in which inflation is fully anticipated, so that many of its effects disappear. Find an unavoidable cost borne by someone as a result of inflation which is not balanced by a benefit to anyone else, except the government that is printing the money. This is a hard problem.)

3. In discussing the relation between the money supply and inflation, I said that a large increase in the general price level *almost* never occurs without a large increase in the money supply. Consider a city under siege. When the siege has lasted long enough so that people start getting hungry, the price of a loaf of bread may be 100 times what it was before the siege. Explain what is happening in terms of the explanation of the relation between money and the price level that was given in the chapter. (Note: You may *not* use the example given in this question to answer Problem 1.)

4. The only cost of holding money which I have discussed is interest lost by holding money instead of lending it out. Another cost is the possibility that if you have money in your wallet, someone may steal it. Suppose the rate of such crimes increases drastically. What will the effect be on the price level, according to the analysis of this chapter? According to the analysis of Chapter 19? Do the two effects work in the same or opposite directions? Explain. (This is a hard problem.)

5. Suppose the inflation rate is 12 percent and the nominal interest rate is 10 percent. Are real interest rates high or low? Assuming that you expect the inflation to continue, is this a good or bad time to borrow money and buy a house? Discuss.

6. Under current tax law, interest payments are deductible and interest income is taxable. How does this affect the relation between real and nominal interest rates—assuming that real rates are defined after tax rather than before tax? How does it affect your answer to Problem 5?

7. In discussing the effects of an unexpected increase in the inflation rate, I claimed that the resulting decrease in the unemployment rate was a cost not a benefit, since workers were being fooled into "inefficiently short" searches. Does this imply that the increased unemployment due to an unexpected decrease in the inflation rate is a benefit? Discuss.

8. If, as I argue, minimum wage laws result in unemployment for unskilled workers, who, if anyone, benefits from such laws? You may want to use the ideas of Chapter 13 in answering this. (This is a hard problem.)

9. How might you test the correctness of your answer to Problem 8? You may wish to use ideas from Chapter 18. (This is a hard problem.)

10. Laws setting maximum interest rates are called *usury laws*. What effect would you expect such laws to have? What relation would you anticipate between inflation and difficulties associated with usury laws?

The following problems refer to the optional section:

11. Assume that all consumers are identical. Consider a single consumer in Year 1 and Year 2. In Year 1, he has income I. He consumes only two goods—quantity x of good X and quantity y of good Y. The prices of X and Y are different in the two years.
    a. Use an indifference curve diagram to show that the Laspeyres price index for Year 2 based on Year 1 is greater than the percentage increase in income necessary to make the consumer as well off in Year 2 as he was in Year 1.
    b. Use an indifference curve diagram to show that the Paasche price index for Year 2 based on Year 1 is less than the percentage increase in income necessary to make the customer as well off in Year 2 as he was in Year 1.
    (Hint: The answers to this problem and Problem 12 are closely related to the explanation of the housing paradox in Chapter 3.)

12. Redo Problem 11 for a consumer consuming many goods, using a verbal analysis rather than an indifference curve diagram.

13. You see the following two advertisements on the same day in the same city:
— "Mrs. Jones went into her local A&P store to do her weeking shopping. After she finished, she duplicated her purchases at the Kroger's down the block. It cost 5 percent more at Kroger's than at A&P. Shop A&P; the P stands for better prices."
— "Mrs. Smith did her weekly shopping at Kroger's then went over to the A&P and bought exactly the same things. It cost her 6 percent less at Kroger's. For better prices, shop Kroger's."
Assume that the advertisements are both accurate and both involved the same stores.
a. Explain how the results of the two "experiments" could turn out as reported.
b. Explain why, if prices on average are really about the same in both stores, you would *expect* the results to turn out as reported.
c. Explain the connection between this problem, Problem 12, and the housing paradox of Chapter 3.

FOR FURTHER READING

There is at least one real cost of fully anticipated inflation which I have not discussed—the cost of individuals holding inefficiently low cash balances because high nominal interest rates make it costly to hold cash. This is analyzed in Milton Friedman, "The Optimum Quantity of Money," in his *The Optimum Quantity of Money and Other Essays* (Hawthorne, N.Y.: Aldine Publishing Co., 1969).

For a statistical study of the effects of minimum wage legislation on various sorts of workers, you may want to look at P. Linneman, "The Economic Impact of Minimum Wage Legislation," *Journal of Political Economy*, Vol. 90, No. 3 (1982), pp. 443-469.

One book on macroeconomics which you might want to read is Michael R. Darby, *Intermediate Macroeconomics* (New York: McGraw-Hill, 1979). Another and much easier one is J. Huston McCulloch, *Money and Inflation: A Monetarist Approach* (2nd ed.; Orlando: Academic Press, 1981).

A more advanced discussion of these issues can be found in Edmund S. Phelps (ed.), *Microeconomic Foundations of Employment and Inflation Theory* (New York: W. W. Norton and Co., 1973).

Two important papers on the economics of search and information, with implications for search unemployment, are George Stigler, "The Economics of Information," *Journal of Political Economy*, Vol. 69, No. 3 (June, 1961), pp. 213-225 and his "Information in the Labor Market," *Journal of Political Economy*, Vol. 70, No. 5, Part 2 (Supplement: October, 1962), pp. 94-105.

Section VI

Why You Should Buy This Book

Chapter 23

Final Words

One defect of many economics textbooks, especially at the elementary level, is that they teach you about economics instead of teaching you economics. The result is to produce students who may be equipped to talk about economics but certainly not to do any—a sort of academic equivalent of learning what names to drop at cocktail parties.

You have now spent 22 chapters learning to do economics. In this final chapter, I shall try to tell you something about economics—what it is good for, how it is done, and to what degree economists know anything.

WHAT IS ECONOMICS GOOD FOR ANYWAY?

Looking at the title of this section, it may occur to you that it belongs in the first chapter of the book, not the last. As a believer in rational behavior, I should perhaps have explained to you why economics was worth learning before expecting you to spend a lot of time and trouble learning it. Unfortunately, if I had told you what economics was good for before you read the book, you would have had no way of judging whether or not I was telling the truth and might rationally enough have dismissed my claims as no more than deceptive advertising. You may still come to that conclusion, but at least you now have some evidence on which to base your conclusion.

There are at least four different reasons to learn economics. The first is that economists, in the process of developing a theory of human behavior based on rationality, have done quite a lot of useful thinking about how it is rational to behave. While we may know very little about what your objectives are or should be, we know quite a lot about how, given a set of objectives, they can best be attained. Once you understand concepts such as marginal cost, marginal value, sunk cost, and present value, you should find them to be useful tools in making decisions about how to organize your life. When you finally realize that you have invested six months of effort and heartache pursuing a member of the opposite

542

sex who has no interest at all in you, you can sum up your situation—and reluctantly reach the correct conclusion concerning what to do about it—with the observation that "Sunk costs are sunk costs." When deciding whether to spend another few weeks looking for a better buy in a house or a car, you can put the issue more clearly by asking, not whether you have found the best possible buy, but whether the expected return from additional search is greater or less than its marginal cost. When deciding whether to buy or rent a house, you can, with some effort, combine the ideas of present value from Chapter 11 with the analysis of real and nominal interest rates in Chapter 22 to figure out which is the better alternative.

A second reason to learn economics is in order to understand and predict the behavior of other people, especially the effects of the behavior of large numbers of people, in order to take account of it in planning your own life. This should be useful whether you are an investor trying to make money on the stock market, a general trying to figure out how to keep his soldiers from running away, a homeowner trying to discourage burglars, or a student trying to predict future wages in different professions. In none of these cases will a knowledge of economics by itself be enough to answer your questions—you always need facts and judgment as well. But in all of those cases and many more, economics provides the essential framework within which knowledge and judgment can be combined to reach, perhaps, a correct conclusion—or at least a better conclusion than could be reached without economics.

A third reason to study economics may be that you expect to be a professional economist—someone employed to teach economics, to create economic theory, or to apply economic theory to questions that your employer wants answered. Obviously I believe that being an economist is an attractive profession; if I did not, I would be doing something else for a living. As a missionary, I hope some of you have come to the same conclusion. Of course, as an individual concerned with his rational self-interest, I hope that I have not persuaded enough of you to become economists to significantly reduce my income—or that if I have, you will have the consideration not to enter the field until after I have retired, or at least signed a long-term contract.

The fourth reason to learn economics is that it is fun. Once you understand the logic of economics, you can make sense out of elements of the world around you that you could not otherwise understand—which is fun as well as useful. You can also make the process of extracting a rational pattern from apparent chaos into a game played for its own sake—even in cases where it is likely enough that there is no pattern there to be extracted.

It may occur to you that I have omitted a fifth reason to learn economics, one that many textbooks would put first—to make yourself a better citizen and a better informed voter. It is true that understanding economics makes you much more likely to perceive correctly the consequences of actual or proposed government policy. But while that may be a good reason for me to teach you economics, it is not, unless you are quite an extraordinary individual, a good reason for you to learn it. In a society as large as ours, your vote, as I have pointed out several times, has a very small chance of affecting anything. If you are extraordinarily altruistic, the large number of people benefited by an improvement in government policy may balance, for you, the tiny chance that your actions will produce such an improvement. If you expect to be unusually influential—perhaps because your name is Kennedy or Rockefeller—you may conclude that the public benefit of making yourself an informed citizen justifies the cost. If neither is the case, it is very unlikely that the effect on you of the public benefits produced by your improved understanding of economics will be worth the private costs.

WHAT ECONOMISTS DO

So far as I can tell, economists employed in business or government have two functions. One is to use economic theory to answer questions their employers want answered—to tell Ford what the demand for autos will be next quarter or to estimate for the Treasury what effect a change in the tax laws will have on tax revenues. The other is to use economic language to construct plausible and professional-sounding arguments in favor of whatever their employers want.

Since I am myself an academic economist, I have a somewhat more detailed picture of what academic economists do. What academic economists do is to teach courses like the one you are taking, write books such as the one you are reading, and write articles and do research designed to use economics to explain, predict, and prescribe.

Of the three activities, the research is the one with which you have the least contact; it is also the hardest to explain. I commented in an earlier chapter that economics involves, in practice, a continual balance between unrealistic simplification and unworkable complication. I might have added that striking that balance—producing pictures of reality simple enough so that they can be analyzed and understood and accurate enough, in their essential structure, to tell us something useful about the real world—is an art, not a mechanical process that can be learned from this book or any other. One discovers whether the attempt has been successful by seeing whether the theory generates predictions about the real world which are not obvious and are true.

This raises a problem: How can we distinguish between things a theory logically implies and things it "predicts" only because its author knew they were true before constructing the theory? There is a fine line between using knowledge of the real world to construct a correct theory and constructing a theory which is no more than a complicated restatement of things you already know.

One solution to this problem is to predict things you do not know—preferably things you cannot know because they have not happened yet. This is a very convincing way of demonstrating the usefulness of your theory—especially if other people with other theories are making different predictions, and theirs turn out to be wrong and yours right. Unfortunately, this way of testing a theory only works for theories whose implications can be tested over a fairly short period of time and under conditions that currently exist. The first article I ever published in an economics journal was entitled "An Economic Theory of the Size and Shape of Nations." Its predictions were tested against the changing political map of Europe, from the fall of the Roman Empire to the present. If I had restricted myself to testing my theory against future events, the first tentative results might have come in during the lifetime of my great grandchildren.

One way to stay on the right side of the line dividing prediction from description is to only predict the future. Another way is to adopt what appears to be an unreasonably rigid insistence on following out the logic of complete rationality. Most of us believe that actual behavior is a mixture of rational and irrational elements. It is tempting, in constructing an economic theory, to start out with a model based on rationality and then introduce elements of irrationality whenever they are needed to resolve a conflict between the predictions of the model and what is actually observed. The resulting "theory" looks more like a description of the real world than would a theory which assumed rationality everywhere, but it is very much less useful. If you feel free to assume irrationality wherever convenient, you can explain anything—and having done so, there is no easy way for either you or anyone else to know whether your theory works because it is right or because you knew the answers before you started and modified the theory accordingly.

If, instead, one insists on assuming rationality everywhere—even in the behavior of small children deciding whether or not to kick their siblings—one has much less freedom to alter the predictions to fit the facts. Once the basic assumptions have been set up, the model is driven by its own internal logic. It takes you wherever that logic leads, whether or not you want to go there. One advantage of this is that it may take you to conclusions that you know are false—thus providing evidence that the initial model was wrong. Another advantage is that it may take you to conclusions you thought you knew were false—thus showing you something you did not already know and would never have learned from a "theory" constructed to fit what you thought were the facts.

Seen in this way, the economist's assumption that individuals are rational is, in part, as I argued in Chapter 1, a way of deducing the predictable element in human behavior and, in part, a way of keeping the economic theorist honest.

MODEL, MODEL, AND MODEL

The term "model" is used, in economics, to describe three quite different things. Explaining the different sorts of models prevents confusion among them; it is also a way of sketching out three quite different things that economists—especially but not exclusively academic economists—do.

One kind of model is a simplified picture designed to make it easier to analyze the logic of a situation while ignoring inessential complications. Models of this sort have been used repeatedly in the previous 22 chapters. One example is the discussion in Chapter 7 of the effect on landlords and tenants of legal restrictions on rental contracts. I assumed that all landlords were identical, that all tenants were identical, and that the restriction affected cost (to the landlord) and value (to the tenant) in a way similar to the effect of a tax or subsidy. I made these assumptions not because I believed they were true, but because they made the problem simple enough to be analyzed, without changing the essential logic of the situation. Once one has used this sort of model to figure out what is happening in the simple situation and why, one is prepared to analyze more realistic—and difficult—cases. Other examples in this book would be the barbershop problem in Chapter 10 and the analysis of the effect of tariffs—in a world where wheat is the only export and autos the only import—in Chapter 18.

A second and different sort of model is used in mathematical economics. In many ways, this sort of model is just as complicated as the real world it describes. A typical example might start by assuming "a world of N commodities and M consumers"—where the numbers might be 10, 100, or a billion. Simplifying assumptions are then made, not about the number of goods or participants but about the mathematical characteristics of elements of the model such as utility functions and production functions. These assumptions are useful not to solve the model—nobody expects to solve that sort of model anyway, in the sense of plugging numbers in and getting numbers out—but to prove theorems about what the solution must be like. I have not done any of that sort of rigorous mathematical economics in this book, but I referred to it in Chapter 8, when I explained how, in principle, one would solve an economy, and again in Chapter 15, when I suggested that my proof of the efficiency of a competitive market could be translated into a more precise form. One of the things which mathematical economists prove theorems about is under what circumstances an economy is efficient.

The third sort of model, which I have not discussed at all in this book, is an econometric model. Unlike the other two, an econometric model attempts to give a quantitatively accurate picture of a particular economy—say, the U.S. in January of 1987. It does this by first simplifying the real situation—rather as I simplified it in Chapter 13 when I reduced everything to three factors of production, although not quite that drastically—and then using real-world data and statistics to estimate actual numbers for the quantities and relationships of the model. It is thus a crude picture of a real economy. Its objective is not so much understanding as prediction.

As you probably realize by now, a real economy—say, the U.S. in January of 1987—is an enormously complicated interacting system. Econometric models generally take the form of computer programs, run on very large and expensive computers. Even with the best computers available, any model simple enough to produce a prediction of what will happen next year and take less than a year producing it, has to ignore most of what is really happening in the economy being modeled. Econometric modeling is then the art of building models simple enough to be useful but with enough resemblance to the real economy being modeled to be of some use for predicting what will happen. Seen from the perspective of an economic theorist, it is an art made up of roughly equal parts of economic theory, statistics, and witchcraft.

Econometric modeling survives and prospers, despite the difficulty of doing it and the unreliability of its predictions, because of the immense value of the information it is trying to generate. If you knew what was going to happen to interest rates for the next year, you could make a very large fortune playing the bond markets. Even if the predictions of such models are not very good, knowing a little bit—having a prediction which may well be wrong but has a slightly better than random chance of being right—is worth enough to pay the cost of many hours of computer time and the salaries of many econometricians and programmers.

IS ECONOMICS A SCIENCE?

One side effect of econometric modeling, unfortunately, is to encourage the idea that economists are people who spend their time "trying to predict what the economy will do next" and that economics is either a confidence game or a very primitive science, since "economists never agree with one another." It would make about as much sense to say similar things about physics and physicists and to cite as evidence the poor performance of weather forecasters. On questions of economics, economists often—perhaps even usually—agree with each other. They disagree about quantitative predictions of the outcomes of systems much too complicated to be solved in any other than a very approximate sense.

A second cause of the popular belief that economics is a highly unscientific endeavor is that economic theory often concerns issues of considerable real-world importance. An economist who says, for example, that we would be better off if tariffs were abolished is making a statement which several large and wealthy organizations—General Motors and the United Auto Workers, for example—would like to believe is false, or would at least like other people to believe is false. In such a situation, the publicity given to opposing views has very little relation to the percentage of the profession that supports them. If 99 percent of all economists agree that tariffs should be lowered (only a slight exaggeration of the real situation), the supporters of tariffs will surely be able to find at least one articulate member of the remaining one percent to represent their views. The public impression will then be that "Some economists are for tariffs; some are against them."

The same thing happens in other fields. Physics is generally regarded as one of the most "scientific" of sciences. But when it comes to issues about which many people feel deeply—and in different directions—it rapidly begins to seem as though physicists too "never agree with each other." Consider the controversies over whether nuclear reactors are safe, what the long-term effects are of nuclear war, or whether space-based defenses against a nuclear attack are practical. For all I (or, probably, you) know, there is a "right" answer to each of these questions, subscribed to by the great bulk of those competent to hold an opinion. But as long as there are at least a few people on the "wrong" side equipped with the right credentials, and as long as large and influential groups support both sides, the impression received by the general public will be that the profession is more or less evenly divided.

Several years ago, the *American Economic Review* published the results of an opinion poll sent to a large number of economists, some academic, some employed by business or government. The questions—and the results—divided fairly clearly into three categories. One consisted of reasonably straightforward issues of price theory—the effect of rent control, of minimum wage laws, of tariffs. On those questions, there was general agreement, often by more than 90 percent of those polled. The second category involved questions, mostly "macroeconomic" questions, in areas where there is considerable professional controversy; as one would expect, opinion on those questions was divided. The third category consisted of questions where the answer depended in large part not on economics but on issues of moral philosophy—what one believes to be a good or just world. An example would be the question "Should the income distribution of the U.S. be made more equal?" In this category too, there was widespread disagreement. My conclusion from the results of the poll was that economists—like physicists—generally agreed about the "solved" questions of their science, disagreed about areas where work was still going on, and disagreed on issues where their conclusions depended largely on things other than economics.

PROBLEMS

1. In discussing reasons for learning economics, I asserted that making you into a rational voter was not a good reason for you to learn economics but might be a good reason for me to teach it. Explain. In order to justify the statement, you may have to take a very optimistic view (from my standpoint) of how successful this book is going to be.
2. Apply economics in an original way to something that has not been analyzed in this book. Ideally, your analysis should use one or more of the ideas developed in this book to provide some nonobvious explanations of or predictions about real-world phenomena. Some possible subjects are: professional sports, college sports, intramural sports, sex, mental illness, dieting, the relation between students' GPA's and other characteristics, religion, landscaping of different campuses, attractiveness of female students at different campuses with different majors, attractiveness of male students at different campuses with different majors, dorm food, climates and the people who live in them, pet ownership, the notorious inability of Americans to speak foreign languages, why drivers are more courteous in some cities than in others, relation between amounts of partying engaged in by students and other characteristics of themselves or their campuses, and differences between the attitudes and behavior of residents of small towns and those of inhabitants of big cities.
3. Give a consistent and plausible-sounding economic explanation of something which you are sure cannot be explained economically.
4. Reread your answer to Problem 3. Are you still *sure* your explanation is wrong? Discuss.

FOR FURTHER READING

My first economics article, referred to in this chapter, is David Friedman, "An Economic Theory of the Size and Shape of Nations," *Journal of Political Economy*, Vol. 85, No. 1 (February, 1977), pp. 59-77.

The poll of economists is reported in J. R. Kearl, et al., "A Confusion of Economists?" *American Economic Review: Papers and Proceedings*, Vol. 69, No. 2 (May, 1979), pp. 28-37.

Students who are interested in the history of economics and would like to read the works of the inventors of economics should read Adam Smith, *An Inquiry into the Nature and Causes of the Wealth of Nations* (New York: Oxford University Press, 1976); David Ricardo, *The Principles of Political Economy and Taxation* (Totowa, N.J.: Biblio Distribution Centre, 1977); and Alfred Marshall, *The Principles of Economics* (8th ed., London: Macmillan, 1920).

The three books are very different. Smith's is the most far ranging and entertaining. Ricardo's is the most difficult; in it he works out the essential logic of economics—what we would now call general equilibrium theory—without any of the mathematical tools which a modern economist would consider essential for doing so. The modern economist reading Ricardo's *Principles* feels rather as a member of one of the Mount Everest expeditions would feel if, arriving at the top of the mountain, he encountered a hiker clad in T-shirt and tennis shoes. Marshall's *Principles* is the book in which modern economics was first put together; it is the only one of the three which could, for a sufficiently ambitious reader, serve as an alternative to a modern textbook.

Students who would like the help of a modern discussion of the classics of economics should read Mark Blaug, *Economic Theory in Retrospect* (New York: Cambridge University Press, 1978).

For a series of interesting essays on the economics of past societies, I recommend Carlo Cipolla, *Money, Prices and Civilization in the Mediterranean World* (Staten Island, N.Y.: Gordian Press, 1967).

Two books which I can recommend as alternatives or supplements to this one, covering much the same materials in a different and interesting way, are Milton Friedman, *Price Theory* (Hawthorne, N.Y.: Aldine Publishing Co., 1976) and Armen Alchian and William Allen, *University Economics* (Belmont, Ca.: Wadsworth Publishing, 1964). A shorter version of the latter also exists as Armen Alchian and William Allen, *Exchange and Production: Competition, Coordination, and Control* (Belmont, Ca.: Wadsworth Publishing, 1983).

Index

F

inflation, 522, 525, 526
  anticipated, 526
  consequences of, 526
  deficit spending and, 535
  double digit, 526
  government as beneficiary of, 534
  as source of revenue, 535
  unanticipated, 527
  uncertain, 529
  unemployment and, 532
  why it happens, 533
information, as public good, 426
input efficient, 347
input inprovement, 347
insurance, 307
interest rate:
  market, 262
  money, 524
  nominal, 265, 524
  real, 265
  time and, 262
interior solution, 11, 45
internal discount rate, 274
Interstate Commerce Commission (ICC), 232, 382
intransitive ordering, 359
invisible demand curve, 158
involuntary unemployment, 531
iron law of wages, 330
isoquant, 182

J

joint products, 373
judgment-proof, 469

K

Kaldor improvement, 356
Krueger, Anne, 449

L

labor:
  backward-bending supply curve for, 105
  as factor of production, 329
labor, supply of, 100
  and indifference curves, 107
Laffer, Arthur, 409
Laffer Curve, 107, 409
Lagrange multiplier, 60
land, as factor of production, 330
land-use restrictions, 339
Laspeyres index, 538
law, economics of, 452
law breaking, economics of, 452
law enforcement:
  private, 468
  public, 468
law of diminishing returns, 184
laws, usury, 539
least cost bundle, 185
legalization, of polygyny and polyandry, 476
legislation, market for, 441
liability rules, 401
long-run costs, 287
long-run supply curve, 290
lottery, compound, 311
lottery-insurance puzzle, 308
love:
  economics of, 473
  marriage and, 486

M

Malthus, Thomas, 16, 330
marginal cost, 92
marginal firm, 201
marginal physical product, 322
marginal product, 183
marginal rate of substitution, 46
marginal rate of transformation, 46
marginal revenue, 217

marginal revenue product, 322
marginal unit, 74
marginal utility, 70
  declining, 72
  vs marginal value, 106
  principle of declining, 39, 60
marginal value, 73, 183
  declining, 74, 75
  demand and, 76
  vs marginal utility, 106
market, 136
  allocation, distribution, and effects of in-
    tervention in, 403
  captive, 244
  failures of, 411
  illegal, 457
  interference in, 390
  lack of in production, 110
  for legislation, 441
  political, economic analysis of and public
    choice, 440
  with and without price, 483
market interest rate, 262
marketplace, political, 432
market segmentation, discriminatory pricing and, 228
marriage, 412
  costs of bilateral monopoly and, 485
  decline and fall of American, 487
  economics of, 473
  enforcement problems of, 486
  as firm, 484
  love and, 486
  monogamous, 473
  polyandrous, 473
  polygynous, 473
  what and why, 484
Marshall, Alfred, 37, 228, 352, 360
Marshallian efficiency, 351
Marshallian quasi-rents, 287
Marshall improvement, Pareto improvement and, 354
mechanism, vs equilibrium, 156
median voter model of public choice, 446
metastable equilibrium, 138, 243
middlemen, 204

minority, privileged, 419
model:
  econometric, 546
  economic, 545
money:
  barter vs, 411
  changing price of, 525
  gift vs, 494
  price of, 523
  supply of, 523
  value, prices, and, 86
money interest rate, 524
money prices, 522
monogamous marriages, 473
monopolist, America as, 438
monopolistic competition, 216, 235
monopolistic industry, 375
monopoly, 215, 245, 374
  artificial, 233, 252, 377
  discriminating, 215, 383
  government enforced, 232
  nationalized, 382
  natural, 231
  regulation and, 378
  single-price, 215, 216, 375
  why it exists, 230
monopoly, bilateral, 126, 245
  costs of and marriage, 485
monopoly power, 230
monopoly profit, 220, 233
monopsony, 234, 245
Morgenstern, Oskar, 246, 310

N

naive price theory, 30, 153, 520
nationalized monopoly, 382
natural cartel, 231
natural monopoly, 231
necessity, 25
needs, 23
negative feedback, 14
net advantage, equal, 341

net nominal assets, 528
New Deal, 337
Niskanen, William, 447
nominal cash balances, 525
nominal interest rate, 265, 524
non-excludability, 422
nonlinear production, 112
nonpecuniary costs, 392
non-satiation, 24
non-sunk costs, 280
normative statements, positive statements vs, 346

O

oligopoly, 216, 245
  bilateral, 245
oligopsony, 216, 245
opportunity cost, 40, 200
optimal bundling, 52
output efficient, 347
output improvement, 347

P

Paasche index, 538
Paretian efficiency, 351
Pareto, Vilfredo, 350
Pareto efficient, 350
Pareto improvement, 350
  Marshall improvement and, 354
  potential, 356
partial equilibrium, 170
patents, efficiency and, 387
pecuniary, 411
pecuniary externality, 195, 372, 425
percentage change, 222
perfect discriminatory pricing, 224
physics, of heating, 499
plea bargain, 415

political business cycle, 536
political market, economic analysis of, and public choice, 440
political marketplace, 432
pollution, 423
polyandrous marriages, 473
polyandry, effect of legalizing, 476
polygynous marriages, 473
polygyny, effect of legalizing, 476
positive statements, normative statements vs, 346
present values, 265
price, 40, 333
  changing, of money, 525
  cost, value, and, 36
  equilibrium level of, 524
  markets with and without, 483
  money, 522
  of money, 523
  money, value, and, 86
  relative, 49
  value equals, 46
price control, 28, 30, 390
  of gasoline, 29
  summary schema of, 398
price index, 537
price searcher, 216
  price taker vs, 219
price searching, other forms, 245
price taker, 215, 216
  price searcher vs, 219
price-taking firm, 216
price theory, 27, 151
  naive, 30, 153
pricing:
  perfect discriminatory, 224
  two-part, 224
pricing, discriminatory, 222
  market segmentation and, 228
Principle of Comparative Advantage, 123
Principle of Declining Marginal Utility, 39, 60, 72
Principle of Revealed Preference, 24
prisoner's dilemma, 414
private express statutes, 230
privileged minority, 419

Q

R

risk preferrer, 305
robbery, 459

S

search unemployment, 529
shortages, 157
short-run costs, 287
short-run supply curve, factory size and, 288
simple trade, 118
single-price monopoly, 215, 216, 375
single tax, 332
small-numbers problems, monopoly and, 215
Smith, Adam, 107, 207, 330, 409
social alternatives, 358
social welfare function, 351, 358
sociobiology, 487
speculation, 296
stable equilibrium, 19, 138
substitutes, 166
substitution effect, 49
   income and, 47
sunk cost, 279
superior, 347
supply, and demand, 156
supply curve, 190
   long-run, 290
   short-run, factory size and, 288
   upward-sloped, 200
supply curve, industry:
   and closed entry, 194
   free entry, 198
supply of money, 523
supply-side economics, 107
surpluses, 157

T

tariffs, 432
   good, 438

protective, 123
in real world, 444
why undesirable, 433
tax, single, 332
temperature, profit-maximizing, 509
time:
   economics and, 85
   interest rates and, 262
total cost, 288
total cost function, 183
trade:
   potential gains from, 118
   without production, 118
   production and, 121, 124
   simple, 118
   two-person, complications of, 126
trading, Edgeworth Box and, 130
traffic jams, 416
transaction costs, 166, 373, 411
transfer externality, 425
two-part pricing, 224
two-person trade, complications of, 126

U

unanticipated inflation, 527
uncertain inflation, 529
unemployment, 522, 529
   disequilibrium, 531
   fictitious, 530
   inflation and, 532
   involuntary, 531
   kinds of, 529
   search, 529
unemployment rate, 529
unit elastic curve, 222
unstable equilibrium, 138
usury laws, 539
utiles, 72
utilitarianism, 360
utilities, summing, 350
utility, 38, 58
   expected, 301

marginal, 70
   Von Neumann, 310
utility efficient, 349
utility function, 36, 58, 311
   indifference curves and, 62
   risk preference and, 303
utility improvement, 349

V

value, 24, 40
   economic, 25
   marginal, 73, 183 ·
   money, prices, and, 86
   price, cost, and, 36
   price equals, 46
values, 346
   present, 265
variable cost, 290
Von Neumann, John, 246, 310

Von Neumann utility, 310
voting, 413

W

wage, equilibrium, 330
wage differentials, 339
wages, iron law of, 330
wants, 23
Wealth of Nations, 107

X

x-efficient, 347

Z

zero sum game, 204